James and Bradley

James and Bradley
American Truth and British Reality

T. L. S. Sprigge

OPEN COURT
Chicago and La Salle, Illinois

Cover photo of William James is by Pach, 1898? (Harvard shelf mark pfMS Am 1092), and is reproduced by permission of the Houghton Library, Harvard University.
Cover painting of F. H. Bradley is by R. G. Edes, c. 1924–1929, from the collection of Merton College, Oxford. The photograph of the painting is reproduced by permission of Thomas-Photos, Oxford.

OPEN COURT and the above logo are registered in the U.S. Patent and Trademark Office

© 1993 by Open Court Publishing Company

First printing 1993

Printed and bound in the United States of America.

Library of Congress Cataloging-in-Publication Data

Sprigge, Timothy L. S.
  James and Bradley : American truth and British reality / T.L.S. Sprigge
    p. cm.
  Includes bibliographical references and index.
  ISBN 0-8126-9226-8 (hard). — ISBN 0-8126-9227-6 (paper)
  1. James, William. 1842–1910. 2. Bradley, F. H. (Francis
Herbert), 1846–1924. 3. Truth—History. 4. Reality—History.
  I. Title.
  B945.J24S66 1993
  191—dc20   93=1275
                                                     CIP

To
ANTHONY GRAYLING
and
LEEMON McHENRY
one time students of mine and life long friends

The world of our experience consists at all times of two parts, an objective and a subjective part, of which the former may be incalculably more extensive than the latter, and yet the latter can never be omitted or suppressed. The objective part is the sum total of whatsoever at any given time we may be thinking of, the subjective part is the inner 'state' in which the thinking comes to pass. What we think of may be enormous—the cosmic times and spaces, for example—whereas the inner state may be the most fugitive and paltry activity of mind. Yet the cosmic objects, so far as the experience yields them, are but ideal pictures of something whose existence we do not inwardly possess but only point at outwardly, while the inner state is our very experience itself; its reality and that of our experience are one. A conscious field *plus* its object as felt or thought of *plus* our attitude towards the object *plus* the sense of a self to whom the attitude belongs—such a concrete bit of personal experience may be a small bit, but it is a solid bit as long as it lasts; not hollow, not a mere abstract element of experience, such as the 'object' is when taken all alone. It is a *full* fact, even though it be an insignificant fact; it is of the *kind* to which all realities whatsoever must belong; the motor currents of the world run through the like of it; it is on the line connecting real events with real events. That unsharable feeling which each one of us has of the pinch of his individual destiny as he privately feels it rolling out on fortune's wheel may be disparaged for its egotism, may be sneered at as unscientific, but it is the one thing that fills up the measure of our concrete actuality, and any would-be existent that should lack such a feeling or its analogue, would be a piece of reality only half made up. (Compare Lotze's doctrine that the only meaning we can attach to the notion of a thing as it is 'in itself' is by conceiving it as it is *for* itself; i.e. as a piece of full experience with a private sense of 'pinch' or inner activity of some sort going with it.)

JAMES, VRE, p. 499

My way of contact with Reality is through a limited aperture. For I cannot get at it directly except through the felt 'this', and our immediate interchange and transfluence takes place through one small opening. Everything beyond, though not less real, is an expansion of the common essence which we feel burningly in this one focus. And so, in the end, to know the Universe, we must fall back upon our personal experience and sensation.

BRADLEY, AR, p. 229

[H]owever erring man's ideas may be, so long as they admit the existence of discipline in life, of something external really existing, which it is the duty of man to bring his will into harmony with, there is hope for him.

WILLIAM JAMES, 1869 (in Perry, I, p. 296)

Now what does all this rest on? Observation of *our* experience, that of a few passing parasites on a speck of dust?

BRADLEY in a letter to James criticising 'humanism' (Perry, II, p. 492)

Grau, teurer Freund, ist alle Theorie
Und grün des Lebens goldner Baum

GOETHE, *Faust*, Part 1, Scene IV, lines 2038–39

In philosophy we must not seek for an absolute satisfaction. Philosophy at its best is but an understanding of its object, and it is not an experience in which that object is contained wholly and possessed. . . . The shades nowhere speak without blood, and the ghosts of Metaphysic accept no substitute. They reveal themselves only to that victim whose life they have drained, and, to converse with shadows, he himself must become a shade.

BRADLEY, ETR, p. 13 and note on p. 14

My dear Bradley,

I duly got your highly interesting letter of Nov. 25th, but delayed answering it till I should be able to send also a reprint of an article criticizing *you*, the bogey and bugbear of most of my beliefs.

JAMES to Bradley, January 22, 1905

CONTENTS

Preface

William James (1842–1910) and Francis Herbert Bradley (1846–1924) were the dominating philosophers of the U.S.A. and of Britain respectively in their time. They were also, what is far from the same thing, the most important in my opinion. The two philosophers never met, but they did correspond. (I provide some account of the letters they are known to have exchanged in an Appendix.) They also commented on each other's work frequently.

There are two extremes in writing about the work of historical philosophers. One extreme is that of a book on, say, Spinoza which treats him as a contributor to the latest issue of *Mind* and evaluates what he says as the supposedly atemporal attempt at truth he expects there. Another extreme is that of the historian of ideas who treats his subjects simply as historical phenomena, with no suggestion that they may be addressing him or his contemporaries in any way worth responding to.

The philosophers studied in this book are much nearer in time than Spinoza and, in fact, were regular contributors to *Mind*. Nonetheless, the two extremes are still possible and, in fact, exemplified, sometimes in very good studies. I see this book as lying between the two. It does not assume that to get anything philosophically worthwhile out of our two thinkers one must first translate it into some more fashionable idiom; rather, it tries to understand them in their own terms (which I find very congenial). On the other hand, it is written in the belief that what they had to say was of permanent philosophical importance, and something which theorists of truth and metaphysicians should come to terms with.

This work aims to provide a comparative exposition and personal evaluation of their main views on truth and on the general nature of reality. The reasons why I think a comparative study of their work so fruitful will emerge and are adumbrated in the Introduction. Originally I planned to organize the book on a topic-by-topic basis, giving each philosopher's views on a given matter in the same chapter. However, in order to examine their two systems thoroughly, it has proved more satisfactory to devote a separate Part to each. Instead, there are frequent comparisons along the way. The bulk of such comparison is in Part Two, where James's position is already before us. Part Two also includes a discussion of the one great set-piece dispute between them in *Mind*, on resemblance and identity. It will be found that I see the work of each philosopher as offering the main alternative solution to the problems the other thought himself to have solved, and that the position of each is best understood in this light.

In approaching them neither as philosophers whose ideas need modernizing in order to be interesting, nor as merely historical phenomena of which it is our task simply to seek the causes and effects, I pay more attention to some of the contemporary criticisms of their work than representatives of the first extreme are likely to do and less than do the latter.

I have provided very little biographical detail. That on James is abundant, on Bradley less so. My purpose has been to capture (in a necessarily selective way) the nature and grounds of their main claims about the meaning of truth and the general character of reality. This includes treatment of most of their philosophy, the main gap being that their distinctively ethical views are only dealt with in passing.

For all sorts of help and encouragement in completing this work I would like to thank especially my wife, Giglia, and four valued philosophical friends, Tony Grayling, Leemon McHenry, Dory Scaltsas, and George Davie, with whom I have had many stimulating discussions. I should also thank the many students at Edinburgh who have listened to my lectures on Bradley and James with a surprising degree of sympathy with my somewhat unfashionable stances.

Quotations from the letters from Bradley to James held in the Houghton Library is by permission of the Houghton Library insofar as the rights of the Library extend. I should also like to thank the Houghton Library for providing photocopies of these letters for my personal use.

Passages quoted from unpublished manuscripts held in the Bradley Collection at Merton College, Oxford, are used by kind permission of the Warden and Fellows of Merton College. I thank Merton College warmly for this and particularly Mr J. Burgass for his help when I consulted the manuscripts there on various occasions. There is much there that awaits a really scholarly treatment.

I should also like to express my appreciation of the new Harvard edition of the works of William James which has made so much James material readily available that previously was only accessible to the most energetic of scholars. This is particularly true of the two volumes, *Manuscript Essays and Notes* and *Essays, Comments and Reviews*.

Some material has been used, with kind permission of the editors and publishers of the original volumes, from the following three essays of mine: 'Bradley and Russell on Relations' in *Bertrand Russell Memorial Volume*, ed. George Roberts, Allen and Unwin, 1979; 'The Self and Its World in Bradley and Russell' in *The Philosophy of F. H. Bradley*, ed. A. Manser and G. Stock, Clarendon Press, Oxford, 1984; 'Refined and Crass Supernaturalism' in *Philosophy, Religion and the Spiritual Life*, ed. Michael McGhee, Cambridge University Press, 1992 (Royal Institute of Philosophy Supplement: 32).

Introduction

William James once wrote an essay called 'Bradley or Bergson?'. He saw these two thinkers as basing their philosophies on the same great insight but as drawing quite different lessons from it. Each realized that discursive reason, so far from imposing unity on a world which without it would be a thing of disconnected fragments, as Kant and others had thought, breaks up the essential wholeness of reality by discrete concepts. From this Bergson concluded that we must look for the deepest sort of understanding in intuition rather than in rational thought while it drove Bradley to the desperate pursuit of the will o' the wisp of a higher form of rationality.

My own philosophising has more and more taken the form of asking 'Bradley or James?'. For I see them, just as James saw Bradley and Bergson, as arriving at opposed metaphysical systems on the basis of very similar initial insights. In fact one of the main contrasts I find between them is that very same one. For the Bergson James described was that side of Bergson which coincided with James himself, and personally I think James upon the whole a better representative of that sort of thinking than is Bergson.

The common ground between James and Bergson is considerable.[1] Both believed in the essentially creative nature of the flow of consciousness, and in the impossibility of doing justice to genuine reality through spatial and mathematical concepts. And ethically there was much in common between them.

---

1   It was once controversial which of the two had priority in the 'conception of consciousness as a continuous stream constituting reality itself, but one which the intellect distorts for practical ends by solidifying it and cutting it up into distinct and static fragments'. Flournoy, p. 199. It was evidently James. See Flournoy, pp. 199–203. Flournoy points out that despite much that is common James's tendency was to see the universe as a chaos becoming a unity, and Bergson's to see it as a unity developing itself into a plurality. See also Perry, II, p. 600.

Each, for example, believed that a new kind of asceticism might be the great need of the age.[2]

Seeing James and Bradley in this way I have written this comparative study of their views on truth and reality. Its purpose is to clarify the main claims and arguments of two thinkers who, in my opinion, are often badly misunderstood and misrepresented by commentators, to bring out both the historical and, still more, the purely conceptual relations between their philosophies; to draw attention to the importance and, as I see it, essential truth, of the main positions they held in common, and to explore the alternative metaphysical constructions they built upon partly common foundations.

Among the more important positions which James and Bradley held in common are the following:

1. Our states of consciousness at any one moment are wholes such that every element within them is so coloured by the totality that they could not occur again without difference in another state of consciousness.

2. These momentary states of consciousness, together with other realities similar to them in their more abstract generic nature, are the basic building blocks of the universe.

3. There is something about the concreteness of fact to which concepts can never do justice.

In addition:

4. They both inclined to reject the idea of a permanent ego and to think of consciousness as a scene in which different groups of ideas tend to dominate at different times, each functioning for its time as the agent of action. They both tended to conceive mental phenomena as 'mental weather' in which certain ideas are blown into the control tower each for its turn, to just that style of psychological thought, in fact, which Sartre later castigated for substituting mental mechanisms for the choices of a unitary for-itself. (This is true of James more especially in *The Varieties of Religious Experience*.) Although, unlike Bradley, James was a committed believer in a contra-causal freedom of the will, it is remarkable how far, at times, particularly when looking at things in this way in *The Varieties of Religious Experience*, he lets the notion of free will drop out of sight and is content to look at things in the light of 'mechanical analogies' or other physical models.[3] Thus the phenomena of religious conversion are explained as a gradual buildup in the subliminal mind of idea and feeling systems which eventually grow so strong that they burst forth and expel the previously dominating moods. However, both thinkers also tried to free themselves from too full an endorsement of this approach—James, in a way not far from Sartre, by ascribing to the individual moment of consciousness a certain radical spontaneity in its dealing with what past experience has delivered to it,

2   See VRE, pp. 360–78, and Bergson, *Les Deux Sources*, in Bergson, p. 1230 et ff.
3   See VRE, p. 271, note 2, and p. 262.

Bradley by seeing the whole as imposing a character on the parts which is not derived in any predictable way from their interaction.

It is more particularly in their psychological theorising that they tend to be at one with each other, though this extends also to much of their more specifically metaphysical thinking. To some extent this reflects the mood of that time common to many thinkers of the period.[4] Even so, they would be worth comparing for the different uses to which they put this common background, especially as they are probably the most important proponents of these shared views.

Among the most striking differences between James and Bradley are:

(1) their opposing views on free will;

(2) James's pluralism versus Bradley's monism;

(3) the divergence of their views on time and eternity.

I have concentrated on what I consider to be the strongest aspects of the work of each philosopher, paying less attention to what seems to me of less intrinsic value. I have been persuaded by each of them of a good deal of what they have to say, but besides positions which I actually endorse there are others which I find persuasive enough to deserve serious consideration from philosophers with a genuine interest in the nature of truth and reality. I have not wanted to spend too much time on parts of their work which I find less satisfactory.

With Bradley, in particular, I have concentrated on what I wish especially to commend and by-passed examination of what I find of more doubtful value, in particular some of his arguments about space and causation, or more tortuous investigations of the relation between the possible, the actual, and the necessary. But of course there is much of value in both thinkers which I have passed by.[5]

That much of Bradley's reasoning seems sophistical cannot be denied. However, there are special difficulties with Bradley in deciding what is so and what not. For his endeavour, after all, is to show that ordinary thought uses concepts to understand the world which are radically incoherent. But he also acknowledges that our conceptual system contains devices by which we blind ourselves to these incoherences. So how can we decide what is a proper way of unravelling an apparent incoherence in a concept and what is employment of one of our devices for hiding it? To do so, it seems, we must step out of a conceptual scheme, which is quite satisfactory judged by its own criteria, and judge it from outside. But this we can hardly do if the concepts are the essential tools of all our thinking, as the ones Bradley attacks admittedly are.

These difficulties make it hard to evaluate such central Bradleyan arguments as those meant to establish the unreality of relations. Thus it has been thought

---

4   See, e.g., F. C. S. Schiller in Sturt, p. 75.

5   Of course, this work is concerned with the squarely philosophical part of James's work, not with his psychology as such, nor for that matter with the less important psychology of Bradley.

a sufficient reply to his arguments to say that they turn on not accepting relations for what they are, *relations* whose whole mode of being is to relate, and perversely blaming them for being unintelligible as *things*. (This misses a point or two, but let that pass for now.)

Such ways of dealing with his problems dig themselves in on the adequacy of our ordinary locutions and emphasise how they can be used without raising them. But this may only show that, at a purely verbal level, we have, as Bradley himself allows, ways of defusing them. So even if Bradley is right in essentials, his arguments are bound to seem sophistical. For if he is right, they point to problems which ordinary language has developed devices for obscuring. The difficulty is to know whether a reply to Bradley is merely such a device for obscuring a problem which he has cut through ordinary language to identify or whether it is a demonstration of its speciousness.

A similar difficulty arose when J. L. Austin accused sense-datum philosophers of basing their positions on pseudo-problems. To some, this approach seemed to resolve the matter, but for others it only appeared to do so by avoiding important problems. Austin was often right that ordinary language can fend off these problems without any ontology of sense data; what he was not prepared to acknowledge was that the less ordinary way of talking in which philosophers engage does not so much create false problems as draw attention to ones disguised by ordinary language.[6]

In short, ordinary language and ordinary concepts may work for many practical purposes and may provide verbal answers to all the paradoxes of disruptive metaphysicians, and yet this may be merely through devices which obscure questions which one must break away from it to ask. Bradley, I suspect, was often asking such questions but underrated the devices which ordinary thought and language had to meet them uncomprehendingly. If so, it may be better to delve down to his deeper message than engage in endless debate over the surface argument.

Returning to comparison of our two thinkers, I might remark that to me James seems more often right on points of detail than Bradley but Bradley nearer the truth on more general points. Consequently I shall suggest ways in which an essentially Bradleyan position might be developed on the basis of ideas taken from James. For oddly enough, from the point of view of their explicit positions on the role of conceptual thought, I think it is James who often develops novel concepts which can replace the old ones of which Bradley has pointed up the inadequacies, while it is Bradley who in practice washes his hands of conceptual thought much more quickly and completely than does James.

Part One of the work is devoted to James's views, and Part Two to Bradley's. Originally I planned a third part in which I would offer my comparisons. However, it turned out better to incorporate these into the main study of each

---

6   See Austin, e.g., p. 98.

thinker, more particularly Part Two, where the discussion of Bradley's views on a topic could be related to what had already been said about James. I have treated James first because, as I have just suggested, I believe that the details of Bradley's metaphysics can often be improved by use of his ideas. I realize that James might not relish being so used.

The degree of attention given to different topics is dictated by their relevance to each philosopher's overall picture of reality. The part of their philosophies most neglected here is ethics. I shall not excuse this solely on grounds of my title. One reason is that although any two moral philosophies can doubtless be fruitfully compared I do not see any special reason to compare these two thinkers' moral philosophy in detail. But I have touched on ethics, as was almost inevitable when discussing their religious views. I would emphasise that I admire both of them as moral thinkers.

There is little here on how their thought relates to the general culture of their time. There has been a wealth of discussion of James, in particular, from this point of view. Such studies can be of considerable importance, but those who interpret major philosophers primarily on this basis are often given to badly misunderstanding them. One must first be sure one grasps what they thought before studying the way in which this arose from large historical trends. James's pragmatism is seen by some as an expression of the pioneering spirit of America; if so, it is notable that his family circumstances hardly brought him much in touch with it, unlike Josiah Royce, whose philosophy, however, is much closer to Bradley's. So if one ventures into such interpretations, one may swim in a sea of unverifiable claims much wilder than that of metaphysics.

> There is a sense, then, in which pragmatic philosophy is a report of actual social life; in the same sense it is true of any philosophy that is not a private and quickly forgotten intellectual excrescence. Not that philosophies set out to frame such reports. They are usually too much preoccupied with the special traditions within which their work is done to permit the assumption of any such task. They are concerned with doing the best they can with problems and issues which come to them from the conflict of their professional traditions, which, therefore, are specialized and technical, and through which they see the affairs of the contemporary scene only indirectly and, alas, darkly. Nevertheless, being human they may retain enough humanity to be, subconsciously at least, sensitive to the nontechnical, nonprofessional, tendencies and issues of their own civilizations, and to find in the peculiar characteristics of this civilization subjects for inquiry and analysis. In any case, if it is as necessary as it is legitimate that their methods and results should, in their leading features, be translated out of their proper technical context and set in freer and more public landscape, the product of the dislocation may surprise no one more than the author of the technical doctrines. But without it the ulterior and significant meaning of the doctrines is neither liberated nor tested. The office of the literary and social critic in dealing with the broader human relationship of specialized philosophical thinking is, accordingly, to be cherished. But the office is a difficult one to perform, more difficult to do well than that of technical philosophising itself, just as any truly liberal human work is harder to achieve than is a technical task. Preconceptions, fixed patterns, the too urgent desire to

point a moral, are almost fatal. A pattern is implied in such critical interpretation, but it must be tridimensional and flowing, not linear and tight.[7]

Certainly the metaphysics of each is tied up with their vision of human good.
But to relate that vision to their own peculiar circumstances or that of their time
and country is not the task of this work. It will be concerned rather to point out
that in their work which will be worth pondering in any age for its present
relevance.

Likewise there will not be much comment on how they stood to various other
thinkers. The possibilities of such comparison are endless. Here I concentrate
on the content and merits of my chosen philosophers' actual view and only
consider other philosophers insofar as doing so forwards that main task. Thus
there will only be limited reference to other pragmatists or absolute idealists.

My most serious neglect, in this respect, is of Bernard Bosanquet. Bosanquet
had a great influence on Bradley and was strongly influenced in turn. They
often read as echoes of each other. It would be a substantial historical task to
work out their mutual debts precisely. However, I do not think that the
influence of Bosanquet on Bradley was always fortunate; certainly its tendency
was to pull him away from those doctrines which I find it most fruitful to
compare to James's. My excuse for the minimal attention to other pragmatists,
in particular Peirce and Dewey, is that James's pragmatism is much better
understood if kept clearly distinct from these.[8]

---

7   John Dewey in Kennedy, p. 51. He is defending pragmatism against charges by
     Lewis Mumford which associate James and Dewey and pragmatism generally
     with alleged American over-concern with technology and characterise it as the
     philosophy of commercialism on the grounds of its concern with the cash value of
     ideas. Such a criticism is, indeed, somewhat ludicrous in the case of James, and one
     against which Dewey defends himself with vigour. (I should apologize here that
     the task of this work has made it impracticable to attempt any comparison of
     James's pragmatism with Dewey's instrumentalism.) However, it must be admit-
     ted that such a view of pragmatism has been endorsed at the highest philosophical
     level. [See Russell, 1910, p. 108.]
8   For a vast attempt to set pragmatism in the context of the whole history of Western
     philosophy see Thayer, 1968.

PART ONE

WILLIAM JAMES ON TRUTH AND REALITY

1

The Pragmatic Conception of Truth

§1. James's Shocking Statement

> *'The true,' to put it very briefly, is only the expedient in the way of our thinking, just as 'the right' is only the expedient in the way of our behaving.* Expedient in almost any fashion; and expedient in the long run and on the whole of course; for what meets expediently all the experience in sight won't necessarily meet all farther experiences equally satisfactorily.
>
> PRAG, p. 222

These and other such statements (mainly in *Pragmatism* and in the essays collected in *The Meaning of Truth*) have shocked many ever since they were first published. For it seems that by identifying the truth of ideas with their utility, James is repudiating the very meaningfulness of what has been thought one of humanity's sublimest enterprises, the quest to know how things really are, replacing it by the quest to find ideas which are merely useful. And things tend to look worse rather than better to many people when they realize that the utility in question includes not only the better technological handling of nature, but also the merely emotional effects that an idea can produce in us, whether by way of comfort or of vitalisation, so that the truth about such matters as the existence of God, or an afterlife, is identified with what it is most emotionally satisfying or vitalising to believe about them. Nor are those who react like this reconciled to pragmatism by James's emphasis in such passages as the present on long-term, as opposed to short-term, utility, for it seems to ignore the fact that the real truth about various matters, which it is our intellectual duty, and perhaps the special glory of the human mind, to pursue may be emotionally less satisfying than are various infantile myths which we ought to be abandoning. If there is emotional value in knowing the real truth, such critics of pragmatism insist, it is the satisfaction in having within our minds what we have good reason to take as a transcript of how things really are, in a manner of which pragmatism denies either the desirability or intelligibility.

And in any case the whole concept of truth as what it is expedient to believe seems maddeningly incoherent to many philosophers. For it seems to imply that to find out whether an idea is true we must find out whether it is useful to believe it. But that, it is objected, must mean either finding out whether it really is thus useful, that is, whether it is true that it is useful, in a realist sense of truth dismissed by pragmatism, or deciding whether the belief that it is useful to believe it is itself a useful belief, which in turn will be a matter of deciding whether it is useful to believe that it is useful and so on forever in a futile regress. Besides, it is often much more straightforward to find out whether a proposition is true or not than to find out whether it is useful to believe it, so that the idea, which is given as one reason in favour of pragmatism, that it brings truth down to the earth of the practically discoverable and away from the clouds of speculation, is quite mistaken. Surely it is easier to know whether one slept well last night than whether one will fare better in the day by believing that one did or believing that one did not.[1]

One puzzle about James's espousal of the pragmatic view of truth is that if ever there was a man who wanted to know how things really were it was surely James. It may well be that some who have become pragmatists have not had the yearning for a real understanding of things, and have wanted simply a convenient set of beliefs to live by, but that was certainly not the way with James. So how did such a man come to hold such strange views about truth?

Sometimes pragmatism, and its view of truth, seems not so much the thesis that the truth of an idea is the expediency of believing it as that the meaning of an idea lies in its empirically testable implications and that its truth, if it be true, consists in the actuality or possibility of finding that they actually hold.

> "Grant an idea or belief to be true," it [pragmatism] says, "what concrete difference will its being true make in anyone's actual life? How will the truth be realized? What experiences will be different from those which would obtain if the belief were false? What, in short, is the truth's cash-value in experiential terms?"
>
> PRAG, p. 200

Put like this (as it often is) pragmatism seems basically the same doctrine as the verification principle of logical positivists. Comparison, however, is complicated at a verbal level by the fact that logical positivists used 'verifiable' to mean 'the kind of idea (or proposition) of which positive empirical confirmation or disconfirmation is conceivable' while James used it to mean 'an idea empirical testing of which will give a positive result'. In the first sense the existence of, say, unicorns is verifiable while in the second it is not. I shall stick to James's sense.

---

1   See Russell, *Essays*, pp. 118–19.

Although such a verificationist view of truth and meaning will trouble philosophical realists it does not have the same alarming appearance of saying that any belief is true which its supporters find it convenient to have accepted. But whatever the merits and demerits of verificationism, of the sort advocated by the original logical positivists (and given its classic statement in A. J. Ayer's *Language, Truth and Logic*) statements such as that quoted at the beginning of the chapter (which is not some isolated aberration) show that pragmatism cannot be equated with it. For it would seem that empirical verifiability (in James's sense, not the logical positivists') is at best just one form of the utility with which the pragmatist identifies truth.

Evidently James's pragmatism, and its view of truth, is a doctrine not altogether easy to grasp. And, in fact, we can only do so by realizing that its significance for James lay in its being a synthesis of the following eight themes or key ideas which he developed individually in other works. (Whether it combines these various themes into a coherent whole is something we will have to consider later.)

1. It is proper, in certain contexts, to believe things, not on grounds of sufficient evidence or demonstration, but because it is emotionally useful or vitalising to do so.

2. Many disputes, especially in metaphysics, turn on a lack of clarity as to what precisely is at issue.

3. The human mind deals with reality in a selective way, picking out what is relevant for its purposes, organizing phenomena into patterns, and carving out units, which as much reflect its own biological and other interests as the one way in which its environment is independently organized.

4. The symbols which flow through one's consciousness when one is thinking that things are thus and so, have the sense and reference they do, not in virtue of their intrinsic nature as elements of subjectivity, but in virtue of their external relations.

5. Concepts are only intelligible insofar as they have an experiential cash value and this holds in the case of the concept of truth as much as of any other.

6. Facts which do not concern actual or possible experiences are vacuous.

7. Without thinking there is no truth, since truth is a property of thoughts and cannot be there in the world apart from it.

8. The point of thought is not to copy reality but to relate us to it fruitfully.

I add a ninth proposition which I do not think James really held, but which he gives the impression of holding, and which is what critics chiefly fasten on.

9. There is no way things really are, just the way humans, more or less usefully to themselves, think they are.

§2. *James and Tarskian T-sentences*

A neat way of bringing out what is often found so wrong-headed in James's treatment of truth is that it seems to offend against a certain requirement which, it is often thought, must be met by any account of truth worth taking seriously.

Consider the two propositions:

(1) It is true that snow is white if and only if snow is white.

(2) It is true that God exists if and only if God exists.

These propositions are instances of a certain pattern which I shall call the T pattern:

(3) It is true that P if and only if P.

It seems obvious that all propositions of the T pattern are true, and that a definition of 'true' which implied that there may be false propositions of that pattern must have gone wrong. Indeed, it seems that a satisfactory definition of 'true' must explain why they are all true. And yet, so it may be thought, so far from explaining this, James's account of truth implies that there may perfectly well be false propositions of the T pattern. For suppose it is much more expedient to believe that there is an afterlife than either to believe some contrary of that proposition or to have no belief on the matter. Then it appears that on James's account it is true that there is an afterlife. But this seems something which might well be so even though there is no afterlife. For it is surely quite conceivable, first, that beings which have no afterlife may find it emotionally satisfying or vitalising to believe that they do, and, second, that these benefits are not accompanied by any evils which outweigh them. In that case it would seem that on the pragmatist conception of truth it is true that these beings will live hereafter although they will not live hereafter.

It may be said that the pragmatist has no notion of something simply being true. It is beliefs which are true or false and we should distinguish between the question, Which beliefs of those individuals are true? and the question, Which beliefs of ours about them are so? That is so, but it does not affect the essential point. For even if 'true' is only properly predicated of some definite individual's (or perhaps group's) belief, we will still want to accept a requirement on satisfactory accounts of truth of the same essential sort as we have been considering. Thus we might revise the requirement somewhat and say that an adequate account of truth must show that and why all propositions of the following pattern are true, taken as meaning that every belief with such a proposition as its content must be true:

(4) Someone's belief that P is true if and only if P.

So an adequate account of truth must imply the proposition (that is, hold that any belief of which it is the content must be true).

Someone's belief that there is an afterlife for members of his species is true if and only if there is an afterlife for members of his species. (This is not strictly of the right pattern, since 'his' after the biconditional expression refers back to what preceded it, but it would be pedantic to put this right in an informal discussion.)

But we have just seen that it may well be the case that a belief that members of one's species have an afterlife is a very useful belief even though no members of the species do have such an afterlife. So it seems that pragmatism implies rejection of a principle with which an adequate account of truth should not merely be compatible but of which it should provide the rationale.

The idea of the T pattern requirement is, of course, borrowed from the preliminaries of Tarski's statement of his semantic theory of truth.[2] However, I have adapted it so that it becomes a suitable instrument in the discussion of James's views and would request the reader to concern himself only with its relevance as thus adapted. However, the rest of this section (which can be skipped by the uninterested) offers a word or so on the contrast between Tarski's language-centred approach and the idea- or judgement-centred approach common to both James and Bradley.

Tarski was looking for a definition of truth which would explain the sense in which *sentences* could be said to be true or false. (In fact, he thought there were puzzles about applying the predicates 'true' and 'false' to any sentences except those which pertained to certain sorts of ideal language, but we can ignore this point.) For James, in contrast, truth was a property of beliefs, or ideas, as he sometimes called them; presumably he would have said that a sentence is true if and only if (or when and only when) it is functioning as the expression of a true belief.

To me it seems clear that James's view as to the kinds of items which are true or false, in the most basic sense, is much more satisfactory than Tarski's from the point of view of fundamental philosophical questioning. The main ground for objecting to it is that there would still be a truth as to how things are even if the universe contained no thought. But if this is so, I doubt if matters are best put right by conceiving of unthought truth as composed of true sentences somehow existing in an unthinking void.

Be that as it may, Tarski's approach was to specify a class of so-called T sentences conforming to the pattern:

(5) 'S' is true if and only if S,

giving as his famous example

(6) 'Snow is white' is true if and only if snow is white.

Now one might think that one could use this as the basis for a definition of truth along the following lines.

(7) *Definition*: For every sentence 'S', 'S' is true if and only if S.

However, there are various reasons why this was rightly seen as impossible.

First, when Tarski conceives of truth as a property of sentences, he thinks of sentences as strings of words of a certain syntactical character. It is not, so to speak, built into the identity of the sentence that it has a certain meaning or even that it belongs to a certain language. Thus theoretically the sentence 'Snow is white' could occur in two different languages, and be true in one, and false in the other, as for example if one were English and the other an otherwise similar language in which 'white' meant black. Therefore we should not say that the sentence is true, but rather that it is true in L, where 'L' names a language, such as say English, or some idealised form thereof. So the kind of T sentence we really want is something such as

(8) 'Snow is white' is true in L if and only if snow is white.

---

2   See Tarski, *Formalized* and *Semantic*.

However, (8) is only true itself in a language suitably related to L. For (8) belongs to a meta-language in which "'snow is white'" names a sentence in the object language, and if 'snow', 'white', and the other words do not have an appropriate meaning in the meta-language, (8) will not be true.

A more important objection to using (7) as a definition of 'true' is that it requires a highly debatable use of the variable 'S' so that its values can either be names of sentences or sentences themselves. For in (6) the words 'snow is white' occur first as the name of a certain sentence in L and secondly as a sentence actually being used as a subordinate clause. Consider in contrast the sentence which would really result if we replaced 'S' in (7) by a name for the sentence 'Snow is white'. It would be:

(9) 'Snow is white' is true if and only if 'snow is white'.

The trouble is that the second clause has no main verb, only a name dangling in the air waiting for a predicate. If we try to supply it, we will probably end up with the unhelpful

(10) 'Snow is white' is true if and only if 'Snow is white' is true.

If, on the other hand, we try to replace it throughout by a sentence, rather than a name of a sentence, we will get

(11) Snow is white is true if and only if snow is white

and this will be nonsense because 'is true' must be predicated of something named (or of a quantified variable) not just hang in the air at the end of a complete clause. In any case, it is not really proper to have a variable whose values (or substituends) are something other than names.

There are ways of looking at variables which are supposed to avoid these difficulties. However that may be, Tarski himself thought that nothing along the lines of (7) itself could work as a definition.

As to the sort of definition he did offer, that is a technical matter beyond our concern. Basically it consists in finding for any language L a formula from which can be deduced, for each sentence it allows, an appropriate T sentence which will occur in a certain meta-language. This formula trades on knowledge of the precise conditions under which certain sentences taken as basic will be regarded as true or false by speakers of the language (in effect, therefore, on knowledge of the specific meaning of these basic sentences). Or more truly, it trades on the fact that we can pretend to a kind of bogus knowledge of what any sentence 'S' means by saying that it means S, pretending, if need be, that we know what we are saying when we say 'S'.

§3. *Confrontation between James and G. E. Moore*

The precise semantic theory of truth which Tarski develops on this basis seems to me deeply unhelpful though it is doubtless a fine technical achievement. For first, it is not satisfactory to think of truth as a property of sentences, and secondly, it cannot be satisfactory to say that 'true' has no definite meaning in natural languages. But the general idea that a satisfactory account of truth must explain why all T sentences are true, when revamped to meet a different conception of the kinds of item of which 'true' and 'false' are to be predicated, is an altogether compelling one. For our purposes it is best taken as the claim that an adequate account of truth must explain the need we feel to endorse (3) (It is true that P if and only if P) and (4) (Someone's belief that P is true if and only if P) above. For further reference I shall formulate and label these proposed requirements to be satisfied by a theory of truth as follows:

(A) The requirement of compatibility with, and of explaining the need we feel to endorse, any proposition of the form: It is true that P if and only if P.

(B) The requirement of compatibility with, and of explaining the need we feel to endorse, any proposition of the form: Someone's belief that P is true if and only if P.

The horror many thinkers have felt towards the pragmatic conception of truth might be dispelled if it turned out that after all it does satisfy one or both of these requirements. (If it only strictly satisfies one of them, the other can still be thought of as a rough and ready way of stating that one.)

Let us say that conceptions of truth which satisfy either the A or the B requirement (or both) satisfy the equivalence requirement. It will be helpful also to regard any theory of truth as satisfying the equivalence requirement which endorses any similarly patterned statement of which (A) or (B) can be conceived as a rough and ready statement, even if it contains grounds for not finding those formulations quite satisfactory as they stand.

Among the sharpest critics of James's pragmatism was G. E. Moore in his 'Professor James's "Pragmatism" ', 1907–8.[3] Moore (who was constantly in the position of defending common sense, as he conceived it, against the outrageous suggestions of his fellow philosophers) was appalled by what he took to be James's denial of the most basic facts about truth.[4] And upon the whole it does

---

3   Moore, *Studies, chapter III.*

4   The debate between James and Moore was discussed by Richard A. Hertz in his 'James and Moore: Two Perspectives on Truth'. I hope that my subsequent discussion adds some further light to the nature of the clash, which Hertz, like others, is rather too apt to see as merely reflecting a contrasting type of interest rather than as a confrontation between opposing views.

A much more sympathetic criticism of James's pragmatism than Moore's written from the point of view of a correspondence theorist is that of J. B. Pratt. [See Pratt, *Pragmatism*, lectures 2 and 3.] He insists on the misleadingness of assuming that a correspondence theorist, for whom someone's thought is true if and only if 'the object of which one is thinking is as one thinks it' must suppose that our Ideas are like their objects. [See Pratt, pp. 67–70.] However, James may, as I shall be contending, in the end be going deeper than such thinkers in insisting that such formulations leave 'as' unexplained. [See 'Professor Pratt on Truth' and Pratt's comment on it in Pratt, p. 69.] Still, upon the whole Pratt's book has never been surpassed as an outstanding common-sense critique of James's pragmatism. It shows a far better sense of what James, Dewey, and Schiller were about than do Moore or Russell in their criticisms, and is a good deal clearer than Bradley's criticisms which take rather the same direction. [Bradley's critique of James on

seem that Moore was right to think of his view of truth as the common-sense one, that is, as an articulation of what unphilosophical people implicitly believe about it. It will be a good way of considering how far James really did depart from common sense, and how far any such departure matters, to consider how far criticisms of his conception of truth from a perspective such as Moore's are to the point, and if so, how damaging. Although Moore made his own explicit attack upon the pragmatist conception of truth, my concern here is not with the details of that but with showing in a more general way how his positive views about truth can be used to mount a criticism of James's.

Moore at one time held a view of truth which very neatly meets the equivalence requirement.[5] He said that a belief was true if and only if it stood in a certain relation of correspondence to a fact. As to what correspondence was, exactly, he allowed that it was difficult to analyse, but suggested that we can indicate its general nature by pointing out first that it is a relation which any belief can have only to one fact, and second that its holding is a matter of a connection between the belief and the fact, which makes it possible to give an exact specification of each of them by the use of the same sentential expression. Thus when a belief corresponds to a fact there will be a sentential expression 'P' (indeed various alternative such expressions) such that the belief can be described as 'the belief that P' and the fact as 'the fact that P'. The fact that the best way of describing each of them will be in this same form of words does not mean that they are somehow just one entity, but that the belief has a peculiarly intimate relation to the fact, of which 'corresponds to' serves as a label.

What of a false belief? Moore might well have said that a false belief is simply one which does not correspond to any fact. In fact, he said that it is one such that the fact to which it corresponds does not exist. In the light of this, we must qualify what I have just said, and say that for Moore a true belief is one which corresponds to a fact which exists. But perhaps it would have been better to have said that a true belief is one which corresponds to a fact, and a false one which fails to correspond to any fact, though it will be evident what a fact would have to be like for the belief to correspond to it.

Whichever way we take it, it is clear enough that it offers an explanation of why, say, Cardinal Newman's belief that God exists is true if and only if God exists. (To be more precise, we should perhaps say, instead, something like: 'Granted Cardinal Newman had the belief, then his belief is true if and only if God exists' but I hope the looser formulation, which glides over certain problems, will pass.) For we can explain it by considering the conditions under which each of the clauses would be true, or if it seems too question begging to use that word here, would rightly be asserted. The antecedent is properly asserted if and only if there is a fact to the effect that Cardinal Newman's belief

---

truth is discussed in Part Two, Chapter Two below. For Russell's criticisms, which are quite similar to Moore's, see Russell, *Essays*, IV and V.]

5   See his 1910–11 lectures, *Main Problems*.

that God existed corresponded to a fact, and the consequent is properly asserted only if there is a fact to the effect that God exists (that being the only fact which could play the role of having the Cardinal's belief corresponding to it).

To see how well Moore's position copes with the equivalence requirement, compare it with another theory of truth which does so, but only at the expense of depriving the concept of truth of any real role in human thought.

I refer to the redundancy theory of truth.[6] This says that sentences of such patterns as 'It is true that P' really say nothing more nor less than does the corresponding sentence 'P'. The most that 'It is true that. . .' does is make the assertion of what follows more emphatic or show that it is said to support someone else's statement. Thus nothing is said by use of the word 'true' which could not be as well expressed without it, and the word 'true', and any equivalents to it, are redundant.

One objection to this view is that it cannot easily explain such assertions as 'I'm sure he said something true in his lecture though I don't know what'. The suggestion that it means 'For some p, he said p in his lecture, and p' is open to the kind of objection considered in the previous section to the generalisation of the pattern as a way of defining truth, namely, that the sorts of substituend that the variable invites in each case are of quite different sorts, the name of a proposition and a proposition.

But even if that objection could be met (as I do not think it can be), it would surely not begin to explain our sense that our beliefs divide into the true and the false in virtue of some relation in which they stand to something beyond themselves. Thus though both the redundancy theory and Moore's theory satisfy the equivalence requirement, only Moore's does justice to the common-sense idea that a true belief is one reality and that which makes it true another. What is so appealing about Moore's account is that it does this while also insisting on such an intimate relation between the belief and what makes it true that the equivalence requirement is fully met.

So I am inclined to think that Moore succeeded in providing an account of truth which can serve as a common-sense foil to James's. However, the fact that Moore's is the more common-sense one does not mean that it is necessarily the finally most adequate. And I shall be suggesting that in fact James's view when properly understood meets the equivalence requirement while confronting what is puzzling about truth in a more profound way than does Moore's account.

§4. *Where There Is* **Prima** **Facie** *Clash between the Pragmatic Conception of Truth and the Equivalence Requirement and Where There Is Not*

If we look at the eight themes which, so I have claimed, underlie James's

---

6   For a classic statement see Ayer, *Language,* chapter V.

pragmatic conception of truth, and the ninth theme which may or may not do so, we will see that they divide into two groups, those which do not even initially seem to clash with the equivalence requirement or with Moore's common-sense correspondence view and those which either do or at least initially seem to.

(1) (it is proper, in certain contexts, to believe things not on grounds of sufficient evidence or demonstration, but because it is emotionally useful or vitalising to do so) and (2) (many disputes, especially in metaphysics, turn on a lack of clarity as to what precisely is at issue) do not even *prima facie* clash with either of these. One could hold, with (1), that we can properly have beliefs on emotional rather than rational grounds, without doubting that truth consists in correspondence to fact in something like the way Moore thought. Undoubtedly theme (1) was anathema to Moore but it does not clash with a correspondence theory of truth of his sort. As for (2), few would disagree with it, though one might disagree as to how much of metaphysical dispute rested on such misunderstanding.

Leading idea (3) was that the human mind deals with reality in a selective way, picking out what is relevant for its purposes, organizing phenomena into patterns and carving out units, which as much reflect its own biological and other interests as the one way in which its environment is independently organized. If this is simply the obvious point that we cannot think about everything or even all aspects of any one subject, and that our selection of what we do think about, will reflect our own particular interests, it may not seem at first to conflict either with the equivalence requirement or with Moore's correspondence view; however, even so much as this may have some potentiality for disrupting them.

James pointed out that the constellation named 'the plough' is an entity which is hardly there in nature as a unit, and is only a unit for us in virtue of our particular position in the cosmos relative to the stars which compose it and particular patterning habits of the human mind. The patterning of phenomena by the selective activity of the mind is also illustrated well by examples of historical truth. Even an account of some historical process, such as the French Revolution, which got right every precise matter of fact it considered, would have to select what was covered so as to produce the picture of a certain overall pattern (even if that pattern was of a chaotic nature), and it seems obvious that an alternative account quite as correct in a narrow factual sense would by different selection and emphasis produce a different pattern. Moore himself could hardly object to so much. And yet this obvious fact contains an element of threat to Moore's simplistic position. For while the ideas yielded by such patterning purport to be true, it is a little difficult to see how they can correspond to facts which were simply waiting there for our attention without in any sense being created by our mental activity. If a correspondence theorist like Moore claims that such facts are just there waiting to be registered by mind, how is it that different ways of patterning what are in some sense the same phenomena seem to be incompatible? It hardly seems satisfactory to say that each way of patterning the phenomena corresponds to its own fact. For to call them alternative patternings is to suggest that they are in some sense rivals and that one cannot easily accept both as equally good, and the correspondence theorist is unlikely to be happy with the idea that real existent facts can be rivals of each other. So here is the beginning of a pragmatist critique of Moore's sort of correspondence view, which starts out from considerations which even he would hardly want to deny. Yet the whole drift of such a correspondence view is that the world contains sharply distinct facts which are in no sense the work of thought, but which thought can simply register by corresponding to them in its own peculiar way; as against this James is insisting that the division into distinct facts is itself the work of thought and it is hard to disagree, even apart from the Darwinist concept of consciousness as a survival instrument with which James tended to associate it.[7]

As for (4) (the symbols which flow through one's consciousness when one is thinking that things are thus and so, have the sense and reference they do, not in virtue of their intrinsic nature as elements of subjectivity, but in virtue of their external relations) it may not directly clash with the equivalence requirement but it certainly clashes with Moore's way of satisfying it. For on Moore's account each belief has a nature which dictates the nature of the fact with which it must correspond to be true, and it is, we may feel confident, assumed that that nature is a matter of what the belief is strictly like as a mental event, not a matter of its mere external relations. I shall be suggesting that it is in virtue of its denial of this that the pragmatic conception of truth may satisfy the equivalence requirement but only in a way which turns on a view of mental events quite alien to a common-sense philosopher like Moore.

(5) (concepts are only intelligible insofar as they have an experiential cash value and this holds in the case of the concept of truth as much as of any other) and (6) (facts which do not concern actual or possible experiences are vacuous) can be understood either as resting primarily on an ontological conviction or on a theory of meaning. They may, especially (6), be taken as resting on an ontological conviction that experience is the only thing there is, and that therefore all genuine facts are about experience. Moore would disagree, but it does not challenge his view of belief and truth as such. But if it is taken as resting on a rule of meaning, there are incipient clashes with the kind of realist account of truth and fact given by Moore, for it points to an equation of truth and positive verifiability which has no place on his scheme.

(7) (without thinking there is no truth, since truth is a property of thoughts and cannot be there in the world apart from it) on the other hand, is a position

---

7   As a quintessential statement of the copy theory of truth under attack from James, consider: 'That philosophy only is the true one which reproduces most faithfully the statements of nature, and is written down, as it were, from nature's dictation, so that it is nothing but a copy and reflection of nature, and adds nothing of its own, but is merely a repetition and an echo.' (Francis Bacon in *De Augmentis Scientiarum* 1. 2, c. 13. as quoted in Schopenhauer, I, p. 15).

which Moore himself at times seems to have held, and which fits in very well with that view of truth of his which I have been considering.

(8) (the point of thought is not to copy reality but to relate us to it fruitfully) indicates James's main negative target, what he calls the copy theory of truth, of which he would certainly have taken Moore as an adherent. Moore himself would have insisted on clarifications of 'copy' and of 'point' before responding to it, but certainly if 'copy' means 'correspond to' and 'point' means 'main value' or 'only possible reasonable goal' or anything like that, he was strongly opposed to (8). Note how naturally (1), which a realist can regard as quite harmless, may slide into what he must regard as the thoroughly objectionable (8).

As for (9) (there is no way things really are, just the way humans, more or less usefully to themselves, think they are), it is because this is so often thought to be its central message that pragmatism has seemed so appalling a theory to philosophers like Moore. But we must suspend judgement as to whether (9) really is a component in James's pragmatism.

I shall now consider how these eight (perhaps nine) themes were developed by James in various different writings and then consider how far they are tied up consistently in the pragmatic doctrine of truth.

§5. *The Will to Believe*

The suggestion (formulated in (1) above) that it is proper, in certain contexts, to believe things not on grounds of sufficient evidence or demonstration, but because it is emotionally satisfying or vitalising to do so, is put forward in James's famous essay 'The Will to Believe' (1896) in WB.[8] He had, indeed, already reached this view in 1875 (clearly distinguishing it from a theory as to what it is for the belief actually to *be* true).[9]

The argument of this is rather well known and I will not spend too long on it. James claims that there are certain cases where we have to decide between two hypotheses (James says two, but there seems no reason why it should not be between more than two) and our decision has the four characteristics of being live, forced, momentous, and not intellectually decidable.

Such an option is (1) *live* in the sense that each alternative makes some appeal to our belief; (2) *forced* or *compulsory*, in the sense that we must, in effect, give an answer to it by our whole way of life, and any theoretically agnostic position really amounts to answering it in one particular way; (3) *momentous* in the sense that it makes a great difference to us which hypothesis we adopt; (4) *not intellectually decidable* in the sense that neither empirical evidence nor demonstrative argument is sufficient to settle the matter. (I have slightly amplified James's own definitions to take account of points made elsewhere.)

---

8   See also 'Is Life Worth Living?', also in WB.
9   See Perry, I, p. 529.

When a question is of this sort, James thinks it legitimate and indeed desirable that we let our 'passional nature' decide the answer we give to it. Perhaps there is a certain ambiguity in what James means here. Does he mean that we should give that answer to it which has the most emotional appeal for us, or that which we judge will be the most subjectively effective for us, in the sense of providing us with the emotions and stimuli which will lead to the most satisfactory life? Although the word 'passional' suggests the former, I suspect he sometimes has in mind rather the latter. It could make quite a difference which is meant. The answer with most emotional appeal may not be the one which does us most emotional good.

James's main concern is with the basic religious question 'Does God exist?' which he thinks precisely fits these conditions for most of his likely audience and himself. To be agnostic about it is effectively to live as an atheist; purely intellectual considerations balance each other out and leave the matter open, while it will make an immense difference to the whole quality of our life whether we give a positive or a negative answer. But there are other questions which may satisfy the same conditions, such as that of the existence of free will or of an afterlife.

A question much discussed in relation to James's proposal concerns the very possibility of someone choosing to believe something in the way which seems to be required.[10]

Do I not, after reflecting on the matter, simply find myself convinced or otherwise that something is so, without the option? If one decides to believe that God exists, because although intellectual considerations leave one open-minded, one thinks one will feel and act better if one does so believe, is one not simply deciding to pretend to oneself to believe in God? Santayana said in this connection that 'James did not really believe; he merely believed in the right of believing that you might be right if you believed'.[11] But others say that one can make oneself believe that something is so, by initially pretending to believe it, and then eventually finding that one believes it.

Perhaps the answer is that one cannot directly say to oneself: 'I will believe this' and thereby find oneself doing so, but that one can initiate conditions as a result of which one is likely to acquire a belief. But there is much that is odd about this. If the conditions which will produce the belief do so in a basically non-rational way, then surely when one realizes that they are of this sort, one's belief will waver. If, on the other hand, they are of a rational sort, then in anticipating that exposure to them will produce the belief, one is virtually presupposing the rationality of the belief as something capable of that kind of

---

10   See, for example, Bird, p. 164, and Williams, 'Deciding to Believe' in Williams, pp. 136–52. Compare James himself at PP, II, pp. 321–22. On pp. 307–11 he emphasises the influence of our passional nature on what we believe in a way which does not seem to commend it.

11   Santayana, *Character*, p. 77.

support. So I take it that the way in which one decides to let the belief be produced in one is essentially non-rational. And that seems to imply that the beliefs we decide to give ourselves in this way are likely to be rather insecure. Still, it does seem both logically and factually possible for someone to kid himself into believing something, and even into overlooking the weakness of its cognitive basis, though the extent to which it can be done probably varies greatly from person to person. How far it is ever desirable is another matter.

How does belief adopted in this deliberate way, without adequate rational support, relate to 'faith', for example, as traditionally understood by Christians? Well, perhaps this is what 'faith' sometimes means, but it may be better understood rather as a readiness to stand by a belief once it has been adopted without falling into a state of doubt whenever things arise which might seem to count against it. Those who can never settle down to a settled way of looking at things may suffer from a kind of disease of the intellect and will, which is perhaps well dealt with by a decision, stuck to with some determination, not constantly to think things out from the bottom up, but to rest on beliefs arrived at after one's most determined efforts to reach a true or probable view of things in a certain area of enquiry. But this is a much weaker claim than the one that James urges.

In putting forward his thesis of the *right to believe* in such cases as this (he later wished he had said 'right' rather than 'will'), James was very much the psychologist, concerned for the emotional health both of those who might listen to him, and also (and not least) his own. He is not exactly discussing the nature of truth, which is fairly much taken for granted. However, insofar as he is urging that we do not feel bound to restrict our beliefs to matters on which there is decisive rational evidence, when we will be healthier for the holding of beliefs which go beyond this, he is talking of something very like what Jung was later to call psychological truth. But most philosophers have thought this a rather unsatisfactory way of using the word 'truth' and seriously misleading if identified with truth in a more proper sense.

Be that as it may, since truth is typically conceived of as the goal of thought, and James is saying that psychological healthfulness is one goal of thought, it is understandable that the doctrine of the will to believe should be among the factors leading James to the view that truth does not consist in correspondence to fact but in any kind of valuable service a belief can do for us, even if it was not originally associated with this view.[12]

One can construct an argument which might have led James from the

---

12 Certainly when he wrote that essay he had no wish to challenge the most strictly objective approach to science. Thus he says: 'But in our dealings with objective nature we obviously are recorders, not makers, of the truth; and decisions for the mere sake of deciding promptly and getting on to the next business would be wholly out of place. Throughout the breadth of physical nature facts are what they are quite independently of us.' [WB, p. 20] How far the pragmatic conception of truth moves away from this remains to be seen.

doctrine of the will to believe to a pragmatist conception of truth as useful thought along the following lines:

(1) The goal of thought is truth.

(2) Sometimes, the goal of thought is not to have thoughts which there is rational ground for thinking 'copy' reality, but for having thoughts of emotional value.

(3) So truth does not always consist in copying but sometimes in emotional value.

(4) So truth consists in various sorts of good which thought can do for us.

But though such a drift of thought is intelligible—and seems to be one of the streams which fed the flood of the pragmatic conception of truth—it is doubtful whether it is reasonable. For it seems likely that 'goal' is used in somewhat different senses. Really to have a thought (in the relevant sense of a belief) is in some sense to hold it for true. (There are, indeed, puzzles here, since it can hardly be the case that every thought involves a judgement about its own status.) Truth, one might say, is the internal goal of thought, and thought can only be stable if it takes itself to have reached it. But that leaves open a wide range of external goals which would-be-true thought may aim at. It may aim at truth because truth on a certain matter will be technologically useful, or it may aim at it because it is supposed that finding the truth about something will be emotionally rewarding. And it may aim at truth for its own sake, in which case there is no distinction between internal and external goal. It seems that the above argument infers from the fact that thought may sometimes have the external goal of emotional value that this somehow constitutes the truth, which is the internal goal of thought, and this is a *non sequitur*. As for the role of 'copying' in the above argument our attitude to it will depend on whether we think the truth, which is the internal goal of thought, is best thus characterised.

I conclude that the doctrine of the will to believe does not give good logical grounds for a view of truth which runs counter to the equivalence requirement but that it is understandable that one should pass from one view to the other through confusion between the internal and the external goals of thought.

If this confusion is avoided, the doctrine of the will to believe seems to be that thought should abandon its internal goal. I suggest that to do this in respect of a belief being currently entertained is impossible, for to have a belief in consciousness is to think of what it asserts as true. What one can do, however, is set out to have beliefs in the future which promote certain external goals, whether or not they meet their internal goal.

My own view is almost the opposite of James's. For it seems to me that it is quite satisfactory to go for beliefs which work well in practice for the purposes of daily life, without much bothering about their real truth, but much less desirable to do so in matters of great religious and moral moment. But this is to anticipate points which will only fully emerge when we come to Bradley. My present purpose is simply to show the bearing of James's doctrine of the will to believe on his pragmatist conception of truth. (For a remark which links them closely see letter to T. S. Perry in Perry, II, p. 468.)

§6. *Selective Interest, the Hallmark of Mind According to* The Principles of Psychology

§ In PP James contends that it had been a defect of psychology to date that it had taken cognition as the most basic feature of mind, and had tagged on studies of will as a kind of extra, whereas the truth, as James saw it, was that cognition could only be understood in connection with will or interest. This is closely associated with the third leading idea listed above as lying behind the pragmatic doctrine of truth.

The view that the presence of mind is to be determined above all by behaviour of an irreducibly goal-seeking nature is enunciated in the very first chapter of PP.

> *The pursuance of future ends and the choice of means for their attainment are thus the mark and criterion of the presence of mentality* in a phenomenon.
>
> PP, I, p. 8

An early statement of the same essential point is to be found in his 1878 article 'Remarks on Spencer's Definition of Mind as Correspondence' .

Herbert Spencer, then an immensely influential thinker, had said that the most essential feature of mental evolution lay in the increasing 'adjustment of inner to outer relations'. To this James objects initially by asking

> what right has one, in a formula embracing professedly the "entire process of mental evolution," to mention only phenomena of cognition, and to omit all sentiments, all aesthetic impulses, all religious emotions and personal affections?
>
> EP, p. 8

He goes on to argue that the very concept of the adjustment of inner to outer relations is unclear and can only be explained by reference to purposes ascribed to the organism. For it can only mean that the organism becomes more suited to achieving certain ends in the environment to which it is said to be adjusted. Otherwise any distinctive way in which it reflects environmental influences can be called 'adjustment'. What Spencer presumably had in mind was the increase of skills which assist survival and comfort. But this is straight away to see the mind as essentially a survival- and interest-serving tool. So, as he says elsewhere, in the course of more positive remarks about Spencer, 'fundamentally, the mental life is for the sake of action of a preservative sort'.[13]

There is a certain analogy to Schopenhauer here. Schopenhauer had said that most previous philosophy had erred in seeing thought as the essence of man, whereas this lay rather in will, of which thought was essentially the mere

---

13   BC, p. 4. Compare EP, pp. 34, 370; Perry 1948, p. 195, etc.

instrument. However, James was not claiming, as did Schopenhauer, some ultimate metaphysical status for will, only looking at cognition in the excitingly new way which Darwinism appeared to have opened up, according to which the main features of the human mind have developed as a result of natural selection. In the light of this, he contended that the first thing to do in understanding mental phenomena is to grasp how they have helped the organism survive and prosper. This approach, however, was qualified by James's (quite Darwinian) insistence that much that was not itself useful had developed as a side-effect of what was.

There is a plausible line of thought leading from this Darwinist approach to thinking to a pragmatist conception of truth. 'True' is the main success word applicable to thought, and, if thought is essentially a survival instrument, surely it is its success as such that it should mark.

Although something along these lines seems to have been one of the several tributaries leading to James's pragmatism, it is doubtful how far it really favours a pragmatist conception of truth over a more common-sense correspondence one. The correspondence theorist may grant that conscious thought has developed as a survival instrument, but he will claim that it is useful precisely to the extent that it provides the organism with a map of the world in which it must behave in ways which help it prosper. Thus, since its particular utility to the organism lies in its correspondence to the environment, there will be a strong tendency for truth and survival value to the organism to go together, but this, so far from making them identical, depends on the fact that the first is a means to the second. That is, indeed, Spencer's position.

James, however, has a reply to this, namely, that a mere isomorphism between something in the head or mind and what lies outside would not be thought about it, true or false, unless it somehow served to promote useful dealings with it on the part of the organism. And though an element of isomorphism between thought and reality may sometimes be useful in this regard, it is a highly selective kind of isomorphism that will be so, in which what is strictly relevant to our purposes is picked out, or put together, from the total flux of stimuli which reach us, in a manner that goes well beyond any merely passive reflecting of the environment in the medium of thought. What matters in our ideas is that they should put us into appropriate relations with aspects of reality relevant to our interests (whether basically biological or those developed by culture); if there is some 'copying' here it has arisen only as a means to this.

Although this partly Darwinian critique of the view that it is the function of thought to copy reality is a main source of James's pragmatic conception of truth, it is, in the end, the far more purely logical considerations of the fourth leading idea, to be discussed in the next section, which are ultimately most crucial. These do, however, fit neatly together with the Darwinian point.

§7. *Intentionality and Royce*

§ A proper understanding of James's thought requires some knowledge of how he viewed the philosophy of his colleague Josiah Royce, who, I believe, was a much more important influence on him than was C. S. Peirce. This is particularly true in connection with what I have listed as the fourth key idea lying at the base of pragmatism, namely, that the symbols which flow through one's consciousness when one is thinking that things are thus and so have the sense and reference they do, not in virtue of their intrinsic nature as elements of subjectivity, but in virtue of their external relations.

Josiah Royce—whose philosophy deserves to be more widely known than it is today—was an absolute idealist who believed that the being of things of any kind whatever consists in their being thought or experienced by an absolute mind. His viewpoint is upon the whole quite similar to Bradley's, though there are also important differences between them.

In his first philosophical work, *The Religious Aspect of Philosophy*, Royce had offered a new demonstration of the existence of God or the Absolute (unlike Bradley he identified these two).[14] Only the existence of an absolute mind in which all things are included, so he argued, could make sense of the existence of error, and error certainly exists (one can't be wrong in thinking that there is error, for if one is wrong one is right).

Santayana commented:

> It is characteristic of Royce that in his proof of something sublime, like the existence of God, his premiss should be something sad and troublesome, the existence of error. Error exists, he tells us, and common sense will readily agree, although the fact is not unquestionable, and pure mystics and pure sensualists deny it. But if error exists, Royce continues, there must be a truth from which it differs; and the existence of truth (according to the principle of idealism, that nothing can exist except for a mind that knows it) implies that some one knows the truth; but as to know the truth thoroughly, and supply the corrective to every possible error, involves omniscience, we have proved the existence of an omniscient mind or universal thought; and this is almost, if not quite, equivalent to the existence of God.
>
> Santayana, *Character*, pp. 100–101

This is something of a simplification of Royce's argument, doing it less than justice. What Royce says is that in order for error to exist two conditions must be satisfied. First, a mind must identify an object as that of which it is thinking, and secondly, it must ascribe some character to it which it does not, in fact, possess. And there is a problem as to how these two conditions can be satisfied.

For consider, first, that the object that the mind identifies must either be a content of its own consciousness, such as one of its own ideas, or something outside it. In the former case it can hardly be mistaken about it, so it seems that when thought is erroneous it must be concerned with something other than and lying beyond its own contents.

If the mind identifies some object beyond itself, it must presumably do so as

---

14   See Royce, *Aspect*, chapter XI.

that which answers to some idea it possesses, that is, as answering to some description which the mind gives to itself. But if there is an object which answers to that idea or description, then that mind is in possession of the truth about it. To suppose that it does not answer to that idea is to suppose that the mind is not thinking about that object. Rather is it thinking about whatever object it is which answers to its idea, and about that object it must be right. Hence there is no possibility of error.

Since, however, there is such a thing as error, there must be some deficiency in this account of how the mind can home in on something lying beyond its own bounds. This deficiency can only be remedied, according to Royce, by recognizing that both the individual mind and its object are contents of one overarching absolute mind.

To see how this would remedy the deficiency consider that, although one cannot be in error about a content of one's own consciousness, one can entertain a false thought about it. Thus I can direct my attention upon a blue shape in my visual field, and think the thought that it is red, though realizing, of course, its falsehood. Similarly an infinite mind which includes absolutely everything as a content of its consciousness could contain all sorts of false thoughts about such contents. To it the falsehood of these thoughts would be evident. However, a finite mind which was only part of the absolute mind might contain one of these false thoughts without containing that direct confrontation with its object in virtue of which it is that which it is about and which reveals it as erroneous. And the only possible explanation of our capacity to have false thoughts is that we are just such fragments of an absolute mind.

Thus when I think falsely, the absolute mind unites the ascription of a predicate with a definite object to which it is falsely ascribed. However, my consciousness is only a fragment of that totality and contains only the faulty ascription, though it is continuous in the Absolute with a direct confrontation with its object. This is what error, granted it exists, must really be. As to why there is such a thing, Royce holds that the Absolute's grasp of the character of its own contents is enriched by the correction it contains of what is thought about them in these fragments of itself. And that correction of our false thoughts in the Absolute, in which their true object and its character are fully displayed, is a deeper version of ourselves, whose gradually fuller realization in our lives, here and hereafter, is what gives them significance.

§ My concern here is not with Royce's argument for its own sake, but as an influence on James.[15]

The argument will strike many readers as so strange that they will find it hard to credit that for many years James, very much against his inclinations, found it quite irresistible.[16] Its effect, however, was to make him think that absolute idealism must be true, much as he disliked some of its implications.

---

15   See, in this connection, his review of Royce's book in ECR, pp. 383–88.
16   See MT, p. 23, note 6; also Kuklick, pp. 181–84 and 259.

Of these the most objectionable was the conclusion that all evil is somehow ultimately good as an element in the one perfect absolute mind. (Its perfection is supposed to be demonstrable from the fact that a mind which is the whole of things, having no external frustrations, must be at peace with itself. Things would only have been mildly improved for James if we were part of an absolute mind which, because at peace with the evils in the world, must be called imperfect.)

But whatever may be thought of the argument, that certainly was its effect on James. And though it is not very satisfactory, just as it stands, there is more to it than impatience with its conclusion may allow some contemporary philosophers to recognize.

Its defects as it stands are indeed several. First, it rests on the supposition that falsehood always consists of wrongly ascribing a predicate to a subject. But this is not evidently so of false existential beliefs, positive or negative. To believe that there are such things as unicorns, or that there are not such things as horses, is not to believe of certain things that they do or do not answer to a certain predicate (or at least it would require some argument to show that this was so).

But even if recognition of this point would reduce the snappiness of Royce's proof, its main thrust could be preserved, provided he could win our agreement to the fact that there are false beliefs of the subject-predicate type he requires. He could not, indeed, claim to prove that there are errors of this sort, since statements about the existence or non-existence of error are not subject-predicate, but he might still take it as a premiss everyone will in practice grant.

Consider any erroneous belief of the required kind, say, the belief, on my part, that my friend Sandy Freshman is honest (although in fact he is not). Royce will say that there is a problem as to how it is *that* Sandy Freshman of whom I am thinking. For the idea I have in my mind is of a man, who, along with other things, is honest, and this is an idea to which Sandy Freshman does not answer. How then can it be of him that I am thinking? But if I am not thinking of him, I cannot be wrong about him. (Royce, indeed, says that I am simply right about my own Sandy Freshman—neglecting the point that I am also wrong in thinking that such a person exists. However, this is not essential to his contention that I cannot be wrong about Sandy Freshman himself.)

There is, however, a rather obvious reply to Royce's argument even thus reconstructed. For surely I can identify Sandy Freshman by a description which does uniquely identify him and which does not include the erroneous predicate. Thus I may identify him as the man who looks a certain way, lives in a certain place, whom I have met on certain occasions, etc., all of which do truly identify him, and then go on to think falsely that the man thus identified is honest. This is essentially to reduce subject-predicate propositions, at least ones of the kind to which Royce might appeal, to a conjunction of existential ones, along the lines of Russell's theory of descriptions, already anticipated by Bradley.

§ Until quite recently such a reply would have seemed the end of the matter to most analytical philosophers. However, recent discussions of *de re* thoughts and beliefs may encourage us to regard Royce's argument with more respect.

For many philosophers have come to think the Russellian account of how our thoughts may refer to things other than immediate contents of consciousness inadequate, as putting us at too much of a distance from the world. Surely, they argue, when I have a thought about some particular person or thing in my environment, I am not just thinking that just some one otherwise-unidentified something answers to a certain description, and that whatever does so also answers to another. Rather am I thinking about precisely that thing, and could not have had that thought without being appropriately related to just that thing. Thus something else which might have answered instead to the same identifying description would not have done. Thus suppose I think that a certain rock which is blocking the road would be hard to lift. Surely I could not have had just that very thought if instead of that rock there had been another one there just like it, even if my purely subjective state would have been the same in either case.

Elaborate arguments have been given for this claim. And more generally, there is a widespread feeling that only *genuinely de re* beliefs can put us into the kind of direct touch with the environment which it seems reasonable to suppose that we have, and can serve in the explanation of behaviour towards particular objects in the way in which our beliefs should do.[17]

There is much to be said for the claim that an adequate account of belief will show that the mind is often put thereby in a more direct relation to particular things beyond its own contents than that of simply containing a description which they match. Yet on most contemporary accounts of *de re* belief one's relation to what one is thinking about remains strangely external. The picture is of some kind of inchoate mental activity occurring within one, which is only the belief or thought it is, or even belief or thought at all, because it occurs in the right spatial or causal relation to be described as about it. It could have been just the same subjectively, that is, so far as what it was like to live through it went, without having been the same thought or even a proper thought at all.

In contrast, Royce can be taken as giving an account of genuinely *de re* thought which does not make its being about what it is about so extrinsic to what it feels like to have it. For if I am a component in an absolute mind in which my thought directly confronts that which it is about, then perhaps something of the nature of that direct confrontation permeates my thought even within its own bounds. In short, on Royce's view there is no hard-and-fast divide between what is in my mind and what lies beyond it. Doubtless there is much that is mysterious in this, but perhaps there *is* something essentially mysterious about the directedness of thoughts on *things beyond* which cannot be captured in more common-sense accounts. Even if we are determined to fight our way out of such mysteries, as James was eventually to satisfy himself he had done, we should recognize the force of Royce's case and why James took it so seriously.

§ Be all that as it may, James took Royce's argument very seriously and his

---

17   See Evans, *Varieties;* Kripke, *Naming;* McGinn, *Thought;* and various authors, such as Tyler Burge in Woodfield, *Thought,* and Pettit and McDowell, *Thought.*

efforts to find an alternative way of explaining how our thoughts can be about what they are about played an important part in the development both of his pragmatism and of his radical empiricism. And in the present climate of interest in *de re* thought we can look on the struggles of Royce and James with more sympathy than when most philosophers were prepared to accept something like Russell's theory of descriptions as the basis for an adequate account of how thought can relate to things beyond itself. For both were concerned to offer an account of thought which could explain its ability to be genuinely *de re*.

James usually posed the problem as to how mind can *intend* its objects insofar as they are not merely its own contents. And it is important to grasp the meaning of 'intend' here. It does not stand for the relation in which a mind stands to its intentional objects, as this phrase is usually understood today (in a manner deriving from Brentano). For the whole idea of an intentional object is that it is something which may not exist. But James and Royce assumed that one can have thoughts about things in a way which cannot be fully cashed by saying that they answer to some description one gives of them. In the light of this assumption they used 'intend' to stand for the relation between two fully real, existent things, namely, a thought and the real thing it is about, when there is such a thing.

One might divide philosophers into those who, in effect, suppose that intending has to be explained in terms of intentionality and those who suppose that intentionality has to be explained in terms of intending. The more usual answer, associated with Brentano and Husserl, is that to intend a really existing object one must have a certain intentional object which is somehow realized in that intended object. On this view one must first say what it is to be thinking about something (in the sense of having it as an intentional object) and then deal with the question of intending by saying how some actual object must be related to the intentional object to be its actually existing version. Most discussions of intentionality (at least till quite recently) in analytical philosophy have approached things on this assumption, usually explaining it by a development of Russell's theory of descriptions .

The alternative approach is to take intending as basic. Cases of thought where there is no intended object, only a so-called intentional one, can then be explained as failed cases of intending; to specify the intentional object is saying what there would have had to be in the world for the mental activity in question to have intended something, or, if the thought is of a type which does not postulate the actual existence of its object, as one where the subject gives himself some kind of impression of intending something. On this view, the primary case of thinking about something will be that in which one is in the intending relation to some actual thing, and thought which is about something which does not exist, or descriptions of thought which leave it open whether there is, are to be explained as deficient cases of this or as cases described in a way which does not rule out some such deficiency. This is how James, like Royce, effectively approaches the question of the aboutness of thought.

Not indeed that he sets the matter out thus explicitly. Although he was certainly aware of Brentano's position, the first approach was not then a norm departure from which required explanation. But if we are to evaluate his position fairly, we must recognize that this is the logic of it. One must not simply suppose that, when he assumes that aboutness is a relation between a thought and an existing something beyond it, he is failing to recognize facts about the logic of intentionality which only need to be pointed out to be obvious.

Once the two approaches are fairly distinguished, some argument is required in favour of whichever one one adopts. However, this may mainly take the form of offering an account of thought in terms of it for which one claims success. And that is how one should evaluate James's approach (to the way in which thoughts can mean and refer and be true or false) for which the notion of intending is basic. Present interest in *de re* thought should provide a climate sympathetic to such an approach. (The same goes for Santayana's valuable discussion of intending in Santayana, *Scepticism,* chapter XVIII. When we come to Bradley, we will see that, different as is his account from James's, it too is likely to get less than a fair hearing by those who take the status of intentional objects, rather than the relation of the mind to its intended objects, as the primary issue.)

§ A seminal struggle of James's with the problem of intending is his 1885 article 'The Function of Cognition' which, as he tells us in a note sprang directly from his struggles with Royce's argument (known to him from Royce's not-yet-published text).[18] (In fact this very condensed article, written at a high level of abstraction, foreshadows much of both his later pragmatism and his radical empiricism.) Although when he first wrote the article he doubted the adequacy of its psychological and practical solution as an alternative to Royce's more mystical one, he eventually thought it only required a more thorough working out to provide an adequate philosophical riposte thereto.[19]

James asks how one bit of reality, such as we might call a mental state, can know or be about another. ('Know' covers effectively both intending something and being right about it, matters not very distinct for James.) First, he says, there must be another bit of reality for it to know—a mental state which was the only reality there was could not be about anything. Perhaps then a mental state knows any other bit of reality which there is, provided only it sufficiently resembles it. James does not entirely reject this answer. Insofar as the mental state has a quality which is actualised in other instances too, it can be said to know the quality as something which outstrips its private being. But that does not mean that it knows any other particular instance of that quality as a particular. If it did, there would be no contrast between knower and known, since likeness is symmetrical. What is required, James says, in addition to their

---

18   MT, pp. 13–32; the note is on p. 23.
19   Bruce Kuklick has dealt with this aspect of James's development well, suggesting that James's not-very-convincing claim to avoid metaphysics in PP was really an avoidance of the ultimate encounter required with Royce. [See Kuklick, chapter 14.]

sharing a quality, is that the first bit of reality, the mental state which is said to know the other, is the cause of behaviour which operates upon it. *'The feeling of q knows whatever reality it resembles, and either directly or indirectly operates on'.*[20]

In a note added to the reprint of the article in *The Meaning of Truth*, James speaks of it as an early adumbration of the pragmatic account of the truth-function, deficient mainly in its too great stress on the need for a resemblance between knowing thought and thing known.[21] That dropped, we virtually get at least one version of the pragmatist conception of truth. True, James is not very clear about the relation between intending and truth, but the upshot of his position is evidently this. To be about a particular object a thought must prompt, or be liable to prompt, action which helps the individual cope with it; to the extent that the coping is successful it is called a true idea of it, and to the extent that it is less so it is called a more or less false idea of it.[22]

When we realize how basic this idea was to James's pragmatism we see why he found it so incomprehensible that his critics supposed that on his account truth did not require any kind of correspondence to a real object. For if a true idea is one which promotes successful dealings with something real, then that is a kind of correspondence with it. What James was attacking was the assumption that the correspondence required for truth needed no analysis or one solely in terms of some kind of copying.

§ This whole account of intending seems on the face of it more concerned with how whatever in our mental processes corresponds to the subject of a proposition has reference than with the meaning of whatever corresponds to the predicate. Perhaps one could interpret the original position of 'The Function of Cognition' by taking the operative efficacy of the idea as giving it its subject and its quality as giving it its predicate. But if that is so, its later development surely interprets both aspects of the thought in terms of their efficacy. Thus one might say that on the pragmatist account of meaning the subject component of a thought denotes whatever object it directs one's behaviour towards while the predicative component connotes that possible property of it to which it would help one adjust.

It is, in fact, difficult to know how far we can press James on what he has to say about essentially linguistic categories, like 'subject' and 'predicate'. For he is talking of 'ideas' not verbal statements. But though ideas are not meant necessarily to consist in words, they certainly may do so. It appears, then, that one may legitimately ask for his theory's bearings on the parts of an idea which is verbal. A possible answer might be something like this. The subject helps the idea as a whole orientate our behaviour towards some definite object while the predicate makes it the kind of behaviour which will be successful if and only if it possesses a certain character. Thus to know the meaning of the subject term

---

20   MT, p. 26.
21   MT, p. 32.
22   See, e.g., MT, pp. 51 and 130.

is to know what object would have had to exist for there to have been orientation towards anything definite, while to know the meaning of the predicate is to know what character the thing to which the idea orientates us must have if the resultant behaviour is to be successful. There will be something less than complete truth to the extent to which either of these fail to do their job. And a similar account could be given of the subject and predicate element in a non-verbal idea to whatever extent one can distinguish aspects within them playing these different roles.

It seems to follow that the meaning of the predicate is a matter of the real nature which things must possess if it is to mediate successful encounters with them. It is interesting that such a claim could be developed in a way supportive of Hilary Putnam's account of the meaning of words for real kinds.[23] But perhaps that would have been too far removed from the verificationist pull of pragmatism ever to have been taken on board by James. He might have tried to resist it by saying that it is the more obvious surface properties of things, whatever their deeper physical basis, which determine the success of our actions. But it is doubtful that that is so. However, one cannot really work out a Jamesian answer to such questions apart from an investigation of his conception of the nature of the physical world, such as we shall be conducting later. The matter turns to a great extent on whether the causes and success of our action lie in what we directly confront in perception. For the pragmatist account of thought is an account of thought, not of the knowledge which perception brings. In the latter case, for James, the object of awareness is transparent to our consciousness, not something with which we are merely interacting causally.

But however it may be with perception, the whole tendency of his account of thought is to make what one is thinking about less and less a matter of one's actual subjective state and more and more a matter of its effects. Thus its *de re*-ness tends to have for him that external character which we complained of above in recent accounts. It seems doubtful whether James was ever happy to go the whole way in this anti-Cartesian direction. There certainly remains some tendency towards the view, effectively assumed in PP, that the very nature of one's conscious state settles what one is thinking at any time. Moreover, we shall see how he made efforts to modify the externality of the relation by emphasising that the way in which it leads to behaviour is something we actually live through experientially. Nonetheless, the main upshot of his grappling with the problem of intending, as presented to him by Royce's argument, is to deny that thought can be self-transcendent in the magical way that seems to imply. Rather its power to be about what lies beyond the present contents of consciousness turns on its actual or potential effects in effective behaviour towards what it can therefore be said to be about. And this idea, that thought is about that to which it promotes adaptive behaviour, leads almost inevitably to the equation of the truth of the thought with the success of that behaviour.

---

23   See Putnam, *Mind.*

For after all, 'true' is a success word and should surely mark the kind of success it is the function of thought to gain.

§8. *Against the Copy Theory, Or, Concepts Are Only Intelligible Insofar as They Have an Experiential Cash Value, and This Holds in the Case of the Concept of Truth as Much as of Any Other*

§ The fact that James's pragmatic view of meaning and truth arose partly from his wish to find an account of intending which would enable him to escape Royce's argument for absolute idealism suggests that it is somewhat misleading to see it as a form of verificationism akin to logical positivism. For, while the logical positivist is contemptuous of metaphysical questioning as such, James was concerned rather to escape one particular type of metaphysics, that of absolute idealism, than metaphysics as such. Yet the complex tapestry of James's pragmatism does contain a verificationist thread, under the influence of Peirce's famous first statement of the pragmatic principle in his article 'How To Make Our Ideas Clear' (1878)[24] (though Peirce, taken *in toto*, is certainly no less of a speculative metaphysician than James).

> Consider what effects, that might conceivably have practical bearings, we conceive the object of our conception to have. Then, our conception of these effects is the whole of our conception of the object.
>
> Peirce, V, p. 258

§ However, there are, on the face of it, two ways in which pragmatism leads to a verificationist approach to the concept of truth. First, one may see it as the result of applying a pragmatic account of concepts to one particular concept, that of truth. Secondly, one may see a verificationist account of truth as part of, rather than as merely one special application of, the basic pragmatist doctrine. Surely the second approach is nearer to the heart of the matter. However, in *Pragmatism*, especially chapter 6, he professes to approach the nature of truth in the first way. (This is primarily associated with what I have called key ideas (2), (5), and (8), but (6) is also relevant.) Thus the following passage from chapter 1 introduces pragmatism as a method for clarifying the meaning of concepts which is then applied, in chapter 6, to the meaning of truth. (Talk of the meaning of a concept or idea may seem bad grammar. However, it is in line with James's approach. For, as we shall see he tends to think of concepts or ideas as symbols in experience which have a meaning in something like the same sense as words do. Indeed verbal concepts or ideas *are* strings of words.)

---

24   Peirce, V, pp. 248–55.

A glance at the history of the idea will show you still better what pragmatism means.... It was first introduced into philosophy by Mr Charles Peirce in 1878. In an article entitled 'How To Make Our Ideas Clear,' in the 'Popular Science Monthly' for January of that year Mr. Peirce, after pointing out that our beliefs are really rules for action, said that, to develop a thought's meaning, we need only determine what conduct it is fitted to produce: that conduct is for us its sole significance. And the tangible fact at the root of all our thought-distinctions, however subtle, is that there is no one of them so fine as to consist in anything but a possible difference of practice. To attain perfect clearness in our thoughts of an object, then, we need only consider what conceivable effects of a practical kind the object may involve—what sensations we are to expect from it, and what reactions we must prepare. Our conception of these effects, whether immediate or remote, is then for us the whole of our conception of the object, so far as that conception has positive significance at all.

PRAG, p. 46

When he comes to apply this method to the clarification of the concept of truth he begins by saying that there is general agreement that truth is a property of certain human ideas consisting in their 'agreement with reality'.[25] However, the pragmatist will want to know what such agreement really amounts to in practical terms.

We may note in passing that James seems to use the word 'idea' very flexibly, so that sometimes it is equivalent to 'belief' or 'thought' (as an occurrent mental event), sometimes 'proposition', sometimes rather to 'concept' or 'predicate' (said to be 'true' when true of something) either in an occurrent sense to mean one's present conception of something or in some more abstract sense. It would be rather misleading to attempt to put James's position in some more regimented terminology which might emphasise distinctions he would think unhelpful. However, upon the whole the basic truth bearers for him are certain mental states, types or tokens, most often referred to as 'ideas', whose occurrence constitutes one's thinking that something or other is the case.

Saying that a true idea is one which agrees with reality is fair enough, but it really gets us nowhere until we can explain what agreement means here. The popular answer is that agreement is copying. However, it is only a very limited number of ideas whose truth could consist in their being copies of reality. Perhaps our visual images may be, but most of our theories about the world are not simply sensory images of that sort occurring in our minds. Besides, even where our thoughts are in images it is most unsatisfactory to say that they are ever true simply because they are like something out there beyond our minds. There may be all sorts of resemblances between our images and what lies beyond which are quite irrelevant to any truth they may possess.

So expressions like 'agreement' and 'copying' take us little way in understanding the genuine differentia of true ideas. To arrive at this we must take the pragmatic approach.

---

25   See PRAG, p. 198.

Pragmatism . . . asks its usual question. "Grant an idea or belief to be true," it says, "what concrete difference will its being true make in any one's actual life? How will the truth be realized? What experiences will be different from those which would obtain if the belief were false? What, in short, is the truth's cash-value in experiential terms?"

The moment pragmatism asks this question, it sees the answer: *True ideas are those that we can assimilate, validate, corroborate and verify. False ideas are those that we can not.* That is the practical difference it makes to us to have true ideas; that, therefore, is the meaning of truth, for it is all that truth is known-as.

                                                                    PRAG, pp. 200–201

How the notions of validation, corroboration, and verification stand to each other is not crystal clear but the general drift is clear enough, namely, that when we classify ideas as true or false, we do so, not by considering whether they copy, agree, or correspond with anything standing apart from them with which they may be compared, but by considering (1) how far they have led to correct predictions of what there is to be observed under various conditions, (2) how far they have been supported by what has been discovered in other related fields, and (3) how far it has been possible to assimilate them into the main body of knowledge. Closely connected with this is the thought that ideas are classified as true if they imply instructions, which have been found to work, as to what we need to do to get certain desired results. Thus Newton's theory of gravitation is properly called true not because what goes on in the minds of those who affirm it is a likeness of anything out there, but because it promotes their ability to anticipate future experience and deal effectively with the environment, and meshes in harmoniously with the mental activity corresponding to other theories to produce further such successes.

§ So officially this theory of truth is just one special application of the pragmatic theory of meaning on a par with its use to clarify such other problematic concepts as those of energy, matter, soul, or God. However, there is something distinctly odd about this. For what does this special application of the theory add to the theory as it stands at first? In short, what does the pragmatist account of truth add to the pragmatist account of meaning? The former professes to help us grasp what it is for an idea to be true, but has not all it has to tell us in this connection already been said when it told us how to grasp what an idea means?

The trouble arises from the fact that while the concepts of energy, matter, soul, and God do not have to occur in the formulation of the general pragmatist theory of the meaning of concepts, that of truth seemingly does. For pragmatism is 'a method of carrying on abstract discussion', derived from Peirce, according to which '[t]he serious meaning of a concept . . . lies in the concrete difference to someone which its being true will make'.[26] Even if formulations of the pragmatist conception of meaning are possible which do not use the

---

26   MT, p. 37. See also EP, p. 94.

concept of truth explicitly, it is certainly there in the background. Thus if the pragmatist account of the meaning of a concept is formulated as the claim that our concept of an object or phenomenon consists in what sensations we are to expect from it and what reactions we must prepare towards it, that must mean that to understand the concept of the object we must know what to expect in this way if it is true that the object exists, or true that it is present in a certain locus.

Even if it is possible to formulate a pragmatic conception of meaning without express use of the concept of truth James shows no particular concern to do so. Thus he considers a formula of the chemist Ostwald's, which involves the notion of truth, as equivalent to Peirce's.

> To táke in the importance of Peirce's principle, one must get accustomed to applying it to concrete cases. I found a few years ago that Ostwald, the illustrious Leipzig chemist, had been making a perfectly distinct use of the principle of pragmatism in his lectures on the philosophy of science, though he had not called it by that name.
>
> "All realities influence our practice," he wrote me, "and that influence is their meaning for us. I am accustomed to put questions to my classes in this way: In what respects would the world be different if this alternative or that were true? If I can find nothing that would become different, then the alternative has no sense."
>
> PRAG, p. 48[27]

But if the concept of truth must be used in the formulation of the pragmatist conception of truth, it is problematic how it can be one of the concepts whose meaning is to be clarified by the pragmatic method. Thus if one uses the pragmatic method to determine what it means to say that a proposition is true, the answer will be something like this: Ask yourself what difference it makes to expected experience or required action whether it is true that it is true. That can hardly be satisfactory, and, so far as intelligible at all, seems equivalent to saying that the meaning of a proposition is the difference it makes to expected experience or required action whether it is true or not. It is doubtful, then, how far James had a right to approach the question of truth, as he professes to do, as just one more problem for the pragmatic method to resolve.[28]

I am not arguing, as some have done, that the pragmatist conception of meaning depends upon some conception of truth (such as a correspondence one) which implicitly undermines the pragmatic point of view. My point is rather that the pragmatist must find some way, consistent with his general approach, of showing that the concept of truth is not just one concept among others to be analysed by its methods. It must present itself somehow as at once

---

27 Ostwald's formulation only has any bite if 'world' is taken, as doubtless it is meant to be, as equivalent to 'world as we experience it', but this begging of the question is endemic to most verificationism. See section 11 below.

28 See PRAG, pp. 200–201.

a theory of meaning and truth offering a unitary explication of each as part of its central doctrine.

Thus it might be advanced as the thesis that 'true' is the success word applicable to propositions, that the meaning of a proposition is to be identified with the kind of success which is its goal, and that this goal in all acceptable cases is the correct prediction of experiences available or action required in a range of possible experientially identifiable conditions. Something along those lines would recognize the concepts both of truth and meaning as belonging to a different level from those which the pragmatic method is to be used to clarify.

Something of that sort does seem to be the underlying drift of James's thought. But on the surface, at any rate, there is some confusion as to the relation of the theory of truth to that of meaning, especially in PRAG. In the papers collected in MT James is closer to presenting pragmatism as a combined theory of both truth and meaning in a way not far from what I have suggested.

Another way of putting it would be to say that the view at which James is implicitly aiming is one in which the notions of truth (and reference) are basic, and that the meaning of an 'idea' is a matter of the conditions under which it is true. This is perhaps somewhat similar to the views of Donald Davidson, though I cannot explore the matter here.[29] James's main point would then emerge as the claim that ideas are true when they work, while specification of an idea's meaning is specification of the circumstances under which such working will occur.

§ To some extent this combined theory is simply part of that great wave of operationalist and verificationist accounts of meaning and truth which have been so pervasive from the late nineteenth century till quite recently.

James, like others, tends to support pragmatism, on its more verificationist side, by inferring, from the obvious fact that a proposition whose truth or falsehood did not make any difference at all to anything beyond itself must be vacuous, that a proposition whose truth or falsehood does not make a difference to me, in the sense of making a difference to the kind of experience I can expect to have, definitely or conditionally on some other experience, must be vacuous from my point of view. But this is a thoroughly question-begging move from the obvious to the contentious. What is more it only needs to be pushed a little further to lead to the unacceptable solipsism implied in saying that I cannot attach sense to a proposition whose truth or falsehood only makes a difference to the experiences another can expect or have without making a difference to me. One may try to palliate this by saying that facts which are about someone else's experience can make a difference to me insofar as they involve my sympathetic feelings, as facts about, say, mere matter cannot, but this is hardly satisfactory; if states of unexperienced matter can be conceived,

---

29   Certainly his interests are far from the primarily technical one of theorists like Davidson, but partly just for that reason he may get more straightforwardly to the heart of the really philosophical issues.

why should not one care about them? In truth, if a fact about another person's experience can be said to make a difference to me, simply because I may react to my grasp of it or to its manifestations in my experience, then one can say that the existence or otherwise of unexperienceable matter can make a difference to me in the same sense. It will be seen that I endorse James's rejection of the idea of there being things which are utterly unexperienceable (indeed, I would add, as he eventually did 'or utterly unexperienced'), but one cannot base this on grounds as slender as the present.

§ However, James's verificationism and operationalism have deeper sources than this. For one thing, it is just one application of a larger view not shared, or nearly so prominent, in other streams of verificationist thought, that of understanding 'ideas' as biologically or psychologically useful states of the human organism. Thought would not have developed in our species into the complex forms it has unless it was doing us some good, and the promotion of successful prediction and practical know-how is the most obvious benefit it confers. For James, however, there are also other benefits.

For if we ask more generally what the main benefit is which we gain from the ideas we call true, the general answer must be that it lies in their enabling us to cope better with reality. This may be because they advise us of what needs to be done to get, or to avoid, experiences of a type which interest us positively or negatively. But it may also lie in the way in which they provide us with comfort when we feel low or galvanize us into fruitful activity when our spirits are slack. And if ideas which are good for us in the first way are fit to receive the accolade of the success word 'true', why not also the second which can be just as valuable for us? Thus do the grounds for verificationism become grounds for calling ideas true in virtue of other less 'cognitive' services which they may perform.

It is common to contrast James's tough verificationist account of scientific truth with his tender-minded endorsement of forms of religious truth and to see the latter as the weak way out of someone unwilling to be consistently verificationist. But to see James in this way as a kind of failed logical positivist is to ignore the basic consistency of his position. For both follow quite straightforwardly from the basic premiss that ideas are there in the mind to perform a function and are true to the extent that they perform that function effectively.

Although the inspiration behind this functional approach to ideas is partly Darwinian, that is not the whole story. We should remember that James trained as a doctor and had a great concern with problems of health, physical and mental (not least with his own). It is not surprising, then, that he should have favoured an approach to the values to be sought in thinking which stressed their contribution to psychological health.

One could sum up much of this as follows:

1. The truth of an idea must be something worth aiming at.

2. Since it is not worth aiming at what is of no practical benefit, an idea's truth in any reasonable sense must be something somehow thus beneficial.

3. Truth would not be worth aiming at if it consisted in the mere copying of outside things within one's head.

4. It is worth aiming at if it helps us predict and control experience, and ideas which do this deserve the accolade of being called true.

5. It is worth aiming at if it helps comfort or galvanize us, and ideas which do this deserve the accolade of being called true.

6. It is even up to a point worth aiming at if it is simply pleasing. So ideas which are simply pleasing have some *prima facie* case for being called true.

7. However, none of these things are worth achieving at too great a cost to the rest of what we need for a satisfactory life, so ideas which are beneficial in any of these ways only in the very short term, and which frustrate longer-term benefits obtainable from other ideas, should be rejected and stigmatized as false. This is as much as to say that true ideas must be assimilable into a total system of ideas which is beneficial as a whole. This is unlikely to be true of ideas whose only positive benefit is their immediate pleasurableness. So this provides only the slightest *prima facie* case for calling them true.

We may add that James seems somewhat ambivalent as to the extent to which calling someone's idea true implies only that it is beneficial for him in the long term, or whether it implies that it is in the long-term interests of society as a whole that he or others should have such an idea. Upon the whole, he seems to think that we can form the concept of a kind of absolute truth consisting in ideas which, once discovered, will remain forever afterwards of benefit to humanity, but that for most purposes we should be content to look for ideas of benefit to ourselves and those with whom we share them in the shorter term. Such ideas are now true in the sense most appropriate for ordinary purposes and we can call them so without claiming that they will always remain so. (However, we will see later that James effectively also had room for a much more realist conception of a truth which would be absolute in contrast to the merely work-a-day value which is good enough for most purposes.)

§9. *No Truth without Thinking: No Need to Think of an Unthought Truth Lurking over Reality*

The seventh key idea which I listed as contributory to the development of James's pragmatic conception of truth was to the effect that truth is a property of thoughts and, therefore, cannot exist apart from thinking. According to James, those who insist that it can are simply confusing truth and reality. There may well be realities with their own independent being and character such as are not adequately grasped in any thought, but there cannot be unthought truth about them. To suppose that the mere being of things brings truth with it is to imagine some kind of ghostly transcript of reality looming over it and copying it in another medium in a manner of which we can form no clear conception. The only report upon a reality which can be called a truth about it is that which exists as an idea in a mind.[30]

---

30   However, James does not stick consistently to this sharp contrast between reality

This is a very differently flavoured leading idea from most of the others. In itself it poses no threat to the equivalence requirement and is, indeed, common ground with a realist like G. E. Moore.

The challenge to a correspondence theory only comes when James insists further that the truth of an idea cannot consist merely in its somehow copying its object. (Put in this way ideas figure as concepts true of objects rather than true propositions. However, if ideas are taken as propositions, the point will be that their truth does not consist in their copying something external to them called a 'fact'.) Why would truth matter, either to us or as an enrichment to the universe, if it were the mere reproduction inside us of something already there outside? If truth is the significant value it is normally considered, it must pertain to ideas in virtue of some more worthwhile feature than that. It must turn, in fact, upon their somehow helping us cope with the realities with which they are said to agree. Certainly this may sometimes be because they copy them in a map-like way (though even then they are only true, just as maps are only maps, because we use them as a guide to coping with what they copy). But in other cases they fulfil the same role of helping us cope with the realities they concern without being in any sense copies thereof, for example by stimulating helpful behavioural responses to them.

§10. *Ideas May Help Bring About Their Own Truth Conditions*

§ The eighth leading idea (that the point of thought is not to copy reality but to relate us to it fruitfully) has cropped up continually in our discussion of the others.[31] But there is an aspect of it which requires further attention, namely James's enthusiastic belief in the power of hopeful and vigorous thought to make radical changes in people's personalities. Here James was the psychologist with a message of personal improvement by optimistic styles of thought.

---

and truth. See, for example, 'Does Consciousness Exist?' in ERE, p. 24. Such inconsistency is probably inadvertent. Certainly his dominant view is that truth, as something other than true thought with a real psychological existence, is a vaguely conceived third form of being whose postulation is vacuous. To say, as Marcus Ford does (in his excellent commentary on James), that he is simply confusing truth with knowledge does not do justice to the force of this point. [See Ford, p. 66.] Ford is mainly concerned to argue that James's conception of truth is at bottom a realist one. I agree that it is more 'realist' than is sometimes supposed, as I try to bring out in this chapter. But this is a separate question. To say that truth can only exist in the form of actual thought leaves it open what it is for thought to be true.

31   This leading idea is given a classic expression in 'Reflex Action and Theism'. 'The willing department of our nature, in short, dominates both the conceiving department and the feeling department; or, in plainer English, perception and thinking are only there for behavior's sake.' [WB, p. 114]

James, indeed, had considerable sympathy with the Mind Cure or New Thought movement of his day (a popular philosophy of self-improvement with an appeal comparable to that of Transcendental Meditation today) which urged people to deal with their troubles by cheerful positive thinking and optimistic meditation.[32] The belief was that you can become a more competent and confident person by thinking that you are so. Although James stressed that there were limitations to this gospel of healthy-mindedness (akin in some respects to the muscular Christianity of Charles Kingsley) he shared a good deal of its contempt for 'the pining, puling, mumping mood' of the dissatis-fied.[33] Thus when James contended that thought is not so much there to report the world as to mould it, he was closer to this psychology of personal self improvement than to any Marxist recommendation concerning the social goals of thought.

Thus in thinking about what sort of person one is, one should not simply try to register some pre-existent fact. For it is part of the process whereby one makes oneself what one is. The same is true of facts about one's relation to others. If in thinking about the degree of one's friendship with another, one tries merely to register pre-existent fact, one loses the chance of making the relationship nearer to what it should be, as experienced by the other as well as oneself. This suggestion has wide ramifications. It suggests the dangers of educational streaming which produces the facts it purports to be based on and in general the importance of individuals and institutions being guided by self-images of a desirable kind.

Probably James's position on these matters exaggerates the effectiveness of such positive thinking. More important, for the theory of truth, these facts, such as they are, can be stated in ways which do not threaten a correspondence theory of truth. It is important, however, to recognize this as another source of the pragmatist conception thereof.

§ It is arguable that James is concerned here with facts about the psychology of *will* rather than of cognition. For in *will* we do have ideas which tend to make themselves true by passing into activity likely to actualise them. Or such is James's own account of *will* (and that of Bradley too), and personally I agree with it. However, it is only certain sorts of ideas which have this power; the standard assumption, at least, is that it is possessed only by ideas which (a) are about the future and (b) are about events which can arise or not according as to how my body moves about. Perhaps what James is really doing when he insists that we should not think of truth as pre-existent but rather as something to be made, is insisting that the power of the *will* extends further than we commonly realize, and that we commonly fail to tap it by not appreciating its extent. For example, to a great extent the truth about our own personality and relationships with others may be produced by our ideas of them.

---

32   See VRE, IV and V, particularly pp. 118–26; also WB, p. 259 et ff.
33   See VRE, p. 89.

Not that saying this necessarily conflicts with the standard conception of the power of *will*. For if our ideas of our own personality and relationship with others can realize themselves, they must do this largely through the mediation of standard bodily movements. Still, a conventional account of *will* may overlook this, and in any case there are aspects of our self-creation which may not be thus mediated by overt movement (even if the alteration will ultimately express itself in this).

At any rate, if *will* consists in ideas which make themselves true, James is not wrong to relate this point to his account of truth. However, he confuses things by not distinguishing clearly between the claim that the power of *will* in a quite ordinary sense is much greater than is ordinarily thought and the much bolder claim that cognitive enquiry quite properly as much creates its object as discovers it.

§ James does, however, want to make this bolder claim too. For he is also concerned to claim that in forming our conception of the reality in which we live we are to some great extent creating a world out of raw material which could have been used to create quite different worlds, and that our desires should have their say in this task if we are to have the one most worth living in.

His suggestion that even the truth of one religious hypothesis as against another can be a matter for us to decide, is certainly surprising. Can the existence or nonexistence of God really be open to settlement by our way of thinking about the world? Is this not too reminiscent of Tinker Bell's appeal in *Peter Pan* to children to believe in fairies in order to save them from extinction?[34]

Of course, it depends what is meant by the existence of God. If God is supposed to be a genuine mind or spirit with his own independent thoughts and experiences, the idea that he can be created by our belief in him is absurd. If on the other hand his existence means something like the final victory of good, then perhaps it can partly be created by our belief in it as can sometimes the rosiness or otherwise of our personal futures. Considerable confusion follows from James's shifting between these two different interpretations of the theistic claim.

The idea that thought may create its own truth has another striking application to the facts of history. We may agree that there is indeed much in the idea that choice between rival interpretations of the past is not so much a matter of surmising which duplicates something already there but of constructing alternative *gestalten* with different messages for the future. But surely one cannot dissolve the past entirely into subsequent interpretation. That there were individuals who thought, felt, and moved in certain definite ways is a matter of known or unknown fact about which our judgements are simply right or wrong, however much what it all added up to may be a matter which can only be determined subsequently. (Even though there are views about the content

---

34   See, for example, WB, p. 61.

of thought, not too far from James's own, which make this a matter of subsequent interpretation or upshot, there must be some level at which what
occurred in a stream of consciousness is a matter of sheer fact, though this has
been denied, amazingly enough, in our own time.[35]) Thus here again James
rides roughshod over too many important distinctions when he insists on the
extent to which it is for thought to decide, rather than find out, what shall be
true.

There is something in common between this aspect of James's pragmatism
and the views of Sartre. For Sartre it is human projects which settle how things
were and are, by carving out units in reality relevant to our projects. But the
rather breezy optimism of James is alien to Sartre, who would surely consider
that James's enthusiasm for positive thinking often showed a failure to note the
dangers of 'bad faith'.

Though James often sounds the note of thought as reality-creating, he also
warns against the excesses of such an approach on the part of such fellow
pragmatists or humanists as F. C. S. Schiller.

> I myself have never thought of humanism as being subjectivist farther than to
> this extent, that, inasmuch as it treats the thinker as being himself one portion
> of reality, it must also allow that *some* of the realities that he declares for true
> are created by his being there. Such realities of course are either acts of his, or
> relations between other things and him or relations between things, which, but
> for him, would never have been traced. Humanists are subjectivistic, also in
> this, that, unlike rationalists (who think they carry a warrant for the absolute
> truth of what they now believe in in their present pocket), they hold all present
> beliefs as subject to revision in the light of future experience. The future
> experience, however, may be of things outside the thinker; and that this is so
> the humanist may believe as freely as any other kind of empiricist philosopher.
> 'Humanism and Truth Once More' (1905), ERE, p. 251

§11. *There Is Nothing but Experience*

The sixth key idea affirmed that facts which do not concern actual or possible
experiences are vacuous. James seems to hover between taking this as ontology
and taking it as a principle of meaningfulness, as a factual claim about the world
and as a claim about what it is to understand a factual statement.

Thus at times he appears to hold by the verificationist idea that to think of
any way things might be is to think of the kinds of experiences its being so
would make available for oneself, or at least for someone whose experiences
one can imagine. Thus taken, it is rather one way of interpreting what pragmatism is than a source of it. What it comes to is that to think something is the case
simply is to have certain expectations as to what one would experience under

---

35   See Dennett, chapters IV and V, e.g., at p. 136.

a variety of specifiable circumstances. This is close to the logical positivism of such thinkers as Schlick and Ayer, who would have always denied that it amounted to an ontological thesis. A good formulation is the following:

> The pragmatic rule is that the meaning of a concept may always be found, if not in some sensible particular which it directly designates, then in some particular difference in the course of human experience which its being true will make. Test every concept by the question "What sensible difference to anybody will its truth make?" and you are in the best possible position for understanding what it means and for discussing its importance.
>
> SPP, p. 60

James differs, however, from logical positivists in his readiness to relate his pragmatism to an explicitly ontological claim to the effect that reality is entirely composed of experience, or at least that any reality in which we have any good reason for believing is so. The expression 'radical empiricism' is sometimes used as a name for this doctrine, but since it also has other meanings, I shall for now call this doctrine 'panexperientialism'. According to this doctrine, if one concentrates one's attention on the flow of one's own experience, one will find an exemplar of the basic nature of the stuff of reality in general. All else that there is is stuff of the same general sort, however different in detail. The most general characteristics we can find of our experience are echoed in everything real.

Such a contention is, of course, at the heart of most forms of idealism. It is certainly central to Bradley's form thereof and the respective uses to which our two philosophers put this common commitment is one main subject of this book. Our main investigation of James's version of it will be in chapters 3 and 4. We shall see that there are two rather different directions in which this thesis leads him. At times it points him towards a tough-minded pragmatic account of truth and meaning close to the verificationism of logical positivists. But at other times it points him towards a bold metaphysics, quite remote from anything which a verificationist would favour, according to which nature at large is somehow experiential in its inner being. (Which path is followed turns largely on how far it is being supposed that one can make sense of the idea of experiences of a type one could not live through while remaining oneself.) At present we are concerned with it only as a background to the pragmatic account of meaning and truth.

A useful statement of the relation between pragmatism and panexperientialism is this:

> The pragmatic method starts from the postulate that there is no difference of truth that doesn't make a difference of fact somewhere; and it seeks to determine the meaning of all differences of opinion by making the discussion hinge as soon as possible upon some practical or particular issue. The principle of pure experience is also a methodical postulate. Nothing shall be admitted as fact, it says, except what can be experienced at some definite time by some experient; and for every feature of fact ever so experienced, a definite place

must be found somewhere in the final system of reality. In other words: Everything real must be experienceable somewhere, and every kind of thing experienced must somewhere be real.

'The Experience of Activity' (January 1905), ERE, pp. 159–60

Even when primarily associated with the pragmatic doctrine of truth and meaning James's panexperientialism is not so much a misleadingly ontological way of presenting it as it is a metaphysical view which he holds on partly independent grounds and which lends added support to it. But what are these grounds? Well, essentially it seems that James regards it as a postulate, or hypothesis, through which we make the best sense of the universe we can. Thus he is not a dogmatic panexperientialist, dismissing all possibility of there being anything other than experience. Yet he insists that we have no ground for believing in anything not composed of experience and that there is nothing else which can be of any conceivable concern to us. If there is anything else, it need not figure in as theoretically complete and as practically comprehensive an account of reality as we can have any grounds for seeking. We may add, I believe, that despite his explicitly allowing the bare possibility of things in themselves of a non-experiential nature he is strongly inclined to regard the very idea of *being* as inseparable from that of *being felt* and the postulation of any other type of being as vacuous. (If the ontological claim is based partly on the vacuity of any alternative, it may be said that it is being derived from a theory of meaning. But the claim that one thinks nothing genuine, and therefore nothing which can be true, if one affirms the existence of what is in no way experienced, need not derive from a theory of meaning laid down in advance as a method for clarifying meanings or exposing nonsense.)

Insofar as panexperientialism and pragmatism are associated it is hard to say which is the premiss and which the conclusion. Is it because truth has to be useful in a way which this precludes that propositions not cashable in experiential terms are dismissed as meaningless? Or is it because there is nothing but experience that propositions which profess to guide us in our relations with anything else are without point? The answer must be surely that each reinforces the other without either having priority. If so, panexperientialism functions partly as one source of the pragmatic account of truth.

It might lead to it through the following reflections. If there is nothing but experience, then there is nothing which true ideas can tell us about except experiential facts. Now assume that there are no experiential facts except those which concern the actual or possible experiences of beings such as ourselves. Then true ideas will be those which can inform us of such facts. It is not a long step from this to saying that true ideas are those which might serve us (or might have done so in the past) as useful guides (and false ideas those which would let us down as such) to what experiences we may expect absolutely, or on condition of having had or given ourselves certain other experiences, and that ideas are only meaningful if they can be assessed for their truth or falsehood in this sense.

It is to be noted that such a formulation allows that ideas can be true not merely as telling us what we will experience but as telling us what we *would* experience under various experiential circumstances more or less under our control. It follows that an exhaustive account of all experiences to come, or perhaps present, past, and future, would not exhaust truth. In short, some truths, expressed in basic experiential terms, are irreducibly conditional. This is formally compatible with the experientialist thesis that there is nothing actual but actual experience, yet it does not sit altogether easily with it. After all, a possibility, or the holding of a conditional truth, is not an experience and in a world of nothing but actual experience it is not clear to what reality propositions of an irreducibly conditional character are relating. One who thinks that nothing actual exists except actual experience, on the ground that nothing else is imaginable, is likely to find possibilities suspect too. Certainly there is considerable difficulty in knowing how their kind of quasi-being is to be imagined.[36] For Peirce, indeed, belief in irreducible conditionals was an important part of pragmatism. And James himself often goes along with the appeal to conditionals to elucidate the meaning of various ordinary statements. Yet he seems never to have been quite at ease with this. That, as we shall see, is one reason why his panexperientialism developed into panpsychism.[37] (It is worth recalling, in this connection that Peirce tended to identify realism with a belief in the holding of irreducible conditionals—though confusingly enough he was more keen to represent it as realism about the physical than about conditionals.)

§12. *Does Pragmatism Deny that There Is a Way Things Really Are?*

The ninth proposition listed on page 11 was this:

(9) There is no way things really are, just the way humans, more or less usefully to themselves, think they are.

However, I did not list this as one of the actual sources of pragmatism but only as a view which James sometimes seems to have held, leaving it open whether he really did so. We must now consider whether he did hold it.

It would certainly be wrong to ascribe any opinion to James which implied that thought is wholly the creator of its objects in the way in which it is possibly for some extreme idealists (Fichte perhaps). For the basic doctrine of pragma-

---

36　See Sprigge, *Facts*, pp. 274–96.
37　An alternative might have been to invoke the perceptions of a Berkeleyan God as the categorical basis of these conditionals. See Grayling, *Berkeley*, pp. 102–6. But James seems never to have found this option attractive; perhaps such a God seemed too like the Absolute for comfort; he certainly poses in some ways an even more resistant problem of evil. See my *Vindication*, pp. 90–92.

tism is that the point of thought is to promote adjustment to reality in whatever character it possesses, and that it is true to the extent that this adjustment is successful.

Still, there are three claims of James's which might be said to support some version of proposition (9).

(a) First, there is the point discussed in section 10, that our ideas have much more to do with determining how things are than we are inclined to allow. Sometimes this is put in a way which suggests that nature is so much in the making that we should not think in terms of there being a way things are which it is the job of our ideas to copy.

That those ideas of the future which constitute our volitions partly create their objects is obvious enough but we saw that James contends that many ideas which are normally thought of as cognitive rather than conative are similarly creative (at least to an extent) of their objects. This claim is not too perplexing when it is only a reminder of such facts as that moral laziness may encourage us to think of our own personality or relations with others as more fixed in character than it is. However, we saw him moving into stranger waters with his suggestion that even the overall character of the cosmos may be in process of determination by how we react upon it. This is fair enough if it is only the common-sense point that history is still in the making and that as a result even the significance of what has already occurred is not yet settled. However, James seems to think, more strangely, that religious belief may somehow help bring about the reality of its own objects. We have sufficiently considered this point already. It certainly does not represent any kind of wholesale support for proposition (9).

(b) The expression 'a way things are' suggests that the reality to which thought adjusts us exists in a propositional form properly caught in 'that' clauses, apart from our thinking. James certainly rejects this, holding rather that reality is just there, being what it is, and only takes on propositional form in our ideas of it. This does perhaps give a sense in which he asserts proposition (9).

This is closely related to the selective character of thought in virtue of which it cannot attend to everything but must carve reality up or organize its phenomena into patterns in ways which reflect its own concerns rather than any independently possessed articulation. And since our concerns differ we tend to different, often equally legitimate, ways of conceiving the world, which cannot be synthesised into one single theory. James emphasises this particularly in relation to the contrast between scientific and religious accounts of reality, adding in a note to the following passage that it is an open question whether there might ever be a single conceptual scheme holding all such presently alternative systems in unity.

> What, in the end, are all our verifications but experiences that agree with more or less isolated systems of ideas (conceptual systems) that our minds have framed? But why in the name of common-sense need we assume that only one such system of ideas can be true? The obvious outcome of our total experience is that the world can be handled according to many systems of ideas, and is so handled by different men, and will each time give some characteristic kind of

profit, for which he cares, to the handler, while at the same time some other kind of profit has to be omitted or postponed. Science gives to all of us telegraphy, electric lighting, and diagnosis, and succeeds in preventing and curing a certain amount of disease. Religion in the shape of mind-cure [a type of religious movement he is discussing] gives to some of us serenity, moral poise, and happiness, and prevents certain forms of disease as well as science does, or even better in a certain class of persons. Evidently, then, the science and the religion are both of them genuine keys for unlocking the world's treasure-house to him who can use either of them practically. Just as evidently neither is exhaustive or exclusive of the other's simultaneous use. And why after all, may not the world be so complex as to consist of many interpenetrating spheres of reality, which we can thus approach in alternation by using different conceptions and assuming different attitudes . . . ? On this view religion and science, each verified in its own way from hour to hour and from life to life, would be co-eternal.

VRE, pp. 122–23

If his opinion that reality lends itself to radically different forms of conceptualisation and is not propositionally organized in itself means that James in a manner affirms proposition (9), he does so in a form of it which is quite compatible with the following realistic sounding proposition.

(10) Thought is for the most part concerned with a reality which possesses its own being and character independently of it.

It would be a mistake to see James's panexperientialism as inimical to proposition (10). The experience which James thinks the fundamental reality is not some kind of cosmic thought which creates its own objects.[38]

(c) A third way in which James might seem to affirm proposition (9) is in his insistence that thought is not merely the reproduction of its object but a fresh reality in its own right. In thinking about a reality we do not live through it but through our own symbolic processes, and these are as much a fresh contribution to what there is as a copy of that which they concern. Here again, even if this represents a partial affirmation of (9), it is in a form which leaves the realist proposition (10) unchallenged. There is no question of his contending that thinking is the determinant of how things are in any radically subjectivist manner.

---

38 The matter is somewhat complicated however. When panexperientialism leads James to think of the existence of physical objects as constituted by the holding of conditional propositions, physical reality does seem to become inherently propositional in character. And if propositions can only exist for thought, that would seem to make physical reality thought dependent. However, his discontent with appeal to conditional truths in this connection can be seen as reflecting a much more basic commitment to proposition (10), taken as concerning an independent reality which is not inherently propositional.

If one wishes to see a pragmatist theory which really did get close to denying that thought is ever concerned with a reality with its own independent character, one should turn to James's one conspicuous British disciple, F. C. S. Schiller. For Schiller

> the truth is that the nature of things is not *determinate* but *determinable*, like that of our fellow-men. Previously to trial it is indeterminate, not merely for our ignorance, but really and from every point of view, within limits which it is our business to discover. It grows determinate by our experiments, like human character.
>
> Schiller, Humanism, p. 12, note

James liked to see pragmatism as a great transforming movement sweeping all in its path in every philosophising country. Thus he exchanged continual chortles of mutual praise with Schiller and other pragmatists (such as Papini in Italy) across the world.[39] In consequence, affinities were emphasised and contrasts played down. In fact, Schiller give a much more sweeping licence for believing what one wishes and calling it true than James ever did.

Of the various background ideas which developed together into James's pragmatic account of meaning and truth the one I would most stress is the account of intending which James developed partly to meet Royce's challenge.[40] This account certainly disturbs our usual sense of the way in which thought stands to its objects, for it seems to render its relation to them singularly opaque, but it is not a challenge to the idea that it has independent objects. (Quite what the independent objects are, in the light of the sixth of the background ideas I have listed, is another matter, which we will consider more fully in chapters 3 and 4.)

§13. *Formulation of the Pragmatic Theory of Truth*

§ If these seemingly rather disparate ideas are the sources of James's pragmatic conception of truth (and also meaning and reference), how far is the resultant theory coherent, and how far satisfactory?

At its heart is the belief that human thought consists in the occurrence in consciousness of certain mental items which we can call ideas. These may consist in images or they may consist in verbal noises, externally vocalised or internally felt.[41] And maybe there are other sorts of ideas too. However, there is nothing to these ideas, considered just as elements in the stream of conscious-

---

39   See Perry, II, chapters LXXVII, LXXVIII, LXXIX, LXXX, LXXXIV.
40   See section 7 above.
41   See PP, I, pp. 265–66, 269; PP, II, chapter XVIII; BC, chapter XIX, e.g., p. 309; ERE, p. 30; SPP, pp 58–60. See also letter to Helen Keller, Perry, II, p. 455. For a contrasting emphasis on the superior adequacy of imagery see, for example, ER, p. 30.

ness, which gives them any meaning or any reference, specific or general, to things beyond them.[42] They are just experiences which we live through as we do through dumb aches and pains and other sensory experiences. Thus they have no inherent aboutness or 'intentionality' (though we have seen that these should not be identified too readily).[43] Yet they do have meaning and reference. A naive view would be that this turns on their resemblance to things beyond present consciousness; however, resemblance to their objects is just an occasional aid to the factors which really determine their relation to them. These factors are their causal powers, in virtue of which each prepares us to behave in certain ways should we be confronted with a certain object, objects, or sort of object (to which in virtue of this they refer) as well as promoting or otherwise such confrontation. And insofar as the action for which they thus prepare us actually occurs and represents a successful adaptation to the relevant objects they merit the title of 'true' in a primary sense, while insofar as there is reason to think that it would be successful if it did occur they merit that title in a secondary sense. (The implication seems to be that all ideas are true to some degree. For an idea can only have a definite reference and meaning, and thus be an idea, if it is sufficiently helpful in preparing us for encounters with some object or type of object to be about it. Falsehood must consist in a balance of harm in the adaptive behaviour for which an idea prepares us.)

This is a fair summary of the upshot of much that James says (though it partly resolves and partly leaves standing certain vaguenesses or ambiguities in

---

42   Hilary Putnam says that Wittgenstein was the first to realize the enormous significance of the fact that even mental images are not inherently referential. [See Putnam, *Reason*, p. 3.] However, this fact, or claim, is central to James's pragmatism. James is attacking what Putnam calls a 'magical theory of reference' and reaching conclusions quite like Putnam's. And Bradley raised objections with which arguably neither has the resources to cope, though James at least makes an effort to do so. See further at note 149 to Part Two, Chapter Two.

43   The brunt of Pratt's excellent critique of James [see note 4 above] is the perverseness of the pragmatist's attempt to explain truth and knowledge without granting genuine transcendency or aboutness to thought. For Pratt, in contrast, ideas are judgements with an assertive force and a self-transcendency which belongs to their inherent nature. He notes that the peculiarities of pragmatism stem from its thinking of the ideas which are the bearers of truth not as judgements but as mere psychical events but he thinks of this as an obvious mistake on the pragmatist's part and apparently did not think that it posed any deep challenge to the notion of an intrinsic aboutness. [See Pratt, pp. 112 and 139–41.] As a result he fails to appreciate the brilliance with which James tries to develop a view of thought, truth, and knowledge which refuses to take aboutness for granted. There is a real analogy in James's view of the meaning, reference, and truth of ideas with the Wittgensteinian view, supported by more recent so-called externalist views of mental content, that the fact that I am thinking something is not a fact about what is going on inside me either physically or mentally, but about how what is going on inside me relates in a behavioural way to what lies beyond.

James's formulations). And unless further qualifications are added it has some strange implications. In particular it suggests the idea (which Wittgenstein supported explicitly) that even God could not read off what one is thinking merely from the contents of one's current consciousness.

§ Although James is bound to the thesis that the full sense and reference of an idea is not displayed in our experience in its initial occurrence he sometimes tries to palliate the conclusion that it is settled by something quite external to the way in which we experience it.[44] He does so by claiming that insofar as this meaning and reference are actually cashed, we actually do experience the passage from idea to object (and our response thereto) and the control which the idea has over the whole process. Thus there is a felt continuity of feeling between the original idea and the consummatory behaviour in virtue of which it has the meaning and reference which it does have.

The main problem about this theory is as to exactly *when* the passage from the idea to this consummatory experience of encounter with its object is felt (in those primary cases where the reference is actually cashed). Consider the idea as it first occurs. The theory is meant to explain what it is for that idea to be the thought that such and such is the case, as well as what it is for such a thought to be true. Call the idea on its first occurrence A, and call the final consummatory encounter and behaviour Q. Then James's claim is that we actually experience the passage from A to Q through the intervening experiences B, C, D . . .

But surely we can only be said to actually experience this passage in the quite untypical case in which it falls within a single specious present. Even if we somehow experience the passage from one specious present to another, we can hardly experience a series of such passages. So it is difficult to see how the passage from original thought to the objects it concerns can really be said to be experienced in such cases as must provide the paradigm of an idea putting us into relation with an object.[45]

James would reply by claiming that the experience of next to next over a long passage constitutes a real experience of that passage. I do not think this satisfactory, for, as has often been said, a series of experiences is not an experience of a series; indeed, it is not an experience at all. But be this as it may, James believed that the continuity of experience was such that he could qualify an account which otherwise seems to make the relation between thought and its object excessively external by insisting that we can actually experience the passage from idea to a consummatory encounter with its object. Thus the position he is aiming for lies mid-way between the view common in his time—that thought somehow leaps beyond itself to its object by some mysteri-

---

44   More substantial qualifications to this thesis are considered in later chapters.
45   James would have surely resisted inclusion of idea and its referent in one specious present as the paradigm, for that would have been to play straight back into Royce's claim that truth, sense, and meaning can only be explained by the inclusion of all thoughts and their objects in a single state of absolute consciousness.

ous self-transcendency—and certain views of our own time about *de re* thought for which its reference to its object is not a feature of our subjectivity at all.

§ If an idea is a psychological occurrent then two people cannot have the same idea. And if ideas are beliefs, the same applies to beliefs. But such an implication seems unacceptable and there is little suggestion that James wished to promote it. So it seems that for an exact statement of his view he should have distinguished between idea tokens and idea types and said that two people have the same belief when they have idea tokens of the same idea type. However, it would not be enough that they were of some identical type or other. Being of the same sensory type would not do. They must be of the same meaning type.

For James there are both verbal ideas and image ideas. Superficially the problem of sorting out verbal tokens seems easier than sorting out image tokens. But that is only because we readily assume that with speakers of the same language linguistic tokens of the same sensory type will be tokens of the same meaning type. The real question, then, is what it is for two idea or belief tokens to be so much the same in meaning that they can both count as the same idea or belief in a type sense. From James's point of view this would have to consist in the fact that they promote the same sort of behaviour towards the same sort of objects. Thus two tokens very different in sensory character could be instances of the same idea or belief in the type sense. This is, indeed, a point which James himself especially emphasised in PP.[46]

A full elaboration of a James-type theory of ideas and beliefs would have to go into such matters much more fully. It would need to take into account not simply the behavioural effects of each 'idea' taken singly, but the way in which our ideas make up a system position within which is crucial to the identity of each. It would also need to take account of the sense in which an idea may be a historical continuant with a characteristic influence on the life of an individual or community as a whole. But although James is very vague on matters of this sort, that does not show that his conception of ideas or beliefs is wrong in principle.

However, explicit appeal to the type/token distinction would have clarified certain points. Thus he insists at times on its being a contingent fact that an idea has the meaning and reference which it does. Here he must mean an idea token, specified not in terms of the meaning type to which it belongs, but simply as a sensory occurrence in the stream of consciousness. Thus the item in my stream of consciousness which is my occurrent thought that James (for most of his life) had a beard is a sensory item which only has that meaning in virtue of certain external and contingent behavioural effects which in some way (only vaguely suggested in James's account) adapt me suitably to that feature of James and, were my locus in the world different, could have guided me to a successful encounter with it.

---

46   See chapter IX, pp. 264–71 and chapter XVIII passim.

§ Escaping from these subtleties, we may sum up by saying that ideas (on James's view) have meaning, reference, and truth or falsehood in virtue of the way in which they mould behaviour in more or less successful ways towards certain things. This does not depend on their copying or mapping their objects, although sometimes—as often in the case of images—their doing so may be an ingredient in the way in which they adjust our behaviour to them.

Prima facie, the successful adaptive behaviour promoted by ideas which are true may be of two different types. First, it seems that they may be successful by pointing us to the means most effective for pursuing our goals. Secondly, they may be successful in the sense of promoting emotions either satisfying in themselves or invigorating behaviourally. Commentators on James often conclude that he believes in two different sorts of truth, appropriate to two different sorts of idea, which may be called cognitive and non-cognitive ideas respectively. To the first class are supposed to belong scientific theories and much matter of fact opinion. To the second class are supposed to belong moral and religious beliefs.

Such an interpretation is given by A. J. Ayer, and by Graham Bird in their commentaries on James.[47]

Ayer rightly emphasises the point that James thought of pragmatism as a compromise between, or synthesis of, tough-mindedness and tender-mindedness and that central to this goal was his wishing to allow a place to religious belief.[48] As Ayer sees it, James is able to do this because he effectively thinks of there being three kinds of truth: (1) that which pertains to a proposition because it is empirically verifiable—this is the kind of truth proper to scientific claims and ordinary statements of fact; (2) that which pertains to a proposition because it follows from our concern with consistency—this is the kind of truth proper to logic and mathematics; (3) that which pertains to a proposition because it satisfies our emotional and practical natures—this is the kind of truth proper in morality and religion.

This interpretation brings James quite near to logical positivism (understood in a broad sense to cover, for example, Ayer's work as a whole) on the meaning and possible truth of propositions of the first two types. (Provided we remember that, as noted above, James uses 'verifiable' to mean such as *would* be confirmed as true by observation, while the logical positivist uses it to mean what *could* be found true by observation.) In fact, if the logical positivist countenances emotive meaning, perhaps their views would not be so very different on the third type.

Such an account is designed to clear James of the charge that he thought one

---

47   See Ayer, *Origins*, and Bird.
48   The distinction between tough-minded and tender-minded philosophers and the role of pragmatism as mediator between them is made in chapter one of PRAG. Incidentally, I have examined the extent to which Ayer is a paradigm case of the former in 'A. J. Ayer: An Appreciation of his Philosophy' in *Utilitas*, Spring, 1990.

could properly call true any belief which was emotionally satisfying. It has always seemed easy to make pragmatism look absurd taken like this. If Ayer is right, James would agree as to the absurdity of this in the case of straight factual statements and claim it at most (and in fact with various qualifications) for religious and moral claims.

But this reading of James is hardly correct. There is no sign that James did, in fact, think religious or moral propositions of a quite different kind from scientific ones; indeed, he argues explicitly for the contrary. On the one hand, he insists on the relevance of experience, that is, religious and moral experience, to the determination of truth in religion and morality. And on the other, he is concerned to interpret both the meaning and truth of the claims Ayer would regard as factual by reference to their function as instruments for helping us obtain the kinds of experiences we want.

The truth seems to be that what Ayer lists as three types of truth are for James rather three conditions which are relevant to the assessment of the truth of any idea whatever. And that James speaks rather of 'ideas' than propositions is important, for truth-bearers for him are essentially certain mental phenomena which help the individual deal with the environment in ways which forward its welfare. The way in which scientific and religious ideas are true, so far as they are true, is not essentially different. None have meaning except as mental events which promote certain behavioural patterns, and to speak of them as true or false is to opine as to the helpfulness to the individual's welfare of the behaviour they promote.

The fact is that there is a failure here to see how bound up James's account of truth is with a view of reference and meaning designed to counter Royce's claim that they can only be explained by appeal to the unity of our thought and its objects in the Absolute.

Bird similarly makes constant use of a distinction between so-called cognitive and so-called non-cognitive beliefs in discussing James. Thus he claims that, when James says that the pragmatic difference between materialism and spiritualism is that the latter is a doctrine of promise, he is making the difference between them affective rather than cognitive.[49] This misses the point in the particular case, that there is an empirical difference, as James sees it, between a universe which will finally fulfil our main hopes and one which will not, so that the difference is not just how we feel about a universe whose character is not in question.

However, the attempt to foist a distinction between cognitive and non-cognitive ideas on James is more deeply flawed than merely inadequate for certain examples, and there is little sign that James wished to make any sharp distinction of this kind.[50] What is more, his general theory seems neither to require it or even to supply a comfortable home for it.

---

49 See Bird, p. 25.
50 In this connection consider the quotation from VRE in the last section. See further

If such a distinction were to be made in terms acceptable to James, it would have to be done somewhat like this. Some ideas put us in effective contact with (what are therefore) their objects because they prompt us to pursue our goals in ways which take account of their character. Thus someone who has correct ideas of how his car works is more likely to get to the end of his journey successfully (when the car goes wrong) than someone who does not. Or again someone is more likely to get to the end of his journey correctly if he has correct ideas as to the geographical relations between his starting point and destination. Ideas which are candidates for a success of this kind can be called cognitive and cognitively true if they actually are thus successful or have the potential for being so.

In contrast would stand ideas of another kind which may be called non-cognitive. From a Jamesian perspective the success which would earn them the title of truth would be of two not sharply distinct types. First they may be of value to us simply in the sense that they produce feelings of satisfaction not outweighed by any harm they do. (Since the harm would most obviously consist in damaging misinformation of a cognitive kind, reference to it already breaks down the cognitive/non-cognitive distinction.) Second, they might produce emotions which energise us to more vigorous and confident, and therefore effective, behaviour in pursuit of our goals, without pointing out the means to these. Of these two James would certainly think the second the more important.

If James had meant to distinguish between cognitive and non-cognitive truth, his use of the same word in each case would not be unjustifiable. For in each case the idea's truth would consist in its promotion, actual or potential, of successful action. Still, there would be an important difference in the way in which they did this.

But it is doubtful if his pragmatism can make much final sense of the distinction. Its intention is to contrast ideas which are useful because they provide correct information about what must be done to get a certain result, and those which are useful as energizing stimuli to action. But both these seem equally a matter of the ideas promoting activity which will be successful in getting us what we want. Correct ideas about the workings of a car are true because they promote movements with one of the characteristics conducive to the end, and ideas which help us to obtain what we want by being more energetic promote activity which has another characteristic conducive to the end. If drying the sparking plugs (or working on the engine in some more technically informed way) is necessary to the right result, so is doing it with a requisite degree of energy.

It may be said that the cases are different in the following way. Ideas which are cognitively true provide information about how it will or would be useful to act in certain circumstances and, as essentially bound up with this, something about the character of the objects onto which such action would be directed. In

---

VRE, pp. 118–26 in toto.

contrast non-cognitive ideas simply stimulate useful emotional propensities without telling us that or why they are useful. Thus if belief in God really is a non-cognitive idea, it does not tell us of the character of any separately existing divine being, or even of the utility of certain emotions; it simply prompts them.

But such a distinction is not available to the pragmatist. For it depends upon a contrast between thinking that something is the case and behaving in a way which will be successful if it is the case, while it is the whole point of pragmatism to analyse the second in terms of the first. For him the informational content of an idea consists in the power it has to produce behaviour which will be successful to the extent that things are thus and so. This is the only way in which even the most 'cognitive' of ideas can depict things as being thus and so; they have no peculiar perspicuity, as representations of reality, such as could not be ascribed equally to so-called 'non-cognitive' ideas. There are not two things, understanding and believing in a reality, on the one hand, and an adjustment of our behaviour in the light of this, on the other. It follows that the distinction between cognitive ideas and non-cognitive ideas is unavailable to the pragmatist. So-called non-cognitive ideas are simply our grasp of the utility of certain emotions.

It is common in much the same connection to charge James with confusing two sorts of satisfactory idea: ideas whose consequences are emotionally satisfactory and those which are cognitively satisfactory 'in the sense of being born out by experience'. Thus Israel Scheffler says that if James had managed to confine his attention to the latter he would have identified truth with predictive adequacy which is, at any rate, better than identifying it with emotional pleasingness. [51] But an idea is emotionally satisfactory only if it brings us agreeable feelings when confronted with the objects to which it leads, and this depends on how they are, and therefore represents an adjustment to their being thus and our knowledge of that as a fact. Thus even where an idea is only true in virtue of bringing a simple but helpful emotional feeling it is, for James, an adjustment to real fact. Or if on rare occasions James implies that it is just the feeling it brings and not the propensity to feel in a beneficial way in one's encounter with certain aspects of reality, that is a very minor aspect of his pragmatic conception of truth.

It seems to me, then, that James is quite right not to build a distinction between cognitive and non-cognitive ideas into pragmatism, and to treat both scientific beliefs and religious truth as on a level, even when he seems to be interpreting religious ideas in a way which appears to drain them of factual content.

We may note in passing (what we will consider fully later) that religious ideas can be understood in two very different ways by the pragmatist. Pragmatism sits happily with a view according to which ideas about God are really true, so far as they are true, of nature, telling us how it will respond to certain

---

51   See Scheffler, p. 109.

ways of dealing with it. But it also sits happily with a more conventional supernaturalistic account of them according to which the reality to which they primarily adjust us is a creative spirit behind the scenes of this world. James said things pointing in each direction, though he clearly did have full-fledged supernatural beliefs. Either way the pragmatist can speak of certain religious ideas being true; the difference will be as to the nature of the reality to which they adjust us. Of course, to make this distinction one must be able to step outside the language of religion in order to characterize the reality to which it adjusts us in other terms and some would think this a questionable possibility.

A pragmatist who wanted to distinguish between informational and merely energizing ideas might perhaps argue that the former adjust us to the nature of the objects we are dealing with, while the latter affect the vigour of our own action without relating it to any characteristics of that on which we are acting. But why is the energy required in order to deal with something not a fact about it? Perhaps it will be said that religious ideas, to the extent that they can be interpreted in the first more naturalistic manner do not prompt adjustments to any particular features of reality, but just energize us generally in getting on with whatever we happen to be about. But that suggests not that they are peculiarly non-cognitive but only that their object is the character of the universe as a whole as repaying a certain general emotional stance towards it.

Thus the distinction between cognitive and non-cognitive ideas seems to be foisted on pragmatism by commentators like Ayer and Bird from a philosophical perspective quite alien to it.

§ A difficulty in the pragmatist conception to be noted in passing is this. Its most natural formulations take it for granted that a person has certain aims, and say that ideas are true if they will prompt behaviour which is suited to their achievement. But what makes it true that we have those aims? For the fully fledged pragmatist it cannot consist in the ideas we have of those ends, for the meaning and reference of an idea have to be explained on the basis of the circumstances in which it will promote our ends. Either he must explain the sense in which ideas adjust us to reality by identifying their success with certain upshots, such as survival, pleasant feeling, and reduction of distress, without calling these our ends, or he must make it definitional that these are our ends.

But why should survival and satisfactory feeling be the criteria of that success on the part of ideas which earns them the title 'true' if it is not because we want these in a genuinely intentional sense not available to the pragmatist? Why not choose some quite different upshots, if there is nothing in particular which people are genuinely aiming at? [52]

Perhaps it will be said that survival (and pleasant rather than unpleasant feeling as a guide to what will promote it) necessarily provides the criterion which will in fact weed out ideas which will endure from those which will not,

---

52   James himself posed a rather similar challenge to Herbert Spencer. See his 1879
      review of his *The Data of Ethics*, ECR, pp. 347–53.

and therefore the ones which we have come to mark by the success word 'true'. But it is doubtful how convincing an answer that really is, and, in fact, I do not think that James ever deals with this question very adequately.

§ So the meaning and reference of an idea are determined by the conditions which must hold if it is to promote, or be liable to promote, a successful encounter with a reality or successful dealings with reality in general. Such a semi-behavioural account of reference is inevitable once a magical pointing, or unity in the Absolute, is rejected as an account thereof. Having seen this, we can hardly think of its truth as anything but an idea's promotion of successful feeling or behaviour.

We can now see that this account of truth satisfies the equivalence requirement we formulated in section 2 of this chapter, for an idea will only be successful under the circumstances which must hold if it is to be so. What makes it correct to call my 'idea' a 'belief that P' is that the expression 'P' stands for precisely those conditions which must hold if the idea is to do its job of relating me usefully to some part or aspect of reality. It will, therefore, be true, will 'work', just under those conditions. G. E. Moore said that on James's account his belief that James existed could be true even if James did not exist.[53] But what made Moore's idea a belief to the effect that James existed was (on the pragmatic theory of reference, meaning, and truth) that its usefulness depended on James actually existing. One's idea intends an object if and only if it prepares one to cope with it, and its characterisation of that object is the character it must have if the idea is to enable one to cope with it successfully. The belief that birds sing is true if and only if birds sing because only if they do are the conditions met to which ideas thus describable are ready to adjust us. It is only in virtue of this readiness that they are beliefs to the effect that birds sing. In themselves they are just bits of what James calls 'flat' bits of experience.[54]

The key to all this lies in the fourth leading idea which I have identified among the sources of James's pragmatism. And the source of this lies in James's wish to meet Royce's argument for the Absolute as necessary to make the reference of our ideas intelligible. Although Royce was concerned with the reference of the 'subject' of an idea, rather than the meaning of the 'predicate', James, who did not distinguish carefully between reference and meaning took it as a challenge to find a more naturalistic account of both reference and meaning along lines I have tried to explain and develop. We see then that the usual objection to James's pragmatism, that it implies that ideas can be true

---

53   See Moore, *Studies*, p. 127.
54   ERE, p. 57. MT, p. 63. True, the lack of intrinsic relation between an idea as a psychological existent and its object is qualified by the insistence that when an idea is verified it is so by a series of actually lived-through mediating experiences terminating in direct experience of its object. Thereby James makes its reference intrinsic to our experience *over time* as it is not for the somewhat similar later theories of philosophers like Hilary Putnam. Nonetheless the idea is not really about anything simply in virtue of what it inherently is at the time of its occurrence.

even if what they posit does not exist or hold, fails because it does not recognize that for him ideas, qua tokens, are not inherently intentional or propositional but only so in virtue of the fact that they prepare us to deal with the things or conditions which they are therefore said to concern. One can, indeed, look at the matter in two different ways. The belief that P can be said to be 'that P' because 'P' specifies what must hold if the effects it produces are to be useful, or one can say that 'P' specifies those conditions because those who say 'P' have ideas which are calculated to make them cope with them.

So pragmatism satisfies the equivalence requirement and even explains why it is a requirement. However, for the Jamesian pragmatist, a definition of truth merely in terms of that requirement tends to hide the point that what makes an idea, as a psychological event, true is not its being a transcript of something beyond it but its prompting a successful adjustment to its existence and character.

It follows, as James sees it, that to understand an idea or evaluate it for truth we must consider how acceptance of it would affect our expectations, feelings, and behaviour. And in fact if 'expectation' is not to have a question-beggingly intentional sense, it must simply refer to the circumstances under which the effects on feeling and behaviour will be successful in terms of survival and pleasant rather than unpleasant feeling.

Some rough distinction may be made perhaps between two appropriate questions when we assess an idea for truth. (1) What sensations will holding the idea lead us to expect and to prepare ourselves for under various different circumstances and will those sensations be forthcoming? (2) What sorts of responses will we make to the sensations which come our way? But there is no sharp distinction between them since the basic question is always 'What responses to what sorts of realities is the idea liable to produce and how useful will these be?' This is in effect what James means by the cash value of an idea.

§ However, James has been charged with confusing two distinct things: what would follow from an idea's being true and, second, what would follow from its being thought to be true. Thereby he is said to have confused the difference between determining the meaning of a scientific proposition by reference to the observable difference it makes to the world whether it is true or false and determining that of a religious proposition by the difference it will make to our behaviour and feeling whether we think of it as true or false.

This complaint simply echoes the insistence that James should have distinguished clearly between cognitive and non-cognitive ideas and fails in the same way to come to terms with the essence of James's position. For one who has different expectations, as a result of holding a certain idea, from what he would have if he had not held it, is one who is ready to behave in appropriate ways (from the point of view of survival and comfort) when the relevant sensations come along, while one who has different patterns of behaviour as a result of holding a certain idea from what he would have otherwise is thinking that the world has characteristics of such sorts as make that behaviour appropriate from the point of view of survival and comfort.

To the extent that the difference can be made in Jamesian terms it will be between the specificness of that to which an idea adjusts us. A scientific idea, if true, will prompt a very fine-tuned adjustment to certain features of reality, while a religious or moral idea is likely to represent an adjustment of a more generic sort to something very pervasive about the universe (or at least the human universe).[55] But that is much less of a difference than that supposed by those who charge James with this confusion. For the distinction can be made only on the basis of a challenge to the adequacy of a pragmatic account of meaning and truth as a whole.

§ Later we will see James entertaining notions which heavily qualify the notion that our ideas are only extrinsically connected with their objects. Thus not only will we see him claiming that in perception the very object itself is present as an ingredient in our experience, but we will also see him insisting that the same may be true in thought. The first point simply rounds out the nature of those encounters with the objects of our thought which must be successful if the thought is to be true, but the second is doubtfully consistent with some of the ideas we have been ascribing to him in this chapter. In this development one might almost compare his conception to that of Heidegger's doctrine of truth as the uncoveredness of being to us. But though this theme is importantly present in James, it represents at most a strong qualification of the approach to thought which is the key to his more distinctively pragmatist ideas.

§ If James's theory of meaning and truth is right at all, it is only as a bold gesture in the right direction requiring a great deal of tidying up and further development to be satisfactory. And there are, in fact, certain developments in philosophy in quite recent times which can be taken as attempts to work out a similarly pragmatic approach to these issues more exactly.

An obvious name here is that of W. V. O. Quine.[56] But Quine's approach would have to be broadened to cover non-verbal as well as verbal meanings to meet all the phenomena with which James was concerned. Moreover, both Quine's physicalism and his holism set him quite apart from James. (We will be finding that a useful but similarly qualified comparison of Quine with Bradley can be helpful.)

A self-proclaimed pragmatist of our own time is Richard Rorty, who often invokes James, but I believe the views he ascribes to James are often quite distant from what I find in his work, even that very small part of it to which Rorty gives references.[57] Indeed, Rorty speaks of *Essays in Radical Empiricism*

---

55 This way of making the distinction may be queried on the ground that laws of nature are very pervasive facts. But grasp of the law of gravity is useful for making very finely tuned adjustments to reality, say in the design of space ships, whereas religious ideas, naturalistically interpreted, determine only such very general attitudes as that of a willingness to go along with events in an optimistic manner.
56 See Quine, *Methods*, Introduction, and *View*, chapter II.
57 See especially Rorty, *Consequences*.

as belonging to the bad 'metaphysical' part of James.[58] Rorty's own pragmatism seems to make the following main claims.[59]

(1) There is no valid distinction between bottom level statements which are true or false by correspondence to fact and others which are in some sense expressive—in particular, the analytic/synthetic distinction is to be rejected; (2) the epistemic status of what we say turns on behavioural facts about the practices of the community to which we belong, not on some culture-transcendent eternal truths; (3) these practices cannot be explained, except in a quite bogus way, by the nature of the objects to which items in our language refer; (4) there is no such thing as knowledge derivable from a direct confrontation with objects, whether these be sense data or meanings; (5) this is because meaning is holistic so that each affirmation is subject to test by coherence with other parts of our belief system.

James's pragmatism approximates to this position so far as most discourse of a type which is not deeply metaphysical goes. But we shall be seeing in subsequent chapters that his philosophy clashes with Rorty's in fundamental respects. (1) He believes that in perception there is a direct and infallible confrontation with the reality with which our ordinary affirmations are there to enable us to cope more or less successfully. There are, doubtless, no incorrigible statements to be made about these percepts; nonetheless the point of what is called knowledge is to promote immediate perceptual encounters of a desirable kind. (2) For James, there is a realm of concepts or ideas the eternal relations between which must be respected by our ordinary knowledge claims. (3) Though James cannot be said to have a holistic view of meaning, something of the sort accords quite well with much that he says, but what we think and say is, for him, still ultimately true or false in virtue of its use in guiding us in a world of genuinely independent realities. (4) James's tendency is to treat the meaning and reference of my thoughts as turning on how they relate to the reality I am in the midst of. The control exercised on me by the verbal habits of the community is just one important case of this. Certainly I learn most of my concepts from my community, but the meaning they have for me consists in the way they guide me personally in my dealings with the environment. Thus James has an essentially individualist view of thinking. (5) He believes that there is something deeper than ordinary truth, namely, an intimate grasp, direct or imaginative, of the ceaseless flow of the pure experience which constitutes the world.

James, then, believes that, though our true statements cannot, and should not be expected to, correspond to sharply distinct items in the world, the point of ordinary thought is to make certain direct encounters with distinct bits of the world fruitful, and that metaphysics can clarify the real nature of what we thus encounter, even though the cognitive message of such an encounter cannot be

---

58   Op. cit., p. 214.
59   See Kraut.

tabulated in an atomic statement describing its object. For Rorty in contrast, all talk about such direct encounter with reality is absurd.

Upon the whole Rorty's pragmatism represents the outlook of a mind poles apart from James. While it masquerades as a genial tolerance of all types of contribution to the human conversation, provided that they do not claim to correspond with how things are in some deep sense, it is really a hasty intolerance of all philosophical views opposed to his own somewhat crude 'eliminative materialism'. James's philosophy, in contrast—though at times cocking a snook at absolute idealism and traditional metaphysics—is essentially that of a philosopher whose life-long concern was to settle 'accounts with the Kosmos' as it really is.

So much perhaps needed to be said as to how James's pragmatism compares with some more recent philosophical positions thus labelled. However, it would take us too far afield to explore them more fully. So let us return to a direct evaluation of the essence of James's own position.

§ There is certainly much to be said for looking at human thought as a natural process which promotes behaviour useful for survival and comfort, and which has developed in ways better and better adapted to this role, by natural and cultural selection and through the reinforcing power at the individual level of pleasure and pain. And if we look at it solely in these terms we are likely to arrive at something like James's pragmatist view of truth, meaning, and reference.

But after all here are we understanding this picture of human life and of the role of thought in it, and it is very difficult to think of our own entertaining of this picture solely in this way. The world, with human beings in it, is somehow there for us, and this cannot be explained in terms merely of the causal effects of the images and feelings which display it to us. If one puts it in terms of images and feelings at all, it must be in terms of images and feelings which are inherently intentional and which display a world to us in a way to which James's account, at least as we have so far explored it, cannot do justice.

For on that account ideas are quite opaque, not the windows from which we look out at the world which they seem to be.[60] And although James tries to

---

60 This sense in which ideas may be regarded as opaque or transparent is quite different from, and almost the opposite of, that in which Quine talked of referential contexts as being transparent or opaque. [See Quine, *Word,* chapter IV.] For Quine 'John was hunting a lion' contains 'a lion' in an opaque context if it does not licence the inference that there was a lion he was hunting and in a transparent context if it does licence such an inference. That usage is common and quite intelligible. But emphasis on the fundamental nature of opaque contexts in that sense suggests that thought is transparent in a more natural sense because its content is not a matter of how the thought is related to something beyond it, while emphasis on the fundamental nature of transparent contexts suggests that the content of a thought is not inherent to it and that it is in that sense opaque, giving no inherent indication of what it is of. In any case my use of 'transparent' and 'opaque' must not be

avoid the more unpalatable consequences of a causal view of their meaning and reference by saying that we experience the way in which they lead to their objects, this still does not allow them to display the way things are supposed to be at the time at which they occur. And in any case, it is difficult to see in what sense the leading of an idea to its object is genuinely experienced when the whole process, as is normal, extends far beyond the specious present within which alone anything is genuinely experienced.

Of course James is no vulgar behaviourist denying the individual consciousness. How could the great prophet of the stream of consciousness be so? But his denial, in his more tough-minded moods, that the elements of the stream of consciousness have any inherent aboutness brings him in sight of being so. And although this denial is belied by much of what he says elsewhere it does play an important part in the foundations of pragmatism.

My own suggestion on these matters is that we distinguish two ways in which ideas can have meaning and be true or false. I shall explain this with reference to truth alone, since its extension to meaning is fairly obvious.

An idea may be true because it puts one into effective behavioural contact with some thing, or feature of the world, and about which therefore it reports or is a truth. That is the kind of truth to which pragmatism draws our attention and which it tries to explicate. True ideas of that sort do not display their objects or their characters to us in any genuine way.

But in other cases an idea may be true in a deeper way which we may call that of literal truth.[61] Such a literally true idea presents us with some aspect of the character of the object we are thinking about so that it is actualised not only in the object but in our consciousness (not only formally in the scholastic sense but also objectively).

That does, indeed, raise Royce's problem: How does the idea pick out a particular object in the world as that the nature of which it is displaying? I answer that there are two cases—that in which our specific relation to that particular (as opposed to its character) is the rather external one of behavioural adjustment, and that in which there is a much more intimate feeling of linkage with that particular unique object. But this is not the time to develop this point.

I do not say that ideas divide neatly into those susceptible at best of pragmatic truth and those susceptible also or instead of literal truth. An idea whose truth consists primarily in its effectiveness as a guide to suitable feeling and behaviour towards its object may also possess an element of literal truth through the faint whiff it brings into our minds of its character. Moreover, even those ideas which, from an external perspective, should be regarded as possessing only (at best) pragmatic truth are lived through in much the same way as

---

confused with Quine's.

61   The contrast here is not between literal and metaphorical truth but between literal and pragmatic truth. Literal truth is often better expressed in metaphor than in prosaic language. The latter is often capable of conveying only pragmatic truth.

are ideas susceptible of a more literal truth. Both help provide that felt environment in which we live and have our being.

The main point to insist on is that if we are ever really to grasp any fact about the world, including the occurrence in it of creatures with ideas which are pragmatically true, we must sometimes have ideas which display such facts to us in a way which cannot be captured in a purely pragmatic account. To that extent I must regard pragmatism as a one-sided theory.

Perhaps James would never have agreed in so many words to this, but we shall see below that in fact he held views which come close to it. For he came to think that philosophy should seek a deeper and more intuitive grasp of reality than can be given by ideas which are true in the manner pragmatism describes.[62] But however that may be, his pragmatism stands out as a gallant attempt to think through a determinedly naturalist account of meaning and truth of a basically extensional type, which is certainly superior to such as merely appeal lazily to notions of intentionality without any deep explanation of its nature.

With this chapter I conclude my main discussion of James's views on truth, so far as these pertain to his pragmatism, and turn to his views on reality. First, I shall consider the view of reality implied in his *Principles of Psychology*, then turn to two later positions I shall characterize as radical empiricism and mystical pluralism.

---

62   See below at Chapter Four, §1(c) and (d).

2

The Metaphysics of *The Principles of Psychology*

My main concern in this book is with the metaphysical positions espoused in James's latest work. There are two main strands to this. First, there is the doctrine of radical empiricism; second, there is what one might call the mystical pluralistic metaphysic developed mainly in *A Pluralistic Universe, The Problems of Philosophy*, and *The Varieties of Religious Experience*. But, before we turn to these, some consideration should be given to the metaphysical views expressed or implicit in *The Principles of Psychology*, more particularly on the relations between the mental and the physical. Such will be the task of the present chapter.

In the preface to this work (first published in 1890) James tells us that it will keep 'close to the point of view of natural science' and eschew metaphysics. He continues:

> Every natural science assumes certain data uncritically, and declines to chal-
> lenge the elements between which its own 'laws' obtain, and from which its
> own deductions are carried on. Psychology, the science of finite individual
> minds, assumes as its data (1) *thoughts and feelings*, and (2) *a physical world* in
> time and space with which they coexist and which (3) *they know*. Of course these
> data themselves are discussable; but the discussion of them (as of other
> elements) is called metaphysics and falls outside the province of this book. This
> book, assuming that thoughts and feelings exist and are vehicles of knowledge,
> thereupon contends that psychology when she has ascertained the empirical
> correlation of the various sorts of thought or feeling with definite conditions
> of the brain, can go no farther—can go no farther, that is, as a natural science.
> If she goes farther she becomes metaphysical.
>
> PP, I, pp. v–vi

Thus he plans to avoid 'both the associationist and the spiritualist theories' each of which confuses psychology with metaphysics, and not very good metaphysics at that. 'Spiritualism' here simply means the postulation of a substantial non-physical spirit or soul as the object of psychology and it is not surprising to have it dismissed as unduly metaphysical, but associationism might seem to be more 'scientific'. However, James thinks that the so-called 'ideas' with which it deals are metaphysical items explanation by reference to which runs counter to the truly scientific psychology which he is here thinking of as concerned primarily with the physical basis of mental phenomena.[1]

It was not James's intention to denigrate metaphysics in general, though he did not have a high opinion of these two forms of it, but only to distinguish its task from that of the scientific psychology with which he purports to be engaged in this book. In the event, however, there is a great deal in James's book that is more like metaphysics than scientific psychology even if we adopt a more generous conception of the task of the latter than that James takes.

Bruce Kuklick has suggested that what James was mainly intent to exclude from psychology, when he set out to avoid metaphysics, were the doctrines of absolute idealism, a philosophy which in many ways he disliked, but suspected to be true because he could not satisfactorily meet Royce's arguments in favour of it.[2] Its truth, however, was of a kind not suitable for inclusion in a purely scientific study of the mind. Thus much that seems highly metaphysical in the work still avoids the ban on metaphysics in the main sense intended, though it could be included in metaphysics itself once James's own metaphysics became more naturalistic.

There is a good deal in this, I suspect, though James may also have been aiming to steer clear of anything like the neutral monism, with its reductive view not only of the physical but of the intentionality of mind, to which he was quietly moving in metaphysics. The main point is that it is to be taken for

---

1   Bradley too recommended that psychology should operate independently of metaphysics and use ideas with which metaphysics finds fault conceived as final truth. But for Bradley scientific psychology meant precisely associationism, which he contrasted with the ultimate truth presented in absolute idealism.

2   See Kuklick, p. 179. This is an indispensable work on James and related thinkers, philosophically first class as well as historically fascinating.
      A strong suggestion of absolute idealism as the doctrine to which humanity will eventually attain is given in PP, II, p. 317. Here his attitude to it seems quite positive. See also PP, I, p. 272, and Perry, I, pp. 577–85.
      For a treatment of James's psychology from the point of view of its broader cultural implications see Browning. This is sometimes weak on philosophic detail but provides an excellent comparison of the philosophy of life implied by James's psychology with those implied by such more recent psychological theories as those of Freud, Maslow, Skinner, and Erikson. He is, however, one of many authors who exaggerates the similarity of James's introspective approach with that of the phenomenologists and still more misleadingly treats radical empiricism as a step nearer to their position. However, he places more emphasis than some of the others on the broader naturalistic setting of James's introspective enquiries.

granted, throughout the book, that there is a non-mental physical world and that one of the things which exist within it are human organisms containing brains which generate mental events, called thoughts, which 'know' things besides themselves, both physical and mental.

Even if such a view of the world, and of the place of mind within it, is not thought of as the final metaphysical truth by James, he does in fact sketch a metaphysic of mind and matter on this basis which is worth considering. I shall examine it under four heads.

1. Relation between brain and mind;
2. Characteristics of the stream of thought or consciousness;
3. The nature of the Self;
4. Free Will.

§1. *Relation between Brain and Mind*

Most of the time James seems to use such words as 'mind', 'consciousness', and 'thought' as more or less synonymous. Where there is not some special reason to contrast them it seems we can take them as interchangeable. Thus his most famous characterisation of consciousness occurs in a chapter called 'The Stream of Thought', though its equivalent in *The Briefer Course* (a partly rewritten digest of the work for students) is called 'The Stream of Consciousness'. Likewise he uses 'thoughts' in the plural to cover all contents of consciousness, including sensory feelings of every sort, a rather unfortunate usage. I shall stick mainly to 'consciousness', 'state of consciousness', and 'content of consciousness' in my discussion.

How is consciousness related to the brain, for the James of PP? Certainly it is not identified with any brain process. James thinks of consciousness as a fresh reality in the world, additional to anything occurring physically in space. However, every state of a person's consciousness somehow precisely corresponds to the state of his brain at that moment. Every time one's state of consciousness changes there is a somehow corresponding change in the state of one's brain.[3] It is implied that granted the precise state of the brain at any moment the precise state of consciousness of the individual is settled.

Yet James is not an epiphenomenalist for whom all true causation is physical, for he allows consciousness its own efficacy and even a kind of free will. How can this combine with the idea that a given state of the brain determines the precise present form of consciousness?

Perhaps James really wishes to qualify this idea somewhat as follows. States of the brain follow on one another in ways which are mainly determined at a purely physical level and these largely determine the state of consciousness at each moment. (He speculates in a rather general way about the physical

3   See, e.g., PP, I, p. 232.

processes in question, particularly in his chapter on 'The Association of Ideas', PP, chapter XIV.) However, as each state of consciousness occurs it includes a direction of the attention to some of its contents rather than others, the nature and comparative degree of which is not determined either by the present or the previous state of the brain or by previous states of consciousness; rather is it freely or spontaneously chosen. And this freely chosen direction of attention is an additional factor in determining the next state of the brain, a state which will settle the character of the next state of consciousness in every detail apart from the precise degrees of freely chosen attention which it will contain to the various ideas included within it. (However, he does not rule out some slight influence of one state of consciousness on the next which does not operate through the intermediary of a brain state.)

Such a theory is not without difficulties. What exactly is it which chooses how much attention to give any particular content of consciousness? James does not want to invoke a soul to do the choosing; rather is it an event which occurs within the stream of consciousness. But when does it occur—before the state of consciousness in which that attention is given or as a part of it? Presumably the latter, but that suggests a kind of partial self-creation of a state of consciousness, which is certainly a puzzling conception (though it became central to the thought of Whitehead). However, we may postpone consideration of such problems for now.

At any rate, the general picture of what goes on seems to be something like this. At any one moment there is brain state N1 and a simultaneous state of consciousness C1, the nature of which is largely but not entirely settled by the character of N1 but is partly somehow self-chosen (in virtue of the different degrees of attention given to the various contents of C1 which are settled by N1). Then at the next moment there is a brain state N2, the character of which is largely due to N1, and various purely physical inputs to the brain, but is also influenced by the self-chosen features of C1. Simultaneous to N2 is a state of consciousness C2 related to it as C1 was to N1. And N2 and C2 are followed, God willing, by an N3 and C3 which stand in the same way to them as they did to N1 and C1. And so the process goes on. (However, as I said, James does not rule out some direct influence from C1 to C2—if this is an alternative with any real meaning.)

One of the less serious objections which might be made to this account is that it treats the change of brain and consciousness as consisting in the replacement of total units one by another and ignores the continuity of change. We shall see later that James gave a great deal of attention to the nature of such continuity. For the present it is sufficient to say that if the account is defective on this ground, that is only because of some oversimplification in our presentation of it.

James is thus in an important sense a dualist; not only is consciousness a reality distinct from its physical basis, it also produces its own distinctive results in the physical world. However, the general tone of PP is opposed to any stronger form of dualism, such as would postulate a spiritual substance which could exist apart from a brain. Consciousness is simply a stream of conscious states and the only substantial thing involved is the organism itself. It arises from states of the brain, and somehow corresponds to them; however, it reacts back upon them, so that the brain, and eventually the organism as a whole, behaves in ways in which it would not do without its presence. Thus what goes on in the brain is not entirely explicable in terms of physical causation. James's view is, in fact much the same as that advocated today by the neuro-physiologist Roger Sperry.[4]

In defending his own view James gives some consideration to what he takes to be the other main alternative views of the status of mind or consciousness. These are (1) interactionism, in which consciousness is the activity of a spiritual substance or pure ego which interacts with the brain as a quite distinct reality therefrom; (2) epiphenomenalism or the 'automaton theory' as James usually calls it; (3) the mind dust theory. He only refers in passing to the fourth main type of alternative provided by idealisms of one kind or another, wherein he may have suspected the ultimate truth to lie.

(1) *Interactionism.* Of the three interactionism seems the most promising, and James even thinks it looks initially more plausible than his own hypothesis and can be expected to remain an appropriate way of looking at things for some purposes. However, he says that even if there were a spiritual substance which possessed our passing states of consciousness, it would remain these passing states, not that substance, which alone concern scientific psychology.

> I confess therefore, that to posit a soul influenced in some mysterious way by the brain-states and responding to them by conscious affections of its own, seems to me the line of least logical resistance, so far as we yet have attained. If it does not strictly *explain* anything, it is at any rate less positively objectionable than either mind-stuff or a material-monad creed.
>
> PP, I, p. 181

He goes on, however, to say that

> *The bare PHENOMENON, however, the IMMEDIATELY KNOWN thing which on the mental side is in apposition with the entire brain-process is the state of consciousness and not the soul itself.*
>
> PP, I, p. 182

And it is in favour of that as the sole mental reality that James finally comes down.

However, as James might himself have agreed, it is not at all clear how much real difference in meaning there is between the thesis of a soul substance and the thesis that there is a stream of consciousness distinct from anything strictly in the physical world. For it is doubtful to what belief in a soul substance amounts beyond the claim that the stream of consciousness has its own peculiar

---

4   See Sperry.

form of continuity. The view only seems to have any distinct meaning if it is meant that this substance could exist apart from the brain. And in saying that it could do so, something stronger than mere logical possibility must be intended. For the mere logical possibility might be acknowledged by any believer in a stream of consciousness. It can hardly be logically impossible that the stream of consciousness should continue after dissolution of the brain, or that one with some claim to belong to part of the same stream should have preceded it. Still, as we shall see, James gives a reductive account of the self which proponents of a soul substance or pure ego are usually reluctant to accept as an adequate analysis of the whole meaningful content of their own position and which he himself thinks of as an alternative to it.

(2) Epiphenomenalism. This is discussed by James, under the label of 'the automaton theory', as a position advocated by Shadworth Hodgson, Douglas Spalding, T. H. Huxley, and W. K. Clifford.[5] For this theory the only true causation is physical causation, and brain states succeed each other according to purely physical laws, while producing states of consciousness as a kind of by-product with no effects of their own either on brain or subsequent states of consciousness. James has a number of reasons for rejecting this.[6]

First, he finds it hard to believe that the automaton theory can give an adequate account of how anything other than consciousness can steer the organism towards its goal states through behaviour with the degree of flexibility found in higher animals and men. Such flexibility is not easily explained in purely physical terms. Rather does it seem to require the peculiar causal influence of the conscious envisagement of certain goals felt to be desirable and of the means which could lead to them. This argument seems less persuasive in the age of artificial intelligence research.

However, there is, I think, something to be said for his claim that pleasure and pain would not be associated, as they are, primarily with beneficial and

---

5   James does not actually use the phrase 'epiphenomenalism' for this theory which seems to have acquired this label somewhat later. He does, however, speak of the automaton theory as regarding consciousness as an epiphenomenon [See PP, I, p. 129, also VRE, at p. 495, where he says the expression comes from W. K. Clifford.] At one stage James himself had inclined to such a view. See MEN, p. xlvi, and Perry, II, p. 26.

C. A. Strong in his *Why the Mind has a Body*, a book to which James paid a good deal of attention, argued later that it was a mistake (though he does not actually name James here) to assimilate the parallelism of Clifford, for which the mental and physical are parallel but not causally connected, and the automatism theory of Huxley for which there is a one way causal dependence of the mental on the physical. [See Strong, p. 78 and passim.] For T. H. Huxley's epiphenomenalism see his 'On the hypothesis that animals are automata' in Huxley, Methods, at pp. 237–44. However, Huxley combined this doctrine in a curious way with a kind of idealism.

6   See PP, I, pp. 143–44.

harmful experiences respectively if they were not efficacious.[7] This argument does, however, seem to presuppose that it is true a priori that if pleasure and pain were to be efficacious at all it would have to be in the familiar way as respectively positive and negative reinforcers. Personally I am inclined to accept that that is indeed an *a priori* truth, though I am doubtful how far even James's generous type of empiricism can regard it as such.[8]

A second objection is that if there is to be an evolutionary explanation of how consciousness developed, it must have some survival value. Regarding it as assisting the organism to survive by more subtle adjustments to the environment than would otherwise be possible is the obvious candidate for this.

James comes close to the argument, of which Santayana has shown the fallacy, that if consciousness were merely a passive spectator of our behaviour, without any real efficacy of its own, it would not have been preserved and developed by natural selection. Surely a peculiarity of certain organisms of no positive survival benefit to them would have simply died out. But this is no argument against epiphenomenalism. For if it is, or follows from, a law of nature that certain sorts of brain state are accompanied by certain sorts of consciousness, then any evolutionary pressures which sustained brain states of that sort would sustain consciousness, even if the consciousness itself performs no useful role. So if what James thought the work of consciousness was really done by physical mechanisms which underpin it, then consciousness itself would be an idling extra bound to be selected and sustained along with them. Hence we do not have any extra objection of any weight to epiphenomenalism here. However, James is not perhaps arguing precisely in this way, only claiming that far the most natural way of interpreting the situation is to see consciousness as having the survival value it seems to itself to have of helping the organism adapt flexibly to circumstances.

More impressive, perhaps, is James's contention that epiphenomenalism is an unnecessarily far-fetched departure from ordinary modes of thought which only finds favour because it fits in with not very well-founded prejudices about the nature of scientific explanation.[9] It quite clashes with our sense that consciousness is no mere idle spectator of what the organism is up to but a *'fighter for ends'*.[10] And clearly James was particularly concerned with its incompatibility with conceptions of free will which are too important to us simply to be jettisoned on the basis of any such mere dogma.

(3) *The Mind Dust Theory.* The third theory to which he gives some attention is what he calls the 'mind dust' (or 'mind stuff') theory.[11] Proponents of this think it problematic how consciousness could arise in human brains if it were

---

7   See PP, I, pp. 143–44.
8   See Sprigge, *Ethics,* chapter V.
9   See PP, I, pp. 137–38 and passim.
10   See PP, I, p. 141.
11   See PP, I, chapter VI.

something quite different from and alien to physical reality. Surely the laws of nature could only bring forth fresh combinations of physical particles or physical stuff, if that was all there was in the first place. If, however, every physical particle has a certain simple form of sentience or consciousness to it, then it is intelligible that, as particles of matter arrange themselves in ever more complex, larger functioning units, the charge of sentience associated with each particle should combine with that pertaining to the others to make up a complex total consciousness of their aggregate. This can be assumed to have reached its highest form in human brains. Thus the ultimate units of the physical world must be a kind of mind dust which becomes mind proper when the dust particles are aggregated in certain ways.

I suggest that such a theory may take either of two forms. On the first, the mental charge pertaining to each particle is in ultimate truth precisely what that particle really is or, better put, is the thing in itself which presents itself to scientific enquiry as the particle. Alternatively it may be assumed that there is no more ultimate answer to the question what the ultimate particles of matter really are than one couched in irreducibly physical terms so that the mental charge pertaining to each particle is an extra reality, not the inner essence of the particle itself. The first view gives an account of what matter really is, claiming that its inner essence is always mental. Thus the higher order forms of mind are complexes of units which considered externally are physical particles, while each is, in itself, a kind of mind-kin. The second theory offers no special explanation of the nature of matter but only seeks to explain how human and animal consciousness could arise in an originally lifeless world without presenting some radical break in the continuity of things. James does not distinguish at this stage between the two theories but his concern at this point is evidently with the second. However, his main criticisms, so far as well taken, would apply equally to either form of the theory, importantly different as they are from a metaphysical point of view.

James's main criticism of the theory is that a single state of consciousness is not a totality made up of elements with a distinct reality in their own right. Elementary feelings cannot come together so that *en masse* they actually are a complex feeling. Twenty-six consciousnesses each cognizing a single letter of the alphabet cannot combine to constitute a consciousness of the alphabet as a whole. That would have to be a twenty-seventh state of consciousness, as much a single unit as any of the others. For we must distinguish between the complexity of a content of a state of consciousness and the complexity of the state of consciousness itself. Even if states of consciousness are typically themselves in a certain sense complex, that is not through having parts each with its own distinct felt being.

James's argument is surely a strong one, whether it is conclusive or not. We shall see that reflection upon its main point, that units of consciousness cannot combine to make a 'larger' consciousness, was a central element in his metaphysical thinking throughout his career, and that finally he was inclined to abandon, or at least drastically qualify, it, even if not quite in favour of the mind dust theory.

James infers from this that the physical determination of a state of consciousness cannot consist in separate bits of the brain determining the existence and nature of separate bits of our state of consciousness. For this is a unitary whole, the overall character of which pervades the character of each of its constituent elements, so far as we can talk about its elements at all. The state of consciousness one enjoys at any moment must be a product, insofar as it is a product of the physical at all, of the whole state of the brain at that moment. (Perhaps he should have said, of some substantial aspect of the brain state, for it is not clear why absolutely everything occurring in the brain should have any specific influence on our state of consciousness.)

James considers, as an alternative hypothesis to its being the brain state as a whole (or at least some substantial aspect thereof) which determines the state of consciousness, that it may be one particular unit in the brain, say one particular cell, the state of which does so. That would provide a very neat solution to the difficulty of how the simplicity, or at least peculiar unity, of the mind relates to the complexity of its physical base but it is not very plausible physiologically. In any case, really to do the trick the unit in question would have to be not a cell, which is itself a complex unit, but some ultimate physical particle within the brain. Such a theory has a certain metaphysical attraction but it is not likely to appeal to the scientific mind.[12]

Before turning to some more detailed aspects of the philosophy of mind and matter found in PP, a word should be said about what are sometimes thought certain 'materialist' tendencies within it.[13]

If by a materialist approach to mind or consciousness is meant a naturalistic one in which it is seen as a feature of animals which has emerged in the course of evolution, rather than as the ultimate basis of reality as in idealism, then the general tone of PP is indeed materialistic. Certainly it was maintained there that the goal of a scientific psychology was discovery of the detailed basis of all aspects of mind in facts about the brain and preliminary descriptions which would assist that discovery. That was at least the official programme of PP even if it was not consistently adhered to. However, it is much clearer today to call such an approach to mind naturalistic rather than materialist.

For philosophers, at any rate, now usually mean by materialism the thesis that there is strictly no reality besides the physical. Such is typically the view of modern proponents of the brain-mind identity theory as also of the still more extreme so-called eliminative materialists. Such a materialism had no proponents in James's time since people had not managed to unlearn the better part of Descartes's arguments.[14] Certainly the epiphenomenalism which was then

---

12   See PP, I, pp. 179–80.
13   See Čapek, p. 528.
14   In earlier times the Greek atomists were materialists in the strong modern sense, and so evidently was Hobbes. But materialism on the lips of those who have never really grasped what they are denying, because a Descartes had not arisen to mark out its distinctive nature, or was too contemporary a thinker for his strange

often called a materialist theory was not materialist in the strict modern sense, for it recognized consciousness as a reality distinct from the brain activity to which it corresponded. However, calling it a materialist theory was natural enough at that time, as was then common, since there was no more extreme doctrine to capture the name. But James was neither a materialist in the modern sense nor an epiphenomenalist.

However, there is a very different sense in which James did show strong materialist tendencies in PP and elsewhere. The thesis in question here might be called phenomenological materialism. This does not try to reduce mind to matter as physicists conceive it, but interprets much or all of the mental, even the most spiritual aspects of mind, as the consciousness of physical processes. A chief example of this is his introspective report that, 'in one person at least, the Self of selves, when carefully examined, is found to consist mainly of' a 'collection of . . . peculiar motions in the head or between the head and throat'[15] and his later reduction of the 'I think' of Descartes to the 'I breathe'.[16] Similar is his account of emotions (the famous so-called James-Lange theory) as the consciousness of certain bodily processes.[17]

Such a phenomenological materialism does not imply that the consciousness of these physical processes is itself a physical process in any ordinary sense. It claims rather that our mode of 'being in the world' is through and through a physical one. I shall have more to say about this later.

§2. *Characteristics of the Stream of Thought or Consciousness*

Chapter IX of *The Principles of Psychology* is called 'The Stream of Thought'. James tells us there that *'The first fact for us . . . as psychologists, is that thinking of some sort goes on'* and reminds us that he uses the word 'thinking' for 'every form of consciousness indiscriminately'.

James lists five main characteristics of thought or consciousness:

1) Every thought tends to be part of a personal consciousness.
2) Within each personal consciousness thought is always changing.
3) Within each personal consciousness thought is sensibly continuous.
4) It always appears to deal with objects independent of itself.

---

challenges to be properly understood, is a very different kettle of fish from materialism in a post-Cartesian age. Wilful blindness on the matter seems a unique feature of our own time.

15   PP, I, p. 301.
16   ERE, p. 37.
17   See PP, II, pp. 449–68.

5) It is interested in some parts of these objects to the exclusion of others, and welcomes or rejects—*chooses* from among them, in a word—all the while.

PP, I, p. 225

James's initial account of these characteristics is somewhat modified as he goes on. I shall consider briefly the main upshot of his discussion of each characteristic, making use of other chapters too. There is no need to provide a substitute for this highly accessible chapter.

(1) *Every thought tends to be part of a personal consciousness.*

James's view of this characteristic is closely bound up with his views about the third. There are two main points.

First, at any one moment every thought or feeling which is occurring then belongs to a particular total state of consciousness which is distinct from every other state of consciousness. When a hundred people are sitting in a room there will be many human thoughts and feelings associated with their presence there. One could conceptually group these thoughts and feelings into bundles on a variety of different principles, for example, in terms of their moral quality. However, the most fundamental way in which two thoughts or feelings can belong together is as aspects of one single state of consciousness. Simultaneous thoughts or feelings which do not belong to one state of consciousness are as separate from each other as any two simultaneous things can be. (This is one way in which James's individualism contrasts with Bradley's collectivism; for Bradley the significant units in the Absolute may be drawn from different total centres of experience.)

Secondly, a state of consciousness normally occurs as part of a series of such states in which each is succeeded by another which it, so to speak, flows into (until the series is finished). Those which we call your states flow into each other as mine never flow into yours. For each momentary state can only flow from one predecessor and into one successor. Thus they form distinct streams.

We ordinarily report or explain these facts by saying that the states of consciousness belong to different persons. But the empirical fact at the heart of the matter concerns the states of consciousness themselves, and how they stand to each other, rather than something called a person to which they belong. And this fact has two aspects, the distinctness of total states of consciousness at a moment, and the separateness of the streams of consciousness formed by the flowing of one such state into another. It is this basic empirical fact (rather than any explanation of it, which may or may not be acceptable, by reference to persons conceived as something more than their conscious states) which James means by the first characteristic of consciousness. And the third characteristic is simply the second component of this fact more fully described.

Actually, as it turns out, that is rather the normal situation, or the situation as we tend initially to take it, than the only one. For James believes that the existence of secondary personalities, and of feelings which are in some sense unconscious or subliminal, complicate the picture. Thus in states of disassociation or secondary personality there seem to be feelings related to what we may call one person's dominant state of consciousness more intimately than any feelings of another person, while not exactly belonging to it as do its contents proper. Rather do such feelings seem to be components in their own to some extent distinct, total state of consciousness, which belongs to a subsidiary stream whose contents colour those of the main one and sometimes spill more fully over into it.

(2) Within each consciousness thought is always changing.

This seems rather obvious. However, James is not merely saying that the totality of thoughts and feelings within our consciousness changes from moment to moment but that the same such element can never really figure in it twice.

Does he mean merely that a thought or feeling occurring at one time is always a different particular event from that occurring at another, or does he mean that it cannot be quite the same in character as a previous one? To be of much interest he must mean the second, and this, it seems clear, is what he does mean. For his point is that each element of a state of consciousness is so coloured by the rest, and the synthesising character of the whole, that it can never be quite the same as an element in any other state of consciousness. We may ask, What if those total states were duplicates of each other? I think James would dismiss this possibility on the grounds that not only are the elements of a momentary state of consciousness thus conditioned by the whole, but so also is the whole by the earlier parts of the stream and the physical conditions of its production. And James takes it for granted, not unreasonably, that these cannot be duplicated. (His concern is more down to earth than that of the status of the identity of indiscernibles as a logical principle.)

Each unique overall state of consciousness, with its unique constituents, corresponds to one unrepeatable total state of the brain. Thus its determination by that brain state is not via a separable determination of each of its elements by some more particular event in the brain. James is not denying the special dependence of certain aspects of a conscious state on what is occurring in particular parts of the brain, only denying that any particular part of the brain determines separately the whole character of any one such aspect. Thus he believes that the brain state as a whole produces a unique state of consciousness at each moment whose character is not simply a combination of qualities of thought and feeling which have occurred before or may occur again.

> A permanently existing 'idea' or 'Vorstellung' which makes its appearance before the footlights of consciousness at periodical intervals, is as mythological an entity as the Jack of Spades.
>
> PP, I, p. 236

Thus it can only be true that one had the same thought or feeling twice in the sense that one had thoughts and feelings similar enough to bear the same name. As just remarked, the claim is not just that they are different particular events, occurring at different times, but the much stronger claim that they can never be precisely the same in character.

The basic idea is that the different contents of consciousness so run into each other that you cannot sharply separate them. The context provided by the rest of what is present in consciousness always bites into the individual nature of any particular element therein. James thinks that this account is reinforced by the most plausible hypothesis as to how brain states produce states of consciousness.

James suggests that one thing which leads us to think we can have just the same thought or feeling twice is that we confuse the thought or feeling with its object. He is not denying the obvious fact that we can apprehend the same object twice. But even in the case of feelings of quality or sensations we should distinguish the sensation from its object. Thus the particular sensation by which we experience some shade of green is not the shade of green itself. (It is none too clear how James understands this distinction, however, which is abandoned in his later radical empiricism.) That can be reapprehended on many different occasions, but the sensation by which we apprehend it will always have its own unique quality determined by the state of consciousness to which it belongs and the conditions of its emergence. (Thus just as for Bradley, as we shall see, it is apprehended universals which are repeated over time but never particular psychic elements, so for James it is the objects of thought or sensation, never the thoughts or sensations themselves, which are repeated.)

The claim that we confuse the identity of the object of two thoughts or feelings with a non-existent identity holding between themselves is bound up with James's emphasis on the fourth characterisation of consciousness, that it is always about something. But we must now turn to the third characterisation which is that:

(3) Within each personal consciousness thought is sensibly continuous.

> Consciousness . . . does not appear to itself chopped up in bits. Such words as 'chain' or 'train' do not describe it fitly as it presents itself in the first instance. It is nothing jointed; it flows. A 'river' or a 'stream' are the metaphors by which it is most naturally described.
>
> PP, I, p. 239

The precise sense in which consciousness is continuous was a problem which puzzled James over many years. It became particularly important when, in his later metaphysics, our own streams of consciousness were made the model for his view of reality in general. There are two points to which he always strives to do justice, but which are apt to pull in rather different directions. One is that the stream of consciousness is not a series of sharply distinct states. The other is that a change which falls within the so-called specious present is experienced as a unity.

There are, I suggest, three main possible views as to how this problem should be dealt with. None is without difficulties, nor do they exhaust the possibilities.

(i) A stretch of normal continuous waking experience may be represented by a line with no divisions marked along it. A cross-section of the line is an artificial abstraction which does not stand for anything which can be called a single experience. A real experience is always some stretch of the line. For a real and normal experience is always of change and that means that it must itself be in process of change. However, there is no stretch of the line especially privileged to be called a single state of experience. We may say either that the whole line is one experience or such shorter segment of it as is convenient; there is no real truth of the matter. Still, since a cross-section of the line does not represent anything which can properly be called an experience, any actual experience will incorporate a change. On this theory any experience is itself undergoing change and is thereby an experience of that change.

(ii) A stretch of continuous waking experience is again represented by a line. But this theory separates from the former on two related points. It allows a cross-section of the line to count as an experience, and it distinguishes between the change which an experience undergoes and the change of which it is an experience. We may mean by an experience either the whole line, some segment of the line, or a cross-section of it according to convenience; whichever we choose, a normal experience will always be an experience of change.

(iii) A stretch of continuous experience consists of a definite number of states of consciousness which take over from each other. (Thus if we think of this stretch of experience as represented by a line, we must think of the line as intrinsically divided into natural segments, and each of these segments as a single state of consciousness in a way in which other arbitrarily made segments would not be.) However, each state of consciousness, as it comes into existence, feels itself as having emerged from the previous state, the nature of which somehow qualifies its own felt character, and as passing into a next state for which it is preparing the ground. Thus there is no sharp divide between it and the experiences which flank it. Moreover, each state of consciousness does in a manner incorporate a change, but this change is part of a unitary experience. It is therefore a different sort of change from that which consists in one state of consciousness being replaced by another.

A fourth possible theory would relate to (iii) rather as (i) does to (ii). It would postulate such states of consciousness, but deny that they incorporated change within them, insisting that they were only experiences of change. But I do not think this theory is one to which James ever tends, so I shall ignore it.

In his later thought James definitely adopted the third theory. It is difficult to say whether he held it in PP or not. Some of what he says suggests it, but there are also strong suggestions that one of the other two theories is intended. Of these the distinction James makes between experience and its objects might seem to favour the second. Nonetheless, I think he is nearer to the first. For the change with which each of these theories is concerned is that which is directly presented in a specious present, not a change postulated in a judgement, and upon the whole I think James would think that such directly presented change could not be distinguished from the change which the experience itself undergoes.

Whichever of these theories James came nearest to holding in PP, his main concern, when he gives continuity as the third characteristic of consciousness, is not to press its merits as against those of the others. For his main point is compatible with each of them. And that is that whatever we mean by a single state of consciousness it has somehow emerged from a previous experience from which it is not sharply divided, and has a sense of itself as having emerged out of previous experiences which belong to the same stream. Indeed, it is essentially this which constitutes its being in the same stream as them.

James says that this continuity can link experiences which are divided by a period of unconsciousness, as in sleep. On waking after sleep we have an experience which feels to itself to be continuous with experiences we had when last awake. And James suggests that in fact there are many such breaks in a stretch of what we take to be unbroken consciousness, but which in virtue of the feeling which each experience has of carrying on from previous ones are continuous in the sense of his main concern.

It is in the context of his discussion of continuity that James develops his notion of the 'fringe', 'the influence of a faint brain-process upon our thought, as it makes it aware of relations and objects but dimly perceived'.[18] He uses this notion to elucidate the distinction he has previously made between knowledge by acquaintance and knowledge about.[19] In the former we are merely presented with something; in the latter we have thoughts about it. The difference, suggests James, consists in the fact that in the latter our awareness of the object is suffused with a dim sense of its relations, real or ideal, to other things, relations which, in principle, we could follow up in a flow of continuous consciousness until we had acquaintance with them too.

James's account of these matters is none too clear in PP, because he has foresworn coming to terms with the full metaphysical question of how the mind stands to an object presented in perception. The aboutness of both thought and perception is said to consist in likeness to their object combined with utility in prompting effective dealing with it, the difference seeming to be simply the degree of the likeness and the directness of operative control.[20] In all perception or thought one is acquainted with something, and one has propositional knowledge about it according to the richness of the fringe. Or rather this is what the commenting psychologist will say about a state of mind he is studying, while for the state of mind itself the problem does not arise.[21] We will see that in his radical empiricist phase James substituted for this the view that in perception the object itself swims into our state of consciousness, and that the meaning and reference of thought is determined by the way in which it prepares us for such direct perceptual encounter with its object (or at least its 'associates'). And his conception of the continuity of consciousness plays an important role in the way in which he explains this.

---

18   PP, I, p. 258.
19   See PP, I, p. 258 et ff.; also p. 221.
20   See PP, I, pp. 216–28.
21   See PP, I, p. 217.

(4) It always appears to deal with objects independent of itself.

We have followed James in anticipating discussion of this characteristic of thought in the discussion of its continuity. And however problematic it may be, it is, says James, an essential feature of the mental as we ordinarily think of it. Yet many theorists of mind do it scant justice.

For example, empiricist philosophers and psychologists have tended to examine consciousness as a series of 'impressions' and 'ideas', conceived as mere bits of the universe complete in themselves. James is insisting as against this that the study of the mental must take account of the unique way in which it is about or of something. In doing he so comes close to Brentano's claim that it is distinctive of the mental that it is intentional.

For Brentano there is always some object which 'inexists' in a mental act, an object which may or may not exist independently.[22] We have seen that in his later pragmatist and radical empiricist philosophy, James largely rejected the notion of intentionality conceived as something intrinsic to every mental occurrence. However, at the time of PP he seems to endorse the notion without qualification. Although he does not give any very clear idea of the nature of intentionality, its pervasive presence as a feature of the mental is important for his treatment of a number of issues (e.g., his discussion of the so-called 'psychologist's fallacy').[23]

In giving this fourth characterisation of consciousness James is also contending that the presumption is against idealism, absolute or otherwise. Even if it were the final metaphysical truth that the physical world is somehow mind's creation, that is not how it seems to ordinary consciousness. And a scientific

---

22   See Brentano, book 2, chapter I, §5, pp. 88–89. Later Brentano thought the scholastic term 'inexistence' somewhat misleading as suggesting a kind of existence, when the point is that what thought is about need not exist at all.

23   Chapter XXI, The Perception of Reality, contains James's main discussion of belief in PP and thus is in a way the main locus for considering James's then views on intentionality. This is a chapter which was dropped in *The Briefer Course* and that may suggest that he was not too satisfied with it. In some ways it contrasts sharply with his radical empiricist account of intending, since belief is treated as a kind of specific sensation which accompanies those of our ideas which represent realities for us. However, James is here arguably inclined to confuse ideas and their objects. He holds that everything we think of does thereby in a broad sense exist and can quite correctly be regarded as real if only we fit it into the right 'world', whether that of the sensorily giveable on the one hand, or the world of some novelist or myth on the other. There is a certain tendency to go along too easily with this view as a result of confusing the idea, which certainly does exist, with its object, and thereby concluding that its object must exist in some world or other. Such a view can indeed be defended without any such confusion, but James may nonetheless go for it too readily on this basis.

psychology must side with the ordinary view here. Its purpose is to study consciousness as a phenomenon arising out of the natural world, and assisting the organism in its dealings with it. That implies that it knows it without having created it.

(5) *It is interested in some parts of these objects to the exclusion of others, and welcomes or rejects—chooses from among them, in a word—all the while.*

In his discussion of this characteristic James examines some of the phenomena later prominent in Gestalt psychology but conceives them as reflecting our particular interests rather than as an inherited sensory mechanism. Objects are experienced in holistic patterns which reflect our particular interests. More generally, the fifth characterisation of consciousness indicates that its function is to present biologically suitable goals to the organism and to steer it towards them. As such it helps organisms survive and has therefore been sustained and developed by natural selection.

It was in this connection that James spoke so often with enthusiasm of the conception of the reflex arc as the great new key to psychology.

Writing in 1888 he had said:

> The only conception at the same time renovating and fundamental with which biology has enriched psychology, the only *essential* point in which 'the new psychology' is an advance upon the old, is, it seems to me, the very general, and by this time very familiar notion, that all our activity belongs at bottom to the type of reflex action, and that all our consciousness accompanies a chain of events of which the first was an incoming current in some sensory nerve, and of which the last will be a discharge into some muscle, blood-vessel, or gland. . . . Viewed in this light, the thinking and feeling portions of our life seem little more than half-way houses towards behavior; and recent Psychology accordingly tends to treat consciousness more and more as if it existed only for the sake of the conduct which it seems to introduce, and tries to explain its peculiarities (so far as they can be explained at all) by their practical utility.
>
> Perry, II, pp. 75–76; [Perry is quoting from 'What the Will Effects' in *Scribner's*, III (1888)]

Although he does not invoke the concept of the reflex arc in PP, chapter IX, he is making the same essential point, namely, that consciousness exists for the sake of practice and is to be understood in terms of its teleological function. Psychologies of cognition apart from will (like those of some empiricists) are bound to deal inadequately even with their own domain.

Those who see will as more fundamental than cognition often attack what are called presentationalist accounts of willing for which willing is identified with the experience of a particular sort of idea. It was on these grounds that James Ward and others attacked Bradley's treatment of volition. One might expect James to be on Ward's side here. However, when we turn to James's treatment of will in PP we shall see that this is only so to a very limited extent.

§3. *The View of the Self Taken in* The Principles of Psychology

§ James contrasts two aspects of the 'self'—the self as known (the 'Me') and the self as knower (the 'I' or 'Ego'). The former is the object of self-interest and self-concern of all types; the latter is the ultimate knower of the Me and of all other things.

In the shortened version of the work James says that common sense thinks that the Me and the I are the same item, and that his initial distinction between them is not meant to preclude this.[24] For it would remain helpful to distinguish the self qua object of someone's selfish concerns, and the self qua ultimate knower and doer. However, seeing that the material Me includes my possessions it is difficult to believe that there is even a *prima facie* case for confusing this aspect of the Me and the I. At any rate, James's conclusion is that the distinction is fundamental for psychology and metaphysics.

James distinguishes the 'Me' into three components, though he emphasises that what belongs to the Me, and what belongs to the not-Me varies over time, the Me always being that in which the I takes a selfish interest. (This seems to beg the question against the identity of Me and I.) Selfish concern divides into two main types, self-appreciation and self-preservation. Anything in which I take personal pride, or for which I feel shame, belongs to the Me, as does anything the preservation of which is among my most ultimate motives. Understood in this broad sense the Me, or self-as-object, has three main components: (1) the material Me; (2) the social Me; (3) the spiritual Me. A main task of youth is to choose which of these Me's, taken with which of its unstable contents, is to be that with which 'I' most fully identify myself and which must be dropped as incompatible therewith.

The most obvious part of the material Me is my body. Thus in caring for myself I may simply be concerned with the fate of my body. However, James includes under the Me also my material possessions insofar as they are the objects of emotions of the essentially same self-regarding type. One's clothes also belong to it, along with all those material possessions which swell what I am for myself so that I would feel depleted if I were deprived of them. One's house, for instance, or today one's car, may be a part of that self whose presentability concerns one just as much as that of one's body.

James says that our family are typically part of our material Me.

> Our father and mother, our wife and babes, are bone of our bone and flesh of our flesh.
>
> PP, I, p. 292

---

24   See BC, p. 176. I quote indifferently from BC and PP on the self, as there seem to be no important differences.

It seems odd to describe these as part of my material self. If I am proud of my children it is likely to be for their attainments, mental or otherwise, rather than for their physical properties. If so are they not rather an extension of my spiritual 'Me' than of my material 'Me'? Altogether, there is much that is insightful in James's quite influential discussion of these different Me's, but there is also a certain amount that is questionable in its detail.

By the 'social Me' James means the image of myself which exists in the minds of other people or perhaps the image which I believe thus to exist; either way it defines the same sense of self-concern. A special development of this occurs when my interest is not in how other people perceive or think of me but in how I am appearing to my God, or even how I would appear to some ideal knower who personifies the moral law for me. This social self may become more important for me (=I) than that which figures in the minds of my fellows.

Next comes the 'spiritual Me'. This must not be confused with the 'I' conceived as the ultimate subject of all my thoughts.

James begins by describing the spiritual self as consisting in

> the entire collection of my states of consciousness, my psychic faculties and dispositions taken concretely.
>
> BC, p. 181; see PP, I, p. 296

Otherwise put, it is the sum of my cultural, intellectual, and spiritual achievements and the supposed merit I have won through them. This self is the object of its own special sort of selfish feeling.

However, taken more concretely, James says that the spiritual self is a kind of 'innermost centre' of our consciousness which is the ultimate source of thought, effort, and action.[25] In attempting to introspect what this central core of consciousness really is James decides that, in himself at least, this

> *'Self of selves', when carefully examined, is found to consist mainly of the collection of ... peculiar motions in the head or between the head and throat....* If the dim portions which I cannot yet define should prove to be like unto these distinct portions in me, and I like other men, *it would follow that our entire feeling of spiritual activity, or what commonly passes by that name, is really a feeling of bodily activities whose exact nature is by most men overlooked.*
>
> PP, I, pp. 301–2

This is an example of the phenomenological materialist tendencies I noted at the end of the first section of this chapter. However, James professes to be open-minded as to whether there is also something more purely spiritual to this inner core of the self, or whether it may take a different form in different persons. But it would not be very surprising, he thinks, if it were to consist more or less wholly in such bodily feelings. For they may be our sense of the bodily

---

25   PP, I, p. 297.

processes by which we most constantly make the most subtle of those adjustments to incoming stimuli which determine what we do or say.[26]

There is something rather confusing, as it seems to me, in lumping together
under the heading of the 'spiritual self' one's distinctively mental or spiritual
talents, and this inner core from which they seem to spring. Be that as it may,
the spiritual self is not to be confused with the pure ego, if there is such a thing.
For they are its presentations just as much as are the more objective constituents
of consciousness. The truth is rather that what is presented divides into a self
and a not-self aspect, and both these contrast with that to which these contents
are presented, if there be any such thing. Whether there is any such thing is left
as an open question; perhaps there is just the flow of consciousness (or 'sciousness') and nothing at all which can be said to be aware of it. Maybe it should
not even be said to be aware of itself, but just there. However, though James
will not dismiss this idea, he will continue to assume that there is, if not
necessarily a subject of awareness which binds all the contents of present
consciousness together, at least a unifying act of awareness which does so.[27]

§ James says that there is no *a priori* reason why the I (whatever exactly that
is) should have directed the special sort of interest it does at one particular Me
of any of these sorts rather than of another. Selfish feelings are directed at one
of the Me's or at their collection, not at the pure I which has the feelings or the
consciousness in which they are lodged. My 'I' might have been directed at the
welfare of another's body as directly as it is in fact at mine, and indeed often is
so where the other is my child.

> I might conceivably be as much fascinated, and as primitively so, by the care
> of my neighbour's body as by the care of my own. I *am* thus fascinated by the
> care of my child's body.
>
> BC, pp. 194–95; cf. PP, I, p. 325

The fact that the core of the material Me might have been a different body
from that which houses the knowing I helps us see, according to James, that
ordinary self-love is not the concern of the knowing I with itself but with
something in the world presented to it. Thus there is no difference in principle
between altruism and egoism, merely a difference in the presented objects upon
which they are directed.

I doubt whether this is quite satisfactory as it stands. It may be true enough
so far as the Me is that of which one is proud or ashamed; doubtless there are
those who take pride in the Miss X of their nation! However, the more basic
and crude sort of physical selfishness is concerned with the kinds of 'physical'
content which will be present in the same stream of consciousness as that of the
concern. The body at which this is directed is that which will be present in or
to that consciousness as the home of feelings more or less comfortable. Con-

---

26   See PP, I, pp. 302–3.
27   See PP, I, pp. 304–5.

ceivably that could have been other than the one which houses the I (whether phenomenologically as the perspective from which the distance senses present the world or physically as containing the brain-producing consciousness). But this is not what James has in mind. He is simply insisting that I might have had the same direct concern with your bodily welfare as I do with mine without any strangeness in the location of my sensations. And that seems impossible. For the concern with a body in which I do not feel pleasure and pain cannot be the same as that with one in which I do.

James is claiming that in physical self-concern (as in all other forms of self-concern) the I is not directed at its own well being, but at a particular object in the world to which its relation is not essentially different from that in which it stands to other objects. That it is directed at what it calls its own body rather than another's is explicable in terms of natural selection but is not a deep necessity.

But there must be something wrong here. Physical self-concern is with that body which is presented as incorporating feelings of pleasure and pain. Since such presentation, as James himself insisted later, is something which is actually included within consciousness, it is misleading to say that consciousness is here concerned with something beyond itself. Whether the body thus presented is or is not the seat of consciousness, ordinary physical self-concern is concern with it as a constituent of consciousness and cannot be directed in the same way at a body presented merely from the outside. Your concern with your child's sufferings may be greater than with your own but it is directed at what can only occur in the stream of consciousness to which the concern itself belongs by vivid representation and thus contrasts with self-directed worry.

There seem in fact to be three relations between an individual consciousness and its body. That body contains the brain on which consciousness depends, it determines the point of view upon external things given by the external senses, and it is the locus of felt bodily pleasure and pain. These relations might perhaps have linked one consciousness to two or three different bodies but in fact they link it only to one. But, whatever may or may not be in principle possible here, the essence of ordinary physical self-concern remains the same, namely that *this* consciousness should be filled with pleasant rather than unpleasant bodily feelings. The only thing which would radically alter the nature of that kind of physical concern would be a break-down of the division of consciousness into distinct personal streams, and that is not what James has in mind.

Thus it is at the best misleading of James to say that selfish feeling is not the pure ego's concern with itself but always with an object in the external world presented to it. Doubtless if there is no such thing as the pure ego (as we will see James arguing) selfishness is not the pure ego's concern with itself. But that does not affect the fact, which James would seem to be denying along with this, that the most basic sort of physical self-concern is distinct from the concern one can have with another's physical well being. For its object is the kind of physical sensations which will occur in the stream of consciousness to which it belongs, whatever their 'objective' location. So James's attempt to assimilate egoism and altruism, as being both the direction of consciousness upon something other than itself, cannot stand. And this applies equally to selfishness which is not merely physical. The object of selfish concern is the quality of the experiences which will be sensibly continuous with itself, while altruistic concern can only flow into representations of its object. The division between them can only break down if the sensible continuity which divides experiences into streams allows these to merge or bifurcate. James had an increasing tendency to think this possible, but that is not what is at issue here.

§ We must now turn more directly to James's treatment of the ultimate I. After much discussion of views which postulate a pure ego, self-identical with itself over time in some non-natural way, James contends that the only I we need postulate is the passing thought itself. The thinker at any moment is simply the thought then occurring. What gives the impression of there being a permanent I is that the thought as of now has a very peculiar attitude to certain thoughts which have occurred in the past and less directly to whatever they had that attitude towards, what that had that attitude towards, and so on. Thereby the passing thought gives itself a history and constitutes itself the present state of an enduring I. There is, as James finally concludes, no other sense in which there is any such I.[28]

A convenient way of putting the essence of James's view is this. This presently occurring thought is a sort of momentary self which looks back upon various past momentary selves as being past versions of itself, and thereby makes them belong to its past. These momentary selves are either momentary passing thoughts or series of such which have melted into each other by gradual degrees and which are conceived now as units. And not only this. In looking back upon them as past versions of itself it also accepts as past versions of itself whatever momentary selves they regarded as past versions of themselves, and also what these regarded as belonging to their past, and so on. Thus my past is whatever I look upon as a past self of mine and whatever a past self of mine (made such either by my own present attitude to it or by the attitude to it of a momentary self which this rule makes a past self of mine) looks upon as a past self of itself.

James's precise position is not without its obscurities but its general gist is very convincing. The main objection I would raise is that he is too inclined to present his view as the thesis that the idea of an enduring self is an illusion. Surely it would have been better to present it as an account of what it is for there to be an enduring self.[29] Certainly from the later pragmatist perspective it

---

28   But there are some unclarities in this claim. Are the past thoughts with which it thus identifies itself necessarily ones with which it is sensibly continuous? Or is it even this identification in which sensible continuity partly consists? Answers to these questions are complicated by the fact that James effectively includes two distinct things under the heading of sensible continuity: (1) the peculiar way in which one moment of experience melts into the next; (2) the retrospective identification of itself of one passing thought with previous ones. See PP, I, p. 334.

29   Still, he does say: 'The sense of our own personal identity, then, is exactly like any one of

should be taken as an analysis of the whole real meaning of the claim that there is such a thing and this is the position sometimes taken up in PP.[30] But he also tends to give the impression that people normally believe in a something more than this with which he is dispensing.[31] (If this something more is some distinctive personal essence reactualised in one's own experience from moment to moment, then it is, indeed, an empirically significant claim which James may mean to challenge, as we shall see below, by stressing the extent to which personality alters over time. But so far as what is in question is a substance whose identity does not depend on any repeatable characteristic, his view should surely be that its only real meaning is one captured in his account.)

§ Does the present passing thought, or momentary I, only identify itself with past Me's, or does it identify itself also, or rather, with past I's? Some of James's remarks might suggest the former. For example, he speaks of the present thought as appropriating 'the content' of the previous ones (which seems different from appropriating them).[32]

However, if what is collected are past Me's, rather than past I's, then personal identity is not a relation between experiences as James surely intends it to be. For past Me's include not just elements of past states of consciousness but objects which are only intended by them. Thus, as we have seen, my clothes and my family are typically part of my material Me. These are not experiences but objects intended by my mental states. Or at least that is the obvious view which James espouses in PP. But perhaps when past Me's are collected it is as they were for past consciousness rather than as objective things. However,

---

our other perceptions of sameness among phenomena. It is a conclusion grounded either on the resemblance in a fundamental respect, or on the continuity before the mind, of the phenomena compared' (PP, I, p. 334). But he goes on to emphasise how this sort of empirical identity does not 'mean more than these grounds warrant' and is compatible with differences as real as the identity. The question whether a philosopher is denying the existence of something most people believe in, or explaining the real content of their belief, quite often arises with what are commonly described as reductionist approaches to a topic. James, Ayer (in various works), and Parfit [see Parfit] agree almost entirely on what the facts are about us on this matter, but Ayer thinks those facts answer to the whole of the common meaning of the concept of personal identity, Parfit thinks they fail to do so, and James is ambivalent. James does not draw the kind of ethical conclusion from his views on this matter (his moral position being that of individualism qualified by empathy) that Parfit does from his similar ones. If anything, it is Bradley who, at times, comes nearer to Parfit on this matter. Of American classic philosophers the nearest to Parfit is perhaps Santayana. See *Reason: Science*, pp. 250–51. To me it seems that there cannot be any great moral significance to the failure of a type of identity to exist the concept of which is incoherent, unless, indeed, the assertion of such an identity is really just a way of asserting a moral view.

30   E.g., PP, I, p. 345.
31   See PP, I, p. 348.
32   See PP, I, pp. 344, 371–73.

complete clarity on this point would require a clearer view of mind's intention-ality (characteristic five of the stream of consciousness) than I believe James had attained at that point. In any case, I shall assume that in this connection we must mean by the Me what might be called the not-self side of the state of conscious-ness, rather than the presumed external objects which correspond to this, if these are to be distinguished therefrom.[33]

In any case, why should the passing thought or momentary I not collect past I's, or perhaps a combination of past I's and past Me's? The reasons for saying that the momentary I or passing thought cannot make itself an object do not seem reasons for saying that it cannot make previous I's or passing thoughts its object.

Why should not what was merely lived through, without being made object at its own time, become an object later? How indeed could we gain any sense of what a passing thought is if our previous ones could not be made objects of attention by subsequent recall? (Bradley's ETR, chapter VI, is important in this connection.) The conclusion would seem to be that the present I, although it cannot make an object of itself, can make an object of a past I. And I think this is, in fact, James's position.[34] The thought or 'I' of each moment appropriates the past I's, together with their Me's, and appropriates too whatever they appropriate.[35]

§ Another possible objection to James's account is that the passing thought can hardly identify itself with past selves, whether I's or Me's, without making itself an object to itself. James deals with this objection effectively by saying that it is really just verbal. For what is meant by its identification with past selves is simply the special warmth with which it feels them, not a discursive judgement connecting them with itself.[36]

§ Actually I suspect that there is some ambiguity or oscillation in the meaning attached to such phrases as 'the passing thought' in PP and BC. This is related to his indecision as to whether he really is postulating some kind of ultimate, even if only momentary, subject of experience or just a stream of conscious states which are just there. Thus sometimes the expression seems to denote whole states of consciousness as they occur at any one moment, sometimes only certain elements therein. At one stage he speaks of the passing thought which

---

33 Actually, I think that this distinction between the I and the Me is dealt with more effectively by Bradley than by James. This is partly because James's treatment of intentionality is so ill-developed in PP that he does not make clear the contrast between elements of the Me which are actually components of my consciousness and those which are not. (However, Bradley's treatment of it can itself gain by being associated with James's main position regarding identity across time, which is more satisfactory than Bradley's. For further discussion see Part Two, Chapter One, §3.)

34 See, for example, PP, pp. 354, 359–60, 400, etc.

35 See PP, I, pp. 400–401.

36 PP, I, p. 341 note.

does the collecting as the 'identifying "section" of the stream'[37] but at other times a passing thought seems to be a whole momentary state of consciousness.[38]

Perhaps nothing much hangs on this ambiguity if it is one. For on James's holistic view of consciousness (as it is at any one moment) anything less than the whole state of consciousness, such as an identifying component thereof, is simply a convenient conceptual abstraction not a real entity with an independent character of its own of which there could be a duplicate in another state.

One reason, however, for wishing to know just what the expression 'the passing thought' stands for is that towards the end of BC James suggests that the very notion of such a thing may be a superstition. (This corresponds to his wondering in PP, at pp. 304–5, whether there is just the flow of consciousness [or 'sciousness'] and nothing at all which can be said to be aware of it.)

What he seems to have in mind here is the passing thought, conceived neither as merely one among other elements in the total state of consciousness, nor merely the total state of consciousness itself, but an overarching act which collects all the other contents to make of them one state. For he seems to be contending that they may not need to be unified by any such overarching cognitive act.

> Neither common-sense, nor psychology so far as it has yet been written, has ever doubted that the states of consciousness which that science studies are immediate data of experience. 'Things' have been doubted, but thoughts and feelings have never been doubted. The outer world, but never the inner world has been denied. [Happy days, the present reader may think!] Everyone assumes that we have direct introspective acquaintance with our thinking activity as such, with our consciousness as something inward and contrasted with the outer objects which it knows. Yet I must confess that for my part I cannot feel sure of this conclusion. Whenever I try to become sensible of my thinking activity as such, what I catch is some bodily fact, an impression coming from my brow, or head, or throat, or nose. It seems as if consciousness as an inner activity were rather a *postulate* than a sensibly given fact, the postulate, namely, of a knower as correlative to all this known; and as if '*sciousness*' might be a better word by which to describe it. But 'sciousness postulated as a hypothesis' is practically a very different thing from 'states of consciousness apprehended with infallible certainty by an inner sense.' For one thing, it throws the question of *who the knower really is* wide open again, and makes the answer which we gave to it at the end of Chapter XII [namely the view of the

---

37   PP, I, p. 338.
38   For example at BC, p. 464, the 'entire thought' evidently means a whole current state of consciousness, not some overarching mental act which apprehends it. And the formulation on p. 341 of the point that the thought which collects past experiences can only be apprehended retrospectively seems to treat it as the whole present state of consciousness.

passing thought just discussed] a mere provisional statement from a popular and prejudiced point of view.

BC, p. 467

This seems to point in various possible directions. It may signify only that what unites a person's experiences at any one moment is not their presence to a distinct synthesising thought but their being aspects of a unitary totality (the passing thought qua total state of consciousness). Or it may point to the view, with which James toyed later in the radical empiricism of 1904–5, for which the unity of consciousness at any one moment is virtually dropped, and its contents, which are not be distinguished from the objects said to be immediately presented to it, only belong together for a retrospective act (itself only in unity with the rest of current experience retrospectively by a later act directed at it).[39] Or again a hint may be intended that the true answer may lie with absolute idealism for which what holds experiences together is their presence to the absolute mind (though it is not clear that this would supply any immediate answer to the question of why at our level the experience occurring at any one time falls into distinct personal unities).[40]

§ Despite such problems as to the precise meaning of the expression 'the passing thought' the main thrust of the dominant PP account of personal identity over time is clear enough. Within each total state of consciousness there is an activity of 'collecting' past Me's which links that state to those Me's and to the past states of consciousness in or for which they figured (however, exactly, such figuring is interpreted). This collecting has two main features.

First it is a way of knowing them with a very special kind of fullness to it. It is no mere knowledge of a set of discrete propositional facts about them. Rather do the past experiences seem to re-present themselves in a manner as inexhaustible by verbal description as are the contents of the present perceptual field. Secondly there is a special kind of emotional aura which these past Me's have for present awareness which does not attach to events which one knows or believes have happened in connection with other people. James sums this up as their presenting themselves in a manner especially 'warm and intimate' and with a special kind of 'glow'.

> Each thought, out of a multitude of other thoughts of which it may think, is able to distinguish those which belong to its own Ego from those which do not. The former have a warmth and intimacy about them of which the latter are completely devoid, being merely conceived, in a cold and foreign fashion, and not appearing as blood-relatives, bringing their greetings to us from out of the past.

PP, I, p. 331. See also p. 333

---

39   See 'How Two Minds Can Know One Thing', ERE, chapter IV.
40   For some hints in this direction see PP, I, p. 367, and the reference to a possible *anima mundi* on p. 346.

§ There are two main types of objection which have been raised to any such account.[41]

First, there are objections from those sympathetic to the main idea but who see certain difficulties in explicating personal identity along these lines so that it conforms to a reasonable extent with what normally counts as identity of the same person across time. A. J. Ayer's discussions of James on personal identity fall into this category.[42]

The main difficulty he raises is that there may be cases where we have physically the same person over time and yet amnesia has caused such a gap in memory that James's criteria of personal identity are not satisfied. Ayer thinks that in most such cases we would still talk of the same person. From this he infers that relation to the same body (by way of somatic sensations pertaining to it) must be regarded as the crucial factor in determining personal identity.[43]

§ The second, more radical type of objection to an account of personal identity along James's lines goes back to Joseph Butler's objection to Locke's somewhat similar account, by which James was certainly influenced.[44] It is that words like 'memory', 'pride' and so forth, can only be correctly used for knowledge or feelings a person has about himself. Thus one must know whether it is with himself that the knowledge and feelings are concerned before one knows whether they can be described as memory, pride, or whatever.

This second objection is rather superficial. James's claim is that there is a special phenomenological quality to the awareness I have of my own past feelings and that this is what makes them mine. There is nothing circular in this if that quality is in principle describable, or at least introspectively identifiable on the basis of appropriate verbal cues, without presupposing the notion of personal identity. One cannot establish that this is impossible merely by pointing out that there is no pure way of referring to it in ordinary language such as does not carry the conceptual load of the notion of personal identity. It does not even matter if he himself uses words which normally carry this load if he manages thereby to direct our attention to a special quality of awareness on the basis of which we can explicate it. The only real question is whether James has

---

41   Milič Čapek raises rather different objections to the PP position, supposedly from the perspective of James's own latest position in which one's self is somehow one's real past creatively entering into the present. See Čapek. But this is much nearer the PP position than Čapek allows, for that implied a not dissimilar real presence of the past in the creative work of the present passing thought. Altogether Čapek does less than justice to the PP position and makes other claims about James's development which I would question. However, I agree, on the whole, with the contrast he draws between PU and the radical empiricism of around 1904.

42   See Ayer, 1968.

43   See Ayer, 1968, p. 270 et ff.

44   See Perry, I, p. 549.

identified the most promising candidate for such a role and, if so, whether its candidacy is successful.

But though this criticism is superficial it must be admitted that James does sometimes beg the question of personal identity and thereby weaken his account. He does so, not because there is anything question begging about his account of the special quality of our awareness of our own past experiences (our own experiences, if he is right, because of this special quality pertaining to our awareness of them), but on account of the detailed explanation he offers of why some experiences are objects of this kind of awareness and others not. For he suggests that the 'distant selves' which fulfil the condition of warmth and intimacy, are distinguished from others (i.e. the past Me's of other people) as those

> which fulfilled it when they were alive. *Them* we shall imagine with the animal warmth upon them, to them may possibly cling the aroma, the echo of the thinking taken in the act.
>
> PP, I, p. 333

This certainly is question begging. For it is obvious that the past selves of other people, as those people experienced them, had warmth and intimacy for them. It is only in relation to oneself that they can be said to have lacked warmth and intimacy. So James is saying that I identify with the past selves which were experienced warmly by me, through conceiving them with a warmth akin to that with which I first experienced them directly. But that presupposes that persons are distinguished one from another apart from these feelings of warmth and intimacy.

Does James perhaps mean that they are the object of a warm and intimate recollection now because the brain and body from which this present consciousness springs is one associated with the direct experience of them in a warm and intimate manner in their original occurrence? If so, he would be saying that while personal identity is constituted by the retrospective awareness of experiences in that special manner the cause of such personal identity lies in the sameness of the relation of these experiences to the same body.

That would fit in with the naturalistic approach of PP quite well, though there is no explicit formulation of it. At other times, however, it is clear that he would not wish to insist on the rooting of personal identity in the sameness of the body. However, he could still say that the ordinary naturalistic explanation of the ordinary facts of personal identity is of this sort but that, since the essence of personal identity consists in relatedness by warm and intimate recollection, it may in principle exist even without its usual physical basis.

However, upon the whole this 'explanation' of why some past experiences re-present themselves in this especially warm and intimate way, and thereby on James's view are mine, tends to confuse the issue which is whether that view of what makes them mine is adequate. To me it seems that he is right that it is this special sort of awareness of my past experiences which makes them mine (and indirectly makes mine those pertaining to, or similarly presented to, the state of consciousness to which they belonged, and so on) but that there is a good deal more to be said about the character of this special mode of awareness.

For example, one should surely extend the description of the special aura which tends to attach to the past Me's collected by the present passing thought to take more account of the variety of peculiarly self-directed feelings involved, such as pride, shame, nostalgia, and so forth. James certainly refers to these as attitudes which one has towards one's Me but he does not specifically invoke them as among the determinants of personal identity over time. However, it is fully in tune with his account of personal identity to supplement it by a fuller description along these lines. For these are as much feelings, directed to past Me's, which one does not have to events which one knows or believes have happened in connection with other people as those bathing their objects in the special kind of affectionate glow of which he speaks.

The crucial issue is whether my past experiences are the object of a unique kind of cognizance and emotion which is what ultimately makes them mine, or whether there is nothing that distinguishes them from feelings I have towards the experiences of others except that I use a different word when I know on more objective grounds that they were not mine. The former seems to me clearly the case. Both the emotional quality and the intimacy of the non-conceptual knowing with which my own past is presented are distinct from the presentation of anyone else's past experiences. If 'someone else's' experiences were presented in that way, there would be good ground for saying that that someone else was merely another physical incarnation of myself. And, if that means that cases of fission and fusion are a logical possibility, I see nothing there to conflict with personal identity as ordinarily understood. For it is not at all clear that that is incompatible with the logical possibility that identity might have been a less rigid affair than it normally is.[45]

James suggests that his view of the self's transtemporal identity is ultimately the same as must be given of that of anything else, a combination of a particular kind of resemblance and continuity.[46] The continuity consists in the way in which one experience flows into another without any sharp separation between them. It unites long stretches of experience quite apart from any retrospective 'collecting'. However, for any very full identity the past experiences have to be collected together in virtue of the special warmth and intimacy with which they present themselves in retrospect. James treats this second factor in personal identity as a form of resemblance because what is felt to be thus warm and intimate is what has a certain resemblance in its way of looking at things with what is going on now, both in respect of bodily feeling (the special quality of my own body) and emotional kinship

We will see how Bradley rages against any view which would reduce identity

---

45   See Sprigge, 'Personal and Impersonal Identity'.
46   See PP, I, p. 334.

to resemblance rather than vice versa.[47] Without necessarily siding with him on this, we may object that James's talk of resemblance here is not very satisfactory. Surely if resemblance is to figure in a theory of personal identity it must be in some more objective manner. Sameness of person must depend upon sameness of personality, whether it is registered in feelings of retrospective warmth or not. The specially intimate awareness which I have of my own past certainly has all the importance James attributes to it, but it is rather constitutive of the relevant kind of continuity than of the necessary resemblance.

In short, while we may agree that resemblance should have figured as a main factor in his account of personal identity, it does not do so just as it stands. Rooting personal identity in the warmth and intimacy with which our past experiences present themselves is not rooting it in resemblance. Perhaps James would claim that, if I am to think of those past experiences now, there must be a present image resembling them as they were. Even so, it is misleading to treat this intentional relation as merely one of resemblance, for resemblance can hold without it. Rather is it the fact that they are thought of, and as thought of have a special glow about them, which matters on James's view. If personal identity involves an element of distinctive resemblance between my experiences at different times, it must be because there is some distinctive personal way in which each of us experiences the world in virtue of which my experiences resemble each other as they do not yours. James himself recognizes this when he says finally that

> the identity which the [sc. momentary] *I* discovers . . . can only be a relative identity, that of a slow shifting in which there is always some common ingredient retained.
>
> PP, I, p. 372

This is true, he thinks, even in the normal run of events. It is much more strikingly true in cases of multiple personality.[48]

The conclusion seems to be that personal identity only exists in the fullest sense so far as there is not merely a string of experiences related by warm recollection, but a common personality exhibited (or at least in the offing in the sense that the stream of consciousness has flowed from and/or will flow back into it) throughout and that how far this is so in particular cases is an empirical question.

§ It may be objected that I have been taking James's treatment of personal identity too much as an effort at conceptual analysis, or metaphysical theory, rather than as simply a psychologist's description of the distinctive character of self feelings. Thus Graham Bird, after finding various difficulties in it as a full analysis of the concept of the identity of the self across time, suggests that James was only concerned to describe our 'sense' of personal identity,

---

47   See pp. 389–93, 554.
48   See PP, I, pp. 373–400.

leaving it open how much more there might be to the full concept of the thing. [49] However, while it is probably true that Ayer, for example, assimilates it too closely to conceptual analysis in his own style, James did explicitly indicate that his concern was with what personal identity amounts to in fact.[50] That his concern was thus to a great extent philosophical is confirmed by his long discussion of the views of such thinkers as Hume and Kant.[51] So it seems quite appropriate to take it as an answer to the philosophical question: In what does our personal identity really consist, so far as it is a reality?

§4. *Will, and Free Will, as Treated in* The Principles of Psychology

§ The problem of free will was of immense personal significance to James. He was rescued, as a young man, from a belief in determinism (which he found the bleakest of views) by the thought of the French neo-Kantian philosopher, Charles Renouvier.[52] In *The Principles of Psychology* James says that a scientific

---

49   See Bird, p. 87.
50   See Ayer, 1968, pp. 263–88; cf. PP, I, p. 332.
51   See PP, I, pp. 342–70.
52   See Perry, I, chapters XL–XLIII. The work of Renouvier which had such an immense influence on James as a young man was his *Psychologie rationelle* in *Essais de Critique Générale* (1854–64; 2nd ed. 1875). [See SPP, p. 165; Perry, I, p. 655.] Renouvier's definition of free will as 'the sustaining of a thought because I choose to when I might have other thoughts' played a key role in James's recovery from a long period of depression in 1879 [see the famous diary entry in Perry, I, p. 323.] and also clearly influenced the treatment of 'effort' in PP. Not only was Renouvier a free-will-ist, cognitive voluntarist, and metaphysical pluralist, but also his philosophy is founded on a denial of a real infinite, something with which James did not fully agree, but with which he was always sympathetic. [See Chapter Four, p. 214–25, below.] Later James came to think Renouvier's philosophy too scholastic or rationalistic, drawing hard and fast divisions between aspects of mind and reality which flowed into each other. [See, for example, SPP, p. 165.] However, Perry may be right that 'Renouvier's was the greatest individual influence upon the development of James's thought cannot be doubted'. [Perry, I, p. 655.] His respect for and gratitude to him is expressed in the dedication of SPP. '[Charles Renouvier] was one of the greatest of philosophical characters, and but for the decisive impression made on me in the seventies by his masterly advocacy of pluralism, I might never have got free from the monistic superstition under which I had grown up. The present volume, in short, might never have been written. This is why, feeling endlessly thankful as I do, I dedicate this text-book to the great Renouvier's memory.'
      I find that experts on French philosophy today are usually quite ignorant of the important position Charles Renouvier had during his long life (1815–1903) among French philosophers. Renouvier started a journal, *L'Année Philosophique*, largely as a platform for his own type of neo-Kantian philosophy to which James often

psychology must take determinism as a working principle. Nevertheless it cannot tell us that determinism is actually true, and James's own belief is that it is not true. What a scientific psychology can do, however, is cast some light on what the *modus operandi* of free will might be if there were such a thing.

But before we turn to free will we must consider James's account of will in general in PP, II, chapter XXVI. This is not always easy to follow since he tends to lay down positions which are subjected later to substantial qualifications.

He begins by insisting, against a common assumption, that no special act of willing, no special *fiat*, is required in order that we shall do something deliberately or voluntarily.[53] This sounds like the point much emphasised by some later philosophers, such as Gilbert Ryle, that there need be no preceding mental act of will in voluntary action. But these philosophers mean that there need be no causing mental event at all for an action to be voluntary. James, in contrast, assumes that a voluntary act must spring from some kind of triggering mental event. (Otherwise we have merely one of those instinctive or reflex responses which form the necessary background of action proper.) His point is rather that the mental event which triggers the action need not involve any special element of will. Rather is the mere idea of a movement of a kind performed in the past often the only mental element in the causation of a voluntary action. More frequently still it is the mere idea of some state of affairs X, when X has in fact been produced by such a movement in the past, which produces the movement now.

Such action is of the type which James calls ideo-motor. Its occurrence, easily detectable in most people's introspection, shows that the ideas of past movements, or the past results of such movements, have a direct tendency to produce them again and that no special act of will nor envisaging of the object of action as especially good is required in voluntary action.

§ The movements performed in ideo-motor action must have been made in the past without any prior idea either of them or of their consequences.[54] For both of these are ideas of certain sensations, either the sensation of the body as it moves in that way, or the sensation of perceiving some upshot of the movement, and they can only have become associated with the movement itself as a result of past experience.

Thus everything we perform voluntarily must first have occurred as an instinctive or unconditioned reflex response to a stimulus. Only thereby do we gain ideas of our possible movements or of their consequences. But when such an idea has once been acquired in association with a particular sort of move-

---

contributed. He was a close friend of its later editor, and disciple of Renouvier, François Pillon, to whom PP is dedicated. Renouvier's main work is *Essais de critique Générale*, 4 vols., Paris, 1854–1864, with several revised editions concluding with one in 1897.

53   See PP, II, p. 522.
54   See PP, II, p. 487.

ment, then the idea itself acquires a tendency to produce that movement. So we cannot do anything deliberately which we have not done first instinctively.

This is evidently grossly over-simplified. It is obvious that I can do something for the first time and it be a completely deliberate action. James must mean that whenever we do something voluntarily for the first time our action could be decomposed into a complex of more ultimate actions, the sensory nature and results of which were originally learnt from their reflex occurrence. Our idea of them must be a complex idea whose elements and form of combination are simple ideas which have come to cause the ultimate movements which contribute to the action as the result of past experience of them in distinct reflex responses.

§ So, according to the ideo-motor theory of action, voluntary action may consist in movements whose cause is the mere idea of that movement or of some result it has had in the past. Or it may consist in a complex of actions each of which is individually of this type. (The movements I make in taking a piece of chocolate and eating it may be caused by ideas such as I had of what I was up to in a piece of instinctive or reflex seizing and eating in infancy or by ideas which are the combination of ideas of seizing and ideas of chewing which were acquired separately and are now first combined.)

One sometimes gets the impression that for James we have a case of ideo-motor action wherever an idea causes a movement through having been associated with it in the past. If so, we would have ideo-motor action when, because the idea of going to bed has become associated with drinking a cup of hot chocolate, that idea acts as an immediate stimulus for movements likely to produce hot chocolate for me, even though there is nothing else about it which makes it the idea of drinking hot chocolate. We would have it again if, because Latin lessons in childhood, and hence the idea of them, have been associated with yawning, the idea of Latin words now causes me to yawn, though they can hardly be called an idea of yawning. Yet these seem scarcely deliberate actions even to the extent that James thinks of ideo-motor action as being so. So perhaps they are not meant to be covered by the term. However, he sometimes seems to deny any real distinction between ideo-motor and any activity caused by states of consciousness, where there is no special *fiat*, implying that it is merely a case of the general propulsiveness of consciousness.[55] But how far is it distinct from other cases of this? That is, how far does James mean to distinguish cases (1) where ideas cause activity without being ideas either of that activity or of its likely results, and (2) where they cause that of which they are genuinely the idea?

A possible answer might be that for James no idea is really *of* anything except in the sense of being associated with activity relating to it. If so, the distinction could not be made. But it is doubtful whether James is operating with any such reductive account of the aboutness of ideas in his PP discussion of will,

---

55   See PP, II, pp. 526–27.

whatever may be his later views on the topic. Thus upon the whole his discussion of will in PP seems to assume that in ideo-motor action ideas cause behaviour the movements and results of which they can be said to be *of* independently of this causal power and that the cases I have instanced would be a sort of conditioned ideational reflex rather than ideo-motor action proper.

Perhaps, then, his position is this. In ideo-motor action the ideas are intrinsically of the sensations *produced by* the movement, or the effects of the movement, which they cause, but only as a result of association ideas of the movement and its effects *itself*, while in what I have called a conditioned ideational reflex they are not even of the sensations of what they cause. However, I doubt whether James would really have been happy to accept such a sharp contrast between ideas of physical facts and ideas of the sensations they produce; certainly it clashes strongly with some aspects of his later radical empiricism.

What does seem clear is that if the relation between the ideas and their objects were, in ideo-action, simply that of being somehow associated with them, it would be difficult to distinguish between the kind of case where an idea of Latin words or of going to bed causes me to yawn or make hot chocolate and the case where an idea of yawning or of making hot chocolate does so. For such an account would risk making any idea which caused yawning or the making of hot chocolate, as a result of some kind of association between them set up by past experience, an idea of yawning or of making hot chocolate. Since it seems fairly clear that in ideo-motor action, as James conceives it, the idea is in some independent sense of the movement, or the likely results of the movement, which it causes, we must take it that he is presupposing some account of the relation between idea and its object which allows for this distinction. Basically what he has in mind, it would seem, is that the idea must in some genuine sense envisage either the movement made or its likely results. (But what of ideas which consist of words rather than images? However, we must leave such questions alone for now.)

For it is surely only in the case of behaviour whose character or likely results are envisaged in the triggering idea that we have anything approximating to will, and ideo-motor action is supposed to be the most basic sort of will. When the idea of some past event merely produces an action like that which it produced before (the Latin words producing a yawn) we do not have a case of voluntary action at all, as we do when an action is caused by an idea which is genuinely of it or of its results. Some distinction is required, then, between ideas which produce behaviour which actualises their content and those which produce behaviour with which they have no direct intentional connection.

However, since James's account of the relation between ideas and their objects is so ill-developed in PP, I shall not attempt to explore further what view of this relation best fits the text as it stands.

§ The main point of the ideo-motor account of voluntary action is to deny that it turns on the occurrence of anything which can be called an act of will, conceived as something extra to the idea of the thing to be done or achieved. Another is to challenge the doctrine of psychological hedonism. In its simplest form this claims that voluntary action is caused by anticipations of pleasure to come from doing the action, or pain to come if the action is not done. In a more subtle form it says that pleasant ideas have a tendency to *promote* activity which will actualise what they envisage, unpleasant to promote activity which will *prevent* what they envisage, although what they envisage need not consist in pleasure or pain for oneself or indeed for anyone. As against hedonistic psychology of either type James insists on the tendency of ideas to produce the movements or situations they are of apart from any pleasure or pain pertaining to them or their objects.[56] Pleasure and pain serve at most to reinforce the power to produce action which belongs to ideas in general. Thus an alcoholic may be driven by the mere idea of heavy drinking without either the idea or the drinking bout as it envisages it being pleasurable.

§ Granted much voluntary action is of this ideo-motor kind, is there also a kind of action which is produced not by the mere idea of a movement or its likely effects, but by that in conjunction with some special *fiat* of the will? James's answer to this is not altogether clear.

Initially he seems to answer the question affirmatively.[57] And he suggests that the extra ingredient provided by this special *fiat* is required where an idea is checked from producing its associated action by the presence of another idea prompting to contrary action.[58] However, as his examination proceeds, his view seems to be rather that, though in a sense there is such a *fiat*, it is not really something with a positive nature of its own. It consists rather in the falling away of some factor (such as the presence of other ideas tending to produce contrary behaviour) inhibiting the idea from producing its standard effects. However, one could take it as his view that there is a *fiat* with a positive character of its own, but that this is merely an explosive feel which pertains to an idea when it bursts through inhibitions which have up till now prevented it from producing its usual effects.

§ Thus James has listed three types of action.

(1) Purely instinctive actions which occur as innately determined reflexes to certain stimuli. (They are distinguished from merely physiological occurrences by the fact that they can later be produced by the ideas of themselves or their previously experienced results, that is, are the basis of ideo-motor action.)

(2) Ideo-motor actions produced by the ideas of the movements in which they consist or of their results, such ideas having been acquired through the making of such movements in the past, or others from which these ideas have been derived. (If I am right, reference should also be made to actions which are caused by ideas which, not being of them, do not exemplify ideo-motor actions proper.).

(3) More explicitly deliberate actions produced by ideas operating in con-

---

56   See PP, II, pp. 549–59.
57   See PP, II, p. 526.
58   See PP, II, p. 528.

junction with a distinct *fiat* which breaks down some obstruction to their standard efficacy.

James's more detailed phenomenological descriptions of all this are as fascinating as one might expect, but we must stick to the bare bones of the matter.

§ Insofar as the theory of ideo-motor action is the theory that *will* consists in ideas actualising themselves in action, there is, as we shall see, some affinity between it and Bradley's theory of will, though they differ in detail. James's particular working out of the idea includes, moreover, the rather striking suggestion that there is no inherent distinction between the character of the ideas which thus tend to realize themselves through our movements and those which do not. Thus it is, he says, merely an empirical fact that ideas of my own body's movements, or what they can bring about, cause my body to move as ideas of a table which I see before me moving in certain ways do not.

James even claims that the difference between will and belief is merely that (for reasons which do not affect their intrinsic nature as psychological states) ideas belonging to the first tend to actualise themselves while the second do not.

> We shall see . . . that will consists in nothing but a manner of attending to certain objects, or consenting to their stable presence before the mind. The objects, in the case of will, are those whose existence depends on our thought, movements of our own body for example, or facts which such movements executed in future may make real. Objects of belief, on the contrary, are those which do not change according as we think regarding them. . . . I *will* that my foreign bookseller in Boston shall procure me a German book and write to him to that effect. I *believe* that he will make me pay three dollars for it when it comes, etc. Now the important thing to notice is that this difference between the objects of will and belief is entirely immaterial, as far as the relation of mind to them goes. All that the mind does is in both cases the same; it looks at the object and consents to its existence, espouses it, says 'it shall be my reality'. It turns to it, in short, in the interested active emotional way. The rest is done by nature, which in some cases *makes* the objects real which we think of in this manner, and in other cases does not. Nature cannot change the past to suit our thinking. She cannot change the stars or the winds; but she *does* change our bodies to suit our thinking, and through their instrumentality changes much besides; so the great practical distinction between objects which we may will or unwill, and objects which we can merely believe or disbelieve, grows up, and is of course one of the most important distinctions in the world. Its roots, however, do not lie in psychology, but in physiology; as the chapter on Volition will abundantly make plain. *Will and Belief, in short, meaning a certain relation between objects and the Self, are two names for one and the same PSYCHOLOGICAL phenomenon.* All the questions which arise concerning one are questions which arise concerning the other.
>
> PP, II, p. 320

It is to be noted that explaining the contrast between ideas pertaining to will and those pertaining to belief in this way, points to a further need for an account of what ideas are *of*, which does not link it too closely with their behavioural effects. For James certainly believed that all or at the least most ideas influence behaviour, and if they are *of* the actions they produce, or *of* their results, simply in virtue of producing them, then all or most ideas will exemplify ideo-motor action, and be cases of will in this sense. Thus the distinction made in the passage quoted only makes sense if ideas are *of* something in some more intrinsic way.

§ But is James right in holding that there is no inherent difference in the mental state of one who believes in the existence or occurrence of something and one who wills its existence or occurrence, so that what distinguishes will from belief is a psycho-physical connection extrinsic to their own mental natures? One objection to this lies in the apparent possibility of having mere beliefs about matters on which one could exert one's will, as for instance if I merely anticipate the outcome of some quarrel between my friends in which I could intervene. If willing is merely having ideas of a type which tend to realize themselves in action what prevents such ideas realizing themselves? Perhaps some special blockage. But simply anticipating such a result without intervening seems different from voluntarily taking up the role of a mere spectator.

Moreover, James's arguments against hedonistic psychology leave him with no clear account of the difference between those ideas which produce behaviour calculated to *promote* what they envisage, and those which produce behaviour calculated to *prevent* it.[59] If I have an idea of myself being burnt through picking up a dish just removed from the oven, that does not make me pick it up and get burnt but makes me desist from doing so. In contrast, if I have an idea of a warm relaxing bath, that is likely to make me run one for myself. Why does one of these ideas cause what it envisages and the other idea prevent it? To me it seems that the hedonist answer is essentially right, namely that the difference is that one idea is pleasurable or of something pleasurable, while the other is unpleasant or of something unpleasant. But James explicitly rejects this. (But see Perry, II, p. 97 for a second thought upon the matter.)

James says, in this connection, that even thinking of something unpleasant gives us some tendency to do it.[60] There are peculiar cases in which something of the sort seems to hold but I suggest that there is always either some overriding pleasurable fascination in what is thus envisaged or it is seen as offering a release from the struggle against it. Thus the alcoholic for whom, James says, the prospect of drinking may still move to action, though it has become more unpleasant than pleasant, surely anticipates it as assuaging the unpleasantness of his present tension.[61] And when we go on tugging at a sore tooth, another example James gives of counter-hedonic action, are we not trying to find true the idea that it no longer hurts?

> If one must have a single name for the condition upon which the impulsive and inhibitive quality of objects depends, one had better call it their *interest*. 'The interesting' is a title which covers not only the pleasant and the painful,

---

59   See PP, II, pp. 549–59.
60   See PP, II, pp. 553–54; BC, pp. 447–48.
61   See PP, II, pp. 541–45.

but also the morbidly fascinating, the tediously haunting, and even the simply habitual, inasmuch as the attention usually travels on habitual lines, and what-we-attend-to and what-interests-us are synonymous terms.

PP, II, pp. 558–59

But this does not explain the difference between those of these interesting ideas which lead to activity calculated to actualise their objects and those which lead to activity calculated to prevent it. (I have offered an account of will, somewhat influenced by James, but much more hedonistic in character in Sprigge, *Foundations*, chapter 5.)

§ Such might seem to be James's complete account of the nature of will. However in the course of classifying a variety of different kinds of willing James eventually brings another character upon the stage called 'effort'.[62] And having introduced it he even suggests that it is only when it is present that we have will in the very fullest sense.[63]

Effort is a force which can push us into actions in what seems the line of most resistance. Its operation is not reducible to ideo-motor action, and it is something more than the *fiat* which marks, or consists in, the collapse of inhibitions to the self-realization of an idea.

The role of effort is not to convert ideas into action but to sustain certain ideas rather than others in consciousness by directing attention at them.[64] This done, ideo-motor action does the rest. Thus effort does not directly act on anything physical but only on ideas. It directs attention at certain ideas, once they are there, and away from others, so that eventually the former have the field to themselves. Effort acts intra-mentally on the ideas, and it is the ideas themselves whose tendency to realize themselves in action affects the transition from the purely mental to the behavioural.

§ If there is such a thing as free will, in the important sense in which free will is incompatible with determinism, it is, says James, a property of effort.[65] For he is confident that which ideas come into the mind is settled deterministically, as also is their passage into action. No non-deterministic account of either seems conceivable. Moreover when ideas struggle for dominance the outcome is also an entirely deterministic matter, so far as this turns on their own intrinsic natures, such as the greater interestingness of one than another. So whether we do or do not possess genuinely contra-causal freedom, at the level of effort, we are certainly not thus free to determine which ideas will come into our minds of things we might do. It is only insofar as effortful attention at one of various rival ideas makes it so dominate the field of consciousness that rival ideas fade away, that there is any possible room for any real freedom of the will. Not that the existence of effort is equivalent to the existence of free will. Effort exists as

---

62   See PP, II, p. 548; BC, p. 442.
63   See PP, II, p. 562; BC, p. 450.
64   See PP, I, pp. 447–54; PP, II, p. 576; BC, pp. 452–53.
65   See PP, II, p. 571; BC, pp. 455–58.

a reality additional to ideas, their degree of interestingness, and their results through ideo-motor action, whether causally determined or free. However, if we possess free will, then, the amount of effort is not settled by past facts and laws of mind and matter.[66]

So the only contra-causal freedom possible is that of sustaining or expelling ideas, once they are there, by letting our attention dwell on them or turning it away from them to other ideas. But scientific psychology cannot show whether we do or do not possess a real contra-causal freedom of this type.[67] It will always be arguable, and never provable, that there is a sufficient cause in a physically determined state of the brain for the degree of attention we direct at each idea. However, since we are likely to lead better lives if we believe that we do possess such a freedom, the sensible path is to hold it for true that we do.

§ To believe this, we may note, is an exercise of that will or right to believe something on passional rather than evidential or rational grounds of which James was to defend the propriety in his 'The Will to Believe' (1896). For it satisfies each of the requirements he lays down for this. (1) Affirmation or denial of free will is a forced option. Not believing in it amounts virtually to thinking of ourselves as determined. (2) It is a momentous option. Our whole conception of ourselves will be affected by our decision. (3) It can neither be established nor refuted on evidential or rational grounds.

§ But what, we may now ask, exactly is this activity of attending to ideas which is the only possible locus of contra-causal freedom? James's account is none too clear. It must be something more than the fact that these ideas tend to feel more interesting than others and as a result to dominate over them and eventually expunge them from consciousness. But it's not clear what more. What, after all, is attention? And how is the attention itself related to the effort to sustain it?

James's main account of attention, in PP, I, chapter X, is not too helpful in this connection. For there he reduces attention to external objects to accommodation of the sense organs together with 'preperception' (a term borrowed from G. H. Lewes) of what we are about to perceive.[68] Thus it consists in having an idea of what we are about to perceive in advance of the perception, and this idea added to the perception gives the latter a special strength. It is difficult to see how attention thus understood (as a perception strengthened by a preceding idea) can be directed at the ideas themselves which produce movements, since here attention is not a perception at all but an act directed at certain of our ideas. Nor is it easy to see how effort conceived along these lines can constitute a distinct force which modifies the results which ideas would have left to themselves. Still, however precisely it is to be understood, James does think that there is an activity of effortful attention to one idea rather than another, and

---

66   See PP, II, pp. 571–72; BC, p. 456.
67   See PP, II, p. 572; BC, pp. 456–57.
68   See PP, I, pp. 434–46.

that it is in this that the free choice to do something which goes against the grain, in the possibility of which he believes as a moralist if not as a scientist, consists.

§ Sometimes James expressed the point by reference to the concept of the reflex arc.[69] According to this the brain is a centre to which impulses come from the sense organs and which responds to them by sending out impulses along the efferent nerves to the muscles resulting in some so-called voluntary movement. There is a continuous stream of energy travelling along the afferent nerves from the sense organs, reaching the brain and somehow processed there, and then travelling out from the brain through the efferent nerves to the muscles causing contractions productive of so-called voluntary behaviour.[70] The function of the brain is to process this energy so that the actions it produces are of an appropriate kind. The conscious analogue of this processing consists in conscious ideas and the ideas themselves play a part in settling just what sort of processing it shall be, each exerting its own particular influence on how it develops.[71]

If we ask how there might be any real free will in the situation, we must answer that it can only come as an influence on the extent to which the ideas which are thrown up into consciousness by the initial stage of this processing are sustained. If they are ideas of a kind which produce good or bad actions, our moral quality is shown in our capacity to preserve them in consciousness, or expunge them, and thereby allow them to do their peculiar job in influencing the processing and its results in behaviour.[72]

§ Why is James so sure that the only thing which can be free is the degree of effort that we direct at ideas already in the mind so that free will must be an energy working on ideas rather than on physical movements? There seem to be two essentially *a priori* answers. First, free will must involve some sort of choice, and the alternatives between which we choose cannot themselves be produced freely but must already be there. Secondly, the alternatives must present themselves in the form of ideas, since if they presented themselves as objective facts, the choice would already have been settled. One might object to this that attention could work on an external piece of behaviour and sustain it or otherwise, so that it does or does not consummate itself. For James's point does not rest on any confinement of the mind within the circle of its own ideas;

---

69   See particularly the 1881 'Reflex Action and Theism' in WB, pp. 111–44.
70   James was much concerned with the question whether there is any sensation corresponding to the outflow of energy through the efferent nerves, the so-called feeling of innervation, or whether all sensation is determined by the input of the afferent nerves. Wundt and others had associated the experience of voluntary movement with sensation of the former kind. James concluded that such sensation is a fiction and that our experience of moving is of the sensorial (kinaesthetic and perceptual) consequences of the movement, as supplied by the input of the efferent nerves. I take it that he was right in this. See PP, II, pp. 493–518.
71   See, e.g., WB, p. 114.
72   See PP, I, p. 453.

mostly he assumes that ideas themselves are directly of a reality beyond them, and it would seem that effort could be directed at what the ideas present to the mind rather than at the ideas themselves. However, James would presumably reply that, if you are really to know what you are up to, what you sustain or otherwise must be the idea of the end state, which may or may not occur, to which it tends.

§ James presents his position as though it were the claim that you cannot will external actions and their results, only ideas of them.[73] But he need not have done so. It is better put as the claim that to will an external action and its results is, where the willing is truly free, the attending to the idea of it with an effortfulness the strength of which is not causally determined. However, to me the notion of free will in this sense seems doubtfully intelligible. If ideas must come into the mind without being chosen beforehand, is not the same true of the attention directed at them? However, I doubt if there is any alternative account of contra-causal free will which is any more intelligible, at least if free will is not to be equated with sheer randomness.[74]

Actually, in certain moods James himself hardly minds equating free will with randomness, for elsewhere he seems mainly to cherish the notion as implying that there is an element of unpredictable spontaneity in the universe, an idea satisfying in itself and freeing us from the horrific claim that the good in the world is necessarily bound up with the evil there, and thus furnishes a justification for it as a feature of a perfect Absolute. (This is a main theme in the 1884 'The Dilemma of Determinism' in WB.) But that will hardly suffice for the more personally moralistic reasons which he seems to have in mind here.

§ Such must serve as an account of the general view of reality taken in PP. Of the other metaphysical topics treated there which I have not considered, the most important is the discussion of the nature of necessary truth in Chapter XXVIII. I shall touch briefly on that later. It is time now to turn to James's late philosophy, above all to his radical empiricism.

---

73   See PP, II, pp. 567–68; BC, p. 449.
74   The main official alternative is that free acts are caused by a timeless self or ego. Both James and Bradley took a dim view of any such idea. See, for example, PP, I, pp. 342–50; AR, pp. 74–75. For one thing it can only intervene in time if it performs acts of choice which are, in effect, events in time, and it will be the character of these events which must determine which of various alternatives open to that self in principle are chosen. But if these acts are events in time, it would seem that their occurrence must either be causally determined or, to whatever extent they are not, be merely random. To say that the self chooses between them is nonsense since they are its choices.

3

The Metaphysics of Radical Empiricism

§1. *What Radical Empiricism Is*

§ I turn now to the metaphysical investigations which absorbed much of James's later years. And I make no apology for considering him as a metaphysician. There are, indeed, those who think this quite inappropriate. Thus H. S. Levinson says: 'If ontological statements amount to statements that make categorical claims about what there is, then James simply does not make any'. And, he goes on, '[d]oing metaphysics, for him, amounts to "making a picture of the whole world," and results in a kind of esthetic stance, or roughly, a place from which to view "things" in the broadest sense of the term'.[1]

Such remarks seriously underestimate James's concern with how things really are, even if that concern squares a little oddly with some of his more aggressively pragmatist pronouncements. (In fact, there is a problem akin to that which arises with Nietzsche. A somewhat relativistic conception of the status of ontological claims is itself rooted in an ontology the absoluteness of which it seems to undermine.) Fortunately there are other commentators, such as Kuklick and Ford, who recognize the thoroughly metaphysical goals of James's thinking.

§ Our investigation of James's late metaphysics will start with his 'radical empiricism'. By this James sometimes means the thesis that the universe, or at least the totality of what we can know or even properly speculate about, is experiential through and through, so that the clue to its generic nature is to be

---

1   Levinson, *Religious Investigations*, pp. 111–12.

found in our own streams of consciousness or experience. He was consistently a radical empiricist in this sense from 1885, or earlier, till his death. However, the writings most explicitly presented as statements of radical empiricism (in particular, in the 1904–5 essays brought together as *Essays in Radical Empiricism*) present a much more specific set of doctrines, and it is these which I shall mostly use the term to cover and which are the topic of this chapter. The core of them is a highly individual form of direct realism which exists in tension with the importantly different system, to be considered in the next chapter, to which he moved finally, and which I shall call mystical pluralism. I shall not attempt to chart the precise chronology of James's shifting between these systems (a difficult scholarly task); the important thing is that they are sufficiently distinct to demand separate treatment.

§ The first main presentation of radical empiricism is the 1904 essay 'Does Consciousness Exist?', reprinted as the first essay in the posthumous *Essays in Radical Empiricism*. It is carried further in a 'A World of Pure Experience', and in other articles written shortly after.[2]

It is important to realize that the apparently negative answer the first of these gives to the question its title poses does not represent (as is sometimes supposed) an amazing jettisoning of that whole realm which had been the main subject matter of PP. James is not denying that there is a stream of sentient experiences constituting the 'what it is like being us' of each of us. It is nearer the truth to say that the radical empiricism presented here takes the stream of consciousness of PP as the paradigm of the nature of reality at large. However, there is a certain shift in the view taken of this stream, inasmuch as while earlier he had been content to take it as being somehow at each moment intrinsically *about* something, radical empiricism denies this straightforward conception of its intentionality. Rather is its *aboutness* a function which it only performs by way of its consequences in further experience.

What is now denied, then, is that consciousness exists as some unanalysable mental act or state which is somehow *of* or *about* things. For James wishes to replace what he regards as the mysterious notion of intentionality by a series of experienced relations of transition between different sensory items within the stream of experience. We have already seen this aim at work in the background of pragmatism and will return to the theme again later. However, this view of consciousness is an application rather than a formulation of the doctrines definitive of radical empiricism, and it is these which will be the concern of the present section.

§ James provided a convenient summary statement of what he means by

---

2   The crucial documents of radical empiricism are those of 1904–5 included in ERE. Closely related to these are the following ones in MT: 'The Function of Cognition' (1885); 'The Tigers in India' (1895); and the preface to *The Meaning of Truth*. Some of these could also be classified as statements of pragmatism, and often it is difficult to say which claims are considered more definitive of pragmatism, which of radical empiricism and which of what he sometimes called 'humanism'.

radical empiricism in the preface to *The Meaning of Truth* (1909). He also tells us here that the pragmatic theory of truth was for him 'a step of first-rate importance in making radical empiricism prevail.' In spite of that it is very hard to say just how pragmatism and radical empiricism do, or are supposed to, relate to each other logically. The present remark suggests that pragmatism provides a foundation for radical empiricism, but the converse would seem equally true. Certainly the pragmatic conception of truth is much less perplexing when it is seen as a development of radical empiricism.

It is possible that James found it easier strategically to advocate pragmatism first, even though the full pragmatic doctrine can only properly be understood in the context of radical empiricism. For he may have thought that pragmatism would (at least in a simplified form) be more acceptable to many people than full-blown radical empiricism and that this is best recommended as a rounding out of it. Still, some people, myself among them, find radical empiricism the more immediately appealing doctrine and can only sympathise with pragmatism, more particularly its conception of truth, when they see it as a development thereof. All in all, it must be said that James is not very clear as to how the two doctrines stand to each other, or as to what belongs to which.

However that may be, James here formulates the basic doctrine of radical empiricism thus:

> Radical empiricism consists first of a postulate, next of a statement of fact, and finally of a generalized conclusion.
>
> The postulate is that the only things that shall be debatable among philosophers shall be things definable in terms drawn from experience. (Things of an unexperienceable nature may exist ad libitum, but they form no part of the material for philosophic debate.)
>
> The statement of fact is that the relations between things, conjunctive as well as disjunctive, are just as much matters of direct particular experience, neither more nor less so, than the things themselves.
>
> The generalized conclusion is that therefore the parts of experience hold together from next to next by relations that are themselves parts of experience. The directly apprehended universe needs, in short, no extraneous trans-empirical connective support, but possesses in its own right a concatenated or continuous structure.
>
> MT, 1909 Preface, pp. 6–7

So the radical empiricist seeks an account of reality which uses no concepts not explicable in terms drawn from experience while not denying the possibility that 'noumenal' realities may exist. The claim is rather that it is

> wise not to *consider* any thing or action of that nature, and to restrict our universe of philosophic discourse to what is experienced, or at least, experienceable.
>
> 'A Reply to Mr Pitkin' in ERE, p. 243

§ We should avoid putting too much emphasis on James's saying that noumenal unexperienceable realities may exist ad libitum. For in spite of this qualification it is clear that radical empiricism is committed to the possibility of an account of reality in purely experiential terms which is complete, in the sense of providing a coherent account of what *may* be the sum of all things, and *is certainly* the sum of all things which humans can sensibly think about. Thus he rejects any view which affirms that the totality of experiential reality must depend on something non-experiential (whether its nature be otherwise knowable or not).

Thus radical empiricism is a strong positive metaphysical position about the completeness of an experiential account of things. And it seems reasonable, in expounding it, to talk of the *universe* or *reality* as consisting only of the experiential. For, as James saw it, if there is anything beyond reality or the universe in this sense, it is no part of the most comprehensive totality which could be the business of any conscious being. And indeed sometimes James shows less patience than here with a supposed noumenal realm.

§ There is some uncertainty, it must be said, as to whether the elements of a radically empiricist universe must each be experienced, or whether it is enough that they are experienceable.

A first thing to note in this connection is that the expression 'experienceable' here could be misleading. For some might agree that there is nothing which is not experienceable while denying that there is nothing except actual, and perhaps possible, experience. For, some will say, it is not true that all we ever experience is itself experience. (Some may even say that it is never experiences which we experience.) But whatever the merits of this view, it is not James's. For him what one experiences is itself an experience, and to the extent that he acknowledges a realm of the experienceable which is not actually experienced, it seems clear that what he has in mind is that besides actual experiences, there are experiences which have a definite possibility of occurring. It is not supposed that they are somehow lurking there as actualities waiting to be experienced.

So I think one may interpret the basic claim of radical empiricism as this. There is nothing strictly actual except what is experienced and nothing properly speaking describable as possible except possible experience. Thus actual things, and the actual relations between them, must not only be experienceable but actual parts of experience. The only doubt raised by reference to the experienceable is as to how far the truth about the universe may need to refer to possibilities of experience as well as actual experience. Either way, we have a much stronger form of empiricism than one which merely insists that our conceptions be derived from elements present in our own experience, without ruling out that they may apply to actual things which are not the elements of any actual experience.

§ That this is the *key* claim of radical empiricism is clear from such statements as these:

> My thesis is that if we start with the supposition that there is only one primal stuff or material in the world, a stuff of which everything is composed, and if we call that stuff 'pure experience' then knowing can easily be explained as a

particular sort of relation towards one another into which portions of pure experience may enter.

'Does Consciousness Exist?' (1904), ERE, p. 4

And elsewhere he talks of 'pure experience' as the name he has given to the *materia prima* of everything.[3]

§ What precisely does reference to the experienceable, or to possible experience, add to the conception of a universe containing nothing actual but actual experience? This is a matter on which James seems to have had some difficulty in coming to a conclusion, but he was clear enough that if possible experience adds something to reality not provided by actual experience, it is not some further stuff of reality but something whose existence as a possibility is simply the holding of certain conditional statements to the effect that if experiences of one sort should occur, such as those of our doing something, then experiences of some other sort will or would occur, such as our perceiving something. This implies that there is more to truth than an account of what actually is, but not that there is more to what is than actual experience.

§ It is an important feature of radical empiricism for James that it holds that the universe is held together by connections between things which are themselves 'parts' of experience.

> To be radical, an empiricism must neither admit into its constructions any element that is not directly experienced, nor exclude from them any element that is directly experienced. For such a philosophy, *the relations that connect experiences must themselves be experienced relations, and any kind of relation experienced must be accounted as 'real' as anything else in the system.* Elements may indeed be redistributed, the original placing of things getting corrected, but a real place must be found for every kind of thing experienced, whether term or relation, in the final philosophic arrangement.
>
> 'A World of Pure Experience' (1904), ERE, p. 42

§ This enables radical to agree with traditional empiricism in a primarily anti-holistic conception of the universe. (We will see that it even represents something of a retreat from the holistic treatment of the individual consciousness, as opposed to the universe, typical of PP.)

> Empiricism is known as the opposite of rationalism. Rationalism tends to emphasize universals and to make wholes prior to parts in the order of logic as well as in that of being. Empiricism, on the contrary, lays the explanatory stress upon the part, the element, the individual, and treats the whole as a collection and the universal as an abstraction. My description of things, accord-

---

3   'The Place of Affectional Facts in a World of Pure Experience' (May 1905), ERE, p. 138.

ingly, starts with the parts and makes of the whole a being of the second order.
It is essentially a mosaic philosophy.

'A World of Pure Experience' (1904), ERE, pp. 41–42

However, James thinks that the older empiricism of Hume, Mill, and others
gave undue emphasis to the reality of what he calls disjunctive relations, which
separate things from one another, at the expense of conjunctive relations which
hold things together. In particular, it did not do justice to the continuity of
personal experience, not realizing that '[p]ersonal histories are processes of
change in time, and *the change itself is one of the things immediately experienced'*.[4]
Thus it pictures a world of sharply distinct sensory atoms, inviting the claim
on the part of rationalists and absolute idealists that transcendental egos or the
Absolute must be postulated as what holds the atoms together.

We may note that on the topic of the transcendental ego James and Bradley
are at one. Both thought it quite vacuous to see the unity of experience as
depending on, or explicable in terms of, its pertaining to a single ego or soul,
claiming rather that the unity of experience is itself an experience. Thus the
point of the Absolute, for Bradley, is not to unify supposedly distinct elements
present in finite consciousness at any time but to unify the larger reality to
which such finite consciousness belongs. We shall have more to say about this
when we come to James's views on relations and on absolute idealism.

§ There are three main questions to be asked about this radical empiricist
doctrine:

(1) Why does James hold that there is nothing but pure experience? Are there
good reasons for holding it?

(2) What exactly is this pure experience which is supposed to be the stuff of
all things?

(3) How does radical empiricism, in the more specific sense here in question,
deal with such main metaphysical questions, as that of the nature of physical
things and minds? And how acceptable are its answers? (These questions will
concern us in later sections.)

§ (1) He does not offer much justification for it. Personally I think there is
much by way of justification that he could have offered, but I will not pursue
that now. For James I think there are several main things in its favour.

First we never come across anything except pure experience, and therefore
there is no point in postulating anything more unless it is required to explain
pure experience, and James thinks that it is not. In short, since we never come
across anything but pure experience, the burden of proof is on those who claim
that there is something more.

Second, it is difficult to see how we can form any conception of anything
other than pure experience, since we have no materials adequate to construct

---

4   Ibid, p. 48.

any such conception. That we seem to is only because we give a faulty account of our own meanings.

Third, the main metaphysical problems find a more elegant solution when approached on the basis of this ontology.

In general, James seems to regard it as a promising hypothesis which we will accept or not according as to whether it provides a satisfying basis for solving the metaphysical problems which we think important.

§ (2) The view that nothing that concerns us exists except experience seems to stand in striking contrast with many ordinary opinions. Normally we assume that there is a physical world which is certainly not 'composed of experience' and many of us think of minds as things which have experiences without themselves being, or being made up of, experiences. Again some of us think that there are abstract entities like numbers and would deny that these are in any sense experiential. Thus the view that nothing exists except experience is quite radical and quite properly contrasted with other empiricisms by this epithet. Certainly it seems much more strange than the common form of empiricism for which all knowledge derives from experience without necessarily being limited to a subject matter which is exclusively experiential.

What, then, is this pure experience which is supposed to be the stuff of reality, or at least of all reality which can in any way concern us? Note, first, the contrast between the passage quoted above on p. 112–13 from 'Does Consciousness Exist?', where he speaks of 'pure experience' as the stuff of which everything is composed, and the following:

> 'Pure experience' is the name which I give to the immediate flux of life which furnishes the material to our later reflexion with its conceptual categories. Only new-born babes, or men in semi-coma from sleep, drugs, illnesses, or blows may be assumed to have an experience pure in the literal sense, of a *that* which is not yet any definite *what*, though ready to be all sorts of whats.
> 'The Thing and its Relations' (January 1905), ERE, p. 93

> [And also: It is only virtually or potentially either object or subject as yet. For the time being it is plain unqualified actuality or existence, a simple *that*. ERE, p. 23.]

These passages are *prima facie* in conflict, one implying that there is nothing other than pure experience (and systems made of pure experiences in relation) and the other implying that in addition to pure experience there is something else which supersedes it to form the consciousness of adult human beings. Speaking in the latter vein he says elsewhere:

> Its purity is only a relative term, meaning the proportional amount of unverbalized sensation which it still embodies.
> 'The Thing and its Relations' (January 1905), ERE, p. 94

(We shall see that almost exactly the same conflict occurs between different statements of Bradley's about *immediate* experience.)

Presumably we must take the first sense as the primary one when considering the basic ontology of radical empiricism. And in this sense 'pure experience' stands for all reality which is of the same essential sort as that which makes up what he would once have called the stream of consciousness of human beings and animals. It does not follow that for radical empiricism nothing exists except human and animal streams of consciousness. There may be streams of experience not forming the consciousness of any conscious subject or at least any commonly recognized one. Radical empiricism must claim, however, that these are made of the same generic stuff as our streams of consciousness are.

In the light of the account of consciousness in 'Does Consciousness Exist?' it might seem better to avoid the word in this context. But, after all, he did not deny that there is a reality properly called our 'stream of consciousness', but only insisted that what made it 'consciousness' rather than mere 'experience' is its function rather than its nature. The radical empiricist claim is that reality in general consists of stuff of the same sort as in us performs that function and James himself sometimes refers to all such stuff as a species of consciousness. So I shall not myself attempt any rigid consistency in my use of 'experience' and 'consciousness', though I shall often talk of a 'stream of experience' rather than of 'consciousness' to emphasise that not all such streams carry symbols performing the 'function of consciousness'. (Sometimes I may use James's expression, a 'personal biography' instead of 'a stream of experience or consciousness'.[5])

§ But although James made reality of the kind we all encounter in our own streams of consciousness or experience the very stuff of all things, such streams, as we have noted, are now conceived in a much less holistic manner than they were in PP, and this is essential, as we shall see, for the direct realism he now espouses. (Its being so is also a main reason why he eventually abandoned the latter.) Thus he no longer claims that its constituents at any one time cannot be identical with, but only akin to, items belonging to another time or stream and are inseparable from the precise felt context to which they belong. Rather are our streams of consciousness made up of items, sometimes known as 'natures', which can enter into all sorts of different sorts of arrangements without any inherent change. This represents something of a return to the psychological atomism of the traditional empiricists which he had previously attacked. However, he still distanced himself from it in his own eyes by recognizing that these experiential atoms are held together by conjunctive relations, not merely held apart by the disjunctive ones which haunted their imaginations.

§ Sometimes James uses the idea of such 'natures' to suggest that radical empiricism does not really claim that there is just one sort of reality. Rather is 'experience' just a collective term for the variety of different 'natures' which we speak of as making it up.

---

5   See ERE, p. 13.

Although for fluency's sake I myself spoke early in this article of a stuff of pure experience, I have now to say that there is no *general* stuff of which experience at large is made. There are as many stuffs as there are 'natures' in the things experienced. If you ask what any one bit of pure experience is made of, the answer is always the same: "It is made of *that*, of just what appears, of space, of intensity, of flatness, brownness, heaviness, or what not." Shadworth Hodgson's analysis here leaves nothing to be desired. Experience is only a collective name for all these sensible natures, and save for time and space (and, if you like, for 'being') there appears no universal element of which all things are made.

ERE, pp. 26–27

Some commentators have sought to tame James's radical empiricism in the light of remarks like this. Thus Graham Bird claims that James's radical empiricism is not an extreme, but a more 'generous, tolerant version' of empiricism.[6] It is more generous because it takes such a large view of what can be experienced, and therefore does not have to be so reductive as to what we can know empirically.

There is a modicum of truth in this. James holds that experience immediately delivers various sorts of relational facts which had seemed problematic to earlier, as to later, empiricists. Nonetheless, taken as a whole, his radical empiricism is certainly not less disruptive of ordinary views than most more traditional empiricisms. For it makes the striking metaphysical claim that there is nothing in the world except ingredients of the sort which go together to make up the flow of our personal streams of experience. This is a far from obvious ontological claim, and certainly not a merely verbal decision to label everything 'experience'.

§ But what exactly are these 'natures', or whatever, which form the ingredients of our streams of consciousness and the filling of the world in general? James makes no obvious distinction between them and what he at other times calls 'percepts', though these terms are meant to cover not only the usual sorts of 'sense-data' but other items of an obscurer sort, and even space and time, as we shall see. Upon the whole they seem to be much what C. I. Lewis later called 'qualia', definite somethings occurring as distinguishable items in streams of personal and, by hypothesis, of impersonal, experience.[7]

One problem about James's conception of them is as to whether they are primarily conceived as particulars or as universals. Are they characters or things which possess characters? Sometimes James seems to say that they are mere *that*'s which neither have nor are characters until classified by an act which is extrinsic to them. But he can hardly mean quite this, since they are obviously meant to be distinct from each other.

It might seem that the fact that they can re-occur in a variety of different

---

6   See Bird, p. 69.
7   See Lewis, *World*, p. 60 et ff.

contexts shows that they are universals. However, James does not distinguish too clearly between the kind of occurrence in different contexts distinctive of universals and that possible for particulars.

At a common-sense level we would distinguish between cases where a particular (e.g., a car in motion) continues to exist although its context changes and cases where a universal (e.g., a type of car) occurs in many different instances. Upon the whole it is not the first kind of re-occurrence in different contexts which pertains to 'natures', since they are not conceived as continuants. But that does not necessarily show that they are universals rather than momentary particulars or events. For there is still a distinction between the occurrence of the same event-type in different contexts (e.g., a song sung on different occasions) and the belonging to two different sequences of one quite particular event (as a certain battle may be an event in the history of two nations). And when James insists that his natures may remain the same in different contexts, he seems to run these cases together. Yet one kind of case suggests that natures are universals, the other that they are particulars.

Doubtless James thinks it quite legitimate to take them either way according to context. Yet unclarity on the matter weakens his argument at times. Thus some of his remarks about the basic elements of pure experience must concern particulars if they are to serve his purpose. For, as we shall see, he associates the claim that we live in a genuinely public world with the possibility of the very same 'percept' belonging to different contexts. But, if the identity is only between percept-types, then the thesis that each of us can only encounter particulars belonging to his own private world has not been countered, as James thinks it has been. Yet the difficulties in supposing that the same percept may belong to different contexts are glossed over by reference to considerations which only obviously apply to percepts qua universals.

Perhaps James would say that these natures belong to an ontological level more basic than that at which such a distinction applies. A. J. Ayer has said the same things about the qualia out of which he constructs the world in a system he has developed in relation to James's.[8] But it is doubtful if the question can properly be avoided thus.

Another question about these natures is whether, qua universals, they are all capable of presence in our experience prior to any conceptualisation or whether, after infancy, the natures which occur in our experience incorporate a conceptual element. Here again James might take refuge in the suggestion that until we classify them they are mere *that*'s and that it is only when thoughts occur which place them in a context or compare them with each other, that they become *what*'s for us.

But, one may ask, even if they are not *what*'s for us until we have thoughts about them, must they not already have or be distinct characteristics with a distinctive individuality? For, surely, it is their very point to be, each of them,

---

8   See Ayer, *Origins*, p. 308 et ff.; Ayer, *Questions*, pp. 93–94.

a qualitatively distinct something. But if each is a something of a definite character before they are conceptualised, the question may be pressed how far it remains the same something when it is conceptualised and how far it is thereby replaced by something else with a certain affinity to it. And the same question arises when a nature is reconceptualised, rather than first conceptualised. According to PP, in effect, there is a fresh nature with any change of conceptual context. And James, as radical empiricist, still sometimes repeats this point.[9] Yet it is also essential to radical empiricism (in its narrower sense) that the natures keep their individual identity and character unsullied by the different contexts, perceptual or conceptual, into which they enter. Only thus can he make the claims we will see him making about the possibility of two minds being confronted with one thing, or of the same thing existing unchanged when out of and in a mind.

A related problem, as we saw above, is that James sometimes uses 'pure experience' to denote something peculiar to infancy, sometimes to denote the stuff of all our experience and ultimately of all reality. Perhaps the point is that it is only in infancy that natures are merely objects of acquaintance, rather than things known about, though when 'knowledge about' comes on the scene both knowing and known are still composed of these same natures. But are the natures which occur in infantile experience ever quite the same as those which occur in maturity? Or are they so modified by the thoughts which accompany them in maturity as to be different from what they were in infancy? More accurately: Does maturity experience the same, or only somewhat kindred, natures to those experienced in infancy?

The matter is of some importance for the direct realism which is distinctive of radical empiricism in the narrower sense. For, according to this, the physical world, in its independent being, consists in percepts existing for the most part apart from streams of personal experience. Now if we deny that the adult can experience the same percepts as a baby, we may ask which kind of percept pertains to the physical world as it exists apart from us. To say that it is the percepts of the adult suggests that the physical world only exists as conceptualised which is surely not James's meaning. Yet the idea that it is the baby who experiences the physical world as it really is is a somewhat peculiar one. To avoid this dilemma James must stick by the view that natures do not alter as they are conceptualised. Thus radical empiricism seems to require abandonment of that whole holistic approach to mind so central to PP. This may be one of the reasons why James could never be quite satisfied with it. However, we must now consider how he deals with various more particular issues in terms of the radical empiricist view that the world is composed of 'pure experience'.

---

9   See, for example, ERE, pp. 29–30.

§2. *The Radical Empiricist View of the Nature of the Physical*

One of the main implications of radical empiricism is said to be a certain conception of the nature of physical reality and of its relation to mental reality. This conception is a form of DIRECT REALISM for which, in perception, we are immediately acquainted with the portion of the physical world perceived, not merely with a representation of it.

The view is explained in such articles as 'Does Consciousness Exist?' (1904) and 'How Two Minds Can Know One Thing' (1905) and may be summarised somewhat as follows.

When I perceive, say an apple, or the monitor of my word processor, there is a certain element in the present cross-section of my stream of experience which, as well as belonging to that stream, also belongs to another historical process, that of the history of the apple or word processor. Take the apple as the easier case. There is a historical process which we may call the history of the apple running from its original growth on the tree to its being plucked, transported, displayed in the shop, bought there by me, placed on this table, a process which will doubtless continue awhile till the apple is eaten and di-gested, at which point it will end as a distinct process and merge with various others. There is also another historical process, that of my stream of experience, or 'personal biography'. At the present moment these two historical processes partly intermingle, so that the apple occurs at one and the very same moment as an element in each. Thus the real apple is not something which my percept merely represents to me. Rather, when I see or otherwise perceive an apple it is the very apple itself which belongs for a moment as an actual element in my experiential stream.[10] At that moment the stream of my consciousness crosses and partly overlaps with a historical process in the physical world which constitutes the physical life of the apple. Thus whenever a conscious being perceives something, that something is temporarily an actual part of his state of consciousness, that is, of the present cross-section of the stream of his experience. It is this view which the expression DIRECT REALISM will stand for throughout this chapter, exclusive of any other position which might be so called.

Does my consciousness of the apple consist solely in its for the moment swimming into my stream of experience? No, for if there is to be anything worthy of the name 'consciousness' of it, I must have some sense that this temporary visitor in my stream of experience has a certain sort of more or less fully surmised history in a process beyond it. In short, as James puts it, I must

---

10   Inasmuch as he thinks that in perception there is an absolute identity between knowledge and thing known James's position contrasts with fallibilism as usually understood and as argued for by Peirce. It seems to me that a writer such as Levinson who sees Peirce and James as fellow opponents of any notion of the absolutely given is therefore wrong about James. See Levinson, *Science*, p. 61.

not merely be acquainted with it as a *that* but must have some sense of *what* it is. That must mean, to use the language of PP, that when it comes to figure in my stream it tends to be surrounded by a fringe which constitutes its being known about rather than being merely an object of acquaintance. This does not affect the point that consciousness does not need to make a mysterious leap beyond itself to be about the apple. Rather, there is an absolute coincidence between a pure experience which belongs to the stuff of my consciousness and the sensory content which is an element in what the apple actually is. At the heart of aboutness in this case is an absolute identity.

All the same, we are conscious of many things which are not a part of our present experiential state in this way. Indeed, to think about the apple, and thus be properly speaking conscious of it, we must have thoughts about past states of the apple and of the tree from which it came, and neither of these are literally part of my present experience. We have already said a good deal about how this happens in our discussion of James's views on intentionality in our first chapter. Our thoughts (which consist in 'pieces' of pure experience) are about the things they are about because they are states of mind which prompt us towards behaviour which will constitute more or less useful adaptation to them, or at least have the capacity to do this.

James does not reject the usual view that one's thought is about certain things because it consists in concepts which apply to them. However, he effectively identifies concepts with such sensory items as images and words which occur as elements in the stream of experience as prompters of behavioural tendencies which, if followed through, would lead one to some more or less successful encounter with the things of which, in virtue of this, they are one's concepts. Such encounters, if they occur, will involve the same kind of absolute coincidence, of some part of the object thought of with some part of one's experiential stream, as holds between the apple perceived and the perception of it.

One difficulty about this account is that it seems to imply that what our thoughts are really about must always lie in the future. For that with which they promote more or less successful encounters are things as they will be when they enter directly into our experience.

Perhaps we can regard the behavioural adjustment as equally to the thing as it is now and as it will be when we actually perceptually encounter it. For perhaps it is to the thing as it is developing over a period of time which spans the interval between the start of the adjustment and its more or less successful termination. But it is rather difficult to see how on this account thoughts can be about things as they were in the quite distant past, e.g., about the apple as it was when it was originally growing on the tree. James must suppose that somehow images and words can produce behaviour which takes account of those things as they were. Thus he sometimes indicates rather vaguely that thought can be about a thing because it brings us to a direct confrontation with its associates or surroundings.

Actually, James grew more and more attached to a view according to which this was not, after all, the only way in which thoughts about things relate to them, suggesting that there may sometimes be an actual identity between the present thought or concept, as an element of consciousness, and the object thought of, quite parallel to the identity of the perception of a thing and the thing perceived. On this view, thoughts are not simply stimuli towards adaptive behaviour towards their objects. Rather our concept of something may be the thing itself swum into our mind in a notional rather than perceptual form. On this view, thought can relate to its object either as leading to it or as the actual presence of the thing in the mind.

That is a puzzling view and complicates the initial contrast between the immediacy of our perceptual contact with physical reality and the purely preparatory role of conceptual thought. I shall, therefore, set it aside for the present and assume that it is only in perception that there is an actual identity between the object cognized and what presents it in the stream of consciousness.

The claim that the apple simply is the same as our sensory presentation of it seems to entail total rejection of such traditional distinctions as that between primary and secondary qualities. For colour and shape and so forth are all on a par as elements in what is actually given in perception. It seems, then, that, according to radical empiricism, we are under no illusion when we picture physical things carrying on in the absence of observers with all the qualities they display to us when we see, touch, hear, smell, and taste them. (Unless perhaps the identity of percept and object perceived is restricted to the deliverances only of certain of the sensory modalities, e.g., sight and touch, and does not cover others, e.g., taste.)

Such a form of DIRECT REALISM raises many puzzling questions: How does this jolly round apple, which is just what swims into my stream of experience when I see it or eat it, manage to possess the properties scientists ascribe to it, of being made up of molecules composed of atoms and so on? And again how does the apple presented from the point of view in which I saw it relate to the apple as you did or might have seen it, at the same time, from a different angle and perhaps a different distance? For one cannot really imagine a single entity which is both the apple seen near to and the apple seen from further away, or which is both the apple with its smooth coloured continuous surface and the apple as made up of lots of molecules.

Whatever may be thought of such appeals to what one can or cannot imagine as a method of philosophical clarification in general they are certainly absolutely relevant to understanding James here. For the whole point of his thought is to equate physical reality with what we do encounter directly in our own experience and can imagine clearly as going on without it. And the baffling thing is that one simply cannot do this.

One cannot do it, at least, in any coherent manner. On the other hand, I think that this actually is how we think of the physical world at the level of quite ordinary unsophisticated and uncritical thought. For on this conception the physical world consists in a system of sense impressions, some of which are experienced and some are not. And that is just the view which Hume, quite rightly as it seems to me, regarded as the ordinary naive way of conceiving the physical world, in spite of its obvious clashes with the more sophisticated view of things to which we are forced by science or even by a little pre-scientific reflection.[11]

It is one thing for a philosopher to say that this conception of the physical world is that of naive common sense and the one in terms of which we inevitably conduct most of our daily business, another to say that it is a coherent concept which can be used in an adequate metaphysical account of how things really are. I believe the former claim to be correct but that it raises far too may insoluble puzzles to be taken up into an adequate metaphysics (though Russell at one time took the possibility seriously.[12]) Ordinary thought is not troubled by these problems because it concentrates on that aspect of the thing which suits its present purposes and ignores those which clash with it. But we cannot be content to do this when we are trying to form a serious metaphysical view of physical reality.

Among the many real or apparent objections to a serious metaphysical endorsement of this conception are these.

§ First, the very idea of an unexperienced sense impression may be thought absurd. However, there is an at least initially promising reply (stemming from Hume) to this that since the elements of a stream of consciousness are distinct existences, each must be able to exist apart from the relations which make it a part of a personal stream of experience. (To say that these would not be 'sense impressions' is a merely verbal point.)

§ Second, the object itself seems to be fragmented into a variety of different perspectives on it and of data from different sensory modalities (including all our different modes of handling it). Do these have any kind of real belonging together beyond the fact that their changes are correlated with one another? It is hard to see how, yet it is also hard to believe that single objects are made up of mere isolated fragments.

It is difficult even to see how the different perspectival sense impressions of one object (in a sense of 'perspectival' suited to the sensory modality to which it belongs) can belong in a common space, since it seems that each must belong to a space which exists only from the same perspective as itself. Yet James supposes that they do so[13] and this would indeed seem essential to their forming a real independent object together.

One solution might be to think of them as existing not just *at* places, but *from* and *at* a place, whether or not there is any observer at the place from which they exist.[14] But it is very difficult to imagine the content of this suggestion without effectively imagining an observing subject which somehow synthesises all perspectives, thus moving towards Berkeleyism. The alternative is to seal the sense impressions off from each other in distinct vistas which make up no larger

---

11   Hume, *Treatise*, p. 202.
12   See Russell, *External*, pp. 94–100.
13   See ERE, p. 84.
14   Cf. Broad, *Mind*, p. 162.

vista. But that seems quite destructive of the notion of there being a single physical world at all and hardly suitable for a theory which purports to capture and endorse a common-sense view of things.

§ Then, thirdly, there is the problem of the 'size' of the unsensed sense fields to which these presentations belong. The visual presentation of a chair can hardly exist merely on its own, with no sort of background, but the size of the background which goes with it is most problematic, if this is not determined by the sensory apparatus of a perceiver.

§ A fourth objection is that it tends to give the object only surface properties. For it is difficult to understand what sorts of perspectives can exist on its inside. Perhaps we must suppose that as well as the familiar perspectives on opaque objects there are others with an X-ray character which reveal their insides (from outside). But that multiplies the bewildering variety of panoramas into which any single bit of physical reality breaks up.

§ This leads naturally into the fifth difficulty in DIRECT REALISM, that of the way in which scientific entities fit into its picture of the world. It is an extraordinary form of realism which makes these less really there than the most superficial character of the objects, yet if they are really there you have to postulate not merely a fragmentation of perspectives on the object depending on the viewing or perceiving point, but also a fragmentation from each point of view depending on the scale on which the object is given and the degree to which it presents what lies behind the surface.

These problems are perplexing enough in themselves. It is particularly difficult to understand how James, of all people, can take them so lightly, after insisting so strongly in PP on the way in which our impressions of the world are the end result of light and sound waves and so forth stimulating our sense organs and those acting on the brain, and on the way in which it is the part of the brain stimulated rather than the nature of the original source of the stimulation which determines the kind of sensory quality we will experience.

The fact that James saw such points as supporting idealism hardly helps matters, for they lend little support to the position he advocates as a radical empiricist.

Consider in this connection the following:

> . . . as matters actually stand in any adult individual, it is safe to say that, more than anything else, the *place* excited in his cortex decides what kind of thing he shall feel. Whether we press the retina, or prick, cut, pinch, or galvanize the living optic nerve, the Subject always feels flashes of light, since the ultimate result of our operations is to stimulate the cortex of his occipital region. Our habitual ways of feeling outer things thus depend on which convolutions happen to be connected with the particular end-organs which those things impress. We *see* the sunshine and the fire, simply because the only peripheral end-organ susceptible of taking up the ether-waves which these objects radiate excites those particular fibres which run to the centres of sight. If we could interchange the inward connections, we should feel the world in altogether new ways. If, for instance, we could splice the outer extremity of our optic nerves to our ears, and that of our auditory nerves to our eyes, we should hear the lightning and see the thunder, see the symphony and hear the conductor's

movements. Such hypotheses as these form a good training for neophytes in the idealistic philosophy!

BC, p. 12

§ And then, sixthly, there is the problem touched on in the last section: Does the physical world, in its independent being, consist of sense impressions such as babies experience or such as we experience? When James distinguished sensation and perception in PP, he contended that as adults we hardly ever have that knowledge of mere acquaintance which the baby may have with the sense qualities sensory stimulation presents him with.[15] And yet it would seem to be in the case of mere acquaintance that the physical world swims into a stream of personal experience with least modification to itself. The implication that it is the baby, not the adult, who confronts the physical world as it really is is rather unsatisfactory for those who hope to have gained something with the years. The only solution for the DIRECT REALIST is to deny that sense impressions are affected in their own character by the conceptual scheme in terms of which we interpret them, a solution strikingly counter to the holistic conception of consciousness of PP.

§ Seventhly, a similar problem is posed by the way in which sensible qualities seem to alter with the context in which they are perceived, something stressed in PP.[16] Thus, to take just the case of sight, when an object can be seen by us either in association or apart from some neighbouring object, in which case do we apprehend the sensory impressions which constitute its independent being? To try to save the day by saying that all these sense impressions exist independently of our awareness of them, and that this is purely selective in its operation, makes the physical world even more fantastically crammed with different versions of what we thought the same object than it had seemed already. This is a fragmentation of things additional to that made by the multiplicity of points of view on things. For even when the point of view is fixed, the extent to which we are aware of what environs it may change.

It is hard to suppose that the sense impression of an object which we see from a given point of view when, say, we close off from sight what is to the left of it, ceases to be (what it was before) the object in its independent character. For, after all, there is always an immense amount of environment of which we are unaware, and if only sense impressions appropriately modified by the environment belong to the genuine external world, then none of our sense impressions do, and the whole doctrine collapses. But it is equally hard to think that a thing can only figure in consciousness in its independent nature when there is no influence from the environment, for then all presented complexity will deprive its elements of their genuinely independent character.

§ An eighth possible objection is that the tendency of this view is to lead to an excessive emphasis upon the distance senses, more especially sight, as

---

15   See PP, II pp. 7–8; BC, pp. 12–15.
16   See PP, II, p. 28; BC pp. 24–27.

revelations of the world, thus downplaying the contribution of other senses to the proper conception of it. For it is these which it is least problematic to think of existing unsensed; it is much more difficult, for example, to conceive of percepts of taste and swallowing as doing so, despite the fact that eating can seem our most intimate way of apprehending things. This is because it is only with visual and auditory percepts that we find a firm phenomenological distinction between the object perceived and some state of our consciousness as we encounter it.

However, if it is true (and I am inclined to agree with James and Hume that it is) that we do ordinarily conceive the world somewhat along these lines, it would seem that we do ordinarily somehow manage to think of it as including unsensed percepts of all sensory modalities. What is true, however, is that when one examines the matter theoretically it is much more difficult to think out in full what independently occurring percepts would be like with some such modalities than others. Since vision is the easiest case, philosophers who endorse this conception tend therefore to an excessively visual conception of the world. (Yet they are right that the visual is in some respects peculiarly basic; witness the primarily visual metaphors in which we couch most of our 'views', 'theories', 'speculations', and 'revelations' as to how things are.)

But direct realism of James's kind must certainly take the independent world as including non-visual percepts too. They, especially the tactile ones (presumably including the various feels of things as we handle them—roughness, smoothness, heaviness, lightness, etc.), must figure along with visual percepts in those flows of impersonal experience which make up the independent physical world. For the feel of something gives us a much stronger awareness of it as something real with real powers than does the sight of it and to suppose that the real independent world is merely visual would render it a curiously ghostly affair (with the odd implication that the blind are quite cut off from reality). Yet there are peculiar difficulties in knowing which tactile presentations are supposed to exist independently, since the ones we experience depend so much on how we handle things.

It might be better to abandon the idea that the different senses provide quite distinct presentations. For subjectively, surely, we experience things as unitary visuo-tactile solids, replete, as we handle them, with all sorts of resistances, heaviness, lightness, roughness, and softness, etc., and permeated by qualities presented through the other senses and hints of their power to act on other things. (More precise properties of a measurable kind seem—at this simple level of thought—more a matter of how things act on each other, and align with various measuring devices, than part of what the objects are individually.) Then one could say that what exists independently are percepts mixed in their sensory modality. Yet this, it must be allowed, would clash with James's inclination to think of 'pure experience' as composed of distinct 'natures' repeating themselves in different contexts.

§ However, such difficulties need not be seriously perplexing if it is not maintained that these unsensed sense impressions really exist, but only that our ordinary way of conceiving the physical world supposes them to do so, and that this supposition is the best way of conceiving it for most of our more ordinary practical purposes, however much it breaks down into incoherence once you press it too far. Nor would they arise if what is really meant is that, insofar as they are not perceived, the sense impressions in which physical things consist exist only as possibilities and are there only in the sense that they are what some conscious subject will experience if it gives itself certain appropriate experiences of locomotion, etc. So although James certainly writes as though he was committed to this DIRECT REALIST view in a very straightforward form, perhaps it should not be taken at face value. And, in fact, so taken, it seems only one of several views of the physical world which one can find in his writings of this period. Indeed, there seem to be five different views which one might reasonably suppose him to be putting forward in his radical empiricist writings.

1. That physical things consist of percepts, most of which exist outside of any conscious being's experience. (This is DIRECT REALISM taken at face value, and, in the light of its influence on the American new realists, may be called the NEW REALIST version of DIRECT REALISM.)

2. That we ordinarily conceive of physical things as systems of percepts which can exist unperceived but that, as philosophers, we do not have to endorse the existence of physical objects in this sense as literal truth and may see it rather as useful fiction or illusion. (I shall call this the PHENOMENOLOGICAL version of DIRECT REALISM.)

3. That this is the view of the physical world we ordinarily take and that since it works it is true in the only sense in which any belief can be true. (I shall call this the AGGRESSIVELY PRAGMATIST version of DIRECT REALISM.)

4. That physical things consist in possible sense impressions in a sense which makes James's position akin to that of phenomenalists such as J. S. Mill, C. I. Lewis and early A. J. Ayer. (I shall call this the PHENOMENALIST version of DIRECT REALISM.)

5. PANPSYCHISM. (This is the one theory which can hardly be called a form of DIRECT REALISM, though it falls with the others under the common heading of NEUTRAL MONISM. I shall be suggesting that this was James's final position and one to which he always had a strong inclination.)

1. NEW REALISM

If you take what he says just as it most obviously seems to stand, he would seem to be holding the first view and claiming that the very thing which, when you perceive it, figures as an element in your consciousness is a member of a series of similar things most of which do not pertain to your consciousness or to anyone else's, when it is not being perceived. Take the simplest case, that of visual perception. On this view the visual presentation, presence of which in your consciousness constitutes your seeing an object, is a phase, not only in your stream of consciousness, but in the duration of the object itself. What can this mean, if not that there has been, and will be, a series of similar visual percepts (altering only so far as the object alters with time), most of which were not, or will not be, the elements of anyone's consciousness, but which exist independently in a perfectly straightforward way and together with other

unperceived percepts of various types and from various points of view somehow combine to constitute the object? These percepts, it would seem, must
occur in a kind of impersonal flow or flows of world experience.

> On the principles which I am defending, a 'mind' or 'personal consciousness'
> is the name for a series of experiences run together by certain definite transi-
> tions, and an objective reality is a series of similar experiences, knit by different
> transitions.
>
> ERE, p. 80

We have just been seeing the very serious difficulties there are in the claim
that this is the real metaphysical truth about the world. However, the school of
new realists, including such figures as E. B. Holt and R. B. Perry, were influenced by James to develop a view along these lines, which accepted some of its
most peculiar implications, as the literal truth about the world.[17]

2. PHENOMENOLOGICAL DIRECT REALISM

These difficulties make it well nigh impossible to take this seriously as a view
of how things really are. It seems much more promising if we interpret it, not
as a metaphysician's view of how things really are but as a phenomenological
psychologist's account of how things are for us, that is, of how and into what
our conception of the physical world, and its relation to the mental, develops
from infancy.

That the doctrine is much more satisfactory taken in this way emerges
particularly from James's discussion of what he calls 'affectional facts'. In 'The
Place of Affectional Facts in a World of Pure Experience', first published in May
1905,[18] he speaks of an initial stage in infancy where there is just pure experience undifferentiated into 'inner' and 'outer', or 'mental' and 'physical', and
how this is gradually differentiated into an 'active' group, which constitutes
the physical, and an 'inactive' group which constitutes the mental.[19] (I discuss
the oddness of James classifying the mental here as 'inactive' in the next
section.) There are, however, certain elements which do not seem ever finally
to get sorted out into one group or another, namely the affectional elements
such as pleasure, beauty, love, and all other sorts of pleasantness, painfulness,
and value, positive or negative. While some critics, according to James,[20] have
claimed that the existence of our affections form a class which is so distinctly
spiritual that they cannot be accounted for on the basis of a radical empiricism
which regards the stuff of the mental and the physical as the same, James sees
them as precisely supporting his doctrine. For only when we see that the

17 The school produced a manifesto volume in 1912 called *The New Realism: Compara-
    tive Studies in Philosophy* by Edwin B. Holt and others.
18 ERE, pp. 137–54.
19 See ERE, p. 141.
20 ERE, p. 138.

distinction between the mental and the physical is a classification of the same essential stuff into different groups to suit different purposes can we explain how there are elements which do not fit neatly into either group. For some purposes, and in some cases, affectional facts count as mental, and for others as physical.

> [I]t is a mistake to say . . . that anger, love and fear are affections purely of the mind. That, to a great extent at any rate, they are simultaneously affections of the body is proved by the whole literature of the James-Lange theory of emotion. All our pains, moreover, are local, and we are always free to speak of them in objective as well as in subjective terms. . . . All our adjectives of worth are similarly ambiguous . . . Is the preciousness of a diamond a quality of the gem? or is it a feeling in our mind? Practically we treat it as both or as either, according to the temporary direction of our thought. 'Beauty' says Professor Santayana, 'is pleasure objectified'; and in Sections 10 and 11 of his work, *The Sense of Beauty*, he treats in a masterly way of this equivocal realm. The various pleasures we receive from an object may count as 'feelings' when we take them singly, but when they combine in a total richness, we call the result the 'beauty' of the object, and treat it as an outer attribute which our mind perceives. . . . Shall we say an 'agreeable degree of heat' or an 'agreeable feeling' occasioned by the degree of heat? Either will do; and language would lose most of its esthetic and rhetorical value were we forbidden to project words primarily connoting our affections upon the objects by which the affections are aroused. The man is really hateful; the action really mean; the situation really tragic—all in themselves and quite apart from our opinion. We even go so far as to talk of a weary road, a giddy height, a jocund morning or a sullen sky.
>
> ERE, pp. 142–44

After this he speaks of the secondary qualities, and how in older styles of thought they were considered as physical because it was supposed that

> things act on each other as well as on us by means of their secondary qualities. Sound, as such, goes through the air and can be intercepted. The heat of the fire passes over, as such, into the water which it sets a-boiling.
>
> ERE, pp. 146–47

Now, however, we put down all the efficacy to underlying primary qualities and regard these sensory qualities as inactive effects in our mind. And, James continues, even the standard primary qualities are gradually being treated as subjective, on Kantian principles, with the real efficacy left with things in themselves which alone exist outside consciousness. However, there are persisting ways in which we are bound to regard even the most affectional facts as having effects in the wider world of physical nature. The disgustingness of a mass of carion will not affect its interaction with most physical things, but it does affect our stomach when this 'turns'. Indeed our body, and what goes on it, is a

> . . . palmary instance of the ambiguous. Sometimes I treat my body purely as a part of outer nature. Sometimes, again, I think of it as 'mine', I sort it with the 'me', and then certain local changes and determinations in it pass for spiritual happenings. Its breathing is my 'thinking', its sensorial adjustments are my

'attention', its kinesthetic alterations are my 'efforts,' its visceral perturbations are my 'emotions.' The obstinate controversies that have arisen over such statements as these . . . prove how hard it is to decide by bare introspection what it is in experiences that shall make them either spiritual or material.

ERE, pp. 153–54

The references to the body and to the James-Lange theory of the emotions which he had advocated in PP support my contention that the seeming materialism of parts of that work is phenomenological rather than metaphysical materialism. And the whole treatment of affectional facts in this article suggest that he is not proposing an ultimately realistic account of the constitution of a physical world which is supposed to exist apart from human consciousness, or experience, of it but giving a phenomenological account of how we ordinarily conceive the distinction between the physical and the mental without claiming objective validity for it.

So perhaps the radical empiricist account of the physical is meant as a phenomenological account of the genesis and nature of our ordinary conception of physical reality, the main point being that for our ordinary thought, there is no fixed contrast dividing the mental and the physical, only a gradual, and never final, sorting out of the basic stuff of pure experience into two groups according as where we see fundamental efficacy at work.

3. AGGRESSIVELY PRAGMATIST DIRECT REALISM

It may be objected that the contrast between the view that physical things really exist as systems of unexperienced percepts, and the view that it is only our usual and practically effective way of thinking of things to suppose that they do, turns on a distinction between literal truth and practically useful ideas which is meaningless for James as a pragmatist. For are not ideas true (on that view) just insofar as they work, and if these ideas work, are they not therefore literally true because true in the only sense in which any idea can be true? If another conception of the physical world is to be preferred for science or even metaphysics, it cannot be because its ideas correspond more accurately to an independent reality but only because they work better for certain technological or theoretical purposes.

So perhaps James only claims for DIRECT REALISM that it is the ordinary view of physical reality and that it works quite well enough to be called 'true' and endorsed as such by the philosopher.

One may object to this that, even if we sometimes think of physical reality like this, it is not a very useful conception of it and should not be given the degree of endorsement which calling it true, even on the lips of a pragmatist, implies. Surely for any adequate practical handling of things, something which gives more place to the scientific picture and less to the manifest image would be better. Moreover, such a view, it may be said, is altogether unsatisfying to the intellect, since it is both incoherent in itself and incapable of coherent combination with even a modicum of science. So if it is to be called true at all, by a pragmatist, it must be acknowledged that it only possesses truth of a very low grade.

We will see that such an evaluation is not so far from that which Bradley gives of common sense realism. But James surely wants to endorse it more enthusiastically than this. Certainly he is commending it over the usual philosophical alternatives. For he sees it as rescuing us from the problems which beset purely representationalist accounts of perception by not cutting us off from the physical world in the unsatisfactory way in which they do. So whether we agree with him or not, we must understand James as both thinking of this view as the ordinary one, and as giving a high degree of personal endorsement to it. The question is: does he endorse it (1) as literally true, (2) as useful but not literally true, or (3) as true in the only possible sense in which any idea can be true, that of being useful?

It may seem that it is only the third alternative which makes sense for a pragmatist. However, throughout his radical empiricism James displays the true passion of the metaphysician for knowing how things really are. (Let him who doubts this consult especially the Miller-Bode notebook.) And there can be no serious doubt that James wants radical empiricism to help us grasp how things really are. So while I admit that the more positivistic aspect of James's pragmatism may have complicated his quest for a satisfactory view of the literal truth about reality by inclining him at times to suppose that there was nothing more to be discovered than which ideas work best in practice, I shall persist in asking how far we are supposed to take him as endorsing DIRECT REALISM as true in some literal sense.

4. PHENOMENALIST DIRECT REALISM

An interpretation of James of this fourth kind seems to be supported by his suggestion that in knowledge there are three standard sorts of situations, those in which

> the knower and the known are:
> (1) the self-same piece of experience taken twice over in different contexts, or they are
> (2) two pieces of *actual* experience belonging to the same subject, with definite tracts of conjunctive transitional experience between them; or
> (3) the known is a *possible* experience either of that subject or another, to which the said conjunctive transitions *would* lead, if sufficiently prolonged.
> 'A World of Pure Experience' (1904), ERE, p. 53

Thus understood James's account of the relation between the mental and the physical becomes the view that the perceived aspect of a physical thing belongs to two different streams of being; on the one hand it is a phase in that stream of actual being, which constitutes someone's consciousness, while on the other it belongs to what is mainly only a stream of possible being. That is, the physical object at any moment consists of a group of appearances which are actual insofar as they are perceptually present to an observer and merely possible insofar as they are not. Those which are actual are events in the streams of consciousness of the relevant observers, while both actual and merely possible ones belong to streams of physical process in which they follow on one another in a sequence which changes only according to rules which are distinctive of that kind of physical thing, or of that kind of physical thing when subject to certain environmental pressures.

What exactly are those appearances which are merely possible and which constitute things insofar as they are not perceived, according to this phenomenalist interpretation of James's radical empiricist account of the physical? Clearly they are not merely logically possible. Presumably they are possible in the sense that they could occur, or could have occurred, as the termini to acts of exploration which might have been undertaken by various conscious subjects. Thus their existence as possibilities consists in the fact that there would have been actual appearances of the relevant sort if subjects of experience had given themselves certain experiences of going to certain places, etc.

There *is* a host of problems here. Do these possible appearances have to be termini of possible explorations on the part of actual subjects, or are the possible explorations of possible subjects allowed? And either way, in what sense do these explorations have to be possible? I shall have to pass such problems by.[21] I shall, however, note one interesting objection which seems to me not very well taken, namely, that if a thing, when unperceived, consists of merely possible appearances, then the actual appearances of it which occur when it is perceived cannot be constituents of its being in the same sense, since possibilities have a different status from actualities.

This, I suggest, may be met by insisting that actual appearances are not something other than possible appearances, but those possible appearances actualised. Thus we need not think of the constituents of a physical thing as of two different kinds, possible and actual appearances, but only of possible appearances which may or may not be actualised.

It may be countered that possibilities may be of various different levels of specificity, and that if the possible appearances which constitute a physical

---

21   The status of possibilities, in effect of if-then propositions, was quite a problem for James, as indeed it is for all philosophers worth their salt. On the one hand, he was convinced that 'possibility, as distinguished from necessity on the one hand and impossibility on the other, is an essential category of human thinking' (SPP, p. 139). Moreover, it is a category central to his conception of the pointfulness of action: 'The melioristic universe is conceived after a *social* analogy, as a pluralism of independent powers. . . . Its destiny thus hangs on an *if*, or on a lot of *ifs* which amounts to saying (in the technical language of logic) that, the world being as yet unfinished, its total character can be expressed only by *hypothetical* and not by *categorical* propositions' (SPP, pp. 228–29). But on the other hand, he had some uneasiness both as to the real nature of possibility and as to the reduction of most of the apparent actuality of the physical world to the level of merely possible sensations. Perhaps the truth of the matter is that he steps forward as a champion of the reality of possibility when the alternative seems to be necessity of some kind but at the same time was uneasy at a notion of possibility which did not somehow explain it by reference to actuality. At times he urges a view of possibility not very different from Bradley's (e.g., PRAG, p. 283 et ff.). For my own views see Sprigge, 1983, pp. 51–64.

object are less than absolutely specific, then any actualisation of them will have more to its nature than they do. From this it would seem to follow that actual appearances cannot merely be said to be the possible appearances actualised. But surely the actualisation of a possibility in one absolutely specific form is compatible with admission that it might have been actualised in an alternative absolutely specific form. In any case, we need not attempt to clear up all the problems which may arise for this phenomenalist view of physical things. The general spirit of such a view is clear enough and our concern is not with working it out in detail but with deciding whether James's position was of this type.

In their conception of what there really is, there is little or no difference between this phenomenalist version of direct realism and the phenomenological one. The difference lies in their interpretation of how what we ordinarily believe stands to this conception. The phenomenological version encourages us to engage in a fiction which puts us in touch with the possibilities of experience which are open for us; the phenomenalist version encourages us to think directly of these facts about possibilities of experience. Thus the phenomenalist account gives an interpretation of ordinary thought about the physical world in which it has a literal truth rather than merely that of a pragmatic fiction. Or rather it can be accepted as doing so by anyone who is not unduly troubled by the status of if-then statements of the required sort, and recognizes that not all truth is pragmatic. Much of what James says suggests the phenomenalist view. But his uneasiness about the nature of conditional statements and thus of possibility checked his complete commitment to it. And the most prominent ERE texts are certainly most naturally read in the first NEW REALIST fashion.

Each of the four positions so far considered regards the percept of a perceived object, which is that with which we are immediately acquainted, not as a representation of the object perceived, but as the object itself (or at least a component thereof). Thus each of them is a form of direct realism. And it was doubtless because his main concern was to establish this in some form that James stresses what is common to these views, without distinguishing very clearly between them.

Some will be surprised at my treating phenomenalism as a form of direct realism.[22] However, it is not only James's possible version of it which fits this description perfectly, but also the phenomenalism of logical positivists such as Moritz Schlick and, earlier, Richard Avenarius.[23] The idea that the prime aim

---

22 Graham Bird is one who contrasts phenomenalism and realism in what I think a misleading way. See Bird, pp. 119–20. Incidentally James talks about his position at times as 'phenomenism' but his use of this expression only implies that the given phenomenon is a constituent of the physical world itself, and does not settle whether he understood this doctrine phenomenalistically or otherwise as I am taking the term.

23 Thus James's phenomenalism is very much in the spirit of Schlick's characterisation of it as 'one of the main theses of true positivism: that the naive

of phenomenalism is to drive a wedge between the physical thing and the sense data presented of it is either a misunderstanding or a wrong emphasis. Its essential thrust is rather to oppose what A. J. Ayer used to call the 'iron curtain' theory of perception, and exhibit physical objects as directly accessible to consciousness. For it regards a physical object not as something other than its appearances, somehow lurking behind them, but as composed of them. Thus in coming across them one comes across the physical thing itself. True, no one sense datum is identical with the physical object it presents, it cannot even be identical with any one *physical* part of it, but it is, nonetheless, for phenomenalism, a genuine element of what the physical object is, and, in a quite decent sense of the word, a part of it.

Of the first four positions it is indeed the first which is direct realist in the most straightforward way. But each of the first four, including phenomenalism, avoids those representationalist views which

> violate [our] . . . sense of life, which knows no intervening mental image but seems to see the room and the book immediately just as they physically exist.
>
> 'Does Consciousness Exist?', ERE, p. 12

It is in this spirit that he says that radical empiricism:

> has, in fact, more affinities with natural realism than with the views of Berkeley or of Mill.
>
> 'A World of Pure Experience', ERE, p. 76

And it may well be its seeming to reintroduce the notion that we only know the real object we say we are perceiving in a representational manner that held him back from a complete endorsement of panpsychism for so long.

5. PANPSYCHISM

However, there are more or less obvious reasons why none of these views, when properly spelt out, could have been accepted as altogether satisfactory by James, and he shows increasing awareness of this. New realism makes objects only exist from, so to speak, outside themselves. For it identifies them with what they are from external perspectives upon them. The phenomenalist and pragmatist interpretations of direct realism do not slake the thirst which

---

representation of the world, as the man in the street sees it, is perfectly correct; and that the solution of the great philosophical issues consists in returning to this original world-view, after having shown that the troublesome problems arose only from an inadequate description of the world by means of a faulty language.' See 'Meaning and Verification' by Moritz Schlick, in Feigl and Sellars, p. 170. For an account of Avenarius's views on this see A. E. Taylor, *Elements,* pp. 80–81; 121 note; pp. 298–301.

James, for all his pragmatism, obviously had for gaining a grasp of how things really are. And the phenomenalist version rests heavily on counterfactual conditionals without any evident grounding in categorical fact, something about which James was rightly uneasy.

There is, however, a view which squares perfectly with the view that nothing exists except experience and which does not raise any of these problems, namely a panpsychism for which each physical thing is a stream of experience developing both according to its own momentum and in ways which reflect its interaction with other streams. James was impressed by C. A. Strong's (and evidently Morton Prince's) development of this position.[24]

> The beyond must, of course, always in our philosophy be itself of an experiential nature. If not a future experience of our own or a present one of our neighbor, it must be a thing in itself in Dr. Prince's and Professor Strong's sense of the term—that is, it must be an experience *for* itself whose relation to other things we translate into the action of molecules, ether-waves, or whatever else the physical symbols may be. [James's footnote: Our minds and these ejective realities would still have space (or pseudo-space, as I believe Professor Strong calls the medium of interaction between 'things-in-themselves') in common. These would exist *where*, and begin to act *where*, we locate the molecules etc., and *where* we perceive the sensible phenomena explained thereby. (Cf Morton Prince: *The Nature of Mind, and Human Automatism*, part 1, ch. III, IV; C. A. Strong: *Why the Mind has a Body*, ch. XII.)] This opens the chapter of the relations of radical empiricism to panpsychism, into which I can not enter now.
>
> ERE, pp. 88–99

And I believe that it was to this that James finally tended more and more, but that he fought against it because it threatened the direct realism which had initially seemed to him one of the most attractive features of radical empiricism.[25] For on this view, it would seem that we are only acquainted with representations of real objects in perception.

Still some compromise with direct realism is possible for the panpsychist, if he distinguishes between things as they are for us, and things as they are in themselves. For then he can say that the thing, as it is for us, does actually swim into our consciousness. But he will have either (a) to regard the view that the

---

24 For more on Strong see section 7 below and note 74.
25 Compare CER, pp. 443–44; ERE, pp. 188–89; SPP, pp. 218–19, etc. Commentators who have recognized that James's final position was panpsychic in character include Bruce Kuklick and Marcus Ford. See especially chapter five of Ford which marshals the evidence for James's panpsychic convictions both before and after the phenomenist period. James's friend Flournoy thought James sympathetic to, without ever having quite adopted, panpsychism. See Flournoy, pp. 95–96. My own commitment to this interpretation, and indeed to panpsychism itself, has been long standing. The foremost proponent of panpsychism today, is, of course, Charles Hartshorne.

appearances, which are the thing as it is for us, continue to exist when we are not perceiving it, as something of a pragmatic fiction, or (b) contrast the phenomenal thing, conceived à la phenomenalism, as a system of possible appearances, with the thing in itself. There are suggestions of such a view in the later writings of that period of frenetic intellectual activity in which he wrote his radical empiricist articles. For example, in the 1905 'The Essence of Humanism' he says that common sense is

> a perfectly definite halting-place of thought, primarily for purposes of action
> ERE, p. 197

but that there

> is a stage of thought that goes beyond common sense
> ERE, p. 197

for which the percepts we each have when we are said to see the same thing rather carry us some way towards, than actually give, convergence on some one and the same entity.[26] This may initially be conceived physicalistically as a complex of atoms. However, these atoms will have to be defined as percepts which we might share under certain ideal conditions, of confluence between our two minds, which are practically impossible. And in the end, James suggests, it may be better to suppose that our experiences are somehow continuous with, and on the verge of flowing into, the mind stuff which is the reality behind the object as we perceive it, without ever quite actually doing so, though they might do so in principle. (If James had distinguished more carefully between continuants and momentary events, he would have said that the present experience is of its nature separated from the inner mind stuff of the thing perceived but that in principle the main streams to which each belongs could flow into each other, and are sometimes on the brink of doing so.)

James sometimes suggests that prior to the development of a distinctively scientific conception of the world there was no cause to regard our percept of a thing as an appearance of something deeper, rather than as a thing in its own right. For it is only when we have the scientist's atoms to be the reality behind the sensory scenery provided by our percepts that there is any reason to speak of what is immediately given as a mere *representation* of the real object. But, in fact, since the atoms are themselves only further possible perceptions which we might obtain, which of them we dignify as the reality is a matter of choice, depending on current purposes. It is only, he seems to be suggesting at times, if there is some ultimate flow of experience at the heart of the thing itself, which cannot be reduced to the observer's possible sensations, that we have anything

---

26   See ERE, p. 199.

more absolutely entitled to be called the reality which our percepts only represent.[27]

But even if James's radical empiricism often pointed him in the direction of panpsychism, it is not the dominant position in the phase of his thought we are now investigating. He was held back from it, I suggest, partly because the more positivistic side of his pragmatism left him with some scruples about adopting so apparently unverifiable a position, and partly because he was so much in love with a direct realism which eschewed any taint of representationalism. Altogether a certain amount of obscurity in James's position seems to have stemmed from his having commitments which could not be jointly satisfied in a fully coherent fashion.

A plausible chronology of James's developing commitment to panpsychism is that given by Marcus Ford, that he was a panpsychist from 1900 to 1904 and again from 1905 till his death in 1910, but that the position I have called direct realism was a briefly attempted alternative which intervened for a time.[28] Perhaps the correct view is that James had more or less settled on a panpsychist view of nature in the years 1900 to 1904 but that he attempted to develop an alternative to it during the years 1904 and 1905 when he elaborated the direct realist position we have been discussing, and that then he turned back again to panpsychism with still greater conviction.

§3. *The Differentia of the Physical*

§ Whatever attractions panpsychism may have already had for him as an ultimate solution, it belongs rather to the final system we shall be discussing in the next chapter than to his main radical empiricist phase. The centrepiece of that was DIRECT REALISM of the kind we have described. James was fascinated in working this position out, and I shall now consider some further details of his attempt to do so. Since he managed to discuss it, while leaving it unclear which of the four interpretations of its claims which I have distinguished he favoured, I shall often attempt to follow him in this. To me it seems that the most promising way for a philosopher to take it is the PHENOMENOLOGICAL for which the DIRECT REALISM, which NEW REALISM takes as literal truth, is endorsed as our ordinary way of conceiving things. In any case we can try to work out the details of such a DIRECT REALISM without deciding whether to interpret it as literal truth, or as the way we ordinarily conceive things, or as true but only pragmatically so. (It is only PHENOMENALISM which affects the actual content of the theory and this in a way which we can ignore for much of the time.)

For James's DIRECT REALISM the perception of a physical thing is its literal

---

27   See ERE, p. 215 et ff.
28   See Ford.

presence as an element in the perceiver's stream of consciousness. If the perceiver understands to any extent what he is perceiving, it will occur there together with other elements which constitute the knowing of some facts about it. His realization that it is a real physical thing is the realization that it also belongs to a stream of process with its own history which only coincides every now and then with his or any stream of personal consciousness. What we must now ask is this: How do we normally determine which elements in the stream of personal consciousness do and which do not also have a history and a future in an independent physical world? For it is only some elements in the stream of consciousness which are thought of as doing so.

James's answer is rather surprising. It is that those elements are regarded as physical which are 'energetic' or efficacious, while those elements which lack efficacy are regarded as purely mental. Thus we are told that

> The central point of the pure-experience theory is that 'outer' and 'inner' are names for two groups into which we sort experiences according to the way in which they act upon their neighbors. Any one 'content', such as *hard*, let us say, can be assigned to either group. In the outer group it is 'strong', it acts 'energetically' and aggressively. Here whatever is hard interferes with the space its neighbors occupy. It dents them; is impenetrable by them; and we call the hardness then a physical hardness. In the mind, on the contrary, the hard thing is nowhere in particular, it dents nothing.
> 'The Place of Affectional Facts in a World of Pure Experience' (May 1905)
> ERE, p. 139

Thus 'mental fire' doesn't burn sticks, or rather it may burn 'mental sticks', but equally it may not. Hence it is not subject to the laws of physical efficacy.

This seems to contrast strangely with James's emphasis elsewhere on the potency of mind and enthusiasm for 'the strenuous life'.

James takes note of this objection and qualifies his statement by saying that it is not every kind of efficacy which the mental lacks, but only 'physical' efficacy. If this is somewhat question begging, James thinks that 'physical efficacy' can be defined in a way which avoids circularity. A rough definition might say that it is the efficacy by which the world process is carried on beyond personal consciousness. And elsewhere James supplements his account of mental efficacy by reference to its special mnemic features.

In a footnote to the 1904–5 'The Experience of Activity' he says

> Let me not be told that this [the view that in the experience of our own activity we have 'creation in its first intention, [and that] here is causality at work'] contradicts. . . . 'Does consciousness exist?'. . . in which it was said that while 'thoughts' and 'things' have the same natures, the natures work 'energetically' on each other in the things (fire burns, water wets etc.) but not in the thoughts. Mental activity-trains are composed of thoughts, yet their members do work on each other, they check, sustain, and introduce. They do so when the activity is merely associational as well as when effort is there. But, and this is my reply, they do so by other parts of their nature than those that energize physically. One thought in every developed activity-series is a desire or thought of

purpose, and all the other thoughts acquire a feeling tone from their relation of harmony or oppugnancy to this. The interplay of these secondary tones (among which 'interest,' 'difficulty,' and 'effort' figure) runs the drama in the mental series. In what we term the physical drama these qualities play absolutely no part. The subject needs careful working out; but I can see no inconsistency.

ERE, p. 184

But even if there is no actual inconsistency with his special stress elsewhere on the efficacy of the mental, it must be admitted that a strong impression is given at this point that the mental is that which does not work effectively in the world.

The general group of our experiences that *act*, that do not only possess their natures intrinsically, but wear them adjectively and energetically, turning them against one another, comes inevitably to be contrasted with the group whose members, having identically the same natures, fail to manifest them in the 'energetic' way. I make for myself now an experience of blazing fire; I place it near my body; but it does not warm me in the least. I lay a stick upon it, and the stick either burns or remains green, as I please. I call up water and pour it on the fire, and absolutely no difference ensues. . . . Mental fire is what won't burn real sticks, mental water is what won't necessarily (though of course it may) put out even a mental fire.

'Does Consciousness Exist?', ERE, pp. 32–33

If one were to make an evolutionary construction of how a lot of originally chaotic pure experiences became gradually differentiated into an orderly inner and outer world, the whole theory would turn upon one's success in explaining how or why the quality of an experience, once active, could become less so, and, from being an energetic attribute in some cases, elsewhere lapse into the status of an inert or merely internal [that is, merely 'mental'] 'nature'. This would be the 'evolution' of the psychical from the bosom of the physical, in which the esthetic, moral and otherwise emotional experiences would represent a half way stage.

Ibid, pp. 35–36

The special efficacy of the mental is given more prominence in the two essays 'The Place of Affectional Facts in a World of Pure Experience' and 'The Experience of Activity' than in the earlier essays 'Does Consciousness Exist?' and 'A World of Pure Experience'. The distinctive sorts of quality, which we may call the values and interest of things as they present themselves, are increasingly found, as thought advances, to be inactive taken as features of physical things but they do their own special kind of work in the mental sphere. We will consider this point further in the next section.

It should be noted that James does not express his view quite accurately when he says that the mental is what lacks physical efficacy. For, according to him, many mental contents are also physical—that is, after all, the main point of the doctrine. So what he must mean is that the 'merely mental' lacks it, while what is both physical and mental has physical efficacy within the physical stream of being to which it belongs, and efficacy of the valuational and mnemic kind in the mental stream to which it belongs. [29]

§ James's form of DIRECT REALISM is sometimes called NEUTRAL MONISM, or a species thereof, since it regards the basic stuff of the world, pure experience, as in itself neutral between the mental and the physical, only counting as one or the other in virtue of the type of context in which we are currently considering its occurrence.

A certain ambiguity exists as to which of the following propositions is asserted by neutral monism:

(1) Every 'content' or element of pure experience which is physical is also mental and vice versa since every element of pure experience belongs both to a physical and to a mental context. So the same element is properly treated either as physical or as mental according to which context is the one of interest to us.

(2) Some 'contents' or elements of pure experience are both physical and mental because they belong both to a physical and a mental context, while some (though still things of the same generic kind) only belong in one of these contexts and so are only physical or only mental.

Some of James's statements suggest the first proposition, but upon the whole we must take him as intending only the second. Actually, the two statements shift their meaning according as to whether these 'contents', are supposed to be particulars or universals, a matter on which James seems ambiguous, as we noted above. The talk of 'hard' in the passage quoted at the beginning of this section suggests that he is talking of repeatable universal qualities, and saying that the same quality may have instances some of which are physical, some mental. But elsewhere he is evidently concerned to say that the very same instance of a quality may be both mental and physical. In general it would seem that he switches from talking of the various contents which make up 'pure experience' as universals to talking of them as particular instances thereof without much warning. Even if (as I suggested was possible above) they are meant to be below the level of such a distinction, one needs to have some idea of the force of 'same' when it is said that the 'same' content can occur in both a physical and a mental context.

---

29   In 'Does Consciousness Exist?', ERE, pp. 13–14, he contrasts the perceived room taken physically with the same room taken mentally and says that in the one case it must be destroyed if fire plays over it while this is not so in the other case. He must mean that the momentary percept can be continuous in my mental life with a series of images in which fire plays over them harmlessly whereas in the physical history of the room it carries on into a series of appearances in which fire can only be present destructively. James's statements do not make a sharp distinction between the momentary percepts or images and the series or streams of such which can be regarded as constituting the enduring of one and the same percept or image over time.

If we take them as universals, so that there cannot be two exactly similar ones, but only the same one occurring on two different occasions, then the chances for every content to be both physical and mental are increased (though perhaps not to the extent of making proposition 1 acceptable). However, even thus taken as universals, it seems doubtful whether James's considered view is that every such content belongs to both a physical and a mental context. For he seems to think that, as the mind matures, various contents, such as the affectional, and, at a later stage, the usual secondary qualities, are treated as only having a home in mental contexts. In contrast, it seems likely that no nature will belong only to purely physical contexts. For whenever it is perceived it belongs also to a mental context, and when it is imagined it belongs only to a mental context.

If we take these contents as more of the nature of particulars (as seems James's more usual practice), then it must be the second statement which gives his position. For he holds that there are particular mental images which belong only to the mental realm, and presumably there are also elements of unperceived physical reality which belong only to the physical realm.

So, upon the whole, it seems best to take James's neutral monism as the view that while many contents, qua universals, belong to both physical and mental contexts, their particular instances may belong either to both or to just one or other of them.

Thus some particular percepts belong only to physical streams of being, some only to mental streams of being, and some to both. All streams of the first kind are parts of one vast process of physical being in which the elements interact according to a system known as the laws of physical nature. Some of the contents in a mental stream of being have flowed in from the physical stream and initially belong at once to both streams. However, once within the mental stream they enter into processes in which they may continue themselves (in memory) or have effects which continue to develop according to a specifically mental kind of causation, all of which is 'mnemic' in a broad sense. One main form of this is that of positive and negative reinforcers of those mental ideas which function as acts of will.

§ We have already seen some of the peculiarities which this type of direct realism exhibits if we try to make a coherent theory of it. It may appear stranger still if we ask what account it can give of the relation between consciousness and the brain (a central issue in PP which falls rather into the background in the ERE writings). It would presumably run somewhat as follows.

A person's brain is a process in the physical world consisting in a complex of streams of being constituting the lives of the individual cells. If a scientist could see one of these cells, his percept of it would be both something in his own mental stream and something in the physical stream of being of the cell. But while they remain unobserved, the events which make up the existence of the brain are not mental at all. However, when the brain is in a certain state a personal stream of consciousness occurs and may (if we go along with the qualified dualism of PP) interact back on the events in the brain.

This stream of consciousness, however, contains many events which are not generated by the brain. For many of them are percepts which are elements in the physical stream of being of perceived objects, and would be such whether they belonged to a mental stream or not. So it seems that what the brain must do is, not *produce* percepts, but *select* certain of those percepts which occur in that stream of impersonal experience which constitutes the environing world for entry into the personal stream of consciousness which it subtends. In short, the role of the brain will be to bring together (in response to promptings which reach it from the sense organs) in a mental stream what otherwise would just exist physically, while also helping to generate (in combination with a more purely intra-mental generation within the mental stream) various other elements (private images and feelings) which belong only to the mental stream. For the identity between the elements of the mental and the physical postulated by this kind of neutral monism is not between brain event and subtended mental event, but between things perceived and mental events.

This view of the brain as a selector from a system of impersonal 'images' which make up the physical world (and itself, of course, a part of this system), for entry into personal consciousness as a guide to the organism's behaviour, was argued for by Bergson in *Matière et Memoire*.[30] Although James does not advance it expressly, he does advert to it in his notebooks[31] and it seems to be an essential ingredient of DIRECT REALISM.

Such, at least, is how DIRECT REALISM, taken in the NEW REALIST fashion, must conceive the relation between brain and consciousness. If, however, it is taken phenomenalistically, or treated as a pragmatic fiction, then matters are complicated by the fact that the mental streams and their contents will be the only literally existing categorical things. So the brain which selects the parts of the physical world which are going to flow into personal consciousness will, along with the realm from which it selects, either consist in mere possibilities of sensory occurrence in the mental realm or exist only as part of a pragmatic fiction. It would follow that, as things really are, personal streams of experience occur in a kind of void with nothing really there to explain why they take the course they do, for the world as it is conceived within them, including the brain which is supposed to subtend them, is either a system of mostly merely possible appearances or a mere pragmatic fiction. This is so strange a view that the NEW REALIST version of direct realism, with all its oddities, may well seem preferable.

Things are very different, indeed, if these possibilities, or the appropriateness of that pragmatic fiction, have a categorical basis in something actual. And it would seem that only a panpsychist view can provide this for a philosophy for which experience is the only actuality. That James was aware of this is shown by various adumbrations of panpsychism in the course of the main ERE

---

30   See esp. chapter 1, Bergson, pp. 169–223.
31   MSN, pp. 58, 61, 90, 93, 121.

essays.[32] But James was so charmed by his DIRECT REALISM that he struggled hard not to abandon or qualify it thus, and I shall continue to follow his efforts to think this theory out. For it is certainly a most intriguing theory and one always likely to retain some attraction.

§4. *Radical Empiricism and Space*

§ What fascinated James about his form of direct realism was that it purported to show how we are in direct contact with the physical world. This gave him the same kind of excitement as Moore and Russell felt when they escaped from absolute idealism, as they conceived it, and found themselves able to believe that, after all, grass was green.[33]

But the excitement of direct realism for James also lay in the directness of the contact in which it allowed us to suppose ourselves with each other. For most of the contents of my consciousness exist in the very same physical world as yours. Does that mean that the very same physical thing can both be an element in your consciousness and in mine? If so, the streams of being or impersonal experience which make up the physical world not only criss-cross with our streams of personal experience, but your stream of experience and mine can both merge, at least partially, with the stream of process which makes up the independent being of some physical object which we both perceive. Is this really possible and can it occur simultaneously? Can the very same element of the physical world occur at once both in your stream and mine when we perceive the same thing?

James tried desperately to give a positive answer to this last question. For unless our consciousnesses sometimes so intermingle that there is an element literally present in both our minds, it would seem that we do not really share a common world but are quite cut off from each other. Moreover, since thinking about something is having symbols in one's mind which can lead to it, it seems that we cannot even think about the same thing if there is not the possibility of our symbols leading us to experiences in which the very same reality occurs in both our consciousnesses. And this seems to require at least the possibility that the same momentary phase of some real physical process should be immediately present *to*, which for James means *in*, each of our consciousnesses.

Still, James is constrained to admit that, since we always see things from a different perspective, there never is, in actual fact, such a complete identity between our percepts as seems required for this. However, he insists that it is logically possible, and that therefore it makes sense to say that sometimes our consciousnesses come nearer to such a complete convergence than at other

---

32   See, for example, 'The Experience of Activity' (given as a lecture in December 1905) which is essay VI of ERE.

33   See Passmore, p. 207.

times. So we can interpret our concern with the same object as the fact that our streams of experience are in movement towards a common destination even though convergence on it will never be complete.

But how can it even be logically possible that the same percept should occur in different minds, and actually true that there is often a movement towards this situation? In 'A World of Pure Experience' (and elsewhere) James suggests that, even if the same sensory percept is never present as an identical content in two minds, they may be closely connected with something which can occur as such a common element.[34] This is space, and specific parts thereof. For even if your sensory percepts and mine are perspectivally different and so not identical, the space in which they are present is identical. Here our minds do actually meet, and in principle the difference of our perspectives on the world might fade away if matters were pushed just a little bit further. This answer stems from some reflections of James's on the meaning of *identity*.

Although there are empirical grounds (in terms of perspectival and other differences in character) for saying that your percepts are never numerically identical with mine, it remains true that, if they were both qualitatively the same and each responsive equally to the will of each of us, there could be no ground for calling them different. For difference without a difference is meaningless, and precise sameness of character together with causal equivalence seems to give all the meaning we can ever find in claims for the identity of A and B. Now the empirical reasons for saying that our actual percepts are numerically different do not apply to the space in which we experience them as occurring. Here there is in fact qualitative identity, and, since there is also causal equivalence, we may conclude that the very same parts of space are present as elements in your consciousness and in mine. To insist that there is, all the same, a numerical difference is to speak of sameness and difference in an empirically meaningless fashion.

§ Surely this is very unsatisfactory. For, first, the idea that one can single out a given element in perceptual presentation which is the space in which the percepts occur, but which is not infected with their perspectival character, seems rather dubious. And secondly it is irreconcilable with the point on which James had so much insisted in his earlier work, that the character of any element of consciousness is permeated by the total character of the whole mental state (and even by the past features of the stream to which it belongs). One can say, at least, that James's radical empiricism here forces him to take just that atomistic view of consciousness, as made up of elements which are the same whatever their experienced context, which he had previously spoken against so strongly.[35] So this notion that the percepts of different people belong to a common space is a deeply problematic one.

§ There is a sympathetic discussion of this matter in A. J. Ayer's work on

---

34   See ERE, pp. 85–86.
35   See again ERE, pp. 85–86.

James. Ayer equates James's discussion here with what he had said about spatial consciousness in PP at chapters XVII and XX (though perhaps he is a little too inclined to treat James as already having held a radical empiricist view then). His general conclusion is that James can only give sense to the notion of two minds confronting the same space by reference to the criteria we normally use for saying that they are perceiving the same thing, and cannot legitimately use it to resolve problems in making sense of the latter.

It is hard not to agree with Ayer's general conclusion that the precise meaning James attaches to the location of the percepts of different minds in the same space remains unclear.[36] But perhaps Ayer is too inclined to suppose that James is concerned with just the same project of analysis, and should have the same concern with verifiability, as typifies his own philosophy. For though James's radical empiricism was intended to explain everything in terms of experiences and the relations between them, he was prepared to make much more transcendent claims about how things really are than Ayer has ever been, otherwise he would not so much as have dallied with panpsychism. So maybe James did at one time think of there being some sort of enveloping space in which the percepts of different persons exist without reducing their mutual belonging to it to anything strictly verifiable. The claim would be that each of us can grasp what space is by examining the fragments of it present in his own experience, not that we can reduce its existence as a whole to facts about the fragments of it which we experience. Its existence would then be a transcendent

---

36   See Ayer, *Origins*, pp. 233–43. Ayer also offers a valuable discussion of the way in which James treats the construction in infancy of a single perceptual space out of the supposedly originally distinct spaces of the different senses. However, Ayer converts James's account in PP of the way in which the infant comes to form the conception of a common space into an account of the meaning which it has for us, or at least of its epistemological foundations. This suggests that Ayer tends to think of our different senses as still providing us with percepts belonging to distinct sensory spaces. This seems to me wrong phenomenologically, just as is the Berkeleyan view that three-dimensional space is not given sensorily, a position challenged both by James and Ayer. Whatever the causation of such an experience, we experience visual and tangible qualities immediately as in the same given space. Thus we do not now have to construct their togetherness out of anything, it is given to us automatically. But James may be right that this sort of experience is a result of correlations which occurred in infancy between sensory fields not initially united.

However, Ayer is right to stress the importance in James, and in truth, of the overlap in content of our shifting perceptual fields when we move in providing us with our sense of one great space of which all our perceptual fields are fragments. That overlap is the basis of the judgements which Bradley called synthetic judgements of sense. We will see that James and Bradley were at one in thinking of the physical world, as we ordinarily conceive it, as a *more* of the same sort as our given perceptual fields of which they are regarded as fragments.

hypothesis not strictly verifiable, though intelligible to each of us in terms drawn from his own experience.[37]

§ I do not have the verificationist worries about such a claim which Ayer does. But I do find the idea deeply problematic. For if I try to imagine the percepts of different people existing together in a common space, together with further percepts not experienced by anyone, I find myself trying to imagine them either as parts of a common sensory field, or as components in a single state of mind (which experiences a totality of distinct sense fields in one unitary super-sensory consciousness). But I find I cannot do the first. For the percepts of an object from a certain point of view can belong only to a sense field which presents things as a whole from that point of view and which therefore cannot contain percepts of them from another one. The other alternative is less problematic. We have some experiences ourselves which suggest what it might be like to experience diverse sense fields. For I can see the world around me, while at the same time imagining a scene which I do not place in any spatial relation to it. But this is to replace the notion of a common space by that of a universal consciousness. And that is perilously close to introducing that Absolute which it was one main point of radical empiricism to keep at bay.[38]

Be all this as it may, James was certainly at times satisfied with the idea that what brings our different percepts together in a common world is 'the great enveloping Unit, which we believe in and call real Space' (together with real Time). [39] The trouble is, as we have seen, that space can only be the great container of all things physical if the real physical exists in a non-perspectival form and is therefore distinct from the perspectives on it which occur in our streams of consciousness.

§ Sometimes James seems to be struggling for a view of space for which the spatial relations between things are a matter of the patterns of immediate or mediated causal relation possible between them. But I am not sure how sharply he distinguishes the conception of space as a system of possible causal relations between things from the claim that it is only because they are co-present in the same space that things can interact (or rather that interacting things must either be in, or each separately continuous with what is in, such a universal container.[40])

§ The difficulty in understanding this is considerable if James intended his DIRECT REALISM to be literally true in a NEW REALIST fashion. If, however, the world of direct realism is the world as it is conceived by us (rather than an independent reality in which the philosopher is invited seriously to believe) or if it exists in large part only as a system of possibilities, then the incoherences

---

37   It would, however, itself have to be a 'pure experience' in James's sense, if it was to be consistent with the basic doctrine of radical empiricism.
38   See ERE, p. 86, etc.
39   See ERE, p. 31 and pp. 84–86.
40   See, for example, ERE, pp. 84–86 and p. 89, note 1.

can either be regarded as elements of the fiction, not damaging to its practical utility or as not arising because the possibilities are never totally actualised and the contradictions would only belong to them if they were.

§ So let us return to the question as to which form it was in which James intended his DIRECT REALISM. One consideration which suggests that perhaps the phenomenological interpretation is the closest to his intentions is that he came to think that the same identity holds between the thing thought of and our conceptual representation of it as holds between a thing perceived and our perception of it.

Such a view is expressed in one of the earlier radical empiricist essays 'Does Consciousness Exist?' (1904).[41] He there quotes with approval his colleague Hugo Münsterberg who had said that things thought of stand before one 'exactly as perceived objects . . . do, no matter how different the two ways of apprehending them may be in their genesis'.[42] Now when James endorses this and says that just as our perception of an object and the object are one, so is our thought of the object and the object, is he really supporting the identification of our mental activity as we think with an externally existing object thought of, as a metaphysical truth or only as a good phenomenological account of how things are for us? It seems to me so implausible as the former in the case of thought— how can my thought of a far away place be that place?—and so plausible as phenomenology that it suggests that it is only intended as phenomenology in the case both of thinking and perception. If so, the puzzling notion of space as a real container containing the percepts of different persons appears less problematic as essentially only a phenomenological point too.

§ But convenient as it might be to close the matter thus, it must be said that James's introduction of space as the great container of the 'physical' percepts of all persons, together with others not belonging to any personal consciousness, seems to be intended in a much more straightforwardly realist way, à la new realism, and as an alternative to the Absolute. And this is confirmed by his continuing inclination to think of it as a great container even when he moves to a panpsychism which is clearly meant with full metaphysical seriousness. Indeed, the way in which he does so even suggests a kind of reconciliation between direct realism and panpsychism. For he hints that your percepts and mine may exist together with a perceived thing's own experience of itself, also existing at the very same place. Thus if you and I both see a cake, our percepts of it may be at the same place as the cake's experience of its own bodily presence.[43] That suggests that our percepts are not mere representations of the cake in our minds, but are elements of what the cake becomes for us. That is,

---

41   At ERE, pp. 15–25.
42   ERE, p. 18, quoting Münsterberg.
43   Eating it might be thought a better candidate for my experience's merging with the cake's own experience of itself; but since you and I cannot eat the same piece of cake (at least at the same time!) that would preclude this as a way of our experiencing exactly the same thing.

our percepts of the cake are so united with the cake's experience of itself that, while we perceive it, the cake is a bundle of our percepts and its own experiences all lying side by side in the same bit of space. At times James does seem to be suggesting such a thing.[44] But sympathetic as I personally am to panpsychism, I doubt if it can really take on such a view of space. Even if it could, it would still only satisfy James's hankering after direct realism in a very partial way, since anything of the nature of our percepts would only belong to the thing perceived when it was being perceived. We would, in fact, have a doctrine very like that ascribed to Protagoras and Heracleitus in the *Theaetetus*, where sensible qualities are produced in the object and in the perceiver when the motions which constitute each of them merge. It is much better to treat direct realism as giving a phenomenological account of how things are for us, and panpsychism as giving a metaphysical account of the underlying reality responsible for our experiences. Of course, a serious panpsychism will not suppose that objects like cakes have an over all experience of themselves but only that their ultimate physical constituents, such as the sub-atomic particles within them, do.[45]

§ Be that as it may, James's own hope was to place different minds in a common world by giving them the possibility of directly experiencing the very same things. Only thus, he sometimes felt, can radical empiricism escape the snares of absolute idealism, for which contact between different minds can only occur within a universal consciousness.

§ However, James also proposes a quite different solution to the problem of how different minds can encounter the same reality. In 'How Two Minds Can Know One Thing' (March 1905).[46] which is specifically directed at this problem, he offers another account of the matter which is even more remarkable, and I shall end this section with some account of this.

James refers first to various general 'dialectical' difficulties which monistic philosophers such as Bradley have raised about the very possibility of one thing standing in two different relations and claims to have met these thoroughly sophistical arguments in a previous paper, 'The Thing and Its Relations' (1905).[47]

Yet, he allows, there are special difficulties in understanding how one element can be simultaneously present in two streams of consciousness.[48] For in the case of a state of consciousness, its

> *esse* is *sentiri*; it is only so far as it is felt; and it is unambiguously and unequivocally exactly *what* is felt. The hypothesis under consideration would, however, oblige it to be felt equivocally, felt now as part of my mind and again at the same time *not* as a part of my mind, but of yours (for my mind is *not*

---

44   See, for example, ERE, pp. 85–86, and 89 as quoted above.
45   As emphasised by Hartshorne, e.g., Hartshorne, *Creative*, p. 141.
46   ERE, pp. 123–36.
47   PU, pp. 347–69.
48   See ERE, pp. 125–27.

yours), and this would seem impossible without doubling it into two distinct things.

'How Two Minds Can Know One Thing', ERE, p. 127

He now offers to resolve the problem by the suggestion that the fact that various distinct contents fall within a single consciousness is not strictly something which happens at the time, but consists in their being recalled and gathered together by a later mental act. Thus there is no special unity linking my visual and auditory sense impressions as of now. They are only linked retrospectively by being recalled (or perhaps by the possibility of their being recalled) together with later mental acts. In that case, if the same content is recalled later by two distinct mental acts, which do not belong to the same consciousness (because they cannot be recalled together), it belongs to two different consciousnesses.

The extent of the departure here from PP's holistic conception of consciousness is quite amazing, and the idea is most far-fetched in itself.[49] Superficially, indeed, it may look rather similar to the PP conception of the unity of the self as a matter of earlier moments of consciousness being held together by the retrospective gathering of them together in a later one. But that was supposed to explain the unity of the self across time, not the unity of the elements of a single state of consciousness at a moment. In PP James rejected any view for which the elements of a single state of consciousness need to be glued together by something external to them, and the view that they are glued together by a retrospective act directed on them is a particularly far-fetched view of just that kind. In fact, this suggestion seems to me an ingenious if desperate strait into which James was thrown in his Herculean efforts to find a form of direct realism which would achieve all he wanted, including the real presence of the same physical reality in two minds.

§ We must conclude from the various problems discussed in this section that James was deeply committed to certain ideas which it was difficult to unify. He believed strongly that a final account of reality must be in experiential terms, and he also felt that there must be something wrong in accounts of perception for which we never directly encounter the things perceived. Direct realism of the radical empiricist sort seemed to give him much of what he wanted, but it threw up a variety of difficulties. He became fascinated with trying to find a formula which would resolve these and in doing so played at times with views which were extremely strange ones for such a person to hold.

§5. *The Experience of Activity*

The sixth essay in *Essays in Radical Empiricism* is 'The Experience of Activity'

---

49   For something oddly similar see Dennett, chapters V and VI. I comment on this in an issue of *Inquiry* devoted to Dennett to be published in 1993.

(January 1905). It is expressly given as an example of pragmatic method and of the radical empiricist principle. In fact, it represents something of a fresh development in James's radical empiricism. For it adumbrates a radical empiricist account of the relation between brain and mind (or consciousness) which points towards panpsychist developments.

In this essay James effectively considers three questions (though he himself tabulates its concerns somewhat differently):

(1) What is activity?
(2) What are the efficaciously active agencies involved in human action?
(3) What fundamentally makes things go in the world?

(1) What is activity?

James says that, in one sense, any change whatever is a case of activity. However, most thinkers contrast active and passive change and consider conscious human willing the prime case of the former. But as to what is distinctively active about it there is angry disagreement. Bradley has called the question of activity a scandal to philosophy, and it is, indeed, scandalous, says James, that writers like Bradley and James Ward describe each other's efforts in the contemptuous terms they do.

As James sees it, there certainly is a distinctive type of experience properly called the experience of activity (or alternatively there is a definite range of such types of experience). And various writers have managed to capture something of its nature in their descriptions. However, such descriptions do little to advance human knowledge, for we all know well enough already what this type of experience is like. And since there is no obvious stopping place at which to cease adding detail upon detail to one's descriptions, the whole effort is directed at no very certain aim. James admits to much wasted effort of his own in this respect in PP.[50]

One defence of such phenomenological efforts might be that they aim to pick out necessary and sufficient conditions of what we recognize as genuinely active willing from the mass of varying detail. But however that may be, James is here quite dismissive of such phenomenological investigation. It is enough, he says, for his purposes to point out that such experiences always (or typically?) include the envisagement of certain future contingencies which they are felt to be on the way to bringing about in spite of certain resistances.

Granted that there are experiences like this and that they are the source of our very idea of 'activity', the radical empiricist will not wonder whether there is some sort of *real* activity which they manifest, but will take it that by 'activity' we precisely mean a process of the character we find in them. It is senseless to suppose that there could be something more truly worthy of the name of which the actual existence is problematic. In the experience of activity we encounter activity in as good and genuine a sense as there could be.

---

50   See note 65 below; also Perry, I, p. 176.

Two things would seem to follow. First, that if someone has the experience of activity, then it follows deductively that he is genuinely active and that therefore we all are genuinely active beings. Second, that other things, e.g., merely physical processes in inanimate nature, can only be active if they contain within them an experience with some analogy to what in us is called the experience of activity.

James does draw the second conclusion, or is within an inch of doing so. In particular he suggests that the efficacy of brain cells implies that they have a dim prevision of something they are up to. But surprisingly enough he does not draw the first. For he says that while the fact that there is an *experience* of activity shows that there is such a *thing* as activity, it does not show that we always locate the thing correctly. There must be activity somewhere, but its real locus may be somewhere else than we think it to be. Perhaps its true locus is not in us but somewhere else. This he says follows from the radical empiricist principle that

> [n]othing shall be admitted as fact, it says, except what can be experienced at some definite time by some experient; and for every feature of fact ever so experienced, a definite place must be found somewhere in the final system of reality. In other words: Everything real must be experienceable somewhere, and every kind of thing experienced must somewhere be real.
>
> ERE, p. 160

Both the principle here enunciated and the conclusion drawn seem strange. It is not uncommon, indeed, for philosophers to distinguish between the source from which we draw the raw materials out of which we construct a concept and the subject to which it can truly be applied. But for empiricists that typically means that we encounter the basic elements of our concept in several different loci and combine them to form a complex concept of something we have not actually encountered. However, James has said that it is the overall character of experiences which we all actually have from which we obtain our concept of activity. From this it is no step at all to saying that we are all in a position to know that we are among the genuinely active agents in the world.

Perhaps what he means is that it is an open philosophical question whether the real home of what 'we' call 'our' *experience* of activity is not really in individual persons but in something else (the Absolute, for example). He does say things which suggest this meaning. Yet he also seems to be concerned with the question whether these experiences are really cases of genuine efficacy at all, and that seems unintelligible granted his view that there is nothing else we can properly mean by activity than what has the character of these experiences. Surely he should conclude immediately, what indeed he clearly believes, that we, or at least our experiences, are genuinely active agents. However, let us consider how he deals with the other two questions.

(2) What are the efficaciously active agencies involved in human action?

James says that there are three main views as to what are the primary, or even the only, efficaciously active agents involved in human action: (1) there is a divine mind of some kind which is efficaciously active through us; (2) what is really efficaciously active in us are the ideas which pass through our mind; (3) it is our brain cells which are the genuinely efficacious agents.

James is more concerned in this article to clarify the pragmatic *meaning* of the question (and of various answers to it) 'which are the primary or only genuinely efficacious active agencies at work in human life?' than to answer it.[51] And this lies, so he tells us, in the difference between the results implied by the final dominance of one kind of agency rather than another in the world. (James was already approaching the question of where efficacy really lies in this 'pragmatic' way as early as 1875.[52])

If it is God who is the real agent, then we can expect our higher purposes to move gradually towards some kind of fulfilment, if not in our lives, then in the course of history. If it is brain cells, then the fact that their activity combines together to produce the behaviour typifying some individual, or humanity at large, is an accidental upshot of particular combinations, and there is no reason to expect its apparent purposes to have more than a very temporary influence on how the world develops. And if it is ideas, then that suggests that there is no real unity to each of us, and that different ideas may take over from each other and have upshots which do not combine into any coherent whole.

It is not altogether clear whether James thinks that the naive view that it is oneself who is active represents a fourth alternative or whether it is a pre-philosophical account waiting to be analyzed in one of these three ways. Upon the whole the subsequent discussion makes better sense if the fundamental efficacy of persons, or at least of unitary states of personal consciousness, is one of the possible alternatives. Moreover, since each of the three alternatives he lists is disintegrative of the individualist values dear to him James presumably did want to leave the fourth possibility standing that each of us, qua an individual person with a fairly coherent set of purposes, is a primary agent, not in some vacuous metaphysical sense of 'person' but in the way developed in PP for which our consciousness consists in a series of units which are so. For the whole discussion was introduced by reference to the sense each of us has of his own activity as a sensible element in our personal streams of consciousness.[53] I take it that the 'pragmatic meaning' of taking this sense as veridical would lie in the prospect, encouraging for the heroic or strenuous life which was for James the human best, that firm long-term commitments and strivings tend to reach their goals.

It remains a puzzle how the question can arise whether personal consciousness is a real agent in the world, granted that activity and the experience of activity are one. Perhaps we have here an admission that it cannot be simply

---

51   See ERE, pp. 155 and 176–78.
52   See Perry, I, pp. 523–24.
53   See ERE, p. 168, and the preliminary discussion leading up to it.

the internal quality of an experience which constitutes its activity. In fact, James admits as much himself in his discussion of the third question, as we shall see below.

And a second puzzle is this. The pragmatic meaning of a question and its answers are for the pragmatist the whole of what they really mean. But can James really think that the consequences which he suggests are implied by the different answers to the second question give them their whole meaning? Surely the contrast between them is what gives *importance* rather than *meaning* to the question.

Perhaps James's view is really this: There is a weak sense in which there is activity wherever and only where there is the relevant experience. (This may mean that it is at least the locus of the emergence of new real being in the world. But is this not equally true of every experience?) However, there is another sense in which such experiences are not *truly efficacious* unless they envisage results which they actually make more likely of occurrence.

His point would then be that if, say, it is in the brain cells that true efficacy lies, then it is the small-scale immediate effects they have on each other which constitute the real purposes their existence sustains, so that what seem to be our purposes are just the result of relations between them liable to break down at any moment. If, on the other hand, the purposes envisaged by our overall consciousness carry a likelihood of being realized which does not turn entirely on the way the brain cells are arranged and are acting on each other (so that what would otherwise happen simply as a result of interaction between brain cells, each seeking merely its own ends, is modified by the influence of the overall purposes of the dominant stream of consciousness), they can be expected to be sustained over a much longer period.

For, James suggests, the ultimate question is how different levels of efficacious process relate to each other. One such level is that dealt with by standard physical science, and one usual modern view is that what goes on in the brain is entirely explicable by this. In that case, the brain cells are the *truly efficacious* agents, and the apparent efficacy of our consciousness a mere reflection thereof. However, if we are the agents we think of ourselves as being, then the stream of our conscious experience must interact somehow with the streams of experience which are the inner life of the neurons as they interact, perhaps by damping down the action of certain of the neurons and somehow promoting others.[54] And in the same way it is possible that a divine stream of consciousness somehow interacts with our stream of experience, damping down some of what goes on there, and promoting other things.

(3) What fundamentally makes things go in the world?

Finally, James asks what really makes experience (which for radical empiricism

---

54　This is very much the view advocated by Sperry in our own time. [See Sperry.] For some suggestions of my own see my *Vindication*, chapter III.

means any sort of process in the world) unfold. Why, so to speak, does anything happen at all? Why is there not 'far rather nothing at all' (as Heidegger puts it) or not a merely static something? James suggests that perhaps we should not look further than precisely to experiences of activity. May it not be, he asks, that here we actually find reality in the making? When we introspect or sympathetically imagine the experience of activity are we not perhaps confronted with the very bringing of new fact into existence out of nothing? Here James again seems to be suggesting that there is something not quite captured in the pragmatic meaning ascribed above to the question of what is *truly efficacious*, and that there is some deeper ontological insight to be gained from inspecting the experience of activity.

§ There is much that is obscure here and much groping for, rather than reaching of, conclusions. But perhaps the upshot is this:

We can all identify experiences of our own which are difficult to describe quite satisfactorily but which we know as experiences of really doing something, of really acting, as opposed to merely being acted on. They include the envisagement of certain future eventualities which they seem to us to make more likely of occurrence by their possession of the phenomenal quality of effortfulness. The existence of efficacy, in a weak sense, is established by the mere existence of such experiences, but if we are to accept such experiences as *truly efficacious* in a stronger sense, we must suppose that they satisfy two further conditions. (1) We must think that they really do make it more likely that the eventualities they envisage will occur. They must be more than mere registers of the fact that they are likely, and must be part of what actually does make them more likely. (2) We must think that it is the existence of experiences like these which alone makes things happen in the world at all. Insofar as there is real agency in things non-human it must be because something of this sort goes on at the heart of them as something subjectively felt there.

Unfortunately this second condition makes use of that notion of real efficacy whereby one thing makes another happen, the meaning of which was supposed to be manifested to us by the inherent nature of these experiences. Yet the fact that this condition has to be added as an extra suggests that it does not really do so. For without this further condition, according to James, we only have apparent, not real efficacy.

However, it is here that the peculiarly pragmatic elucidation he has offered of the concept of real efficacy is supposed to help. According to this, the real meaning of the question where real efficacy is to be located lies in the effect on our life hopes (in Ted Honderich's expression[55]) of the answer.

But here, at least, he can hardly suppose that the pragmatic meaning, in this sense, is a full elucidation of what the question asks. (Indeed he explicitly dissociates himself from a suggestion of Royce's somewhat to that effect.[56]) His

---

55   See Honderich, chapter VII.
56   See ERE, p. 187.

view seems to be rather that it is of the very nature of the experience of efficacy that it is the feeling a process has for itself, or for its subject, that it is making certain eventualities which it envisages more likely to happen than they would be without it. It is thus part of its own inherent felt character that it points beyond itself to something that it goes some way to necessitating. (The idea that experiences can have such an inherent intentionality is an idea which alternatively attracts and repels James throughout his work.) The two further conditions tell us how far this necessitation is basic or derivative from other deeper necessitations. The so-called pragmatic meaning of the question how far it is so is really an explanation of why it matters.

§ The main drift of the discussion in this chapter seems to be in line with that of the treatment of *will* in PP. There is simply the further suggestion that the brain processes with which our own personal conscious willing interacts really consist in the interactions of the inner felt willings of our individual brain cells.

Yet there does seem to be some change of position. The theory of purely ideo-motor action, advanced in PP, implied that in many cases there is no difference between mere speculative ideas and those which produce action, except that the latter happen to be about things (namely, those which relate to the movement of our own limbs, etc.) which as a matter of brute fact tend to occur as we ideate them. Distinctive feelings of effort were supposed only to occur under special circumstances where some special internal obstacle needed to be overcome. If his position is now that there can be no real efficacy without the feeling of effort, it would seem that there can be no genuine ideo-motor action. At least, if mere ideas are followed by action in the way described in PP, the explanation must be an epiphenomenalist one, and we are only real agents when the distinctive experience of efficacy occurs. Upon the whole, this seems an improvement on the position of PP, for surely there is a distinct phenomenological quality to the way in which ideas are entertained in willing, which sets it apart from mere thought (though I would explain this myself, contra James, by reference to the pleasure or pain with which it envisages its goals).

§ This article has more far-reaching metaphysical implications than may at first appear. For it presents in effect an unorthodox account of the nature of causation in general. To make this clear I shall tabulate four main claims implied in it:

(1) Efficacy or causation is a concept derived from experience, not an *a priori* concept applied to it *ab extra* and irreducible to anything observable or sensible as Kant claimed.

(2) Efficacy or causation is not, however, reducible to the mere following of one thing on another in accordance with universal law, especially if universal law is understood merely as the constant holding of a certain generalisation, as Hume, or at least his subsequent followers, held.

(3) Efficacy is not something more than what the experience of activity reveals to introspection and yet it is not merely a sensible characteristic of the experience but the fact that the experience is a real force at work in the world. (It is not clear whether James would think that such efficacy yields universal

laws. At any rate causation, on this view, is a real fact about the individual case as such, not just the fact that what holds in this case, holds in others too.)

(4) 'Efficacy' has no meaning except as a word for the sort of experience mentioned in (3), so that efficacy in the physical world can only be interpreted as meaning the presence there of experiences of generically the same sort as our experience of activity.

§ Propositions (1) and (2) are examples of James's tendency to meet Kantian claims that a concept cannot be derived from experience by granting that this would be so if experience were such as traditional empiricism describes it, but wrong as experience actually is. Proposition (4) represents an agreement with Berkeley that true causation must be conceived psychically. Proposition (3) looks like an attempt to have one's cake and eat it but perhaps the attempt is successful. At any rate, he seems to hold both that efficacy is just a particular quality of experience and that, all the same, its pertaining to an experience is inseparable from its exerting a real pressure on things beyond itself. All four propositions show James adumbrating claims central to the metaphysics of Whitehead.

§ On the face of it this represents a complete *volte face* on the relations between the mental and the physical. For we saw above that in earlier ERE articles the mental was distinguished from the physical by its non-efficacious or energetic character; while now the physical is only allowed to be efficacious if supposed to be psychic or at least psychic-like at its heart.

James, indeed, denied, as we saw, that there was any conflict.[57] But certainly there is some difference of mood. And if the conflict can be resolved, it must be with more care, as James admits, than he bestows on it here.

It could be resolved, for example, by distinguishing the phenomenal physical world from the reality which underlies it. Then we could say that causation in the former means only that events follow each other in conformity to inductively establishable laws and that it is as belonging to sequences governed by these that presentations are characterised as physical. In contrast, presentations are dismissed as merely 'mental' if they do not fall under these laws, while those which do so are said to belong also to the 'mental sphere' when they are considered rather as elements in the distinct patterns of process in the personal stream of consciousness where those laws do not apply. It is, however, precisely in this mental sphere that the metaphysician must look for the real efficacy which will give him that deeper understanding of the world process which he craves. And he must suppose a similar efficacy present in the reality underlying the physical. I have already contended that this was the kind of position into which James's radical empiricism was developing, to culminate in the panpsychist metaphysics which we shall be exploring in the next chapter.

We may anticipate our discussion of that by noting that one of the reasons why James came to favour a panpsychist view of nature was that he thought genuine causation must be conceived as always involving something like the experienced activity situations from which we get the idea of it. This point is developed in what may be the last thing James wrote, Chapter XIII of the unfinished *Some Problems of Philosophy*.[58]

> No matter what 'efficacies' there may really be in this extraordinary universe it is impossible to conceive of any one of them being either lived through or authentically known otherwise than in this dramatic shape of something sustaining a felt purpose against felt obstacles, and overcoming or being overcome.
>
> SPP, p. 212

If nature does not contain something of this sort, it does not contain the genuine causation we must assume it does. The view of nature to which these reflections lead is quite unlike that James espouses in his promotion of 'direct realism'.

§6. *Radical Empiricism vs. Phenomenology*

§ Several commentators have presented James as a proto-phenomenologist. Just as philosophers of a Whiteheadian persuasion (with a good deal of justification) see James as the herald of process philosophy so (with less justification) do some American philosophers who believe that phenomenology has been the great philosophical development of the century like to claim their native James as its previously unrecognized prophet.[59]

The affinity with Whitehead is, I believe, much greater than that with Husserl and other phenomenologists. Comparisons with Whitehead are made on various occasions in this book. Here I venture some brief remarks on how James's radical empiricism stands to the phenomenology of Husserl. If one is especially struck by the contrast between each of James and Husserl with the more external approaches to human reality of some other philosophers, especially in our own day, one may see them as kindred spirits. Likewise they both belong to that great class of thinkers who believe that genuine concepts must be capable of some sort of intuitive fulfilment.[60] There are very great differences between them nonetheless.

---

58   See SPP, pp. 210–14.
59   For Whiteheadian interpretations of James see Ford and Eisendrath. (The latter is a somewhat uncritical summary of positions held in common by the two thinkers, but the author sometimes takes them as agreeing when they are saying almost the opposite. See p. 42 where both are said to see consciousness as a synthesis of elements, missing the point that for James in the PP passage quoted there is no question of the synthesised elements being actual components of the unifying consciousness. Likewise different senses of 'possibility' are run together on p. 182.) For phenomenological interpretations see Wild, Wilshire, and Stevens.
60   Thus James said in PP 'that all conceptual knowledge stands for intuitive knowl-

If phenomenology means the study of consciousness as such then certainly much of James's work is phenomenology. But if it means the doctrines and methods of Husserl and his followers, then, despite some overlap in viewpoint, on the whole James (at least in his radical empiricist period) must be regarded as a deliberate opponent of its most distinctive doctrines, as he encountered them in such kindred writers as Brentano.

§ To say that the claim, in 'Does Consciousness Exist?', that consciousness is a function rather than an entity, sets James apart from phenomenology may seem to turn on that very mistake I warned against above. For we have seen how misleading James's deliberately startling statements (such as that consciousness does not exist as an entity, but only occurs as a function)[61] in this connection can be. This is especially true for readers today. For we live in the midst of people who seem to deny the existence of that stream of personal experience which is for James both what has that function and in the end our best clue to the nature of reality in general. Thus if we hear today that a philosopher maintains that consciousness is a function and not a thing, we may ascribe to him a view like that of modern functionalism for which consciousness is whatever in the brain performs a certain function and the whole notion of consciousness as the 'what it is like to be it' of an organism a superstition. Nothing could be further from this than James's radical empiricism, which was quite as far from any kind of physicalism or behaviourism as is Husserl's phenomenology.

Nonetheless, when he declares that he believes that 'consciousness (as it is commonly represented, either as an entity, or as pure activity, but in any case as being fluid, inextended, diaphonous, devoid of self-content, but directly self-knowing—spiritual, in short) . . . is pure fancy',[62] that of which he is denying the existence is precisely consciousness in Husserl's or Sartre's sense. If one is determined to assimilate his position to some philosopher in that tradition Heidegger would be a better choice. For one could describe James, like Heidegger, as replacing the notion of our being conscious of things by a notion of our being in the midst of them. But I doubt if such a comparison will be of much help in understanding James, if only because it would be explanation of the less by the more obscure.

James was, in fact, attacking two distinct ideas when he said that consciousness was not an entity, though perhaps he did not distinguish them. (One could, indeed, combine the two, taking the first as an account of perceptual consciousness, the second as an account of conceptual—or imaginational—consciousness. Even so, they specify two quite different ways in which consciousness may be supposed to relate to its objects.)

First, he was attacking the view that consciousness is a kind of search light

---

edge, and terminates therein' (PP, II, p. 649, note).
61   ERE, p. 13.
62   McDermott, p. 190; McDermott's translation of James's French at ETR, p. 222.

which picks out things which are otherwise in darkness while remaining distinct from what it plays upon, or, to use another metaphor expressing essentially the same point, that it is something purely diaphanous which as it were lies over the object and can only be distinguished from it with difficulty. This is the view of consciousness of which Moore's 'The Refutation of Idealism' (1903)[63] is the most famous statement.

Secondly, he was attacking the notion of consciousness as a mysterious leap the mind makes outside its own boundaries to something which is precisely not present to it in the immediate way of the first view or as an element of its own being. This is very similar to the view which Hilary Putnam has called 'the magical theory of reference'.[64] On the face of it, Brentano held some such view, though his full position is, naturally, a good deal subtler.

If James had had to choose between these two views, he might have preferred the Moore view, for the specially basic case of perception. For it makes the object of which one is conscious in perception the very thing which sensibly fills one's perceptual field as Husserl's view, with its distinction between the hyletic datum in consciousness, and the thing perceived, does not. Even so, he certainly rejected it, both for perception and other cases, and indeed quotes Moore's article as an example of precisely what he is arguing against.[65]

> Now my contention is exactly the reverse of this [Moore's view that consciousness is a diaphonous medium which with careful introspection we can distinguish from what is presented to it]. *Experience, I believe, has no such inner duplicity; and the separation of it into consciousness and content comes, not by way of subtraction, but by way of addition.*
>
> 'Does Consciousness Exist?' (1904), ERE, p. 9

He was certainly equally or more opposed to the Brentano type of view which he seems to have thought an idle, merely verbal, answer to the problem of the aboutness of thought. His view of consciousness is thus quite different from that of Husserl for whom mental acts are inherently intentional. True, Husserl's view of the objects of consciousness does tend in the end to be idealist in character. Thus he certainly came to identify the existence of physical objects with their perceivability. Nonetheless, he was absolutely committed to the view that consciousness (when it is more than merely introspective) inherently presents something which is not a literal component of one's present state of mind or experience. Consciousness, thus conceived, is neither the 'function' which, according to James, one part of absolute experience has of leading fruitfully to another, nor that absolute experience itself.

§ James was rather nearer to Husserl in certain respects in PP. But if much of that work is taken up with descriptions which are phenomenological in a

---

63 *Studies*, pp. 1–30.
64 See Putnam, *Reason*, pp. 3–5.
65 See ERE, pp. 6–9.

sense sometimes approximating to Husserl's, it must be borne in mind that for James these are only a preliminary to the real task of a scientific psychology, the biological explanation of mental life by reference to brain physiology and survival value. Thus in a most un-Husserlian way he is apt to cut such descriptions short with the remark that the reader knows the experience perfectly well himself. And periodic impatience with thinkers who merely try to describe the character of experiences which everyone knows quite well enough already, recurs in his later writings too (as we noted above in relation to the 'experience of activity') and shows only a limited sympathy with the goals of Husserlian phenomenology.[66]

Nonetheless some commentators, such as John Wild, try to present radical empiricism as an advance to a more completely phenomenological point of view. This is true, up to a point, so far as subject matter goes, for the concern of the ERE writings is, as we have seen, best interpreted as description of our 'life world' and turning away from speculation on the 'physical' underpinning thereof. But if the goal is to some extent the same as that of Husserlian phenomenology, it is pursued on the basis of explicit rejection of two ideas which are the very hallmark of the latter, namely, (1) that consciousness must be distinguished from its objects, (2) that it contrasts sharply with physical reality, by being inextended and intrinsically outward pointing, while physical things are extended and wrapped up in their own being without essential continuity with one another.

> As 'subjective' we say that the experience represents; as 'objective' it is represented. What represents and what is represented is here numerically the same; but we must remember that no dualism of being represented and representing resides in the experience *per se*. In its pure state, or when isolated, there is no self-splitting of it into consciousness and what the consciousness is 'of'.
>
> ERE, p. 23

And he goes on to say

> Descartes for the first time defined thought as the absolutely unextended, and later philosophers have accepted the description as correct. But what possible meaning has it to say that, when we think of a foot-rule or a square yard,

---

66   Thus in 'The Experience of Activity' he says of various descriptions which have been given of what it feels like to be active: 'Every hour of human life could contribute to the picture gallery; and this is the only fault that one can find with such descriptive industry—where is it going to stop? Ought we to listen forever to verbal pictures of what we have already in concrete form in our own breasts? They never take us off the superficial plane. We knew the facts already—less spread out and separated, to be sure—but we knew them still' (1905, ERE, pp. 164–65). James adds the note: 'I ought myself to cry *peccavi*, having been a voluminous sinner in my own chapter on the will.' Compare Perry, I, p. 176.

extension is not attributable to our thought? Of every extended object the *adequate* mental picture must have all the extension of the object itself.

ERE, p. 30

§ The partly shared goal and the enormous difference in its working out shows itself in the contrast between James's (radical empiricist) and Husserl's account of perception. The common goal is the restoration of the ordinary conception of things presenting themselves *in propria persona* in perception, as opposed to philosophical views for which they only present themselves disguised by secondary qualities and other subject-related properties which they do not really possess. The difference is that for James the perceived object is actually a component in our stream of consciousness or personal experience, while Husserl insists that it is a bad mistake to think of it as *ein reelles Bestandstück des Bewusstseins*. Rather, the perceptual act somehow uses the hyletic datum which is *in* consciousness to present the physical object *to* consciousness.

Personally I doubt whether Husserl can reconcile the claim that the object is somehow directly present *in propria persona* with the insistence that it is distinct from anything which actually enters into the flow of consciousness. But certainly he means to assert both. James, in contrast, thinks that the perceived object can only itself be there for us if it is an actual element in our stream of experience.

In some respects perception is, for Husserl, just one among a variety of mental acts, through which the world is presented to us, all of which have the same basic structure. Thus we can imagine things or remember them just as we can perceive them. In each case there is a subjective 'hyletic' datum which the mental act 'animates' in order that it shall serve as the vehicle for the presentation of the object imagined, remembered, or perceived.[67] And in each case what we are imagining, remembering, or perceiving is not the hyletic datum but the physical (or other) thing which it serves to present to us. This applies even where the thing perceived, imagined, or remembered does not in fact exist; indeed it applies even in that type of imagination where the likely non-existence of the thing imagined is of its evident essence.[68] (This insistence that it is the thing, and not the subjective datum which presents it, which is perceived, remembered, or imagined is not merely a point about normal linguistic usage. The point is rather that our mind is not directed at the datum but through it to the object which, as animated by the mental act, it presents to us.)

But in spite of this common structure to acts of perception, memory, and imagination, there is (for Husserl) something special about perception, namely, that in its case alone is the object of the act in some sense bodily present, or present *in propria persona*. But it is none too easy to say in what this direct presence of the object in perception is. For he contends that the same contrast

---

67 See Husserl, *Logic*, Investigations I, §23 and VI, §14 (b); *Ideas*, §§41–46 and most importantly §85.

68 See Husserl, *Ideas*, §23.

holds between the hyletic datum, which is an actual component of consciousness, and the object presented which is not, just as in memory and imagination.

Though he cannot explain it satisfactorily Husserl is surely right that, as we ordinarily conceive the matter, a perceived object is present *in propria persona*, as something merely remembered or imagined is not. However, as an elucidation of this ordinary conception James's radically empiricist direct realism seems much more promising.

On this view, the thing perceived is an actual ingredient in our perceptual experience of it or, more accurately, consists in elements one of which is so. This is close to Hume's view that the physical thing of common sense actually consists in our sense impressions, thought of as capable of going on outside our consciousness. And we shall see (in Part Two, Chapter Five, §5) that Bradley's position is also quite similar, granted he would take a much less atomistic view of the various ingredients within a single whole of experience than Hume, and than James in his ERE phase. The position of each of these three thinkers contrasts sharply with Husserl's insistence that the physical thing is something which can never be an actual element of our experience and, as I see it, is much better as phenomenology. It only seems to clash with common sense because when presented explicitly as theory it confronts us with puzzles which we manage to ignore when we simply presuppose it in daily life.

To accept it as an account of our ordinary most primitive conceptions is to leave metaphysical questions as to how far it is correct, or even coherent, quite open. It is just because James seems to keep such metaphysical questions at bay that one is so inclined to interpret his enterprise as phenomenological, in a non-doctrinaire sense. But unlike Husserl he could not stop there and is pushed towards panpsychist metaphysics.

§ Let us consider now how far Husserl and James describe non-perceptual consciousness in similar ways. James tends to lump all these together as *thought*, and I shall follow him in this.

James gives two different accounts of thought, which are never very satisfactorily combined.

(1) On the first, thought's being of or about an object not present in experience is its having the potential of leading to it by a train of continuous experiences.

This is sometimes developed in a way with some affinity with Husserl's notion of how an 'empty' intention gets fulfilment in imagination or verification in perception through a felt continuity between the two and a sense of the terminus as fulfilling what was dimly adumbrated in the intention.

However, there is considerable hesitation on James's part as to how far the fact that the encounter with some definite object is the terminus to which an idea has led us as its object requires an intrinsic fit between their characters. Thus sometimes he seems to see it as a quite external causal transaction, sometimes as the filling out by the object, as we encounter it, of a content already implicit in the idea. If the second approach has a real affinity to Husserl's, the first stands in complete contrast to it.

James sometimes seems to suggest that any apparent tension here arises only if we think of experience as chopped up into discrete bits.[69] This is the same misconception as leads to the invocation of a magical leap of empirically inexplicable self-transcendence on the part of thought. In truth, the only leap is that of the felt unbroken flow of experience from the thought to the object to which it leads us and there cannot be an adequate description of either end which does not refer to the other.

But this, one may think, can only be true, if at all, where thought leads very quickly to its object. Surely when there is a long interval of intervening uncon-sciousness between the initial thought and the verifying encounter with the object the original thought is undeniably a thing in its own right, with its own distinct character, a mere 'flat piece of substantive experience like any other, with no self-transcendency about it'.[70] And the question should not be ducked whether the leading of the thought to its object is to be conceived only as a causal relation which can link things whose characters have no special fit with each other, or whether part of what is meant by such a leading is that the character of the object completes something adumbrated in the character of the idea. James seems to oscillate between these two views. (An extremely faint analogy holds here to the contrast between descriptivist and causal accounts of refer-ence, like Kripke's, in recent philosophical literature.)

Some of these tensions are exhibited in the following statement of his view in 'Is Radical Empiricism Solipsistic?' in ERE in reply to Henry Bode who had objected to the lack of real connection on James's view of thought with its object.

> I very much fear—so difficult does mutual understanding seem in these exalted regions—that my able critic has failed to understand that doctrine as it is meant to be understood. I suspect that he performs on all these conjunctive relations (of which the aforesaid 'pointing' is only one) the usual rationalistic act of substitution—he takes them not as they are given in their first intention, as parts constitutive of experience's living flow, but only as they appear in retrospect, each fixed as a determinate object of conception, static, therefore, and contained within itself.
>
> Against this rationalistic tendency to treat experience as chopped up into discontinuous static objects, radical empiricism protests. It insists on taking conjunctions at their 'face-value,' just as they come. Consider, for example such conjunctions as 'and,' 'with,' 'near,' '*plus*,' 'towards.' While we live in such conjunctions our state is one of *transition* in the most literal sense. We are expectant of a 'more' to come, and before the more *has* come, the transition, nevertheless, is directed *towards* it. I fail otherwise to see how, if one kind of more comes, there should be satisfaction and feeling of fulfilment; but disap-pointment if the more comes in another shape. One more will continue, another more will arrest or deflect the direction, in which our experience is moving even now. We can not, it is true, *name* our different living 'ands' or 'withs'

---

69   See ERE, p. 69 et ff; ERE, p. 95 et ff; MT, p. 63 et ff.
70   MT, p. 63.

except by naming the different terms towards which they are moving us, but we *live* their specifications and differences before those terms explicitly arrive. Thus, though the various 'ands' are all bilateral relations, each requiring a term *ad quem* to define it when viewed in retrospect and articulately conceived, yet in its living moment any one of them may be treated as if it 'stuck out' from its term *a quo* and pointed in a special direction, much as a compass-needle (to use Mr. Bode's excellent simile) points at the pole, even though it stirs not from its box.

                                                                ERE, pp. 236–38

There are many difficulties in this account to which we shall return when we consider Bradley's criticisms of it. The present point is simply that there is, indeed, something in common with Husserl in James's account whenever (as happens only sometimes) it insists that the verifying encounter is somehow felt as a fulfilment of what was dimly presaged in the original thought. But that still leaves a radical opposition between them as to what happens in the fulfilling perceptual encounter with an object originally only intended in thought.

§ (2) Let us turn now to James's second account, from a radical empiricist point of view, of the relation between thought and its object. This treats it in very much the same way as perception. Thus it claims that when we think of something, our 'thought stuff' is the very thing itself as it exists currently in our consciousness (though it may exist there precisely as something at a great temporal or spatial distance). Or rather, that is how it is for us at the time; later we will classify it either as the thought of the thing or as the thing itself according as to whether it is its place in the system of physical or of mental causation that interests us.

We saw in section 4 how difficult it is to take this in a strong metaphysical sense but that, if the point is that in our 'life world' the things we think of are as truly 'there for us' as are the things we perceive (and that our thoughts are for us rather the distant things themselves, than representations of them), it is good phenomenology. But it may not be very Husserlian, for it presents a further challenge to that contrast between the hyletic data which present the objects of intentional acts to us and the objects presented on which Husserl laid such stress.

If those who associate James with Husserlian phenomenology only mean that they both attempted descriptions of perception and thought and so forth which try to capture their felt essence, they are right enough. But the actual result of their attempts is more interesting for its contrasts than its affinities.

§ Finally, there is the fact that James, in a way which some have found surprising, affirmed a form of conceptual realism according to which universals, or at least universal concepts, have their own sort of being, apart from particular instances to which they apply, and their own necessary relations to one another. Although he calls them concepts he seems to think of them as having a being independent of our use of them in thought. For example, in SPP he describes himself as

affirming here . . . the platonic doctrine that concepts are singulars, that concept-stuff is inalterable, and that physical realities are constituted by various concept-stuffs of which they 'partake'.

SPP, p. 106

Since Husserl is famous for his concern with essences, this may seem to be an important affinity between them. But it is hardly greater than that between any philosophers with Platonic sympathies. At most one might say that both thought universals were somehow constituted in consciousness but once constituted display relations over which we have no choice. But the details of the way in which they worked this out are not very close.[71]

Both James and his commentators bring this Platonism under the same head as the account of thought we have just been considering. This is somewhat confusing, for they seem to be concerned with different questions.

(1) What is the status of concepts either qua abstract or general ideas or qua objective universals?

(2) How is thinking about a thing (thus having a concept of it) related to the thing and how does the relation between a thing and the thought of it compare with the relation between a thing and the perception of it?

His answers to both questions do, however, have something in common. Each represents a qualification of the typically pragmatist idea that the sole point of concepts is to lead to success in the world of perception. His answer to the first insists that there is a world of universal abstractions of interest on its own account and not just as a guide to the realm of particulars. His answer to the second establishes that the world composed of things thought of has its own independent interest, and is not just a guide to perceptual encounters.

James salves his pragmatic conscience by insisting that concern with merely thought-of objects and universal concepts is a luxury when we rest from our coping with the more threatening world of percepts. Thus the compulsory task of thought, whether of particulars or universals, is to mediate prosperous dealings with the perceptual world, but it also provides us with a realm to enjoy and enquire into which is an end in itself.

§7. *The Miller-Bode Notebook*

James's radical empiricism was subjected to some quite penetrating criticism shortly after the main set of articles expounding it were published. James was deeply perplexed as to how his theories could best be developed to meet them. These puzzlings were set down (in the course of 1905–8) in a set of private notes which he did not publish but which have long been known as 'The Miller-Bode objections'. R. B. Perry quoted largely from them in Perry, and other scholars have made use of them. (They were deposited after James's death in the

---

71   For James's view see particularly the last chapter of PP.

Houghton Library at Harvard.) They have recently been published in the new Harvard edition of James in the volume called *Manuscript Essays and Notes*. The published essays expounding radical empiricism which we have been considering are just early stages in an adventure of ideas continued through this notebook into PU and SPP.

Thus most of the ideas developed there are to be found in these works. However the last few pages (in particular pp. 123 to 127 of the Harvard edition) provide perhaps the best statement he ever made of his ultimate metaphysics while some of the more puzzled sections show how troubled he was about the adequacy of views advocated with such apparent confidence in published articles.

The criticisms which they concern stem from Henry Bode and from James's friend and one time student, Dickinson Miller, the former in published articles,[72] the latter in private communications.[73]

Dickinson Miller's objections turn on the problem radical empiricism has in explaining how two minds can confront the same thing and Bode raises the same problem as part of a more general critique of the radical empiricist account of thought's aboutness. Thus he claims that it cannot explain how two minds can 'point' to, that is have thoughts about, the very same object. For this requires that our mental activity can somehow point to what can never be a part of our conscious state. If I can only point to what can become an element in my own conscious state, then you and I cannot think about the same thing, since it is impossible for the same thing ever to be an element literally present in two different minds either in turn or at once.

We have seen how James attempted to cope with this problem in the published ERE corpus by claiming that, in principle, the same thing can be a part of the mental state of two different persons. In a sense this is so whenever we perceive the same object, for that object is then partially present as an actual ingredient in the mental state of each of us. If, in fact, we never incorporate precisely the same elements of its being, because we perceive it from a different point of view, we can at least be on the way to doing so. For it is the ideal terminus of a process which is under way.

However this terminus must be a logical possibility if it is something we can even thus move towards, and James continues to worry over the grave difficulties there are in seeing how it can be so. For the object, as it is experienced in my consciousness, will have accompaniments which are different from those

---

72   Bode, 1, 2, and 3.
73   Dickinson Miller (1868–1963) was a philosopher who wrote little but well. His 'Is there not a Clear Solution of the Knowledge Problem' (1937) has a good deal of relevance to James, and he also wrote various critical pieces on James. His most famous piece is 'Freewill as Involving Determination and Inconceivable Without It' written pseudonymously as R. E. Hobart, *Mind* 43, 1934. Most of his work has been published in Miller, 1975. There is a good deal of correspondence between him and James in *Letters*.

which it has in yours, while in yours it will lack some of the accompaniments which it has in mine. The trouble is that an experience is what it is felt to be, and the accompaniments it is experienced as having seem to be as much a part of what it is as is any other feature of it. So how can it exist as the very same item in two different consciousnesses where its accompaniments are different? Yet, unless it can do so, the radical empiricist view of intending seems unworkable and we are pushed back on the mysterious self-transcendency of mind which radical empiricism aimed to make more intelligible. In the notebook James put the problem thus:

> Then can we point to *the same*? . . . [The difficulty is] that in a philosophy of pure experience, the terminus must be represented as a possible *terminating experience*. As such it must (whatever it may be actually before we get there) potentially and finally be an experience conterminous to us both. . . . [But h]ow *can our two fields be units, if they contain this common part*? . . . Bode would say that the apperceiving 'part' of our respective fields, cannot both of them include the common terminus entitatively, but they (or the selves to which they belong) can *know* it by self transcendency. On my theory, self transcendency can only mean *eventual* incorporation by confluence. Now assume two experiences to be originally distinct:—*can* they grow confluent, yet still retain their entitative identity? If so, "composition" is possible in minds. If not, then what grows confluent is not the original terminus, but two substitutes for it, one which my mind runs into and another which your mind runs into.
>
> MEN, pp. 65–66

In the course of his discussion James reflects at length on the treatment of these matters by two other philosophers he had been reading recently. One was Bergson, the other C. A. Strong (later a leading, if not typical, member of the 'critical realist' movement). The whole series of notes could well have been written as an inconclusive Platonic dialogue between spokesmen for these and other alternative viewpoints on these problems which suggest themselves to James as he agonizes over them.

Strong held a panpsychist view of nature, and contended that the brain, or rather the cerebral cortex, as ordinarily conceived is the phenomenal appearance of what in itself is the series of our own experiences, while there is a psychical in itself of every other physical item too.[74] He was well aware,

---

74 See Strong, *Why the Mind.* Perhaps I might note that I first read Strong's *Why the Mind has a Body*, which is not easy to obtain, in a late stage of writing this present work, though I knew something of Strong's association with Santayana. I mention this because there is a remarkable similarity in point of view, and even in turns of expression, between that book and my *The Vindication of Absolute Idealism.* The strong affinity doubtless stems from the strong influence of William James on both books and the sheer internal logic of the line of thought we both pursue. There are, indeed, differences. Strong does not develop the position on relations which I do, and he has no doctrine of the Absolute. But the arguments for first postulating

however, that the great problem for any conception of the world as composed of experiences is how such experiences as are not felt in the unity of one consciousness can have any real relations to each other at all. To resolve it he postulated a quasi-space in which they relate to each other in a manner of which the spatial relations between objects is a phenomenal rendering. James saw much to attract him in this doctrine (which has affinities with his own appeal to a common space containing all physically real percepts), but he was also fascinated by the view of Bergson that the primal condition of all things psychic is one in which they are all felt together (whatever mind they belong to, or, once they have occurred, to whatever time) and that the brain functions as a selector which blocks off, for a finite consciousness, that with which it does not need to feel itself united for its present practical purposes. The great advantage of this view is that it frees us from the need to find a principle of togetherness between mental items, suggesting rather that what is needed is an explanation of how they can ever be separate, something supposed to be simpler.[75]

Both these theories, like James's own various positions, were seen by James as important, above all, because they showed possible ways of escaping the ever-present threat that one must in the end postulate a Roycean or Bradleyan Absolute if there is to be any togetherness of things psychical or experiential at all (which for radical empiricism means the togetherness of anything with anything). There are quite a few references to the force of the Bradleyan position here.

The problem for a pluralistic system is how there can be any kind of togetherness of things. Relationship within a totality of experience is reasonably straightforward, but relations between distinct total fields of consciousness or experience, or between elements belonging to different fields, is deeply puzzling. The absolutist solves it by saying that the different fields belong to one total cosmic field, the one absolute consciousness. But that is what James is trying to avoid.

On p. 116 he puts the problem to himself thus

Whence the *co* if we start pluralistically?
   "   " *ex* " "   " mon   "   ?

By the 'co' he means the occurring of experiences together (coconsciously),

---

'things in themselves' and then interpreting these panpsychistically are remarkably like the line of thought I pursued without having read Strong. Naturally I now think that Strong has been undeservedly neglected and sympathize with him in this. For James's high opinion of him see *Letters*, pp. 198, 229–30, 301, 310.

75   Thus on pp. 92–93 he plays with the idea of Bergson that really the fundamental fact is the togetherness of everything with everything and that the function of the brain is to filter out for one bit of agency in the world those bits of the all-together world which alone should be dealt with at this present pass.

by the 'ex' he means the relation between experiences which do not belong to one field.

Gradually he moves towards the outline of a solution with the following features.

(1) The account of physical things which identifies the thing perceived with the percept is taken as an account of the common-sense way of looking at things. This will do for many ordinary purposes but it becomes deeply problematic if we press the question how the same perceived thing can belong to the mental states of two different persons.

> Similarly in the pen-problem, or rather still worse. If mental fields are units, as my Psychology pretends, pen co my mind can't be the same as pen-co-your-mind. And if they be not units, what makes the flux co in either case? and then what stops it from extending throughout?
>
> MEN, p. 101

(2) Although James is troubled as to how the same percept (and thus perceived thing) could occur as an element in the consciousness of two perceivers, he is less concerned as to what its status is when not perceived at all. He seems fairly content with thinking of it as a pure possibility, and suggests that it may be unnecessary to look for any genuinely categorical basis for this.[76]

(3) However, the fact that we are in a common world does require that we exist in some kind of common medium, and James moves towards the conviction that that consists in a larger world of experience which, à la Strong, somehow underlies the ordinary things of the phenomenal world.

(4) This common medium might be thought of as a quasi-space of a kind that Strong suggested. But upon the whole James prefers to think that experiences may relate to each other by being, of their own nature, rather than through mere juxtaposition in an external medium, 'next' to each other, allowing other experiences to be less directly linked by a chain of intermediaries running from next to next.

(5) There is a great deal of discussion of what this relation of nextness can really be. Thus he oscillates between an introspectionist or phenomenological sense that nextness implies unity in a felt whole, so that it cannot hold between what is felt as distinct, and a 'pragmatic' view for which things are next if they work as one, so that the nextness can be retrospective.[77] He is even still tempted by the bizarre view that the togetherness of even simultaneous experiences is retrospectively bestowed on them by a subsequent act of synthesis. On this view it is only by being recollected that two experiences come retrospectively together in a common field of consciousness. We have seen how this view was adumbrated in 'How Two Minds can Know One Thing' as a solution to the problem.

---

76   See MEN, p. 97.
77   See MEN, p. 113.

I suggested in section 4 that this view is quite unsatisfactory in virtue of that inherent unity of each moment of consciousness of which James himself makes so much elsewhere. Aware of this he gradually works round to the view that nextness must be conceived as a kind of merging of experiences into each other so that the distinctness between neighbours is not a sharp one.

(6) James is concerned, at any rate, that nextness should not be conceived as something non-empirical. Rather is it what we directly feel when one experience shifts into another in the stream of our own experience. However, he shows himself very sensitive to the fact that it is much easier to see how this can link the elements of successive distinct total moments of experience than those of distinct simultaneous ones.[78]

> The successive is supposed to be entitatively so distinct from what preceded as to have no consubstantiality with it. Hence, if one successor can come with a certain relation to an original datum, there seems no reason why any number mightn't come, so long as the terms and relations themselves were not mutually incompatible.
>
> When, however, the related terms are simultaneous, there are relations that seem to lock them together so solidly that the term pen, e.g., can't relate itself to *you* without dragging *me* (to which it is also related) along with it, so that *you* and *I* also grow co-conscious. In the case of successive appropriation of the pen by you and me, the consciousness of it by each of us is not immediate, but representative. We and it are entitatively 3 things. Can this be the case where the pen is in its immediacy a constituent of both our knowledges? Keeping of course a purely abstract case in view.
>
> The *you* and the *me* here have to be taken as ready-made apperceiving masses.
>
> MEN, p. 109

James is trying to conceive the units of experience as pervading each other in a way which allows A to pervade each of B and C without B and C pervading each other. He thinks this quite readily intelligible where A comes before B and C, much less so when they are all three simultaneous.

(7) However, in the end he thinks it may only be intellectualism which prevents our granting its possibility in the simultaneous case.

> Is the whole trouble over the fact that connexions do obtain, that the logically distinct nevertheless does diffuse, that you can't pen reality in, that its nature is to spread, and *affect*, and that this applies to relations as well as to terms, so that it is impossible to call them absolutely external to each other? The only difficulty in admitting this kind of constitution of reality is our inveterate intellectualism, and its idolatry of the concept.

---

78   He might have moved to Whitehead's position that contemporary totalities of experience are not related to each other, but only linked up by successor experiences which draw on them both. This may sound similar to the view I have dubbed bizarre, but the difference is that it concerns the relations between simultaneous totalities of experience, not those between their elements.

> If it were admitted, how would the 'compounding' of the psychical occur?
> That which is *ex* in one relation would become *con* in another und zwar by an event outside of itself, or at any rate by things outside apperceiving it, which apperception doesn't 'count' for it or for its other relations. In discussing this, one must absolutely abandon, seriously *suppress* the logic-chopping procedure indulged in by Royce and others.
>
> MEN, p. 121

The problem was to combine the view that the world consists of a multiplicity of distinct pulses of experience each with its own individual sense of its own being with an adequate sense of the togetherness of things. For

> [t]he most general peculiarity of fact is that it consists of things in environments.
>
> MEN, p. 122

The continuity of one pulse of experience with the next in a stream of consciousness may be conceptually problematic, but at least we are confident enough that somehow we experience it. The relation between simultaneous pulses of experience is more problematic, but still we do somehow experience ourselves as in relation to other minds and other things, even if we can only express how we do so metaphorically.

> I find that I involuntarily think of *co*-ness under the physical image of a sort of lateral suffusion from one thing into another, like a gas, or warmth, or light. The *places* involved are fixed, but what fills one place radiates and suffuses into the other by lateral movement, "endosmosis".
>
> This seems to ally itself with the fact that all consciousness is *positional*, is a "point of view," measures things for a *here*, etc. Will the notion that co-ness-with-me is apperception *by* me work along these lines? And can one limit the suffusion to the "between"—experience that makes continuity or rather that continuity *is*.
>
> MEN, pp. 91–92

Much of this is covered in the published papers which we have already considered, and most of the remainder occurs in work to which we shall be turning. But in the course of these notes we find a definite turning towards a panpsychic doctrine, remarkably like Whitehead's and Hartshorne's, and a clear tendency to take the direct realism distinctive of the earlier statements of radical empiricism as a phenomenological account of how things are for us which needs to be rooted in a metaphysical account of how things are for themselves.

4

Towards a Mystical Pluralism

§1. *Critique of Absolute Idealism*

(a) What James Meant by Absolute Idealism

Much of James's positive metaphysical thinking was devoted to refuting what he thought the sillier mistakes of absolute idealism, to learning something from its worthier arguments, and to finding an alternative to it.

The absolute idealist for whom he had the most respect was his colleague Josiah Royce, whose career he largely launched. When Royce, then teaching English literature at Berkeley, California, wrote to him in despair at his isolation from other philosophers James managed to have him brought over to Harvard, first as his own replacement when he was on leave in 1882 (when Royce was twenty-seven and James forty), and then as a permanent colleague.[1]

His opinions on the value of Royce's thought varied over the years. Upon the whole he thought him a major thinker whose version and defence of absolute idealism was the best there had been.

However, James also took a considerable interest in the philosophy of Bradley, though he approaches it less sympathetically than he does Royce's, and it is these two together who are the main targets of his critique of absolute idealism. As for Hegel, James had little to say in his favour, though his lively chapter on him in *A Pluralistic Universe* shows some appreciation.[2] James

---

1   The best account of the personal and philosophical relations between James and Royce is to be found in Parts 2 and 3 of Kuklick. See also Perry, I, chapters XLIX–LI.
2   James's view of Hegel is discussed interestingly in Cook.

also took some notice of the absolute idealisms of such other figures as Lotze and T. H. Green. We should bear in mind too that his father had advanced a philosophy which can be seen as a version of it. This doubtless added to the emotional need he had of coming to terms with it.

For James the core of absolute idealism was the thesis that ultimately there is just one great fact, a certain total state of static consciousness, of which every ordinary thing is a component which we (or the Absolute through us) misconceive as a thing in its own right with a being to some extent independent of its precise position therein. (James does not seem too aware of the difference between this and another version of absolute idealism for which there is one cosmic spirit to which everything else is present as something it thinks and wills. On this version, finite things are not so much parts of the cosmic spirit as presentations to it.)

One implication of this is that the future is not genuinely open. For Royce and Bradley the Absolute comprises or cognizes all moments of time at once and the unrolling of time as we experience it is something of an illusion. Thus there is no ultimate distinction for the Absolute, and hence none in literal truth, in the contrast between past, present, and future. It must be said that James often seems to confuse this with the simpler (though less satisfactory) view that the Absolute has somehow settled every detail of the future in advance and then watches it unroll. However, in terms of James's particular concerns, the difference between these might not have seemed too important. Both, he would doubtless say, have the objectionable implication that there has never been any real alternative to what has happened or will happen, whether because the Absolute includes all times in an eternal *Nunc Stans* or because it has always already settled every detail of what is to come.

There are some important differences between the absolute idealisms of Royce and of Bradley. In particular, while for Royce the Absolute is essentially a personal God who lives out his life through us, for Bradley it is something much more impersonal. Both views, however, have, from James's perspective, much the same unwelcome implications: the denial of an open future and such a mutual implication of every detail of the universe with every other that there can be no ultimately valid distinction between what is good and what should be recognized as irredeemably evil.

Before considering James's response to absolute idealism further we may note that there was one heterodox version thereof for which he showed considerable enthusiasm. While he thought the work of Gustav Fechner on psychophysics had led psychologists on a wild-goose chase, he was strongly attracted to his metaphysical speculations.[3]

Fechner was like other absolute idealists in thinking that the essence of the world was spiritual and that ultimately there was one total world spirit in which

---

3   See PU, chapter IV, and introduction to Fechner, *Little Book*. Bradley also took some interest in Fechner's panpsychist view of nature. See AR, chapter XXII.

all things were contained. But whereas most such idealists thought that there were just two levels of unified consciousness, that of our finite minds and that of the cosmic mind, for Fechner consciousness was unified at many different levels and was pervasive throughout the physical universe. Thus for him every genuine unit in nature was sentient. At the bottom level were the ultimate physical units of nature, each having their own unitary sentience, at the next level these units (or some of them, for presumably some missed out a level, coming in again only higher up the scale) combined to form higher-level units of sentience, at the next level these were again combined to form further such units, and so on till the one unitary consciousness of the universe was reached. Thus there was an earth consciousness, uniting all finite consciousness on the earth, which united with the individual consciousness of every other planet (and of the sun?) to form the consciousness of the solar system, and so forth on ever larger scales, until ultimately all were united in God, conceived as the consciousness of nature as a whole. James praises this system for its 'thickness' in contrast to the 'thinness' of most absolute idealist philosophy.[4] By this he meant that it did not reduce the richness of reality to the level of the threadbare stock concepts of philosophy. (Actually in a note to his discussion of Fechner, James partially excludes Bradley from the charge of thinness levelled at other absolute idealists[5] though at other times it is rather Royce who is made the partial exception to this generalization.[6]) Bradley, we might note, acknowledged some justice in the charge that his philosophy was 'thin'.[7]

In making this charge against most absolute idealists, James, it seems to me, confuses views for which the universe itself is a thin affair, lacking the richness it presents to a more empirical investigation, with views which only purport to say something about its more general characteristics without pretending to do justice to its actual richness. After all his own radical-empiricist and other metaphysical doctrines are developed at a high level of abstraction.

(b) James's Shift of Attitude towards Absolute Idealism

It would be close to the truth to say that James moved from a position in which he thought absolute idealism both logically compulsive and logically impossible to a position in which he thought it logically optional but empirically false. Accompanying these changes was a constant belief that it was morally objec-

---

4   He jokingly derived these concepts from a philosophical crank of his past acquaintance of whose philosophical views he could only remember one which 'had she been born in the Ionian Archipelago some three thousand years ago . . . would probably have made her name sure of a place in every university curriculum and examination paper. The world, she said, is composed of only two elements, the Thick, namely, and the Thin.' PU, p. 136.
5   See PU, p. 338, note 4.
6   See PU, p. 265.
7   See Perry, II, pp. 492–93.

tionable. This being so, he thought that it should be rejected on the basis of our will or right to believe what we find makes the best moral sense of things wherever purely rational considerations leave equally acceptable alternatives.

It was around the time of PP that James appears to have thought it (i) logically compulsive and (ii) logically impossible, and that it therefore posed an unsolved problem.[8]

(i) Its *logically compulsive character* arose from considerations which Royce had articulated with most success. We considered Royce's argument in chapter one, pointing out that the notion of intending central to James's pragmatism arose from his wish to meet it but let us recall the argument briefly here. In order to think truly or falsely I must apply a predicate, the sense of which is present to my mind directly, to some reality which my thought is about. However, its being about that reality must not consist simply in the fact that it answers to the predicates I apply to it. For unless what my thought is about is identified in some other way I cannot refer to something to which my predicates apply falsely and thus can have no false beliefs about anything. But the suggestion that I have no false beliefs is absurd. It must itself be false since, if it is not, then my usual belief that there are such is so.

Now this problem does not apply when I think about things which are actual components in my present state of consciousness. Here I can notice the properties that component actually has, and although I cannot seriously judge falsely of its given character I can entertain false ideas about it, ascribing to it properties contrary to those it manifestly has. In the light of this I can make sense of the idea of false thinking by postulating a universal consciousness in which both my thinking and my objects figure. For I can interpret my false thinking as the absolute consciousness's own similar hypothesising, within a fragment of itself, about another element of its total conscious state. The essential deficiency of finite thought is its illusory sense of separateness. This cuts it off from that appreciation of its own falsehood which, for the Absolute, is compresent with it.

The essential point is that the absolute spirit which contains both me and my thoughts chooses the objects to which my thought shall refer other than by way of the predicates present to my consciousness and that only so can I refer to what does not answer to them.

As remarked above, there are various objections which might be raised to the argument so far. For one thing Royce plays down the possibility that falsehood may turn on the total non-existence of the object I specify—or for that matter on the existence of what a negative existential belief specifies. However, if taken as a problem as to how there can be false beliefs about particular things, and supported by considerations according to which there must be genuinely *de re* beliefs not reducible to existential form, it can perhaps be revised in such a way as to give it some force.

---

8   On this see especially Perry, I, pp. 703–5.

At any rate, as we saw, James thought it very strong and struggled over it for many years, seeking a characterisation of the relation between a thought and its object which made it a genuinely experienced one, while still leaving a gap between them which allows for falsehood. Thence the view that thinking connects with its object by leading to it through intermediate experiences which terminate in a verifying or falsifying experience thereof. Thereby he eventually escaped from the fear that absolute idealism was logically compulsive.

(ii) The main reason for thinking it *logically impossible* was that it required that states of consciousness could compound in a way which James originally believed inconceivable.[9] According to absolute idealism, at least of the type James took seriously as a challenge, your present state of consciousness and mine, together with those of all other sentient beings, are elements in the one absolute consciousness, just as are the pain which I now feel in my back and my present thoughts about William James elements in my present state of mind. But, thought James at the time of PP, this is to think of consciousness in misleadingly physical terms. For a state of consciousness is not made up of its constituents as a house from bricks. The sensations, thoughts, and feelings which it includes are not separable bits which could belong in other states of consciousness. When a sensation, feeling, or thought in one state of consciousness is said to be the same as that in another, all that can really be true is that they have a certain affinity or that they are of the same object without themselves being identical. They are certainly not the same particular and, I think James also wants to hold, even their characters are never identical. Thus a state of consciousness may have distinguishable aspects but it does not have parts in any proper sense.

Yet the notion that the absolute consciousness literally contains each of our states of consciousness implies that it has parts in just that sense in which consciousness cannot. For it is supposed that the very same particular conscious state which I feel as my whole present state is included in the Absolute as a part. True, the absolute idealist may call it an aspect or an appearance of that whole rather than a part thereof. Nonetheless, the feeling that a total finite conscious state has of its own being is incompatible with its being merely an aspect of the Absolute's own feeling of itself.

James's point was that if twenty-six people each think of a letter of the alphabet, their thoughts cannot be put together to constitute a thought of the alphabet as a whole.[10] The thought of the alphabet as a whole requires a fresh state of consciousness with a sufficiently rich specious present to comprehend the whole series at once. Furthermore a state of mind as a whole cannot be otherwise than it feels *itself* to be and its elements can only be what it feels *them*

---

9   James describes his old position and his present abandonment of it in PU, chapter
     V. For statements of the earlier arguments see PP, I, pp. 158–62, also Perry, I, pp.
     808–9.

10   See PP, I, p. 160.

to be. My state of mind feels itself as having certain contents and certain limitations, such perhaps as not knowing the way to somewhere I am trying to reach, and these must really pertain to it. It cannot thus be a constituent in a state of mind which knows all things. For such a constituent would be known by that state of mind as an element in its total knowledge of all things, and could not have its own rival knowledge of its own being. If it did, it would be another state of mind with a content echoing that component in the larger state of consciousness, but not itself literally included therein.

James sometimes put his objection to the absolute idealist's conception of how we stand to the Absolute in a rather different way, suggesting that creatures which are only the objects for an absolute mind could be for themselves no less and no more than what they are for that universal knower and could not have even a sense of doing things on their own account.[11] This seems a pretty effective objection to the view that we are simply the Absolute's intentional objects with no more substantial an existence than Mr Pickwick. However, on the face of it, the view of Royce and Bradley on how we stand to the Absolute is different. For them we are not merely elements in a story the Absolute tells itself but genuinely existent components of its consciousness, related to it rather as our thoughts, images, and feelings are to us than as our postulated or feigned objects are.

How different these two views of our relation to the Absolute are depends on how one thinks consciousness stands to what it presents or feigns. If one thinks of Mr Pickwick as a kind of aspect of Dickens's own state of mind as he wrote, then our relation to the Absolute as Royce and Bradley conceive it may be much the same. Conceived thus as a kind of process in Dickens's mind, Mr Pickwick was perhaps a psychical existent with an element of independence, and perhaps the same is true of us within the Absolute to an even greater extent. Still, James could plausibly argue that an element within a larger state of mind cannot have a sense of itself as a separate being. This seems initially persuasive, but we shall see that even James came to doubt the point.

The heart of James's logical objection to absolute idealism was much the same as he had had to the mind dust theory, criticised in chapter VI of PP, for which all consciousness arises from the combination of particles of sentience derived from a kind of cosmic mental dust so that our states of mind are combinations of little bits of sentience present in each of our brain cells, and these of little bits of sentience in the atoms. Both, he thought, postulate a meaningless compounding together of individual states of consciousness to form a single larger one, depending on a misleadingly physical conception of the way in which a state of consciousness can have parts. (This he saw as especially odd on the part of absolute idealists who insist strongly on the misleadingness of physical conceptions for a proper understanding of reality.)

In PU James still complained that absolute idealists have never adequately

---

11   See PU, pp. 193–94; also Perry, I, p. 705.

faced up to these difficulties. For this Fechner may be forgiven, for they had apparently never occurred to him, but Royce could plead no such excuse.[12] Unfortunately James ignores Bradley's own heroic efforts to take on just such objections in chapter XIX ('The This and the Mine') of *Appearance and Reality*. This is a pity because the holistic conception of consciousness which gives rise to them is very much one which Bradley shares with James.

In any case, by the time of PU James himself had come to think this argument against the Absolute unsatisfactory. Indeed he decided that it turned on that 'intellectualist logic' reliance on which was one of the main faults of absolute idealism itself.[13] For its underlying principle is that the same thing cannot answer to different predicates, and this is derived from the implicit assumption that the contexts in which a real thing can exist are limited by the definition of the concept by which we refer to it. Thus the concept of a feeling existing merely as my personal state seems to clash with the concept of a feeling existing as part of a larger unity. But, argues James in PU, the fact that these two concepts are different does not show that the same thing cannot answer to both. So James decided that it was a mistake to rule out the Absolute on the basis of that old argument. (I have discussed James's objections to this aspect of absolute idealism in more detail in Sprigge, *Vindication*, chapter VI, section 2.)

True, he still thought it difficult to understand 'how a collective experience of any grade whatever can be treated as logically identical with a lot of distributive experiences'.[14] This, indeed, was but one aspect of a more general problem as to how there could be any sort of continuity or togetherness between things at all.

> What has so troubled my logical conscience is not so much the absolute by itself as the whole class of suppositions of which it is the supreme example, collective experiences namely, claiming identity with their constituent parts, yet experiencing things quite differently from these latter. If *any* such collective experience can be, then of course, so far as the mere logic of the case goes, the absolute may be. . . . I don't logically see how a collective experience of any grade whatever can be treated as logically identical with a lot of distributive experiences. . . . The absolute happens to be the only collective experience concerning which Oxford idealists have urged the identity [but] . . . Fechner's earth-soul, or any stage of being below or above that, would have served my purpose just as well: the same logical objection applies to these collective experiences as to the absolute. . . .
>
> So now for the directer question. Shall we say that every complex mental

---

12 See PU, p. 196.
13 'Intellectualist' was used both by James and his ally F. C. S. Schiller as a derogatory term for philosophical opponents. However, while for James 'intellectualism' referred to the tendency to confuse reality itself with our concepts of it, for Schiller it referred primarily to the tendency to think of cognitive, rather than volitional, activity as basic. See his essay in Sturt, p. 65.
14 PU, p. 204.

fact is a separate psychic entity succeeding upon a lot of other psychic entities which are erroneously called its parts, and superseding them in function, but not literally being composed of them? This was the course I took in my psychology; and if followed in theology, we should have to deny the absolute as usually conceived, and replace it by the 'God' of theism. We should also have to deny Fechner's 'earth-soul' and all other superhuman collections of experience of every grade, so far at least as these are held to be compounded of our simpler souls in the way Fechner believed in; and we should have to make all these denials in the name of the incorruptible logic of self-identity, teaching us that to call a thing and its other the same is to commit the crime of self-contradiction.

But if we realize the whole philosophic situation thus produced, we see that it is almost intolerable. Loyal to the logical kind of rationality, it is disloyal to every other kind. It makes the universe discontinuous. These fields of experience that replace each other so punctually, each knowing the same matter, but in ever-widening contexts, from simplest feeling up to absolute knowledge, *can* they have no *being* in common when their cognitive function is so manifestly common? The regular succession of them is on such terms an unintelligible miracle. If you reply that their common *object* is of itself enough to make the many witnesses continuous, the same implacable logic follows you—how *can* one and the same object appear so variously? Its diverse appearances break up into plurality; and our world of objects then falls into discontinuous pieces quite as much as did our world of subjects. The resultant irrationality is really intolerable.

PU, pp. 203–6

We shall be looking into this turn in James's thought more fully shortly. For now it is sufficient to say that James's solution was that the successive states of consciousness through which we live are, on the one hand, each distinct from each other and, on the other hand, inter-penetrate and belong together. Thus there is a togetherness of things which allows each mental state to belong to a larger whole than that which is fully given in its own feeling.

James spoke of himself as thus having come to believe in the possibility of a compounding of consciousness. There is, however, a certain ambiguity in what he says. Did he now think that there could be a single state of consciousness made out of lesser ones, or only that states of consciousness could be continuous with each other in a way which would justify us in saying that they form larger wholes together, without these larger wholes having any unitary feeling of themselves as wholes? His own positive conception of the unity of the world seems an exploration of the second conception rather than the first but it is not too clear whether he has abandoned his basic logical objections to the first or only concluded that they do not rule out the kind of compounding of consciousness postulated in the second.

Certainly he still saw difficulties in the idea of a collective experience which is 'logically identical with a lot of distributive experiences'.[15] But he also felt

---

15   PU, p. 204.

that if such an idea is ruled out as absurd, we risk making all continuity in the universe seem impossible. So there must be some way in which distinct experiences can combine together to make larger units.

But does this have to be after the fashion in which absolute idealists suppose finite experiences combine to form the Absolute? Although he does not always make the point very clear, it seems that the compounding of which he made primary use in his own late metaphysical construction was of a rather different type, in which experiences combine into larger units by relations of continuity between them internal to the character of each term but not necessarily implying that they are parts of any inclusive feeling of them in unity. However, it seems that he now regarded even this as logically possible and perhaps even as sometimes a fact.

With the logical reasons both for and against absolute idealism removed, James's attitude turned more and more on its moral implications, which he found repellent. For the absolute idealist thinks that his Absolute is good, promoting his concept of it as a more sophisticated version of the traditional conception of God, and therefore as an appropriate object of religious adoration. (This, we may note, is more true of Royce than Bradley.) But it includes all evil, and has (for Royce, at least) in a manner willed it. Thus absolute idealism forces us to think that all partial evil is greater good misunderstood. And to think thus, in James's opinion (as in Santayana's) is morally corrupting.

Nor is this the only moral blemish in absolute idealism. It is also quite as destructive as materialism of the belief in free will or an element of personal spontaneity within us.

(c) The Critique of 'Intellectualist Logic'

§ So in his last few years James decided that his old argument against absolute idealism, based on the impossibility of a compounding of consciousness, rested on intellectualist logic just as did many of the unconvincing arguments of its exponents. And one of James's main aims now became the unveiling of the pretensions of intellectualist logic and exhibition (to say 'demonstration' would be too intellectualistic) of its limitations as a way of reaching truth. This done, absolute idealism emerges as a possible, but far from proven, hypothesis. Its claims must, therefore, be assessed empirically rather than argued over intellectualistically. Or if empirical evidence is insufficient we may quite properly use our will, or right, to believe, to determine its acceptability according to the satisfaction it gives to our passional or moral nature.

§ Intellectualist logic, James explains, is reasoning which rests upon confusing things with our concepts of them. Typically it treats what holds of the concept by which we identify something in our thought as holding of the thing itself. It may also exploit, or fall victim to, other ways in which conceptual thinking inevitably distorts our sense of reality. Such distortion must be corrected by directing our attention freshly at perceptual reality and grasping features thereof which lie beyond successful capture in concepts.

§ The central mistake of intellectualist logic, he sometimes says, is to hold that only that can be true of a reality which is implied by its name or concept.

The treating of a name as excluding from the fact named what the name's definition fails positively to include is what I call 'vicious intellectualism'.

PU, p. 60

Thus the real intellectualist will think that a rider cannot dismount and walk since being a rider implies being on horseback. He will reason as though there are two different things, the rider and the pedestrian, and will think it a puzzle how they are related.

According to James, then, it is this confusion, between our verbal labels (or those abstract features of things in virtue of which they apply) with the things they stand for, which breeds most of the problems the Absolute is called on to solve, such, for example, as to how a thing, or the universe itself, can be truly one thing and yet have many properties or relations. The truth of the matter, argues James, is that while abstract features are indeed closed off from each other and are no more than is implied in the meanings of the words which stand for them, this is not true of concrete things.

To construe any one of their abstract names as *making their total nature impossible* is a misuse of the function of naming. The real way of rescue from the abstract consequences of one name is not to fly to an opposite name, equally abstract, but rather to correct the first name by qualifying adjectives that restore some concreteness to the case.

PU, p. 59

§ James's discussion of this point would have been clearer if he had distinguished more emphatically between the question how something can answer to different predicates at different times and the question how it can do so at the same time. Many philosophers have answered the first question by substituting for the notion of identical things which endure through time that of a series of distinct temporal phases thereof, thus providing distinct subjects for the different predicates. That was indeed how James himself regarded the self in PP and the whole drift of his radical empiricism is to extend it to all continuants, since its fundamental units are momentary pulses of experience. And even if one sticks with the category of enduring things, the more serious question raised by the absolute idealist is how something can answer to different predicates at the same time, while James's solutions too often seem only directed to showing that they can do so at different times. For example, he says that for pluralism things can at one time have their relations to certain other things riding high, and at other times their relations to other things. Thus everything may be related to everything else, directly or indirectly, and more or less distantly, but it is not required that all these relations be realized at once. A thing

is thus at all times in many possible connexions which are not necessarily actualized at the moment.

PU, p. 324

Such reference to the varying prominence of a thing's relations at different times, distracts attention from the question how a momentary thing, or an enduring thing at any one moment, can answer to different predicates. And it is in relation to this question that James primarily needs to make his criticism of 'intellectualism', that it exploits perplexities which arise from a confusion between things and concepts, stick.

§ James sometimes suggests that Royce's great argument about intending rests on this basis. For Royce seems to think that if a cat sees a king then the king cannot exist except insofar as seen by the cat, it being of his essence to be seen by it.[16] Here again, James rather confuses the question how a thing can change its relations to other things with the more fundamental question how the thing, with its own separate character at any one moment, stands to the thing as an element in a relational situation. (However, elsewhere he makes the more relevant point that it is only the intellectualist's confusion between concepts and things which raises a problem as to how the same thing can be seen by different people at once.[17])

It cannot be denied that in *The World and the Individual*, especially in the crucial third chapter, Royce uses arguments which seem thoroughly sophistical in very much the way James describes. But, for all Royce's intensive studies of modern logic in the interval between them, the level of argument there is far below that of *The Religious Aspect of Philosophy*, whose great argument about intending is much more profound and would, indeed, never have been so stimulating for James if it had not been.

§ It is Bradley, however, rather than Royce, who is mainly represented as the victim of the confusion between things and concepts. It leads him to raise sophistical problems about the nature of the simplest predication. How can one say that a man is good? For surely the man is not just his goodness.

> Mr Bradley is the pattern champion of this philosophy *in extremis*, as we might call it. . . . His reasoning exemplifies every where what I call the vice of intellectualism, for abstract terms are used by him as positively excluding all that their definition fails to include. Some Greek sophists could deny that we can say that man is good, for man, they said, means only man, and good means only good, and the word *is* can't be construed to identify such disparate meanings. Mr Bradley revels in the same type of argument.
>
> PU, pp. 68–69

The whole puzzle, according to James, arises simply from failing to see that 'good' applies to the man in virtue of just one feature of his total concrete reality.

§ The same confusion (according to James) underlies Bradley's puzzlement about relations. Thus he is perplexed as to how these three things can somehow be the same thing (the example is mine): this green saucer, this saucer on the

---

16   The example of the cat and the king is used by Royce in *World*, I, p. 117.
17   See SPP, p. 89.

table, this saucer below the cup. James replies that the concept we form of this green saucer, if we concentrate just on it, is indeed different from the concept of the saucer as on the table, and different again from the concept of the saucer as below the cup. So if we confuse concept and thing, we will think that there must be three things here, and will wonder what holds them together. But, he believes, the whole problem arises from the elementary mistake of identifying the concept by which we identify a thing, on the basis of just one of its aspects, with the thing itself. That does not consist in three units which have to be joined but in one thing which answers at once to all those concepts.

§ It must be said that this is a rather superficial interpretation of Bradley's concerns. Bradley would say that the thing answers to more than one concept because it has more than one feature, and the difficulty is as to how these features relate to each other. (He also thinks that there is a difficulty as to how a feature identified in abstract thought can be the same as a feature which figures in the fullness of concrete reality.) If the relation is distinct from the terms related, it needs to be related to each in turn by a further relation, but if it is not distinct from them, then the relation and its terms collapse into a unity in which there are no distinct terms to be related. Thus there is a problem in conceiving a togetherness which is compatible with the independent in-itself-ness which we normally imagine things as possessing.

James, however, is inclined to dismiss this as just a further example of the follies of intellectualist logic.

> Any conjunctive relation between two phenomenal experiences a and b must, in the intellectualist philosophy of these authors, be itself a third entity; as such, instead of bridging the one original chasm it can only create two smaller chasms, each to be freshly bridged. Instead of hooking a to b, it needs itself to be hooked by a fresh relation r' to a and by another r" to b. These new relations are but two more entities which require to be hitched in turn by four still newer relations—so behold the vertiginous *regressus ad infinitum* in full career.
>
> Since a *regressus ad infinitum* is deemed absurd, the notion that relations come 'between' their terms must be given up. No mere external go-between can logically connect. What occurs must be more intimate. The hooking must be a penetration, a possession. The relation must *involve* the terms, each term must involve *it*, and merging thus their being in it, they must somehow merge their being in each other, tho, as they seem still phenomenally so separate, we can never conceive exactly how it is that they are inwardly one. The absolute, however, must be supposed able to perform the unifying feat in his own inscrutable fashion.
>
> PU, pp. 69–70

We will be seeing, however, that James was really well aware that the problem of relations, as absolute idealists like Bradley and Lotze mainly saw it, does not arise from any such trite confusion of things and concepts.

§ However, I expect that many a philosopher today will agree with the main gist of these criticisms of Bradley. Where he may disagree is as to whether the fault lies in conceptual thought or only in bad conceptual thought.[18]

It is well within the resources of conceptual thinking, he may say, to draw the needed distinction between a concrete thing and the concepts under which it falls. For conceptual thinking is not simply thinking about concepts. Thus we can recognize 'at a purely conceptual level' where Bradley went wrong. The fact that the thing which answers to a verbal definition or specification has properties which cannot be deduced therefrom only shows that not all truths are analytic. It is hardly baffling to conceptual thought that the prime minister of Britain is also a father, or even that there is more to being a father than can be captured in a verbal definition of paternity. Bradley's is a fault in logic not of logic.[19]

We may agree that if the intellectualist were arguing in ways as easily corrected as this, and corrected well within the confines of discursive conceptual thought, he would hardly be exploiting that real impossibility of concepts doing justice to reality on which James came more and more to insist. But James is here vastly over-simplifying both Bradley and the nature of his own more serious charges against him.

§ Actually, James himself hovered between regarding the absolute idealist's intellectualism as bad conceptual thinking and as an exploitation of the defects of conceptual thinking as such. But his eventual view was certainly that it is conceptual thinking as such which gives rise to paradoxes which baffle the intellect and which can only be resolved by a quite other mode of understanding things.

> I see the intellectualistic criticism destroying the immediately given coherence of the phenomenal world, but unable to make its own conceptual substitutes cohere, and I see the resort to the absolute for a coherence of a higher type. . . . [But may] not the remedy lie rather in revising the intellectualistic criticism than in first adopting it and then trying to undo its consequences by an arbitrary act of faith in an unintelligible agent. May not the flux of sensible experience itself contain a rationality that has been overlooked, so that the real remedy would consist in harking back to it more intelligently, and not in advancing in the opposite direction . . . to the pseudo-rationality of the supposed absolute point of view[?]
>
> PU, pp. 72–73

§ In saying that concepts cannot do justice to reality James may sometimes seem merely to be making the point that normally propositions are not the same thing as their subject matter. To complain about this seems rather, as Ayer put it, like complaining that the menu at the restaurant does not taste very nice. So far as such a complaint has any point at all it is simply as an insistence, à la Goethe, that theory is secondary to life, and that books are not everything.

---

18   For various remonstrations on this point with James at the time see Perry, II, pp. 593–98.

19   Or would have been if he had really argued in this way.

But surely, it may be said, if we once recognize that the point of true propositions is not to provide a substitute for non-verbal reality, but simply to say in words how it is, we will see no grounds here for saying that there is anything in reality which cannot be told in words. If our usual concepts do not serve as an adequate instrument for saying how things are, should we not seek others rather than despair of conceptual thought? That, indeed, was the spirit in which Whitehead developed his alternative to the concepts of substance and attribute which he thought the root of so many problems.[20] The upshot is a metaphysics very close to James's, but presented as a conceptual reform rather than as an alternative to conceptual thought as such.

§ But it is not as simple as that. For I believe that James's sense of the limitations of conceptual thought is related to his pragmatic conception of truth in a somewhat curious manner. Truth, he argued, as a pragmatist, is no mere copy of reality in another conceptual or verbal medium. There would be little point in it if it were, and we should regard the conceptual symbols in which it consists rather as tools for dealing with (and perhaps sometimes as a worthwhile addition to) reality than as revelations of its essence. Nonetheless, James did hanker for something which could provide a sense of the real essence of things and, since concepts and truth were precluded from this role, it had to be sought in a metaphysics which turns us towards reality in some more intimate way than they do. And here the logic by which we organize our concepts is more an obstacle than an aid. Thus the fault of the intellectualist is to look for a revelation of reality from what are merely tools for dealing with it.

This is much the account that Bergson gives of the relation between James's pragmatism and his anti-intellectualism.[21] And in the next section we shall see how James identified himself with Bergson on this matter.

§ That conceptual thought cannot do this, arises, largely from the fact that it can only provide a static picture of a world which is essentially dynamic. (This is all right so long as that static picture is used to guide our dynamic dealings with things, but it leads to trouble when we expect it to provide a real grasp of the nature of its object.) Such rationalizing of a mass of perceptual fact consists in aligning it with the conceptual order, that is aligning what is in flux with what is essentially static.[22] For nothing happens in the world of concepts, it being a timeless order in which items are arranged once and for all on the basis of relations of likeness and unlikeness, more and less. As such it simply cannot give an account which is satisfying, even within its own terms, of the way in which the world really unrolls itself in time. The conceptual order is a practical necessity as a guide to the sensible flux, and there is even a place for Platonic

---

20   See Whitehead, *Process* passim.
21   See 'Sur le Pragmatisme de William James: Verité et Réalité', pp. 1440–50 of Bergson, *Oeuvres, especially p. 1449. This first appeared as a preface to the French translation of Pragmatism* by E. Le Brun, Paris, 1911.
22   See SSP, chapter IV.

delight in it for its own sake, but it remains for ever inadequate to the flow and richness of concrete reality and inevitably generates problems like Zeno's which tease the intellect. This need no longer trouble us once we give up expecting our concepts to mirror the concrete world in any exact way, and take them either as tools for dealing with it or as objects of contemplation in their own right.

So James moved towards the view that it is the limitations of conceptual thinking as such which lead to the paradoxes which absolute idealists exploit. And from this he concluded that conceptual thinking, though a fine tool for dealing with things for practical purposes, deceives if taken as a window on reality. The fault of the intellectualist lies in taking it as the latter.

§ James says, in PU, that he owes the insight that it is conceptual thinking itself, rather than defective versions of it, which is flawed as a way of understanding reality, to Bergson, though one may suspect that he was moving towards it unaided. At any rate, Bergson had contended that concepts have a static nature in virtue of which they cannot capture the true essence of that continuous flux in which genuine reality consists and James enthusiastically endorses this.

> When conceptualism summons life to justify itself in conceptual terms, it is like a challenge addressed in a foreign language to some one who is absorbed in his own business.
>
> PU, p. 291

So James tells us that while he used to try to deal with intellectualist problems in intellectualist terms, now he simply submerges himself in life, to which language can only point.

I conclude that James really means two different things by 'intellectualism'. First, the intellectualist is one who confuses concepts and things and thereby makes false steps in reasoning which reasoning is adequate to correct. Second, the intellectualist is one who supposes that the true nature of reality can be grasped conceptually and thereby deprives himself of the insights which can only be gained intuitively.

Clearly intellectualism in the first sense is to be rejected; whether it is so in the second is more disputable. Either way, it is somewhat strange to pick out Bradley as a prime example of it, and Bradley himself found it 'very funny' to be so called.[23] For Bradley, as much as James and Bergson, thought that concepts necessarily distort reality and the arguments which James calls intellectualist are largely concerned to demonstrate the paradoxes inherent in conceptual thought in virtue of which what it postulates is only, in his special sense, 'appearance'.

(d) Bradley or Bergson?

James is not unaware that in some respects Bradley is an ally of Bergson and

---

23   See Bradley to James, May 14, 1909, in Perry, II, p. 640.

himself in the critique of intellectualism. All three hold that concepts distort reality. But he insists on an important difference. Bradley sees the need to correct conceptual thinking, or perhaps rather dream that it is corrected at the level of the Absolute, by a higher form of intellect, while Bergson and James think it can only be corrected by a plunge into the sensory flux which will remind us what reality is really like. Finding that concepts cannot do justice to perceptual reality and convinced that truth cannot be found in feeling, Bradley seeks truth and reality in a mysterious intellectual world beyond both. Bergson, in contrast, says: 'Recognize concepts as useful instruments but get your sense of reality from feeling.'

> [C]oncepts . . . being thin extracts from perception, are always insufficient representatives thereof; and, although they yield wider information, must never be treated after the rationalistic fashion as if they gave a deeper quality of truth. The deeper features of reality are found only in perceptual experience. Here alone do we acquaint ourselves with continuity, or the immersion of one thing in another, here alone with self, with substance, with qualities, with activity in its various modes, with time, with cause, with change, with novelty, with tendency, and with freedom. Against all such features of reality the method of conceptual translation, when candidly and critically followed out, can only raise its *non possumus*, and brand them as unreal or absurd.
>
> SPP, p. 97

James devoted a fascinating article to a comparison of Bradley and Bergson, called 'Bradley or Bergson?' (1910)[24] which should be read together with chapter VI of PU. Bradley seems to have thought that James's difficulties in understanding Bradley, and Bradley's in understanding Bergson, made it useless for him to discuss the article.[25] This is a pity for, of all absolute idealism's critics, James had the best grasp of it.

Both Bradley and Bergson, says James, reject the traditional idealist view

> that feelings, aboriginally discontinuous, are woven into continuity by the various synthetic concepts which the intellect applies
>
> EP, p. 151

and that

> conception is essentially a unifying process.
>
> EP, p. 151

---

24 *Journal of Philosophy, Psychology, and Scientific Methods,* 7 (January 20, 1910). Reprinted in EP, pp. 151–56. It is presented as a comment on Bradley's 'Coherence and Contradiction' [ETR, chapter VIII], which had appeared in *Mind* in October 1909.
25 See Perry, II, p. 436.

Instead they see the grid of discrete concepts we apply to the world as breaking it up, for our thought, into sharply distinct bits the connectedness of which it cannot exhibit. Thus the harder we think the less we can understand how things hang together and the more are we caught up in such hopeless paradoxes as Bradley's about relations, Zeno's about motion, and such traditional puzzles as how qualities stand to things.

Thus the two philosophers give much the same diagnosis of our intellectual ills. But when it comes to the solution offered they move in different directions. Arrived at the realization that conceptual thinking is a useful tool which breaks down when we expect it to be more than useful and to give a deep understanding of reality

> Bergson *drops* conception—which apparently has done all the good it can do; and, turning back towards perception with its transparent multiplicity-in-union, he takes its data integrally up into philosophy, as a kind of material which nothing else can replace. The fault of our perceptual data, he tells us, is not of nature, but only of extent; and the way to know reality intimately is, according to this philosopher, to sink into those data and get *our sympathetic imagination to enlarge their bounds. Deep* knowledge is not of the conceptually mediated, but of the immediate type. Bergson thus allies himself with old-fashioned empiricism, on the one hand, and with mysticism, on the other. His breach with rationalism could not possibly be more thorough than it is.
>
> EP, p. 152

Bradley is quite as fully aware that

> '[c]oncepts are an organ of misunderstanding rather than of understanding; they turn the 'reality' which we 'encounter' into an 'appearance' which we 'think'.
>
> EP, p. 152

He believes that the

> form of oneness in the flow of feeling is an attribute of reality which even the absolute must preserve.

But for Bradley the philosopher is one who has abandoned feeling for ideas or concepts. The goal of philosophy is a purely conceptual understanding of reality, and if it sank back into mere feeling it would betray its defining ideal. So we must stick to concepts, when philosophising, however inadequate the grasp of reality they can provide. For example, Bradley says that the propositions which philosophy takes seriously must not use mere 'designation' (i.e., token reflexives or indicator words) but must capture their subject matter in a purely conceptual form. Certainly its refusal to accept the help of mere feeling makes philosophy one-sided, but such one-sidedness is essential to its task. The merely conceptual understanding sought by philosophy is not the way of life, but the only conclusion is 'so much the worse for life' so far as philosophy is concerned. For its goal is truth rather than reality, and it will stick to the first even if it distorts the second. But for James this is like a hungry person saying

> that the way of starvation is not the way of life, but to the starveling it is all there is.
>
> EP, p. 154

> The wise and natural course [for one who has realized, like Bradley, the inadequacies of conceptual thinking] . . . would seem to be to drop the notion that truth is a *thoroughgoing* improvement on reality, to confess that its value is limited, and to hark back [to immediate feeling]. But there is nothing that Mr. Bradley, religiously loyal to the direction of development once entered upon, will not do sooner than this. Forward, forward, let us range! He makes the desperate transconceptual leap, assumes *beyond* the whole ideal perspective an ultimate 'suprarelational' and transconceptual reality in which somehow the wholeness and certainty and unity of feeling, which we turned our backs on forever when we committed ourselves to the leading of ideas, are supposed to be resurgent in transfigured form; and shows us as the only authentic objects of philosophy, with its 'way of ideas', an absolute which 'can be' and 'must be' and therefore 'is'. 'It *shall* be' is the only candid way of stating its relation to belief; and Mr. Bradley's statement comes very near to that.
>
> EP, p. 154

We can only understand Bradley's insistence on sticking to the way of ideas rather than of 'life' as an exercise of his personal will-to-believe, for there is certainly no rational or other obligation upon him to do so. The will-to-believe of Bergson in contrast is to

> tumble to life's call, and turn into the valley where the green pastures and the clear waters always were. If in sensible particulars reality reveals the manyness-in-oneness of its constitution in so convincing a way, why then withhold, if you will, the name of 'philosophy' from perceptual knowledge, but recognize that perceptual knowledge is at any rate the *only complete kind of knowledge*, and let 'philosophy' in Bradley's sense pass for the one sided affair which he candidly confesses that it is. When the alternative lies between knowing life in its full thickness and activity, as one acquainted with its *me's* and *thee's* and *now's* and *here's*, on the one hand, and knowing a transconceptual evaporation like the absolute, on the other, it seems to me that to choose the latter knowledge merely because it has been named 'philosophy' is to be superstitiously loyal to a name. But if names are to be used eulogistically, rather let us give that of philosophy to the fuller kind of knowledge, the kind in which perception and conception mix their lights.
>
> EP, p. 155

James ends by urging the reader who has followed Bergson and Bradley on the road they travel together (in the course of which his trust in the adequacy of conceptual thinking to do justice to reality has been shaken) to follow Bergson at the point where their paths divide. He ends with the pious hope that Bradley will see the light too and lead 'english thought' to a new day in which it lays 'post-kantian rationalism permanently underground.'

Thus James does not abandon the thesis that truth consists in useful ideas. But he claims that there is a deeper way of understanding reality than knowing truth about it and that it is this, rather than truth, which philosophy should especially seek. This is a transmutation of James's pragmatism which must surprise those who take it as implying that there is no reality other than that posited in useful thinking.

There is certainly something problematic in the ideal of philosophy which James now favours. It is perceptual rather than conceptual, and gathers how things are from feeling rather than from thinking. Yet philosophers like James and Bergson are respected for their books, their lectures, and for those with the luck to have heard it, their talk, not for how they felt as they registered reality in some more immediate way. It may be better to feel reality richly in dancing, or in ecstatic religious meditation, but surely Bradley is right that that is not philosophy.

Nevertheless James is saying something valuable, even if he has overstated it. Philosophy is, of course, inevitably a species of conceptual thinking, and James's philosophy cannot avoid being an attempt to catch reality in concepts. What he must be seeking is not something altogether non-conceptual but concepts which do better justice to reality in its actual essence than ordinary ones, and thus do not alienate our thought from reality but keep it more fully in touch therewith. And he is saying that we can only obtain these concepts by continually checking our more discursive thought by the immediate sense we have of reality in perception and feeling.

To say that such a philosophy summons us to immerse ourselves in reality rather than in concepts is still puzzling. For, after all, we cannot very well help being immersed in reality, as long as we are on the scene at all, though we can experience more or less satisfying forms of it. Reality—at least as James and Bergson understand the matter—is just what one inevitably continually lives through. The task of philosophy must, then, be either the better understanding of this reality, or the improvement of the form of it we live through. The conclusion to which James and Bergson seem to point is that philosophy has two main goals which need to be distinguished: (1) thought with a purely pragmatic truth of the most useful kind for the improvement of our lot; (2) thought with a more deeply literal sort of truth. (However, one should surely not deny that the latter may also have a more practical utility and needs to be incorporated as an element within the otherwise largely pragmatic truth of everyday life.) In effect, I think this is James's position, but for a really satisfactory statement of it he would have had to withdraw some of the more strident assertions of his pragmatist writings.

(e) Relations

§ In spite of his critique of intellectualist logic, James saw absolute idealism as pointing to some genuine problems and as having its own genuine insights. These problems come from expecting our ordinary concepts to be a better guide to the real essence of reality than they are, but James's more considered position does not depict them as arising from the kind of elementary howler exhibited in the suggestion that a rider can never dismount and become a pedestrian. Rather the idealists had the real insight that the traditional view, that each ultimate finite thing in the universe (whether these are experiences, atoms, souls, or whatever) is a nugget of being with a character independent of how it stands to other things, leaves it problematic how they can hang together to form any larger reality together. Thus, in spite of his impatient way with them at times, he saw Bradley and Royce as posing a real problem about relations. What could not be accepted was the claim that absolute idealism offered the only possibly solution to it. James hoped to find a more adequate answer by plunging into the heart of experience and bringing back a better sense of what relationship is than our usual concepts convey.

> That vital comprehension [of Hegel, which, as Royce says is what will endure, however specious the details] we have already seen. It is that there is a sense in which real things are not merely their own bare selves, but may vaguely be treated as also their own others, and that ordinary logic, since it denies this, must be overcome. Ordinary logic denies this because it substitutes concepts for real things, and concepts *are* their own bare selves and nothing else. What Royce calls Hegel's 'system' was Hegel's attempt to make us believe that he was working by concepts and grinding out a higher style of logic, when in reality sensible experiences, hypotheses, and passion furnished him with all his results.
>
> What I myself may mean by things being their own others, we shall see in a later lecture.
>
> PU, p. 143

The essential problem, then, posed by the absolute idealist was how something can be an entity in its own right without being sealed off from other things with no real communion with them. Thus Bradley holds that the way in which distinct items are supposed to be related in the world is unintelligible. If the terms are distinct from each other and from the relation linking them, the relation is a third something standing between them, and this third something needs to be related to the original terms by further relations which pose the same problem over again. Yet if the terms are either not distinct from each other or not distinct from the relation, then really we do not have distinct things at all, but just a single ONE. And, since this will apply wherever we suppose there are distinct things, it follows that there is but one Reality, not many things in relation.

§ According to James it was its inadequate conception of relationship which was the main reason for the problems which had so far beset the development of a satisfactory empiricist philosophy. The point had been made already in PP. Experience contains two different sorts of item, he had there said: (i) substantive elements corresponding to nouns, adjectives, and most verbs; (ii) non-substantive relational aspects which are the flights or leaps which thought makes between these.[26] Traditional empiricism only took account of disjunctive relations and was thereby landed with that highly atomistic picture of the world which invited the rationalist and idealist claim that the atoms could only be put together by a pure ego, a soul, or what not.

In his discussion of relations in PP James takes these as including the supposed referents of connectives like 'and', 'if, 'then', as much as of expressions like 'in', 'above', 'loves', 'is brother of'. And he says that we should talk of a feeling of 'if' as much as of a feeling of 'blue' or 'sweet'.[27] His whole treatment of the matter looks a bit naive from the perspective of precise logical analyses of these expressions. What merit it has would need reconsidering in the light of the more formal explications of the meanings of these words provided by their analysis as truth functions.

Perhaps James would say that this charge rests on confusing our ideas of relations with the relations themselves. He is writing as a psychologist about the former; logical ontologists are considering the latter. Such a reply fits in with his insistence that we distinguish between successive ideas of the same thing and the reoccurrence of the same idea[28] and his rejection of the 'psychologist's fallacy'. (This is not, it should be noted, the same error as 'intellectualists' are later charged with. The one is a confusion of ideas, qua mental events, with both their meanings and their referents, the other of things with meanings.)

However, I doubt if such a reply is really available to James, for it is hard to avoid interpreting his talk of the feeling of 'if' and of other terms he calls relational as supposedly casting light on both their sense and their reference. Thus he is not so free as he should be, on his own account, from the confusion with which he charges others. The trouble is that there is no very clear idea in PP of how an idea relates to what it is of, and so none of how our idea of a relation stands to the relation itself.

§ Some of these confusions linger in later discussions of relations, but though it is not put forward in any set way as a general theory of relations, he does, in effect, develop, in ERE, PU, and SPP, a positive view of relations of some interest which is supposed to offer an escape for the true empiricist from the problems about them raised by the absolute idealists. We have already encountered it to some extent. Relations on this view, are either conjunctive or disjunctive.[29] The former are the various different ways in which one thing flows into another; the latter the various different ways in which such flows are blocked.

Here again no very clear distinction is made between the question: 'What goes on when one thinks about the relations between things?' and 'What actually is it for things to be related?' For example, he says that we encounter

---

26   See PP, I, p. 243 et ff., and BC, pp. 160–63.
27   See PP, I, pp. 245–46, and BC, p. 162.
28   See PP, I, p. 231.
29   See especially ERE, pp. 44–52.

a disjunctive relation when we try to think of someone else's experience in connection with one's own.[30] One's thought encounters a kind of blockage in passing from the thought of the one to the other. But surely the blockage we may experience in passing from the thought of one to the thought of the other is not itself the chasm which divides your consciousness from mine; at most it somehow symbolises it. James seems to confuse saying that what makes the relation between our consciousnesses disjunctive is the blockage between the thought of the one and of the other and saying that it is the blockage of any real flowing of one into the other.

His later view of relations is closely bound up with the panexperientialist ontology of his later thought and hardly concerns itself with relations between anything other than experiences. It is an attempt to explain how a world composed of experiences can be a single world without all experiences being absorbed into a single absolute feeling. For, at the most fundamental level, these are what the world consists in and the kinds of relations which make the world both one and many are those which can hold between experiences. James does not say much as to how we should think about the relational facts we conceive as holding in the world of daily life posited in pragmatic useful thinking. Perhaps he thought there was nothing much to be said here of deep philosophical importance and that it could be covered by the psychological account of relational thinking in PP.

At the more ultimate level, in any case, the only relations required are those which hold between experiences. And these, on his view, are a matter of the way in which one experience passes into another or is prevented from doing so. The crucial point which must be established to escape either excessive monism or excessive pluralism is the possibility of both of these. And the problem concerns mainly the former, for if we can understand what a conjunctive relation is we can presumably understand what a blockage to one is. We must suppose, however, that there is some kind of conjunctive relation, direct or indirect, between any two items in the universe, else they would be utterly disconnected.

If there are to be conjunctive relations between experiences they must be capable of flowing into one another in a way which makes for something less than complete difference between them and more than complete identity. Each experience is in a sense its own other, for it is of the very nature of the one that it is in passage to the other, yet each has its own separate character. The extent to which this occurs is James's key to the real presence both of connectedness and disconnectedness in the universe. Even the experience of what are to a great extent distinct streams of consciousness may flow into those of other streams, and streams which do not flow into each other, can be related mediately by a third stream into which each flows. Still more indirect but real relations are possible through a longer chain of such intermediary streams of experience.

---

30   See ERE, p. 49.

If this is what conjunctive relations essentially are, my consciousness can only be related positively to anything beyond it if it flows into other streams of experience. But what are these other streams? There are three main possible cases, it would seem.

§ First, there must be some flow between it and those streams of experience which constitute the inner states of all the various processes which make up my bodily being, including that of my brain cells. (James, we have seen, in sections 5 and 7 of the last chapter, remained ambivalent as to whether C. A. Strong was right that my conscious states are the inner being of certain physical processes in the brain or a different level of experience which interacts therewith; either way there needs to be a flow between my experience and those experiences which are the inner being of such brain process as it is not.) James only hints at this view, developed later by Whitehead and Hartshorne, but it is implied in what he does say.[31] It would normally only be via the relatedness in this manner of my dominant stream of consciousness with the various flows of feeling constituting the inner nature of my body that I can enter into my less direct relations with the rest of the physical world, conceived as consisting ultimately in a vast system of sequences of experience flowing into and out of one another. (The more direct-realist forms of radical empiricism, discussed in the last chapter, would have to put this rather differently. But James's final view can only be understood panpsychistically.)

Secondly, there are probably various streams of consciousness which constitute my own so-called unconscious, or better, subliminal experiences. Normally one only dimly feels the presence and influence of these as they flow into and out of that dominant stream which is what one is for oneself and which expresses itself in one's ordinary voluntary action. In cases of multiple personality, however, such streams enter into a more vigorous rivalry for dominance and hold the controls in turn. In such cases the flow between them may be such that the ones greeted by other persons at any time as me may recognize the others as partially being me as well.

Thirdly, there is the possible flowing of a divine stream of consciousness into one's personal stream of feeling. Mystics may have a vivid sense of this but it may occur less obviously in all of us. And there may be influence back from our experience onto the divine consciousness too.[32]

§ Thus James came to think that the basic type of relatedness is that which holds between one state of consciousness and the next in the stream of one personal consciousness. That my stream of consciousness is not completely isolated from the rest of things can only be because relations of that sort hold not just within it but between some of its elements and experiences belonging to other streams. And the same must be true of all those streams of experience which make up the inner being of concrete reality at large if each is not to be

---

31   See, for example, PU, pp. 386 and 394.
32   See section 3(f) of this chapter below.

hermetically sealed within its own limits with no commerce with what lies beyond them. Yet these streams can be distinct from each other in virtue of the various sorts and degrees of blockage which prevent their intermingling and the number of intermediaries by whose relations of this sort to each other they are connected indirectly.

Such flowing of one experience into another, will involve some *influence* of the predecessor experience on the character of its successor. And, indeed (as we effectively saw in Chapter Three, §5) James tends to think that this is the only sort of influence there is, from which it follows that the influence of one thing upon another requires the partial merging at times of the streams of experience which are their inner being. This will happen when an experience occurs which belongs primarily to one stream but is in the next-to-next relation not only to its predecessor there but also to one belonging to another stream. The pragmatist account of truth fits in here as the view that the truths known within a stream of consciousness are symbols occurring within it with the potential for channelling it towards a successful such merging with the stream of being of the object it concerns.

Everything, in this scheme, hangs on the nature of that relation of next-to-next which holds between the successive total experiences which succeed each other in those streams of experience of which one's own stream of experience must be one's paradigm example. James had already worked hard at developing a satisfactory view of this relation in PP, at a time when its metaphysical importance was not so great. And in §7 of Chapter Three we have seen him working at it in something of a frenzy of intellectual excitement in the Miller-Bode notebook. His later published writings offer a further series of attacks upon the problem. We shall consider what seems to have been his eventual conclusion in section 2(e) of this chapter on continuity.

(f) Absolute Idealism One Hypothesis among Others

The conclusion to be drawn, thought James, from the inadequacies of intellectualist logic as a way of reaching truth, and the possibility of an alternative conception of the togetherness of things than that of the absolute idealist, is that both absolute idealism and his own pluralistic metaphysics are permissible hypotheses. It is possible that all finite experiences belong together in a final unity and that what we conceive as the relations between them are reducible to their common inherence in a single totality of cosmic feeling, but it is also possible that they are only related in that more strung-along fashion of which the relations between the successive phases in our stream of consciousness are an example. Neither metaphysic can conquer simply on the basis of logic and each provides an answer to the main intellectual problems of metaphysics. Moreover, each has the advantage of making some sense of our religious feelings. The choice between them is, therefore, of just that kind specified in

'The Will to Believe' as giving us the right to believe what we find most personally helpful.

Absolute idealism has the appeal to our passional nature of providing us with what James notoriously called 'moral holidays'.[33]

If we think of all the evils of the world, or even of our own personal problems, we may be overcome by the terrible demands these seem to impose upon us if we are to play any part in putting them right. If we have grown up in a Protestant tradition which emphasises our need to escape from sin, we may be overcome by a sense of personal inadequacy. Absolute idealism, with its message that everything which occurs is just what is required by the rational purposes or nature of an absolute mind, allows us to relax a little, and to feel that things will be all right in the end even if we lose our own grip on life and morality from time to time.

James thought this a genuine good, but one in the end outweighed by the evils it brings with it.[34] For it forces us to think of the terrible things of the world as somehow required by the final good, and that is bound to blunt our sense of outrage at them and urge to put them right. Therefore absolute idealists are likely to contribute less than they might to human progress.

However, the same may be even more true of materialists whose bleak view, that the course of history is determined by mechanical causation occurring below the level of human planning and ideals, is likely to produce an inactive cynicism. It was because he saw Santayana's philosophy as only a refined version of such a materialism that he sometimes spoke so sharply of his work. Of course, James was hardly familiar with a Marxist materialism for which material laws have a teleological drive towards an ultimate human good whose operations we can only delay or hasten but not finally prevent.

Thus neither of these philosophies, he thought, can give us the sense that our own moral struggles have any real point. Moreover, it is only on the basis of a pluralistic metaphysics that we can have a morally reputable theism. For the 'finite God', who is the only possible God for such a metaphysics, need not be responsible for evil, and we can believe in him without that corruption of our moral sense which must ensue upon either the absolutist's deification of the Universe or orthodoxy's conception of a God responsible for its every detail. Rather is he the great cosmic fighter for goodness whose cause we can genuinely help or hinder. That suggests the wisdom of using our will to believe to accept such a pluralism and such a theism, if reasoning and evidence show them to be no less coherent and probable than absolute idealism or materialism. To see how James argued that this was so, I shall now turn to his positive final positions.

---

33   See PRAG, pp. 73–75.
34   See, for example, Perry, II, pp. 473–74.

§2. *Steps towards a Positive Alternative*

(a) The Nature of Continuity

§ In PP and ever after James insisted on continuity as one of the essential features of the stream of consciousness. Indeed it is one of the main features of consciousness which the metaphor of the 'stream' is meant to express. The experience of any one moment is not made up of sharply discrete units, nor is one's total experience of each moment a complete fresh existence which vanishes, to be replaced by another complete total experience. Rather do the experiences of any one moment overlap with those of immediately following moments. Experience is not a series of distinct total states but a perpetual flux. Embroidering a little on James's metaphor one might put it thus. The present moment is a bridge over one's stream of consciousness and one's present experience is the water below the bridge. Thus there is no sharp break between the water of consciousness which belongs to the present and that which belongs to the past or future. The flow of consciousness never stops to produce a definite static state.

By depicting the present as a bridge across the stream of consciousness rather than as a line, we also bring out the point that, as James conceives it, there is no such thing as the experience of an instant. Present experience always contains a temporal stretch including items before and after each other. The minimal unit of experience is a specious present with some duration. It is a two-dimensional band of the stream, not a line across it. (For simplicity I take it that it is merely the surface of the stream which represents one's experience, though it would be more apt to think of it as including the water below as well.)

Thus there are two leading ideas in James's account of consciousness, that of the continuity of consciousness and that of the specious present. Some version of these ideas always remained important for him, but the precise meaning given to them is not altogether clear in PP and seems to have changed in his later work. Certainly they seem to have been interpreted in a rather different way in PU and SPP. They are topics which gave James a good deal of trouble.

Some of the difficulties may spring from a failure to be clear as to just what in detail the metaphor of the stream is meant to convey. It is certainly very suggestive but it is so ubiquitous in James and others of a similar outlook that its point needs more investigation than it usually receives.

Altogether James is much clearer about these issues in his later work. But the position in PP deserves investigation both for its own sake and as a background for following his later thought, so I shall start with some account of that. I shall round out what James actually says in an effort to clarify what I believe to be his main point. It would take too long to defend my account by a detailed exegesis of the text, and it will have to be judged as a whole by Jamesian scholars. (In this section I use 'experience' and 'consciousness' as synonyms for the sake of 'elegant variation'.)

§ According to PP (in chapters IX and X) the stream of experience consists in a continuous flow of what we might call consciousness-water flowing under the bridge of the present moment. The band of water below the bridge at any one moment is the specious present and contains the totality of what is actually experienced at that moment. The consciousness-water in the stream which has already passed under the bridge is one's past experience, that which is yet to pass under it is one's future experience.

This may seem straightforward but now we must ask just what is meant by the phrase 'at any one moment'. Does it refer to an instant without temporal duration? Any appeal to the notion of an instant may seem to go against James's conception of experienced time. However, although he did later develop views which were meant to challenge the very notion of an instant, it is not clear that, at the time of PP, he meant to deny that there actually is such a thing as the instantaneous present, and until we find ways of avoiding it, it seems such an obvious notion that we can hardly dismiss what seem reasonable enough questions just because they presuppose it. And one question which presents itself is this: Which straight line represents the instantaneous present? Is it, for example, the edge of the bridge on the upstream side or is it somewhere below the bridge?

Before dealing with this question it is necessary to distinguish two senses of 'instant'. First, there is a sense in which history is composed of instants one of which is present and others of which are past (whether there are really also future ones is more problematic). These are represented by straight lines across the stream of water-consciousness which move along the bank with it, and which we may call 'moving instants'. These flow past instants in the second sense, which we may call 'standing instants', and which are represented by fixed straight lines at right angles to the stream's banks. One of these will presumably be the instantaneous present and the others the infinitude of positions represented by different degrees of pastness (and perhaps futurity). Thus the upstream edge of the bridge (towards the stream's source) will represent one standing instant, and its downstream edge (towards its mouth) another. And there will be an infinite number of standing instants represented by lines across the water under the bridge. Since the series of instants is usually thought of as compact in a mathematical sense, there will be no adjacent instants (in either sense of 'instant'), but between any two there will be an infinity of other instants.

Of the two senses of 'instant' it is perhaps the first which is more usual. But it will be more convenient to use 'instant' in the second sense (that of 'standing instant') when dealing with the question just raised. For that concerns the relation between the specious present and the instantaneous present, supposing the ordinary view that there is such a thing, and since we are conceiving of the former as a static stretch of the river bed through which experiences flow we must think similarly of the present instant as a line past which they flow. So for this reason, and because it allows some other questions to be raised in a more convenient way, where there is no contrary indication 'instant' will henceforth mean a 'standing instant'. (Thus by an instant we will not be meaning a dated event. Rather are instants fixed points which dated events slide past. The river of events is conceived as moving past fixed positions in time. It is the events which flow past these positions which are dated; the instants are positions in time which do not change. An alternative way of looking at is to regard the series of dated events as staying still and the present, together with all the different degrees of futurity and pastness, as moving up to a dated event and past it toward events as yet future. But that way of looking at it fits less well with the metaphor of the stream of experience and James himself uses the other. For the moving stream is meant to represent the fact that concrete experience is on the move, not some kind of abstract form of time. McTaggart gives a good account of how these two ways of looking at it stand to each other.[35])

However, we are not at the end of our troubles in attempting to give a precise sense to the metaphor. For we seem obliged to think in terms of there being an instant at which any one moving instant (together with the experiences which belong to it) occupies the first instant of the specious present, and other instants at which it occupies each of the others.

This difficulty is intrinsic to the metaphor and reveals its limitations. I shall deal with it by talking of *the state of affairs* in which any one instantaneous experiential event is at the first or present instant of the specious present, that is the first state of affairs in which it is experienced at all. Pertaining to the same state of affairs will be the precise position in the river bed of each instantaneous experiential event, both those occupying a position in the specious present, under the bridge, and those which have flowed past the bridge or are still due to do so. It seems that we must think of there being an infinite number of states of affairs which succeed each other, and which form a compact series, in which strictly there are no neighbours. These states of affairs are instants in a third sense, and I shall call them 'instants of real time'.

§ We may now turn to the question: Where is the straight line across the river bank which represents the instantaneous present? Two main answers suggest themselves. (1) The instantaneous present is a line across the water somewhere well under the bridge. (2) The instantaneous present is represented by the upstream edge of the bridge.

These alternatives give two different conceptions of the specious present, consisting in the span of the bridge as a whole. On both views the specious present contains a stretch of duration, but on the first it contains something of the future, while on the second view it only contains the instantaneous present and something of the past.

There is a third view with a good deal to be said for it. (3) On this view the positions within the specious present are not well described in terms of present, past, and future. Rather, the experience represented by water under the bridge is all present, but not all simultaneous. Some items within it are before others. And there may be one standing instant pertaining to the specious present where experience is maximally present, so that other instants within it are less, though quite as truly, present, and nearer to being, without actually being, past (or perhaps future). This line might either be that of the upstream edge of the bridge or somewhere under the bridge. This third view has some attractions and is

---

35   See McTaggart, *Studies,* p. 126 note.

somewhat nearer to James's final position (though it does not do justice to his later 'epochal' view of time). However, it strongly suggests that there is no such thing as the instantaneous present, and I am doubtful whether James would have embraced it at the time of PP.

Each of these does justice to the main point of the specious present in that it represents it as a stretch of duration within which real relations of before and after can hold. And, for the main issues I wish to raise, it does not matter which view is taken. But it will be clearer to couch our discussion in terms of just one of them. James himself would seem to take the first view. But upon the whole I think it is the second which fits in best with his general tendency to conceive the future as unsettled and the present a point of real becoming, and I shall couch my account in terms of that.[36] This may seem high-handed, but it will aid my attempt to get a reasonably clear version from PP of the two leading ideas of our concern. So I shall take it for now that the specious present is a stretch of duration which includes the instantaneous present and a short stretch of the immediate past, while not including any of the future.

§ A conception of the specious present along these lines (whether in the second version, in which we shall take it, or in either of the other two) is not the only one that can be found in PP, but it does seem to be the dominant view implied by James's statements. And there seem to be two main reasons in its favour.

(1) First, it seems that some such doctrine is required if we are to give an empiricist account of how we have any conception of time at all and of the difference between the past and the future.[37] An empiricist supposes, to put it in Hume's terms, that an idea must be derived from some impression, that is, that our basic concepts must be derived from something we actually experience. Now if we are to have a concept of time, we must have a concept of the earlier-later relation which, for the empiricist, implies that we must actually sometimes experience one event as being earlier than another. And it seems that this can only happen if there are experiences which embrace a stretch of time.

It may be suggested that no notion of a specious present is required to explain this. It is now eleven A.M. and I got up at eight o'clock and have not been unconscious in between. Have I not experienced the series of events which have unrolled in my felt life during that period? So have I not experienced the earlier-later relation as holding between the drinking of a cup of coffee when I got up and the experience of hammering these words out on my word processor?

The proponent of the specious present will reply that there has not really

---

36   Ayer suggests that James's own view is the first (that the specious present contains present, past, and future) but that it should have been the third (according to which it only contains the present). This is only denied through a lingering belief in the instantaneous present. But I am inclined, for the reasons given in the text, to a slightly different position. See Ayer, *Origins*, pp. 246–48.

37   See PP, I, p. 631.

been any such experience as the experience of the events which I have lived through during those hours. You might as well say that I have experienced my life up till now, though with breaks. Certainly there is a sense in which I have lived through both this morning and through my life till now, but I have not experienced them as a unit containing elements between which I note relations.

What then do I strictly experience, in that important sense in which I do not experience events lasting three hours? Do I perhaps only experience instantaneous events? No, so the proponent of the specious present will argue, for there can be no change within an instant, and thus no items between which I can experience the earlier-later relation. So there must be a short stretch of time which is experienced as a whole and contains a before and after within it. This is the specious present and everything which I genuinely experience must occur within it. It is only because we experience such a specious present, and can derive from it a concept of before and after, that we can make sense of the past and future in general as what lies before or after a given experienced event, distanced from it by whatever number of intervening events of some standard sort is necessary to give it a sufficiently precise position in time for our purposes.

But if there *must* be a specious present, can we not investigate it and ask how long it lasts? Yet this seems very difficult. However, this, it may be replied, is not surprising. Obviously I cannot stop a specious present to examine it more closely. Nor can one time it with a stop watch. Yet one certainly seems to oneself to experience short stretches of time as a unit. And, in fact, there are psychological tests which suggest that it lasts a few seconds.[38]

(2) Besides this somewhat *a priori* ground for postulating a specious present, there is the directly phenomenological point that it does seem that we can actually see or otherwise perceive short stretches of process, and that this is quite different from the case where we simply infer that there has been change from the fact that we remember things as having been different from what they are now. This second phenomenological ground was perhaps the consideration which weighed primarily with James.

There are, indeed, other ways in which people have tried to explain the direct experience of change which do not appeal to the specious present. However, I do not think any has been successful. (I shall briefly consider the attempts of Husserl and of Bergson at the end of this section.) This is not to say that the specious present has to be conceived in the way James seems to conceive it in PP. Indeed, we shall be seeing that he himself moved to a rather different view of it later.

Let us now consider some difficulties in the notion of the specious present conceived in the way we have outlined.

§ (1) We seem to be assuming that any one state of affairs includes the parts of the moving stream which have not yet come under the bridge, as well as those which have done so; that is, the state of affairs seems to be one in which each

---

38   See PP, I, pp. 611–19.

experience has its definite position in time whether it is in, before, or after the specious present. But that suggests a definite future waiting to come under the bridge and a definite past still there though no longer under it. Common opinion would seem to support this way of conceiving the past (though it finds it hard to say what sort of being it possesses). But it rejects a similar supposition about the future, and James agrees with it. For he always conceived of the future as open rather than as a definite reality awaiting its moment of presentness.

Perhaps we could accommodate this by supposing that the parts of the river in the future are somehow there, but only in an indeterminate form. It is simpler, however, to alter our metaphor and think of the upstream edge of the bridge as lying above a spring where water flows up to start the river. And to make the metaphor more accurate we must think of the water as actually created at that spring and spurting up, so to speak, out of nothing, as a line or, rather, sheet. Or one can think of it as an absolutely smooth waterfall in which a sheet of water flows down in a plane from a sheer nothingness above. At any rate one must suppose that the instantaneous experiential event, which, in any one state of affairs, occupies the upstream instantaneous position in the specious present, did not exist before, but is at the very point where the water springs up from nothingness.

§ (2) We may now note a rather curious feature of the conception of experienced time depicted by this image. Consider a stretch of experience which is more than instantaneous but shorter than the specious present. It seems that it must be experienced an infinity of times. It will first be experienced in the state of affairs which occurs immediately it has passed as a whole below the bridge. But as the consciousness-water flows on, it will be experienced within an infinite series of different positions within the specious present until at last some of it has passed out of it.

The same will be true of those cross-sections of the stream of experience which each pertain to just one moving instant, as they move through the specious present. For each must occupy in turn each of the standing instants represented by the cross-sections of the bridge (or rather of the bed beneath it) in turn, and thus be experienced an infinite number of times, first as a present event, with no given successors, but with predecessors presently experienced as past, then an infinite number of times as a just-past event, both with experienced predecessors and successors, then finally with experienced predecessors but no successors. After that it is no longer experienced, but at most remembered.[39]

Whether it is stretches or instants of experience that are in question this seems a very strange idea and hard to square with introspection. Yet it seems an unavoidable feature of the fact which our metaphor purports to represent.

---

39 Note that essentially the same point can be made if the specious present contains some of the future as well as of the past, or if these distinctions do not apply within it.

Here I must insist that one must not think of the past end of the specious present as containing merely remembered experiences. It is supposed to explain how a stretch of time can actually be experienced, not merely occur as something in part only remembered. (Sometimes James does seem to think of the past part of the specious present as an object of 'primary' memory, as opposed to that 'secondary' memory which 'memory' usually denotes. But it is misleading to think of anything within the specious present as either remembered or anticipated. It must all actually be there as an object of immediate experience if the specious present is to do its job, as we shall now see more fully.)

§ What is objectionable here is not primarily the idea that each experience falling within the specious present is repeated an infinite number of times but that there is any such repetition at all. It would remain discordant with introspection, mine at least, to say that I have every experience falling within a specious present several times, as it occupies different positions within it, even if one somehow managed only to allow only a finite number of these.

It is not, indeed, implausible, or even false, that what is experienced initially as fully present is gradually experienced as fading away so that finally we only have a kind of echo or after-image of it. But this cannot be the main fact to which the doctrine of the specious present refers, if it is to explain how we genuinely experience the passage of time. For if its later aspects were merely such echoes or after-images occurring simultaneously with those which are fully present, there would be no real experience of time. If the changing position which a sensation occupies in the specious present were simply a degree of vividness, we would not really experience an earlier-later relation but simply a contrast between degrees of vividness. In hearing a tune, for example, we would not experience a succession of notes, in a certain rhythmic pattern, but only chords, in which the fainter sounds would echo sounds heard earlier. Real experience of a series of sounds requires that it be heard somehow 'at once' as part of a pattern over time, not that instant by instant we hear echoes of what occurred just previously, or that the character of what is heard now is influenced by what went before. In hearing a long piece of music, what is heard towards the end may be influenced in an intimate way by the whole of what went before, but this is different from the way in which we hear a short phrase as a whole.

James's language does, indeed, sometimes suggest an inadequate idea of the specious present as consisting in a contrast between the quality of experiences which are dawning and those which are fading. But I do not think he means to reduce it to this. For the real point of the specious present (as that within which we experience stretches of real process) is lost if this means simply a contrast in their vividness. Perhaps the objection that that would make it impossible to distinguish between temporal relations and contrasts of vividness can be met by identifying the former with a unique type of degree of vividness. Even so, they would not be real temporal relations.

There are two ways in which one might attempt to avoid this problem of the repeated experience of each event which falls within a specious present.

First, one might say that it arises from thinking of the successive states of affairs in which the specious present is differently occupied (through the entry of real instantaneous experiential events and the passage of old ones across it till they are pushed off at its final edge) as sharply distinct events. But we should think, not so much in terms of a compact series as of a phenomenological continuum without sharp breaks, so that there is no series of distinct states of affairs in which the same sensation is repeated in different positions. However, this idea is not very clear and still seems to imply that there is some kind of continuous repetition of each sensation as the continuum unfolds.

A second more radical solution would be to say that we are confusing the flow of experience with the mind which attends to it. We should think, so it may be suggested, of the band across the river representing the specious present as the base of a triangle whose apex is the attending mind. This attending mind stays as it were motionless with a continuously changing base as the line of process attended to sweeps across it at the bottom. (Or alternatively one can think of the apex and two upper sides of the triangle moving over a straight line which stays motionless. The apex of the triangle is then not so much an attending mind as successive acts of attention, forming a compact series.)

It is doubtful if James could embrace such a view. For he seems to think that the attention directed at the stream of sensory stuff is simply a way in which that stuff itself comes. And anyway it does not promise any real solution to the problem. The point would be, presumably, that the mind, or an act of attention, only ever sees successive overlapping segments of the line which form the base of the successive triangles. So it is not acquainted with its own passage from awareness of one such segment to another and is thus oblivious of the fact that it has had most of the matter of the present segment an infinite number of times before. But it has memory presumably and should be aware of the matter through this.

It must be admitted that there are extreme difficulties in attending to the experience of time in order to give a satisfactory account of the specious present and that this is compounded by more purely conceptual problems. But it does seem hard to get over difficulties such as the present one, and perhaps the next, without moving, as indeed James did, to a rather different account of the whole matter from that of PP.

§ (3) A third difficulty of this account of the specious present is that it falls foul of those problems about the nature of time which have dogged human thought since Zeno. Many suppose that modern mathematics has resolved all these difficulties. But in showing how the matter may be represented mathematically it is doubtful if the real problems about the phenomenology and metaphysics of temporal experience have been answered.

The puzzle is simply this. On the account given we have to think of each state of affairs (in which the specious present is occupied by a certain stretch of the sensory series) as coming into being and then being succeeded by others. But a later state of affairs can only replace an earlier one after each of an infinite set of intermediaries has done so. For there are no strictly next members of the series. Call one of these states of affairs A, and another B. In between A and B there will be state of affairs A1, and in between A and A1 there will be A01 and so forth. So B cannot follow on A until A1 has come in between, while A1 cannot follow on A until A01 has come in between, and so on. If we think of A as emerging out of nothing, then it seems that a new one can never emerge, for before it emerges an intervening one must emerge, and so on before that can emerge. If a state of affairs cannot emerge into being before another does, and the same is true of that other one, and so on, it seems that no new state of affairs can ever emerge. So our account makes it impossible for one state of affairs to follow on another.

The problem is not the absurd one it is sometimes taken to be as to whether there is time enough for the infinite series of new states of affairs which must arise between A and B to occur. For we are concerned with the growing of time itself, not with some timeable event. And the same will apply if we do not think of B as emerging out of nothing to replace A (and all that came between A and B) but as coming into some sort of present actuality out of a state of mere futurity.

There are various fairly standard solutions to this puzzle. It may be said that, after all, there is no real contradiction in the notion of an infinite series of states of affairs coming into being, or into present actuality, and that rejection of such an idea is only the result of ignorant prejudice. Or it may be said that talk of the infinite number of states of affairs is only a way in which we can think of a continuous line as being theoretically breakable up into smaller and smaller units. and does not imply that they exist or occur as distinct items. I shall say something about these claims later. For the present it is enough to say that James saw a puzzle here, and did not feel it could be satisfactorily solved along such lines. As a result he moved towards what has subsequently been called an epochal view of temporal process.

§ The reader may think that I have foisted problems on James by taking the metaphor of the stream too seriously, thus arriving at the notions (1) of the specious present as a kind of static band which is filled up differently from 'moment to moment', then (2) of instantaneous cross-sections both of (3) the stream which passes through this band and (4) instantaneous cross-sections of the band, then (4) of the moment or 'state of affairs' at which the stream is in each of what it seems must be an infinite number of positions vis-à-vis the specious present.

However, this metaphor is the main clue we have to what James is asserting to hold as a matter of literal truth and I have tried to clarify the nature of the literal truth it is supposed to represent. I cannot see how any less metaphorical form of statement could resolve these problems, without moving to the somewhat altered conception of these matters which James himself developed later.[40]

---

40   One might attempt to put the matter in a would-be more literal manner somewhat as follows. Real time consists in an infinite compact series of instants (instants of real time roughly as explained above). These instants come into being first as present instants and thereafter retain some kind of being as past instants.

Let us now turn to the view to which James came later, largely as a result of reflection on the difficulties we have seen in the earlier position.

In PU, especially chapters VII, and IX–XIII, and more fully in SPP, in chapters X and XI, James takes Zeno's paradoxes very seriously, as we will see more fully in the next section. With a brief statement of the paradox of the arrow, and a fuller account of that of Achilles and the tortoise, James suggests that the fundamental problem is how new being of any sort comes into the world. For if this is the world of real change which it seems to be, something must literally emerge into being out of nothing.

Applying this principle to the stream of a person's experience this means that new experience is always being added to old. James seems to assume that once an experience has occurred it belongs to reality forever after, however far it slips into the past, but that before it occurs as a present experience it is simply not there at all. Thus our stream of experience has a growing end and the last part of it is the experience which is present. Then it sinks into the past and it is another experience which is there at the growing point of my personal reality. This is a view very like the doctrine of absolute becoming as developed by C. D. Broad.[41] My account of James's view owes something to Broad's statement of it, but remains, I think, true to James's intentions.

Since James, at this stage, thought that our own personal experience is the type of all concrete reality, points made about its temporality apply to temporal processes in general. He is not, perhaps, too clear as to how the temporality pertaining to distinguishable processes, such as a stream of consciousness, relates to the temporality of the world as a whole, but he seems bound to hold that the universe is added to all at once across all distinct processes, your subjective experience and mine, and the innumerable processes of experience which underpin the rest of nature. For otherwise there would be no sense in which there is a reality with a definite content which has or has not had certain particular items added to it as yet, and whether something has or has not been added would be in the eyes of the beholder. Whether or not the theory of

---

Since instants of real time are just instants there is no real before and after within them, yet at each such instant of real time there is a specious present which contains its own specious before and after within it. And in spite of the word 'specious' the earlier-later relation as it holds within the specious present is quite real enough to provide us with a proper concept of before and after in general.

I do not see that this attempt at a more literal statement of the matter resolves any of the problems we have encountered. How can one instant of real time be followed by another, granted an infinite series of intervening instants must occur in between? And can it really be accepted, as seems implied on this account, that each stretch of sensory time which is at its own instant a specious present (or as we put it before, the occupant of the specious present) will have each smaller sensory event in a just slightly different position from what it occupied in earlier or later ones?

41   See Broad, 1923, Part I, chapter II.

relativity now obliges us to think differently of the matter, it would be hard to combine James's position with the denial of a universal common now. For if what is 'now' is 'frame relative' rather than absolute, it cannot possess the unique kind of concreteness which separates it off from what has been and will be as the growing point of reality.[42]

All this is quite consistent with the metaphysics or phenomenology of PP. The new development is the claim that reality must be added to all at once by experiences which have a certain temporal spread to them. For, so James now argues, if every stretch of experience with some temporal duration came into being piecemeal, by the occurrence first of earlier parts of its stretch, and then of later parts, no experience with duration could come into being at all. For the coming into complete being of every stretch of experience would need to be preceded by the coming into being of its first half, and the same would be true of *its* first half and so on *ad infinitum*. Thus no experience with a temporal stretch can come into being unless some stretches of experience come into being with their own duration all at once. And it will be equally true of nature as a whole that it can only develop because some processes stretched out in time come into existence as complete buds added to reality all at once. And since James thinks of all these complete buds of process, which are added all at once, on the analogy of our own specious present of experience, the specious present now emerges as the only *real* sort of present. (If there is a universal now of a kind I have suggested James's own outlook requires, it would seem that the specious presents of all different streams of experience or being enter into reality all at once. The phenomenologically unpersuasive character of such a claim, implying as it does that the specious present of all creatures has the same span, seems a real difficulty for James's view, and alien to other aspects of his thinking.)

So James now rules out two views of temporal process, which the PP position, given a wider metaphysical application, might suggest.

(1) Reality cannot grow by *the coming into being* one at a time of cross-sections of a stream of consciousness or other such real process pertaining to a single moving instant. These can only come into being as elements of a stretch of the stream (presumably of the length of a specious present) which comes into being all at once.

(2) Reality cannot grow by *the becoming present* (in successive states of affairs or instants of real time) of cross-sections of a stream of consciousness or other such real process as they come under the bridge of the specious present (or some more cosmic equivalent).

Thus entry into the specious present cannot be merely at the upstream edge of the bridge but must somehow occur all at once in a two-dimensional band across it. Otherwise no band of the stream can ever become present, since this requires that its earlier half has done so, and that requires that the earlier half of that has already done so, and so on. If James had had to choose between the

---

42   Compare Johnston, pp. 114–15.

two views thus ruled out, he would surely have chosen the former, but he is now convinced by Zeno's arguments that neither can be true (though perhaps he does not make much distinction between them).

What James concludes, in effect, is that reality is added to by increments which do not form a compact series, and can be genuine neighbours to each other. One increment occurs, and then another. However, he is still committed to the notion of a specious present which contains a before and an after, so that it is not a static instant which is added all at once, but a stretch of time with its own internal duration. Thus real moments of time, including a stretch of duration within them, replace the real instants of time of our previous discussion. This means that the metaphor of the stream now becomes unworkable if pressed and should only be used in connection with James's later position as a sleeping one (though I shall be considering another aspect of James's watery metaphors in the final section of this chapter).

How far does this leave us with anything like an instant? Well, perhaps James could have allowed real instants of which each real moment would contain an infinite number in a compact series. But I think his view was rather that, while a real moment has a temporal dimension stretched out in time, its intensive unity is such that it is mere conceptual mythology to suppose that there are real cross-sections constituting distinct instants. But should we regard the becoming of a moment of process as a whole as instantaneous? I doubt if that would be helpful. Rather should we think of the whole moment of process as coming into being as a single unit, but with a certain duration in scientific clock time, it making no sense to ask how long it takes for this fresh stretch of duration to be added to reality.

This model allows for two possibilities. Let the alphabet represent a series of successive stretches of experience shorter than a specious present. Consider now two successive specious presents, or moments of process, and let us call the contents of the first 'FGHIJ'. Now we have two alternative possibilities as to the character of the preceding and succeeding total units of becoming. On the first view, the preceding unit was ABCDE and the succeeding one was KLMNO. On the second view, the preceding unit was EFGHI and the succeeding unit will be GHIJK.

Which was James's view and which is the preferable view? The second may seem nearer to James's actual view, for he is anxious to insist on the intimacy of the link between the successive experiences. But it has the disadvantage we found in the PP position, that the same sensation has to be experienced more than once in successive different positions. Moreover, the first view seems to do more justice to whatever we may want to retain of the notion of consciousness as a stream.

Perhaps the best, and James's own, view lies between these two. Perhaps we first have DEFGH, then HIJKL, then LMNOP so that the successive moments match at their edges without every item occupying every position (on some plausible level of discrimination, since instants are now abandoned). Phenomenologically this seems to me to make fairly good sense.

It is likely to be objected that in coming to this view James gives up his essential claims about the continuity of the stream of consciousness. But is this true, and if so does it matter?

James himself says that, though, on this view, process is not continuous in the sense of consisting of instants which form a mathematically compact series, it is continuous in the more ordinary sense of containing no breaks. Nothing comes between one unitary stretch of process and the next one which replaces it. Nor is there a kind of intervening nothingness in which nothing occurs. Rather the end of one moment of process absolutely touches the beginning of the next. But what does touching mean? It means that somehow one just takes over from the other.

However, James holds that they do not merely touch but are somehow mixed up with each other. They are their own others as he puts it echoing Hegel; there is a kind of identity between them in spite of the difference. For when things are 'conjunctively' related in an immediate fashion James holds that there is a partial identity between them.[43] Thus while they are two in number they are not totally distinct existences in the traditional empiricist sense but rather flow into one another. (Disjunctive relations, it will be recalled, consist, in contrast, in various kinds of block to such a flowing of one experience into another.)

I have already suggested that successive real moments of process overlap by saying that what follows DEFGH is HIJKL. But one feels bound to put the question: Is the H which is present in each a universal or a particular? In short, is it a certain universal sensory quality which is exemplified at the end bit of the first and the beginning bit of the second specious present, or real moment of process, or is there an actual sensory particular common to both?

Perhaps James would reply that to press the question is mere scholasticism, resting on an undue contrast between identity and difference. For this is a matter on which he is quite close to Bradley.[44] However, insofar as the question has an answer he would, surely, have to regard H as the same particular in each case, for he is wanting to establish a real community between the successive moments. But this is highly problematic. For, after all, the second moment is supposed to come as a quite novel addition to reality, and how can it do so if some of it is already there? Perhaps it is a novelty with a bit of the old in it. But if H is as intimately a part of HIJKL, as James holds, it is difficult to see how it can occur first without it. James may reject this as intellectualist logic. But it is certainly no merely verbal fallacy. It is supposed to be of the very essence of the feel of H, as it occurs in the second moment, that it is leading into I, and it is hard to see how a particular with that essence can also be a particular which exists in DEFGH, without that feel.

The difficulties of interpretation here are akin to ones which arise in White-head's philosophy. For with Whitehead it is problematic whether what passes from one 'actual occasion' into another is strictly a particular present in the

---

43   See PU, p. 282.
44   See below at Part Two, Chapter Three, §4.

former, or a universal qualifying such a particular. Each philosopher regards the basic units of the world as specious presents in a stream of human consciousness, or some other process of a generically similar kind, of such mutual involvement that they do not need to be hitched onto each other by external relations. But each also insists that they are not so intimately one that they lose all distinctness. Both philosophers appreciate the force of the Bradleyan critique of relations but seek to avoid a complete monism. Whitehead thinks he can do so by improving our concepts, James by finding how to grasp things in a way more intimate than that of conceptual thought.

To me it seems that neither thinker's view of this most basic sort of relationship, or togetherness of one occurrence with another, is quite satisfactory. But perhaps James's position is the stronger, since he only regards his concepts as an inadequate pointer to what must be grasped non-conceptually. For a deeper understanding, he insists, we must fix our attention on the flux and not bother about the precise conceptualisation of it. Concepts are a static grid which cannot do justice to the real flux. True, we can improve them to some extent by relaxing the logic of identity in a somewhat Hegelian fashion, and seeing each total moment as its own other, that is as somehow identical, as well as different from, the one which follows it. But, in the end, conceptual thinking inevitably distorts reality to some extent.

Personally, while agreeing with James to a great extent on this aspect of reality, I am less ready to despair of conceptual thought. But I doubt if Whitehead has found quite the right way of conceptualising it. My own suggestion would be that H, as something which occurs in both real moments, is a universal, but that it occurs in the second in a specific version which intrinsically points to its having just occurred as a quality pertaining to the end bit of the previous one. (Thus the specific form of H is not only modified by the fact that it is at the beginning, rather than at the end, of a specious present, but by the fact that it follows on one at the end of a specious present with the unique character of the previous one.)

The main objection to the view of real temporal process as a series of intrinsically related moments is that it seems to ascribe a jerky quality to the stream of consciousness which conflicts with the deliverance of introspection. A possible answer is that, since what we strictly experience, is always what lies within one moment, we do not actually experience the transition from one to another, so do not experience the jerk.[45] But perhaps the real answer is that

---

45   Marcus Ford thinks that James's trouble over this can be avoided if we allow that the jerks take place at an unconscious level and that James's theory therefore requires the notion of unconscious experience in a manner the legitimacy of which Ford endorses. But it is not much of a solution to introduce the notion of unconscious experience. Even if there is such a thing, it is implausible to dissolve a problem in describing conscious experience by reference to its unconscious extensions. That is to return to that compositional view of consciousness against which James argued so well. In any case, I believe he is wrong in suggesting James ever

it is misleading to say that the moments follow on each other in jerks. That suggests an irregularity in the movement of something through a constant medium. But there is no such medium, for there is no time other than that which either falls within a moment or consists in one moment replacing another. There is nothing jerky in either case. The replacement is better called smooth than jerky but neither expression means much, since it makes no sense to talk of the time in which one follows from another. Time is the line formed by all the moments yet in being and these meet smoothly at their edges.

However, although this seems to me the best way of looking at it, it might not have satisfied James. For he seems to have believed that we do experience the transitions, we do somehow experience the one moment being taken over by the next. Thus he says that conjunctive relations are as much experienced as disjunctive relations. And, in spite of the doctrine of the specious present, James says that we do experience the way in which an idea leads to its object through some great stretch of time, far longer than a specious present. Perhaps we can make sense of this by allowing that each moment of sensory experience, as it comes all at once as an increment to reality, also comes with a sense of how it is carrying on from the previous moment, and more vaguely from earlier moments still.

Thus James's final view is that a stream of consciousness is added to by increments which come all at once with a sensible temporal spread, that these increments match at their edges and are in some sense partially identical, and that somehow the sequence of one from another is experienced inasmuch as its emerging from the earlier one, and from its predecessors, is included in the sense the next one has of its own being. And the processes which are the underlying reality of the physical world are of the same basic sort.

It may help clarify some of the issues to compare James's treatment of time consciousness with that of Edmund Husserl. This was probably influenced by the earlier PP doctrine of the stream of consciousness and can in fact be seen as an elaboration of the view of the specious present given there.[46]

Husserl seems to hold that we can only genuinely be conscious of something if we can be conscious of it for an instant.[47] Of course, we can be continually conscious of something over a period, but that requires being conscious of it at every instant of that stretch of time. This being so, the problem arises how we can be conscious at an instant of a change which cannot occur within that instant. The problem is especially sharp in the most basic case of all—that of

---

went back on his denial of unconscious experience. What he believed in, later and indeed then, were different consciousnesses going on in connection with one brain.

46   See Husserl, 1928. Richard Stevens writes of James's doctrine of the specious present as an anticipation of Husserl's account of our basic consciousness of time mainly in Husserl, *Time.* But he shows no awareness that, while the PP account can be interpreted in this way, James later moved to what was certainly a different view. See Stevens, pp. 62–65.

47   See Husserl, *Time,* p. 49 et passim.

our awareness of the temporality of our own consciousness, of the temporal flow of our own experiences, rather than of the objective processes they present.

Thus he reminds us that some have explained this by supposing that the earlier phases of the change of which we are perceptually conscious are present to us in the form of faded images. On this view I see or hear ABCD by seeing or hearing D together with a faded image of C, a rather more faded image of B, and a still more faded one of A. These are not like images of absent things in the normal sense, but have a special perceptual quality to them; still they are but images. That was roughly Brentano's view.

Husserl rejects such a view on the ground that it would not give us any real consciousness of a temporal pattern, but only a simultaneous situation with components having different degrees of vividness. It would mean, as we noted above, that a tune would be heard as a chord, an objection which Husserl notes as Brentano's against cruder versions of the same type of view.

Husserl's own view is that there is a special mental act, which he calls 'retention', through which we hark back to something as having been sensorily given just now. It is not awareness of an *image* of what is just past, but of what actually is just past, and of it as just past. For example, in hearing a continuous noise our sense that it has gone on for some time turns on its being presented both to perception and to retention.

Our perceptual experience is also always accompanied by a 'protention', a sense of what is to come. These acts contrast in that protention can be disappointed while retention is, so Husserl seems to claim, infallible.[48]

That there is something of the nature of retention and protention in our consciousness seems to me true. (Indeed my own suggestion that each real moment repeats the character of the end of its predecessor, in a form which points back to its occurrence there, could be taken as an alternative way of referring to it.) But surely retention cannot explain the awareness of change fully. Retention is a present act which points to something at a distance in the past. In the direct experience of change, in contrast, nothing is merely pointed to, but the whole change is given perceptually. It is a direct all-at-once experience of a temporal pattern, comparable to the direct experience of a spatial pattern.

The sight of a spatial array does not derive from distinct perceptions of spatial points somehow brought together. Even if something of the sort is true physiologically, it is not correct as an account of how any experiential realities are related. Rather is there a single experience of that total pattern as a unity. It is just the same with the brief changes we actually perceive. These are not a series of instantaneous perceptions glued together by their joint retention at a later instant but a single experience of a temporal pattern. Though there is such a thing as 'retention' in something like Husserl's sense it is not what provides our direct experience of change. All in all, it seems to me that James's is the

---

48   See Husserl, 1928, pp. 56–57, 72, 76, 80.

more convincing as an account of the direct experience of time than Husserl's, even though it is not without its difficulties.

Another philosopher for whom the nature of our experience of time is a central concern was Bergson.[49] Indeed his whole philosophy derives from views about the contrast between time as experienced and time as conceived. Lived time is in continual growth, but as it grows it is replete with the past, which never really disappears but is still present at the growing end of time. There is a wholeness to an action as we actually live through it. Somehow the action simply occurs in a unitary fashion and gets itself done all at once. To split up Achilles's passing the tortoise into a number of distinct actions distorts a process which occurs in one unitary sweep. That our concepts cannot do justice to this yields Zeno's paradoxes.

This is very close to James and was, indeed, an important influence on him. However, Bergson thought that duration grew in a continuous fashion, not by the successive addition of total increments in the way James supposes. It seems to me that James is right that Bergson was not quite satisfactory at this point.

As already suggested, it is Whitehead who, of all other philosophers, is closest to James on this topic. But though his epochal theory of time is developed with a mathematic thoroughness alien to James, I believe James's position the better. But James would certainly have been grateful for the endorsement by a mathematician of the impossibility of fully resolving Zeno's paradoxes by reference to developments in the mathematical understanding of the infinite and consequent need for a view of time akin to his.[50] The next section considers James's reflections on this topic.

(b) James, Bergson, and Zeno

§ So far is James from being the anti-metaphysical thinker he is often represented as, that his last work, *Some Problems of Philosophy* was intended to round out his metaphysical system. Sadly it was not completed but there is quite enough to make clear the essentially unpositivistic nature of his mind. Thus he shows a keen interest in that most basic and most scoffed at of metaphysical questions: Why is there anything at all rather than nothing? He does not even rule out the (epistemic) possibility that the answer may lie in something like an ontological proof. However, he thinks a question we may get further with is this: Is new being added bit by bit to the world, or is all being given once and for all in one single great block as absolute idealists believe? If it is the first, as it certainly seems to be, the further question arises: Is what is added essentially novel or just a fresh arrangement of what has already been given?

If the time-content of the world be not one monistic block of being, if some part,

---

49   See especially *Essai sur les données immédiates de la Conscience* (1889), *Matière et mémoire* (1896) and *L'Évolution créatrice* (1907), in Bergson.

50   See Whitehead, 1978, pp. 35, 68–69.

at least, of the future, is added to the past without being virtually one therewith, or implicitly contained therein, then it is absent really as well as phenomenally and may be called an absolute novelty in the world's history in so far forth.

Towards this issue of the reality or unreality of the novelty that thus appears, the pragmatic difference between monism and pluralism seems to converge. That we ourselves may be authors of genuine novelty is the thesis of the doctrine of free-will. That genuine novelties can occur means that from the point of view of what is already given, what comes may have to be treated as a matter of *chance*. We are thus led to the question: In what manner does new being come? Is it through and through the consequence of older being or is a matter of chance so far as older being goes?—which is the same thing as asking: Is it original, in the strict sense of the word?

We connect here again with what was said at the end of Chapter III. We there agreed that being is a datum or gift and has to be begged by the philosopher; but we left the question open as to whether we must beg it all at once or beg it bit by bit or in instalments. The latter is the more consistently empiricist view, and I shall begin to defend it in the chapter that follows.

SPP, pp. 145–46

§ To defend the idea that there is real novelty in the world against both absolute idealist and materialists is, indeed, one of James's main philosophical concerns. And he virtually identifies this question with that of the existence of free will, something which, we have seen, always had great emotional significance for him. Against the belief in the emerging of real novelty in the world there are two main opposing positions. Materialists think that the perceptual flux is an illusion, resulting from the unceasing re-combination, in new forms of mixture, of unalterable elements 'coeval with the world'[51] while absolute idealists think that everything is there at once in one eternal moment. Both views clash with our own direct realization that genuine novelty is continually coming into the world as our life develops. And as our personal consciousness is the best clue to the nature of reality in general, the reasonable belief is that genuinely novel being is continually arising in the world.[52] However, the question how it does so is complicated by conceptual problems about the infinite divisibility of time.

Actually it seems to me a mistake for James to tie up the two questions he is interested in so closely. First he has the question: Do things change by infinitely shaded gradations or by total increments added all at once? Secondly he has the question: Does change bring genuine novelty into being, or is it never more than a fresh arrangement of old material? If the answer to the first question is, as James thinks it, then the second question becomes: How genuinely novel is each such increment? But that is surely a matter of degree; it must be novel to some extent, since a fresh arrangement of old material is itself a novelty. And if reality could change by continuous gradation, in the way James thinks

---

51   SPP, p. 141.
52   See SPP, p. 151.

impossible, it could presumably change towards something as novel or as old hat as could be. However, even if it is a mistake to identify it with the question whether there is real novelty or only rearrangement of old materials, his discussion of the question whether change is continuous or incremental is of great interest.

§ We have already seen that James thinks that human experience increases by buds or drops which come all at once and that the same should be taken as true of all those processes which constitute the history of the world. This view rests partly on phenomenological grounds, but is also advanced as a solution to Zeno type problems. So let us now turn to James's discussion of those paradoxes, in particular that of Achilles and the tortoise.

James is sceptical of the claim made by Bertrand Russell and others that the new mathematics of the infinite has solved the Zeno paradoxes. In disagreeing with such 'superior minds' James confesses his mathematical incompetence and his foolhardiness in venturing into this territory. (These superior minds must include C. S. Peirce who, after James's death, wrote of his despair of clarifying the nature of 'this ridiculous little catch' to him.[53])

> Being almost blind mathematically and logically, I feel considerable shyness in differing from such superior minds, yet what can one do but follow one's own dim light?
>
> SPP, p. 183 (note 2)

I suppose one answer would be not to write upon the topic, but James would, of course, feel that he had something to communicate on it and I suspect he is right. I myself am still more mathematically incompetent than James, and should perhaps leave this part of his philosophy aside. However, it is so central to James's metaphysics that I must examine it, especially as I suspect that James may be right about the matter. I am encouraged in doing so by the fact that his approach is so similar to that of Whitehead who was certainly not chargeable with mathematical incompetence.

§ James describes the Achilles paradox clearly. The tortoise has a start in the race, and when Achilles reaches the tortoise's starting place, the tortoise has moved on to a further place. When Achilles reaches that place the tortoise has reached a further place again, and so on for ever. Each stretch Achilles has to run in this way is shorter than previous ones, but it seems he can only catch up with the tortoise by accomplishing an infinity of tasks of this sort.

The problem is not, so James insists, that Achilles would need an infinitely long time to overtake, so 'solutions' which point out the absurdity of this are besides the point. It is no good pointing out that if time is infinitely divisible any length of time supplies enough units. The point is rather that he must

---

53   See Perry, I, pp. 539–40.

accomplish an infinite number of tasks, not about how long he has in which to do this.

So James takes the paradox as posing a serious problem. But this is not because he thinks the idea of an infinite number of things of a certain sort is itself paradoxical. He does not even claim that it is only abstractions or possible things, rather than actual concrete individuals, which can be infinite in number. He is not unhappy, for example, with the supposition that the number of stars is infinite (nor, presumably, that the number of conscious individuals is so). And he does not agree with the Kantian view that this is because a star only exists until perceived as a possibility of experience, so that if the number of stars is infinite it is only in the form of an infinity of possibilities. Kant was right, according to James, that there cannot be an infinity of concrete things existing in what James calls the 'all form'. What he failed to see was that an infinity of such things can exist in what he calls the 'each form'.

James's point seems to be that an infinity of actual things cannot come together to make up a genuine concrete individual such as could be presented as a whole. To say that there is an infinite number of standing each-es is to say that the growing whole of counting them could never be completed however long one took. If one completed the count, the numerals used in doing so would have occurred in the all form and that is what James thinks impossible.

> The reader will note how emphatically in all this discussion, I am insisting on the distributive or piecemeal point of view. The distributive is identical with the pluralistic, as the collective is with the monistic conception. We shall, I think, perceive more and more clearly as this book proceeds, that *piecemeal existence is independent of complete collectibility*, and that some facts, at any rate, exist only distributively, or in form of a set of eaches which (even if infinite in number) need not in any intelligible sense either experience themselves, or get experienced by anything else, as members of an All.
>
> SPP, p. 170

It is not easy to be quite sure what James means by his contrast between the existence of a number of things in the all form as opposed to the each form. Sometimes, as the passage quoted suggests, he seems to mean by existence in the all form occurrence as a presentation to consciousness. However, that seems rather too restrictive an account of his meaning and existence in the all form seems to cover occurrence together in any sort of genuine concrete individual.

One immediate implication of this is that a physical thing, if it is a genuine individual, cannot be made up of an infinity of real parts. It would also follow that the universe is either made up of a finite number of real individuals or is not a genuine individual. This is a conclusion welcome to James, for part of what he means by his doctrine of a pluralistic universe is that the universe is not an individual thing. (Yet there are some aspects of his thought which seem to clash with such a position, for certainly he often talks of philosophy as having as its goal some kind of adjustment of the mind to the universe as a whole.) It is also a conclusion quite acceptable to a monist like Bradley who thought the notion of a real infinite absurd. But it would be fatal for a monism for which the universe is both a real, indeed the one real, individual, and composed of an infinite number of real parts. It would be possible to see Spinoza's as a monism of this sort, though perhaps his somewhat Bergsonian doctrine of the infinite distances him from such a position.

James sums his point up thus:

> So long as we keep taking such facts piecemeal and talk of them distributively as 'any' or 'each', the existence of them in infinite form offers no logical difficulty. But there is a psychological tendency to slip from the distributive to the collective way of talking, and this produces a sort of mental flicker and dazzle out of which the dialectic difficulties emerge. 'If each condition be there',—we say, 'then all are there, for there cannot be eaches that do not make an all.' Rightly taken, the phrase 'all are there', means only that 'not one is absent'. But in the mouths of most people, it surreptitiously foists in the wholly irrelevant notion of a bounded total.
>
> SPP, pp. 168–69

§ I once heard R. B. Braithwaite say, in reply to a monistically toned paper of my own, that the only proper sense of 'all' was that expressed by the universal quantifier. Perhaps this was a way of saying that proper statements about all things of a kind take them in what James would call the 'each' form. James, in contrast, has two uses for statements about all things of a certain kind. In the first they are conceived as making up a totality. In the second no such totality is supposed but something is said which is meant to apply to every such thing which might ever be identified. As James sees it, the things figuring in statements of the first kind cannot be infinite in number; those which figure in the second can be.

One main reason for the impossibility of the first kind of infinity seems to be that the growing act of counting the things in question could never be completed. Thus James's contrast between an infinity of things existing in the all form and one existing in the each form seems closely bound up with a contrast between a standing infinite, which he thinks possible, and a growing infinite, which he thinks impossible. (By a 'growing' infinite he evidently means a completed growing one, that is, a grown infinite.) That strongly suggests a Kantian view of a standing infinite as one which could grow into actuality as you counted it. However, that is not James's meaning, for he insists that there can be a standing infinite of actuals. But I must confess that I personally find it hard to conceive how there can be existing actual things which do not somehow belong in a real 'all together' and in this respect am in the Bradleyan camp.

However that may be, for James there may be an infinite number of stars, but they cannot make up a real unit together. For the same reason the inner articulation of matter must be finite and its ultimate units must be intensive unities without genuine parts (a view, of course, which makes good sense on a panpsychist conception of the physical). Most importantly for our present purposes a stretch of time which is a real individual in its own right cannot be made up of an infinity of shorter stretches of time.

On the discontinuity-theory, time, change etc., would grow by finite buds or drops, either nothing coming at all, or certain units of amount bursting into being 'at a stroke'. Every feature of the universe would on this view have a finite numerical constitution. Just as atoms, not half- or quarter-atoms are the minimum of matter that can be, and every finite amount of matter contains a finite number of atoms, so any amounts of time, space, change, etc., which we might assume would be composed of a finite number of minimal amounts of time, space, and change.

Such a discrete composition is what actually obtains in our perceptual experience. We either perceive nothing, or something already there in sensible amount. This fact is what in psychology is known as the law of the 'threshold'. Either your experience is of no content, of no change, or it is of a perceptible amount of content or change. Your acquaintance with reality grows literally by buds or drops of perception. Intellectually and on reflection you can divide these into components, but as immediately given, they come totally or not at all.

If, however, we take time and space as concepts, not as perceptual data, we don't well see how they can have this atomistic constitution. For if the drops or atoms are themselves without duration or extension it is inconceivable that by adding any number of them together times or spaces should accrue. If, on the other hand, they are minute durations or extentions, it is impossible to treat them as real minima. Each temporal drop must have a later and an earlier half, each spatial unit a right and a left half, and these halves must themselves have halves, and so on *ad infinitum*, so that with the notion that the constitution of things is continuous and not discrete, that of divisibility *ad infinitum* is inseparably bound up. This infinite divisibility of some facts, coupled with the infinite expansibility of others (space, time and number) has given rise to one of the most obstinate of philosophy's dialectic problems.

SPP, p. 154–56

§ The view that time is infinitely divisible has a special difficulty additional to that which arises with space. Thus he says that infinitely conditioned things, or what seem so, may be 'standing' or 'growing'. (By 'infinitely conditioned' he seems to mean simply existing in infinite number). A standing infinite of 'eaches', he has contended, is quite possible. Its meaning is simply that the growing infinity of counting them starting at one could not be completed. They can exist in the each form, that is, with no one of them missing. But a growing infinite is much more problematic, he claims, and indeed thinks it impossible.

If now we turn from static to growing forms of being, we find ourselves confronted by much more serious difficulties. Zeno's and Kant's dialectic holds good wherever, before an end can be reached, a succession of terms, endless by definition, must needs have been *successively* counted out. This is the case with every process of change, however small; with every event which we conceive as unrolling itself continuously.[54] What is continuous must be divis-

---

54   In truth, as Mr Noel Pinnington has explained to me, occupying all the points in

ible *in infinitum* and from division to division here you cannot proceed by addition (or by what Kant calls the successive synthesis of units) and touch a farther limit. You can indeed define what the limit ought to be, but you cannot reach it *by this process*. That Achilles should occupy *in succession* 'all' the points in a single continuous inch of space, is as inadmissible a conception as that he should count the series of whole numbers 1, 2, 3, 4, etc., to infinity and reach an end. The terms are not 'enumerable' in that order; and the order it is that makes the whole difficulty. An infinite 'regression' like the rearward perspective of time offers no such contradiction, for it comes not in that order. Its 'end' is what we start with.

SPP, p. 170–71

§ So James does not, it should be noted, accept the Kantian suggestion that, if time has always existed, there is a problem as to how the world can have ever reached its present state, since it seems that to do so it would have had to complete a real infinity of process. Thus he says that the past is really a static rather than a growing infinite. For we count its units out from our end, and have a definite starting point, and there is no reason to think that our counting its units out backwards, or reconstructing its phases starting from this end, would have an end. The counting out, or reconstructing of the processes which filled it out, is just like counting the stars, and may be something which could not be finished. [55]

I confess to some dissatisfaction with this statement of the matter. It seems to meet an ontological point with an irrelevant epistemological one. But perhaps I am just parading my difficulties with the notion of things existing which belong together in no 'all'. At any rate, James seems to think that the volume, so to speak, of past events is static, just *there*, and need not be supposed to exist in the all form any more than do the stars at any one time; it is only at the end surface where it is being added to that there is process. And it is here where reality is in the making that James thinks the postulation of a real infinite problematic. (I shall be siding with Bradley's criticism of any such notion in Part Two.[56])

---

the line is a greater challenge than this since the number of such points is not even a so-called countable infinite whose members could be put in one-to-one correspondence with the natural numbers.

55   See SPP, p. 171.
56   If, as James seems to hold, all past time is somehow just there, as (on ordinary views of the matter at least) the stars are, then perhaps the volume of past events is in a sense static (apart from the surface at which it is being added to by new events coming into being). In that case perhaps he is right that it is no stranger that there should be an infinite number of such events than that there should be an infinite number of stars. Neither the past events nor the stars form any sort of whole; it is simply that a process of identifying them one by one, according to some method of specification which would eventually catch up with each, would never come to an end. But I shall be arguing later that the view that somehow the past is simply

§ But now we come to Achilles and the tortoise. On the view that space and time are continua in the mathematical sense, Achilles has to accomplish an infinite number of tasks and these must belong together as a real event occurring in the all form. That modern mathematics provides us with a way of describing what happens which avoids merely verbal paradox does not mean that it describes anything we can think of as really occurring in the concrete.

We can get to the rock bottom of the problem, thinks James, if we see it simply as a question as to how some line of real temporal process grows. Suppose my stream of consciousness at one moment ends at T, then the question is how it can ever grow so that it now ends at U. If it is to grow continuously, then it must first add on the length of half TU. But before that it must add on the length of half the half of TU, and before that of half the half of that and so on. In short it can never add on any length because it must first add on half that length. The only solution, according to James, is to suppose that it adds on some length like TU in one indivisible jump. Conceptually TU may still be thought of as infinitely divisible, and it will, indeed, if it is a specious present, have an earlier and a later aspect to it, but it will not consist of genuinely distinct parts which have come into reality one by one.

The conclusion must be that reality grows by buds each of which comes as a whole. The concrete experiences in which it consists can only change by sensible amounts. That this is difficult to put conceptually is, for James, just one of many examples of the way in which the conceptual transformation of experience makes it more puzzling than before. We can only resolve our puzzlement by dipping our minds into the actual flux of experience and noting how nature, in the form of our own conscious lives, does the trick by coming in pulses each of which is an indivisible moment of experience containing its own felt time as a unity within it.

> The antinomy of mathematically continuous growth is thus but one more of those many ways in which our conceptual transformation of perceptual experience makes it less comprehensible than ever. That being should immediately and by finite quantities add itself to being, may indeed be something which an onlooking intellect fails to understand; but that being should be identified with the consummation of an endless chain of units (such as 'points'), no one of which contains any amount whatever of the being (such as 'space') expected to result, this is something which our intellect not only fails to understand, but which it finds absurd.
>
> SPP, pp. 185–86

So James holds an 'ephocal' view of time like that developed later by Whitehead. Such a view has two main merits for him. (1) It solves the real

---

there as a part of reality, continually added to by the coming into being of fresh events in what we call the present, is unsatisfactory, though it does some justice to an aspect of common sense. See Part Two, Chapter Four, section 3(e).

problem posed by Zeno's paradoxes. (2) It explains how we can experience temporal transition. For we can only really experience change if there is change which occurs somehow all at once within a single experience, and the buds or increments which are added to reality all at once, each with its own stretch of duration, may be supposed to be just such single experiences.

§ It would seem that these experiences which come 'all at once' might have a duration in a clock time which is a continuum in a mathematical sense and thus come together, once they are in being, to form a longer continuum. Even so, time in a more ultimate sense would consist in the series of these real moments of process. And since this is not compact it does not constitute a genuine continuum. Does this mean that James has abandoned the idea that consciousness is continuous in the sense in which he originally insisted that it was? James's comment on this is:

> The mathematical definition of continuous quantity as 'that between any two elements or terms of which there is another term' is directly opposed to the more empirical or perceptual notion that anything is continuous when its parts appear as immediate next neighbors, with absolutely nothing between.
>
> SPP, p. 187

In arguing for this epochal view of time by reference to Zeno's paradoxes James admits his uneasiness in seeming to propound a view about the nature of reality on the basis of *a priori* argument just as did Kant and Renouvier, when they used the paradoxes and antinomies of the infinite to support their own view of things. However, James says he is not so much trying to prove his view by abstract argument as formulating an empirical hypothesis which avoids the conceptual puzzles of the main alternatives.

Of Zeno's four paradoxes of motion it is that of Achilles and the tortoise on which James mostly dwells; however, they are all relevant to his position, and he refers briefly also to that of the arrow. The alleged motionlessness of an arrow in flight at any one instant, in which it could not take up more space than its own volume, was meant to show the difficulty of an atomic view of time. Bergson saw Zeno's paradoxes as supporting his view that movement is a total sweep of change not made up of static parts.[57] James would conclude instead that, though there are ultimate units of process, they are not internally timeless. Rather, there is a real change within each which is an indivisible sweep of alteration not made up of static parts. Thus he differs from Bergson in distinguishing between changes which fall within such a unit, and those which consist in or require a series of them.

§ Still, James allies himself with Bergson in holding that Zeno's paradoxes show that our concepts distort reality by imposing a kind of grid upon the world inadequate to real process. And in SPP, chapter XI (pp. 176–88) he examines the claim, as presented in particular by Bertrand Russell in *The Principles of Mathe-*

---

57   See Bergson, pp. 74–77 and 754–62.

matics (1903) that modern mathematics, in particular Cantor's investigations of infinite numbers, resolves these paradoxes at the level of straight conceptual thought and without appeal to an epochal view of time.

James insists that these developments do not affect the main thing to be learnt from Zeno, namely, that time in the ordinary sense cannot be adequately conceptualised. For Russell only resolves the difficulties by moving to just such a static vision of reality as it was precisely Zeno's purpose to support against common sense.

> The point-continuum illustrates beautifully my complaint that the intellectu-
> alist method turns the flowing into the static and discrete. The buds or steps of
> process which perception accepts as primal gifts of being, correspond logically
> to the 'infinitesimals' (minutest *quanta* of motion, change or what not) of which
> the latest mathematics is supposed to have got rid. Mr. Russell accordingly
> finds himself obliged, just like Zeno, to treat motion as an unreality: 'Weier-
> strass,' he says, 'by strictly banishing all infinitesimals has at last shown that
> we live in an unchanging world, and that the arrow, at every moment of its
> flight, is truly at rest (*Philosophy of Mathematics*,[58] p. 347). 'We must entirely
> reject the notion of a state of motion', he says elsewhere; 'motion consists
> merely in the occupation of different places at different times . . . There is no
> transition from place to place, no consecutive moment, or consecutive position,
> no such thing as velocity except in the sense of a real number which is the limit
> of a certain set of quotients' (p. 473). The mathematical 'continuum', so called,
> becomes thus an absolute discontinuum in any physical or experiential sense.
> Extremes meet; and although Russell and Zeno agree in denying perceptual
> motion, for the one a pure unity, for the other a pure multiplicity takes its place.
>
> SPP, p. 186

Although I find James's argument convincing I am not well qualified to give an opinion on it. His main point is that the mathematical treatment of continuous change by the calculus combined with a satisfactory theory of infinite numbers does not meet the point that a real unit cannot be made up of an infinite number of genuinely concretely existing parts.

§ James, as I have said, seems ambivalent as to whether it is standard concepts which fail to do justice to reality, and in particular temporal process, or concepts as such. His official view is the second but one might well see him as groping for a more satisfactory conceptualisation of time. This conceptualisation would not, of course, be the reality, but that is no reason for saying that it does not properly describe it. Some think that such a conceptualisation was accomplished by Whitehead. According to his view, partly echoing Aristotle's, the extensive continua of space and time are infinitely divisible but not infinitely divided. There is in principle no limit to the real units of space or process which could have been included within any part of it, but what is actually included in any such part must be finite. Thus the extensive continuum is in fact articulated

---

58   James, or his editor, here thus misnames Russell's *The Principles of Mathematics*.

into definite units but does not of itself determine how many of these there are. I am inclined to think that this may be the best scheme into which to fit the view that experience comes in complete buds or drops in the manner James describes.

The upshot would seem to be that any real line of process in the world consists in a finite number of real moments, each including an intensive before and after within it, but without real parts. The infinite divisibility of time would consist in the fact that there always could have been, instead, a process, slotting into the same stretch of clock time, consisting in a larger number of such moments than in fact there were.

However, there is some difficulty in squaring this view with the existence of a universal NOW, of a kind to which James was surely committed by his view of time, whether he realized it or not (and the denial of which, I believe, threatens the ultimate coherence of Whitehead's thought). For, as we saw above, it is hard to see how simultaneity can be an absolute if different processes are articulated into units on a different scale. Since personally I accept the view that process consists in a series of such real moments, but do not accept those aspects of the ordinary view of time which point to such a universal NOW, I am not troubled by this problem. For I accept it, not as necessary for the ultimate reality of becoming in the sense which implies the existence of a universal NOW, but as offering the best account of the nature of temporal experience and the best resolution of what I think real problems in the concept of infinite divisibility.

(c) Panpsychism Supported by Panexperientialism and by Considerations about Causation

We have already seen the strong pressures within James's thought moving him towards a panpsychist view of the world. He believed that the only fundamental reality was experience. Besides actual experience there is only possible experience, and this is not an addition to the sum of what strictly is, but only a truth about what may come to be under certain circumstances. (To be quite accurate, his claim was rather that, if there is anything other than experience, it must remain unknowable and can play no part in any satisfactory conception which we can form. It should, therefore, not be invoked to explain anything.)

I do not say that this argument is entirely satisfactory. As a panexperientialist myself I would not deny the logical propriety of postulating something other than experience, if doing so seems necessary to explain it. I would argue rather that (a) we cannot form any positive conception of anything other than experience and (b) we can form a satisfactory view of the world, and have reason to believe it true, which does not appeal to some other-than-experience (of which we can form no positive conception) as what produces our experience in some unknown way. Still, the upshot is that I support James's quest for a panexperientialist account of things.

A panexperientialist is not necessarily a panpsychist. The panexperientialist believes that there is nothing actual except experience, but, *prima facie*, it is open to him to say that a physical object can exist unexperienced as a system of possible experiences. However, that view is not in the end very satisfactory. It leaves human and animal experience as the sole actuality existing in a kind of void, with an inexplicable set of conditional facts about what might come into the actuality of experience if that takes certain turns. James was surely right not to remain satisfied with a phenomenalism which reduces physical reality at large to the category of mere possibility. (Phenomenalists sometimes say that to put it like this is to confuse the level of the physical with that of the sensory and that what is only possible at the latter level may be actual at the former.[59] But it remains the case that at the level of genuine being phenomenalists reduce most physical reality to mere possibility.) If panexperientialism is to avoid this and give physical reality a genuinely categorical being, apart from its presentation to observers, it must conceive it as psychic or experiential in its own inner being. To do so is to supplement panexperientialism with panpsychism.

Panpsychism received further support for James from his reflections on causation.[60] For, as we have seen, he came to think that causation, and indeed relationship in general, could only be understood on an analogy with the experience of efficacy which we ourselves live through. Thus the real causes of our experiences, insofar as they do not lie within our own streams of experience, and those of other similarly conscious individuals, must belong to streams of experience in which causation occurs in something like the same felt sense. Our brains, bodies, and our physical environments must consist in complexes of streams of experience which are of the same generic sort as our own personal streams of consciousness, though they will presumably lack those higher aspects in which thought, in any usual sense, consists.

James thinks that this panpsychist view of things, intellectually compulsive in itself, is somewhat favourable to a religious outlook. For to think along panpsychist lines is to recognize that the world is a rather more personal sort of affair than it seems on that scientific account which so many think the destined final way of understanding things. For panpsychism returns us to that more animistic or spiritual type of explanation usually now dismissed as primitive. It is understandable enough that many should feel that religion is a survival of primitive habits of thought that we should now be growing out of and that scientific understanding has shown that personal animistic ways of understanding the world do not take us to the real truth of things, which is essentially impersonal. That people should first understand nature in a thoroughly personal and animistic way was inevitable. But mature human minds should have moved beyond any such conception by now.

> The extraordinary value, for explanation and prevision, of those mathematical and mechanical modes of conception which science uses, was a result that could not possibly have been expected in advance. Weight, movement, velocity, direction, position, what thin, pallid, uninteresting ideas! How could the

---

59   See Ayer, *Essays*, p. 146 et ff. and *Foundations*, pp. 226–28.
60   See SPP, pp. 210–14 and above at Chapter Three, §5.

richer animistic aspects of Nature, the peculiarities and oddities that make phenomena picturesquely striking or expressive, [and James gives examples of these ways of understanding things in Aristotle, Christian Wolff and others] fail to have been first singled out and followed by philosophy as the more promising avenue to the knowledge of Nature's life? Well, it is still in these richer animistic and dramatic aspects that religion delights to dwell. . . .

Pure anachronism! says the survival-theory [for which religion is a survival of a merely primitive mode of thought]. . . .

In spite of the appeal which this impersonality of the scientific attitude makes to a certain magnanimity of temper, I believe it to be shallow, and I can now state my reason in comparatively few words. That reason is that, so long as we deal with the cosmic and the general, we deal only with the symbols of reality, but *as soon as we deal with private and personal phenomena as such, we deal with realities in the completest sense of the term.* I think I can easily make clear what I mean by these words.

The world of our experience consists at all times of two parts, an objective and a subjective part, of which the former may be incalculably more extensive than the latter, and yet the latter can never be omitted or suppressed. The objective part is the sum total of whatsoever at any given time we may be thinking of, the subjective part is the inner 'state' in which the thinking comes to pass. What we think of may be enormous—the cosmic times and spaces, for example,—whereas the inner state may be the most fugitive and paltry activity of mind. Yet the cosmic objects, so far as the experience yields them, are but ideal pictures of something whose existence we do not inwardly possess but only point at outwardly, while the inner state is our very experience itself; its reality and that of our experience are one. A conscious field *plus* its object as felt or thought of *plus* our attitude towards the object *plus* the sense of a self to whom the attitude belongs—such a concrete bit of personal experience may be a small bit, but it is a solid bit as long as it lasts; not hollow, not a mere abstract element of experience, such as the 'object' is when taken all alone. It is a *full* fact, even though it be an insignificant fact; it is of the *kind* to which all realities whatsoever must belong; the motor currents of the world run through the like of it; it is on the line connecting real events with real events. That unsharable feeling which each one of us has of the pinch of his individual destiny as he privately feels it rolling out on fortune's wheel may be disparaged for its egotism, may be sneered at as unscientific, but it is the one thing that fills up the measure of our concrete actuality, and any would-be existent that should lack such a feeling or its analogue, would be a piece of reality only half made up. [James's footnote: Compare Lotze's doctrine that the only meaning we can attach to the notion of a thing as it is 'in itself' is by conceiving it as it is *for* itself; i.e., as a piece of full experience with a private sense of 'pinch' or inner activity of some sort going with it.]

If this be true, it is absurd for science to say that the egotistic elements of experience should be suppressed. The axis of reality runs solely through the egotistic places,—they are strung upon it like so many beads. To describe the world with all the various feelings of the individual pinch of destiny, all the various spiritual attitudes, left out from the description—they being as describable as anything else—would be something like offering a printed bill of fare as the equivalent for a solid meal. Religion makes no such blunder.

VRE, pp. 497–99

James was not claiming that panpsychism points necessarily to a religious conception of things, only that it coheres well therewith and removes one usual ground of objection thereto, namely, that to move from impersonal scientific explanation to explanation by reference to the divine or supernatural is to abandon the hard won victories of the scientific point of view. For, if panpsychism is right, scientific conceptions and explanations use a system of abstract symbols which depicts the structure of reality in a way very useful for its technological control but telling us little about what it really is that is being thus controlled. Thus even the physical explanation of the most grossly physical of phenomena represents simply our grasp on what in its inner being is psychic. The full account of what is going on would be in terms of a flow of feelings of tension and fulfilment of a variety of qualitative kinds. So when religion insists on explaining its phenomena by reference to divine personality, rather than in reductive physical terms, it is not turning to a reality different in its generic inner nature from that studied by natural science. Rather is it appealing to a type of explanation which must in the end apply pervasively throughout the universe and of which scientific explanation only gives an abstract sketch convenient for purposes of control (and perhaps all that is presently available).

It is thus inept to object to the explanation of religious experiences by reference to a personal divine source on the grounds that it represents a type of personalist explanation which science has taught us to supersede. For rival materialistic explanations of religion, as of anything else, must themselves simply be a symbolic substitute for a more ultimate explanation by reference to something like, even if humbler in content than, personal feeling. Every explanation of a phenomenon must turn in the end on the way in which different streams of experience interact by flowing into each other. What is in question, then, between a naturalistic and a supernatural explanation of religious phenomena is not the use of impersonal or personal categories but explanation by reference only to lower forms of experience versus that which appeals also to higher forms.

Thus whatever the true explanation of things, religious explanations are at least of the type to which all ultimate explanation must belong. Religion, in concerning itself with the personal, is concerning itself with actual reality in its concreteness, whether it gets the details right or wrong. James even suggests that the personalised view of the world, in occultism, may have more to be said for it than the learned now think. Thus

> the rigorously impersonal view of science might one day appear as having been a temporarily useful eccentricity rather than the definitively triumphant position which the sectarian scientist at present so confidently announces it to be.
>
> VRE, p. 501, note

What then is distinctive of a religious view of the world? James lists three beliefs and two psychological characteristics which may serve to define it. The three beliefs are:

1. That the visible world is part of a more spiritual universe from which it draws its chief significance;

2. That union or harmonious relation with that higher universe is our true end;

3. That prayer or inner communion with the spirit thereof—be that spirit 'God' or 'law'—is a process wherein work is really done, and spiritual energy flows in and produces effects, psychological or material, within the phenomenal world.

The two psychological characteristics are:

4. A new zest which adds itself like a gift to life, and takes the form either of lyrical enchantment or of appeal to earnestness and heroism.

5. An assurance of safety and a temper of peace, and, in relation to others, a preponderance of loving affections.

VRE, pp. 485–86

He looked forward to a science of religions which might move modern man to a reasonable assessment of the truth-value of these claims and hence of the degree to which the psychological attitudes can find a secure basis in them. In the next and final section of Part One I shall consider James's own final guess as to its most likely results, and turn again to his claim that in this matter the will to believe has its rights as against a purely intellectual approach.

§3. Religious Conclusions

(a) The Religious Motivation of James's Thought

The most powerful force behind James's philosophising was undoubtedly a religious quest. He wished to come to terms with the whole of things and to find, if possible, a conception of reality which was essentially religious, but which divested religion of pre-scientific aspects and avoided logical sophistry. This conception would also have to be more satisfying to our moral nature (or at least to James's) than was either traditional theism or the spiritual monism of absolute idealists like Bradley, Royce, and his father.

There have been many psychological studies of James's motivations. Those who dwell on them are only following James's own view that one should see a man's philosophy in relation to the man himself. My concern, however, is with his actual claims, and the reasons he gave in their support, or which we may find for or against them, rather than with their psychological dynamics. Moreover, I am concerned with these claims mainly on their more abstract metaphysical side. So in turning now to a consideration of what seem to have been his final conclusions about religion I shall bypass much of what he says about the psychological enrichment which religion brings to human life, important as his study of saintliness and mysticism is. Thus I shall only consider James's theorising about the psychology of religious experience insofar as that bears directly on issues of metaphysics.[61]

The main work for James's religious views is *The Varieties of Religious Experience*, but this should be taken in conjunction with various other writings. Since in many ways James's attitude to religion remained constant, I shall draw on earlier writings as well. My presentation will give an air of formal tidiness to James's thinking about religion not quite true to the original. But in this context, at least, we may agree with James that if truth consisted in a mere copy of the original it would be redundant, and insist that the menu provided here is not the meal of James's own writing. So while claiming truth for my account of James's thought I will not claim that it provides the full resonances of the original.

The religious position which James tentatively supported postulated the existence of a finite God whose consciousness is continuous with our own subliminal consciousness. The latter is thereby the medium through which our consciousness and behavioural orientation is on occasion open to his influence.

James offers two distinct kinds of support for this religious view of things. The first ground is evidential. There is some evidence for it from mystical and other religious experiences. The second ground is passional. Belief in a God of this sort is to be commended, at least to some of us, as emotionally sustaining and morally invigorating. Since it is cognitively a possible view of the world, and evidence and reasoning leave it on a par with such alternatives to it as are not evidentially or conceptually objectionable, we have every right to believe it, and good reason to exercise this right.

Besides evidential and passional grounds, religious beliefs have been recommended on rationalistic or *a priori* grounds. But James thinks these carry little or no weight. *A priori* proofs of God's existence are by and large worthless. We have seen that for James absolute idealist attempts to prove the existence of the Absolute fail and he thought this equally true of *a priori* attempts to prove more traditional forms of theism (though he does not entirely mock the ontological proof). He also rejects such traditional *a posteriori* proofs as the argument from design, to which he thought Darwin had put paid.[62] The sole evidential proof to which he appeals is that of religious experience.

(b) The Argument from Religious Experience

The Varieties of Religious Experience consists largely in descriptions, culled from many sources, of many different forms of religious experience, though the examples are almost entirely Western and Christian. James believes that religious institutions are a derivative from, and a poor substitute for, what really

---

61   A fairly helpful discussion of James's psychology of religion is Levinson, 1981. However, Levinson can be fairly misleading about James's philosophical positions.

62   See, e.g., WB, p. 43; VRE, pp. 437–38.

matters about religion, the direct sense of contact with the divine by individuals.[63]

As is well known, he distinguishes the once born and the twice born type of
religious consciousness. The former experiences a joyous sense of identification
with the divine, without any prior passage through the valley of the shadow of
death, while the latter only reaches it after a sense of abandonment and
desolation. For the first, mystical experiences are the peak of their typical way
of being in the world; for the second, they come as offering salvation from a
complete wreckage of the soul. In both there is the same sense of being
somehow in union with a greater consciousness than their personal one. This
takes its most humanly valuable form when it is the inspiration for saintliness.

Mystical experiences are essentially ineffable, but one can say, at least, that
they carry the sense of being taken over by some larger power from which
saving experiences come. And they do not feel to their subject like merely
subjective feelings. Rather do they carry the irresistible conviction that he is
somehow continuous with a larger whole with which they bring him into a
fuller than normal relationship. Thus he feels 'grasped and held by a superior
power'. And they bring an intense sense that reality is one and good, and that
the individual is simply an element in this divine unity.

Thus mystical experience comes with an apparently noetic quality, presenting itself as informative about reality.[64] And the information it seems to bring
is typically of a monistic and optimistic character, though this may be down-
played by those who interpret it in terms of a religious orthodoxy which this
would threaten.

Of course, the optimism of the twice born is not of the easy type of the once
born. Rather is it the conviction that the apparent badness of the world, and of
oneself, is not the last word. Still, in their different ways, mystical experiences
of both types seem to carry the message that the totality of things is supremely
good.

That, at least, is the message they seem to bring with such force to their
subject. And such a monistic interpretation is certainly the initially most natural
one of what is going on. But it is doubtful, thinks James, that we are bound to
interpret the deliverance of these experiences in quite such a strongly monistic
way even if we acknowledge them as genuinely noetic. For the core content of
the mystical experience is the sense of being part of, or at least continuous with,

---

63   It was this aspect of his approach to religion which led Santayana to charge him
      with religious slumming. For Santayana religion was a cultural tradition rather
      than a weird experience of isolated individuals. Others complained too at James's
      seeming tendency to associate religion so strongly with experiences which are
      properly regarded as pathological. For some defence of James against such then
      current criticisms see Flournoy, 1917. This book is an excellent untechnical expo-
      sition of James's leading ideas by a personal friend.
64   See VRE, pp. 380–81.

a divine life. This does not require that the divine reality be the only reality, and is compatible with its having a resistant other, which we may join with it in fighting. Either way, if mystical experience is not a delusion, there really is a larger world of consciousness than that with which the ordinary facts of nature acquaint us, and the best solution to our woes lies in entering into conscious unity with it.

But mystical experiences are of various types which may call for different explanations. All point to a reality beyond that open to our senses or ordinary thought. But this reality may be complex and various, and different sorts of mysticism may bring contact with different elements of this larger world. Some mysticisms, indeed, seem to put people in touch with the diabolic rather than the divine. But all are either delusive or forms of contact with a larger and more spiritual world than that of ordinary life.

> It is evident that from the point of view of their psychological mechanism, the classic mysticism and these lower mysticisms spring from the same mental level, from that great subliminal or transmarginal region of which science is beginning to admit the existence, but of which so little is really known.
>
> VRE, p. 426

Still, most mystical experiences are of continuity with something appropriately called divine. But do they really establish, in a way which should bring conviction to all reasonable persons, that there really is such a reality? James answers thus:

> I must give my answer to this question as concisely as I can.
>   In brief my answer is this . . .
>   (1) Mystical states, when well developed, usually are, and have the right to be, absolutely authoritative over the individuals to whom they come.
>   (2) No authority emanates from them which should make it a duty for those who stand outside of them to accept their revelations uncritically.
>   (3) They break down the authority of the non-mystical or rationalistic consciousness, based upon the understanding and the senses alone. They show it to be only one kind of consciousness. They open out the possibility of other orders of truth, in which so far as anything in us vitally responds to them we may freely continue to have faith.
>
> VRE, pp. 422–23

So we can sum up the purely evidential aspect of the matter, as James sees it, thus. Mystical experiences inevitably seem to their subject to establish that there is a divine reality of some sort with which he has had contact. But it does not follow that this is really established thereby. The most it can reasonably force the sceptic to acknowledge is that he has no right to be confident that there is no such reality and that a naturalistic account of the world is complete. Thus the existence of mystical experience should check any 'premature closing of our accounts with reality'.

(c) The Passional Grounds for Religious Belief

§ Mystical experience makes religious belief a serious cognitive option but does not prove its claims. Likewise the success of purely naturalistic accounts of so much that was once explained by divine causation favours, without establishing, a purely naturalistic world view. That leaves many of us, so James thought, in precisely that situation where the will or right to believe has place. This, it will be remembered, is the right to choose that one of a pair or set of alternative beliefs, which will best serve our emotional and volitional needs, when there are no adequate empirical or rational grounds for decision, and the option between them is momentous, forced, and live. An option is momentous when it matters greatly to us in which alternative we put our faith, forced when our style of life will inevitably express one of the alternatives, however much we decline any express affirmation, and live when each seriously solicits our assent. These are, in fact, the circumstances in which James thought his contemporaries typically found themselves when they hesitated between a religious and a naturalistic view of the world. So he recommended them to follow him in making the choice on the basis of the promise which each view holds of being helpful morally, volitionally, and emotionally. Moreover, the precise position adopted might properly reflect the comparative value one placed upon such alternative emotional and volitional goods as peace of mind and moral vigour.

Although he does not appeal to this right in set terms in his later discussions of religion, he is frequently guided by it or something very similar. It is in this spirit that *The Varieties of Religious Experience* investigates (and endorses) the claims of saintliness, and other human products of religion, to be a great (indeed the greatest) human good. And in describing what he calls 'the faith ladder' at the end of *Some Problems of Philosophy* he speaks in favour of a very similar way of arriving at beliefs. So rather than bother with minute differences of formulation, I shall express James's final conclusions in terms of the original will or right to believe doctrine.

§ What then is the nature of the religious option which faces our passional nature? Actually James saw the options as fourfold rather than twofold, though the first was decreasingly live. (They are not, I think, ever tabulated as neatly as this, but are pervasively treated as such.[65])

First, there was orthodox theism, as developed in the Christian tradition, and as understood by its philosophical and theological exponents.

Secondly, there was naturalism or materialism.

Thirdly, there was pantheistic absolute idealism.

Fourthly, there was the notion of a finite God. Such a God would be a morally perfect being of enormous, but still only limited, power, with a real resistant other to cope with, whether in the form of the natural world or evil spirits. Thus He would not only provide the supporting arms which the religious person

---

65   See, in particular, VRE, chapter XVIII, and PU, chapter I.

looks for but also that opportunity to join with Him in a real struggle against evil which the more 'masculine' religious consciousness seeks as well. Although this was a novel position in formal philosophy or theology James thought it effectively that of the bulk of religious believers.

§ 1. For James the first option was decreasingly serious.[66] As advocated by scholastic philosophers it became a logomachy with little hold on living reality or on the hearts of men.[67] At best their God was the keystone of a conceptual edifice with an aesthetic appeal to a certain type of mind.[68] (However, James had more sympathy with the ontological argument than one might have expected. His objection seems to have been that it was not too clear what it established if it established anything.[69])

In more recent times orthodox thinkers relied more on empirical considerations than on the *a priori* arguments of the scholastics, appealing primarily to the argument from design.[70] This was certainly an improvement, as James saw it, for it makes the existence of God a hypothesis for the explanation of undoubted empirical facts, such, in particular, as the adaptedness of organisms to their environment. Unfortunately for orthodoxy, however, it is no longer the best hypothesis on offer, since the phenomena are better explained on Darwinist principles.

Traditional theism also suffers from its incapacity to deal adequately with the problem of evil, a problem which seems more serious to the more sensitive modern mind. However, James thought it better off in this respect than the third position. For in some of its versions, at least, it allows that God has produced a real other for himself in giving man free will.

In fact, of course, traditional Christianity has not so much found the evil in the world an intellectual embarrasment as enthusiastically insisted on it. However, James does not pay much attention to the orthodox view that the earth is a vale of tears given over to destructive forces as the consequence of Adam's fall. For him traditional or conventional Christianity is represented rather by the optimistic eighteenth century insistence on the force of the argument from design. As such, it suffers not only from the fact that Darwinism gives a better explanation of the appearance of design in the universe but from the unprepossessing character of nature on the closer look it provides. Nature, for James, was primarily a scene of horrible pointless destructiveness, 'red in tooth and claw', though he certainly also responded to it in a more positive, and late in life even mystical, way.[71]

---

66   See VRE, pp. 436–42, and PU, p. 29.
67   See VRE, pp. 446.
68   See VRE, p. 456.
69   See SPP, chapter 3, but compare ERE, p. 272 et ff.
70   See VRE, p. 438.
71   On the horrors of nature, see, for example, VRE, pp. 163–64; for James's love of wilderness see, for example, Perry, I, 348–51, 355, 377, etc. Regarding our greater sensitivity today James notes '[t]hat the monarchical type of sovereignty was, for

So this first option rests either on vacuous *a priori* conceptualising and reasoning, or on a flawed induction. The upshot is that James thought that orthodox Judaeo-Christian belief had decreasing appeal to those of a questioning mind. (He concerned himself only with the more purely monotheistic element in Christianity, showing little interest either in the figure of Jesus or in the doctrine of the Trinity.) For most it is no longer a living option.

§ 2. Naturalism or materialism, James recognized, was certainly a living option then as never before. Materialism, it should be noted, as the term was understood in James's day, did not affirm the nonexistence of anything non-physical as it does when advocated by modern materialists like D. M. Armstrong and D. C. Dennett. It was the view, rather, that nature develops by natural laws, that it has no purpose, whether in itself or for a God who has created it, and that consciousness is a byproduct of brain activity.

As James saw it, such a view of the world was favoured both by Darwinism and by increasing knowledge of the dependence of consciousness on brain process. Moreover, our increasing sensitivity to the horror of so much human suffering makes it more difficult for us to see the world as having been created by a perfect God. Altogether, then, there is much to dispose modern man to this view of things.

However, James thought such a view of the world by no means proven. It is at most a legitimate hypothesis covering many of the observed facts very well. But while religious experience, and perhaps some of the phenomena investigated by psychical researchers, do not conclusively falsify it, any one of the other hypotheses, each of which is in its own way religious, seem *prima facie* in a better position to make sense of them.

§ 3. Absolute pantheistic idealism was, in James's time, the dominant creed of spiritually minded philosophers. But we have seen that James thought that the proofs they provided on its behalf were flawed. It is simply a hypothesis with a certain amount going for it, but which has considerable difficulty in explaining those aspects of the world which are recalcitrant to spiritual values.

§ 4. Finally, there was the hypothesis of a finite God. This offers an explanation of religious experience, of man's moral aspirations, and of psychical phenomena. It does not offer any final explanation of the being of things, for God is conceived, not as the ultimate explanation of everything, but just as one particularly important one among the various competing forces in the world. But then, according to James, none of the other theories offers any more successful answer to the question of why there is anything at all rather than nothing, so this is not really any special disadvantage on its part. It must be judged like the others as an account of how things are rather than as an ultimate explanation of why they are so.

---

example, so ineradicably planted in the mind of our own forefathers that a dose of cruelty and arbitrariness in their deity seems positively to have been required by their imagination'. [VRE, p. 329.]

As such, its great advantage over both orthodoxy and spiritual monism is that it avoids the problem of evil and does not threaten the sense we have of our own free agency. Moreover, it incorporates the scientific picture of things which led to naturalism, and yet interprets man's religious experience in the way it itself suggests. True, mystics usually interpret their experience monistically, but there is no real ground for thinking that the source of their saving experiences comes from a God either identical with, or the source of, the universe as a whole. They may just as well come from a reality which is the preeminent spiritual force within it.

James held that this conception of God and how man stands to Him was implicitly that of the ordinary religious believer who thinks that he meets God in prayer, that he can join with Him in fighting the good fight to improve the world (a fight in which setbacks, even if they can be overcome, are not merely illusory for things do really happen which God would have preferred should not) and that it is by his own free will (and not as an eternally fated part of God's plan) that he himself does his part well or ill.[72]

James distinguishes two versions of the hypothesis of the finite God. On the first we can feel confident that good is more than likely to triumph in the world, and certainly will do so if sufficient men lend God their wholehearted support, but cannot utterly rule out the possibility that things will end in total wreckage. On the second, God is bound to win in the end, but may do so more slowly and perhaps less fully, if finite moral agents choose wrongly. On this second view, God is like a great chess player who does not settle precisely how the game will develop, because that depends on his opponent as well as on himself, yet is sure to respond to whatever moves are made in a way which will lead to his ultimate victory. (James has been accused of inconsistency in letting his conception of a finite God sometimes go with confidence in a final victory of good. But I do not see that this is so. James hesitates between the two views given in the text, but each is consistent in itself, and each leaves us humans with real free will and a real power to forward or retard a possible or certain triumph of good and to affect the form of that triumph if it comes.)

If, now, we use our 'will to believe' to choose between these four views, or between the three which remain as serious options after the first has been discounted, James has no doubt that the preference should be given to the doctrine of the finite God. It is preferable to naturalism whose disheartening

---

72 He thought his father had been more successful than most in synthesising this view with a more monistic one. See the introduction to *The Literary Remains* of his father, ERM, pp. 60–63. This introduction also contains William James's fullest discussion ever of the doctrine of the creation, though nothing very positive is said. Upon the whole his finite God does not seem to be postulated as a creator, and to that extent surely departs from anything which can be called ordinary theism. But James seems right that it is very much that of at least many ordinary Christian believers, so far as it is the conception of the state of things after creation and of their own present relation to God which is at issue.

picture of the world is likely to sap our moral energies and depress our hopes of happiness for ourselves and others. For not only does naturalism rule out any hope of an afterlife (though this is not of prime importance for James) but it suggests that humanity itself must come to an end with the destruction of the earth in a final cataclysm.[73] It also suggests that free will is an illusion and that our higher aspirations are always liable to be thwarted by chemical changes in our body. And it makes quite illusory that sense of an encounter with what is most significant in the world which men feel in the highest experiences of which they know.

The doctrine of a finite God is also preferable emotionally and volitionally to spiritual monism.

The human value of absolute idealism lies in the peace it can bring to our minds, when we are weary with our struggles, through its assurance that all is always really eternally all right. Thereby it provides us with what James notoriously called a 'moral holiday'. Such a value was fostered not only by the absolute idealism of learned philosophers, but by the various religious movements of the time which made use of transcendentalist and absolute idealist ideas, in particular the Mind Cure or New Thought movement (as expressed in such works as Trine, 1897) a movement which survives today mainly in the form of Christian Science. James, as a psychologist, had a good deal of respect for this movement, in which absolute idealism acquired a more pragmatic edge, as for instance in the faith healing of mind cure-ists.

But the moral holidays which absolute idealism, and transcendentalism, both learned and popular, allow us to take are likely to damage our moral sense if prolonged, by encouraging us to think of the evils of the world as somehow essential elements in its total goodness as the life of absolute spirit. For its claim that everything is inevitably perfect in any case is likely to weaken our struggle to improve things.

Moreover, James thinks that most of us will feel that there is something rather effete in wanting a guarantee that things will go well. The sense that they will go well only if we and others like us lend a hand is far more to the satisfaction of most of us who want to play a genuine role in the world's affairs.

James's enthusiasm for moral heroism and the strenuous life can seem a little over-strident at times.[74] But he had a strong sense of the superficial nature of an approach to life which is confident that everything will be for the best however finite beings act. Thus he objected to the more cheery popular forms of transcendentalism that they encourage us too much to flee those darker experiences which must be lived through if the deeper kind of twice-born religious experience, which can only ensue on periods of bleakness, is to be gained. The highest spiritual states are only won by those who pass through periods of intense sorrow. And it is a recurrent theme how callous one must be

---

73   See PRAG, pp. 103–7.
74   See, for example, WB, pp. 210–15 and elsewhere.

to accept the simple view that God's in his heaven, all's right with the world. However, he objected equally to 'the pining, puling, mumping mood'[75] of all sorts of passive pessimism and doctrines of despair.

The sum of it, then, as James sees it, is that the doctrine of the finite God has most of the advantages of the other two religious conceptions without their disadvantages. If it fails to give us an absolute guarantee that things will go well, that is something most of us do not want. And it is not as though it gives us none of the emotional support of absolute idealism, for it leaves us with the sense of something greater than ourselves on whose help we can depend if we seek it. It is thus a hopeful view of the universe, but one which avoids a specious apology for its imperfections. It is melioristic and progressive; it does not bid us blind ourselves to the badness of the world but it does give us hope that we can bring it steadily nearer to perfection.

James sometimes seems to hope that the evil of the world may finally be brought to nought in the future, and thereby shows his complete conviction of time's reality. We will see, when we turn to Bradley, that one of the biggest differences between them is over this. For Bradley the universe consists ultimately of all times held together in the standing now of the absolute experience. On such a view evil cannot be got rid of in the future but is only redeemable if at all in the one eternal now. James, in contrast, thinks that past evil can eventually somehow just drop out of reality and be as though it had never been. I do not myself think such a view makes sense, but it has a certain emotional force. In any case the main burden of James's doctrine is to insist on the reality of evil and the possibility of overcoming it.

So James recommends his conception of a finite God as on a par evidentially with the others and as preferable on passional grounds.

§ In the postscript to VRE James describes his philosophical and religious position as that of crass or piecemeal, as against refined, supernaturalism. For refined supernaturalism (such as that of most absolute idealists) the supernatural only provides a totalistic explanation for the world as a whole and never explains any particular fact. These are always susceptible of a quite naturalistic explanation at the phenomenal level. For crass supernaturalism, in contrast, the supernatural really intervenes in the natural and provides the proper explanation of certain, but not all, particular facts. And James thinks that despite its unfashionableness and disreputable air, there is good evidence for crass supernaturalism.

He also says that, as a pragmatist, he wants the theistic principle to make a real difference at the level of genuine particular fact. What that difference is is disputable, but minimally it is the real efficacy of prayerful communion with a something MORE than our own consciousness, a communion through which our characters may develop in ways otherwise impossible. So far as immortality goes, which some may think the thing which matters most, James leaves it an

---

75   VRE, p. 89.

open question. Spiritualism may cast light on it eventually but has no certain results as yet. For James it is enough that something will carry on, and be the better for our efforts, whether it is ourselves or another.

(d) Further Remarks on the Sense of 'True' as Applied to Religious Beliefs

§ It must be admitted that James does not always distinguish as clearly as my account makes him do between the evidential and the passional grounds. Sometimes in VRE he distinguishes sharply between the question whether certain beliefs are true or whether they are humanly valuable. But then again the wires seem to become twisted.

However, if one looks at the matter from the perspective of the most challenging of the various ways in which one may take the pragmatist conception of truth, the distinction is not, after all, a sharp one. For the pragmatist will say that if the doctrine of the finite God is more humanly valuable than naturalism or absolute idealism, that shows that its verbal formulas put us in better contact with some component or feature of reality (in virtue of the emotions and behaviour with which they are associated) than do those of the others. And that means that its truth is both a matter of its being humanly valuable and of the genuine existence of that whose existence it affirms. For the expression or concept 'finite God' has no referent, actual or putative, apart from that which is settled by the nature of the reality which must exist if affirmative existential sentences of which it is the subject are to be humanly valuable. So the human value of their effects cannot be separated from the reality of that which they posit. If alternative religious conceptions are not calculated to be so humanly valuable that will likewise constitute their failure to correspond so well with what actually is.

I do not think this a wholly adequate view of thought and truth. I believe that much human thinking only has meaning, and the possibility of truth, of this pragmatic kind, but that we also sometimes think in ways which have meaning and the possibility of truth of a more literal kind. Such thought presents an essence to consciousness as that of some locus in reality and is true if it is that which is in fact actualised there. And I believe it is this more literal truth which James himself is seeking in his more deeply metaphysical investigations. It is what he agrees with Bergson in seeking in the form of an imaginative sympathy with the inner essence of the flux of reality as opposed to the possession of concepts which merely help us handle it effectively. (It should not be supposed, however, that the former is never useful in a practical way.) But although the seeds of this conception of two different sorts of truth are present in James, he constantly harks back to a more purely pragmatist conception of the sole goal of human thought. And from this point of view the contrast between the passional success of a belief and its objective truth is a thin one.

An uneasiness on this matter may be detected in such a statement as the following:

The word 'truth' is here taken to mean something additional to bare value for

life, although the natural propensity of man is to believe that whatever has
great value for life is thereby certified as true.

VRE, p. 509

In fact, there is a good deal of ambivalence in the work as to whether there
are two distinct ways of considering religious beliefs, for their objective truth
and for their human value, or whether these are both aspects of the one
intelligible kind of truth there is.

Contrast, for example, these two passages.

> Let me then propose, as an hypothesis, that whatever it may be on its *farther*
> side, the 'more' with which in religious experience we feel ourselves connected
> is on its *hither* side, the subconscious continuation of our conscious life. . . . [So]
> [d]isregarding the over-beliefs, and confining ourselves to what is common
> and generic, we have in *the fact that the conscious person is continuous with a wider
> self through which saving experiences come*, a positive content of religious experi-
> ence which, it seems to me, is *literally and objectively true* as far as it goes.

VRE, pp. 512 and 515

> We return to the empirical philosophy: the true is what works well, even
> though the qualification 'on the whole' may always have to be added.

VRE, p. 458[76]

(e) God as Continuous with Our Being rather than as External to It

§ So much for the reasons for postulating a finite God, but what exactly is such
a being? Here James's conception of continuity becomes important, for the finite
God is supposed to be a larger consciousness with which each of ours is
continuous.[77] James thought the speculations of F. W. H. Myers important
here.[78] Myers had developed the notion of a subliminal consciousness which
lies beyond our own familiar stream of experience. And James develops this
into the hypothesis that the consciousness of each of us is not only continuous
with a MORE of essentially the same kind, but that this MORE taken together
with one's ordinary consciousness, constitutes a greater self, which in some
sense is one's true self. This true self may have plans and purposes which go
beyond anything present in one's ordinary consciousness, but which present
themselves in prayer or in mystical experience of contact with a greater other.
He then proposes as the heart of the distinctively theistic hypothesis that this
personal MORE is continuous with a larger MORE which is the same for us all.

However, James does not dismiss the alternative possibility that, while we
each have our own separate MORE, there is no greater MORE common to us all
and worthy to be called God (though we must all be continuous with the MORE

---

76   Among other relevant passages see VRE, pp. 327, 331–32, 458, 489, 506–7, 509.
77   See VRE, pp. 483–84, 512.
78   See Myers.

which is nature in its inner aspect and indeed at least indirectly with other finite persons). That would point to a kind of polytheism for which one's own deeper MORE is one's personal guardian god guiding one, in religious experience, towards a closer union with him in which one's salvation, hereafter if not now, must eventually lie. Such a view is, in fact, a fifth alternative to those I listed above. However, though James plays with it, he seems to have thought it both evidentially and passionally inferior to the doctrine of a finite God.

§ It is tempting to equate the personal MORE with the unconscious as conceived by psychoanalysis. But such a comparison is more misleading than otherwise.

Certainly the personal MORE differs from the Freudian unconscious in at least two ways.

First, it is morally superior to one's conscious self. For while James did believe that we also have a subliminal consciousness of a more id-like nature, that was not the religiously significant MORE with which religious experience puts us in better contact.

And, secondly, it is not strictly unconscious; rather is it simply further consciousness, standing somewhat apart from that ordinary stream of consciousness which is what mainly speaks forth from our lips. Indeed it is doubtful whether James ever really moved away from the view that completely unconscious experience, not belonging to a unity which feels its own being, is absurd, as it has sometimes been said that he did.[79]

It is harder to say how far the MORE which constitutes James's finite God is akin to the collective unconscious of Jung. It depends on how one understands the latter. Is it simply a set of shared inherited ways of thinking, or does it have a more substantial being as a mental unit? If it is meant in the latter way, then there is perhaps some similarity, though again James's divine MORE is of a sublime moral character not ascribed to the collective unconscious by Jung.

At any rate, one must avoid thinking of the MORE of James as unconscious. Rather is it the highest form of consciousness which exists. Its life consists in a stream of experience comparable to, though indefinitely richer in content than, ours and it mingles with those streams of felt experience which are our various personal MORE's and via them with the streams of experience which form our ordinary conscious lives.

§ Sometimes James seems to think that one's personal consciousness is literally a part of the larger personal consciousness, and that in turn of the divine consciousness, distinguishing his position from the absolute idealist's only by insisting that the divine MORE which includes one does not include all reality. But most of the time his view is rather that while one's consciousness is continuous (in the sense we discussed in section 2a of this chapter) with the divine MORE, it is not properly speaking a part of it.

It remains somewhat unclear whether he thought the first a possible concep-

---

79   See Ford, p. 22 et ff.

tion of how things might be (as is suggested by some of the strictures on the intellectualist logic which he had wrongly thought counted against the compounding of consciousness) or thought such compounding could only conceivably be of the continuity, rather than the part-whole, type.

§ James believed that his finite God, conceived as a MORE with which our personal MORE is continuous, secured the most important advantages of religious belief. For the basic core of this is

> 1. An uneasiness; and
> 2. its solution.
> 1. The uneasiness, reduced to its simplest terms, is a sense that there is *something wrong about us* as we naturally stand.
> 2. The solution is a sense that *we are saved from the wrongness* by making proper connection with the higher powers.
>
> VRE, p. 508

The essence of what happens is a sense that one's own being has a higher and a lower part, and that

> *the higher part is conterminous and continuous with a MORE of the same quality, which is operative in the universe outside of him, and which he can keep in working touch with, and in a fashion get on board of and save himself when all his lower being has gone to pieces in the wreck.*
>
> VRE, p. 508

§ James sometimes characterises opinions which one cannot expect ever to be universally accepted among all reasonable persons, but which one personally cherishes, as one's over-beliefs. And in VRE he summarises his own religious over-belief (which he acknowledges will seem a slight one to some of the devout among his Edinburgh audience) thus:

> The further limits of our being plunge, it seems to me, into an altogether other dimension of existence from the sensible and merely 'understandable' world. Name it the mystical region, or the supernatural region, whichever you choose. . . . When we commune with it, work is actually done upon our finite personality, for we are turned into new men, and consequences in the way of conduct follow in the natural world upon our regenerative change. But that which produces effects within another reality must be termed a reality itself, so I feel as if we had no philosophic excuse for calling the unseen or mystical world unreal.
>
> VRE, pp. 515–16

And he adds that he agrees with the devout that the MORE with which we are continuous is genuinely active in the world. For as a pragmatist he holds that a MORE, whose existence does not make a real difference to how the world is going, would be no more than a rosy light in which some choose to see things.

What the more characteristically divine facts are, apart from the actual inflow of energy in the faith-state and the prayer-state, I know not. But the over-belief on which I am ready to make my personal venture is that they exist. The whole drift of my education goes to persuade me that the world of our present consciousness is only one of many worlds of consciousness that exist, and that those other worlds must contain experiences which have a meaning for our life also and that although in the main their experiences and those of this world keep discrete, yet the two become continuous at certain points, and higher energies filter in. . . . So my objective and my subjective conscience both hold me to the over-belief which I have expressed. Who knows whether the faithfulness of finite beings to their own poor over-beliefs may not actually help God [which he has decided it is appropriate to call the MORE] in turn to be more effectively faithful to his own great tasks?

VRE, p. 519

(f) The Mother Sea of Consciousness

WATERY METAPHORS

§ In some late statements James speaks of a mother sea of consciousness to which we all somehow belong. This idea is sometimes thought to be in striking contrast with his insistence elsewhere that consciousness is nothing substantial.[80] But I believe that this is less so than it might seem and that, in any case, there is nothing in the concept of the mother sea which clashes with the panpsychist pluralism which we have taken to be his final position. Since he seems to have stuck by the essentially similar views expressed in these two articles it is of some importance to decide whether this is so or whether he remained in two inconsistent minds till the end.

The main statement of this view is in his 1898 Ingersoll lecture 'Human Immortality: Two Supposed Objections to the Doctrine', though a very similar point of view is also expressed in 'Final Investigations of a Psychical Researcher' (1909) in which he summed up his response to psychical research (understood as the investigation of mediumistic phenomena).

Those who remember only that James said that consciousness is not an entity but a function, may be vastly surprised to find him talking of a mother sea of consciousness. However, the *consciousness* of which there may be a 'mother sea' corresponds to the *experience* within which that function is supposed to occur rather than to the function. And since we should be accustomed to the notion of that experience occurring in streams it is not so remarkable that we are now invited to think of those streams as flowing from and back into a sea.

To see whether there is a real change of view we must try to get a hold upon the true significance of these watery metaphors which become bewildering if pressed too far. What does the metaphor of the single sea add to that of the many streams?

Among the interacting streams of the universe of panpsychist pluralism

---

80   See Myers, 1986, p. 382 et ff.

there are the dominant streams of experience of humans and animals. These interact with those streams of dimmer experience which constitute what the physical world is in its inner being, indeed the two are constantly on the verge (at the least) of flowing into each other. And the postulation of a finite God introduced another great stream of experience, with a specially significant, good and powerful role, with which these two sorts of stream also interact.

Talk of experience coming in streams is meant to allow for the possibility of these streams flowing into and out of each other. Indeed only if they can do so is the pluralistic universe a universe at all. Still, the metaphor on the whole stresses the apartness from each other of the experiences which belong to different streams (though it breaks down insofar as this apartness does not require anything corresponding to the land mass which separates real streams of water). When James uses the new metaphor of the mother sea of consciousness he is suggesting that there may be a still closer and more constant connectedness between all forms of consciousness of a kind we must explore. It is not, however, meant to deny the evident distinctness between them emphasised in PP and elsewhere. Connectedness and disconnectedness are for him a matter of degree so that the metaphors are not supposed to carry sharply contradictory messages. But the new metaphor is meant to suggest that there may be closer kinds of connectedness between the experiences belonging to different streams than is obvious on the surface, even when they remain separate and are not actually flowing into each other.

§ I have suggested already that James does not stick either to the language appropriate to an ontology in which enduring things are basic or to that appropriate to one in which events are. The contrast between these may throw some further light on the difference between the metaphor of the sea and that of the streams. Whereas the flow of the stream is meant to represent the unfolding of a series of events, the sea represents a continuant which changes from moment to moment while being made up mostly of the same 'stuff'. Of course, an actual stream is a continuant as much as is a sea. But the metaphors are used differently. A stream of consciousness is something of which only a cross-section, or narrow band, exists at any one moment. The sea of consciousness is something which exists as a whole at any one moment and changes as a whole over time. The metaphor of the sea represents the world as a continuant whose stuff is changing consciousness; the metaphor of a stream of experience represents an individual mind as a series of temporal stages. But it is surely not the point of the new metaphor to represent a move from an event ontology to a thing one, either in general or with reference to conscious experience. So this change threatens merely to confuse the issue.

The difference between a well worked out event and a well worked out continuant ontology is not, in my opinion, a genuinely factual one (not at least, if the contrast between them does not point out a different conception of the sense in which past and future are real, which is not in question here). James, as a pragmatist, would surely have agreed. But it is confusing to move as freely between the two as he does. So let us see what difference there may be between the many streams concept and the single sea concept if we drop this contrast.

It will be easiest to do this by putting the matter in terms of continuants in both cases.

We may then express the panpsychist pluralist view (without the mother sea of consciousness) by the metaphor of a world composed of innumerable distinct lakes of consciousness. (It is true that there will be nothing of the nature of the landmass which must be there to keep one real lake apart from another, but we will have to suppose a kind of earthy nothingness between them if the metaphor is to do its work.) However, we must add that the lakes which are apart at one moment may come together at the next. The earthy nothingness between them may crumble and they may flow into one another and form a single lake. Later the waters in this single lake may separate again to form distinct lakes and each may correspond in virtue of the quality of its water to a particular one of the lakes which existed previously. (We may suppose that even when there was but one lake the different qualities of water were still somehow each distinctly present in it, but it would be pointless to press the metaphor to the extent of asking just in what sense the different kinds of water in the single lake remain distinct.)

Thus the distinct lakes of consciousness are variously related to each other according to the ease and manner in which they do or might flow into and out of each other for a time to form and unform larger lakes. And we must suppose also that even when the lakes are separate the earthy nothingness between them allows trickles of water from the one to flow into and affect the quality of the other. It is on the model of these relations between the lakes that the real relations between distinct consciousnesses are to be understood.

This world of separate lakes, between which there is yet some exchange of fluid, and which may sometimes merge into larger lakes and then separate again, is the world of the pluralistic panpsychism we have taken to be James's final metaphysics.

What does the notion of the mother sea of consciousness add to this? Does it imply that there is never any real separateness of consciousness, no earthy nothingness dividing it into distinct units, but at most a difference in the quality of water in different regions of the unbroken sea? I do not think so. The idea seems to be rather that as well as the many lakes, representing the consciousness of different people and those which constitute the inner life of the other real units of the natural world, there is a much vaster mass of water, worthy to be called a sea, water from which flowed out to form each lake in its turn and to which each in its turn will flow back. In between, however, they are divided from the great sea, and from each other, by an earthy nothingness just as on the metaphor which depicted the pluralist panpsychist world without a mother sea. However, as before, the earthy nothingness between them need not be supposed quite watertight. And this allows for a regular exchange of water between the great sea and each lake by mediating subterranean channels representing its personal MORE.

If this is the right way of developing these metaphors, the notion of the mother sea adds to, rather than emends, the pluralistic panpsychism we have taken to be James's final view. There is no need to see it as representing any departure from the view that different states of consciousness are related to each other in the next to next fashion, rather than by actually being parts of one overarching experience as they are for the absolute idealist. True, we have noted some ambivalence on James's part on this matter but the idea of a mother sea of consciousness does not, of itself, imply a change of view. Reality still comes in the 'each' rather than the 'all' form. We, as we are now, and the mother sea, as it is now, are a group of interacting each-es rather than an all, though we may have once been, and may be again, an all.

But, it may be said, there is this great difference. The idea of the mother sea forces us to think in terms of an enduring stuff of consciousness, represented by water in the metaphor, while there is no such enduring stuff in panpsychist pluralism. But this is again to treat an event ontology and a continuant ontology as contrasting in a more factual way than they do. The event ontologist does without any such stuff. However, he replaces it by talking of the way in which the character of successive events relates to those they have arisen from.

If we try to present the watery metaphors we have been considering in event terms we must reduce both lake and sea to a series of watery events and the talk of the water flowing from the sea into a lake, or vice versa, and similarly between the lakes, will be a matter of the particular way in which the set of events which constitute sea and lakes at one moment, owe their character to a previous set of such events. There is no more (even if, some say, no less) difficulty in doing this with the mother sea than without it. So it is wrong to see the idea of the mother sea as implying that there is an enduring stuff of consciousness in any way incompatible with the main pluralistic position which is typically expressed by reference to a plurality of streams of consciousness.

§ These considerations show how careful one must be in interpreting James's various watery metaphors. We must bear in mind, in particular, that they are meant to convey facts we can conceive more directly by attending to the actual flux of experience within ourselves, even if ordinary language only allows for a metaphorical verbalisation of them. They are not meant, like traditional analogical predications of God, as indirect ways of characterizing something we cannot grasp directly, but to suggest characteristics of reality familiar to us from our own experience. They invite us to grasp, by a mixture of introspection and empathic imagination, how our changing consciousness, conceived as a continuant, may merge and divide from other consciousnesses, and even without complete merging be somehow partially mixed up in its being with them. This is something we must each try to do for ourselves; the facts cannot be set down in some black and white way so that they can be grasped without a special effort to attend to consciousness itself. If James and Bergson are right, our ordinary, mainly physical, concepts are designed for practical use, and simply cannot be treated as adequate renderings of reality as it genuinely is. This must be grasped, with the aid of physical metaphors which break down if pushed too far, by a kind of sympathetic intuition, born of introspection and empathy.

§ The most important feature of the idea of the mother sea (that is, of the possible reality for which that metaphor stands) is the conception with which it provides James of a possible form of immortality. Our various streams (or lakes) of experience may all flow into (as they may once have flowed out of) a common sea the character of which is affected forever after by the inflowing of these tributaries and which thus preserves something of our being within it. Put less metaphorically, the idea is that after my death the series of my states of consciousness may join up with a series of cosmic experiences with which the series of experiences of all other dead persons have joined.

There are clearly a variety of possible patterns of fusion and separation which are conceivable once the general idea is accepted as intelligible. James's metaphysics gives a general account of the universe which allows for all sorts of more detailed possibilities of this sort. What remains ambiguous is the extent to which James may have eventually thought that one greater pulse of experience can somehow actually contain lesser pulses with a feeling of their own being. If he came to think this a possibility and suspected that we persisted in the mother sea as a stream made up of such pulses, then his final position did, indeed, have much in common with that of the absolute idealists. But it is not clear that he did. Our survival in the mother sea may be conceived rather as that of a special quality present in its water, reflecting the experiences we had when alive but without any felt separate being of its own. And even if after death we exist within the mother sea with a sense of our own separate being, James's position would still contrast with that of the absolute idealist. For this will only be something which happens after death; for the present we are not actual parts of the mother sea as we are of the Absolute for the absolute idealist. (Besides which it is not clear that the mother sea is meant to be something from which absolutely everything emerged and to which it will return.) Thus the mother sea is not an all-embracing Absolute but at most the source and destination of finite consciousnesses such as ourselves.

Is the notion of the mother sea, then, simply that of the finite God? Well, clearly James regarded many questions as open, and these expressions are different ways of suggesting merely the general direction in which truth may lie. The metaphor of the mother sea has an emotional resonance which reference to a finite God seems to lack, and James may use it therefore to express his periodic inclination to believe in a more intimate unity between us and a more comprehensive spiritual reality than that does. But they are not meant to be alternative theories, just different hints at how things may be compatibly with a panpsychist metaphysics which stops well short of a spiritual monism like Bradley's or Royce's.

THE INGERSOLL LECTURE

§ As remarked, James's main use of the mother sea of consciousness metaphor is in his 'Human Immortality: Two Supposed Objections to the Doctrine' of 1898. This was one in a series of lectures, by different hands, on the question of a life after death set up by a bequest. James professes himself not so passionately concerned in a personal way with this question as many people are, but as one who wishes to correct the idea that modern knowledge renders the belief incredible.

One objection is that the universe cannot have 'room' for so many spirits as survival would imply. The other objection is that it is now established that consciousness is a function of the brain and cannot survive it.

§ The objection that there is not enough 'room' for so many spirits is not very serious. There is no sense in which consciousness needs room, rather does it bring its own room in the space it contemplates. (Besides, as James does not actually point out, space itself is usually thought of as infinite. However, he is right not to approach the matter in spatial terms.) The most one can say is that with our limited imaginations we just cannot think easily of a totality including so many spirits. But there is nothing which really precludes it or even makes it unlikely.

But perhaps there is more to this objection than meets the eye. We are no longer prepared to think in terms of some elect few in heaven and the rest as doomed for hell or damnation. If we are to survive in happiness, our democratic sense now makes us feel that all men should (and we may even think the same of animals). The trouble is that our sense of the size and variety in nature of the human population over time has itself been much enlarged and we are appalled at the sorts of individuals who will then eternally cram the world, from primitive men with their bloody lives to those who participate in the most unacceptable cultures of our own time.

> We give up our own immortality sooner than believe that all the hosts of Hottentots and Australians that have been, and shall ever be, should share it with us in saecula saeculorum.
>
> ERM, p. 98

James is at his most eloquent in answering this by insisting that much of what looks repulsive is only so as viewed from our own external perspective on it (sounding here a note also present in Bradley). Internally its values are felt as fully and vividly as are ours and can be supposed to matter as much to the Absolute, if there be such, or to an inexhaustibly empathic God. For anything which matters to itself matters truly, however difficult it is for us to grasp this in the case of very alien forms of experience.

> The truth is that we are doomed, by the fact that we are practical beings with very limited tasks to attend to, and special ideals to look after, to be absolutely blind and insensible to the inner feelings, and to the whole inner significance of lives that are different from our own. Our opinion of the worth of such lives is absolutely wide of the mark, and unfit to be counted at all.
>
> ERM, p. 99

This is a theme basic to James's ethical views, as advocated in 'On a Certain Blindness in Human Beings' (1898). Our ethical insight is essentially a matter

of the extent to which we break down this blindness and insensibility. I have
no time to discuss this approach to ethics, with which I almost entirely agree.[81]

§ The other objection to the idea of immortality, that consciousness is a
function of the brain, is more serious. To clarify matters, James points out that
one thing may be a function of another in two different senses. It may be
produced by it or it may merely be transmitted by it. Thus steam is a function
of boiling water and light of an electric circuit in the sense that the one is
produced by the other, but a crossbow 'has a releasing function: it removes the
obstacle that holds the string, and lets the bow fly back to its natural shape'.[82]
The established facts showing that consciousness is a function of the brain can
be interpreted equally well in either way. If consciousness is only a function of
the brain in the second sense, it may well also exist apart from it.

Thus there may be a fuller realm of consciousness apart from any in the
physical world, and the function of the brain may be to let some of that realm
slip into the material world. Brain processes on which consciousness appears
to depend may really only be those necessary to filter it through from the other
world into this. If it is said that we can get no proper grasp of how they might
do this, it is equally true that one can get no proper grasp of how they could
produce consciousness. And indeed the transmission theory has some advantage over the production theory. For it saves us from having to believe in the
mysterious creation or emergence of consciousness out of nothing, or at least
out of nothing at all akin to it. It allows us, rather, to think of it as coeval with
the world and simply filtering into the physical realm at one of its, so to speak,
weak spots, where it is more thin and transparent as a veil behind which the
deeper reality lies.

Such an account looks dualistic. But in a footnote James explains that he is
simply taking on the physiological objection to immortality in the normal terms
in which it is posed, where it is assumed that the physical world is made of stuff
quite different in nature from consciousness. A more finally satisfactory account
might be given from a 'phenomenist' point of view which denies the ultimacy
of any such duality. Looking at the possibilities of a transmission theory from
a dualist point of view, the fuller world of consciousness might be thought of
as essentially atomised, along the lines of the mind dust theory. In that case the
function of the brain might be to combine these particles of consciousness into
a greater unity. Or it might be that the fuller world of consciousness is unitary,
and the function of the brain is to filter it out into sharply distinct personal
consciousnesses. The latter view is the more promising as a basis for postulating
some kind of personal immortality. And the mind dust theory remains open to

81   I regret that I failed to discuss James in my *The Rational Foundations of Ethics*. I had
      not been concerning myself recently with James as an ethicist, and forgot how
      valuable his treatment of it was, within the limit of his very slight excursus into
      distinctively moral philosophy. I was more influenced in ethics by Santayana, who
      in this matter was very similar to James.
82   ERM, pp. 84–85.

the kind of objections James had raised against it in PP, that particles of consciousness cannot make up a larger consciousness.

§ One might suppose that the notion of a unitary consciousness being filtered out into distinct ones raised similar difficulties. But in both cases, the difficulties arise, once more, partly from moving between conceiving the world in terms of an event ontology and in terms of a substance one. It is one thing to say that the particles cannot exist as particles while constituting a single state of consciousness as well. That does not imply that a set of particulate events may not flow into a unitary event or vice versa or, putting it in terms of continuants, that distinct consciousnesses may not combine or single ones break up into many. As transformation of the many into one or of one into many by the brain, and thus a change over time, it is not clear that one is more problematic than the other.

In any case he says (and emphasises still more in the Preface to the second edition) that, even if we reject the mind dust theory, we do not have to think of the mother sea, from which the finite mind is supposed to be strained by the brain, in pantheistic terms as one vast unitary consciousness.

> The plain truth is that one may conceive the mental world behind the veil in as individualist a form as one pleases, without any detriment to the general scheme by which the brain is represented as a transmissive organ.
>
> ERM, p. 76

In that same preface he says that some have objected that if our personal consciousness is filtered out from a mother sea of consciousness by the brain, then the fact that the mother sea remains when the brain is dead does not suggest any personal survival for us. But the mother sea need not, after all, be so unified as this; it may even be that there is a larger mother sea peculiar to each individual consciousness, from which it flows out at birth and back at death with a content enriched by its temporary separation.[83] Besides (as we can gather from his introduction to a translation of Fechner's *Life after Death* [1904]), he thought that even if there is just one unitary mother sea, it may be enriched by a stock of ideas, developed in our personal lives, which enter into richer contexts there and are in a very real sense ourselves, no longer separated off from the totality of the world spirit.

§ Since the lecture only adopts a dualistic view of consciousness and matter in order to meet objections to immortality raised from a perspective more conventional than his own, we cannot weave its suggestions, just as they stand, into a formulation of the final view of things to which he moved. But it only requires slight modification to cohere with a panpsychist ontology and, as thus modified, was surely a view he continued to think a real possibility. Taken thus, it would become the view that the low-level streams of experience which form

---

83   ERM, pp. 75–76 and 89, note.

the inner being of the ordinary natural world, when they combine with each other to form the events which constitute the existence and duration of a suitable brain, become more intimately associated than otherwise with a superior system of streams of experience which normally stand somewhat apart from them. Looked at from the point of view of that system, streams continuous with it issue from and later return to the superior system and are enriched in the interim through their more intimate contact with the lower streams.

This is still a somewhat dualistic picture but is quite consistent with panpsychism. Insofar as there is ground for distinguishing matter from mind, and thinking of our own minds as the temporary sojourn of mind in a material world, it can be conceived along such lines in a manner quite in line with James's basic categories. Equally panpsychism can be developed in a less dualist way. For example, the lower-level streams constituting our physical world and the higher-level streams constituting our minds may be supposed destined to pass into streams where the divisions between them will be less rather than more sharp. Such would be the message, I think, of mysticism of the nature kind, and it is not one which James would have wished entirely to reject.

James says of the transmission theory, that not only is it intelligible in itself, but it makes sense of the phenomena investigated by psychical researchers as the production theory of consciousness cannot. In interpreting these phenomena we can think of the brain's filtering of streams from the higher level into the lower level corresponding to the physical world as depending on a threshold of resistance set up by the latter which may occasionally be lowered for reasons largely unknown. (What lies below the level of entry into our dominant stream of consciousness will presumably include various more banal sorts of secondary consciousness, such as those James discusses in PP, closely associated with the individual brain, as well as this fuller and higher mother sea.)

> A medium, for example, will show knowledge of his sitter's private affairs which it seems impossible he should have acquired through sight or hearing, or inference therefrom. Or you will have an apparition of someone who is now dying hundreds of miles away. On the production theory one does not see from what sensations such odd bits of knowledge are produced. On the transmission-theory, they don't have to be 'produced',—they exist ready-made in the transcendental world, and all that is needed is an abnormal lowering of the brain-threshold to let them through. In cases of conversion, in providential leadings, sudden mental healings, etc., it seems to the subjects themselves of the experience as if a power from without, quite different from the ordinary action of the senses or of the sense-led mind, came into their life, as if the latter suddenly opened into that greater life in which it has its source. The word 'influx', used in Swedenborgian circles, well describes the impression of new insight, of new willingness, sweeping over us like a tide. All such experiences, quite paradoxical and meaningless on the production-theory, fall very naturally into place on the other theory. We need only suppose the continuity of our consciousness with a mother sea, to allow for exceptional waves occasionally pouring over the dam. Of course the causes of these odd lowerings of the brain's threshold still remain a mystery on any terms.
>
> ERM, pp. 93–94

Thus does the doctrine of the mother sea make sense for James of 'psychical' phenomena in a manner eminently suitable for a piece-meal supernaturalist.

I turn now to the 'Impressions of a Psychical Researcher' of 1909, in which very similar ideas are floated and which raises some other points of interest. The article starts with a reference to Henry Sidgwick's remarking that, if he had realized from the start that, after twenty years engagement in psychical research, he would have still been in his same original state of indecision as to the validity and significance of its phenomena, he would have been amazed. James says that his state is similar after his own twenty-five years of investigation, direct and through the literature. Still, he cannot take seriously the suggestion that the whole mass of mediumistic phenomena is sheer fraud. Sometimes, indeed, he wonders half seriously whether the difficulty in determining which, if any, phenomena are genuine, and why they tend to be so absurd in character, may be due to the Creator's wish for 'this department of nature to remain baffling'.[84]

He also plays with another idea as to why so many of the phenomena seem mere bosh. Perhaps, he reflects (echoing Peirce), the universe was once all bosh, disorganized and lawless, and only gradually became lawful and organized. If so, perhaps some wisps of the primordial chaos remain, and interact with the organized universe to make apparent nonsense of solid scientific explanation.

However that may be, what he does feel sure of is that the boshiness of many of the phenomena of psychical research are no reason for dismissing them. To do so is as misplaced as denying the existence of bacteria because they live on dung or putrefaction. The fastidiousness of a T. H. Huxley, who thinks spiritualism false because the reality it purports to report is so absurd, is in its own way as unreasonable a romantic prejudice as the outlook of those for whom its sublimity proves it genuine.

James's assessment of the evidence for mediumistic phenomena are of some interest and show his concern to know the objective truth about them. He says that there is undoubtedly much fraud among mediums. But he thinks that fraud is normally the imitation of a genuine reality. It is difficult to invent phenomena quite unlike anything which ever happens. Thus it seems unlikely that the types of event supposed to occur in séances are those which would have occurred to someone who had decided to invent evidence of survival without a prior model.

I must say that the point seems rather weak to me. It seems very likely that such phenomena as rapping, trumpets floating in the air, and materialisations of the deceased, were hit on because they were the kind of thing which someone found they could fabricate. In any case, they do not suggest great imaginative powers on the part of a first inventor.

---

84   MS, p. 175.

More interesting, is James's view as to whether all phenomena associated with a medium who has once been caught out in fraud must be discounted as fraudulent however well they stand up to investigation. James admits that this may be a good policy for an organization such as the Society of Psychical Research.

> Better a little belief tied fast, better a small investment *salted down*, than a mass of comparative insecurity.
>
> MS, p. 179

However, it is not a sensible basis for personal judgement. It is far too simplistic to divide people into the honest and the dishonest like this. Anyone with some knowledge of scientific men will know that the best of them indulge in a bit of cheating from time to time. James illustrates this with an amusing personal confession of his own faking of a phenomenon, when a turtle's heart would not perform as it should in a physiology lecture.

> To this day the memory of that critical emergency has made me feel charitable towards all mediums who make phenomena come in one way when they won't come easily in another.
>
> MS, pp. 182–83

Moreover, we should avoid assuming that every case is either one of fraud or one in which things are as the medium claims, and perhaps believes, they are. For example what presents itself as a dead person speaking through a medium may be the medium personating them on the basis of information obtained supernormally. (James owes the suggestion to Mrs Sidgwick, Henry Sidgwick's wife.) For, James contends, a will to personate seems to be a feature of the human mind which should be acknowledged in any case.[85]

> Our subconscious region seems, as a rule, to be dominated either by a crazy "will to make-believe", or by some curious external force impelling us to personation.
>
> MS, p. 200

The study of it in mediumistic phenomena is a worthy psychological study whether they involve anything appropriately called 'supernatural' or not. And we must avoid the simplistic assumption that there is a sharp division between honesty and dishonesty.

> There is a hazy penumbra in us all where lying and delusion meet, where passion rules beliefs as well as conduct, and where the term "scoundrel" does not clear up everything to the depths as it did for our forefathers.
>
> MS, p. 199

---

85   See MS, pp. 189–90.

But there is also the more dramatic possibility that the personation is some-times based on information unconsciously obtained by telepathic tapping of the mind of the dead person personated, perhaps without their even being aware of it on the other side. This is a more promising interpretation of many of the phenomena than is the supposition that it is the dead person himself who is delivering the message and may explain why the spirits of the dead often seem so silly. James is not urging this hypothesis, only pointing out that the possi-bilities are not limited to simple fraud and actual communication with the dead.

As for his final conclusion, it is that, amidst all the humbug, at least some of the performances of mediums rest on genuinely supernormal knowledge. As to how this should be interpreted James's own dramatic sense has some tendency

> to picture the situation as an interaction between slumbering faculties in the automatist's mind and a cosmic environment of *other consciousness* of some sort which is able to work upon them. If there were in the universe all sorts of diffuse soul-stuff, unable of itself to get into consistent personal form, or to take permanent possession of an organism, yet always craving to do so, it might get its head into the air, parasitically, so to speak, by profiting by weak spots in the armour of human minds, and slipping in and stirring up there the sleeping tendency to personate. It would induce habits in the subconscious region of the mind it used thus, and would seek above all things to prolong its social opportunities by making itself agreeable and plausible. It would drag stray scraps of truth with it from the wider environment, but would betray its mental inferiority by knowing little how to weave them into any important or signifi-cant story.
>
> MS, p. 201–2

But this is speculation. James remains simply a psychical researcher, 'waiting for more facts before concluding'.[86]

Yet he does draw a vague general conclusion highly relevant to his general metaphysics:

> Out of my experience, such as it is (and it is limited enough) one fixed conclusion dogmatically emerges, and that is this, that we with our lives are like islands in the sea, or like trees in the forest. The maple and the pine may whisper to each other with their leaves, and Conanicut and Newport hear each others' foghorns. But the trees also commingle their roots in the darkness underground, and the islands also hang together through the ocean's bottom. Just so there is a continuum of cosmic consciousness, against which our individuality builds but accidental fences, and into which our several minds plunge as into a mother-sea or reservoir. Our "normal" consciousness is circumscribed for adaptation to our external earthly environment, but the fence is weak in spots, and fitful influences from beyond leak in, showing otherwise unverifiable common connection. Not only psychic research, but metaphysical

---

86   MSN, p. 203.

philosophy and speculative biology are led in their own ways to look with favor on some such "panpsychic" view of the universe as this. Assuming this common reservoir of consciousness to exist, this bank upon which we all draw, and which so many of earth's memories must in some way be stored, or mediums would not get at them as they do, the question is, What is its own structure? What is its inner topography? This question, first squarely formulated by Myers, deserves to be called "Myers' problem" by scientific men hereafter. What are the conditions of individuation or insulation in this mother-sea? To what tracts, to what active systems functioning separately in it, do personalities respond? Are individual "spirits" constituted there? How numerous, and of how many hierarchic orders may these then be? How permanent? How transient? And how confluent with one another may they become?

What again are the relations between the cosmic consciousness and matter? Are there subtler forms of matter which upon occasion may enter into functional connection with the individuations in the psychic sea, and then, and then only, show themselves?—so that our ordinary human experience, on its material as well as on its mental side, would appear to be only an extract from the larger psycho-physical world?

Vast, indeed, and difficult is the inquirer's prospect here, and the most significant data for his purpose will probably be just these dingy little mediumistic facts which the Huxleyan minds of our time find so unworthy of their attention. But when was not the science of the future stirred to its conquering activities by the little rebellious exceptions to the science of the present?

MS, pp. 204–6

It seems to me that this is quite in line with my opening account of the 'mother sea' conception and thus with the metaphysic we have taken to be his final one.

§ James's reputation suffered in his life through his commitment to psychical research, and it may do so with some people today.[87] However that may be, some interesting things emerge from his discussion of it which bear on his general philosophical approach.

§ If James will seem credulous to some, he certainly never showed the extreme gullibility of Conan Doyle, for example, and, in fact, he shows an admirable combination of open-mindedness and caution. But what is most significant from a general philosophical point of view is that he is employing an absolutely straightforward concept of truth in assessing the claims of mediums. He attempts a cool assessment of evidence and selection of hypotheses for testing. This surely undermines any idea that his pragmatism (or even the doctrine of the will to believe) were taken as licensing wishful thinking. This supports my claim that it is rather concerned to identify the reference of words with the kind of reality with which they are calculated to help one cope than to undermine the notion of objective reality.

§ We will see in Part Two that Bradley also, like most philosophers of that time, gave some attention to the claims of spiritualism. And the contrast James

---

87   See Bjork, 1983.

had in mind when he contrasted his own piecemeal supernaturalism with the refined supernaturalism of the absolute idealists comes out clearly in the difference between their approaches. Bradley thought that it was completely irrelevant to any genuine religious (or metaphysical) issue whether the phenomena were faked or real, and what, in the latter case, was really going on. Religion had no concern with the supernatural, understood as something abnormal sometimes intruding into daily life; its concern was, rather, with that absolute reality to which any phenomena must belong. For James, in contrast, a religion not concerned with something that might thus intrude, was empty. Though his own belief in the reality of such intrusion was not derived from mediumistic (but rather from mystical) phenomena, they could certainly bring further information about a religiously (and metaphysically) relevant supernatural realm. True, they both thought religion more a matter of conduct than of belief, but for the one it was conduct in the light of the nature which any reality must necessarily possess, for the other conduct in response to influences from a special realm. The contrast between their approach to the matter also brings out the contrast between the would-be empirical nature of James's metaphysics and the would-be high *a priori* nature of Bradley's.

§ The basic metaphysical positions to which James was settling down in his later years (and which were often adumbrated even in much earlier writings) leave all sorts of more specific possibilities open. What seems clear is that he believed that reality ultimately consisted in innumerable interweaving streams of experience on all sorts of different levels of articulacy, that among these was one stream of peculiar significance which constitutes the divine life, that our own streams are not sharply divided from this, and that there is no one total experience within which everything falls as absolute idealists believe. This last claim meant that evil need not be regarded as an essential element of good, nor need what we at any one time see as the future be supposed part of an eternal totality together with all present and past experience to which there can never have been any real alternative.

I turn now to a thinker who was as much a pan-experientialist as James, who put similar stresses upon the holistic nature of a single state of consciousness, but who, with Josiah Royce, stood pre-eminently for the absolute idealism with which James contended throughout his life. We might well have chosen Royce rather than Bradley as our exemplar of this great alternative, but it was James himself who saw the great choice as between Bradley and Bergson, and I have taken James himself in the role he cast for Bergson. We will have cause to make many further points about James's philosophy in the course of our discussion of Bradley.

PART TWO

F. H. BRADLEY ON TRUTH AND REALITY

1

An Initial Sketch of Bradley's Metaphysics

§1. *Degrees of Reality*

§ Bradley and James are usually thought of as standing at the opposite poles of philosophical opinion. But in fact the common ground between them is considerable as James, at least, was ready to recognize. We have seen how in his article 'Bradley or Bergson?' he praised these two for sharing the same insight into the defects of conceptual thinking as a way of grasping the essence of things and for their explorations of the two great alternative philosophical paths between which we must choose in the light of it. This present book might have been called 'Bradley or James?' in the same spirit. For the affinities and contrasts between them are very similar to those which James found between Bradley and Bergson, and, upon the whole, I think James's philosophy a better version of the Bergsonian alternative to Bradley's than Bergson's own. Moreover, the comparison has more interest inasmuch as there was a certain amount of actual dialogue between these two.

If Bradley is a fine foil for an examination of James's philosophy, one might feel nonetheless that Royce, with whom James was in virtually constant philosophical dialogue, would have been better still. We have already seen that much of James's philosophy can only properly be understood as a response to Royce. But in the end James has more in common with Bradley, for Royce did not share his sense of the basal nature in thought and reality of non-discursive feeling. Thus it is the way in which these two erected such different total systems upon so much common ground which seems to me especially worth examining. Moreover, convinced myself of the firmness of this common ground, my own philosophical thought has consisted mainly in choosing between, or finding a synthesis of, the philosophies of these two.

In this first chapter I shall give a general sketch of Bradley's view of reality. Its purpose is to give as clear and definite a statement as I can of what his overall position really comes to, not to engage in detailed textual analysis of points which are obscure. For Bradley often is obscure, though not to the extent of Hegel or even Kant, and often leaves one to work out for oneself his precise opinion on points of central importance.

§ It is natural to suppose that to ascertain what a philosopher thinks the world is really like is to find what propositions about it he accepts as true. However, we have already seen that one cannot safely make this assumption in the case of James, who thought of truth as consisting in useful ideas, yet reached for a grasp of the essence of things of a deeper nature than such ideas can bring. Something of the same sort applies to Bradley. For he believes in degrees of truth, and holds that a different degree, and in fact kind, of truth is appropriate for different purposes. In fact, all judgements are partially true; there is no such thing as total falsehood. What we call error consists in judgements which are much more false than true. Likewise all ordinary judgements are partially false. The only judgements which are absolutely true are certain metaphysical judgements (and perhaps it is partially false that they are totally true). But one must not represent him as holding that all other more ordinary judgements are simply false.

His position is, rather, that for practical life we must use judgements which metaphysics must reject. And even in highly serious intellectual and spiritual endeavours, in science and religion, for instance, we will do harm rather than good if we seek for absolute truth. We should use ideas which work for the task in hand, and these will include ideas which the metaphysician cannot accept when he seeks for the peculiarly absolute truth which is his province. Thus one cannot straightforwardly say of various propositions that Bradley either did or did not accept them, for his stance towards them may vary according to the task in hand. For example, such a judgement as that a personal God exists may be an essential element of forms of religious consciousness which are much more in tune with reality than that of mere atheism, and therefore be as true as any ordinary judgement needs to be, without possessing the more absolute kind of truth to be sought in metaphysics. And the same applies to all the uncontroversial statements of common sense.

One must avoid thinking of degree of truth, as Bradley understands it, as a matter of amount of truth in the sense in which if p, q, and r are each true, 'p and q and not-r' is more true than 'p and not-q and not-r'. For degree of truth in this sense presupposes that there is a level of analysis at which propositions emerge which are true or false *tout court*. (Moreover, a modern formal logician might object to such an account of degree of truth on the grounds that a conjunction of propositions even one of which was false would itself be false *tout court*. However, I think ordinary thought sanctions such a usage.)

The proper way to take the doctrine of degrees of truth is, rather, as the claim that every judgement (and it is only judgements actually made or such as one can see might have been made, that are in question) is an attempt to form an adequate conception of some aspect of reality, and that this attempt can only ever partially succeed (a) because it asserts something of some specific part or aspect of reality which it can never completely specify and thus adequately distinguish from parts or aspects of reality to which it does not apply; (b) because all conceptions to some extent distort the character even of the aspect of reality to which they do apply, in that we would not apply them in their original sense if we knew sufficiently much more, but (c) that every such judgement is at least partially true in the sense that it represents the mind's response to some feature of reality of which it is taking some sort of notice.

It's not important for now to dwell on the doctrine of degrees of truth so far as it concerns judgements about particular matters of fact. What matters is how it bears on the truth or falsehood of general theoretical statements about the universe. The fact that Bradley thinks that these are normally or always par-tially true and partially false means that you can't say that Bradley either simply accepts or rejects them. He will typically think that they each possess a degree of truth which makes them suitable for some purposes, and unsuitable for others.

Thus Bradley believes that there are different levels of thinking and that judgements, which it is appropriate to accept when one is thinking at one level, should be rejected when one is thinking at other levels. The special task of metaphysics is to seek the nearest to absolute and literal truth that is obtainable. But since all concepts must to some extent distort reality even this final truth would not be quite true.

§ Just as Bradley believes in degrees of truth, so he believes in degrees of reality. Things aren't just real or existent, but are so to different degrees and in different ways. The species, horse, is more real than the species, unicorn, but the species horse is less real than absolute mind. The things and events of the ordinary world of space and time have reality of some kind and degree but it is quite low compared with that of the laws and values which are manifested there. Sometimes Bradley uses 'exist' to stand for this low type of reality and even sometimes inclines to say that such 'existing' things hardly deserve to be called 'real' at all.

Before considering the notion of degrees of reality further we must clear up an ambiguity in the word 'Reality' as Bradley uses it. In one usage it is a noun referring to what Bradley believes to be the one ultimate subject of predication, that which all thought is seeking to characterise. In this sense 'Reality' simply means the whole universe as it truly is. This is not the sense of reality in question when reality is said to be a matter of degree. That is rather a claim about 'real' as a predicate for application to things other than the universe as a whole.

The notion of degrees of reality may seem more puzzling than that of degrees of truth. Surely even if our judgements about things must always use concepts which do less than total justice to them, and can therefore never be absolutely true, the things themselves are either there and real or not there at all. Yet Bradley does want to say that one thing, or type of thing, may be more real than another. And it is fairly obvious that he believes not only in different degrees of reality but in different dimensions of reality so that X may be more real than Y in one dimension, less so in another.

§ Many philosophers have dismissed the notion that reality can be a matter of degree as an absurdity. G. E. Moore made this point with particular vigour and other philosophers have tended to be equally dismissive.[1] But although Bradley could have made his meaning clearer, his view is not vulnerable to these rather simplistic attacks.

For upon the whole one can take degrees of reality as the direct complement of degrees of truth and equate a thing's degree (and kind) of reality with the degree (and kind) of truth pertaining to the judgement that it exists, or perhaps rather that it is real. Thus to say that mind is more real than matter, would be to say that it's more true (in a presently relevant way) that mind is real than that matter is. This account would leave us with our sense that Reality in general (the universe) is just 'there', but would insist that the concepts through which we endeavour to pick out and characterize particular parts or aspects of it never quite succeed, nor ever wholly fail, in doing so.

Much of what Bradley says about 'degrees of reality' lends itself to this interpretation, and this is how I shall take him for the most part. But he also sometimes uses the expression somewhat differently to indicate the extent to which a thing is capable of being understood in terms of its own nature alone without reference to that of other things. Bradley sometimes refers to this as 'individuality' and it is akin to the traditional notion of a substance, an expression he eschews.

The concept of degrees of reality, then, stands or falls with the doctrine of degrees of truth. Critics such as Moore, indeed, reject this also. But it is by no means obvious that they are right to do so. For Bradley's essential point is this. Our thinking is a way of representing reality in concepts. However, all our ordinary concepts reveal incoherences when examined closely, and being thus incoherent, cannot accurately represent reality as it really is. On the other hand, they do give us a limited sense of how things are, which is serviceable in grappling with reality. And usually nothing more free from incoherence can serve our practical purposes more effectively. So they have a high degree of truth or conceptual adequacy, in spite of their incoherence. For example, the conception of the world as shaped objects moving about in space over time certainly guides us helpfully in coping with reality for our ordinary purposes. It may even capture certain features of the essence of the world as it really is. Nonetheless examination reveals so much incoherence in this conception, incoherence which cannot be put right by any amount of philosophical tinkering, that it simply cannot satisfy one who wishes a genuine grasp of the world in which he lives.

One may object to this claim, but it is certainly not the mere naive blunder

---

1   See G. E. Moore in Moore (1953), and in 'The Conception of Reality' in Moore (1922). See also F. C. S. Schiller in Schiller (1903), p. 187. For a more recent vigorously dogmatic dismissal of the ideas of degrees of reality see Geach (1979), pp. 36–37.

about the possible logic of such words as 'true' and 'real' which critics like Moore thought it. And even if Bradley cannot demonstrate his claim as finally as he supposed, it remains a hypothesis with a good deal going for it. Certainly the endless wrangling of philosophers over the correct analysis of almost all our ordinary concepts is well explained by the hypothesis that these concepts are essentially incoherent and that opposed philosophers have fixed on different ones among the clashing elements which constitute them.

§ In Part One of AR Bradley condemns most of the things, in terms of which we typically understand the world, as mere appearances. This must be understood in the light of the theory of degrees of truth and reality. Thus one should avoid identifying appearances in his sense with sense impressions, and the problem of appearance and reality as he conceives it with that of how a physical thing stands to the sense impressions by which it manifests itself. Rather is an appearance simply something which has a low degree of reality compared with what would figure in a finally satisfactory metaphysic.

Sometimes Bradley stigmatizes that low level of reality as 'unreality'. So one should not be too puzzled by his sometimes saying that certain things, though they certainly exist, are only appearances and unreal, for 'existence' is simply his label for one very low type of reality. What he means, in effect, is that judgements, to the effect that there are such things, are necessary for many ordinary purposes and yet only provide a very faulty sense of any actual character pertaining to the universe on which all thought is directed, or even of any aspect or part thereof. Thus a thing is an appearance if the concept of it is one which, for practical purposes, we have to think of as having application but which, being incoherent, could not be applied to anything in a judgement which was absolutely true. So to say that space, time, or physical things are appearances is to claim that, though ordinary thought inevitably thinks in terms of there being such things, we need to get beyond these concepts if we are to attain anything like that more literal truth about Reality which metaphysics seeks.

But what is the use of the metaphysical criticism of our ordinary thoughts about what there is, if we are to go on having them for all ordinary purposes? Bradley, in effect, has two answers. First, some people simply do want to get as near as is possible to a grasp of something of the ultimate way things are for its own sake. Secondly, we may be better morally and intellectually if we occasionally glimpse some of the almost absolutely true truths of metaphysics.

These points may be clearer if we consider the particularly basic case of the alleged unreality of physical things. Bradley regards these as unreal because our concept of them is irredeemably incoherent for such reasons as the following.

(1) There is no coherent answer to the question what properties a thing has in itself, and what properties are merely its subjective effects on us. There is no satisfactory solution, for example, to the problems which surround the distinction between primary and secondary qualities.

(2) We cannot form any proper conception of a thing existing when not perceived, but equally we lose the whole point of our conception of the physical if we don't conceive it as existing unperceived.

(3) All answers to questions as to what makes a thing the same thing after a passage of time involve incoherences—yet we must think of things as persisting both as one and the same and as different.

(4) There is no satisfactory solution to the question how a thing is related to its qualities.

(5) Space and time are riddled with incoherences, as reveals itself, for example, when we consider the kind of inward and outward infinity they seem to possess.

Actually I do not think that Bradley always presents the best worked out assault upon the coherence of ordinary concepts that is possible. Some of the incoherences can be cleared up, so it would seem, by making distinctions he ignores. Still, I think he is largely right in his conclusions and right, in particular, in holding that our ordinary conception of the physical does contain contradictions, and can't be literally true, although it is essential for practical purposes, and even gives a partially correct idea of what the world is like.

However, Bradley's attack upon the coherence of our ordinary concepts is not based merely on piecemeal investigations of them. For he holds that there is something about conceptual thinking as such (essentially, as we shall see, its relational character) which means that it can never finally shake off incoherence. In the light of this he insists that even the best metaphysical system will not attain absolute truth. Nonetheless we may, as metaphysicians, seek concepts which bring us somewhat nearer to reality and away from appearance, through doing better justice to Reality, as the ultimate subject, than does ordinary thought.

§2. *The Absolute*

§ I shall now offer a first bold sketch of Bradley's metaphysical system (for such it surely is despite his disclaimer of its being anything so thorough). This does not aspire to be absolutely coherent and true but only to be more so than most ordinary thought. There is no suggestion that it could supplant more ordinary views for ordinary purposes. Our need is always for the type of thinking most suitable for the task in hand.

Although he does not tabulate it in this neat way, we may distinguish three main sorts of reality which the system recognizes and aims to characterise in general terms.

(1) The Absolute;
(2) Finite centres of experience;
(3) The constructed object world.

The Absolute is simply the totality of all that there truly is. Of course, this characterization does not take us very far. Knowledge is hardly advanced by finding a grand name for the whole of things. What gives point to talk of the Absolute is that in applying this expression to the whole of things one is making certain claims about its nature. The main claims in question would seem to be four.

(1) The Absolute or totality of all things is not a mere aggregate or assemblage of things—it is much more truly one than many. This means both that it is an organized system and that it has, to a supreme degree, those features which make one regard something as a single thing rather than as a collection of things, and has these features in a much higher degree than do what count as ordinary single things in daily life.

(2) The Absolute is a timeless experience or state of mind inconceivably rich in the elements which go to make it up but still having something like the kind of unity which belongs to a human person's experience as it occurs at any moment. It contains every experience which any conscious being has had or will have, and thereby contains everything, since, for Bradley, there is nothing except experience. Just as what a human hears, feels, sees, thinks, etc., at any one moment is fairly multiple, yet makes up one single experience, so does every ingredient of the world go to make up this single vast cosmic experience which is the Absolute, or the Universe as it really is.

(3) The Absolute is not a person. A person must feel itself in contrast to a world, which provides its environment, whereas the Absolute experiences everything as an element in its own being.

(4) Although the Absolute is the *All*, there is a sense in which the *All* or *Whole* is present in each of its *parts* or *aspects*. As a first suggestion of what this means one might say that it is present in all its parts somewhat as someone's personality may be present in all his acts, or in which the total character of a work of art permeates all its elements.

§ Bradley's reason for thinking that the Absolute is the only genuine individual turns almost entirely on his view of relations. We have seen how James viewed his claims in this connection. Sometimes he represents them as turning on the trite fallacy of supposing that what falls under one concept cannot also fall under another. There is little justice in ascribing this mistake to Bradley. His position is a much stronger one and indeed much of James's subtler thought about relations is an attempt to escape it.

That Bradley thought that relations were unreal is the main thing most philosophers know about him. And they usually believe that he did so on the basis of an argument which is, in fact, only a misleading abstraction from what he actually said. (We shall be going into this later.)

A first obvious point to be made about Bradley's denial of the reality of relations is that he was not claiming that things were too lacking in togetherness to be spoken of as related, but that their togetherness was too great to be truly so described. A second point to be made at once is that, though he did deny the reality of relations, just as he did that of most things (in a sense we have examined) he thought there was an underlying truth about how things hang together which we are trying to get at when we think in relational terms. And what he thus advances as the underlying truth of which relational facts are the 'appearance' can be re-interpreted as a proposal about the proper analysis of relational facts without much affecting its role in defence of his metaphysical monism and doctrine of the Absolute. So this is how I shall take it in this chapter, making such correction to my account as is necessary in Chapter Three.

Thus interpreted, Bradley's account of relations amounts to this. Whenever two or more[2] things are related to each other in any way at all, they constitute together, or help along with other things to constitute, a more comprehensive thing which is *more* of a genuine individual than any of the things taken individually. Actually I think Bradley could establish his Absolute even with the aid of the weaker principle that when two or more things are related to each other, this is always a matter of their helping to make up a larger whole which is *as much of* a genuine unitary entity as each of the terms is. I shall call these two principles respectively the stronger and the weaker holistic principle. I shall begin by showing how his point could be developed on the basis of the weaker holistic principle, and then say something about the other stronger one, which is nearer to Bradley's own position.

An initial defence of the weaker principle might rest on an account of what happens in many ordinary simple cases of discovery about the relations in which things stand to each other. Consider a child who knows the street in which his parents' house stands and also knows the street in which his maternal grandparents' house stands, which lies at the other end of a town. The child, however, has the haziest idea of the spatial relations between them, for he is taken there by car and pays scant attention to the route. What happens when he does begin to learn the spatial relations between the two streets is, surely, that he forms the conception of a piece of townscape with a certain overall pattern and sees the two streets as each making its own contribution to the formation of that pattern. Thus it is to see the streets as elements in a totality which is as much a genuine unit as each is individually.

This account may seem too obvious to be interesting. However, once it is admitted we are carried a long way towards the Absolute. For this, perhaps among other reasons, many philosophers, James among them, have implicitly or explicitly denied it.

The spatial relations between the streets are only a thin extract from the totality of relations between them. The child may gradually come to learn such more humanly interesting facts as that a shop in one street is organized by a firm whose head office is in the other, that two shops receive their supplies partly from the same factories, partly from different ones, so that some of the vehicles the child sees visiting them are the same, some different, that many of the cars passing through the one street have already passed through the other because that is a main route to a major destination, and so forth. And he may realize that even what seems to be a fact about just one of the streets, such as that the traffic in it becomes very heavy at certain times, cannot be properly understood without knowing something of these relations.

Reflection on this is suggestive of the stronger version of the holistic princi-

---

2   Bradley actually denies the propriety of talking of relations with more than two
     terms. I shall touch on this briefly later. It seems such an unessential and unhelpful
     ingredient of his position that I shall mostly ignore it.

ple, that to be related requires belonging together in a more genuine whole. For one could say that the streets, understood as the full social realities which they are, belong together in the life of the town, region, or country, and that at some level one of these is going to be more of a genuine individual than the individual streets. It will be more of a genuine individual in that it makes more sense to try to understand it in its own terms. To try to understand one individual street, in the sense of explaining, or even giving much of a description of, what is going on there, while confining oneself simply to what lies within its bounds, would be hopeless; it requires rather a study of the town as a whole, or perhaps of the region or country to which it belongs. Thus if you take the street as a 'concrete' reality, as the whole of one distinguishable part of the universe, then it seems reasonable to say that its relations to other things are always a matter of how it unites with them to constitute something larger which is more of a genuine individual than they are.

Note that the stronger holistic principle does not imply that every larger whole in which the terms are included is a more genuine individual than they are. The individual households may be more genuinely individual than are the streets, considered as social units, and yet it may still be true that the social relations between the individual households are ultimately a matter of the way in which these households belong together in a larger more unitary whole, that say of the nation. But the nation need not be the unit in question; maybe it is human history as a whole. These matters are left open by the principle.

§ The holistic principle is one of the great pillars of Bradley's doctrine of the Absolute, pervasive in his thinking even if not presented as explicitly as in my account. Taken in its stronger form it would establish that the Universe as a whole is *more* of a genuine individual than is anything else; taken in its weaker form it would establish that it is *as* genuine an individual as anything else. It will do so, at least, if it is accepted that every item that there is is related to every other item. Let us call this the principle of universal relatedness.

For suppose A is R to B, then on the stronger principle there must be a whole X containing them which is more genuinely individual than either. But if X is not the whole of things, then it must be related to other things which lie beyond it. Call one of these other things Y. Then X and Y can only be related if there is a larger whole W which is more genuine than either taken separately. The same principle holds again, unless indeed W be the universe. Ultimately there must be either things which are not related at all or the universe must be more of a genuine unit than anything else. The weaker version of the principle will not sustain so strong a conclusion but it will still imply that the Universe must be at least as genuine a reality as any of the included terms. Moving up to the relevant larger wholes one cannot move towards something less genuine as a unit than one started with.

§ It seems to me that it is difficult to resist at least the weaker holistic principle. However, perhaps its formulation should be qualified to meet an objection raised by Russell, that it cannot apply to the part-whole or whole—part relation. For, he asks, if A is a part of B, does this part-whole relation between them turn on their belonging together in a whole other than B or is B itself the whole in question? And he finds difficulties in both alternatives.[3] To meet this objection, it is only necessary to acknowledge that as well as relations, the holding of which turns on the terms helping to constitute larger wholes, there are relations the holding of which turns on the fact that one of the terms goes together with other things to make up the second term. The general point still stands that relations have essentially to do with the constitution of wholes.

§ Could the argument to the Absolute from the holistic principle be resisted by arguing that the series of larger wholes contribution to the formation of which is required for terms to be related may go on infinitely without reaching a final term? For might not particulars at each level be united in larger wholes and these larger wholes united in still larger wholes and so on endlessly without there ever being a final whole such as the Absolute?

Well, that would seem to require that the whole in which related terms belong is logically derivative from the terms and their relations rather than the converse. And that would go against the principle as it must be understood in relation to Bradley. For it is supposed to explain what really is the case when terms are properly said to be related in a certain way, not merely to point out a logical consequence of their being so.

§ To meet these points the stronger holistic principle should perhaps be reformulated as follows (and the weaker correspondingly): For two or more terms to be related is (or at least the reality underlying this relational appearance is) *either* for them to constitute together, or help along with other things to constitute, a more comprehensive thing which is more of a genuine individual than are any of the things taken individually, *or* for one of them to be a more genuine individual than the other which the latter helps along with other things to constitute.

§ One who wishes to avoid the conclusion that the universe is a more genuine individual than anything within it, or at least as much of one, is likely to look for relations which seem to disconfirm the holistic principle. A hopeful example of these are *ideal* relations, that is, relations of *contrast* or *affinity*, and such relations of *more* or *less* as do not require alignment with a common measuring device for their recognition. These are roughly the relations Hume misleadingly called relations between ideas. (The description is misleading because contrasts, say, in geometrical shape, hold between actual shapes just as much or more than between our ideas of them, at least when the latter are understood à la Hume as images.)

Bradley does not distinguish real and ideal relations, in this sense, but it is clear enough that if he did he would hold that the holistic principle applies to the latter too. And all those philosophers ought to agree with him who think that ideal relations rest upon the possibility of a comparison. For it is evident that things can only be compared if they are in real relations to one another.[4]

---

3   See Russell, *Principles*, pp. 225–26.
4   In any case, it is impossible to reduce ideal relations to the results of a merely

But perhaps his main line of thought does not require this claim. It may be enough for him to claim that every two things in the universe are in some real relation to each other, and that, in virtue of this, the universe is as real an individual as, or more so than, anything within it. This could be called the principle of universal real relatedness.

However, it is very natural to suppose that there might be two worlds having nothing whatever to do with each other, but such that there are definite ideal relations between them and the objects they include. For surely things in quite separate worlds, not linked spatially, temporally, psychically, or in any other 'real' way, would still contrast or be akin to each other in quite determinate ways.

Even if that were granted, one could still defend a position close to Bradley's by saying that such totally separated worlds do not belong in the same universe in any proper sense. One might then affirm the holistic principle together with the principle of universal real relatedness of 'our' universe and come to conclusions about this of Bradley's kind.

So even if we admit the possibility of two universes between which there are no relations except ideal ones, and that the holistic principle does not apply to these, one might say that all we can reasonably mean by *the universe* is our universe, the totality of everything to which we ourselves are in any sort of real relation at all, however indirect. And it would be a strong metaphysical claim that this must be as genuine an individual (and on the stronger principle a more genuine individual) than anything within it, even if it were allowed that there might be another universe quite disconnected from anything concerning us.

Bradley, indeed, wants to make the stronger claim that this is true of the universe conceived as including absolutely everything that there is. For this he needs either the holistic principle, affirmed both of real and of ideal relations, in conjunction with an unamended principle of universal relatedness, or affirmed of real relations in conjunction with a principle of universal real relatedness. But even if he has no right to either of these (and I am not suggesting that he does not), the proof that 'our' universe must be as genuine an individual as anything within it, based on a principle of universal real relatedness (applicable to it by definition), in conjunction with the holistic principle would be no mean achievement. For it runs contrary to pluralistic views for which we can

---

possible comparison. To say that A can be compared to B, though they are not being experienced together, means that they could be experienced together and found to have these relations. But that means that A and B, when brought together, must retain the qualitative character they had when apart. But this retention of character must be an ideal relation holding between each of them as it was before and as it is after the comparison, and that cannot itself be a matter of their being able to be compared. Of course, if they ultimately belong to one experience, then their contrasts may indeed be experienced, though not necessarily deliberately compared. But that is to treat ideal relations as having a holistic element. See Sprigge (1983), pp. 188–90 (also pp. 180–87) for a fuller treatment.

be in real relation to things which are not elements in any larger whole as genuine an individual as ourselves and for which even 'our' universe is rather just lots and lots of things rather than a genuine individual in its own right. It would be a stronger claim still if he could show his right to the holistic principle in its stronger form and conclude that 'our' universe must be more of a genuine individual than anything within it, something it is the main aim of pluralism to deny. I shall, however, ignore, for the remainder of this chapter, the complications which a distinction between real and ideal relations bring into the picture and explore Bradley's use of an unqualified holistic principle and principle of universal relatedness.

§ Another sort of relations which may seem to avoid the holistic principle are those of cause and effect. It may seem that one event can cause another without their making up any kind of genuine whole together. But I doubt if that is really so.

Conceptions of causation are of two main types. On the first, the holding of a causal relation between particulars is not really a relation between these particulars but the fact that a certain relation between them instantiates a law. So there is really no such thing as a causal relation between events, simply the fact that certain relations between them conform to a certain universal rule. Such a causal law will imply that wherever there is an A there will be a B related to it in a certain way, and thus presuppose relations between things which do not require causation for their analysis. On this view, then, causal 'relations' are not genuine relations, but consist in the truth of general or nomic propositions about the relations in which events answering to one description must stand to those answering to another. Bradley could then appeal to the holistic principle in respect of these genuine relations which fall under the law and show that they can only hold between things which help make up more comprehensive wholes *as*, or perhaps *more*, genuine as units than they are.[5]

We may note in passing that it is very superficial to suppose (as is often done) that one can answer worries which have arisen in the Cartesian tradition as to how the mental and physical can interact, if they are distinct sorts of reality, by saying that, since causation is simply constant connection, or at most connectedness according to universal law, there is no reason why it should only hold between things which have some kind of common nature. For the worry that mental and physical events cannot be causally related, because they have no common nature, really stems from the difficulty which is found in conceiving them as forming any real whole together and the sense that this is required if

---

5   Could there perhaps be a law that if a thing of a specific nature X exists, then something of a specific nature Y exists, but not in any particular relation, and perhaps in no real relation at all, to each other? I doubt if this makes sense, but if it did, then things whose only connection was through a causal law of such a sort would exist in a state of separation from one another which would be hardly credible. See Sprigge (1983), pp. 239–40 (also pp. 211–13 and pp. 144–45).

they are to be in real relationship. (This is particularly obvious in connection with Spinoza's treatment of the topic.)

For causation, understood as correlation or succession according to law, implies that cause and effect are correlated or temporally related in a way which does not itself need to be explained by reference to causation. And the problem is what this correlation or temporal relation can be between the mental and physical. Correlation is usually understood as implying a spatial relation of some sort, but from a Cartesian point of view, the mental is not in space and it cannot be put there by appeal to causation, unless some other form of connectedness provided by some non-spatial whole can be found which causal laws state to hold universally. And it is doubtful if merely temporal relations will do since that would suggest that there is nothing which determines *where* the effects of a mental event in the physical world (or of a physical in the mental) might take place and that the real togetherness of the mental and the physical has no finer grain than that of one moment of the world's history to another. Besides, it is hard to reject the claim, which the proponent of the holistic principle would make, that we can only make sense of temporal relations as occurring within a unitary process stretched out in time and that it is difficult to conceive such a unitary process combining mental and physical events which are not elements of a common space or of something else which substitutes for this.

Some thinkers, however, reject this whole approach to causation and insist that it is a real relation between particular events. These may all fall under universal laws, but such laws concern the circumstances under which causal relations hold between particular events and thus cannot serve in an analysis of causation. Is there a coherent conception of causation along these lines in which the holistic principle does not apply to it?

The trouble is that it is very difficult to give any real body to such a conception. Most such attempts seem to take for granted that we have some intuitive sense of causation as a relation of influence holding between particular events, which does not amount to the claim that some other relation between them is the instance of a universal law. But it is more than doubtful whether we do. The nearest to a successful account of causation along these lines is the Jamesian and Whiteheadian one which reduces it to a feeling in the effect of having emerged out of the activity of the cause. And I suggest that it is here if anywhere that the opponent of the holistic principle, and of the monistic metaphysics it implies, must hope to escape their embrace. However, he can do so only at the cost of a panpsychism which only some would-be pluralists will be prepared to pay. Moreover, I believe that even if the feeling in such an effect is the registration of a genuine fact, it is one which can only be explained as its sense of belonging intimately together with the cause in a larger whole.

§ With the various understandings and qualifications to which our discussion has pointed, it seems to me that the holistic principle is very compelling and can perhaps be maintained even in its stronger form. It is at any rate a vital element in Bradley's thought. But we must be careful, of course, not to take 'whole' and 'part' in connection with it in a purely spatial sense, nor understand by 'larger' merely 'greater in spatial size'. Thus it may be clearer to substitute 'more comprehensive' for 'greater'. The objector may suspect that these terms do not have a clear meaning when used in a non-spatial sense. However, there is an obvious enough sense in which an ache may be part of my current conscious state, and my conscious state ('as a whole') be a more comprehensive reality than the headache, even if these realities are not spatial. Similarly for other examples.

But actually almost all the relations between items which are the coin of ordinary thought are either spatial, temporal, spatio-temporal relations, or relations, causal or otherwise, which require such relations between their terms. If one asks how one typically conceives family or social relations, there will always be at the basis of them causal relations which consist in interactions going on within a region of space and time to which each term belongs. Other sorts of relations may be grounded in these, but there seem to be none which do not similarly presuppose the basic spatial, temporal, or spatio-temporal relations.

Thus spatial/temporal relations are basic to ordinary thought, and this seems to be one with the fact that our ordinary way of thinking of things cannot work unless we think of related terms as included in a single region of space and time, which is larger or more comprehensive than that occupied by either term considered on its own. Without space and time our ordinary concept of how things are related collapses.

§ To get to Bradley's Absolute (and away from that ordinary concept) one needs to combine a holistic view of relations with a premiss of a quite other sort, namely, that the only genuine reality is sentient experience. According to Bradley experience is the very stuff of being. The idea of something which *is* without either being an experience, or included in one, is incoherent. (One can perhaps interpret his argument as initially allowing that we may be able to conceive also of something composed of experiences in relation without itself being an experience, but rejecting this on the basis of the argument for monism.) Whenever one forms an adequate conception of anything, what one really conceives is either an experience or something which cannot be coherently conceived except as an element, or internal object, of an experience. Physical things can only be conceived in any satisfactory way as the object of certain perceptual or perhaps intellectual experiences, numbers can only be conceived as the internal objects of mathematical operations, and so forth. We will examine all this more precisely later.[6]

The thesis that there is nothing but experience does not of itself establish that the universe is a single experience of the sort Bradley supposes the Absolute to be. It does not even establish it when taken together with the principle of universal relatedness. For without the holistic principle it might be that every experience could be related to every other without their all combining to

---

6   See also Sprigge (1983), pp. 110–40 for a fuller discussion.

constitute any kind of unitary overall experience, let alone one with the unity ascribed to the Absolute. It may be said that, if the thesis is true, then the universe could not *be* without being an experience. However, the pluralist upholder of the thesis may say that strictly there is no such thing as the universe, only lots of individual experiences related to each other in various ways. Or he might temper it enough to let himself say that the universe is *composed* of experiences without itself *being* an experience. We have seen that James's pluralistic panexperientialism takes one or other of these only verbally distinct positions.

But if we combine the thesis that the stuff of the universe is experience with the holistic principle and that of universal relatedness, then we can move swiftly to a proof of the existence of the Absolute. If every genuine item in the universe is an experience or element of experience, and if every such item is related to every other, then all such items must together constitute a whole which is as genuine an individual as any experience it includes. Thus it must be as genuine an individual as those total experiences which make up the state of a human or animal at any particular moment, together with every other kind of units of experience there may be. What kind of whole could this be? To Bradley it seems clear that the only whole which could fill this role would be something which was itself a unified individual experience. And it seems to me that he is right. It seems impossible that such total experiences could belong together in any whole other than an experience in which they are combined in a synthetic unity somewhat as our various individual sensations, ideas, and feelings at any one moment combine to form a single state of consciousness. It seems impossible that the elements of a purely psychical universe could combine to form a whole except in a way analogous to this. A genuine individual composed of experiences can only be conceived as itself a single complex but unified experience.

§ We could sum up this argument in these three propositions:

(1) the basic constituents of reality are experiences;
(2) these are all related to each other so as to form a single universe;
(3) proposition (2) can only be true, if these constituents all belong together as elements of one single cosmic experience.

Objections to the argument are likely to centre on (1) and (3) rather than on (2). And it will be particularly worth our while to concentrate here on the reasons why proposition (3) is likely to leave people uneasy. For this represents the main parting of the ways between James and Bradley's panexperientialist metaphysic. Moreover, it is arguable that the main case for the Absolute would go through even if we replaced (1) by the scarcely contestable proposition (1a) that reality does include such things as our experiences. For one might well argue on the basis of the holistic principle and the principle of universal relatedness that even if there are things other than experiences, still the experiences must belong together with everything else in a whole which is at least as genuine an individual as the most genuinely individual experience, and that this itself can only be an experience. (If this were accepted, one might then attempt to argue back to (1) on the ground that what is included in an experience must itself be an experience.)

Why, then, does (3) remain unconvincing to most people? I suggest it is because they implicitly accept something at least akin to the holistic principle, and the principle of universal relatedness, but secretly assume that experiences are in space and time and that it is these which provide the whole in which they are all contained. For, as has been clear, at least since Kant, the human mind is determinedly spatialising and temporalising and tends to conceive all relations, and all wholes, as of a spatial, temporal, or spatio-temporal nature. Thus if you ask how your experiences now are related to mine, you think most obviously of the spatial relations holding between us, and think of your experiences as in some sense resident in your head, and mine in mine, and thus as related in a manner the same as, or derivative from, that in which our heads are. And if I ask how my experiences are related to Bradley's, I think of his as having led to his writing *Appearance and Reality* and my having read a book physically continuous with his manuscript in specifiable ways, and having been influenced thereby to the thoughts which spill out in the physical activity of writing this. But if there is nothing except experience, we have to take a different view of space and time from the common one.

For once you see the universe as essentially psychical, space and time, as ordinarily conceived, cannot be the great containers. Their role must be played by something more psychical, and the Bradleyan will challenge us as to what that could be but some kind of single cosmic experience.

§ But what are space and time on Bradley's account? Well, for him the common space which is supposed to include all physical things is a construction each of us makes on the basis of our perceptual experience. We think of our perceptual field as an extract from a much larger whole of roughly the same sort, and we suppose that there are other perceptual fields, such as those of other people, which are other extracts from this same great whole. Also we think of our past perceptual fields as extracts from the same great whole as it was in the past. But this construction, though it works splendidly for elaborate practical and intellectual purposes, is not acceptable as finally coherent. For one thing, each perceptual field stretches out from a kind of centre, which means that it cannot really be thought of as an abstract from the same spatial thing as *your* perceptual field which stretches out from another such centre. So space as the great container is only a convenient and finally incoherent construction.

His view of the common time in which all events are supposed to occur is similar, though it is likely to appear more puzzling at first. Thus he holds that time is a construction made within each of our centres of experience, by an act through which we conceive a greater and kindred whole, of which our specious presents are extracts, extending beyond these as the larger space extends beyond our perceptual fields. Thus experiences can only really be in anything like time together if they all pertain to one great experienced specious present which is the universe as a whole.

It follows from this that the absolute experience cannot itself be in time. For it makes no sense to speak of it as changing. That is not because it persists through time without alteration, but because time exists within it, rather than it within time.

> If there is not, present in this passing 'now', a Reality which contains all 'nows' future and past, the whole of our truth and knowledge must be limited to the 'now' that we perceive.
>
> ETR, p. 332

We can best understand this as follows. Every finite experience is, so to speak, from its own point of view the transition point between a preceding and a following experience (ignoring such qualifications as may need to be made regarding experiences at the start or end of a unified stream of consciousness). It feels itself to be in transition; its felt transitoriness and ephemerality is of the essence of its quality as an experience. But the final truth about the Absolute is that it is an eternal experience which comprises all these experiences which feel so transitory to themselves, but does not feel itself as a whole to be a stage in an ongoing process. It can experience change, in that all history lies within it, and it feels the temporal relations between its elements just as we feel, within one specious present, the change going on within that in one single unitary experience. But our specious presents feel themselves to be merely the temporary stopping points of an ongoing process, and it is only at the level of the Absolute that this feeling of their own transitoriness is experienced as an eternal, changeless item in an eternal, changeless reality. Thus every total experiential state, such as constitutes a cross-section of the stream of our experience—to whatever date it belongs—is just eternally there as an element in the one total absolute experience. But to us whose lives consist in a series of such states it seems that each one ceases almost as it comes into existence and gives way to another.

Although the Absolute thus contains time within it, Bradley insists that what falls within it need not all find a place in one single history.[7] For not only may the Absolute contain timeless elements, but even its temporal elements may not all belong to some one single temporal system. There may be a plurality of histories within the Absolute with no time relations to be felt between them, though certainly there will be some relations between them, that is, some manner in which they fall together within the unity of the Absolute.

§ It might be objected to Bradley that even if the only sort of unit which could include all those experiences which form the stuffing of the world is one akin to one of our own specious presents, the real unity of things may nonetheless be something of which we cannot have the glimmering of a conception. Bradley would reply, I think, that we cannot seriously believe that things belong together in the same universe in the absence of any conception at all of how they do so.

Thus the Absolute is a single experience in which everything is contained

---

7   See AR, chapter XVIII.

timelessly. Everything which there really is is either an experience or an element in an experience.

§ Bradley's doctrine of the Absolute is, I believe, the most forceful version of the monism against which we have seen James so constantly struggling. And it is argued for on the basis of principles which had considerable force for him. For the panexperientialist premiss is common to our two philosophers while the conception of the Absolute is modelled on a conception of our single states of consciousness, as they occur moment by moment, which is very close to that to which James mostly adhered (though, revealingly, he abandoned it temporarily in his most extremely pluralistic period; see above at pp. 118–19; 124–26; 149–50). In fact, James's whole treatment of relations, and his eventual conclusion that their nature cannot be adequately captured in conceptual thought, can be seen as his struggle to escape the holistic principle. I shall now turn to another aspect of Bradley's thought which has much in common with James's.

§3. *Finite Centres of Experience*

§ So the Absolute is the whole of things in its true character and its 'matter', as Bradley puts it, is experience. Other putative realities can have existence only in the sense that judgements which posit them are useful for practical purposes, though the concepts they utilise are so riddled with contradictions that they cannot present absolute truth. At best they point to elements of the Absolute which they misrepresent by depicting them as intelligible in their own right rather than mere abstractions from a more concrete whole.

But who (or what), it may be wondered, can it be that makes these judgements, seeing that human subjects, as ordinarily understood, are as riddled with contradictions as anything else? Presumably they occur as elements within the Absolute, or at least there is something in the Absolute to which the concept of such a judgement approximates.

A fuller answer is that they occur in what Bradley often calls *finite centres of experience*. By such a centre is meant a totality of experience such as (to express the matter by way of more ordinary concepts) at any one moment is the world and himself as someone then experiences it. The concept of such a centre contains its own contradictions but it provides something closer to a grasp of the real articulation of the Absolute than do the concepts of ordinary life, including that of a human person, and must be employed in the nearest to a literally true metaphysical account of reality available to us, or rather available to what really corresponds to such centres in the Absolute.

It is these centres which provide the concrete filling of the Absolute. It is constituted— or so it must be said to be in what Bradley thinks the best available metaphysical account—by an inconceivably large multitude of such centres. Each of the experiences which go together to make it up either is itself such a centre, or is included in one, or, more problematically, occurs as a common element in a number of them. (Actually Bradley suggests it as a remote possibility that the Absolute contains a margin of experience which is not filtered through finite centres of experience, but let us leave this qualification aside for now.)

§ Let us consider more closely what these centres are. Probably the best answer, though not given quite in these terms by Bradley, is that a finite centre of experience is the kind of thing you are seeking knowledge of if you ask yourself what it must be like to be some other individual at a certain moment.[8] That at least is what such a centre is if it is conceived as something momentary, so that there is a different such centre pertaining to me in every successive specious present. Bradley also sometimes speaks of finite centres of experience as though they were continuants which change over time, but for the present I shall stick to the conception of them as momentary.

Suppose you look at someone else at some moment of high emotion on his part and you ask yourself what it is really like being him at that time. You are not asking a question about what is going on inside him physically nor about what he is observably doing, or likely to do. It is a question of a quite different sort. And surely it is a perfectly meaningful question, however difficult it may be to be sure one has come anywhere near the right answer.

You can ask yourself the same sort of question about an animal. You look at a seagull soaring through the air and then suddenly plunging down towards some bread which is lying on the ground. You wonder what it is really like being that seagull. That which you want to know about is not the *seagull as a publicly observable physical thing* with a certain outwardly visible form and internal anatomy.[9] If you want to know more about that you go to a zoologist or an anatomist or someone of that sort. But since it is unlikely that the seagull has any idea of the position of its heart and liver you do not have to bring these into the picture at all. What you do have to bring into the picture is its form so far as that, as felt from the inside, is part of what it is like to be the seagull, and such outward things as the bread as it sees it from way above as it plunges down to grab it.

So when you wonder what it is like to be someone else at a certain moment, or a seagull at a certain moment, you are wondering about the character of something which cannot be straightforwardly identified with that individual person or animal as an organism in the public physical world. But there is certainly something which you believe to exist and which you are trying to characterise to yourself. And it is to things of that sort that Bradley is referring when he speaks of finite centres of experience.

---

8   I first proposed this way of characterising consciousness in my 'Final Causes' PASS, XLV (1971), pp. 166 et ff. The same idea was independently developed more fully by Thomas Nagel in 1974 in his 'What Is It Like to Be a Bat?', reprinted as chapter XII of Nagel, *Mortal.*

9   Nor are you concerned with any physical question about its brain, including here questions about any computer-type programme it is running. Knowledge of this might assist an empathically inclined person to form a likely conception of what it is like to be the seagull, but certainly could not constitute such a conception.

A simpler name for such a centre is 'a total state of consciousness'. It is much what James means by a pulse of experience. However, Bradley's views about their role in reality means that his own expression has some special implications of its own.

This account of centres of experience leaves it completely open which organisms and things in the world are associated with them. Most people think that tables have no consciousness, that is, that there is no truth as to *what it is like being* any table. If you think animals are unconscious, that will, in your opinion, apply to animals as well as tables. The only point to be insisted on is that there is a particular sort of wonder, which can be framed as the question what it is like being so and so, as it is at this moment, and that such wondering rests on the belief that there is something such as Bradley calls a centre of experience *there* at that moment and concerns its character. 'There', in this case, does not mean 'discoverable in that part of space' but rather 'existing as an experience of things from the point of view of what occupies that space'.

Some philosophers say they can make little of the use of such an expression as 'what it is like being a certain creature at a certain time' to name a supposed entity. Their trouble is probably that they suppose that what is in question is an ineffable and elusive something having nothing to do with the world of ordinary observation. But this is a great mistake. The conscious state, or centre of experience, which is what it is like being someone, contains the ordinary things around him in his version of them. Thus that of another need not be altogether hidden from me. It may be very near to mine, or at least be something into which I can enter imaginatively. If I want to know what it is like being John Smith now, whom I believe to be at a concert, I need to know just what music he is hearing. If he is just hearing the beginning of a familiar symphony, then the first thing I need to know is what it is like for an ordinarily equipped listener to hear those opening sounds. Doubtless there will be subtle differences in the way they occur as elements in John's finite centre, but I certainly know a good deal about his current experiential state if I know what those sounds are like, that is, what it is like to be someone hearing them. And if you want to know what it is like to be that person over there sitting in a chair and looking out of the window, you need to know, in a quite ordinary way, what there is to be seen there, and have some familiarity in your own person of sitting in such a chair. Knowing what someone is doing and is up to in the normal way goes with some idea of what it is like to be doing and being up to that; the experiential state is not some mysterious ineffable thing which goes along with one's publicly observable situation but with nothing intrinsically to do with it. Indeed, at the level of ordinary non-philosophical thinking knowing the publicly observable facts about someone and having some idea of what it is like being him go naturally together. Philosophically, however, we need to distinguish them. For sometimes one can know exactly what an organism was doing and what stimuli were reaching its brain and not know what it was like being it. Thus a deaf person could know exactly the physical nature of sound, and all physical aspects of hearing, and not know what it was like to hear sound. Moreover, knowing about a person's finite centre of experience, knowing what it is like being him, is knowing something of a kind which simply does not apply to inanimate objects, on the ordinary assumption that they are quite unconscious.

§ Another way of putting it is to say that a centre of experience is some individual's momentary subjective version of the world. This includes the physical environment as perceptually, and perhaps even as conceptually, presented, and his body as he feels it, both as an object of attention and in the form of action. (There is a certain difficulty as to whether what is only conceptually presented can be a literal part of one's centre, which I shall be considering below. What is perceptually presented certainly is so.)

There are, indeed, problems as to how a person's subjective version of the world relates to *the* world but no reasonable view will suppose them to be things quite apart, whose characters do not bear on each other. One sort of idealist will think that the world, in the relevant sense, is a highest common factor of a community of conscious beings' subjective versions thereof; other, more realist, thinkers will think that the subjective versions of the world are *the* world as not always quite correctly represented in different minds. But both views imply that knowledge of another individual's subjective version of the world cannot be known or conceived in detachment from knowledge and conception of the world and that individual's position and activity within it. Still, we do have our different subjective versions of the world. One simple sign of this is that my version gives me a central kind of place in it while yours gives you a central kind of place in it.

It is worth insisting that the knowledge of what it is like to be someone at a certain moment is not a matter of being able to assent to some cut-and-dried verbal statements. Appropriate such assent may occur in its absence and will not, in practice, adequately express it when it is there. It consists rather in properly grasping the character of something in one's imagination. Verbal statements may trigger off successful such imagining in some sympathetic listener, or may refine one's own ability to know this sort of thing through sympathetic imagination, but no statement can capture the 'what it is like to be someone' at a particular moment (or representative facts about what it is like to be them in general) in a way which can be guaranteed to do this job for any ordinary speaker of the language.

It may seem roundabout to explain what momentary centres of experience are as things of the sort of which you are thinking when you try to imagine what it is like being some other conscious individual at some particular moment. Would it not be better to say that one knows best what such a momentary centre is by considering just what it is like being oneself at a particular moment? But there is a good reason for preferring the first approach.

For it is not at all clear that you can direct your attention upon your present centre. For one thing, even as you try to focus your attention on the present centre it is gone. More fundamentally, your very act of attention is an element in the centre of experience of this moment, and can't attend to itself. Thus you can't really direct your attention to your present centre in any proper way, but only to some element in it. Moreover, it is not only the act of attention which can't properly be attended to, for there are always other aspects of the centre which are vaguely felt, but aren't directly before your conscious attention.

So you must learn about these centres either by attending to past ones of your own in memory or by trying to imagine someone else's centre, rather than by thinking about your present one. You cannot examine one when it is actually in being as your state of mind. This is not, of course, to deny that you do *feel* without being exactly *conscious of* your centre as a whole at each moment. Bradley suggests that this vague feeling of your present centre as a whole serves as a guide in the background when you try to form a conception of what such a centre is.[10]

One may say that it is a paradox of these momentary centres that, while our lives as conscious subjects in a sense consist in *being* a series thereof, they cannot really be brought completely before our consciousness. When we try to think about them clearly we find all sorts of paradoxes arise which show that there are incoherences in our conception of them. For this reason Bradley holds that even they are to be regarded as in a sense unreal. Our concept of them certainly points to something real, but it can never do adequate justice to it, since it cannot quite correspond to the best concept of such a centre we can form. For our best such concept is incoherent in a way in which reality itself cannot be.

Certainly for Bradley the concept of a finite centre of experience is a very basic one by reference to which the nature of other more ordinary things is to be explicated. Thus, on his account, a physical thing is a construction based upon certain elements present in centres of experience, while a self (in one main sense) is one particular aspect of such a centre. Doesn't that make it unsatisfactory to explain what a centre of experience is, as I have done, through the use of more ordinary, and for Bradley less ultimate, expressions, such as person or seagull?

It is true that these were rather my own attempts to clarify the concept than Bradley's, but there is nothing in such explanations alien to Bradley's approach; indeed, an adequate presentation of his views requires something of the sort. But that does not show that Bradley has no right to take the concept of such centres as more basic than the concept of persons, things, or animals. To introduce a special metaphysical concept one needs to explain it by reference to concepts of a more ordinary and familiar kind. That does not preclude its being the concept of a more basically intelligible reality in terms of which more ordinary realities have to be explained. So it may both be true that it is the best way of introducing the notion of what a centre of experience is to say that it is the 'what it is like to be it' of an organism at a certain time, and true that the metaphysically most adequate explanation of what an organism is will be by explaining the kind of presentation it is *to* or *in* a finite centre of experience. Thus finite centres of experience may be the fundamental realities of the world,

---

10   See ETR, chapter VI.

and the ordinary objects of the world only exist as presentations or constructions developed within them, in spite of the fact that the notion of such centres has to be introduced by talk presupposing our possession of the concept of these more ordinary things.

Moreover, having introduced the notion of a finite centre of experience as the kind of thing of which one is thinking when one wonders what it is like like being some organism, we may go on to the conception of centres which do not pertain to an organism at all. For once our attention is pointed to that kind of reality one may see that there might be cases of it which are not related to any conscious physical organism in this way. And it seems to me quite possible that there are, as Bradley seems to have believed.

The point I am making is not so much that centres of experience may be ontologically more basic than more familiar things like persons and physical objects, and yet epistemologically less basic. The contrast is rather between what is conceptually basic and what is linguistically so. Both James and Bradley think that sentient experience is something the nature of which is in a manner immediately known to us, while the nature of physical things is something which becomes more and more problematic the more we reflect. But we do not normally have cause to talk of experience as such, and since we think we understand better what a physical thing is, we can indeed best have our thoughts directed to experience itself, by talk which identifies it by reference to its physical context as ordinarily conceived. Nonetheless we may always have known better in an intuitive way what experience is, and the way in which it comes in units such as Bradley's finite centres of experience, than what the physical world is. Thus claiming a certain basicness for this concept in metaphysics is quite compatible with the fact that it must be introduced into our discourse by way of precisely those concepts which are later to be explicated by reference to it.

§ So far I have been taking centres of experience as things with a merely momentary existence. And certainly Bradley does often so take them. In this sense they are just the same as what he sometimes calls *this-nows*. (In fact, 'this-now' is the preferred term in AR: 'finite centre' only becomes part of his regular vocabulary in the essays collected in ETR.) However, Bradley often speaks as though centres of experience were continuants, so that one's conscious life does not consist of a succession of them but of a single one which changes. In fact, he seems to operate with two different concepts of a centre of experience, one in which it is in effect momentary in its existence, another in which it is a continuant.

Sometimes he tries to clarify things by using the word 'soul' to stand for a centre considered as a continuant, of which successive momentary centres are passing states. Such a use of 'soul' is somewhat eccentric, but I shall sometimes follow Bradley in using it as shorthand for 'finite centre of experience considered as a continuant', contrasting it with the term 'momentary centre' (not one used by Bradley) for such a centre considered as momentary. Before we investigate how the notion of a soul, or finite centre conceived as a continuant, relates to the notion of it as something momentary, let us consider in just what sense centres taken in the latter way are, indeed, momentary.

§ Bradley sometimes speaks of a centre of experience as not being in time.[11] Here he is certainly talking of centres of experience conceived as momentary (odd as it may seem that the 'momentary' should be timeless). Why he calls them timeless can be understood if we once grasp that for Bradley 'time', together with 'space' and all the ordinary things *in* space and time, are a construction made within each of these centres (real time being the common element in the constructions of a community of such centres whose constructions coincide because they are all parts of the unitary life of the Absolute). Thus it is less true to say that the centres are in time than that time is in them. Any particular dated event in the object world exists in virtue of the fact that it is either perceptually or conceptually presented or posited within the felt unity of such a centre, being real to the extent that the taking it as such in one centre is borne out by what is presented within other centres. Each centre will present the event from a different spatial and temporal point of view, but as being the locus for the construction of space and time they are, as Bradley sees it, not themselves properly in space and time. They are, so to speak, the individual bits of story telling whereby the Absolute tells itself the story or history of the ordinary world of physical events and are commonly no more in the story than a novelist is commonly in his novel. But it still seems clear that, for Bradley, each is particularly associated with a certain position in the space and time of the object world, from which, so to speak, it looks out at that world. And though we can think of this position as one with which a continuing soul is only momentarily associated, it is more fundamentally true that it is just one of the positions from which the Absolute looks out eternally at the world. Thus it is not in time, but rather one of the foci in which the object world, with its space and time, is presented. (It is, one might say, part of the projector through which the film of life is projected, not something within that film.) Thus they are timeless or eternal as viewpoints on the world rather than events in it, and yet, if we try to bring them under the ordinary concepts which apply to the world on which they are eternal perspectives, we must say that they are but momentary.

Thus their being timeless in their real being is quite compatible with their being momentary qua elements in the world constructed from within them, if eventually they themselves are brought into the story they tell. For ordinary thought, which operates in terms of that construction, they are momentary events in time, with an outlook on the world determined by this, but their more fundamental character is that of eternal pieces of the story about time which the Absolute tells itself.

§ They are *momentary*, but they are not *instantaneous*. Rather do they include a before and after within them. Indeed, Bradley's conception of them would

---

11   See ETR, p. 410.

seem to be quite close to that of James's of one of his individual pulses of experience (or Whitehead's 'actual occasions'.)[12] However, since James's account is so much easier to grasp than Bradley's, it is tempting to seek refuge from the obscurities of Bradley's discussions and assimilate his position more closely to James's than is correct. Certainly to me it seems he would have done well to take over much of what James has to say here, and would thereby have improved the presentation of his own metaphysic.

He is certainly like James in thinking that there is something about the temporality of these momentary centres or this-nows which cannot be satisfactorily conceptualised. That is one reason why he thinks they are not finally real. We seem bound to say that there are such things but we can find no coherent answer to the questions which press upon us about the nature of their internal temporality, and how they take over from each other, as we shall be seeing later.

§ Though Bradley seems most often to mean by 'a finite centre of experience' something which is thus both timeless and momentary in the sense explained we must also examine the less common meaning in which it refers to a continuant or 'soul'. How are these two meanings related?

The most obvious answer would be that to talk of the existence of a soul or centre over time is simply to refer to the fact that there is a series of momentary centres of experience which take over from each other in much the way that the existence of an enduring self for James consists in a series of total 'thoughts' which do so. This series will be a series of what, looked at from the point of view of the ordinary construction of the world, are momentary events, though from a more profound point of view it is a non-temporal series of experiences, each providing its own perspective upon the world they jointly construct. We will see that some qualification of such an interpretation of Bradley's position is required, but it will serve well as a starting point. It should be realized, however, that for Bradley an account of the identity of an enduring soul over time is not, *ipso facto*, an account of an enduring self. The self, enduring or momentary, is only one aspect of a centre of experience, enduring or momentary, facing the not-self as its other aspect. In Bradley's usage it is only the not—self which is an object of consciousness, through being presented to the self; however, both self and not-self and the total centre of experience in which they are unified are experienced. (By whom? At one level by the centre itself, whose *being* and *feeling of its own being* are one and the same fact, at another by the Absolute as one of the ingredients it experiences itself as containing.)

§ In what sense, then, must a momentary centre take over from previous ones if they are to be phases in the life of an enduring soul? One likely suggestion is that it consists in that peculiarly intimate knowledge it has of them which constitutes memory. Sometimes Bradley does seem near to taking this view. It is suggested, for example, by much that he says on the intelligibility or other-

---

12   See CE, p. 695, for a remark by Bradley on his having learnt from Hegel what James thought unknown there.

wise of various conceptions of a life after death.[13] And although the question of personal identity and soul identity are theoretically distinct for him, it is doubtful if much hangs upon the distinction in this connection. However, he often says things which seem to preclude, and to be recognized as doing so, an analysis of the identity either of a soul or a self across time in terms of memory. For one thing, he associates it with a view to which he takes strong objection that memory is a form of immediate non-inferential knowledge of the past, a view which he thinks makes of it a 'miracle' or a 'psychological monster'.[14]

We shall have to investigate all this further. For the present it will be sufficient to take it that the identity of a soul across time is constituted by a special form of influence which passes from one momentary centre to another in a line which constitutes its life.

§ We must be careful, however, not to assimilate Bradley's position too closely to any for which the identity of a soul across time is simply the holding of certain relations between successive momentary centres of experience without there being any genuine identity to it. For Bradley's views on the nature of 'identity' provide a rather different slant on the whole matter from that of the usual proponents of such views.

In PL Bradley says that it takes two to make the same.[15] The idea is that while judgements of the pattern 'A is (identical with) A' seem to be vacuous and to say nothing, judgements of the form 'A is (identical with) B ' would seem bound to be false. So identity truths seem impossible. The answer to this problem, according to Bradley, is that sameness can only occur in combination with difference. Assertions of identity point out that something is the same in spite of a difference. So a genuine identity truth must be of the pattern 'A in context F is identical with A in context G' and that for this to be so these two, as well as being identical, must be different.

This approach to identity derives from Hegel. It is usually now thought to have been superseded by the superior account of Frege whereby the difference lies in the meaning of the expressions whereby we refer to one thing, without there being any real difference between the identical term and that other version of itself with which it is identical. Personally I think this view inadequate. It makes identity statements of any importance somehow the creation of our language, of the fact that we have differently sensed expressions for the same thing. Even if that is a fair account of some identity truths, the Hegelian and Bradleyan view does better justice to identity truths of a more important kind whose significance arises not from the fact that we happen to have two different ways of identifying something, but from the fact that it remains the same when it occurs in different contexts in the real world.[16]

---

13   See, for example, CE, essay XXIX, and ETR, chapter XV, appendix B.
14   See ETR, pp. 451–55; CE, essay XXIX.
15   See PL, p. 141; also pp. 287–88, 291 et ff. and elsewhere.
16   For a fuller discussion see Sprigge, 'Personal and Impersonal Identity'.

This is typically true of universals. A musical theme remains genuinely the same when repeated on different occasions, though it is also different in terms of its context. This is true even when the different context is merely that of being played at a different time and place. However, the element of difference increases when it is repeated in a different musical context or key. Here there is still sameness, but there is a difference which has entered more deeply into it. To say that the theme is the same as itself on just one occasion is saying absolutely nothing. But recognizing it as the same thing which can occur in different contexts, and in different keys, is noticing a genuine fact of identity, one which involves difference too. This applies likewise to spatial forms and patterns. One can recognize the same pattern on the wallpaper in different rooms, and the difference may become more intrinsic when the pattern is repeated in different colours.

The fact that these genuine identity truths involve universals prompts the suggestion that all genuine identity truths do so. But if so, anything which continues as one and the same thing over time must be a universal. And this is precisely Bradley's view of ordinary continuants. They are not, indeed, abstract universals but concrete ones. I take this to mean primarily that their presence at any one time, with various alterations, stands in a special causal linkage to their presence at other times, in a manner not supposed to be true of purely abstract universals.[17]

In the light of this Bradley is able to hold that there can be a real identity between what exists at one time and what at another even though the difference of time also makes them different. This is as true of historical individuals as of things like themes, shapes, and colours.

This suggests that to ask: 'But is the centre of experience at one moment really the same centre as the one it took over from?' is misconceived since identity or sameness is never an all-or-nothing affair. If one wishes to stress the element of difference between the centres, as occurring at different times and, to a great extent, with different contents, one will call them different and regard them as momentary. If, on the other hand, one wants to stress the element of identity or sameness, one will regard them as one and the same enduring centre. As

---

17 See, for example, PL, pp. 186–96. He contends there that both abstract universals and abstract particulars are unreal and that every genuine individual (with one exception) is both universal and particular, and therefore a concrete universal. The universality lies in the fact that it is something which occurs as the same amidst differences, such as in distinguishable elements of its character, or at different times, or perhaps places. Its particularity consists in the fact that it is restricted in the region of reality in which it occurs. The Universe or Absolute is the one thing which is not particular in this sense (p. 195, note 27); however, it is no mere abstract universal but the whole of things which is also immanent in all that it contains. Thus from a Bradleyan point of view, what can be the same in different contexts is always a kind of universal, never a substance in the traditional sense. See further Part Two, Chapter Five, §1, below.

something which can be present as its own identical self at different times, it is a certain sort of universal. So there is no problem in principle in ascribing a real identity to the soul across time.

So it may not be quite accurate to regard Bradley as having used the expression 'centre of experience' in two senses, sometimes to refer to something momentary, sometimes to something enduring. It may be meant to stand rather for something which at any one moment both is and is not identical with something existing also at other times.

However, although his general view of identity permits my present centre of experience to be both genuinely the same and genuinely different from itself at other times, at a more concrete level, Bradley, at least in his later works, takes quite a dim view of how much real sameness there is in this case, doubting whether there is anything distinctively the same over the life of what we commonly recognize as one individual. Though logically there could be, it is doubtful that in fact there is.[18]

§ I have already indicated the considerable common ground between James and Bradley on the nature of consciousness or (since Bradley uses the expression 'consciousness' rather restrictively) sentient experience and the self. The point is worth developing.

Both philosophers have a highly holistic view of a pulse or momentary centre of experience, while tending to a somewhat atomistic view of the sequence of such which constitutes the life of a conscious continuant. Thus both provide much the same riposte to the position of empiricists like Hume.

Hume thought that a mind or a person was a bundle of sensations (or 'impressions') and ideas, but he thought it a grave problem what kept the components of one bundle together and also kept them apart from other bundles.

There are two distinct problems here:

(1) What constitutes the identity of a mind across time?

(2) What binds its elements together at any one time?

We have sufficiently considered Bradley's answer to the first question for the time being, but it is worth saying something more on his answer to the second. Bradley's implied answer is that a momentary centre of experience does not consist of distinct elements held together by problematic relations. For while it is variegated in character, it is not, after all, really made up of parts in relation. So it is only the inadequacies of our concepts which produce the question. The centre of experience is the primary reality and its so-called parts are only conceptually abstracted elements from the whole which have and could have no being except as aspects of its variegated unity.[19] There is not even any

---

18   See Part Two, Chapter Five, §2, for further discussion.

19   He thus utterly rejects Hume's idea that each of our perceptions answers to the criterion of a substance as something which might exist by itself. See Hume, *Treatise*, p. 233.

definite number of them. The experience has a general kind of many-ness and different elements will emerge for different sorts of analysis. But they are only abstractions from the totality convenient as a way of describing it. *Thus a centre of experience is a non-relational many-in-one, not composed of distinct elements in relation to each other.*

Certainly such a centre is normally quite variegated. It is not normally a single unitary feeling. But it is more real than its parts in the sense that, although we may have to refer to these in order to describe it, each one is so coloured in its character by its relation to the others that it is not really describable as a distinct thing in its own right. You distort the character of any element if you try to conceive it in separation from the rest. For the elements are not separate items somehow combined to make it up. Rather are they different but inseparable aspects of the unitary but variegated character of the whole.

All this is very like James except when the requirements of one sort of radical empiricism dragged him temporarily towards another view.

Each philosopher insists that the unity of consciousness or experience at any given moment should be explained by reference to the character of consciousness or experience itself, not by seeking the unity in something else, however spiritual. Thus they objected to the Kantian answer sometimes given to Hume, that experience is unified by some kind of so-called transcendental ego. For James and Bradley experience is unitary of its own nature and does not need to be held together by something else.

Where Bradley differs from James is in thinking that the way in which the elements of a momentary centre belong together, in a fashion which cannot properly be understood as the holding of relations between distinct items, is the key to the only way in which things can hang together in the universe at all. James, while seeing the force of this claim, was concerned to find a less intimate way in which things could belong together while somehow remaining a feature of the experiences themselves, and not a matter of their being held together by something like a transcendental ego. We shall be exploring this opposition between them further as we proceed.

Although Bradley clearly thinks that the answer to philosophers like Hume is along these lines, he did not think it could be satisfactorily formulated in discursive concepts. The unity of experience is not a matter of distinct items being held together by relations, but thought can only conceive the matter thus. And that is a reason for saying that centres of experience, as we conceive them, are not ultimately real. For the conception of them remains riddled with all the problems of relational thinking. And Bradley, as we shall see, thought this was particularly true with reference to the experience of time. Thus he was not quite prepared to move towards the pulselike view of a stream of consciousness favoured by James.

A contrast between our two philosophers is that James was much more ready to frame things, both with reference to consciousness and in general, in terms of an ontology of events rather than continuants. Although it is often convenient and clarifying to express Bradley's views in this mode, it can be somewhat misleading. Partly I think this was because he did not have the distinction between an event and a continuant ontology clear in his mind (something true also, though to a lesser extent, of James, indeed) and partly because his views on identity meant, as we have seen, that his items were neither quite events nor continuants, being describable in either way according as to whether it was their difference from, or their identity to, their successors which needed to be emphasised.

§4. *The Object World*

§I said that for Bradley there are basically three sorts of reality: (1) The Absolute; (2) Finite centres of experience; (3) the constructed object world. Let us now turn to this last.

It must be said that Bradley tends to leave the status of the object world rather vague. His best statement of his position is in 'On My Real World' in Essays on Truth and Reality (ETR). By the object world is meant roughly the world of daily life, above all the physical world. Bradley's view is that this exists only as an object of the perception and thought which goes on in 'souls'. Souls such as ours form a community whose experiences are sufficiently congruent to form the basis for a thought construction in which a physical world like ours is posited. The ideas pertaining to this construction give us a good deal of control over the course of our experience and can be developed into a system which gives considerable intellectual satisfaction.

That the physical world is only a thought construction is clear from the fact that it combines incompatible elements. Reality, so far as it is more than a useful posit, consists in innumerable finite centres of experience (and just possibly of an additional margin of experience not belonging to any such centre), all constituting together a single absolute experience. Among these centres are those which, conceived as continuants, are the souls of the human race, but it is almost certain that there are many others as well.

The construction of the object world is mainly by way of what Bradley calls analytic and synthetic judgements of sense. (His use of these words has almost nothing to do with the more usual sense derived from Kant.) An analytic judgement of sense offers an analysis of the sensorily given into distinguishable elements, as when I distinguish one part of the given scene as an apple. A synthetic judgement of sense treats what is given as a fragment of something larger of the same general sort, not given as a whole, but which it characterises by concepts drawn from what is or has been given. Thus I take the given space of my perceptual field as part of an indefinitely larger space and the given time, in which processes occur short enough to be perceived, as part of an indefinitely longer time stretching before and after it.

Both analytic and synthetic judgements of sense are essential aspects of that conceptualising of the given whereby it is rendered the presentation of a world. The analytic judgements sort what I actually perceive into distinct physical things, while the synthetic ones provide the ordinary belief in a nature most of which I never perceive. But there is a certain ambiguity in Bradley's distinction between them. When I split up, conceptually, what is presented into distinct things which I perceive, I am certainly making an analytic judgement of sense. But what if I judge that the apple is made of atoms? Here I am neither supplementing the given by seeing it as part of larger whole nor simply analysing what is sensibly present. Though Bradley does not deal with the point, it is probably best to take these as a special type of synthetic judgement. For they add to the given rather than merely carve it up conceptually.

§ Surely Bradley is right that our synthetic and analytic judgements of sense cannot give the literal truth about the world. There are many reasons for thinking this, though I do not think Bradley marshalled them very well. There is a problem first as to just in what sense of 'part' my perceptual field at any one time can be part of the physical world. It can hardly be a straight physical part, for it would seem that no physical part of the physical world is wholly given in my perceptual field. Nor does it seem to do justice to the given thickness of things to regard it as containing only their surfaces, arranged stereoscopically around the thickness of our own body, though such an account has its temptations. It seems rather that we think of a part of the physical world as somehow partially present in my consciousness to constitute my multi-sensory perceptual field. (It is a quite misleading account of perceptual experience, once infancy is passed, as having distinct sensory fields for each sense rather than as a single multi-sensory one shot through with suggestions of the causal powers of things.)

Moreover, even if I could coherently conceive of my perceptual field as only an extract from a larger whole, which extends beyond it in all directions, I cannot coherently conceive of that whole as containing your perceptual field. For mine extends outward from a centre at which my body is located, while yours extends outwards from a centre at which your body, as you experience it, is so. No extension of my perceptual field could include your body except as an object at a distance from the centre. Thus the perceptual fields of different persons cannot coherently be part of the same larger spatial whole. Yet it is part of the very conception of the object world that I live in it together with other conscious beings whose perceptions are related to it as mine are.

Similar problems apply to the conception of the world at different times as belonging to the same temporal whole. For the temporal whole which has this present moment as its most vibrantly actual core cannot be, and yet must be, the same temporal whole as contains other moments as they are experienced when present.

Despite all this I think some such incoherent account does specify what we think of the physical world as being at the level of our most ordinary and least theoretical copings with it. Surely we do think of our perceptual field and its components as an actual part of the physical world which has somehow at least partially entered into my consciousness directly and not simply by way of representation (though it shades off in my consciousness into what on reflection we would say was only imagined). No other account seems to capture the essence of our ordinary sense of living in the world.[20]

§ Although this is surely what his position amounts to, Bradley might not be altogether happy with the statement that, while the Absolute and the finite centres of experience included within it really exist, the physical world is merely a useful fiction. For he seems to hold that to exist as a compulsory object of thought is to exist in as good a sense as can be expected of any ordinary thing. What thought creates for itself is in its own way as real as the mental acts through which it manufactures it, at least if such thought is sufficiently coherent and practically effective for its own purposes. If so, the physical world does, in a good sense, really exist inasmuch as we are certainly incapable of avoiding thinking of it as there. Its final incoherence is a ground for saying that its objects are less than absolutely real. But that still leaves them with a considerable degree of reality, inasmuch as the idea of them is a good way, for most purposes, of thinking of reality.

In the light of this it may be misleading to suggest that souls or centres of experience are more real than the world which is constructed through their judgements. There is a sense in which that world may even be more real than them. For, according to Bradley, the important units for the Absolute need not be the centres of experience but the common objects presented to them percep-tually or posited by them in thought. Thus if there are a thousand perceptions in different souls of a single object, the unit which matters for the Absolute, and which is experienced by it as one, may be the common form of that object present in each, rather than any of these souls or their states. It may even be their main point to produce a fuller version of that on which they converge by their varied contributions to its constitution. Similarly certain values, on which the experiences of different souls converge, may be more real than they are.

However, even if Bradley might object to my way of putting it, it remains true that for him the actual filling of the Absolute consists in finite centres of experience, and the physical world, insofar as it is not perceptually present within these, only exists in the sense that it is posited as doing so in a congruent set of their judgements.

§ Thus Bradley, like James (at least in his new realist phase), avoids a representationalist account of perception. The physical world of ordinary thought is not represented by our perceptions; rather are our perceptions the actually given part of it on the basis of which the rest is posited. I have already commended James's insistence on this point as excellent phenomenology.

Many philosophers will deny that what we ordinarily mean by the physical world is something of which certain actual sensory contents, real components of the streams of different persons' experience, are fragments rather than mere representations, because they assume that the physical world must be coher-

---

20   A brief attempt of my own, using the Bradleyan notion of a concrete universal, to clarify this further may be found in my Vindication, chapter 2, §7.

ently conceivable and realize that such a physical world is not. But even if there is a more real physical world than the one we ordinarily believe in, the one in which we all naively believe most of the time is a supposed whole of which our perceptual fields are literal parts. Incoherent as such a whole may be, and incapable therefore of existing except as a useful posit, the conception of it remains a valuable possession and an inevitable tool for dealing with reality as it really is.

And Bradley would certainly argue that we cannot replace it by some alternative conception of the world free from contradictions. If we wish to plumb the reality which is the source of those experiences on the basis of which we construct the physical world of daily life, we will have to do so by developing conceptions which go beyond that of any merely physical world. To do so is the goal of a metaphysics like Bradley's. But it is not its goal to deprive us of our ordinary conceptions. For many ordinary purposes they are better than the deeper truth. Moreover, much of what purports to be a deeper truth is even further from the reality of things. Thus a certain sort of materialism gives us neither an in all ways more useful reality, nor a more deeply true one; at most it gives us a conceptual system which is technologically useful for certain special purposes.

These are themes to be developed in what follows. However, let me anticipate and remark that Bradley, like James, if not to the same extent, was not averse to a panpsychist view for which the source of our perceptual experiences consists in some kind of impersonal experience which can be regarded as the physical world as it is in itself. But he denies that his conclusions require any such thesis. He is content to refer the explanation of the fact that our experiences dovetail, so that we can form the idea of a common physical world on which they each give their perspective, to the fact that it is through centres of experience such as ours that the Absolute gives itself its one total unitary harmonious experience of itself.

2

Bradley on Judgement and Truth

§1. *Bradley and Psychologism*

It will be impossible to discuss all aspects of Bradley's often perplexing treatment of judgement and truth. I shall concentrate on what bears most strongly on the metaphysical positions discussed in other chapters and on how his thought relates to James's. I shall first consider the treatment of these topics in *The Principles of Logic* [PL] and then turn to his later treatment of them in *Essays on Truth and Reality* [ETR]. My special purposes will mean that I only deal quite briefly with what is, in fact, the central topic of PL, the nature of inference.

Bradley is sometimes praised as an early opponent of psychologism, that is, of the treatment of judgement, inference, truth, meaning, the laws of logic and so forth as psychological processes to be studied empirically, usually by way of introspective psychology. Frege is regarded as the great saviour of modern thought from the errors of such psychologism, and there is a risk that people may suppose that the main merit of Bradley's *Logic* is that of a less lucid attack upon the same thing.[1]

That Bradley was in important respects a critic of psychologism is true. Thus he expressly says that in 'England at all events we have lived too long in the psychological attitude'.[2] But pressed too far, and associated with later conceptions of logic as a formal science with no special concern with thinking as a

---

1   See, for example, Wollheim, p. 26. See also Anthony Manser's article in Manser and Stock, and Manser, *Logic*.

2   PL, p. 2. See also PL, pp. 197–99. His essential objection to the empiricists' treatment of thought is their failure to recognize the break between qualities of mere feeling and thought and judgement. See PL, p. 478.

human activity, describing him thus can be seriously misleading. Certainly he believed[3] that the empiricist treatment of thought by people such as James Mill, Bain, J. S. Mill, and others was wrong-headed in that it considered it merely as a psychological phenomenon (a succession of 'impressions and ideas') which could be adequately understood without reference to such normative concepts as those of rationality, truth, and validity. Nonetheless, judgement was for him essentially something which occurred in conscious minds, and truth essentially a property of such judgement; similarly, implication rested on inference as a mental activity which minds perform. The topic of logic is therefore in a sense psychological; it is concerned with the nature of certain psychological states. However, its concern with them is not qua merely psychological states, as natural phenomena to be explained if possible by natural laws. For it does not merely describe them but evaluates them. But that does not mean that the logician can altogether ignore their status as psychological phenomena. In fact, it will be one of his aims to show that even as psychological processes they cannot be understood without bringing them under such normative concepts. For the degree to which they are true or valid will be part of the explanation of why they occur at all.

> Every conclusion [i.e., inference] possesses two characters. . . . It is a psychical event and a logical judgement, and what is true of it in one of these aspects, may be wholly false if you take it in the other.

But you cannot understand it on its logical side, Bradley makes clear, without understanding how its logical features become embodied in actual mental phenomena. There is a complex relationship between psychological phenomena and logical entailment for Bradley. On the one hand, the explanation of sequences of mental phenomena must often be by reference to the logical relation between their contents, while on the other hand propositions and logical principles need actualisation in mind to be a reality. But to some extent, and to some extent only, psychology may abstract from the logical character and content of its phenomena and logic from the psychological features of the principles it studies.[4]

Bradley's conception of the relation between logic and the study of thinking is not really so far from that of Husserl. It is common (and, properly understood,

---

3   Anyone who supposes that Bradley's concern with logic was anti-psychologistic in the same way as Frege's should browse through III, I, VI of PL. For some explicit discussion on the relations between logic and psychology see note 21 to that chapter stretching from p. 495 to p. 498. See also note 1 on p. 515. Also *Terminal Essays*, I, pp. 611–13 where he says that the sharp separation of logic from psychology is an abstraction necessary for specialised work but such as distorts the final truth about the subject matter of each.

4   See CE, essay XXII, for the point about psychology, and PL, note 18, pp. 549–50 for the point about logic.

correct) to say that Husserl was rescued from psychologism by Frege's criticism of his early work on mathematics. But though he was sharply opposed to the conception of logic, influential in the late nineteenth century, as an empirical study of the laws which govern human thought as a contingent phenomenon, and distinguished sharply between the laws of logic which thought must respect if it is to be valid and facts about thought itself, this did not lead him to a conception of logic as standing quite apart from the study of thinking. The phenomenological logician, at any rate, is much concerned with the nature of mental acts and how they refer to their objects.[5] But his concern with them differs from that of an empirical psychologist in that his topic is their essential rather than contingent features. And though Bradley makes no sharp distinction between the necessary and the contingent, the general spirit of his approach is similar.[6]

§2. What Is a Judgement?

(a) The Nature of Judgement

§ The first chapter of PL sets out to answer the question what a judgement is, understood as what occurs in the mind when one thinks that something is the case. To pose this question as about 'judgement' accords with a certain philosophical tradition, one carried on by Russell in his earlier writings. It is much the same issue as others, such as Hume, have raised when they ask what it is to believe something.

Neither the word 'belief' nor 'judgement' seems quite ideal for the purpose. By a *belief* we typically mean a long-standing state of holding something to be the case. And by a *judgement* we typically mean a careful estimation of something doubtful. It is a little odd to call my consciously taking it to be the case that the cat is outside the window, wishing to be let in, a *judgement*. However, there is no more convenient expression for the thought that something is the case understood as an actual occurrent state of mind. Certainly it is a better expression than 'idea' which James often used in this sense.

§ What then really is a judgement so understood? Bradley rejects various views which have been put forward.

One reason why most of them fail is through their neglect of that problem of the self-transcendency of states of mind which we have seen to be central to

---

5   Husserl's most sustained attack on psychologism is in the 'Prolegomena to Pure Logic' which opens his *Logical Investigations*. His fullest account of thinking is in Investigations V and VI of this work, and in *Formal and Transcendental Logic*.

6   W. R. Boyce Gibson, who later translated Husserl's *Ideas*, notes the importance of Bradley's emphasis on meaning as something whose role in psychological explanation is not that of a mere event. See 'The Problem of Freedom' by W. R. Boyce Gibson, p. 178, in Sturt.

James's concerns. Surely these two thinkers were right that it is a great mystery how the mind can escape beyond its own bounds so that its own states are somehow about something not included within them.

The problem here is not the rather tedious one of scepticism, of how we are justified in believing that there is more to the world than our current states of consciousness. It is the question, rather, of how the mind can even set out to concern itself with something beyond itself. Bradley's answer is that in some sense the reality as a whole is already immanent in one's finite consciousness. This is to some extent the same doctrine as that of Royce discussed above (at Part One, Chapter One, §7), though Bradley's approach is nearer to that of the British empiricists and further from Kant's than Royce's. Admittedly Bradley usually speaks harshly of the British empiricist tradition, but I think he simply did not realize the degree of his kinship to it.

Bradley criticises a number of theories including most of the typically empiricist views. Thus he objects to the Lockean view that judgement is the joining of ideas, on the ground that if all the mind does is join its own ideas, it is unclear how it can think about anything beyond its own states and contents. (The problem, I must insist again, is what doing this is, not when it is justified.) The theory also mistakenly assumes that judgement always involves two ideas. This it clearly does not, for example when it simply affirms the existence of something. It is truer to say that there is always just one idea, our total idea of the state of affairs we believe to be real.

Hume thought that belief consisted in vivacious ideas, but such an account is patently inadequate. Imagination, consciously enjoyed as such, can be very vivacious. In general, empiricists like Berkeley and Hume identify judgement with the formation of images, failing to explain what it is for the mind to take these images as representations of something beyond. The tendency to assume that they represent whatever they happen to resemble is evidently hopeless.

Bradley devotes a good deal of attention to the view of Bain that belief consists in having ideas which influence behaviour. This account had some influence on pragmatism, as Bradley himself noted in his later writings. Bradley objects to this view mainly on the ground that a judgement may occur simply as a theoretical opinion, which never has the chance to influence behaviour.

Bradley continues with an examination of some views about judgement which he claims go wrong through taking the traditional distinction between subject and predicate too seriously. He thus initiates a criticism of the traditional Aristotelian logic which is continued, when he comes to inference, in an elaborate critique of the doctrine of the syllogism. Bradley has received some credit for this by modern logicians. It is assumed, however, that his main conclusion, about the inevitable limitations to the possibility of reducing valid reasoning to formal rules, has been largely outdated by the development of a richer type of formal logic since his day. These issues, however, lie largely outside the compass of this book.

The discussion at this point includes some hints of his later treatment of relations. Since one of his main points is that relational propositions cannot be reduced to subject-predicate form but must be recognized as having their own logic, it is rather ironic that he has been criticised for thinking of the subject-predicate form as basic. It is true that he does think of our whole specification of, or concept of, a situation which we believe to exist as a kind of predicate which we apply to reality; however, it is one of the main concerns of PL to show that the internal structure of that specification need not consist in subject, predicate, and copula.

§ Some decades after PL was first published Russell developed a theory of judgement (in *Problems of Philosophy* and other early works) to which Bradley gave some attention in chapter X of ETR. The theory was that when, say, Othello believes that Desdemona loves Cassio, there is a multiple relation relating *Othello, Desdemona, loves,* and *Cassio,* which may hold even though Desdemona and Cassio are not linked by the relation *loves.* Bradley objected that this theory takes a certain relation between the objects believed in and the mind as the essence of the thing, but cannot explain how the holding of this relation is an experienced fact. Also he thought that it entified relations in an unacceptable way.

§ So what was Bradley's own view of the nature of judgement? *Prima facie* there are two distinct questions requiring answers: (1) What gives an act of judgement its content? (2) What makes this content something asserted, rather than merely entertained, questioned, or whatever? And in the first edition of PL Bradley answered them by reference to distinct acts: (i) the abstraction of a part of the character of some current mental content and its conversion into a concept, (ii) the application of this concept to Reality. However, by the time of the second edition he had decided that these acts were indistinguishable and that the act of abstraction by which the concept is constituted precisely is the act of applying it to Reality. Thence he concluded that ideas, or concepts, can only occur in the context of some form of judgement and cannot, as he put it, merely 'float'.

Nonetheless, the basic position remains the same, namely, that in judgement the mind abstracts a universal from the sensory flux of its own contents and takes it as applying to Reality.[7] And even in the first edition judgement and idea are closely related concepts. A judgement is the act of ascribing some quality or form exhibited by an image or other mental content falling within my consciousness to a reality beyond it, and an idea is such a quality or form which we do or might ascribe in such an act. (This formulation of Bradley's position requires qualification to allow for judgements about one's own mental contents, but brings out its main force.)

§ Bradley develops this view by insisting that we distinguish two senses of 'idea'. In the first, ideas are events in time which can never recur, with a wealth of character most of which is irrelevant to determining what it is that one is thinking. I shall call these 'mental ideas'. In the second, an idea is a meaning which may attach to a mental idea, and which it may share with other mental

---

7　See PL, pp. 10, 13, etc.

ideas, such meanings being what we apply as predicates to Reality in judgement. I shall call these 'logical ideas'. I shall also call them 'concepts', not so much to sound more modern as because this has a more suitable adjectival form than 'idea'.

The importance of Bradley's distinction between the 'mental' and the 'logical' idea has been widely recognized. More likely to be questioned is his particular view about the nature of the logical idea as a repeatable character or universal which is part of the *whatness* of the mental idea (and of other mental ideas with the same meaning) abstracted from its nature as a whole and used by the mind to characterise something (believed in or merely thought of) beyond itself which is thereby supposed to possess it as part of its own actual character.

In view of this we should distinguish between two points which Bradley is making: first, the importance of distinguishing ideas in a logical sense from ideas in a psychological sense, and second, a particular view of the nature of logical ideas, namely, that they are abstracted elements of mental ideas ascribed, or ready to be ascribed, to some region of Reality as part of the character thereof. Although Bradley does not distinguish these points himself, some of his discussions only turn on the first, that our ideas, as psychological occurrents, have meanings as well as natures and that it is only their meanings which are of interest from a logical point of view. (And at times he seems to presuppose only a weaker version of the second claim, for which the predicated idea characterises the reality to which it is applied in some more purely symbolic way than that of something supposed actually present there.)

§ It will be seen that, though Bradley saw himself, and is commonly regarded, as an opponent of an empiricist view of thought, he is, in fact, quite in the empiricist tradition in holding that the fullest sort of judgement involves imagery, even if his account of the role of such imagery, with its distinction between the logical and the mental idea, is considerably more sophisticated than that of the traditional empiricists. And despite some qualifications of this in the second edition he continues to think of such iconic thinking as having a certain pre-eminence. Thus he always regarded merely verbal judgements as secondary to ones carried by thought stuff with more sensuous fullness. And he never shows any inclination to believe in judgements which are imageless and wordless.[8]

§ Such an imagistic view of thinking will seem naive and outdated to many philosophers today. And it may reasonably be argued that the meaning of a mental idea cannot be such a 'mutilated content'[9] of its phenomenal character, since two mental occurrences can have the same meaning without having any

---

8   For the qualification see PL, additional notes 8, on p. 38, and 34, on p. 40. For the
     continued strong commitment to the iconic aspect of a genuine idea of something
     see, e.g., CE, pp. 254 and 334–35.

9   PL, p. 584.

such character in common. However, my own view is that unless one can to some extent cash one's thoughts by giving them what Husserl called 'intuitive fulfilment', one really does not know of what one is thinking and that Bradley's account is a promising one of thought which is thus fulfilled. What is true, as Bradley was more ready to emphasise later, is that such fulfilment is usually very slight and in particular that much judgement is purely verbal (though even here one should bear in mind that words themselves may come to possess something of the character of that which they specify).

§ Much of what seem the limitations imposed upon our powers of thought by an imagist view of thinking disappears if we include under the heading of imagining, not only what may be called *direct imagining*, but also *indirect imagining*. One imagines something directly if and only if the universal one ascribes to what one imagines actually qualifies one's image. One imagines it indirectly if and only if one homes in on the universal ascribed through its postulated ideal relation to such a universal. One can then say that a genuinely fulfilled judgement will be one of which one can imagine the content in one or another of these ways.[10] In effect, Bradley uses such a notion himself, for example in discussing the kind of idea we are capable of having of the Absolute.

§ A difficulty for the simpler kind of imagist view of belief is how beliefs can be unspecific in a way that imagery apparently cannot. Thus Berkeley seems to have supposed that one cannot think about a man, without one's thought determining his precise appearance. Or if he avoids this, it is only by qualifications inconsistent with his denial of universals.

This problem does not arise for Bradley. For on his account it is not the image as a particular, or even its total character, which determines the meaning of my thought. The case is rather that in judgement the mind singles out just one element in its total character and takes it as the character of that with which it is presently concerned.

It was its failure to recognize this which condemned empiricism for Bradley. Thus empiricists fail to contrast rational thought with imagination. For imagination, as Bradley understand it, is thought whose movement is not solely determined by the logical relations between the universals predicated of reality but by features of the imagery not part of its logical meaning.[11] (I might add that, in my opinion, the apparent hostility to imagination of the rationalist tradition in philosophy has on the whole been concerned with distinguishing rational thought from imagination in this sense rather than with challenging the view that the universals ascribed in the most full-blooded sort of thought have to be present as features of psychical imagery.)

§ For a more exact grasp of all this we must consider a distinction which Bradley makes between what he calls the *that* and the *what*. The *what* of a thing

---

10   See below at Part Two, Chapter Four, §1, and, for a fuller account, my *Vindication*, pp. 36–37, and indexed references.

11   See PL, p. 445; ETR, pp. 363–64.

is its total character or nature. It is what you try to convey when you describe it. Its *that*, in contrast, is what you insist on when you say that what you have described is an actual fact such as you can only encounter in direct perceptual or other immediate contact.

It is natural to identify this distinction with that between particulars and universals. Yet it is doubtful if this is quite right, since I think Bradley supposes that each total *that* has a distinct *what* which it could not wholly share with any other *that*. The universals a thing exemplifies are rather distinguishable repeatable elements within its *what*, which it could share with the *what* of other things. But its *what* is not the mere sum of such repeatable elements, for there's always something more to it than can be arrived at by listing these, since '[e]verything given . . . is always in some sense itself qualified by its context'.[12] Bradley does not spell things out in quite this way but I believe it is what his view comes to.

At any rate, the logical idea used in an act of judgement is a universal in just this sense. It is an element of the *what* of the mental idea abstracted from the rest and normally used to characterise some other part of Reality, to whose *what*, if the judgement is true, it also belongs. Or at least this is how it is in a fully realized or intuitively fulfilled judgement.

Suppose I have an image in my mind the character of which includes as one of its elements a repeatable shape and colour. Then so long as I just contemplate the image I have no idea, but if my mind singles out this shape and colour and attributes it to something other than the image, then it has become an idea used in judgement.

This might happen for instance if I am waiting for a friend to pick me up in his car, and I remember that his car is red. If looking out for the car is mediated by a car-shaped red image, then something of its shape and colour is treated, not as a mere feature of the image, but as the form and colour of what I am looking out for, and constitutes my current idea of it. And this same repeatable element can occur as an idea in someone else's mind when they are looking out for that or some other similar car.[13]

§ I noted above a certain shift in Bradley's position between the first and second editions of PL. In the first he thinks in terms of two distinct activities: (i) the abstraction of some quality from the total mental idea to become a logical idea; and (ii) the application of this logical idea to reality as a predicate. In the second, the separation of the quality to become the logical idea precisely consists in its being predicated of reality in a judgement. It follows that there cannot be 'floating' ideas not used in a judgement. But what of our undoubted power merely to entertain something as a possibility? Bradley replies that in such cases we still apply the idea to reality, only it is some special region of

---

12   PL, p. 346.
13   Wittgenstein famously pointed out the illusion in supposing that one must envisage mentally that which one is looking out for. It does not follow that one never does so.

reality, distinct from that main region which constitutes what we call the real world. For reality, in the largest sense, contains such sub-regions as that of the doubtful, the imaginary, and so forth, as well as that of 'the real world' and ideas can be applied to each of these regions. This conception of regions of reality had been mooted in the first edition. It was not used there, however, to deny the possibility of merely entertaining ideas of things without making any judgement.[14] But even in the first edition an idea, in the logical sense, is essentially the *kind* of thing which can be referred to a reality beyond the immediate present.

§ So judgement is not merely the presence of ideas in the mind, or their internal manipulation; to think of it as such was one of the main faults of the empiricists. Rather is it the application of ideas to a reality which is not an idea. (One can, indeed, think about one's own state of mind. But to do so one must be able to conceive it as an event in a historical series which goes beyond what is within one's mind in any simple sense.) And that implies that we must have some mode of access to reality other than via our ideas of it. For we could not refer our ideas to a reality beyond the contents of our own consciousness if we had no awareness of that reality except through our ideas of it. Conceptual thought presupposes non-conceptual awareness. Unless we encounter something other than concepts we cannot think of our concepts as applying to anything.[15] But what is this something other than concepts?

We must note first that this pre-conceptual awareness cannot be awareness of any part or region of reality in particular since, as Bradley sees it, we need concepts to distinguish any particular part, region, or aspect of reality. So the pre-conceptual basis of judgement must be a pre-conceptual direction of the mind on Reality at large. It is this which is the something other than a concept or idea to which we apply our concepts and which can therefore be called the ultimate subject of all our judgements. Having this direction upon reality at large, we may need to identify some sub-region as that of which we are mainly thinking, but this, since it is done by ideas, pertains to the predicate rather than to the subject. (In his later treatments of judgement Bradley is inclined to call this sub-region, the special subject of the judgement, but it remains his view that Reality at large is the ultimate subject of all judgement.[16])

---

14 See PL, p. 4, note, p. 42, and additional notes on pp. 38–40.
15 See PL, p. 50.
16 Some dissatisfaction may be felt with Bradley's talk of predicating ideas of reality. Surely if I think that something is a horse, what I predicate of it is not an idea, but a universal for which my idea (whatever exactly that is) stands. However, we may say in defence of Bradley's usage that since for him the idea (at least in the more fully realised kind of judgement) precisely is a universal present in the flux of my own experience but supposed to be present more fully in the reality of which I am thinking, the idea does not stand for, but is, the universal, as something which, if the judgement is true, occurs both as a feature of my mental state and 'out there'. It may be objected that when I think about a horse horseness cannot possibly

But how does the mind manage to direct itself upon this reality which it tries to characterise to itself in judgement? Bradley's answer is that the present state of our mind is somehow intrinsically continuous with, and in some sense identical with, a larger reality beyond itself, and it feels itself as being such. This is not an opinion in the sense of a judgement using ideas or concepts, but the necessary pre-conceptual background of conceptual thinking. (Perhaps there is some faint analogy here to Heidegger's notion of being in the world. For both thinkers we are somehow consciously in the larger world in a manner which is not a matter of having any opinion about what exists or does not exist.)

Thus at the root of thought is a feeling of continuity with a larger whole of which our present state of mind is just a fragment. Our thoughts are an effort to apply ideas to this whole which will carry us beyond this mere dumb acquaintance. At the level of ordinary thought our general sense of the larger whole is such as to force spatio-temporal characterisations of it upon us. As metaphysicians, or in moments of illumination, our sense of it may lead to the replacement of these by more spiritual conceptions. Bradley says in a note to the second edition that in this work he did not manage to stick either with a common-sense nor with any other (such as a metaphysically adequate) concept of Reality (or, we may add, of the way in which our immediate experience is a fragment of the whole, a fragment, however, in which the whole itself is immanent).[17]

§ Bradley says in his initial statements that it is the reality presented in the perceptual manifold, as experienced immediately quite apart from any ideas we form of it, which is the subject of which we predicate our ideas. But, as he makes more clear in some of his later notes, it is not presented only by the perceptually given, but by anything else thus directly presented or experienced. The point is that one's experience as a whole is lived through in a way which is more basic than any conceptualisation. One in a manner knows what one's whole present state of experience is in a fashion which is deeper than that of thinking something about it. For one's whole of experience includes things other than one's thinking, for example a sensory manifold of perceptual presentation and various inward bodily feelings and emotional colourings, all of which may be intertwined and coloured by thought but are still something more than thought or than anything posited by it. (Besides, our thought itself is lived through as an aspect of the total unconceptualised but felt reality.) In

---

qualify my image. Bradley would answer, I think, that the image is not indeed a complete horse but only a hint of one. See, e.g., CE, p. 349. Nonetheless, the sense in which it has a certain shape, moves a certain way, perhaps has a smell, is essentially that in which a real horse would. Whether such a real horse really can exist other than as a presentation to a mind, equine or human, is another matter. The point here is that in making an ordinary judgement about a horse I project this universal upon a reality which is somehow real to me other than via my characterisations of it.

17   See PL, p. 591, note 27, and elsewhere.

short, we feel our own current state of experience, and this is in a manner the subject of any present judgement or rather is our current way of being presented with that subject which we are trying to characterise in all thinking.[18]

The view that the reality we characterise in judgement is what we feel in the immediate experience of our own being is sometimes put in terms which may sound solipsistic. But there is nothing solipsistic in Bradley's true meaning. For the whole of experience which we live through is felt as essentially continuous with, and somehow one with, something infinitely richer in character and contents of which it is just a fragment. As Bradley puts it, it is the whole Reality experienced in a partial manner.[19] It is to this larger whole immanent in the fragment of it which I live through and in a manner presently am that I apply my ideas. And the essential goal of thought is to capture as much of its nature as possible in ideal form.

§ There are intriguing similarities and contrasts in Bradley's position here and that of Russell (not so much in the theory of judgement just mentioned as in his analysis of propositions, especially during his phase of strict logical atomism). For Russell propositions which can be grasped without acquaintance with the particulars with which they are ostensibly concerned are parasitic upon propositions about particulars which can only be grasped by those acquainted with them. If I, as someone who has not directly encountered him, say 'The president of the United States plays the saxophone', I mean that there is some truth of the form 'x is president of the United States and x only and x plays the saxophone' which can only be grasped by one acquainted with him, and in which a logical proper name for him would take the place of the variable.[20] Mere acquaintance with universals under which he falls is not enough. (Ultimately propositions about persons may have to be reduced to propositions about sense-data, just because persons are not things of a kind with which there could be genuine acquaintance.)

Bradley is even more insistent that a kind of acquaintance, which goes beyond its specification in terms of universals, is required if we are to think of something. But for him the reality with which we have this pre-conceptual acquaintance is always the same, namely, the one sensible reality which we encounter non-conceptually through sense experience. Not that the thought had failed to occur to him that we may have a pre-conceptual encounter with particular bits of reality, which we can refer to by such words as 'this' and 'here'; indeed he makes suggestions in this connection which may well have influenced Russell. But although thinking of our ability to locate particular bits of reality by our direct pre-conceptual awareness of them is quite useful at a rather

---

18   See PL, p. 109, note 19, for the point that our contact with the Reality to which we apply our ideas is not only through what is perceptually, or even also through what is introspectively, presented, but through our whole felt state.

19   See PL, pp. 70–71, §29; also ETR, p. 349, note.

20   See Russell, *Logic and Knowledge*, pp. 200–202; 241–54. Cf. PL, p. 64.

superficial level of analysis, it will not, as Bradley sees it, ultimately do. In the end it is always simply Reality, *tout court*, rather than some particular bit of Reality which is the subject of predication. [21]

§ Bradley's account of judgement strongly suggests the view that a judgement is true if and only if the logical idea which functions as its predicate is a universal actually found in the Reality to which it ascribes it. For what else can we be doing in ascribing the character we abstract from our imagery to a reality beyond but supposing that it is actually found there as an actual feature of that reality? And in what other sense could our judgement be true than that it is in fact present there?

Such an account of truth is not far off from the scholastic view that in true thinking an essence *objectively* exemplified in the mind is recognized to be the essence *formally* exemplified by that reality beyond onto which the mind is directed. And though Bradley never presents this explicitly as his account of truth, it seems to be frequently presupposed in what he has to say about how various different sorts of judgement must be taken if they are to give genuine truth about reality.

Admittedly such a view of truth could only apply to judgements of an 'intuitively fulfilled' type. However, for one who thinks, as Bradley does, in effect, that other judgements are a kind of substitute for these, their truth will consist in the truth of the more fulfilled judgements for which they substitute. This view of truth, then, should be taken as the description of some ideal fullness of insightful thought. Thus taken it is compatible with any amount of stress upon the limited extent to which the ideal is actualised in practice, and with insistence upon the merely symbolic or substitutional nature of most of our ordinary thinking.

This certainly seems to be the view of truth most obviously implied by Bradley's theory of judgement as we have so far considered it. We shall have to examine carefully the extent to which he actually held it. I shall be suggesting that he always remained much nearer to it than a good deal of what he says against any so-called copy theory of truth might lead one to believe.

Since Bradley developed his account I do not think (though the many who have written on the topic in recent years will presumably disagree) that there has been much advance in producing a theory of judgement which deals with the mystery of the mind's ability somehow to leap beyond itself. This is often treated as the problem of intentionality, but that begs the question against a solution of Bradley's sort. For when treated in this way, attention tends to centre on the status of so-called intentional objects (objects of the mind's concern which may or may not exist in reality) and it is assumed that the mind can be intentional without being directed on any existing reality at all and that therefore its self-transcendency is not a matter of its real relation to anything beyond itself. But Bradley holds that in thought the mind necessarily goes beyond itself,

---

21   See PL, p. 50.

not merely by having its own intentional objects, but by being directed on actually existing reality at large. Thus it is only if it is somehow really dealing with something existing beyond itself that there is judgement at all. We may put it once more in the idiom fashionable today and say that for Bradley (as for James) *de re* thought is basic, though for Bradley it is essentially just the one great *res* of reality at large which is in question.

(b) Subject and Predicate

However, this idea of the one great *res* has its difficulties. Suppose I judge that 'Peter has a beard'. What is the idea or universal which I am predicating of Reality here? To the extent that the judgement is fully realized there is some universal present in my imagery. But is this universal mere beardedness, or something more like 'Peter with a beard'?

It can hardly be the first, for I am not supposing that possession of a beard is exemplified by reality as a whole or in some pervasive way. But things are not much improved, it may seem, by saying that it is rather the property of 'being Peter and having a beard.' For quite apart from the question what it is to be Peter, it is no more true that reality as a whole or pervasively is Peter in possession of a beard than it is the mere possession of a beard. It seems then that I must be applying my concept to some specific region of reality, rather than to reality as a whole. In short, it would seem that the question of truth or falsehood can only arise, in this kind of case at least, when the idea is applied to a specific subject such as the idea itself is not sufficient to identify. We saw in Part One how his fellow absolute idealist, Royce, used this consideration as an argument for the existence of the Absolute. Bradley's approach is rather different.

We must be clear, at once, that he rejects the usual conception of subject and predicate. Rather, the idea we apply to reality comprises the whole of what is ordinarily thought of as divided into these two.

The usual division between subject and predicate suggests that judgement has these two distinct components:

(1) picking out something to be judged about;

(2) ascribing a predicate or property to it.

For Bradley, in contrast, judgement also has two distinct components, but they are rather these:

(1) directedness upon reality in general or Reality with a capital R.

(2) the ascription of a certain character to it, or to some part of it, where it is the character ascribed which settles to which part of the whole reality it applies.

§ So when I have the thought 'Peter has a beard' it is the meaning which the whole sentence has for me which is both the concept I apply to reality and the specification of that region of it with which I am more particularly concerned. Thus I may be imagining a man of a very specific character and destiny as in possession of a beard. My judgement then is that *Reality* (subject) answers to the description (predicate) of *including a man of such and such a sort, who, in addition to being of that sort, has a beard.*

This amounts to saying that all judgements are of the form 'Reality has such and such a character' or 'Reality is G'. And this in turn amounts to treating all judgements as existential.[22] They all say that a certain kind of situation, which the idea asserted in the judgement specifies, exists as a feature of reality. The subject always remains simply Reality, and specific regions of reality are only specified by way of the idea ascribed to it.

§ It may be objected that we cannot possibly realize in imagination anything sufficient to specify the situation of which we are asserting the existence, since that is always a situation supposed to belong to a particular position in the world which must be picked out somehow other than by our current ideas of it. One line of reply might be that even if we cannot, in one synthetic imaginative act, identify the precise part of Reality to which the situation we are envisaging belongs, we may still have the potential for identifying it to ourselves in a more piecemeal fashion. Suppose I believe that Julius Caesar was killed by a group of conspirators who did not want him to become a king. The most fully realized judgement to this effect which seems possible would presumably present an assembly of men dressed in togas with those in the centre stabbing one more grandly dressed, with faint suggestions of Caesar's supposed features. Perhaps there would also be some appropriate emotional timbre associated with some of the details.

Now certainly no features discriminable in the mental idea can constitute a logical idea specifically concerning Julius Caesar and ancient Rome, unless they give more information about the place and time than follows simply from its immediate appearance (which apart from more fanciful possibilities, could be those of a stage presentation). But perhaps its geographic and historical context can be sufficiently indicated by further imaginative ideas, which I am at least ready to form, which sketch how it stands to my own here-and-now in a single spatio-temporal system.

Bradley seems to be suggesting something of this sort when, in his later works, he qualifies the claim that it is always the single Reality which is the subject of judgement by distinguishing between the ultimate subject which is simply Reality, and the special subject, which is some special 'region' of Reality.[23] On this view the standard form of judgement is not so much 'Reality is G' as 'Reality, insofar as it is F, is G'. (For example, a standard subject-predicate judgement of the surface form 'S is P' becomes 'Reality is P insofar as it is S', where 'S' indicates the 'special subject'. However, on a more fundamental level it still belongs in the predicate place with 'Reality' as the sole ultimate subject.) The trouble is that the content of 'F' can never be fully given.

But perhaps the latter is determined by a larger system of ideas in the background of our minds which direct the predicate in the foreground to its proper locus. The special subject would, then, be settled by something akin to James 'fringe', the dim sense we have of the complex of relationships to which

---

22   Cf. ETR, p. 426, note.
23   See, for example, Terminal Essays, II, and elsewhere, and ETR, pp. 253 et ff.

the subject of our thought belongs. Perhaps Bradley assumed that something of this sort was indeed part of the matter. But he would certainly not have accepted it as a complete account of how thought can adequately target the region of reality which it concerns, for it was a central plank of his treatment of matters to which we shall be turning shortly that no such complete success is possible.

It might seem that Bradley, as an opponent of social individualism, might have developed a view like Hilary Putnam's, that the meaning and/or reference of what we say is determined rather by the experiences and doings, and associated linguistic activities, of our community as a whole than by what occurs within our own mind.[24] However, for all his criticisms of social individualism Bradley's approach was too individualistic for him to have accepted that the content or object of one's thought is settled by something so extrinsic to its own nature as subjective activity.

§ The obvious answer to this problem would seem to be that identification of our subject matter need not be purely descriptive but may employ indicator words, or the special acts of attention they express, like 'this', 'here', and 'now'. Bradley does, in fact, offer a very sensible account of reference along these lines, which anticipates some of what Russell and Strawson said later.[25] On this account, though it is indeed reality as a whole which is present to us in all our experience, it is present, at any one time, by means of elements of it which are more especially given and to which words like 'here' and 'now' can direct our attention, and by whose relation to which other things can be pinned down.[26] Thus the idea which we apply to reality can contain such elements as 'here' and 'now' and we can form such judgements as 'Reality is here and now a dog chasing a cat.'

In developing this point Bradley distinguishes between 'thisness' and 'this'. Thisness is the property of being a unique individual and we can apply it to any particular of which we think but 'this', though it expresses an idea, is an idea which, of its nature, can only be applied to the exclusive focus of present presentation.[27]

This seems sensible and serves as a reply to points Hegel had made about such words. However, it soon leads Bradley to the unfortunate suggestion that since nothing else has the reality of the 'this' everything else must be construction and not reality. That may pass if 'constructed' means 'inferred', but Bradley often writes as though it had a more ontological significance. He thereby seems to assert a solipsism of the present moment. This, however, is held in check by the claim that our attention is always directed through the immediate presentation to a permanent reality.

> The real can not be identical with the content that appears in presentation.
> It for ever transcends it, and gives us a title to make search elsewhere.
>
> PL, p. 71

---

24   See Putnam, *Reason*.
25   See, for example, Strawson, pp. 17–22.
26   See PL, p. 64.
27   See PL, p. 68.

But though this appeal to indicator words as essential to our identification of a special subject seems so sensible, Bradley regards it as only a half truth. Even if for practical purposes we may think of ourselves as directed upon particular bits of reality by this means (which Bradley later regularly refers to as designation) a judgement of such a type cannot be accepted as genuinely true. For truth must remain truth in all circumstances and thus requires an impossible, purely conceptual identification of its subject matter. Thus in thinking we seek for judgements of the form 'Reality insofar as it is F is G' and are for ever balked by the impossibility of an adequate specification of F.

§ However all that may be, Bradley's central thesis is clear. Judgement is the application of an idea as predicate to the Reality we encounter in immediate perceptual or inner experience, as subject, and this Reality remains one and the same infinite totality however fragmentary and different our participation in it may be at different times.

It is its failure to realize this which marks the defect of the traditional view that judgement is the ascription of a predicate to a subject. This view avoids the empiricist error of treating judgement as merely a play of ideas and rightly conceives it as the application of a universal to a concrete reality. Its mistake lies in its association of the universal with the grammatical predicate of a sentence, and the concrete individual with the subject. The truth is rather that the whole sentence expresses an idea which we ascribe to reality as a predicate by affirming it.

Thus the traditional subject-predicate account of judgement is defective even in the case of judgements of a grammatically 'S is P' type. But it is in more serious trouble when it tries to interpret all other judgements along the same lines. This is true in particular, as remarked above, of relational judgements. It is pointless to ask what the subject of the proposition 'The dog is chasing the cat' is, for it no more ascribes a property to the dog than it does to the cat. Rather than think of it as ascribing a property to either, we should think of it as ascribing the property 'dog chasing a cat here and now' to the reality given in perception.

Consider now the judgement that an event A precedes event B. Here again we cannot single out either event A or event B as the subject. Rather are we saying something about Reality in general, namely that it includes an event of the one sort being followed by one of another sort.

> We saw that all judgement is the attribution of an ideal content to reality, and so this reality is the subject of which the content is predicated. Thus in "A precedes B", this whole relation A-B is the predicate, and, in saying that this is true, we treat it as an adjective of the real world. It is a quality of something beyond mere A-B.
>
> PL, p. 28[28]

Another kind of judgement which it is radically misleading to interpret as

---

28   Cf. pp. 13 and 22.

ascribing a predicate to some particular subject are those which explicitly assert or deny the existence of something. (I say explicitly because, as we have seen, for Bradley ordinary subject-predicate judgements are ultimately existential too.) One gets into insuperable difficulties if one treats 'Unicorns do not exist' as ascribing a property (or the lack of one) to all entities of a certain sort. Rather, it says that reality as such cannot accept the feature of being a horse and having a horn in combination. And the same goes for 'Horses do exist'. It does not say something of entities picked out as horses; it says rather that Reality includes certain features in a certain combination.[29]

That it was a mistake on the part of traditional logicians to attempt to force all propositions into the mould of subject-predicate propositions is a familiar enough point to us today. However, Bradley was writing at a time when an essentially Aristotelian and medieval logic, putting the four forms of the syllogism at the centre of the stage, was still normal and he played some part in taking us beyond the confines of that logic.

The conventional view on this is that Bradley performed a genuine service in some of his criticisms of traditional logic. Sometimes he is even mildly praised as a harbinger of Russell's larger contribution to the more satisfactory treatment of such matters, by interpreting the apparent subject of an existential proposition as really a predicative expression.

Thus the seeds of Russell's theory of descriptions are clearly there in Bradley, only instead of a variable, bound by an existential quantifier, functioning as a gap for an unnamed subject, when we cannot name the particular which answers to our specification, we simply have Reality in the subject place. The result is perhaps more like Quine. Russell's 'The King of France is bald' may derive from Bradley's 'The king of Utopia died on Tuesday'.[30] However, appreciation of this having been once expressed, it is usually assumed that there is nothing much that is positive in his discussions of relational and existential propositions which is not dealt with much more effectively on the basis of the more adequate logic available to us now through the efforts of Frege and Russell.

This may be too precipitate. Certainly Bradley's positive positions cannot now be accepted as the only alternative to the logic he was criticising. Nonetheless, his claim that judgement contains two components (first, the concern with reality at large, and second, the ascription to it of some character) and his account of each of these still stands as a possible line of approach to problems which are still very much with us.

§3. *Types of Judgement and Inference*

(a) Categorical and Hypothetical or Conditional Judgements
Some of these points may become clearer after some examination of what

---

29   See PL, p. 42.
30   See PL, p. 124.

Bradley says about the main different sorts of judgement, in particular the distinction he initially makes, and then partly destroys, between categorical and hypothetical judgements.[31]

Categorical judgements divide into two main kinds: analytic judgements of sense and synthetic judgements of sense.[32] (Remember that this distinction has virtually nothing to do with the usual Kantian one between synthetic and analytic judgements—a distinction Bradley describes as useless on grounds with some similarity to Quine's.[33]) The first of these simply ascribe some character to the present sensorily given. Examples offered include: 'It's all so dreary', 'There is a wolf', 'This is a bird', 'The cow, which is now being milked by the milk-maid, is standing to the right of the hawthorn tree, yonder.'[34] In these judgements a part of the total character of the given is mentally separated off from the rest and reascribed to that given. It seems that no imagery or words are required, only this act of abstraction and predication directed at the given. (However, I take it that the discovery that the perceptually given had a character present in my imagery would also count as an analytic judgement of sense.)

Synthetic judgements of sense extend the given fact by supplementation, based on a bond of identity between the edges of the ideas and the edges of the given fact. This linking to given reality makes them assertions about reality, rather than mere imaginings. Moreover, it is because our characterisation of the Reality beyond contains some indication of how it relates to the given this, that our judgement can be about unique individuals.[35] Thus I identify Peter not merely as a man of a certain, in principle, repeatable sort, but as the one man of that sort who stands in a certain relation to this given scene. Bradley has here anticipated a point much emphasised by subsequent philosophers (though for Bradley, as we will see more fully as we continue, this marks a radical flaw in such ordinary judgements).

> In this second class of singular judgements we make generally some assertion about that which appears in a space or time that we do not perceive, and we predicate of a presentation something not got by analysis of its content. If I say 'There is a garden on the other side of that wall' the judgement is synthetic, for it goes beyond perception. And in 'Yesterday was Sunday', 'William con-

---

31   See PL, I and II.
32   See PL, pp. 48–51.
33   See PL, pp. 184– 85, §§27–28. A slight qualification of this judgement in the second edition still shows how profoundly un-Kantian Bradley thought himself. See PL, p. 195, note 23.
34   PL, pp. 56–59.
35   I must omit discussion of his treatment of proper names, beyond remarking that he insisted that they must have intension, meaning, or sense (PL, p. 59 et ff; p. 169, §4). However, he thought the word 'connotation' for this intension a barbarism, mainly, it would seem, on account of its associations with the loathed J. S. Mill. See PL, pp. 168– 69, §§2– 3.

quered England', 'Next month is June', I certainly do not analyze what is merely given. In synthetic judgements there is always an inference, [inference in Bradley's sense covering any thought process which supplements the given] for an ideal content is connected with the sensible qualities that are given us. In other words we have always a construction, which depends on ideas, and which only indirectly is based on perception.

PL, pp. 61–62[36]

These categorical judgements are all singular. (Bradley notes that there may also be judgements which are singular and categorical but concern a reality which is not a sensible thing in space or time, judgements about God, for example.) They assert the existence of some single unitary component of reality, or assert something of some such component. (These come to the same thing for Bradley.) On the face of it there are also universal categorical judgements. But Bradley thinks this a bogus class, and that such judgements are really conditional.[37] Thus 'all birds have wings' says that if anything is a bird, then it will have wings. (He deals similarly with a 'particular' judgement like 'Some birds have wings' interpreting it as saying that if something is a bird, then it may have wings.) Russell, we may note, acknowledged some influence of Bradley on his own analysis of universal propositions.

So the next great class of judgements to consider are hypothetical or conditional judgements. Bradley seems to take it as obvious that these are not directly about the world but about the relations between two possible judgements or ideas. They say that the person who entertains one idea as a supposition, will, at least if he is sufficiently wise and informed, find himself entertaining another idea as somehow following from it. I suspect that today we think of the obvious way of understanding such a conditional proposition as 'If you turn that key, the engine will start' as being directly about the world (whether we take it as a material or subjunctive conditional) even if we eventually arrive at a philosophical position which depicts it rather as concerning the relation between propositions or judgements.

> A supposal is, in short, an ideal experiment. It is the application of a content to the real, with a view to see what the consequence is, and with a tacit reservation that no actual judgement has taken place. The supposed is treated as if it were real, in order to see how the real behaves when qualified thus in a certain manner.
>
> PL, p. 86

It seems, then, that for Bradley 'If p, then q' means 'If you suppose p, then you must suppose q'. The trouble is that if this is supposed to give the very meaning of 'if', and 'then', it leads to a vicious regress, since these words occur

---

36   Cf pp. 48– 49.
37   See PL, pp. 82– 84.

in the analysans.[38] But perhaps the point is rather to reduce 'if . . . then . . . '
judgements which do not involve the concept of supposition to judgements
which do, so that all 'if . . . then . . .' judgements tell us, implicitly or explicitly,
how an adequately wise and informed mind who made one supposition, would
be forced to make another. Thus a conditional judgement is 'an assertion on the
strength of and about a supposition'.[39]

However, Bradley goes on to say that if this were all there were to it,
hypothetical judgements would not be judgements about reality at all, and
hence not really judgements. For a genuine judgement must apply an idea to
reality, not simply connect ideas with each other. Their status as proper judgements, however, can be reaffirmed when we realize that the pressure to move
from one ideal content to another stems from our positing some quality in
reality which makes such a move appropriate. So while ordinary categorical
judgements are all really hypothetical (or at least should be converted into such
in order to have a chance of being true) all hypothetical judgements are in a
sense categorical.[40] They assert a quality of Reality—where reality is still that
whole of which the perceptual or felt given is experienced as a fragment—grasp
of which would compel us to link our ideas in a certain way. 'If p then q' says
that Reality has a quality which connects p with q.[41] For example, if I say 'If you
had asked Jones for that loan, he would have refused it' I am saying that Jones's
character is such that, when it is taken into account one cannot conceive
(contrary to fact) of your asking him for a loan without conceiving of him as
refusing it. Most probably that quality will be Jones's stinginess. However,
Bradley makes it clear that one can assert a hypothetical without claiming to
know what the relevant quality in reality is which supports it, asserting only
that there is some such quality.[42]

---

38   Bradley himself makes much this point against efforts on J. S. Mill's part to offer a
     reductive analysis of hypotheticals in terms of 'inferrability'; see PL, p. 84.
39   PL, p. 83. See also PL, p. 42, though here the view is simply ascribed to Herbart
     rather than endorsed explicitly.
40   See PL, pp. 86–89. For the sense in which categorical judgements are really
     hypothetical see infra.
41   See PL, p. 87.
42   Bradley himself remarked in a note to the second edition that it is not much of an
     explanation of an 'if . . . then . . .' statement to say that it asserts a quality in
     something which connects antecedent and consequent, where that quality is a
     disposition, since a '"disposition" involves a standing "if"'. See PL, pp. 111–12, note
     41. It is unclear whether he sees this as damaging to his whole account of
     hypotheticals or only to a certain illustration of his point. At any rate, he need not
     have worried too much. Certainly if 'stingy' just means 'person of a kind who, if
     asked for a loan, will refuse', one does not get far by invoking it. But perhaps one
     can take it as referring rather to a pattern of actual behaviour (perhaps even as
     some deeper actual fact about the man's brain—though this would hardly be very
     Bradleyan—which there are good reasons for associating with this behaviour) and
     say that this pattern of actual behaviour shows him to be a man, such that a world

Thus hypotheticals say that there is something about reality which makes it appropriate if one supposes one thing, also to suppose another. This is very close to a view which I advocated in my own book *Facts, Words, and Beliefs*[43] and which is better known as the view of David Lewis.[44] In developing this view, Bradley contends that in the end it is always a general feature of the universe, rendering some general connection between ideal contents appropriate, which is asserted even when a conditional is about a particular thing. Thus apparently singular hypotheticals about a person, rather than a type of thing, are really universal. They assert a connection between ideal contents resting upon a general quality. So our judgement about Jones really says that if one asks a man of Jones's type for a loan then one will be refused. Indeed Bradley effectively says, like David Lewis, that a hypothetical judgement about an actual man is really a judgement about a counterpart man in another possible world. However, he would disagree with Lewis over the status of these other possible worlds. For him they are fragmentary compared with the actual world, for they have no more substance than is at some stage given them in actual thought.

§ So far Bradley has developed views which anticipate some more recent views on conditionals and perhaps gives them a better grounding. But now his thought takes a very curious turn. For he says that, although the distinction between categorical and conditional judgements is helpful at a certain level of analysis, in the end all categorical judgements, taken as such, are false, and can only claim to be true if we reinterpret them as hypotheticals. To show this he concentrates his fire first on analytic judgements of sense. Bradley has several reasons for the strange claim that all these are false.

(1) In such a judgement we abstract some element from the given whole and then cast it back upon it in an act of predication. But, according to Bradley, an element considered in the abstract always has a different character from that which it has in the whole of its actual given context. For every detail of the given depends for its character on its way of fusing with every other element. So such judgements as 'This is a blue patch' or 'That is a wolf' are always false for what they characterise (the given) is always more than mere wolfness, or blueness, and this more makes the blueness and wolfness present in the given something other than what is indicated by the concept or idea of them figuring in the judgement. (It is important to realize that Bradley is concerned with judgements about the given, not the mere experience of it, to which neither 'true' nor 'false' apply.)[45]

(2) Secondly, Bradley claims that since the given always points of its very own nature to a larger whole of which it is a fragment, you cannot characterise

in which he is asked for this loan and refuses it is more like the actual one, than is any world in which he is asked for the loan and grants it. The quality is his actual behaviour over his life, which consorts better with 'If p, then q' than otherwise.

43   See Sprigge, chapter 12, §5.
44   See Lewis.
45   See PL, §67, p. 97; also pp. 67–68.

it properly except as an element in what is not given. However, the more we elaborate our concept of the larger whole to which the given belongs, the more we are forced to modify our concept of the latter, in the light thereof, in virtue of the same pervasion of the part by the whole. So the given is the basis for a construction or inference which, as it develops, destroys its base.[46] If you describe it as though it were not just a part of a larger complex of events, you destroy a large aspect of what it is experienced as being, while if you include a reference to the context, you are no longer describing what is strictly given. Thus an attempt to describe the given just as it is must lead to incoherence and thus falsehood.[47] For example, if you say 'that is a book', you imply facts about how the object at which you are pointing has been produced. But as you learn about publishing and printing, your original concept of what a book is turns out to have been in various ways misleading. So your analytic judgement needs to be expanded, and the expansion shows that in its original form it was false.

(3) More generally the given both purports to have a certain completeness and yet is of its very nature incomplete. Thus it is inherently paradoxical and indescribable as a thing in its own right. Moreover, all your descriptions of it are riddled with problems to do with space and time.

(4) More generally and vaguely the fleetingness of the present moment, the fact that we can never concentrate on what is happening just now because we are already at a different now, seems to count against the reality of the present moment of experience for Bradley.

All in all, his view seems to be that a real thing must have a character which can be ascribed to it without any bother about what anything else is like and that the given moment of experience fails this test. In trying to say what it is like, we either say too little about it—and this little is false because saying more would falsify it—or we say too much about it, and thus are no longer merely describing it.

For reasons of this sort Bradley decides that strictly speaking all analytic judgements of sense are false. This is not meant to rescind the claim that perception and immediate feeling give us our prime encounter with that Real, which is the ultimate subject of predication in all judgement. We need that primitive non-conceptual encounter with reality if our ideas are to be about anything. The mistake lies only in supposing that our ideas can characterise that reality just as it immediately presents itself. So judgements which purport to do this are necessarily incoherent and false.

However, it is not just analytic judgements of sense which fail in this way. For synthetic judgements of sense are based upon them and must share the incoherence of their basis. Moreover, synthetic judgements of sense are especially subject to the contradictions contained in the very ideas of temporality

---

46   See PL, III, II, III.
47   See PL, pp. 97–98, §§68– 69.

and spatiality. For they interpret the given as an element of a spatial and temporal totality of which no finally coherent idea can be formed.

Bradley concludes that both main sorts of categorical judgement are ultimately false. (In terms of the later doctrine of degrees of truth, not yet developed, he might have preferred to say that they are only capable of a low degree of truth.) If we want to make them true, we must change them into hypothetical or conditional judgements.

> When we press for the final truth of the [ordinary categorical] judgement, the particular subject becomes an unspecified condition of the content. The assertion is thus hypothetical. It conjoins mere adjectives, though what it conjoins is vague and undetermined. The true subject of the judgement is, not this or that finite person or thing, but the ultimate reality. All the qualities of the ostensible subject pass into the condition of a universal connection of attributes.
>
> PL, pp. 181–82

It is very hard to get a grip on Bradley's precise train of thought here.[48] The main point seems to be this. Once we realize that all attempts to characterise the given are distortions thereof, and that the same applies to all those judgements which extend such characterisations by positing an extension of it beyond what we actually experience, then we will realize that the only real truth available to us is intra-ideal and concerns relations between ideas, though relations which we must suppose are somehow forced on us by reality. We may no longer say that anything is factually so, but can still perhaps say something true as to how one idea or meaning points to another.

The upshot seems to be something like this. A statement like 'There is a cat lying by the fire' is never a genuinely true one. The most that is genuinely true is something more like 'If one thinks of this scene as a room in a house with a fire blazing, one should also think of it as having a cat lying by that fire'. And this, on Bradley's view, may be properly expressed simply as 'If this is a room in a house with a fire blazing, then that is a cat sitting by it'.

§ His thought becomes easier to follow if one takes it that by 'if' he means something like 'qua' or 'insofar as'. (He does, indeed, reject a somewhat similar suggestion that 'if' be replaced by 'because' on the ground that 'q because p' implies that p is true. However, 'qua' does better justice to Bradley's wish to downgrade the status of the antecedent.)

Then one can interpret him as saying that, while it is a conceptual distortion of reality to say that this that I am confronted with is a room with a cat in it lying by the fire, it remains true that, qua being a room with a fire in it, it is a room in which a cat is lying by that fire.

---

48   I know of no commentator who has made adequate sense of it or shown why this is impossible. Wollheim has done the best job yet (see Wollheim, pp. 93–104) while Anthony Manser is rather short on detail (see Manser, Logic, pp. 110–16).

But Bradley denies that even such a judgement is true. For it still employs token indexicals like 'this' and 'that' which purport to pick out a bit of the world (without making clear what distinguishes this from other bits to which they refer in other judgements) and thus incorporates the vain attempt to characterise the given rather than simply to relate ideas. To get something which has a chance of being really true we should say rather 'Reality, qua being a room with a fire in it, is a room in which a cat is lying by the fire'.

However, here a fresh problem breaks out, for such judgement will be just as much false as true. Insofar as there are lots of rooms with fires in them and without cats, it is just as true that reality qua being a room with a fire in it, is a room in which no cat is lying by the fire.

To remedy this we must distinguish this room from all others in a purely descriptive way. Perhaps we may say 'Reality, qua being the main living room with a fire in it in someone called Timothy Sprigge's house on 12 March 1988, is a room in which a cat is lying by the fire.' But Bradley thinks that the possibility that there is another planet existing at some time with kindred people living on it, with a similar dating system, etc., but in which just such a room is catless, shows that it may be equally true that 'Reality, qua being the main living room with a fire in it. . . is a room in which no cat is lying by the fire.' And indeed even if this is not true at any point in the world with which I am spatio-temporally continuous it MAY BE true of some other world. So it seems that I can only home in on the part of reality I mean, and say something which is certainly true, if I use demonstratives. Yet judgements employing these, and thereby professing simply to characterise, or rest on a characterisation of, given reality, have been seen to be incapable of genuine truth.

To this one is inclined to reply that one can surely make such a judgement, and assume that there is not this kind of partial duplication of the situation specified in the antecedent, with at least a strong likelihood of being right. However, Bradley virtually equates this MAY BE with IS, for reasons with some similarity to those of modern realists (like David Lewis) about possible worlds. In effect he thinks that it will be true of some possible world which we can only distinguish from ours by the illegitimate use of a demonstrative. But perhaps it would be enough for his purposes simply to insist that we never have a right to take it that the MAY BE is not an IS and thus never have a right to assert such conditionals as true.

What is the remedy? There is none and this being so it turns out that our judgement is conditional in a further sense. Our translation has already made it into a judgement of the form 'Reality, qua being F, is G' but now we must see it as saying 'Reality qua being F and X, is G' where we do not know what the full nature of X is. So it is conditional not merely on what can be specified, but on what cannot be specified and this, as Bradley puts it, constitutes a double form of conditionality.

Bradley has a further reason for saying that our judgements must all become conditional in this double sense. This is that judgements which purport to link ideas, rather than to report directly on sensible fact, must purport to be necessary, for a linkage between ideas which is not necessary is no proper linkage at all. (Such a concern to find necessary connection is the inspiration of science, according to Bradley. For science, he claims, is concerned with laws and thus with changeless truths.) There must be something in the first idea such that its application to Reality forces on us the second idea. But if we try to spell out how this comes about, we are forced to go on adding further conditions, hoping to produce an idea which is not only sufficient to individuate the relevant bit of the universe, but also act as an antecedent necessarily implying the consequent. So we need to be able to say not only that reality conceived in one way must be conceived in another way, but be able to explain how this 'must' arises from the ideas themselves. And that means that I cannot make a proper judgement of the form 'Reality, qua F, is G' unless there is an intelligible necessary connection between F and G.

§ How does the claim that the ideal of judgement is to be conditional in this sense square with Bradley's insistence, against those who see judgement as the conjoining of two ideas, that a judgement is always the predication of one idea of Reality? Bradley's answer is that 'if x, then y' is a single idea, not merely because to entertain it is to suppose a categorical quality underlying it, but also because in it the ideas of x and y have become inseparable aspects of a unified thought, intrinsically different from what they would be out of it. This, indeed, poses considerable difficulties for his theory of inference as the combining of ideas taken from different judgements, and as presupposing the identity of the ideas throughout this process. However, Bradley was quite aware of this, and it was one of his reasons for thinking that, in the end, there is something suspect at the very heart of inference.[49]

§ On the face of it Bradley confuses at least three distinct reasons he has for saying that our ordinary categorical judgements, that is, synthetic and analytic judgements of sense, are only true if taken as somehow conditional.

First, there is the point that we can never give a categorical characterisation of any region of reality which is literally true of it. If we want literal truth we must say rather that, once we operate with a certain mode of conceptualisation, then this is the particular species of that conceptualisation which reality forces on us in present circumstances. Thus our judgements, even of the given, can only be true in a conditional sense, this meaning here that they should be taken only as apt characterisations on the part of beings with a conceptual scheme which, like every possible conceptual scheme, to some extent distorts the reality it attempts to conceptualise.

Second, there is the point that if we wish our judgements to have the dignity of a truth which will stand on its own in conceptual terms, and not shift its truth value with context, we must abandon indicator words and look for purely conceptual specifications of what we are talking of. Thus analytic and synthetic judgements of sense can only be genuine truths if transformed into 'eternal

---

49   This matter has been discussed most interestingly by James Allard in 'Bradley's Principle of Sufficient Reason' in Manser and Stock.

truths' in Quine's sense. However, this can never be done satisfactorily, on account of the possible duplication of any specified situation. As a result we can only gesture towards the eternal truths for which our ordinary context-dependent judgements about the given environment are our unsatisfactory stand-in.

And, third, there is the point that a genuine judgement should have a certain necessity to it, and that when we put it into the form 'Reality, qua F, is G' the F should somehow necessitate the G, but that we can never find an F which really achieves this. For once we start thinking out a total picture of the world, rather than merely attempt to register sensory facts, we are committed to attempting to understand it, and that implies a search for a kind of necessity in our judgements which, in practice, we find we can never obtain. All that we can do is postulate a deeper system of necessary truth which grounds our thoughts, and on which such truth as they have must be thought of as conditional.

The best I can do to bring these points together on Bradley's behalf is to state his position somewhat as follows.[50]

A. In judgement our concepts are applied to the sensible reality we encounter in perception but are never literally true of it.

B. However, if we are content simply to say that there is something about that reality which makes us think in a certain way, that can be literally true.

C. In learning how reality forces us to think we are learning how various ideas fit together. That is, we are learning that certain ideas have a place in a larger system of ideas which Reality would increasingly force on us if we explored it further.

D. But we never really manage to get a grip on the whole system of ideas to which ideally we are moving. Thus we do not know the position of the central idea which is currently somehow forced on us in the whole system. We cannot even distinguish the specific spatio-temporal world to which it belongs from others in which it may have no place. In attempting to do so we are thrown back on token indexicals, but these belong to the kind of judgement which vainly attempts to deal with the given itself rather than to organize the ideas reality somehow forces on us.

E. For once we have given up expecting our ideas to apply directly to sensible reality, we must dispense with token indexicals like 'this', 'that', 'here', 'now', and 'I' as proper vehicles of truth, and must look rather for context-free truths (what Quine calls eternal truths) in which demonstratives are replaced by definite descriptions. But no actual definite descriptions will do the job. Even if they pick out just one thing in 'our' world, that does not suffice to distinguish them from other things in other worlds.

F. But although genuine truth would simply relate ideas to one another within a rational system, judgement is not simply the organization of a realm of ideas which is sufficient unto itself. What is forcing all these ideas on us is the Reality we meet with in sensory experience and which fills out our own felt

---

50   See especially PL, pp. 181–82.

being. There is some unknown quality in the reality which makes our so-called conditional truths true, something about it which forces the move from the antecedent to the consequent. So while we must replace ordinary categorical by hypothetical judgements, if we want genuine truth, these hypotheticals still have an implicitly categorical character, inasmuch as they ascribe this unknown quality to reality.[51]

G. Bradley often seems unclear whether it forces this move on us in the sense that our sense experience somehow triggers off these idea sequences by way of connections whose only necessity is that of a response to sense experience, or whether sensible reality is somehow one with something like a Rational Mind active within us which deals in intrinsic necessities.[52]

For the pressure of Reality upon us to think in certain ways seems to cover for Bradley both what others would call the lessons of experience and the insight into logical necessity. He often disclaims any idea that the human mind can find out matters of fact without the use of the senses, yet he also seems to think that we have not got very far in understanding something so long as it seems as though matters might have been otherwise. The general idea seems to be that inevitably much of the truth we acknowledge must be contingent, but that it is of the nature of intellect to attempt to develop its judgements until they form a system in which each part is necessary relative to the rest.

Does that mean that intellect aspires to a system of truth to which as a whole there would be no conceivable alternative or only to a system of mutually implying judgements, in which each part is necessitated by the rest, but to which as a whole there are conceivable alternatives, ruled out because contingent experience does not so well sustain them? Bradley's view would seem to be that the ideal of the intellect is a system which would be unique in the extent to which it satisfied the criteria of internal co-implication of all its parts and maximal richness in content. If so, perhaps there are alternatives which are in a manner conceivable but less satisfying because less full. We shall be looking at all this more closely shortly.

H. For practical purposes most of these points can be ignored and we can think of our concepts as sometimes adequately characterising, or extending, given sensible reality with the aid of demonstratives which pick out the parts of reality which are our starting point. Thus the main judgements which figure in ordinary thought, and which are good enough for practical purposes, are analytic and synthetic judgements of sense as initially specified.[53]

---

51 See PL, p. 192, for a pithy statement of this point. However, heaping layer upon layer of complexity, Bradley says that even this quality, as a merely abstract universal, can only be applied truly to reality in a hypothetical way; see PL, pp. 88– 89.

52 Bradley seems to have thought that a properly grasped conjunction of characteristics as given in sense experience is the grasp of a necessity, but it is hard to be clear just how he conceived this necessity. The note to II, II, I of PL (pp. 343– 45) is typical of his obscurity on this point. See my note 54.

53 See PL, pp. 100–101, §72, and p. 106, §80.

I. However, that categorical statements can only hope to become true by turning into hypotheticals asserting relations between universals accords with the fact that the intellect can only be satisfied by judgements which are both changeless and necessary. And this, says Bradley, is shown in the practice of science which is only interested in the given insofar as it can find a necessary connection of universals within it.[54]

In holding that the only truth ordinarily available to us concerns how *ideas* stand to one another, Bradley is, of course, not saying that we only know about *sense data*, and not about what lies beyond them. For his ideas are meanings, and it is precisely sense data about which we cannot speak truth. In some ways his point is more akin to that of philosophers today who say that the only truth available to us falls within a conceptual scheme which we cannot transcend and compare to a reality beyond. But Bradley does not put the emphasis on the linguo-centric predicament typical of such philosophers. His position is, on the whole, more like James's and Bergson's, that concepts cannot capture lived reality. But unlike these he thinks that the reality we live through points to a more static form of being of which it is a misleading fragment and that the nature of this can be captured neither in concepts nor through mere attention to the flux.

It is hard not to sympathise with James in his criticism of absolute idealists, who castigate ordinary truth for not living up to the requirements which they lay down for genuine truth, when they would have done better to take this as showing the pointlessness of these requirements and taken their criteria of truth from ordinary practice. Should not Bradley, then, have used his dialectic to show that the failure of ordinary judgements to meet such supposed ideals of intellect as context-independence, necessity, and perhaps a kind of accurate picturing of experienced reality, is a reason for rejecting these ideals? Certainly it seems strange that after giving such a sensible account of the role of demon-

---

54   See PL, pp. 105–6, §§76–77. One may well object that men are commonly only interested in such connections insofar as they improve our grasp of particular fact. There seems something radically incoherent in the idea that mind has any inclination to deal only with timeless connections between universals. And in any case this should be distinguished from an aspiration it may have to a context-free perspectiveless vision of reality. Bradley seems to run together necessity and timelessness, ignoring the possibility of Quinean eternal sentences about events at a particular time which need have no sort of necessity to them. Bradley's official view of necessity in PL, I should note, is that it is always relative, that is, that something can only be necessary in the sense of being the necessary implication of something else. To the objection that if Q is necessary relative to P, then 'If P, then Q' is absolutely necessary, Bradley replies that it is really Q which is necessary, as necessitated by P. See PL, p. 199. However, he qualifies this reply in an additional note to the second edition. See note 4 on p. 236. I discuss his later views on necessity further in section 5 (c) and (d). The main point is that no one can ever formulate the sum total of what necessitates a judgement, yet the intellect cannot be satisfied till this is done.

stratives in fixing reference, he should have claimed that because this reference is context-dependent the judgements which use it have no role in serious thinking.[55]

Still, Bradley's arguments against the truth of all ordinary judgements turn, in effect, on a concept of truth for which a true judgement ascribes a character imaginatively or symbolically present in the mind to a reality in which it is literally exemplified, which is, it seems to me, much nearer to that of common sense than is James's pragmatic one.

Thus James, one might say, tampers with the intension of 'truth' in order to give it its usually presumed extension, while Bradley insists so much on its ordinary intension that he challenges all ordinary beliefs about its extension.

But is not this to flout the fact that Bradley held a *coherence* theory of truth? Or was this a later development and his position in PL (apart from the addenda to the second edition) more of a *correspondence* one? I shall be going into this shortly. For the moment I shall only suggest that he always effectively believed that, to be true in the deepest sense, an idea must capture imaginatively something of the real character of its object and thus, in a sense, correspond to it. It is because, for a variety of reasons, he thought our ordinary ideas do not do this, that he considered their truth only conditional.

This is not to deny that his view of truth underwent some development. For example, he came to believe in a doctrine of degrees of truth which has little presence in PL, as originally published.

Verbally the doctrine of degrees of truth is explicitly denied in the original first edition text, for he says: 'There are no degrees of truth and falsehood'.[56] But, as a note to the second edition explains,[57] his real point was that assertion does not have degrees (modal qualifications belonging to the content of what is asserted, not to the mode of its assertion), a position which he still expressed in his later work by saying that at the time of making a judgement one must intend it as wholly true, whatever judgement one makes about the character of one's assertion on reflection.[58]

The twin notions of degrees of truth and of the absoluteness of assertion are developed especially in the late essays collected as *Essays in Truth and Reality*. But before discussing his later views there are a few further points in PL which we can hardly pass by.

---

55   See PL, p. 64, §22. Of course, quite apart from the difficulties we have been considering, Bradley could not accept judgements which indicate positions in space and time by their relation to what is actually perceived as ultimately true, because space and time are unreal. Even if there are genuine spatio-temporal relations of a kind within what is sensibly given, the real relations of the given to what lies beyond it cannot be spatio-temporal. So these relations hold only within the world of our own construction.

56   PL, p. 197.

57   p. 236, note 1.

58   See ETR, pp. 381–82.

(b) Negative Judgements and Some Laws of Logic

§ Bradley takes it that a judgement must say something about reality, and that this can only be true of negative judgements if they say that there is something positive about it which excludes the negated concept.[59] This account covers both judgements in which the scope of the negation is a whole proposition and those in which it is only of a predicate within it. If I say 'God does not exist', I am saying *that Reality possesses some character which excludes the presence of God;* if I say 'My cat is not hungry', I am saying *that Reality, qua being my cat, possesses some quality which rules out its being hungry.*[60] Negative judgements thus implicitly ascribe a certain positive quality to Reality which excludes the negated predicate. Sometimes one may not be able adequately to specify this quality, but to whatever extent it is left unclear, the judgement has a certain incompleteness. Bradley modified some of the details of his account of negation between the first and second editions of PL but the central point remains the same.

This view of negation leads Bradley to challenge the importance of the usual distinction between the contrary and the contradictory, between incompatibles which can both be false and incompatibles one of which must be true. (From Bradley's point of view the incompatibles can either be taken as predicates or judgements, since contrary or contradictory judgements are ones which ascribe contrary or contradictory predicates to reality.)

According to traditional logic 'This is red' and 'This is not red' are contradictories, while 'This is red (all over)' and 'This is blue (all over)' are contraries. Similarly 'All men are honest' and 'Some men are not honest' are contradictories, while 'All men are honest' and 'No men are honest' are contraries. But for Bradley the sheer negation of a judgement is an implicit assertion of a contrary, or at least an indication that its truth or applicability is excluded by the holding of some unspecified contrary. It follows that the so-called contradictory of a positive judgement, consisting merely in the blank negation of it, is more the hint of the direction in which a truth is to be found than a genuine truth itself. 'This is not blue' means 'This has some quality incompatible with blue' and 'Some men are not honest' means something like 'Something about reality excludes a race of entirely honest men'.

So we should be dissatisfied when someone rejects a view until we find he has some positive alternative which excludes it, and should regard him as saying something different according as to the nature of this alternative.[61] Thus merely saying 'God does not exist' is an incomplete judgement until we are given a positive characterisation of the universe in virtue of which it is godless; the man who says that there is no God because the through-and-through physical nature of the universe excludes a non-physical infinite spirit is saying something very different from someone, like Bradley, who denies that God

---

59   See PL, I, p. 3.
60   See PL, p. 120 and pp. 123–24.
61   See PL, p. 279.

exists because the universe as a spiritual whole complete in itself cannot have been created by a spirit external to it.

So while present-day philosophers often say that they do not understand a positive theory until they know what it is denying, Bradley says that we do not really understand a negative claim until we know what it is asserting. (A very similar view of negation, and with it of the conception of nothing and of non-existence, was promoted later by Bergson in *L'Évolution Créatrice*.[62] Sigwart, it seems, may have influenced both. Schopenhauer had already made interesting use of a similar idea.)

This sort of view seems to have a good deal going for it. It seems impossible to imagine a negative situation except by imagining something which we recognize as excluding what we are conceiving as negated. It has, indeed, been argued against such a view as Bradley's that 'P is incompatible with Q' means 'P and Q can *not* both be true' and that this account of negation is therefore circular. But why cannot Bradley insist simply that it is the concept of incompatibility which is the more basic?

After discussing negative judgements Bradley turns to disjunctive judgement. It is amusing to find him saying that he would 'despair of human language' if a non-exclusive use of 'or' were permissible.[63] Certainly he shows great ingenuity in arguing that apparent uses of it in this way are, in fact, not such. His account of 'P or Q' is somewhat like that of negation—we are ascribing a quality to Reality which is discriminable into two more determinate forms without an overlap. For example to say that a man or woman entered the room is to say that a human being did, and implying (perhaps wrongly) that being human has just these two divisions.

This is not the place for further discussion of the details of Bradley's treatment of the types of judgement and of their quantity (in the traditional sense relating to 'all', 'some', etc.), their modality, and so forth, or for disentangling what may remain of interest in it after so many changes in the discipline of logic.

Certainly Bradley's account of negation has interesting implications for problems which remain important. Thus it has long been debated what makes certain predicates incompatible where this is not evident from their form. Much energy has been spent, for example, on the question why a thing cannot be both red and blue all over, something troubling to empiricists who wish to see all necessity as analytic.

Bradley's view is that we should not ask so much why some properties are, as to how it is that others are not, incompatible and that the *prima facie* presumption is always that a pair of discrepants are so. For he claims that if reality, in general or in a particular region, is to have two different qualities, it can only be because it consists of two different parts or aspects, related to each other in some distinctive manner, each of which has one of them. A thing which

---

62   Bergson, pp. 737–47.
63   See PL, p. 134.

was in no sense variegated could not have distinct properties. And to recognize that, and how, a thing is variegated is to see it as consisting in distinguishable elements in some specifiable relation to each other. Thus different qualities can only belong to the same thing if that thing divides into distinct aspects which relate together to make it up, and an inconsistent description is one which ascribes different qualities to something while denying any such division or relationship. Thus it seeks to combine qualities without allowing them any *modus vivendi*.[64]

Thus whenever we think clearly of a thing as having two different properties we take it as having two distinguishable parts or elements and have some idea of how these relate to each other. Typically self-contradictory descriptions of a thing are those which offer no satisfactory account of how it thus divides into distinct components in relation, because all the usual ways of dividing it seem to have been ruled out. Thus there is no contradiction in a thing's being red and blue, if we are allowed to think of each colour as belonging to a different spatial part, or as pertaining to the thing at different times. The difficulty is introduced by the expression 'all over' which expressly forbids us to find the usual distinguishable homes for the different qualities.

However, Bradley's account is not without difficulties. When a thing is red and circular what are the two parts one of which has each feature? Perhaps the colour belongs to its internal extension and its shape to its bounding line.[65] At any rate, Bradley's view—which seems to me on the right lines—is that distinct predicates can only apply to a thing if it consists of distinguishable terms in relation, each answering to one of them. Or more strictly (we must surely add), that they are so, unless one is a determinable of which the other is a determinate, like red and scarlet.

It may seem odd that Bradley, the great monist, makes such difficulties over the idea of a single thing having a variety of different properties, for surely monists must conceive the various things in the universe, as did Spinoza, as so many different modes or properties of the ultimate substance.

The answer to this is that Bradley did not think of that sort of monism as finally satisfactory. For it is couched in terms of a distinction between a thing and its properties which does not resolve the basic problems of pluralism any more than does the conception of a world of many distinct items standing in relations of various sorts to one another. In the end the problem of how the many apparently distinct items in the world constitute a single universe must be resolved by the transcendence of all such distinctions. The present discussion belongs to a level of thought which stops short of such a final transcendence.

---

64   Compare Husserl, *Logic,* Investigation VI, §2, chapter IV.
65   I am thinking of a two-dimensional surface here. Its application to three-dimensional objects is complicated by the question whether we should conceive of them as coloured right though or only on their surface. Either way we can perhaps distinguish the colour as a property of something which can be called the filling, whether of surface or object, and the shape as property of a boundary.

Bradley's view of contraries will not seem convincing to those who think of a thing's qualities as distinct items somehow attached to it. For then the presumption would be that distinct qualities can attach to the same thing unless they have some special power to repel each other (landing us with a problem as to the nature of this power and how far its existence in particular cases can be a necessary truth).

But it goes well with the view that a thing is in some sense made up of its qualities, and we shall find that this is, in fact, Bradley's view. The main objection to this is that it seems to confuse particulars and universals, but we shall see that Bradley's position bypasses this problem, or at least can be developed in a way which does so. [66]

Bradley makes a valuable use of these ideas in his discussion of the principle of contradiction or law of non-contradiction.[67] Is this merely vacuous, he asks, or does it give genuine information? Answer: It reminds us that there are features in reality which cannot be combined in certain ways and it warns us off making judgements which seek thus to combine them. Inasmuch as it does not tell us what is uncombinable, but leaves this to be discovered afresh in each case, it is empty, but inasmuch as it reminds us that there are contraries, and bids us steer clear of them, it says something true and gives us good, if very general, advice.[68]

This treatment of the principle of contradiction is dependent on his interpretation of not-P as the implicit assertion of some contrary, Q, of P, that is, as the assertion that there is a true contrary of P which one can be challenged to supply. The principle thus warns us to be careful not to embroil ourselves in any assent to contraries which could induce us to say 'P' and 'not-P' (whose real force would lie in the contrary assertion in the background) but does not tell us anything as to which judgements or predicates actually are contraries. This interpretation of the principle is part of a general position according to which logical thought cannot be reduced to formal rule and for which logic can only give general guidance as to the sort of thing to which we must be alert if we are to think cogently.

Discussing this principle, Bradley makes some eminently sensible remarks about the Hegelian dialectic. While rating its grasp of thought and reality higher than that of usual empiricist views, he thinks it overplays its hand in professing to deny the law of contradiction. It is better presented as the view that features which seem initially discrepant and uncombinable, and which at a surface level work against each other, are often in fact significantly combined in reality. That does not show any fault in the principle of contradiction properly taken, since this does no more than warn us not to attempt combining the uncombinable.[69]

---

66 See Chapter Three, §3, below.
67 See PL, pp. 145–51.
68 See PL, p. 151.
69 See PL, pp. 147–51. See also pp. 408–11.

Bradley is, therefore, careful to distance his own account of negation from too Hegelian an interpretation. The positive basis of the negative shows itself incompatible with the negated predicate when we attempt to apply that, but that does not put every feature of a thing into a significant relation with all that it is not, still less make it somehow incorporate it as its own other. The dialectic's mistake is the false assumption that not-F is always a genuine feature of reality.[70] Bradley allows that there may be negations in reality which are part of its basic dynamics, but this is not implied in his own account which is, he says, strictly logical, not metaphysical.

§ Bradley's treatment of the law of excluded middle is more complicated, and not very easy to grasp, but the upshot is something similar.[71] It is, says Bradley, one sort of disjunctive judgement. We saw above that he takes 'A is F or A is G' as meaning that A has a quality which is 'divided' between F and G, and warns us not to predicate both of anything. 'A is F or A is not-F' is a special case of this. It asserts a common quality of A, which we may call 'general relation to F', which divides into a region which accepts F and one which rejects it, and tells us that there is such a quality for every F, and that it pertains to every object. It also tells us that this division is exhaustive.[72]

But as with the law of contradiction, the real information this law gives is slight. It bids us gird ourselves to make a definite choice between two positions whenever there really is no third alternative. But it does not tell us when this condition holds. To say that in all cases we must either accept 'A is F' or 'A is not-F' (or P or not-P, where each offers some general characterisation of the universe) disguises the fact that this is only so in certain cases. For sometimes 'F or not-F' is not being used successfully to identify such a quality and its articulation into alternatives, one of which accepts F and the other of which rejects it. Such cases lie outside the scope of the law, but the law itself gives us no mechanical guide to these limits to its own scope.

Thus the law of excluded middle should only be used with caution. To take our previous example, both the person who says that God exists and the person who says that he does not exist may be wrong; neither 'godful' nor 'godless' may provide adequate conceptions of the universe. Thus while the theist's 'God exists' may be ultimately unacceptable, the real purport of the atheist's 'God does not exist' may be even more so. For he may be assuming that he has identified a quality of reality, which can be called 'general relation to being a godful universe' which has only two divisions, and using 'no God' to indicate the second, when in fact there is a third in which the truth lies. Thus the law of excluded middle tells us that if, indeed, P and not-P, as we intend them, are the only alternatives, then we must choose between them and not look vainly for some further alternative; however, we must examine each case individually to

---

70   See PL, p. 123.
71   See PL, pp. 152–56.
72   See PL, p. 152.

see whether it really is of this type. Thus we put the law to a bad use if we fail to bear in mind that the positive content we are thinking under not-P may not be the only alternative to what we are thinking under P, and that sometimes 'P or not-P' as it is intended is not therefore right.[73]

§ The chapter in which these two logical laws are discussed opens with a discussion of the principle of identity. Bradley echoes Hegel's view that, as often understood, this says nothing, for 'A is identical with A' is vacuous, unless A be taken as in some way different in each case.

The principle can, however, be interpreted in ways which give it point (indeed, so much point that later Bradley depicts it as one of the main foundations of all reasoning).[74] Thus we may take it as a reminder that one can have the same amidst differences and that the identity is then as genuinely there as are the differences.[75] Or it might be taken as saying that every judgement asserts an identity in difference, either that of a single subject which remains the same as it sustains different predicates or that of some unitary whole within which the judgement makes distinctions.[76] But, says Bradley, its most interesting meaning for him is as the assertion that genuine truth is independent of context and therefore cannot change. Thus the intellect can only be satisfied that it has genuine truth when it can formulate its judgements in a context-independent form.[77] This is a point we have already sufficiently considered.

§ Bradley somewhat modified his views on the matters discussed in this and the previous section in his later years. The modifications are presented in additional notes to the second edition, published in 1922, and the *Terminal Essays* then added.

His later views of negation and disjunction (for which see especially *Terminal Essay* VI), which are strongly influenced by Bernard Bosanquet's *Logic* and his critique of the first edition of PL,[78] take him further away from the logic familiar to us today. A negative judgement properly understood does not merely have as a positive element the implied quality which rejects the quality negated. It also implies that the negated predicate applies elsewhere.[79] Everything has its place in reality; negative judgments merely tell us not to allocate something to the wrong place. The result is some softening of the contrast between positive and negative judgements, since every judgement is a matter of finding both where features of reality do belong to each other and where they do not. (This is related to the later denial of 'floating ideas'.) Similarly, disjunctive judgements tell us that a range of incompatible qualities under a common genus each have their place. 'P or Q or R' means that the universe contains each of them,

---

73   See PL, p. 153.
74   See PL, p. 470.
75   See PL, p. 141, also pp. 287–94 and passim.
76   See PL, p. 141.
77   See PL, pp. 143–45.
78   Bosanquet, *Knowledge* and *Reality*.
79   See PL, pp. 665–67, also p. 127, note 14, etc.

and in its fuller form it locates the right place for each. This realized, we can see (somewhat hazily!) that the negative judgement is an incomplete disjunctive judgement in which we reject a mislocation of a quality but do not indicate its correct location. Quality in all this means any character which can belong to some 'region' of reality.

A region of reality is something which can become the 'special subject' of a judgement and, as already mentioned, in his later work Bradley emphasises that every judgement has its 'special subject' which is one manifestation of the single universe. This may be a limited portion of our space and time, the whole of our space and time, the world of Dickens, the world of mathematics, the world of the comic, and so forth.

> Everything, to be in any sense real, must hold of the one Reality. And the felt "this" is therefore, so far, the real Universe. On the other side, while the Universe is the "this," it also is more and beyond, and it contains within itself other "thises" innumerable. . . .
>
> You can not in the end with truth abstract wholly from the "this now," and indeed there is nothing in the Universe from which in the end you can so abstract. For suppose your "now this" abolished, the predication of any idea, whether of "this" or of anything else, becomes forthwith impossible. The entire real Universe, inseparably one with your "this," would itself have followed its removal. And hence every idea (you may say) is affirmed of your "this," since every idea is true only of that Reality from which your "this" is indivisible. At the same time the Reality, including more than any one of its elements, can naturally accept ideas which hold beyond the limits of your "this". We have found here in principle, I think, the solution of our problem [as to how we can transcend our present 'this']
>
> PL, pp. 660–61

> Every judgement has two aspects. On one side it holds of the ultimate Reality or the whole World. On the other side it judges of that world as appearing in one emphasized feature. Every judgement therefore is selective, and marks a distinction (we may say) singled out from the Universe. We everywhere refer specially to this or that, and "specially" means that we do *not* refer to the rest—at least in the same way.
>
> PL, p. 662

Ingenious as much of the late discussion is, I am, I suspect, like most other modern readers, more at ease with the earlier doctrines, and upon the whole these suffice as background to his metaphysics.

(c) Inference

The main topic of PL, pursued in Books Two and Three, is the nature of inference. Although this is a most important element of Bradley's whole philosophical oeuvre we shall have to pass it largely by. The central thesis is that inference consists in 'ideal experiment' in the form of synthesis and analysis. Typically this consists in synthesising the ideas we have of things into some more comprehensive idea of a whole to which they must or may belong and finding through analysis that the whole or its constituents, as thereby presented in idea, consequently possess certain characteristics, or relations to each other, which must or would belong to these as they exist in external fact. 'Reasoning thus depends on the identity of a content inside a mental experiment with that content outside.'[80]

In many cases the whole is formed by uniting the ideas together at some point where they contain an identical element, at which their objects must meet in fact, and finding that as a result they are depicted as in a certain relation, affirmation of which constitutes the conclusion. But this (though even so much takes us beyond the narrow limits of the traditional syllogism) is by no means the only case. (This is the kind of inference treated in volume one of PL. Volume two extends the account to cover a variety of other cases, some of them quite remote from the inference of then or subsequent standard logic.)

This is somewhat similar to C. S. Peirce's account of inference as the construction of a diagram from the premises, in conformity with a leading inferential principle, in order to read off features from it which become the inference's conclusion.[81]

One of the main themes is the impossibility of reducing all valid inferences to the syllogistic form except perhaps by an act of torture which distorts their significance.[82] Bradley shows carefully how various sorts of inference cannot be thus treated, in particular those which turn on the meaning of relational expressions. Thus inference cannot be reduced to the application of a limited set of standard rules nor can it become such simply by the addition of some extra rules not recognized by traditional logic. Such an aspiration turns on the wholly mistaken view that the validity of inference is determined solely by the form and never by the content of premises and conclusion. Such rules as there are are only general guides, not formulas to be followed mechanically.

It must be born in mind that Bradley uses 'inference' to cover any conceptual interpretation of the sensorily given as the result of past experience as well as the movement from judgement to judgement in a manner of timeless validity. This broad sense stems from his belief that in all these cases we apply one universal to reality in virtue of the presence there of another, and do so because

---

80   PL, p. 436.

81   It seems also quite similar to the views of Kenneth Craik as reported and endorsed in McGinn, pp. 173 et ff.

82   The definitive statement of the point is in III, II, I. See also *Terminal Essay*, I, pp. 618–19. Bradley also makes a point rather like that of Lewis Carroll in his 'What the tortoise said to Achilles'. You may try to reduce all inferences to syllogism by putting their principle down as a premiss. But to do this is to ignore the fact that the principle of an inference works not as a premiss but as the nature of the inferential operation by which premiss leads to conclusion. Bradley allows that there are some repeatable patterns of valid inference, but denies (i) that they can be finally listed, (ii) that we need to know about them to reason on them, and (iii) that we can so dissociate form from content that some new content might not vitiate the validity of some familiar form.

they belong together as features of a more comprehensive universal content, whether their doing so has been learnt empirically or follows from their very nature. Such a usage is rather confusing. Thus, as we shall see, when he describes memory as an inference he is not necessarily denying what others have meant when they call it non-inferential knowledge of the past.

There is much that is of continuing importance in Bradley's treatment of inference and of related themes, though it is often clumsy in comparison with the treatment that modern symbolism makes possible.

Bradley continued to dwell on the subject of inference in his later writings, both in his additional notes and in the *Terminal Essays* appended to later editions of PL and elsewhere, particularly in ETR. The main change is a much greater insistence on the way in which in inference we find some object of thought developing itself in our minds while still retaining an essential identity with its starting point. And he is perhaps still more emphatic than he was on the dependence of ordinary logical reasoning on certain assumptions which cannot be taken as finally true.[83]

The subject of inference will not loom too large in what follows and thereby some of the total significance of Bradley's positions may be lost. However, a complete study of the matter is not practicable in the present work and would distract somewhat from the features of Bradley's thought which I am most concerned to highlight and compare with James's.

§ There is one issue, however, which looms large in PL of too much philosophical significance to pass by. This is the question whether logical expressions apply only to judgements and their relations or whether they apply also to the reality about which judgement is made. How is causation related to logical implication? Can fact as opposed to judgement be necessary? This is the main topic of Book III, from chapter II on.

Inferential reasoning, Bradley says, cannot be true of reality, for there is no equivalent there of the logical processes it involves.[84] This is true, at least, so long as we conceive reality as a series of events in the common-sense world of space and time.

> [T]he movement in our mind remains discursive, symbolic, and abstract. If the facts come together on just the same principle on which we unite our ideal elements, yet they can not come together in just the same way. The real is divided from the mental union by an insuperable difference. The synthesis of facts may be partly the same as our mental construction; but in the end it diverges, for it always has much that we are not able to represent. We can not exhibit in any experiment that enormous detail of sensuous context, that cloud of particulars which enfolds the meeting of actual events. We may say indeed that we have the essential; but that plea reiterates the charge brought against us. It is just because we have *merely* the essence, that we have not got a copy of

---

83   See especially *Terminal Essay* 1.
84   See PL, pp. 585–86.

the facts. The essence does not live in the series of events; it is not one thing that exists among others. If reality is the chain of facts that happen, then the essence is a creature which lives only in the thought which has begotten it. It could not be real, and it can not be true. Our construction is as false as our separate premises.

And our conclusion can hardly fare much better. Begotten of falsehood it can not so far be misbegotten, as to show us in the end the features of fact. The parental disease still vitiates its substance. Abstract and symbolic it mutilates phenomena; it can never give us that tissue of relations, it can not portray those entangled fibres, which give life to the presentations of sense. It offers instead an unshaded outline without a background, a remote and colourless extract of ideas, a preparation which everywhere rests on dissection and recalls the knife, a result which can not, if events are reality, be aught but unreal.

PL, pp. 585–86

But how do matters stand when reality is taken, not as the system of spatial and temporal events, but in a metaphysically more fundamental way? May we say, then, that inferential thought is, or at least can be, true of the genuine Reality in the sense of being an ideal transcript of it? Bradley's answer is none too clear but it seems to be this. An adequate metaphysics can produce accounts of the world and inferences which come nearer to being true in the sense of an ideal transcript of it than truth could be if Reality were the space-time series. But all the same it cannot do this finally, for it still treats in abstract intellectual terms something which is much more than merely conceptual. The proper conclusion is that thought, even at its best, and in that sense truest, is the development in ideal form of the same principle as is at work in the universe as a totality, but cannot reproduce in its own terms what that Reality is genuinely like.

It may be suggested that if Reality consists in a system of divine thought, as some Hegelians believe, our inferential processes may, so far as valid, be transcripts of it. However, Bradley argues that even if that were so, our reasonings could hardly be transcripts of the divine.

I should be sorry to seem to persist in unbelief, but I am compelled once more to repeat the dilemma: If the reality in this way corresponds to logic, then reality itself has been wholly transformed. One may perhaps accustom oneself to regard events as the reasoning sequence of the divine understanding, but it is not so easy to bring under this head any sameness and difference that is thought to exist. We are forced to wonder, if things by themselves are really *not* alike, how God himself can find them the same; or how even God goes on to distinguish them, if they themselves are *not* really different. It is indeed possible here that a distinction might save us, that a sensuous ground which *is* not different, when taken together with a function of the intellect, produces alike both distinction and difference. And yet this solution is partial, and leaves a worse puzzle behind.

We might perhaps agree that reality is the work of a reasoning mind, but how can we submit to the belief that *my* reasoning must represent reality? How can we suppose that each trivial argument, every wretched illustration that we may have used in these discussions, provided only it be free from flaw, must have its direct counterpart in the nature of things. You may suppose that, whenever we reason, we retrace the solidified logic that is organic in the world;

you may believe that a mind, in union with our own, brings out by one process, that to us seems double, the separate sides of existence and truth. But, on either view, we are troubled with this consequence; every possible piece of mere formal argument, every hypothetical deduction from an idle fancy, all disjunctive and negative modes of demonstration, must each have its parallel counterpart in reality. This consequence may be true, and I will not deny it. But, if true, to me at least it is portentous. Our logic will have secured correspondence with fact, but the facts themselves have been strangely translated.

                                                                    PL, pp. 582–83

In any case, Bradley did not think that reality consisted in a system of divine thought. (It is not, at least, the view of AR and there is no reason to think he ever held it.) So it seems that for him inference is neither true of reality conceived in common-sense terms as a system of events in space and time, nor as the best metaphysics conceives it.

The distance that this puts between logic and reality is, however, surely rather less of a challenge to the ordinary presuppositions of logic than Bradley seems to think. For it is the premisses and the conclusion which are supposed to be true or false, not the movement between them. That is supposed to be truth-preserving rather than true. There is no reason why the inferential process (or even the conditional statement in which its principle may be formulated) should itself limn an aspect of the way things hang together in the reality they concern. However, for Bradley every inference is itself a judgement.[85] And the fact that there are no *ifs* and *thens* in reality shows that they can never really be true in the sense ordinary logic must suppose them.

However, even if this is not the defect in logic which Bradley thinks it, it would be a defect if there were no true premisses from which we can deduce true conclusions. And Bradley claims that this is so. For the premisses of an inference can never be true if the conclusion is, since they present supposed facts which can no longer be accepted as they first seemed in isolation when we relate them to the larger context in which their relation to the conclusion puts them. Moreover, the conclusion cannot be true either, for it too is an abstraction from the totality of the reality to which it is supposed to apply, and cannot be true of it as it stands when placed in that larger context.

This treatment of the relation between inference and truth, incidentally, is further evidence for my claim that Bradley's view of truth in PL is of an essentially correspondence kind. For his ground for denying that logic is 'true' is that its ideas do not transcribe reality.

§ In the material added to the second edition Bradley says that the treatment of the relation of thought to reality in the standing original text suffers from its failure to distinguish clearly between reality, taken as the spatio-temporal world, and reality, understood in a metaphysically more satisfactory way, but

---

85   See PL, p. 622.

that the main point applies either way. This gives him the occasion to insist that he never meant to suggest that the world of common sense was genuine Reality.

> The attempt, made at times in this work for the sake of convenience (see on Bk. I.II. §4), to identify reality with the series of facts, and truth with copying—was, I think, misjudged. It arose from my wish to limit the subject, and to avoid metaphysics, since, as is stated in the Preface, I was not prepared there to give a final answer. But the result of this half-hearted attempt was an inconsistency, which in this Chapter [i.e., the last one, III, II, IV] is admitted. The "real world," as the series of facts in time and space, is neither a given presented fact, nor is it a consistent construction. And obviously it can not be taken as ultimate Reality. Hence the "actual process in things," as identified with what is real, depends on an assumption which is more or less arbitrary.
>
> On the other hand the reader was warned, as I thought, sufficiently, that this view of reality, as the "real world" of Common Sense which is copied in truth, was not accepted by myself. And I will now point to warnings in this Chapter which some critics appear to have overlooked.
>
> PL, pp. 591–92, note 1

When this confusion is cleared up we reach the result that an adequate metaphysics can produce accounts of the world and inferences which come nearer to being true in the sense of an ideal transcript of it than truth could be if Reality were the space time series. But all the same it cannot do this finally, for it still treats in abstract intellectual terms something which is much more than merely conceptual.

It is true that Bradley suggests in the passage just quoted that he had been misleading not merely in seeming to identify Reality with the space-time system but also truth with copying. But, as we shall see, it is doubtful whether what is being denied here is the view that truth is, or would be, the imaginative capturing of something of the essence of what we think of in our minds.

The main development bearing on this in the material added to the later edition is the thesis that thought is somehow a distinct development in ideal form of the same principle as is at work in the universe as a totality. As such it cannot reproduce in its own terms what that Reality is genuinely like. But it is not quite clear whether this is because thought, even at its best, cannot be genuinely true, or because truth does not require such reproduction. Upon the whole I think that his position is the first, which does not imply, of course, that thought is not often as true as it is reasonable to wish it. We will come to closer grips with this issue if we turn to his treatment of these matters in AR and ETR.

§4. *Truth in* Appearance and Reality

§ It is time now to turn to Bradley's later views about truth and judgement. He is usually described as having advocated a coherence view of truth in these later writings.[86] And by a coherence view is meant one for which truth consists in a

---

86   Stewart Candlish has argued that Bradley never held a 'coherence' view of truth

harmony holding between propositions or judgements in a unitary system rather than the relation of a judgement to something which it is about. So, if we are right in depicting the view of truth which is dominant in PL as closer to a correspondence view, it seems there must have been some change of mind, and such there is sometimes thought to have been. However, I shall be suggesting that, despite some contrary appearances, his essential view remains the same.

Bradley, like James, tends to identify truth with true thought. We have seen that James took a dim view of propositions conceived as non-mental bearers of truth values, and insisted that without thought there could be reality but no truth about it. Bradley likewise thinks of truth, in the sense of the feature which makes a truth true, as primarily pertaining to judgements, where a judgement is a thought which occurs as an actual psychological event. However, he also wants to give some place to a notion of a judgement, and thus also to that of a truth, which can exist without any actual occurrence in anyone's mind. Indeed, he seems to regard the status of truths which no one has entertained as just one of those inevitable paradoxes which assail us when we try to organize our ordinary concepts.

Doubts on Bradley's part as to whether there can be unthought truths do not extend to the notion of truths which occur in different minds or on different occasions in the same mind. So perhaps we should think of him as operating informally with a notion of judgement types and judgement tokens. However, we come closer to his viewpoint if we remember that for him identity and difference go together and that to allow that two people may make the same judgement is quite consonant with insisting that their judgements are also two different psychological events. In any case, most of what he says about truth is best understood as an account of what it is for someone to think truly about something. Thus when he speaks of truth as having certain aspirations he is speaking of what we (or the Absolute through us) are aiming to do when we aim to think truly. Indeed, there is a strong tendency to identify truth with knowledge.

It would be a mistake to reject such identification on the ground that 'true' must occur in the definition of 'knowledge'. For we can certainly ask what 'true' means when it occurs in such a definition, and that is precisely what Bradley is considering when he considers what truth is qua knowledge.

A more apt objection is that knowledge is not merely true thinking, but true thinking arrived at in some satisfactory way. For, so it is often argued, a thought which is true merely by accident is not a case of knowledge. (Indeed, even a justified true belief is not so if its justification is not related appropriately to external fact, as when evidence in court, though reasonably accepted, was

---

such as is usually attributed to him, and that his actual view was an 'identity' theory of truth. This is somewhat of an over-simplification, but a better one than what it aims to replace. See Stewart Candlish, 'The Truth about F. H. Bradley', *Mind*, XCVIII (July 1989).

planted by the police to gain the conviction of a man they rightly thought guilty.) However, I doubt if Bradley would grant that such wrongly arrived at truth is really truth at all. For he would think that the defect of its justification would jeopardise its identification of its object. However that may be, it is certainly best, in seeking an initial understanding of his position, to bypass the subtleties of whatever distinction there may be between true thought and knowledge. For Bradley (more in tune here with ordinary linguistic practice than most analytic philosophers) rides over it roughshod.

§ With these points in mind, let us now consider briefly the treatment of truth in AR before we pass on to the more elaborate discussions of ETR. The main development is the doctrine of degrees of truth and the more explicit metaphysical context.[87]

§ Judgement is still conceived as the ascription to reality of ideas which are universals abstracted from our own conscious state. But much of the emphasis is now on the incoherent and unstable way in which judgements occur in our consciousness. For the character of the mental states in which they occur is essentially paradoxical, since they both present themselves as complete entities in their own right and as mere fragments of something more complete. It is, indeed, the felt incompleteness of our own experience, its felt possession of properties which imply something beyond, which gives rise to thought. It is the attempt to find something of which we can predicate universals, unstably exemplified in our own mental state, as features belonging there in a more stable way.

In doing so we typically construct pictures of reality which function well enough as guides to practical conduct. These possess what passes for truth in every day life. But when we devote ourselves to the deeper kind of thinking distinctive of metaphysics we realize that nothing of which we can conceive, or which we can directly encounter, really provides the universals we are predicating of reality with the stable home we are trying to find for them. We can fit them into ever more coherent and comprehensive systems of ideas, but to be true of reality they must somehow be present there in some more concrete way. Thought therefore is the attempt to find a home for universals which would abolish their status as truths.

In the end it would seem that the only really stable home they could find would be an infinite experience with a completeness lacking, though vaguely adumbrated, in the mental contents from which we have abstracted them. However, as occurring there they would have become part of that reality's non-conceptual sense of its own being rather than predicates applied in judgement. It is thus that thought commits that happy suicide of which Bradley somewhat notoriously speaks.[88]

Grasping how the universals we apply to reality ultimately belong in this Absolute is beyond us. (Certainly reality is not a hidden thing in itself, but a

---

87   See AR, chapter XXIV.
88   See AR, pp. 148, 150, etc.

totality whose generic essence we know through our own immediate experience of it; nonetheless, the way in which it combines the complex of often conflicting features we ascribe to it in thought must remain mysterious.) But the more coherent and comprehensive the system of universals which we predicate of reality as a whole, the nearer we get to doing so and the more true is our thought. For, since the absolute experience must be coherent and comprehensive, the arrangement of universals in our thought can only increase its approximation to their arrangement there insofar as it likewise becomes more coherent and comprehensive. Thus the building up of truth by the accumulation of separate facts is hopeless because the characterisations which describe reality as it is are ones which can only conceivably occur as elements in a unitary total system.[89] Even the pictures of reality which serve as the truths of every day must possess some degree of coherence and comprehensiveness if they are going to do enough justice to the reality in which we have our being to serve their own limited purposes of guiding us prosperously within it.

§ Thus truth is a matter of degree, of increasing approximation of the occurrence of universals in thought to that occurrence in the Absolute which is no longer truth. If this is right Bradley's basic view, at least of absolute truth, continues to be that it is the ascription of universals to reality which are really exemplified there. And even truth of a more pragmatic kind gives such hints as to its actual character as are necessary for the purposes in hand. Comprehensiveness and coherence are criteria of truth not because they provide a goal for thought other than that of depicting reality as it is but because such depiction requires them.

So AR develops rather than departs from the view of truth implied in PL. If it is not a correspondence view, at least of absolute truth, that is because it rejects any idea of propositions which map a reality from which they stand apart. Truth is thought occurring in intimate unity with a reality in which it succeeds in finding a home for universals which it abstracts from its own psychical character, and which, as thus abstracted, are otherwise homeless. This must be a matter of degree because there can never be more than an approximation to finding the right universal to project onto the right region of reality.

§ I do not say that I find all that Bradley says on these matters as fully intelligible as one has a right to expect. Though I sympathise with much of its upshot I would develop it myself in a less paradoxical fashion. I would agree with him that our experience contains a pre-conceptual sense of itself as a fragment of a larger reality the rest of which holds out various threats and promises to us, with which it tries to deal by thoughts which characterise it on the basis of universals derived from its own resources (very much as traditional empiricism has taught). I agree with him further that the system of universals we thus commonly ascribe to this larger reality is too riddled with incoherences to be its literal character and that this must in fact be that of a psychical whole

---

89   This idea was already there in PL. See, for example, p. 487.

of psychical elements much of the nature of his Absolute. But I am doubtful about Bradley's view that there is something incoherent about our experience because it has a *what* which it cannot coherently actualise. Rather, I think it actualises its *what* in a perfectly coherent manner, and do not see how that could be otherwise. That its *what* exhibits it as intrinsically a fragment of something fuller does not mean that it only possesses that character in a fashion which is somehow incoherent.

§5. The Final View of Truth: Coherence, Comprehensiveness, and Correspondence

§ *Essays in Truth and Reality,* first published in 1914, consists largely of essays published in journals (mainly *Mind*) from 1904 to 1911 (though one goes back to 1899). The arrangement of the articles in a single book with an introduction implies that they advocate a single system of ideas. That impression is for the most part borne out by a close reading, although the emphasis differs from one article to another. Taken as a whole it contains the most definitive treatment by Bradley of a whole range of questions about thought and truth. It also supplies the main evidence for ascription to him of a 'coherence' theory of truth. It may even be said that it contains the classic formulations of such a view. Nonetheless it is doubtful that its intention is to advocate anything quite like the coherence theory of truth of textbooks. In any case, it clearly requires our examination, more especially as it also contains a good deal of explicit criticism of James's pragmatism.

(a) Judgement

§ The basic view of judgement remains the same as in PL. In thinking that something is the case we ascribe an ideal content to reality. Reality is a totality extending indefinitely beyond our own private experience which we yet some-how feel as a whole (though obviously not in detail) in the immediate experience of our own being. 'At bottom the Real is what we feel, and there is no reality outside of feeling.'[90] Ideas (often here called 'ideal contents') in the logical sense are still regarded as the meanings of ideas in the psychological sense. Though Bradley does not elaborate on the sense in which a mental idea has a meaning, the implication is still that the fullest sort of judgement is one in which that meaning is a universal character or whatness of the mental idea which the judgement ascribes to reality as it extends beyond our own mental state.

Our taking the *what* in this way is made possible by the fact that, as a character of the mental idea, it has an essential incompleteness. The mental idea, that is, is experienced as only actualising it in an imperfect way and as therefore

---

90   ETR, p. 315.

pointing beyond itself to a more complete reality. The *what* is thus alienated from its original *that*, and seeks a better *that* in the world beyond. But, the search can never come to a satisfactory end, in our experience at least. For although we have a general direction of the mind upon Reality at large, we have no satisfactory way of identifying the right region within it to which our idea applies, nor of knowing how far it is transformed as a feature actually present there. We cannot identify it conceptually, for all our identifications are incomplete and could, or, as Bradley seems to think, are bound to, apply to more than one such locus. And we cannot encounter it in direct experience, for though that is of our own centre as somehow at one with Reality at large, it does not point to the particular region of Reality to which it belongs.

These rather perplexing contentions are closely related to the view that the ordinary subjects of our judgements are all only appearances. For an appearance is said to be a *what* which has not found an adequate *that*.

But is it the predicated universal or the *that* of which it is predicated which is the appearance? Perhaps Bradley would think the question trifling. For his view is that when I think (say) of Napoleon, I take a certain whatness, which is present in a rather inadequate way in my experience, as having a home beyond. Napoleon, for me (what I refer to as 'Napoleon') is that whatness present in a *that* which gives it a stable home. But it can only be present there in a radically transformed version and the same would be true even if I were one of his closest friends. Thus when I am thinking truly the universals which are my meanings have a more satisfactory home in the objects of which I am thinking than they do in my thoughts. But in that fuller form they can hardly remain altogether themselves, since they are as much distorted as adumbrated by thought. Thus my ideas of reality can never possess the truth to which they aspire, and their objects are but appearances of something with a character as much different from, as the same as, the universals by which I identify them.

(b) Criticisms of Pragmatism and of a Copy Theory of Truth

Such an account of truth implies that ideally it would be just such a correspondence as James attacks under the heading of 'the copy theory'. For it depicts ideas as true insofar as they reproduce within themselves something of the character of the reality to which they are applied. And in one of his most sustained criticisms of the pragmatic view of truth, Bradley seems to be criticising it on just that basis.[91] Thus he says that the fact that a true idea may work

---

91   See chapter IV of ETR, 'On Truth and Practice', first published in *Mind* (1904). This is directed in the first place at certain positions advocated by so-called personal idealists, but amounts to a general critique of the pragmatic conception of truth as advocated by F. C. S. Schiller, Dewey, and James. There are more specific criticisms of James's pragmatism in the two appendices to ETR, chapter V, originally published respectively in *Mind* (1908 and 1911). Appendix III is a critique of James's radical empiricism.

is typically the result of the fact that it corresponds with the reality with which one is dealing, but that such correspondence may occur without serving any practical purpose. Indeed he even says that '[i]f my idea is to work it must correspond to a determinate being which it cannot be said to make. And in this correspondence, I must hold, consists from the very first the essence of truth.'[92]

> It is dusk and the man-eating tiger will be coming, and I do not know how to avoid him whether by this course or that. And surely, in order to find some idea which will 'do', I must before all things consider his nature and what he on his side is likely to do. The same thing is evident again where my enemies are human. My end is practical, but surely my ideas about the means must be dictated to me by something which is clearly not myself. And this forced agreement of my ideas with a nature other than my volition is, I presume, that which in general we understand by truth.
>
> ETR, p. 79.

It is difficult to square such statements with the view that Bradley was an opponent of any correspondence theory.[93] It suggests rather that he never meant to reject the straightforward view that to know the truth about something is to grasp how it is, by having ideas whereby something of its character is directly present to one.

Still, such remarks occur cheek by jowl with what seem to be statements of a quite opposite coherence view. But before investigating the problem of interpretation this raises, let us examine some further comments Bradley makes about pragmatism.

(1) There is a much weaker sort of pragmatism than the one he finds James advocating with which Bradley expresses great sympathy; in fact, he complains that pragmatists have not pushed it further. This is the claim[94] that for practical, and indeed many theoretical, purposes we must and should often use working ideas for which we do not claim any final truth.

When we look at our ideas in this spirit (so Bradley contends) we should pick those which work best for the task in hand without worrying about their internal consistency or fit with ideas we use at other times. If this had been what James was saying, it would have had Bradley's hearty approval. Indeed, he would have advised James, in this context, not to attach the importance to consistency between and within our ideas on which he seems to lay an unnec-

---

92   ETR, p. 76.
93   At ETR, p. 120, note, Bradley objects to those who have taken this as a statement of his view of truth, as opposed to an aspect of truth on which he was insisting against one-sided theories. But these unnamed persons can hardly be blamed for taking him as meaning what he said.
94   This seems to clash with the suggestion that ideas only work insofar as they report or correspond to the relevant reality. The suggestion that science should seek a truth which is recognized as only pragmatic is made as early as PL. See, for example, pp. 340–43.

essary stress.[95] Although such ideas would not be true in the fullest sense of the word, Bradley even sympathises with those who hold that such practically effective working ideas are the nearest we humans can expect to get to truth.

> I have seen, if I may say so, far too much of metaphysics to think of staking vital issues on the result of speculative inquiry. And for practical purposes I hold in reserve a belief, in common, I imagine, with an increasing number of persons, a belief, the advantages of which Pragmatism would, it seems, like to appropriate surreptitiously. According to this practical creed there is in the end no truth for us save that of working ideas. Whatever idea is wanted to satisfy a genuine human need is true, and truth in the end has no other meaning. Our sense of value, and in the end for every man his own sense of value, is ultimate and final. And, since there is no court of appeal, it is idle even to inquire if this sense is fallible. It is this which in the end decides as to human interests, and whatever ideas are needed to serve those interests are true, however much these ideas are in contradiction with one another or even with themselves. The one question in the end is whether the ideas work. But there are degrees of truth, because ideas may work better or worse, and because again the interest which ideas subserve are more or less valuable. The above is scepticism, if you please, but it is not the stupid scepticism which offers itself as positive theoretical doctrine. It is the intelligent refusal to accept as final any theoretical criterion which actually so far exists. And there is here no mutilation of human nature, since every side of life, practical, aesthetic and intellectual, is allowed its full value. We are emancipated once and for all from the narrowness of all one-sided attempts at consistency. . . .
>
> But that Prof James could accept the position I have sketched . . . seems impossible [since he could not then claim the kind of ultimate truth for his pluralistic views against monism which he evidently means to].
>
> ETR, pp. 132–33[96]

(2) Bradley says that when pragmatists contend that truth consists of ideas which are practically useful they are either diminishing the whole point of life by reducing it to practice in some vaguely characterised sense which excludes a disinterested interest in how things are, and much of our culture, or so extending the sense of 'practical' that it is emptied of any interesting meaning. He sees Dewey (surely with justice) as tending to do the first, James the second.[97]

When it takes the first line pragmatism tends to worship the mere changing

---

95   See ETR, p. 67. See also his letter of 14 May 1909 to James in Perry, II, p. 640. For some remarks by James on how far consistency among our ideas is desirable see ERE, pp. 260–65.
96   See also ETR, p. 318.
97   See ETR, p. 72 and notes at p. 98 and 131. Bradley raises this point with James in two letters to him, that of 21 September 1897, at Perry, II, p. 239, and again in that of 28 April 1904, at Perry, II, p. 489. For some remarks of James on this topic see ERE, p. 260 et ff.

of the world from one state to another, without realizing that it makes no sense to place a value upon such 'practice' unless something other than practice, with its own intrinsic value, is brought forth thereby. But once we acknowledge that there is such a thing as intrinsic value, it is foolish to discount the intrinsic value of thought. When it takes the second line it virtually identifies truth with 'satisfying thought'. Bradley sympathises with this suggestion, but only on the understanding that the satisfaction typically sought in thought is of a distinctive kind. And as we shall see, Bradley himself sometimes identifies truth with that which gives the intellect its own particular sort of satisfaction.

These comments can be interpreted in a manner favourable to a *coherence* theory of truth, if we take it that coherence is the special satisfaction sought by the intellect. But the criticism of pragmatism in the passage about the tiger seems to presuppose a view of a more *correspondence* nature such as we have found to be the dominant *motif* in PL. Yet Bradley has even more sharply critical things to say later, especially in chapter V, 'On Truth and Copying', of the notion that truth is a copy of reality than anything James says. There is, however, a certain ambiguity on the part of both James and Bradley as to what is being criticised under such expressions as 'a copy theory of truth'.

(1) Most of the time they both seem to mean by it the supposition that the point of our ideas is to copy, or somehow transcribe in another medium, what we are or have been directly presented with apart from them. Thus when Bradley criticises it he is mainly objecting to the supposition that true ideas just passively register what has been given us more directly, and apart from thought, in perceptual and other sensory experience.

Bradley has many sensible objections to any such view. Thus he contends that, even if some true thoughts are merely reports on what we have perceived, such copying cannot be the essence of truth. For what we perceive is already the work of truth, that is, of true thought (presumably also sometimes of false thought). So a copy of our perceptions would be a copy of what is already truth, and its truth cannot consist in its being a copy of itself. Besides which, thought typically aims to put (by synthetic judgements of sense) what we encounter in perception in a wider context which it presents to us without necessarily copying anything ever given to us directly. And in the case of truths of a more theoretical sort, those, for example, which formulate laws of nature, it is even more obvious that we have no mere transcription or record of our observations.

(2) Surely Bradley is right that thought is seldom a mere copy, from life or memory, of what has been given. If the point seems rather obvious it may still have needed saying in refutation of some over simple forms of empiricism such as we may perhaps dub 'transcript empiricism'. Such a view is perhaps implied by Karl Pearson's description of a law of nature as 'a résumé in mental short-hand, which replaces for us a lengthy description of the sequences among our sense impressions'.[98] But rejection of transcript empiricism should not be

---

98   From Pearson's *Grammar of Science* quoted in Pratt, p. 14. Curiously, but not

treated as an objection to any even slightly less naive version of the view that truth is a conceptual copy of reality. For such a view need not imply that we get our thoughts or propositions to correspond to fact merely by having them mirror immediate experience. Whatever may be meant by saying that true thought copies fact, there is no need to take it as the view that an adequate copy can be made without inference and hypothesis. Thought may aim to be, and even succeed in being, a portrait, without being a portrait from life or even memory; it may use identi-kit methods or fill in the unseen details of the subject by analogy and conjecture based on the sight of other things. Moreover, we have not exhausted the possibility of a copy theory of truth until we have considered the possibility of copies which are not so much pictorial like-nesses as abstract diagrams of their subject matter (though such views have only had their full development since Bradley and James wrote, e.g., in Wittgenstein's *Tractatus*).

Thus some of Bradley's (like James's) criticisms of a copy theory of truth seem to be directed only at transcript empiricism and not at the more intelligent view that truth is a successful transcription of reality in a conceptual medium in which the gaps in the world as we have directly encountered it are filled by fortunate conjecture. And that leaves it after all none too clear how far he really does object to a more serious copy theory of truth. Certainly it does not establish that he is rejecting the view that the absolute truth sought in meta-physics would ideally be a reproduction in the mind of the essence of thought's object.

However, I think Bradley was objecting also to rather more serious sorts of copy theory than transcript empiricism, even if, like James, he sometimes made the mistake of thinking he could dispose of them all by disposing of that. Thus when he says that explanation cannot simply copy the given facts, he is presumably not just saying, rather obviously, that they are no mere transcrip-tions of perceptual data but more debatably that their aim is to fill in the gaps left by perceptual knowledge.[99] For he says that explanation is not a mere picture of reality, but something which 'holds' or 'is valid' of it rather than a mere mimic thereof. 'And we are driven to admit that, at least when we pass from individual truths, our truth no longer represents fact but merely "holds" or "is valid".'

Moreover, he has some arguments against what he calls the copy theory which are apt, if at all, against any view for which truth, however arrived at, must consist in ideas or propositions which somehow transcribe facts distinct from themselves. Thus he says that its essential fault is to divorce truth from reality, and treat them as distinct things.

---

unreasonably, this has been treated as a pragmatist statement.
99   See ETR, p. 109.

The identity of truth knowledge and reality, whatever difficulty that may bring, must be taken as necessary and fundamental.

ETR, p. 113

The basic error here

consists in the division of truth from knowledge and of knowledge from reality. The moment that truth, knowledge, and reality are taken as separate, there is no way in which consistently they can come or be forced together. And since on the other hand truth implies that they are somehow united, we have forthwith on our hands a contradiction in principle.

ETR, p. 110

And he goes on to say that truth fails of its own goal until it wholly incorporates its object, Reality.

Here he is warming to the theme, much emphasised in AR, that, while it is the aspiration of truth (that is, of thought aiming to be true) to be identical with its object, its attainment of that goal would destroy that *aboutness* which is also essential to its nature. And that is, indeed, how it is with the Absolute which knows its own being and all that falls within it by being it rather than thinking it. The same is true, indeed, of each finite centre's pre-conceptual grasp of its own character. But here the grasp lies below, while with the Absolute it stands above, conceptualisation and truth. So even the truest thought is essentially defective. As a way of grasping the character of something it is an advance on the infra-conceptual intimacy of a finite centre's sense of its own being but it still falls short of the supra-conceptual intimacy of the Universe's total sense of what it is up to.

This view that truth (qua knowledge) aspires to a kind of oneness with its object was aptly criticised in Santayana's aphorism that knowledge is a salute and not an embrace. Yet we do feel that another person, or even an insect, concerning whose state of feeling we wonder, knows the truth at which we can only guess because as a conscious being he currently simply is that state. So thought here, at least, does in a manner aspire to be its object.[100]

It was not, however, against such a realist criticism which Bradley thought he must defend himself but against Hegelians for whom thought is all in all, having no other to be about. To think otherwise they held (as Bradley represents them) is to suppose that thought can somehow transcend itself, an idea sup-

---

100 The upshot is something like the identity theory of truth attributed to him by Candlish—a view, he might have pointed out, clearly present in Heidegger. But the claim is rather more subtle than Candlish indicates, namely, that truth, or more straightforwardly the truth seeker, is aspiring to an identity with that which it is the truth about, which, if obtained, would destroy its character as truth. Truth requires both a distance from and an identity with its object. That is why it is finally a contradictory appearance. See Candlish.

posedly self-contradictory. For thought can have no resources on which to direct itself at something other than itself .

On the face of it, there are two questions here: (1) Is all genuine thought *thought about thought*? (2) Is the very notion of a thought being *about anything* a confusion? Bradley does not distinguish these but presumably he would answer both questions negatively. Thought, he held, can be about something beyond itself which is not thought.

He defends this sensible view against such an Hegelian objection by insisting that we are capable of realizing conceptually the limitations of the conceptual. For concepts occur in minds which are not purely conceptual, and are therefore directly in touch with a reality which is something other than sheer thinking. However, Bradley also holds that the lack of any sharp distinction between conception and feeling in our consciousness adumbrates the breakdown of the division between concept and sensible reality which (he holds) occurs at the level of the Absolute.

So truth (true thought) is about something beyond itself and yet aspires to an identification with its object which would destroy its character as thought and thus as truth. And every true thought is part of a totality in which this identification is achieved, so truth is ultimately the same as reality, which as the total Universe is the knowledge and the truth about itself. (Truth and knowledge are identified by Bradley on the ground that the idea of unthought truth is only a convenient way of reminding us that we are ignorant of many things.)

> And, if we are to advance, we must accept once for all the identification of truth with reality. I do not say that we are to conclude that there is to be in no sense any difference between them. But we must, without raising doubts and without looking backwards, follow the guidance of our new principle. We must, that is, accept the claim of truth not to be judged from the outside. We must unhesitatingly assert that truth, if it were satisfied itself, and if for itself it were perfect, would be itself in the fullest sense the entire and absolute Universe.
>
> ETR, pp. 113–14

> Truth is not perfect so long as it fails anywhere to include its reality, and its reality is not whole so long as any of its conditions are left out. Truth, compelled to select, is therefore forced to remain for ever defective. Its purpose, though realized increasingly, is not utterly fulfilled, and to fulfil that purpose would be to pass beyond the proper sphere and limits of truth. . . . Truth in short is about the real, while that which is only 'about' has stopped short of the truth. The complete attainment of truth's end is reached only in that Reality which includes and transcends intelligence.
>
> ETR, p. 330–31

But all that is at the level of the Absolute. And it seems clear that, so far as thought is taken more straightforwardly as a human occurrence, Bradley thinks that it is only partially identical with such reality as it concerns, and may even appropriately be contrasted with it as corresponding to it.

Obscure as some of this may be, one thing is clear. However much Bradley wanted to distance himself from anything called a copy theory of truth, he was also opposed to any view for which thought is sufficient unto itself. And that makes it problematic to treat him as having held a coherence view of truth, as that is usually understood. We must now turn to those statements which are usually taken as advocating such a view and see what can be made of them.

(c) The Coherence View of Truth

§ Bradley's most elaborate formulation of anything suggestive of a coherence view of truth is in chapter VII of ETR, 'On Truth and Coherence'. He there sets out to argue, as against expressions of the contrary view by G. F. Stout and Russell, that there are no immediately certain facts delivered to us either in perception or memory and that every such judgement, like all other judgements, is subject to the test of includability within a total system of acceptable beliefs. (This was already a main theme of Bradley's first publication, *The Presuppositions of Critical History* [1874].[101]) This test includes not merely coherence but also comprehensiveness.

> The test which I advocate is the idea of a whole of knowledge as wide and consistent as may be. In speaking of system I mean always the union of these two aspects, and this is the sense and the only sense in which I am defending coherence.
>
> ETR, p. 202

Are the twin requirements of coherence and comprehensiveness independent of each other? One ground for a negative answer might be the Hegelian view that it is only by placing individual judgements in a larger context that we can resolve the contradictions which they present in isolation.[102] Bradley himself cannot entirely accept that view in its usual form. For it claims not only that the contradictions present in partial views can only be resolved by placing them in a larger context, but also that the appropriate larger view is rationally derivable from the partial views. Bradley accepts the first point but thinks the second over-optimistic about the power of human reason. He holds rather that, in most cases, the appropriate larger context can only be discovered, if at all, empirically.[103] However, this is sufficient ground for regarding coherence and comprehensiveness as two sides of the same coin.[104]

One might object that Bradley is confusing essential incompleteness with self-contradiction. Suppose it true that any fragment of reality points vaguely

---

101 See CE, p. 19 et ff.
102 See ETR, p. 223.
103 In a second edition note to his criticism of J. S. Mill on induction Bradley says that he has no 'independent view on the subject' of 'induction' but that in the main he accepts 'the view advocated by Jevons, with its two main features of Hypothesis and Verification'. PL, p. 369, note 7.
104 See ETR, pp 223–26.

beyond itself to the existence of a larger context in which it figures. Surely that does not show that the character of that fragment contains a contradiction, or, put more satisfactorily, that our concept of it is bound to do so. (Something of this sort is said by Bradley himself in a discussion of Hegelian dialectic.[105]) For why should the concept we form of a reality which is thus essentially incomplete be either self-contradictory or even otherwise incoherent?

The Bradleyan reply, I take it, is that it is bound to be so because we cannot but try to conceive it both as a thing in its own right and as a mere fragment of the larger whole it vaguely implies. [106] To rid ourselves of that contradiction we must gain a clear idea of that larger context and cease the vain attempt to conceptualise the thing in isolation. Thus the essential motivation behind our search for knowledge is the attempt to resolve the unease of holding the contradictory conceptions imposed on us by partial views.[107] But although he thinks that the two requirements have a common source, he believes that in practice we have to treat them as specifying two distinct criteria which our thought must satisfy if it is to be true. Taken together these criteria constitute the notion of membership of a judgement in a system.[108]

Thus if a judgement as to what I am perceiving, or a memory judgement as to what I perceived in the past, cannot fit into the main body of my knowledge (that is, my current system of beliefs), it will be quite proper for me to reject it, and put a different interpretation on my experience.

But does not that suggest that I know for certain what experiences I am having, even if I do not know for certain what interpretation to put upon it? Well, according to Bradley, there is a sense in which experience itself is 'not fallible', but experience in this sense is not a judgement, and every judgement is fallible, in the sense of being corrigible.[109]

§ Bradley shows some concern to meet what has become the standard criticism of coherence as a criterion of truth, namely, that you can have a

---

105 See PL, p. 410.

106 See especially ETR, p. 241.

107 How does this fit in with the account of contradiction which we considered earlier in the chapter? This should become clearer when we turn later to Bradley's view of relations. But the general idea is this. At any given stage of thought we have ideas which do not cohere. This may be because there is a contradiction between two explicit ideas, or because there is a contradiction between an explicit idea and an implicit sense of a *more*, grasp of which would require that idea's modification. Contradiction, we have seen, is supposed to arise when we have discrepant ideas present to us without any satisfactory way of combining them into a unitary idea. To resolve it we must do two things. First we must distinguish reality into elements or aspects which answer respectively to one or other of the discrepant ideas. Then we must find a way of conceiving how these two elements or aspects hang together in some kind of unity. Bradley is now claiming that this can only be done by finding a higher-level idea in which they both figure as elements in a unitary pattern.

108 See ETR, p. 241.

109 See ETR, p. 206.

coherent system of false propositions. But he may not have realized sufficiently the need to remove the misunderstanding which would so often give rise to this objection. For it rests typically on the assumption that the items to be tested for coherence are propositions somehow 'there', whether affirmed (or even entertained) by anyone or not. But clearly the test was meant to be used only on judgements which someone is inclined to affirm. When this is understood, the force of the criticism is largely blunted.[110] And it becomes even less forceful when it is realized that the test of comprehensiveness is to be used jointly with that of coherence. Thus taken it bids us only accept judgements which cohere with the largest body of other beliefs which will continue to solicit us however encyclopaedic our concerns become.

The difference between Bradley's position and that of the coherence view of textbooks may go deeper still.[111] For he sometimes says that it is not only with other judgements that a judgement must cohere to be true, but also with experience (i.e. or e.g., sense experience). Such, at least, seems to be his meaning when he says that the 'idea of system demands the inclusion of all possible material'. That is, the system of judgements you accept must fit in not just with all the judgements you are inclined to make, but also with your actual sense experience as it occurs moment by moment.

But perhaps it is not really meant that the system includes something other than judgements, but only that immediate judgements of sense must be so. I am not sure of this. What is clear, at any rate, is that for Bradley the system of one's judgements does not occupy some purely intellectual part of the mind cut off from sense experience. Rather does it arise from, and remain continually subject to, testing by judgements which are prompted by, and are only intelligible as interpretations of, one's constantly changing sense experience.

> 'Facts' are justified because and as far as, while taking them as real, I am better able to deal with the incoming new 'facts' and in general to make my world wider and more harmonious.
>
> ETR, p. 211

The idea that somehow thought can remove itself from its basis in experience

---

110   This point has been made by various writers. See for example Wollheim, p. 176, and Walker, pp. 3–4.

111   In a fairly standard discussion of the coherence view of truth from the point of view of an analytical philosopher of the ordinary language type, A. R. White speaks of the classic proponents of the coherence theory as sometimes making 'an appeal to experience and reality ... which is inconsistent with the basic features of their theory'. White, p. 116; see also p. 122. But in discussing Bradley and others we must be careful not to saddle them with one of a standard list of alternative theories which the odd remark might suggest that they hold and then treat their fuller explanations as inconsistent with, rather than as clarificatory of, their basic position.

and discover how things are in some quite *a priori*[112] fashion is firmly rejected by Bradley. (Admittedly he does seem to think of empirical enquiry as rather a second best to the arrival at conclusions by sheer reasoning—an attitude with which I have as little sympathy as does James).

> For the sake of clearness let me begin by mentioning some things in which I do *not* believe. I do not believe in any knowledge which is independent of feeling and sensation. On sensation and feeling I am sure that we depend for the material of our knowledge. And as to the facts of perception, I am convinced that (to speak broadly) we cannot anticipate them or ever become independent of that which they give us. And these facts of perception, I further agree, are at least in part irrational, so far as in detail is visible. I do not believe that we can make ourselves independent of these non-rational data.
>
> ETR, p. 203

What Bradley denies, then, is (not that our knowledge or belief system arises from experience and is continually subject to testing thereby, but) that it is based on some hard data supplied by perception which cannot be rejected.

> We have, I should say, the aspect of datum, and we have the aspect of interpretation or construction, or what Prof. Stout calls implication. And why, I ask, for the intelligence must there be datum without interpretation any more than interpretation without datum? To me the opposite holds good, and I therefore conclude that no given fact is sacrosanct. With every fact of perception or memory a modified interpretation is in principle possible, and no such fact therefore is given free from all possibility of error.
>
> ETR, p. 204

§ It has been observed that Bradley's view, especially as developed in this particular essay, is close to currently influential views of Quine's.[113] Certainly Bradley's opposition to the kind of infallible judgements of perception, and perhaps memory, espoused by Stout and Russell as the essential foundations of knowledge is similar to that of Quine to the basic statements of the original logical positivists. And Bradley argues, not unlike Quine, that observation statements can be in a manner foundational in determining our view of how things are, without that view as a whole collapsing because some

---

112 An expression for which, as for its complementary, 'a posteriori' he expressed a certain distaste. (See PL, p. 409, though at PL, p. 561, he does speak of arithmetic as depending on '*a priori* experiment'.) This is partly because he is concerned to distinguish the status of what is learnt from how it is learnt, a point which may commend itself to followers of Kripke. What is learnt empirically can subsequently be grasped by reason as necessary. But I do not think Bradley's discussions of necessity among his greater achievements. III, I, VI of PL is useful for Bradley's views on the relation between experience and reasoning as sources of knowledge; see, especially, p. 478.

113 See, for example, Holdcroft in Manser and Stock.

of these foundations may later be removed. It is a mistake to think the whole building crumbles because its original foundations are not indubitably secure. But the metaphor is misleading.

> The foundation in truth is provisional merely. In order to begin my construction I take the foundation as absolute—so much certainly is true. But that my construction continues to rest on the beginnings of my knowledge is a conclusion which does not follow.
>
> ETR, p. 210

There are, of course, differences. Quine would hardly endorse Bradley's view that, as our system of beliefs grows in coherence and comprehensiveness, the individual judgements are shown to be somehow necessary. But it is hard to say how far there is real divergence between the two thinkers even here. For Quine even logical truths are only necessary in the sense that we would be especially reluctant to give them up.[114] Thereby he makes the sense in which propositions within a system imply each other so much part of the system itself that it is unclear what inconsistency in a system could really come to. However that may be, for Bradley the judgements in a coherent and comprehensive system are not merely consistent or merely displayable as an axiomatic system. Rather they must be organizable in such a way that each judgement implies and is implied by its more immediate neighbours and thereby in a less direct way each judgement must imply and be implied by every other.

That may justify saying that each judgement is necessary relative to the rest. But Bradley goes further than this. For he seems to think that the more every individual judgement is thus related to every other, the more the system as a whole can be described as necessary. Quite what 'necessary' means in this context is none too clear. Does it mean that it is the inevitable ideal limit of an enquiry whose starting point is the judgements experience typically prompts humans to make? Or is it supposed to possess a necessity which is in no sense relative to actual experience? If the latter, there is after all some excuse for the usual strictures on a coherence view. But however that may be, these objections do not apply to the test Bradley recommends, in practice, of membership in the richest and most coherent system into which as many as possible of our spontaneous judgements can be fitted. Not that the final formulation of such a system is envisaged by him as a practical possibility. Rather is it an ideal limit, apparent approach to which must be our actual test of truth. And this is indeed quite close to the viewpoint of Quine.

Of course, when it comes to the actual view of the world, which the two thinkers expect to provide the best overall system, they are far apart. Bradley holds that the body of judgements, by which we specify to ourselves the character of the ordinary physical world to which our bodies belong, is just one part of the total system of thoughts which we should accept as giving us truth

---

114 See Quine, *Methods*, p. xiv; *Point of View*, p. 42.

about the universe. Not only does that ordinary system of judgements have to be qualified by being regarded as simply a convenient construction, when viewed from the standpoint of a deeper metaphysical understanding of the world, but even at the level of ordinary thought this main object world is just one of the worlds with which we have to deal. There are more fragmentary worlds, worlds of fancy, myth, and dream, about which there is also truth, and while, for ordinary purposes, we have to keep the truth about these different worlds apart from each other as quite separate systems, the final truth would have to somehow bind them all together in one larger system. Still, what, for ordinary practical purposes, we call the real world is incomparably richer and better organized than these alternative worlds (for they are not complete alternative possible worlds such as the modern modal logician postulates but worlds only possessing such riches as are implied in intellectual constructions actually made).

> We each of us have a world which we call our 'real' world in space and time. This is an order, how made and based on what, it is impossible here to inquire [surely it is through those 'synthetic judgements of sense', to use the language of PL, which fit into the largest system of such judgements]. But facts of sense are called imaginary or erroneous, when in their offered character they do not belong to this 'real' order in space or time. They all belong to it of course as facts in someone's mental history, but otherwise they do not qualify the 'real' order as they claim to qualify it. We therefore relegate them to the sphere of the erroneous or the imaginary, unless we are able to modify and correct their claim so that it becomes admissible.
>
> ETR, p. 208

Another important difference is that Bradley basically takes our beliefs, or at least our judgements, as inwardly known phenomena in a manner quite unlike Quine's. Indeed, it is unclear in what sense for Quine there really is such a thing as having beliefs.[115] This marks him off still more strikingly from Donald Davidson, who derives a kind of coherence theory of knowledge and truth from complex considerations about what it is to take someone else to be believing something, and from Hilary Putnam, who does so on the basis of the claim that the very meaning of our concepts can only be given from within a conceptual scheme with no intelligible reference beyond itself.[116]

§ The most thorough elaboration of a coherence theory of truth in recent

---

115   This point is well put by R. C. S. Walker. See Walker, pp. 207–8.

116   For a discussion of Davidson and Putnam from this point of view see Walker, *Coherence,* chapter X. Chief works of Davidson and Putnam in this connection are Donald Davidson, 'A Coherence Theory of Truth and Knowledge' in LePore, also 'On the Very Idea of a Conceptual Scheme' in Davidson, *Truth,* and Putnam, *Realism,* and Putnam, *Reason.*

times has been that of Nicholas Rescher, and it may be well to say a word as to how it stands in intention and in fact to Bradley's. [117]

First, we may note that Rescher advocates coherence (coupled up to a point with comprehensiveness) as a criterion of truth, not as a definition, for he accepts a correspondence theory rooted in Tarski's approach as giving the meaning of truth. For Rescher the coherence theory provides a system of techniques for extracting from a body of data, consisting of individual candidates for truth which do not form a consistent body, a system of propositions which it is reasonable to accept as truths. This is done, to put it very roughly, by determining the various maximum consistent sets of propositions contained within the data (sets of consistent propositions which would be rendered inconsistent by the addition of any further data), applying various tests to these maximum consistent sets which will pick out some of them as cognitively preferable, and accepting as true such propositions as are logically deducible from each of these preferred maximum consistent sets. Those propositions which are thereby finally certified as true need not have been data, and it is even possible that none of them were.

In the detailed working out of these ideas Rescher aims to make more exact many of the main claims of such coherence theorists as Bradley, Bosanquet, and Joachim. But though there are real similarities there are also some striking contrasts.

(1) Rescher rightly says that data in his sense are close to what Bradley called 'facts' which we accept as true or not according to the extent to which they can be brought into the most coherent and comprehensive system we can reach by their prompting. [118] But I believe that there is also an important difference. For Rescher there are various tests whereby propositions are or are not accepted as data. That a certain proposition should be 'counted among the data' of a particular problem of truth-determination is not a primitive fact but a rationally supportable contention (albeit one whose support need not go so far as to establish its truth). These tests are not carried out within the coherence theory, for their purpose is to decide what material the coherence theory is to work on. This seems to me quite contrary to Bradley. His facts are rather any ideas which the seeker after truth feels any inclination to think of as true; these are to be tested for truth by the method of the coherence theory, but there are no prior criteria they have to meet before they are even raw material to which this method is to be applied. For such criteria would have to be carried out in the world as we conceive it to be, and this world can only be that yielded to date by the coherence principle working on whatever we have so far felt inclined to believe. Rescher, in contrast, seems to think of this preliminary testing as carried out in a world concerning the status of our conception of which he has nothing special to say. [119] This is related to the fact that Rescher tends to

---

117 See Rescher.
118 See Rescher, p. 67.
119 See Rescher, pp. 63–64.

recommend testing for coherence as a technique to be used in particular circumscribed enquiries with their own particular sets of inconsistent data from which some reasonable view of the truth on that matter is to be derived, whereas for Bradley the emphasis is on the way in which we build up our picture of the world as a whole.

(2) Rescher excludes necessary truths, meaning primarily or only truths of logic and of mathematics, from the range of the standard of coherence and comprehensiveness. This is because they provide that 'machinery of logic'[120] through which application of that standard is implemented. In this connection Rescher is inclined to think that the best position on truth will combine a pragmatic approach to putative truths of logic and a coherence approach to factual propositions.[121] This is certainly profoundly contrary to the spirit of Bradley who thought of the ascertainment of mathematical and logical truth as a paradigm of that search for coherence and comprehensiveness with which he identifies the search for truth in general. Rescher may be right philosophically, of course, but he is certainly not close to Bradley on this matter.

(3) A fundamental difference, at least of mood, from Bradley cannot be displayed without going into details inappropriate here. Rescher illustrates the workings of his coherence test by formulae within the propositional calculus which suggest that the techniques to be used (for example, in deciding what follows from every maximum consistent set) are of a purely formal nature. This certainly clashes with Bradley's insistence that inference cannot be reduced to rule.

For reasons such as these I believe that it is only to a very limited extent that Rescher's enterprise can be regarded as an updated version of Bradley's. That is no criticism of Rescher's own enterprise and no denial that in certain respects, particularly on the nature of data (despite the point made above), he rightly claims to be developing genuinely Bradleyan insights.

§ Since the rise of analytical philosophy writers on truth are inclined to make a firm distinction between theories which provide a criterion of truth and those which define truth.[122] It is a not uncommon view that the coherence theory points in the right direction so far as the first goes, but that a correspondence theory of some sort gives the essence of truth. (This is upon the whole Rescher's view.) Was this really Bradley's view? If so, the apparent clash between formulations of a more correspondence kind and a coherence kind can be resolved. Or does the answer depend on whether it is ultimate metaphysical or more day-to-day truth which is in question?

Verbally Bradley does, in fact, usually invoke coherence and comprehensiveness as the criteria or tests of truth, rather than as giving its essence. And that

---

120   Rescher, p. 46.
121   Rescher, p. 166.
122   See, for example, Rescher, chapter II, and somewhat contrastingly Walker, chapter I.

might encourage one to take the statement quoted above that '[i]f my idea is to work it must correspond to a determinate being which it cannot be said to make. And in this correspondence, I must hold, consists from the very first the essence of truth'[123] as representing his view of the essence of truth, while the later essays simply recommend coherence and comprehensiveness as the best tests of its presence.

A possibility which suggests itself is that Bradley effectively has a correspondence view of metaphysical truth, which really captures the essence of its subject matter, and a coherence-plus-comprehensiveness view of ordinary day-to-day truth. There is something to be said for this interpretation but it must be admitted that the correspondence formulation just referred to is developed with examples of everyday rather than metaphysical thought.

What of the converse suggestion that the essence of metaphysical truth lies in coherence and comprehensiveness while day-to-day truth is a matter of correspondence? Surely that belies the seriousness of metaphysics as an attempt to understand how things really are.

§ Matters are further complicated by the fact that Bradley sometimes depicts the requirements of coherence and comprehensiveness as derivative from a more fundamental criterion, that of providing intellectual satisfaction.

> What in the end is the criterion? The criterion of truth, I should say, as of everything else, is in the end the satisfaction of a want of our nature.
>
> ETR, p. 219

Bradley realizes that this sounds like pragmatism. The difference is, however, that while pragmatism sometimes seems to be the view that ideas are true simply because they satisfy in any sort of way (and that indeed is what James often said), for Bradley truth is only what satisfies a peculiarly intellectual impulse of our nature. And since this impulse seems to be precisely[124] the impulse to have coherent and comprehensive ideas of the universe, we do not really have a distinct criterion here from that of coherence and comprehensiveness.

> Truth to my mind is a satisfaction of a special kind, and, again, it is a satisfaction

---

123 ETR, p. 76.

124 Bradley is zealous in denying that what will satisfy the intellect will necessarily satisfy all sides of our being. Yet all sides of our being must somehow be present to the intellect, and he thinks that in the end that must mean that they cannot be felt there as clamouring complainants if the intellect is to find what it can rightly call truth. That sounds like a vindication of mere wishful thinking. Bradley's reply is essentially that it turns on a cool demonstration (such as is satisfying to the intellect considered as far as possible alone) that the universe must ultimately be harmonious. See ETR, pp. 241–44 for an eloquent discussion of this which upon the whole absolves Bradley from confusion or complacency on this point.

which, at least at first sight, is able to oppose itself to others. But, however that may be, truth seems to differentiate itself clearly from other satisfactions. And philosophy, I at least understand, has to meet specially this special need and want of truth.

ETR, p. 220

The implication seems to be that true ideas simply are those which satisfy the peculiarly intellectual desire for coherence and comprehensiveness in our ideas and that the more realistic view of truth implied in earlier writings has been abandoned. Yet I cannot really accept this interpretation of Bradley's position, especially in relation to metaphysical truth, since it fails to do justice to his commitment to metaphysics as a quest for an understanding of the actual nature of reality. (We had, of course, the same problem in squaring James's pragmatism with his wish to plunge into the very essence of reality as it genuinely is.)

A very similar problem arises as to the view of truth of that other great monist, Spinoza, who sometimes seems to understand truth as an internal property of ideas, sometimes as their adequacy to an external object.[125] Perhaps the same solution applies in both cases, namely, that they thought the universe such that ideas must have certain features if they are to be true of it, and also that in virtue of the irresistibility of ideas with certain internal features the universe must be such as to answer to them.

§ Bradley himself was not unaware, it seems, of a conflict in his thought between a view which makes truth a feature of a system of ideas considered in its own right and one which makes it turn on its relation to something else. For his final answer to the question 'what is truth?' seems to be that '[t]ruth is an ideal expression of the Universe'[126] and this seems designed to meet this very difficulty.

Not that the answer is an easy one to grasp.[127] What Bradley seems to mean is that the Absolute, as somehow present in all its parts, is striving within each part to develop itself into the whole, with the result that the thought pertaining to any part has an initial tendency to develop into ideas which capture something of its total character. Since the whole is coherent and comprehensive this urge takes the form of a nisus towards a coherent and comprehensive system of ideas which will reproduce the character of the Absolute to whatever extent it satisfies itself. However, the ideas do not form a completely closed-off world,

---

125   R. C. S. Walker has argued that Spinoza has a coherence view of truth, but this is somewhat of an over-simplification. See Walker, chapter III.

126   ETR, p. 223.

127   James expressed what he took to be Bradley's view rather well as 'your general conception of truth in the singular as a sort of entity trying to identify itself with reality, and of reality as a *ditto* trying to idealize itself into truth'. James to Bradley, 22 April 1907, Kenna, p. 324.

for the intellectual part of reality to which they pertain is continually fed by experience stemming from the other parts.

This view is somewhat similar to Royce's claim that reference of thought to something beyond itself would be impossible if a thought and its object were complete beings each encapsulated in itself and such that the character of either could have been just what it is without the other existing. Our having true thoughts, says Bradley, in a similar vein, would be unintelligible if truth were an external relation between thought and its object. For surely an external relation could not be aware of itself.

It also has some kinship with C. S. Peirce's claim that the human mind has an innate tendency to interpret its experience by way of ideas which are actually true of nature and that this is only explicable by its oneness with the creative mind which manifests itself in the natural world. There is also some kinship with Leibniz's view that we each have a personal picture of the world which corresponds to the pictures of others, because all stem from God, and that each picture also maps that system in which each of us has a position determined by the special perspective of his own picture. (But such a view makes much better sense if nature is conceived panpsychistically in a manner to which Bradley did not feel himself committed.)

However obscure the notion that Reality is working itself out within the intellect of each of us may be, it may be this which allows Bradley to combine the view that truth consists in ideas which capture something of the essence of the reality of which they are predicated with the view that it consists in the satisfaction of having ideas which are coherent and comprehensive. For if the reality we are thinking about is expressing itself in the way we think of it, then our system of thoughts can best reach a correct characterisation of what they are about by satisfying the internal criteria it imposes on itself.

§ It remains difficult to know how far some of what Bradley says about truth is supposed to apply only to the kind of truth necessary for ordinary purposes, how far only to ultimate metaphysical truth, and how far to both. Sometimes he defends remarks made apparently as general remarks about truth mainly by reference to one of these, sometimes mainly by reference to the other.

Some passages suggest the view that ordinary truth consists simply in pragmatically useful ideas and contrasts with a metaphysical truth in which something of the real essence of the reality they concern is grasped. (Presumably both kinds of truth would still be ways in which the Absolute develops itself in ideal form.) On this view our ordinary ideas should not aspire to truth in anything like a correspondence sense and can, at best, build up a more or less intellectually satisfactory and practically useful way of filling out and bringing under law that with which we are presented in sense experience. (There are two main reasons for this: first that the ideas it uses are full of incoherences; second that it is incapable of singling out in terms appropriate to thought the special region of reality to which the ideas are applied.)

The implication would seem to be that metaphysics seeks a deeper kind of truth, which is more of a correspondence kind, and that such a truth, however inferior for many practical purposes, and however unmanageable for daily use, does come nearer to a transcription of reality in its ultimate nature. Certainly he held that metaphysics is the one enquiry in which it 'is forbidden to employ any fiction or mythology'.[128] Of this final truth we may only be able to catch the broadest outline. Although in its full compass it would cover all the details of the world, for our ordinary purposes detail, as opposed to comprehensive vision, is best dealt with at the level of day to day truth.

One of the main claims Bradley makes about absolute truth relates to his later view of negation.[129] According to this, as we saw, you can only deny an idea of Reality if you can find another region of Reality in which it has application. What an ordinary judgement says can be rejected because one can locate the idea it mislocates elsewhere. But in the case of an absolute truth, no home at all can be found for any contrary to the idea it ascribes.

The claim that an absolute truth is one to which there is no conceivable alternative is not too puzzling. But the suggestion that one can only negate that which one can ascribe to some other region than that of which it is negated is less appealing. You can, indeed, always call the world of what IS NOT a region of reality and say that that is where such negated predicates apply. But any tendency to put such regions of non-being on a par with the actual seems pretty unsatisfactory to me.

However, these considerations seem rather different from those which make Bradley regard most ordinary ideas as only pragmatically true. For the main thrust of Bradley's demonstration, that most of our ordinary ideas are incoherent, would seem to be to the effect that they do not apply literally, as ordinarily taken, to *any* region of reality, not that there is a difficulty in finding their proper home.

The view that ordinary truth is of a pragmatic, and metaphysical truth of a correspondence, nature could treat coherence and comprehensiveness of a suitable kind as marks of either sort of truth. One could then say that while ordinary truths are true because they belong to a coherent and comprehensive construction which guides us effectively for practical purposes in anticipating and controlling our sense experience, metaphysical truths are true because they belong to a coherent and comprehensive system which actually captures the essence of reality.[130] Yet it is doubtful that Bradley means to make as strong a contrast between the two sorts of truth as this. For, upon the whole, he sees the search for metaphysical truth as arising from the same basic urge towards coherence and comprehensiveness which has led to our system of beliefs about the object world. Although these are to be valued in part for their practical utility, they do also satisfy that intellectual quest to some degree.

(d) The Conditional Nature of All Truth

I turn now to Bradley's later version of the doctrine that all our truths are

---

128   PL, p. 342.
129   See especially *Terminal Essay* VIII to the second edition of PL.
130   See PL, pp. 340–43.

'conditional'. (He came to prefer 'conditional' to 'hypothetical', presumably as less suggestive of one particular explicit form of judgement.)

According to this, as we saw, the ultimate subject of every judgement is simply Reality, but there is also a sense in which the subject of a judgement is some limited part or region of Reality, which he refers to as the special subject.[131] A way of putting this is to say that the predicate applies to Reality under a certain condition. Thus if I say that A. J. Ayer is an atheist, I am saying that Reality, under the condition of being A. J. Ayer, is an atheist. Now Bradley thinks that one might seek to get rid of the conditional element by regarding the whole expression 'under the condition of being A. J. Ayer is an atheist' as the predicate and saying that it applies to Reality unconditionally. But he concludes that this is impossible. For this predicate will itself only apply to Reality under certain conditions which we can never hope to specify adequately. Indeed, there may be (and Bradley rapidly equates this with the admission that there is) a world in which there is an A. J. Ayer who is not an atheist, so that in fact the predicate 'under the condition of being A. J. Ayer is not an atheist' applies to Reality too.[132] We can only avoid this by such a specification of the A. J. Ayer to whom we mean to refer as will distinguish him from that one. Thus if we knew the precise conditions under which we meant to apply the original predicate, we could introduce the conditions into the predicate so as to have one which applied to Reality without qualification. However, since we do not, we must be content with a predicate whose application to Reality is only under conditions which we cannot fully specify and therefore cannot put into the predicate to make a judgement which would no longer be 'merely conditional'. In short, any judgement 'P' can be true only under certain conditions which stand in contrast to other conditions in which it does not hold, and since we do not fully know what these conditions are, we cannot make the categorical judgement: 'Under conditions C, P holds'. These conditions may be that of being a particular point in a space-time series, like that of Julius Caesar hesitating whether to march on Rome, or they may be that of a law of nature which only holds within a general type of reality, e.g., a physical world like ours.[133] In either case, we never know quite what the full conditions are under which, or in relation to which, alone our judgement holds.

One is inclined to object: Is it not possible to make the unconditional judgement 'There are conditions under which P holds'? This at least rules out the judgement 'There are no conditions under which P holds.' However, Bradley's implied reply to this is that it is true of every judgement 'P' that it holds under some conditions. Thus 'There are conditions under which P holds' rules out nothing and effectively says nothing. For, so Bradley holds, every

---

131 See ETR, pp. 331–33.
132 See ETR, pp. 264–65, also 229, 233, 252, 255.
133 See ETR, pp. 232 and 264–65.

predicate which we can conceive has some sort of exemplification and thus every judgement we can make would be true if related to the right context. When you say 'Horses exist' you must mean that in our world there are horses, but that does not preclude that there are other worlds in which there are none. Simply to say 'Horses exist' in some world is vacuous, since that is bound to be so. However, one may object that it is still true. Surely the most that Bradley could establish would be that the only judgements worth making are ones which are conditional in his rather peculiar sense.

Bradley's not altogether convincing reason for holding that every predicate (thus every idea ascribed to reality in a judgement) applies to some region of reality is related to his denial of the Kantian view that existence is not a predicate.[134] Typically when we speak of something as existing we mean that it has a place in our standard world, that which is continuous with our body. So when we say that something does not exist, we mean, not that it has no home in Reality at all, but that it has no home in 'our' world. However, since we cannot give an adequate identification of 'our' world we can never adequately distinguish it from all the other worlds in one or more of which the thing we call non-existent is bound to have a home.

Bradley illustrates his position by considering the judgement: 'Julius Caesar crossed the Rubicon'. He insists that this cannot be unconditionally true until we specify (as we cannot) the particular world system in which this is so.[135] For, he says, 'If there are various worlds, it may also be true that Caesar never saw the Rubicon nor indeed existed at all'. And in effect he seems to treat this 'may be' as a 'must be'.

Here again Bradley might seem to be taking the position adopted by the modern logician David Lewis, described as possible-worlds realism, according to which 'our' world is just one of many equally genuine other possible worlds, and even its actuality is nothing special since it is distinctively actual only from its own point of view, something equally true of all the others.[136] But though there are similarities the positions are not the same. (The similarities include something rather like Lewis's 'counterpart' theory.[137]) For Bradley expressly argues that the existent in the ordinary sense is distinguishable from the nonexistent by the comparative poverty of the world in which it exists.[138] His view seems to be, rather, that the very act of thinking of a certain possibility begins the construction of a world in which it is so, and that we can then never adequately distinguish this (and other worlds in which it is so) from the more complete worlds in which it is not so.

It is not hard to grant that there are regions of reality in which Caesar does

---

134 See ETR, p. 42 et ff.
135 See ETR, pp. 261–67.
136 See Lewis, *Counterfactuals*.
137 See PL, p. 90.
138 See ETR, pp. 42–49.

not exist at all (i.e., he does not fall within them). If these are counted as worlds in which 'Caesar crossed the Rubicon' fails of truth, then the claim that it is only true in some special region of reality follows. But can we really be so sure as Bradley seems to be that there are regions of reality in which Caesar *existed* but did not cross the Rubicon? Bradley seems only to establish this on the rather shaky ground that in the world of fancy, at least, we have made this proposition true.

And in any case why cannot I identify the world of which our judgement is supposed to hold as the spatio-temporal system continuous with the body I immediately feel as my own and make my judgement a categorical assertion about this? That is, indeed, Bradley's own account of the way in which our judgements are ordinarily intended. However, judgements taken thus rely on what he calls 'designation', meaning reference by way of demonstratives or indicator words. And Bradley holds that no judgement in which these occur is worthy to be called a genuine truth about the world.[139] For to know a truth is to have a conception of how things are, and if one's subject matter is identified in a manner which is not purely conceptual one does not know a genuine truth; rather one simply has an idea which may be of practical utility.

Thus the special subject, which is a certain region, aspect, or sort of reality, can never be fully identified in ideas, that is, by conceptual descriptions, and so we can never specify the conditions under which our judgements hold in terms appropriate to thought.

> The whole of the conditions are not stated. And hence, according to the way in which you choose to fill in the conditions (and no special way belongs to the judgement), the assertion and its opposite are either of them true.
>
> ETR, p. 257

Identifying the conditions is for Bradley identifying the 'special subject' of the judgement, that is, the part, aspect, or sort of Reality to which the predicate more especially applies.

One may well object, in the spirit of James, that this is asking of thought what there is no call to ask of it. After all, when confronted perceptually with something which one identifies as an apple, one knows a perfectly good truth about it, which does not have to be regarded as a poor substitute for a proposition about something identified in a purely conceptual way . However this may be, the sense that genuine truth must be context free still haunts philosophy.[140]

The alleged conditionality of all truth is given as one of the main grounds

---

139 See ETR, p. 207.
140 Thus one finds much the same note struck in that great anti-metaphysician, A. J. Ayer, e.g., in his *Essays*, chapter I, and for a similar more recent hankering for the identification of that of which we speak without indexicals see, for example, Baldwin, p. 42.

for saying that there is no such thing as sheer truth or sheer error. If there were to be sheer truth, the conditions under which the predicate applies to reality would be adequately specified in the judgement. But we can never get all those conditions into the judgement. The result is that we never exclude the conditions under which it does not apply to reality. Thus there always remains some truth in the opposite judgement.

§ A rather different reason Bradley has for saying that all truth is conditional turns on his supposition that genuine truth must have a certain necessity.[141] We have seen that for Bradley this means that every truth must follow from other truths. In virtue of this he holds that the conditions which we can never make complete are not just the conditions under which the predicate *does* apply to reality, but the conditions in virtue of which it *must* do so. For the intellect, so Bradley thinks, would never be satisfied with the mere *de facto* holding of something under certain conditions.[142]

In reply to the complaint that he treats it as an unargued axiom that truth must be necessary, in the sense of having a 'how' and a 'why', Bradley says that it is not a background axiom of an inquiry like his but its result.[143] At the level of feeling we do not ask for a reason why what is must be so. But once our sense of how the given points beyond itself leads us to break up the primitive unity of feeling by an intellectual analysis in which we relate it to other things, we are embarked on a course in which we will not be satisfied with less. Why not be content with the brute fact? Because once thought has started there is no brute fact, only a theory which seeks of its own impetus to be improved until nothing is left unexplained.

§ The conditions under which a predicate applies, and *must* apply, to reality may be the spatio-temporal context in which there is a particular with a certain character. But Bradley also has in mind the conditions under which some abstract truth holds. Thus even a simple proposition of arithmetic is only true subject to certain background assumptions, all of which influence our thinking though we can never fully specify them.[144] There must be a context in which other background conditions would imply contrary judgements. Or so Bradley thinks, while admitting that he is not competent to argue for this point in detail.

Bradley also believes that, if one could ever fully grasp the conditions under which a judgement applies, one would find that it did not apply even under them in quite the way one thought. For every increase in knowledge transforms the meaning of all other judgements made by the same mind. What the child means by 'Charles I' in 'Charles I had his head cut off' is not the same as what the historian means, nor does he mean the same by 'head' as does the anatomist. Similarly what the mathematician means by '2+2=4' is not quite what the

---

141   See ETR, pp. 363, 315, et passim.
142   See, for example, ETR, p. 276.
143   See ETR, pp. 311–14.
144   See ETR, pp. 266–67.

ordinary person means. And historian and child alike, and ordinary person and mathematician alike, would all understand their judgements somewhat differently if they saw the whole of what makes them true so far as they are true. As Bosanquet put the same point: 'Every judgement is relative to the whole of knowledge, and no judgement entirely escapes modification as this whole is modified'[145] Moreover, our thoughts about Charles I, or the truths of mathematics, could only be totally purged of error by ceasing to be thoughts as we know them, for they would have to lose that distance from their objects which is of thought's essence. This is how it eternally is with the Absolute which knows every detail of its nature as a whole (including all the thoughts it contains and the experiences they interpret and point to) in a way which corrects both the dumbness of mere feeling and the abstractness and paradoxicality of conceptual thought.

§ Bradley's strictures upon conceptual thought have some kinship with James's for whom the reality of Charles's state is best grasped not by the historian describing it at a distance but by himself as he felt it. Thus the best awareness of it by someone else would be in the form of empathy with his sufferings. But for Bradley it is only at the level of the Absolute that immediacy goes with genuine knowledge and we should not try, as James and Bergson urged, to rectify the deficiencies of our concepts by plunging ourselves into an intuitive non-conceptual *rapport* with reality.

§ It is only the pluralist, according to Bradley, who can suppose that any judgement could possess absolute truth. For he thinks that the world is composed of sharply separate items with natures which can be grasped in isolation.[146] Once one realizes the central truth of monism, that things have no such independent natures, one must abandon any such idea. If there is an absolute truth, it must consist in the one single truth about the world, of which all other judgements are fragments floundering for the meaning that only pertains to them as its elements. And this total truth is in the end nothing other than the total Reality itself knowing itself in the very act of being itself.

Since one can never adequately specify the object of which one is thinking, one can never really know precisely what it is nor how its real context gives it a character which falsifies our concept of it. Although he does not quite say so, presumably Bradley would acknowledge that in virtue of one's actual closer relations with one part of the world than another, there usually is a definite something with which one's thought is somehow dealing, but would insist that, so long as we cannot pick it out in a purely conceptual way, we do not really, properly speaking, *know* which that object is. Thus Bradley would not be content with some of our contemporary accounts of *de re* thought where the proposition we assert is determined partly by facts about our situation which are independent of our actual mental activity.

---

145 Bosanquet, *Logic*, II, p. 230.
146 See ETR, pp. 255, 259, 315.

§ There is no denying the difficulty of finding a unitary formula which could be said to sum up Bradley's view of truth. He gives many apparently different accounts of it, the relations between which are often unclear. Nor is this because he changed his mind, for these different themes seem each to be pervasive in his thinking, at least from AR onwards. But perhaps the following may serve as a rough summing up of his position:

A. IN THOUGHT WE ASCRIBE SOME CHARACTER to Reality the idea of which we find within our own experience. Or perhaps better: We ascribe some character to some part, aspect, or sort of reality, which is specified (though in fact never sufficiently) for us by some other character of which we have the idea. (There is no real difference between these formulations, since having the overall character of *possessing one character qua possessing another* is itself a character.)

Such a thought or judgement has some degree of truth provided only that it has some aptness as a way of registering some feature of reality. But it may be true in one or other of three not sharply distinct ways.

(1) It will be true in the most literal possible way if reality actually possesses this overall character, and true in a degree approximating to this if reality possesses something sufficiently akin to it. Since reality is coherent and comprehensive such a quality can pertain to it only if this ascription could figure in a coherent and comprehensive system of ideas.

However, even in the case of a judgement true in this most literal way, Reality will not possess the characteristic predicated of it in quite the way we conceive it as doing. For it will possess it, not as the thin abstraction which it is for our thinking, but in a fuller and more concrete form in which it coheres with other features of Reality with an intimacy beyond thought's grasp but for which it is of its essence to strive. Moreover thought and its object are united in the unitary experience of the Absolute in a way in which neither the thought, nor indeed its object (should that be a conscious subject), can separately grasp.

(2) It will have truth of a less ultimate and more pragmatic kind if it is a way of thinking about Reality which is suitable for current purposes, even though Reality does not actually have the character it ascribes except for such thought.

Such a judgement may still have a high degree of theoretical value. For thinking of reality in that way may be an essential ingredient in the most coherent and comprehensive system of ideas available in certain types of enquiry and thus be the most intellectually satisfactory way of answering certain questions which arise in them.

(3) But a judgement may be of much less theoretical value than this, being recalcitrant to inclusion in any such coherent and comprehensive system of ideas, and yet still be part of a repertoire of ways of thinking which is very useful for dealing with reality for certain purposes (technological, moral, religious, etc.) other than that of intellectual satisfaction. Such judgements possess only the truth of 'working ideas' but in certain contexts they may be essential.

B. THE REALITY WITH WHICH A JUDGEMENT, true (or for that matter false) in any of these ways, is concerned is that total world of which the finite centre of experience to which it belongs feels itself to be a fragment. And though that centre is only a fragment of the whole, the whole is somehow so immanent within it that it reflects something of the whole's total character. It is only in virtue of this immanence of the whole within the centre in which the thought occurs that it can make reality beyond itself the subject of its predications. And such immanence is the source of its striving for a system of ideas whose coherence and comprehensiveness will show it its place within that whole.

C. THE JUDGEMENTS WE DEVELOP, that is, which are developed within our finite centres, upon this basis are not closed off from the rest of our experience. For the coherence and comprehensiveness we seek is one in which all experience, not merely the intellectual experience of thinking, will be included. Thus they are constantly subject to revision on the basis of sensory experiences. Though these respond to rational interpretation they are not produced by rational thought, at least not by our rational thought. The ultimate explanation of why they take the course they do must remain mysterious to us, but it will somehow be a matter of the role our centre is playing in the organized 'life' of Reality as a whole.

§6. *Bradley contra James*

§ The contrasts and affinities between Bradley's and James's treatment of truth are striking. Each attacks what they call a copy theory of truth in a manner which is to some extent, but only to some extent, Kantian. Each recognizes that the mind has to interpret the given with the aid of principles which it must bring to experience rather than learn from it. Yet each thinks the extent to which this must be done can be exaggerated through an insufficiently generous view of what is present in experience itself.

Again each philosopher tends to confuse two targets in his attack upon the so-called copy theory, an easy one according to which truth is a mere transcript in ideas of sensory experience and a more serious one for which truth is a portrait of reality not normally drawn from the life but based on a variety of indirect clues. And each of them, despite their insistence that the success we should ordinarily demand of judgements which we call 'true' is neither more nor less than usefulness for practical and intellectual satisfaction (which seem to make them enemies of any kind of 'realist' view of truth), seems concerned, as a metaphysician, to find a deeper sort of truth than the pragmatic through which we may grasp something of the essence of how things really are. For James this can only be found by imaginative participation in the subjective lives of other individuals; for Bradley by pressing thought to its limits until it recaptures something of the directness of immediate experience.

Bradley, however, goes much further than James in seeing the philosopher as aiming at a kind of truth which stands in strong contrast to the thought which is useful in daily life. And it must be admitted that he gives some ground for James's mockery of the intellectualist's conception of truth as something remote from anything any ordinary person seeks as such in the day-to-day organization of his life.

§ Central to the concern of each in their discussions of truth is the question how thought can relate to its object. This is much the problem which arises in discussions today of *de re* thinking. According to James thought is about that to which it in some sense leads or might lead, and he developed this view precisely to avoid the absolute-idealist argument of Royce that only common presence in an absolute mind can link thought to its object.

This view of James's was the object of some effective criticism by Bradley.[147]

> To pass to another point—judgement really, on my view, involves mediation. This aspect of the matter has not escaped Prof. James, but he has, in my opinion, turned truth here into ruinous error. For he has taken intermediation to consist in a temporal process from the idea to a perceived object. To this conclusion, in spite of much obscurity, he seems committed. Where an idea merely leads to an object, we, according to Prof. James, have knowledge. Whether there is a relation of identity in difference between the idea and the object, a relation which is also for the knower, I am unable to say. The importance of both these questions is obvious, but the answer, if there is an answer, remains to me obscure. Apparently we have truth wherever an idea leads to an object.
>
> ETR, p. 146[148]

And Bradley goes on to mention cases where thought either leads to an object without being in any proper sense about it, or is about something to which it could not possibly lead, as when the object is in the past. It is doubtful, he says, whether James has said anything worthwhile which goes beyond the surely generally admitted point that

> truth, to be true, must be in vital connexion with the world of particular feelings and perceptions, and in some sense [be] . . . verifiable in this world.
>
> ETR, p. 147

Bradley centres his attention on an ambiguity in James's view. Sometimes, he suggests, James treats the leading relation as explicable in terms not drawn from the language of thought, terms such as sensible continuity or causal connection. That raises the obvious objection that when thus understood it seems quite possible for such a relation to hold between a thought and something which it cannot possibly be said to be about. Moreover, it also implies that a thought, taken at the moment of its occurrence, has nothing in or to it in virtue of which it is really *about* anything, so that its being about anything is quite extrinsic to its own inherent character. And this belies what seems an essential feature of what it is to think at all. At other times, however, James speaks of a feeling of fulfilment which occurs as the experience which mediates between

---

147   See especially Appendices II and III to ETR, chapter V.
148   See also pp. 147–49 and 154–56.

thought and its object unrolls. That suggests that there is something about the thought from the start which makes it a thought fitted to be fulfilled by just such an object, and implicitly recognizes what Bradley seems to have in mind here as a 'felt identity in difference', a sameness with differences between the character present in, and attributed by, the thought to its object and the character found in the object on encounter. That is a much more promising account but quite abandons that rejection of any mysterious 'transcendence' on the part of thought, of any power to leap beyond itself, which was advertised as the great achievement of the theory. It amounts, in fact to 'a covert reinstatement in the idea of that symbolical character, that very self-transcendence, which the doctrine denies'.[149]

> Suppose that I know that somewhere near there is a spring of water. Does my present knowledge consist in my actually finding this water? Has it, in order to be knowledge now, got to wait for this future event? Such a contention seems obviously absurd, and it forthwith is covertly modified. . . . What I wish to emphasize here is the point that, while the self-reference of the idea beyond itself is explicitly denied by Prof. James, he uses, and is forced to use, words which re-affirm it. The present idea of water, he says, *leads* to the finding. There is a continuous advance to the object, with an experience of developing progress, and therefore the object was *meant* (*Rad. Emp.* pp. 57,60, 62). But is it not, I ask, obvious that such language implies at the start, and before the finding, a self-transcendent idea of the water? . . .
>
> If the starting-place really *leads*, it is because that place *points*, and, if it really points, then, at once and now, it refers beyond itself. From the very first it plainly is self-transcendent and qualifies an object beyond itself, and it needs no process of waiting for something else to happen to it in the future. Knowledge of what is now is not, we may say, what it *is*, just because something comes later to make the fact that it *was*.
>
> ETR, pp. 154–55

These criticisms are highly effective. It is hard not to agree that no actual leading is necessary for thought to refer beyond itself. Bradley is surely right also that to say that a merely potential leading may suffice ducks the issue. For surely the fact that thought is about what it is about is an actual fact which cannot be helpfully explained by reference to the problematic sphere of the conditional. (Bradley is always scathing about the use by empiricists of the notion of the potential to get round their problems.)

To me Bradley's argument seems almost conclusive. One cannot reduce knowledge of an event E to the mere fact that there is a series of events,

---

149 ETR, p. 154. Bradley's criticisms of James are much the same as those brilliantly made by J. B. Pratt in Pratt, lecture 4. However, Bradley, through his doctrine that Reality as a whole is immanent in its every part, attempts a positive account of the way in which the mind transcends its own states while Pratt can only call it an ultimate and inexplicable fact.

externally related to each other, passing from a so-called idea to its so-called object, where the series itself cannot be experienced as a whole, and could only be known by just such a mysterious self-transcendent power of the mind as the account is supposed to explain away. James only becomes persuasive when he covertly reverts to language which presupposes such self-transcendency.

§ These difficulties confirm Bradley in his conviction that the only possible solution is that, though James is right that there is no reality but experience, there is and must be, immanent within each finite experience, a cosmic experience which holds the different finite experiences together. This view of the matter is close to that of Royce. But Bradley's account has the advantage of not over-intellectualising our 'being in the world', as Royce's does. For Bradley sees thought as emerging in centres of experience which already possess a pre-conceptual feel of their togetherness with reality beyond such as cannot be captured adequately in concepts. Thus the way in which thought leads to its object, in any sense relevant to its being about something, requires that each experience at the very moment of its occurrence already points beyond itself and is thus self-transcendent.[150]

Bradley's objection to James is essentially a common-sense one. And it may be suggested that, while this gives him the advantage at the level of the debating club, philosophically James's approach is more profound in that he invites us to take a deeper look at the nature of the relation in which thought stands to its objects than we can gain by sticking complacently to ordinary locutions. Better run the risk of going wrong, it may be said, by trying to explain what intentionality really amounts to, than pretend to deliver the answer in terms which assume it has been found. However, I think this charge, on James's behalf, would have more application to Brentano and to modern practitioners of intentional logic than to Bradley.

James's determination to dispense with easy, ordinary assumptions about thought has some kinship with Wittgenstein's approach to philosophy of mind. For it is very much in the same spirit as that of James's scepticism about the self-transcendence of thought that Wittgenstein suggested that when one decides to follow a rule nothing really happens here and now with definite implications for the future. In a similar vein it is suggested that even God would not know what one is thinking by examining a cross-section of one's stream of consciousness.

Too many philosophers today, it seems to me, are ready to assume, with James and Wittgenstein, and various contemporary exponents of what they call an 'externalist' view of mental content,[151] that the aboutness of thought turns on the essentially external relations of our subjectivity. It may be said that the Wittgensteinian tradition stresses the internal relations holding between the

---

150   See ETR, p. 155.
151   For an extreme exponent see Davies, *Perceptual*. This also includes a useful bibliography.

language used by different persons. But this internality (at least as usually and not unreasonably interpreted) is *de dicto* rather than *de re*. That is, we can only describe subjective processes as 'thought', or perhaps at all, by reference to the public meanings of the symbols used. The claim is, therefore, not that there is a relation to what lies beyond which genuinely falls within the subjectivity, but only that we may not say that it means anything until we have found out, without its own help, how it is related to what lies beyond it. The only real alternative to this approach which seems to be current is a defence of intentionality without any serious attempt to explain it beyond suggestions for a language in which to chart its formal features.

In either case, it seems to me, Bradley has done better, for he has seen both the irreducibility of aboutness to any merely natural relation, and the depth of the problem which it poses for conventional views about the nature of the world.

§ But how successful is Bradley's own position on this matter? Its basis is the claim that it is of the essence of each moment of experience to be a fragment from a larger whole and to have a pre-conceptual sense of its own incompleteness, an incompleteness which the ideas it predicates in judgement try to remedy. I suspect that here he is in sight of the only possible answer to the ultimate question how thought can be about anything beyond itself. If that is so, only metaphysical monism can explain how thought is possible.[152]

But on Bradley's account, that pre-conceptual *aboutness* of our subjectivity which creates the possibility of thought is directed on to reality at large rather than onto particular objects. Doubtless our synthetic judgements of sense seem to relate the rest of the world to something particular non-conceptually present to us, but really this is rather a matter of their particular contribution to the characterisation of reality as a whole than a matter of their special relation to some genuinely distinct bit of it. There is just reality on the one hand and, on the other hand, the ever-enlarging conceptual scheme with which we characterise it as a whole, initially based on a given with which adequate thought must dispense. In this connection Bradley often suggests that the reference of certain sorts of thought to their objects can only be explained by regarding these as our own constructions.

The talk of construction must not be taken in any solipsistic fashion. For Bradley insists that my construction of objects beyond me (in the past or in distant parts of space) is not my solitary achievement but something which the Universe or Absolute does through me.

It should be noted, however, that Bradley is rather unsympathetic to views for which the world of ordinary life is a social construction made by us all together. Such views, according to Bradley, ignore the fact that each of us has

---

152   See, for example, ETR, 325–34. This does not, of course, mean that only metaphysical monists can think, an opinion which was attributed to me by a reviewer of my *Vindication*.

to construct his own world; that our worlds coincide to serve as versions of the same world is because we belong to the same Universe, which works through each of us, and, presumably, grounds and implicitly justifies our sense that others are sharing our world with us.

But that still suggests that the existence of many of the things which we posit as lying beyond us is only existence *for us* (though sometimes Bradley seems to mean little more by construction than inference). This is reasonable enough for many cases. Some realities are best thought of as our own constructions, whether we think of them as the work of the Absolute present within us or simply as the mental constructions of a human being. But others, surely, are properly regarded as genuinely independent realities (for example, another person's feelings) and Bradley's monism should allow him to grant this much more frankly than he does, for the oneness of each experience with reality as a whole removes most of the difficulty in seeing how our personal experience can point, and be experienced as pointing, to something existing on its own bottom beyond us.

§ So it is doubtful how far Bradley can really be held to be denying any genuine articulation to reality. Certainly all its parts or aspects are inter-connected and could not be themselves except in just that position in just that whole. But that does not prevent some articulation of reality which is not merely constructed. And is it not unrealistic to think that we can never genuinely think about some part or aspect of the whole, in particular, because we can never identify it conceptually?

Many philosophers of our own time (for example, Gareth Evans and Hilary Putnam) insist that our thoughts, or many of them, depend for their meaningfulness and particular content, not just on what occurs within us but on the external context provided both by the physical environment and the society of language-users to which we belong. But these thinkers always seem to make the Wittgensteinian, and frequently Jamesian, assumption just noted, that the relations between the thinker's subjectivity and his environment, physical and social, are purely external, so that the relations, behavioural or merely spatio-temporal, to things outside him which determine just what he is thinking do not genuinely impinge on it. Putnam frankly concludes that phenomenological investigations of thought, meaning, and reference are misguided since they must ignore those behavioural transactions with surrounding things which are what is really relevant.[153] To this it is surely a sufficient objection that, if the flow of my experience is not intrinsically about things, at least in general and perhaps in particular, it cannot become so—in any sense which adds anything genuine to my awareness of the world—because my behaviour, conceived as something external to my experience, interacts with it. (For then my behaviour will itself be quite opaque to consciousness—a mere unknown thing in itself which unwittingly affects my welfare.)

---

153   See Putnam, *Reason,* p. 20.

It seems to follow that, if it is to be the orientation of my behaviour towards real objects or persons which determines just what I am thinking of, and perhaps what I am thinking about it, then that orientation must somehow be a part of what I experience—otherwise it is as good as nothing for me, however much my 'behaviour' takes account of it. This is, indeed, the main point of Bradley's critique of James. But James, in contrast to Putnam and various recent proponents of 'externalism', who deny that the meaning and reference of thought is intrinsic to it as a subjective event or process, at least tried to meet such objections by insisting that we do actually experience the passage from a thought to a direct encounter with what it is about in which the thing itself is an element in our experience. The difficulty is that even if my relation to my objects is therefore internal to my experience over time, it seems to be external to it at the point of thinking and only gets its reference to an object subsequently. Even so, the view that our actual relations to particular things help determine what we are thinking, seems more realistic than Bradley's view that any particular reference must be in terms of concepts present to our mind.

We may concur with James in finding Royce's solution rather too thin and abstract. However, the tension between a view which makes the aboutness of thought internal to it, but which makes identification of particulars purely conceptual, and a more *de re* account which risks making it external to thought's own character, could be resolved if we could accept the view of Whitehead that particular external things can be so immanent in the process of my thinking that it could not be just what it inherently is unless it arose through real relationship to just those things. For then we can hold *both* that the fact I am thinking about a certain particular arises from my genuinely factual relation to it *and* that what I am thinking makes a genuine difference to me, as it could not if that relation were purely external. It seems to me that such a view consorts well with a monism like Bradley's. For surely if the whole is immanent in the parts, the parts can be immanent in each other. This is, indeed, what James thinks happens in perception, and, at least in his panpsychic conception of a convergence between the perceiver's experience and the experience which is the *in itself* of the object, this becomes an encounter with a genuine other.

For myself I am inclined to think that we can experience our own directedness not merely upon reality as a whole, as Bradley seems to think, leaving it to concepts alone to pick out the part of reality in question, but can experience our own directedness upon particular bits of reality through our own pre-conceptual sense of their present or past tug upon us, especially in perception and in personal relationship and in thought felt as derived from these. It is not clear that Bradley really means to deny such a special directedness (as he certainly allows the appearance of it in synthetic judgements of sense); what he does deny is that it can enter into the constitution of an intellectually adequate judgement. But it seems pointless to insist on such an unsatisfiable criterion of adequate thought. And if it is dropped, much of Bradley's case for the conditional nature of all judgement falls, and we can accept that 'designation', 'logically proper names', or 'token indexicals' may at least sometimes determine genuine references which cannot be obtained by pure conceptual description.

Bradley himself, however, either denies this or holds that such immanence of one part or aspect within another is at too primitive a level properly to determine the content of an adequate thought. Thus for him our thought is always directed on that total reality which 'is the Universe itself, which Universe is immanent in the immediate experience, and always itself is actually experienced'.[154] The particular part or region or sort of reality which it more specifically concerns must be picked out simply as that which answers to the universals predicated of it through our ideas. Or if in practice we must use a form of reference not thus mediated that is something with which a really adequate form of thought would dispense. However, this rather forced view tends to drop into the background, thankfully, for much of the time, and for most purposes we can take it that for Bradley thought is an attempt to place what is given in a larger context, whether that of the object world or some more coherent metaphysical notion of the reality we find ourselves in the midst of.

---

154   ETR, p. 153

3

Reality as Necessarily Distorted by Concepts

§1. *Berkeleyan Considerations*

§ *Appearance and Reality*, Bradley's most ambitious statement of his metaphysics, is divided into two 'books'. In Book One, *Appearance*, he seeks to show that all the main ordinary concepts through which we normally think about the world are incoherent, and the consequent inadequacy of accounts of things which treat the objects supposed to answer to them as genuine realities. Book Two, *Reality*, then presents Bradley's own conclusions as to how things really are. Or at least that is the intention, to which he only partly adheres.

In the first chapter he disposes briefly of a position he refers to as 'materialism'. This is often thought to be the view of reality favoured by natural science, and as therefore fated to become the standpoint of informed common sense. It depicts reality as essentially physical and as specifiable solely in terms of the traditional 'primary' qualities. (These are not listed, but presumably they are the usual ones of shape, size, movement, and mass.) Everything else, including secondary qualities and mind, is regarded 'somehow as derivative, and as more or less justifiable appearance'.[1]

Bradley sets out to show that a physical world characterised only by primary qualities is an impossibility and that, if it were possible, it could not be the sufficient basis of everything else. Most of his arguments originated with Berkeley, though as is usual with him he makes no reference to his predecessors. Altogether the discussion is brief and largely unoriginal. One has the impres-

---

1   AR, p. 9.

sion that he thinks his fellow idealists have so decisively refuted 'materialism' that it need hardly detain the serious philosophical enquirer long.

The materialist contends that the real physical world does not possess such secondary qualities as colour, sound, smell, taste, hardness and softness, tangible texture, and heat and cold as we actually feel them. His reason is that things seem to have these secondary qualities only for the appropriate sense organ, and not in themselves. For example, things seem only to have a definite colour in relation to an eye. Evidence for this is that they present a different colour to different spectators. And similar things are true of heat and cold and the rest. Things may feel a different heat to different parts of the skin.

Another point is that secondary qualities are closely linked to pleasure and pain, and can hardly be thought of apart from them. This is especially true of smell and taste. Since it seems obvious that qualities which involve pleasure and pain cannot occur apart from experience, the materialist concludes that the real physical world, as it exists independently of our experience of it, possesses only the primary qualities.

There are two aspects to the materialist position here: first, the denial that secondary qualities pertain to genuine physical reality; second, the assertion that primary qualities do.

Bradley agrees with the materialist that the secondary qualities cannot belong to a physical world which exists independently of our experience of it. However, he mentions a possible objection to this claim. Perhaps the secondary qualities are really there independently of our experience, and the sense organs and brain to which they seem relative are merely conditions which affect the adequacy of our access to them. Thus the real colour of an object may require a certain sort of eye to be present to the mind, while other eyes misrepresent what is there. And even complete delusion may simply indicate the special conditions required for reality to give itself to us as it actually is. But, in the end, Bradley does not think much can be made of this objection.

> For if the qualities impart themselves never except under conditions, how in the end are we to say what they are when unconditioned?
>
> AR, p. 11

There seem to be two claims here, one more initially plausible than the other. The first is that if you never encounter X except under conditions Y, you have no *grounds* for asserting that it exists except under Y. Thus if colour is only encountered under the condition of being presented to eyes, we have no evidence for its existence in their absence. Bradley is rather precipitate in accepting this argument, but it does seem to have some force.

The second claim is that if we never encounter something except under conditions Y, it is *meaningless* to assert that it can exist without Y. This seems a dubious principle. It only becomes persuasive if we take it thus: If you only encounter X in a form in which what it is in itself cannot be distinguished from the conditions under which it is presented, then you can't meaningfully think of X as existing on its own. Use of this principle suggests quite readily that such tangible qualities as hardness, softness, and variations of texture cannot exist apart from our experience of them. For we can hardly distinguish them, as features presented to our experience, from the handling of objects through which they are presented. It is less obvious, but perhaps still true, that the same principle shows that it is meaningless to assert the existence of the other traditional secondary qualities apart from our experience of them.

So Bradley, like Berkeley, is happy to agree with the materialist that the secondary qualities cannot pertain to a physical world existing independently of mind. But, like Berkeley, he thinks that once this is acknowledged the same must be said of the primary qualities. He has several reasons for holding this, some more distinctively his own.

(1) First, there is a problem in the very idea of a purely spatial world. Such a world would consist of spatially extended things in spatial relations to each other, but, as he will be arguing more fully later, it is highly problematic how the things stand to the relations which link them.

(2) Second, there is a problem as to how the real primary qualities are related to the unreal secondary qualities. For the unreal secondary qualities are certainly somehow there. In short a would-be materialist has got to find some home for the secondary qualities, and if that home is mind, then he is landed with the existence of mind and the problem of its relation to matter.

> (3) Thirdly, the line of reasoning which showed that secondary qualities are not real, has equal force as applied to primary.
>
> AR, p. 12

Thus the shape and size of objects only comes to us via sense organs, and evidently depend on their specific nature. Shape is only known as presented to an eye or a feeling hand.

This argument, as it stands, is hardly adequate. For Bradley needs to show that we cannot make any real distinction between the primary qualities and their mode of presentation. Perhaps he would have argued that we can only think of shape as presented visually in a particular perspective and at a certain distance, or tangibly through a particular type of handling, and cannot really conceive it existing detached from some such form of presentation. Personally I think that this is true, and fatal to usual sorts of materialism. However, Bradley only adumbrates this theme.

(4) At the end of the chapter Bradley gives another argument against the materialism for which the physical world possesses only the primary qualities, namely, that we cannot conceive primary qualities without secondary qualities, so cannot conceive, or coherently believe in, the existence of a physical world characterised only by them. This, he tells us, in a somewhat lordly way, is the argument he would stress most if he were writing for the populace.

There are two especially important points here.

(a) Though the argument comes from Berkeley, Bradley, like Husserl a little later, explains more satisfactorily than Berkeley just why it is impossible to think of objects which have only primary qualities. For he points out that when you imagine an extended object you must imagine something which fills up its shape, and this, it seems, can only be some so-called secondary quality.

> And a man may say what he likes, but he cannot think of extension without thinking at the same time of a "what" that is extended.
>
> AR, p. 14

As Husserl put it, the secondary qualities function as the 'filling' of physical things.[2] Thus no physical thing is imaginable, or in any full way conceivable, without some such filling.

(b) One cannot imagine a stretch of the spatial world without imagining it in terms of up and down, right and left, which bear an essential relation to an observer. Thus one cannot imagine it unobserved.

It will be noted that in these arguments Bradley effectively identifies imaginability and conceivability. I shall say something on this later.

(5) Bradley concludes the chapter by examining the claim that primary qualities are the only independently real ones because science can explain everything by reference to them. He has two objections to this. (i) Science has its own purposes, and these do not include the achievement of absolute truth. Rather, it is one particular human activity by which man gains one type of control of the world. It has a right to conceive the world in the way most suitable for its purposes, but that gives no grounds for taking that conception as literally true. (This line of thought is only hinted at here, but is pervasive in Bradley's work.) (ii) Secondly, even if the secondary qualities made no difference to the causal power of physical things, that would only show that it does not matter which specific secondary qualities a thing has, not that it could exist or function without any. A spatial thing may have to have a colour in order that it shall have efficacy or even being, although it makes no difference to its causal powers what its specific colour is.

§ Thus Bradley has briefly given his reasons for claiming that a purely scientific view of the world, couched in terms of spatial or primary qualities, is unacceptable if we are seeking the literal and absolute truth about reality, as we are when we practise metaphysics.

It must be said that the target of his criticism in this chapter is not as clearly defined as one could wish. Does the materialist he is attacking think that nothing really exists at all except physical objects with primary qualities? Presumably not. Although there are philosophers today who make this weird claim, I don't think it was advocated in Bradley's day. Thinkers had not reached the peak of absurdity of denying that there are, for example, qualities of colour the specific individuality of which cannot be reduced to the holding of purely physical facts in a world possessing only primary qualities.[3] So his target is

---

2   See Husserl, *Crisis*, p. 30.
3   For such current denials see Smart, chapters IV and V; Armstrong, *Mind*, chapter XII; Dennett, chapter XII.

presumably the view that mind (together with secondary qualities which exist only as its presentations) is somehow derivative from a physical world possessing only primary qualities, a derivative which may possess its own distinctive essence, but occupies only a very humble role in the world. The most usual version of such a view is epiphenomenalism, for which mind is a side effect of what goes on in animal brains, with no causal efficacy of its own. Although this is not usually called 'materialism' today, it was in Bradley's time. For though it admits a non-physical reality, it denies it any potency.

It is curious that Bradley does not devote any space to criticism of a robust Cartesian dualism, for which each of mind and matter has genuine efficacy, as many would think this the most serious alternative to idealism. In any case, so far as his arguments are sound, such dualism has been refuted in passing. For if they show anything, they show not merely that the physical world, as we ordinarily conceive it, cannot be the whole of reality, or even its main underpinning, but that it cannot be real at all. For we ordinarily conceive of it as something which might exist quite apart from the mental. But, according to Bradley, we cannot form any coherent conception of such a physical world. For either we must think of it as lacking or as possessing secondary qualities. The first is an incoherent conception for the reasons we have been considering, and the second ascribes qualities to it which could not conceivably occur apart from sentient experience. So, in effect, the chapter amounts to an attempted refutation of any view which takes the physical world conceived in any ordinary way as real.

§2. *Things and Their Qualities*

§ Bradley's next target is a much more general characterisation of reality, of which the materialism criticised in the first chapter is just one species. This envisages the world as composed of a whole lot of things, each with its own qualities. He describes this as the view that the world consists of substantives and adjectives, using these expressions ontologically rather than grammatically. The second chapter of AR is devoted to exhibiting some of its paradoxes.

He asks us to consider a lump of sugar. This is supposed to be a thing or substantive with the qualities or adjectives, white, hard, and sweet. The normal way of describing this is to say that the lump IS white, hard, and sweet. But what do we mean when we say that the sugar IS, say, sweet?

We can hardly mean that it IS, in the sense of being one and the same as, sweet(ness). For we want to say that it is white also, and yet white and sweet are not the same thing. Nor can we mean that it is one and the same as whiteness, and also one and the same as each of the others, for it cannot be one and the same as each of them if each is different from the others. Perhaps what is meant then is that it is one and the same as all of them as a unity. However, it's unclear what this can possibly mean. To take the unity as something over and above the qualities themselves introduces the confused idea that there is something to a thing other than its qualities. (The paragraph in which this is said is condensed and obscure but such seems to be its main purport.).

Perhaps (he indicates) speaking of the sugar as the unity of its qualities is a confused way of saying that its existence consists in the fact that its qualities stand in a certain relation to each other. But promising as this may look it does not solve the problem. For that concerned the meaning of 'is'. And all this new suggestion does is change the subject and predicate, while still using the copula 'is'. While previously we had such propositions as 'the sugar is sweet', now we have such propositions as 'white is in a certain relation to sweet'. And we must ask again what this means. Does it mean that the sweetness is one and the same as the entity 'in a certain relation to whiteness'? Surely not, for we want equally to say that 'white is in a certain relation to hard'. Yet 'in a certain relation to sweet' and 'in a certain relation to hard' are not the same thing. But if 'is' does not mean 'is one and the same as', we have advanced no further in understanding what it does mean.

Thus predication is a problem, for it seems to require us to say that one thing is another thing. And the problem is not solved by identifying substantives with their qualities existing in relation to each other. Predicating a relation of a quality raises the problem just as much as does predicating a quality of a substantive. (Bradley does not distinguish verbally between relations and relational properties, as is now customary. We might prefer to say that the switch is from predicating qualities to predicating relational properties.)

§ Now at last Bradley considers what we may think the obvious solution to the problem he has raised, namely that the word 'is' must be understood as meaning 'has'. Surely we are saying that the substantive *has* the quality, or that the quality *has* or *possesses* the relation. Thus when you predicate a quality or a relation of something you are not saying that it is one and the same as the something; you are saying that the something in some sense HAS the quality or relation. The sugar possesses the quality of whiteness, or the quality whiteness possesses a certain relation to hardness. But, says Bradley, introducing the notion of HAS solves nothing. We cannot picture to ourselves or in any way grasp how a thing stands to a quality which it is supposed to have or a quality to a relation it is supposed to possess.

However, although they both raise the problem of predication, Bradley evidently holds that equating the existence of the thing with the holding of relations between its qualities is an advance on the original thing/quality or substantive/adjective view. Although it still leaves us with the problem of predication we are to some extent liberated from the puzzles which dog the idea that the thing is something mysterious somehow lurking behind its presented qualities. So Bradley's further puzzlings over predication take the form of an examination of what it means to speak of qualities as in relation.

§ Before turning to these discussions let us consider the common accusation that Bradley has followed Hegel in seeing problems where there are none by a crude confusion between two senses of 'is'.[4] These two senses are said to be the

---

4   See, for example, Blanshard in Manser and Stock, p. 218.

'is' of identity and the 'is' of predication. If I say 'The prime minister of Great Britain is John Major', I am saying that the P.M. and J. M. are identical, are one and the same entity. If I say that this piece of sugar is white, I am saying that it exemplifies the property of whiteness. Once we distinguish these, so it is said, we have no reason even to entertain the paradox that if the sugar is white, and is sweet, then whiteness and sweetness should be the same thing.

It seems to me that this charge bears only on Bradley's presentation, not on the substance of what he has to say.[5] For Bradley does not himself think that the 'is' of predication stands for that bare identity without difference which such critics take as the meaning of the 'is' of identity. (Nor indeed does he think that 'identity' does so, properly understood, but that does not affect the present point.) He only points out the absurdities of so interpreting it in order to introduce a discussion of what the 'is' of predication does mean. And surely this is a genuinely important question. So the worst one can say of Bradley in this connection is that he gives an undue degree of attention to a view of predication he rejects. The real question is whether he is right in his main positive conclusion about predication (which, it will be seen, is essentially that it involves relational judgements which are ultimately incoherent). Whether he is right or wrong here, the puzzles he raises are not those of someone who has simply made a mistake in grammar. Thus we do not answer the quite legitimate question he is asking about the meaning of predication, by merely insisting on the grammatical difference between the 'is' of identity and that of predication.

So Bradley is asking what goes on in predication, and exhibiting its incoherence by criticising what seem to be the only available alternative accounts of it. 'This lump of sugar is white' does not mean that it is one and the same as white. However, saying that it means that it somehow 'has' the quality of whiteness does not supply much of an explanation of what is going on either. Does it perhaps mean 'This lump of sugar is one and the same as a certain set of qualities in relation of which whiteness is one'? Such a suggestion does advance matters somewhat in Bradley's eyes. It dispels some of the mystery which attaches to the notion of a thing which is somehow more than any of the qualities it presents. However it still leaves us with the more fundamental puzzle about predication. For you are still predicating something of the qualities, namely, that they are in relations of certain sorts to each other, and the problem of explaining the 'is' of predication breaks out again here.

Bradley, then, is raising genuine philosophical questions, which do not turn on some merely grammatical confusion. Indeed, one could come to the main issue he is raising without talking about the meaning of 'is' at all, by simply asking how a thing stands to its qualities or, if one agrees that it is not really

---

5   See, for example, PL, p. 371, and the rest of the somewhat tortuous II, II, IV in this connection. Bradley did, indeed, maintain that every judgement asserts an identity in difference, but this rather flexible claim is precisely aimed to counter the suggestion that some kind of blank identity between subject and predicate is ever what is asserted.

anything over and above their existing in some kind of relation to each other, how these qualities stand to the relations between them.

§ So the problem of predication has resolved itself into the problem of what it is to say of certain items that they are in relations of one sort or another to each other. And here Bradley begins to raise those difficulties about relations for which he is now perhaps best known. I shall expand somewhat upon his very condensed presentation of these in order to clarify what I take to be his main point.

If one quality is related to another, that seems to be itself a kind of quality pertaining to it. And since every quality is related to more than one other quality, each quality itself has various different qualities, and the old problem of how the qualities of a thing relate to it breaks out again in connection with each quality. If we follow the logic of the view that a thing IS its qualities in relation, we will have to say that each quality is the system of its relations to other qualities standing in relation to each other. Thus if the sugar IS *white, hard*, and *sweet* standing in a certain relation R to each other, then *white* IS *being-R-to-hard* and *being-R-to-sweet* standing in a certain relation to each other. And this is a recipe for a hopeless infinite regress.

It will be worse than useless to attempt to resolve the problem again by replacing IS by HAS, for that raises the problem of which of the two qualities HAS the relation. Neither *white* nor *hard* can very well HAVE the relation on its own without the other. But if you say that they have it together and in relation to each other, you've already presupposed that they are in relation to one another, and saying that they have the relation adds nothing.

But perhaps, Bradley suggests, there is a way of conceiving the holding of a relation between qualities which does not make its standing in such a relation a quality of a quality. Treating its relation to other qualities as a quality of a quality is taking the relation, or the standing in the relation, as an element in the quality's being, as a quality is an element in a thing's being. But what if we give this up, and do not make relations qualify qualities in the same intimate way as qualities qualify things?

May we not say rather that relations are something right outside the things they hold between and thus a kind of externally existing link between them? Thus we give up any idea of *occurring together with white* as being an element inherent in *hard*. Instead we think of there being three separate things, *white, hard*, and the relation of *together with* somehow holding between them. However, as Bradley sees it, this poses us with the problem 'what links the relation *together with* to its two terms *white* and *hard*?' They are now conceived as three quite distinct things, and yet we are somehow saying something about how they stand to each other. And that seems to imply that we must postulate another relation to link up *white, hard*, and the relation of *together with*. And that once again invites the question how this new relation is linked up with the original two qualities and the togetherness between them.

So, according to Bradley, we have either to think of the relations between the qualities as themselves a kind of quality pertaining to the relations or as a third item which exists as a link between them. And each account breeds insuperable problems. Either problems arise because each quality breaks up into a whole lot of relations in which it stands to other qualities, and ceases to be a single quality, or we cannot understand how the relation existing between the qualities relates to the qualities on either side of it.

§ We will examine all this in more detail later. My general conclusion will be that Bradley's formal arguments are not successful, inasmuch as those who wish to reject his conclusions have ways of stating their positions which elude them. All the same he is saying something which seems right to me and more important than the details of his possibly sophistical arguments. The point is adumbrated towards the end of the chapter, where he suggests that to be real a relation 'must be so somehow at the expense of the terms'.[6] What he means, essentially, I believe, is that for items A and B to be related requires that there be a more comprehensive whole embracing them, indeed that their forming such a whole is precisely what their being related is, but that such a whole exists at the expense of the related terms in the sense that its existence is incompatible with the distinct existence of the terms as realities in their own right. Thus to understand the relations between different numbers is to see individual numbers as just aspects of a total numerical system which is the true reality, while to chart the spatial relations between things is to see the things as simply fragments from a larger spatial world more real than each of them individually.

From this Bradley concludes that the relational way of thought is essentially unstable and incoherent, since understanding how things are related requires seeing them as not independently real, because simply aspects of a larger whole, while also seeing them as individuals existing in their own right. In short, it requires oscillation between incompatible conceptions, according as to which best suits the needs of the moment, conceiving of one or other, or perhaps each, of the terms as a reality in its own right or conceiving of them as mere elements within a unitary pattern. Thus in learning that A stands in a certain relation R to B, one is coming to see that it is not A or B which is the reality but rather a whole which embraces both, while trying also to retain a sense of the separate reality of A and/or B which is incompatible with this recognition.

This seems to me the single most important point in the whole of Bradley's elaborate discussion of relations, and the one on which his metaphysics really turns.

However, before we consider his views about relations further I should like to raise a question about the sense in which Bradley identifies the existence of an ordinary thing with its qualities in relation, an identification which he apparently endorses while insisting that it does not solve the central problem of the nature of predication. My question is: are the qualities in question universals or particulars?

---

6   AR, p. 18.

§3. *Are Bradley's Qualities Universals or Particulars, or What?*

§ In treating a thing as somehow the complex of its qualities Bradley continues the respectable philosophical tradition of Berkeley and Hume. Yet with Bradley, as with these, there is a difficulty in understanding exactly what is being claimed. For it is not at all clear what is meant by a thing's qualities in this connection, in particular whether they are supposed to be particulars or universals. This is not the place for a discussion of Berkeley and Hume, but we must attempt some clarification of Bradley's position here.

I suggest that there are four main philosophical views which bear especially on what is to be meant by a quality. These views, which may be held implicitly or explicitly, divide first into those which do and those which do not acknowledge the reality of universals. We may call the first *realism* (about universals) and the main form of the second *the resemblance theory*. For rejection of realism typically, and surely necessarily, replaces appeal to universals by appeal to degrees of resemblance between particulars. Or at least it must do so among philosophers who bother to develop any serious ontological view on the matter at all.

For the realist there genuinely are such timeless things as redness, triangularity, and so forth in which the particular things of the temporal world participate. For the resemblance theorist there are only particular things which resemble each other enough to earn a common name. However, both realism about universals and the resemblance theory divide according as to whether they do or do not acknowledge a sort of *particulars* appropriately called 'qualities' such as ontologically precise thinkers have christened either 'particularised qualities' or 'perfect particulars'.

Thus we have four views: realism about universals with or without particularised qualities, and the resemblance theory with or without particularised qualities. These seem the most obvious alternative theories which bear on the meaning of 'a quality' and the positions of most philosophers fall under one or other of them, even if not very explicitly. However, I shall finally suggest that Bradley's own not altogether explicit view is a fifth one. But to grasp it we need to see how it relates to the first four more standard views.

§ For the realist about universals, for a thing to be white, or sweet, or whatever, is for it to somehow instantiate or exemplify a certain universal which various other things exemplify too. This piece of paper is white, and so is this lump of sugar. This means or implies, he says, that there is a certain universal entity *white* present in each particular.

However, there are two views as to how *white* is present in each particular. On one view there is a particular quality pertaining to the sugar and another quality pertaining to the paper, and each of these qualities is an instance of the universal whiteness. Thus the sugar and paper exemplify whiteness only in the sense that they have particular elements, which can be called particularised qualities, or qualities conceived as particulars, pertaining to them, which do so. (The best known proponent of this view was G. F. Stout—though Husserl effectively held it too. Although not explicitly advocated by many other philosophers it has truly been said that it exists as an undercurrent in much philosophical thought.[7]) On the second view, there simply is the universal whiteness on the one hand, and the lump of sugar and the piece of paper on the other. There are no qualities, other than the universal itself.

Thus on the first view, when you have two yellow objects there is a yellow possessed by the one thing, which is not the yellow possessed by the other thing. These two yellows are the particularised qualities of yellowness possessed by each. Note that this holds even if they are of exactly the same shade of yellowness. Consider height as another example. If two people have exactly the same height, then, for the person who believes in particularised qualities, there are two items, the height of the one person and the height of the other. These items are somehow equivalent rather than exactly the same entity. (Perhaps height isn't a genuine quality, but it will serve as an example for present purposes.)

Virtually the same theory is sometimes called the doctrine of 'perfect particulars'. According to this doctrine, when a thing, like a horse, say, exemplifies a universal such as brown, what exemplifies brown more immediately is a certain so-called perfect particular, which is the particular brown-ness of that horse. The horse is brown because it contains (or there somehow pertains to it) a perfect particular which is brown. A perfect particular only exemplifies one universal, whereas an ordinary thing exemplifies lots. A horse is both brown and of a certain shape. For the doctrine of perfect particulars there is one perfect particular which is its brown-ness and another which is its shape, and each of them exemplifies just the one universal. The notion of a perfect particular and that of a particularised quality are essentially identical.

Actually, there is a certain vagueness as to whether it is quite true that a perfect particular exemplifies only one universal. Consider the perfect particular which is the brown-ness of a certain horse, and call the quite specific sort of brown-ness which this horse has 'chestnut brown'. Then it seems reasonable to say that the perfect particular which is the horse's colour, exemplifies these three universals; (1) chestnut brown; (2) brown; (3) colour. There are two ways in which the doctrine of perfect particulars can deal with this. It may say that the perfect particular exemplifies only one absolutely specific universal, but also exemplifies all the more generic universals under which that falls. Alter-

---

7   See D. M. Armstrong's introduction to Seargent, itself a useful guide to Stout's views. Stout's own main presentation is in his 1921 British Academy Lecture *The Nature of Universals and Propositions*. See also 'Are the Characters of Particular Things Universals or Particulars?' in PASS, III (1923). For further references see his posthumous Stout, *God*, p. 77. Grossmann, *Structure*, contains an important discussion of particularised qualities or perfect particulars. For Husserl's commitment to it see, e.g., *Logical Investigations*, p. 376–79 and passim.

natively, it may say that the perfect particular exemplifies just one universal and that there is one perfect particular which is its particular case of chestnut brown, another which is its particular mere brown, another which is its mere colour. I think that probably the first is the claim usually intended.

For the realist, then, the fact that two things are red is a matter of their participating in a common universal: the universal redness is a real one-and-the same entity present in each of them. But the details of how it is present are different according as to whether he does or doesn't postulate particularised qualities or perfect particulars. If he does, he will think that a thing participates in the universal redness because it has an item of this sort which is more directly the particular instance of the universal redness. If he does not believe in such particularised qualities, he will think a particular red thing participates in the universal redness directly, and that the only entity you can call a quality is a universal.

§ Let us now turn to theories which deny the existence of universals and replace reference to them by talk of the resemblances holding between particulars. On this view, there are no universals, but only particulars which resemble each other more or less. Things are put into a single class and covered by a single general name, if they are sufficiently alike, but there is no identical something present in each case.

The resemblance theorist, like the realist, may or may not accept the existence of particularised qualities (though he will only need the word 'particularised' to emphasise his repudiation of universals). If he does, he will think that resemblance between two things turns on each containing one or more particularised qualities which resemble the particularised qualities of the other thing. Thus he will say that we call various objects 'yellow' in virtue of the fact that each possesses its own particularised quality which is sufficiently like the particularised qualities present in the things we first learnt to call 'yellow'. If he does not believe in the existence of these particularised qualities, he will say that there are simply whole things which resemble each other more or less and are called by the same word in virtue of this. Brentano seems to have inclined to this view.[8]

In the light of this discussion we can see that the question how a thing is related to its qualities will have a different meaning according as to which of these four theories is presupposed. (Doubtless there are many philosophers who ask how a thing is related to its qualities without even an implicit commitment to any one of these views, or to any definite alternative to them, and thereby fail to give it any definite meaning.)

(1) For realism *with* particularised qualities, the question is probably concerned with how the thing stands to its particularised qualities (though it could be as to how it stands to the universals under which these qualities fall). Is the

---

8   See, for example, Brentano, *Evident*, p. 64.

thing something besides these particularised qualities, or is it something which 'has' them (where 'has' does not mean 'exemplifies')?

(2) For realism *without* particularised qualities, it must be a question about the exemplification relation or nexus holding between a thing and the quality-type universals it exemplifies.

(3) For the resemblance theory *with* particularised qualities, the same question arises as for (1) : Is the thing to which they pertain composed of them or does it somehow have them? (The tendency is for holders of these views to take the whole particular thing as composed of its particular qualities.)

(4) For the resemblance theory *without* particularised qualities, it is a confused question to be dealt with by an account of how things can be divided on the basis of their resemblances into groups of things answering to the same quality word.

The most plausible versions of the claim that a thing is composed of its qualities will be that of a philosopher holding positions (1) or (3) who maintains that a particular thing is somehow composed of its particularised qualities. These will be its parts in a special sense of 'part' (distinct from that of a physical or analogous part) of which positions (2) and (4) must deny the sense. A much less plausible version of the claim is that of one who holds position (2) and attempts to depict the thing as composed of the (or certain of the) universals it exemplifies.

§ Where then does Bradley stand? When he talks about a thing and its qualities, is he talking of particularised qualities, or universals? And if he is talking about particularised qualities, as much of what he says suggests, is he supposing that, as well as the particularised qualities, there are universals which they exemplify or does he think that they only come under the same word in virtue of resembling each other in a sense which does not require universals?

The answer is that our fourfold classification of positions bearing on the meaning of 'a quality' is not, after all, exhaustive and that Bradley's position is a fifth one. For all these views make an assumption which Bradley does not share, namely, that if there are to be both universals and particulars they must be quite distinct entities which require to be linked by a relation or nexus of 'exemplification'. For Bradley, in contrast, both the particular and the universal are false abstractions made from the one genuine reality, the individual.

> You are given a [false] choice between naked universals, existing as such, and bare particulars. You can not stomach the first, and so you take the last. But why should you take either? Why not adopt the view that the real is the concrete individual, and that the bare particular and abstract universal are distinctions within it, which apart from it, are only two forms of one fiction?
>
> PL, p. 330

In short, every genuine individual is a concrete universal. It is a one in many and a many in one, the many-ness for Bradley, in the case of ordinary finite things, being both a matter of their presence in different moments of time and in the various different aspects of their character.[9]

Bradley's position was well summed up by G. E. Underhill, writing in 1902.

> In other words the individual thing of perception is both a universalised particular and a particularised universal; or, as Mr Bradley puts it, "the individual is both a concrete particular and a concrete universal. . . . So far as it is one against other individuals it is a particular. So far as it is the same throughout its diversity, it is universal."
>
> Sturt, pp. 200–201[10]

So for Bradley, as I understand him, the qualities of which he talks are universals which are repeatable as one and the same in different particular instances.[11] But their particular instances do not merely 'exemplify', 'fall under', or participate in them. Rather they *are* the universals figuring in one particular context and modified thereby in a way which brings out a fresh aspect of their being.

Thus his reduction of whole particular things to their qualities is somewhat like that of those who would reduce them to the particularised qualities pertaining to them. Yet these particularised qualities are not something other than the universals which they exemplify or under which they fall; rather are they the universals themselves which have become particulars by entering into certain particular contexts.

This position rests on the view that identity in any proper sense is something which goes along with difference, and that the supposed absolute identity which does not allow for difference is a bogus notion. It only makes sense to say that things are identical when there is a sameness with difference holding between them.[12] Thus a quality existing *here* is a particular insofar as it is different from itself as it exists *there*, but it is a universal insofar as it is identical with itself in each position.

Suppose that you have two daffodils of what we'd call the same shade of yellow. Then, for Bradley, the question whether they have each their own

---

9   See PL, pp. 186–93 , 291–94, 486–87, etc.

10   Underhill is quoting from PL, 1st ed., p. 175 (p. 188 of 2nd ed.).

11   Upon the whole this seems to be the doctrine urged at PL, pp. 650–53 (in the 1922 *Terminal Essays,* though it comes, as is usual with Bradley, in combination with so many other points that it is hard to disentangle it). Bradley there argues that qualities, both as items with a being all on their own, and as elements in a system of universals detached from particular instances, are unreal abstractions. The topic of that essay is 'uniqueness', but Bradley seems, rather unfortunately, to treat uniqueness as implying independence of anything else and is mainly concerned, with arguments similar to those in AR, to be discussed below, to challenge the idea of a quality without relations while also insisting on the difficulties which pertain to it when conceived as in relationship with other items.

12   See PL, p. 141. Also p. 373.

yellowness or whether there is just the one absolutely identical universal of yellowness in which each participates is misconceived. For what you have is the same thing with a difference. If you think of them with emphasis on the element of sameness, then you have a universal. If you think of them with emphasis on the element of difference, then you have something more like two distinct particularised qualities. So when asked whether the qualities which, for Bradley, relate to each other to make up things, are particulars or universals we must answer that they are both. They are universals, but as entering into these relations in particular contexts they are particulars.

We may add that, for Bradley, the particularity of the context is ultimately a matter of the whole complex of relations in which the quality stands in this particularisation of it. In short the same universal occurs in two different relational contexts, and thereby functions as two particulars, the relational contexts themselves being specifiable ultimately in purely universal terms. Thus Bradley certainly accepts the identity of indiscernibles.

If all this does not come out very clearly in AR, chapter II, that is, doubtless, because Bradley professes to be approaching the matter without presupposing his whole theory. Moreover, he was not advancing it as an alternative to some other clearly defined position about qualities, but taking it fairly much for granted. And perhaps he would have thought that whatever exactly you think qualities are, the thing cannot be anything over and above them, so that it was not necessary to be precise as to what a quality is. Still, it seems clear enough that when he speaks of qualities he is, in fact, thinking of them in these terms.

§ The upshot is that for Bradley qualities are repeatable elements which combine to form things. As such they are from one point of view the same entities in each repetition, and from another point of view different entities. They are universals insofar as they are repeatable, particulars insofar as one can distinguish the different repetitions. (I do not claim to follow Bradley's own terminology in ascribing this view to him, but I believe that it is the gist of his position.)

§4. *James and Bradley on Resemblance and Identity*

§ Bradley's view that identity is always the other side of a difference and a difference always the other side of an identity is given one of its fuller expressions in a controversy in which he engaged with James in the pages of *Mind*.[13]

13　Among other of his presentations of this doctrine see PL, pp. 286–87, and AR, 2nd ed., pp. 533–38. Perhaps I should note that this is not the view associated with Peter Geach that identity is relative to the expressions by which things are referred to and that there is no such thing as identity *tout court* but only relative to some substantival expression. Bradley's notion of identity (and difference) is decidedly *de re* and absolute. That identity of a thing with itself amidst differences, which is the only genuine identity, does not depend on the way we choose to refer to it,

This seems a convenient place to say something about this, the main set-piece battle between the two heroes of this book.

In PP James had claimed that qualitative resemblance does not always consist in partial identity.[14] Rather, qualitative identity is simply the maximal case of resemblance or likeness or, what is the same thing, the minimal case of unlikeness or difference. Likewise difference does not always consist in the presence of an element of sheer sameness together with an element of sheer difference. Qualities may differ without having anything in common, which is not to say that they do not resemble, for significant difference involves resemblance. But neither resemblance nor difference necessarily involve identity.

Some have thought that when two objects resemble, without being exactly alike, their resemblance is a matter of their sharing an absolutely identical quality, while its failure to be exact consists in their also possessing two or more absolutely different qualities. Or perhaps it is claimed rather that, though things may resemble without sharing anything properly called a *quality*, they must have qualities which share an absolutely identical element. (James seems to be concerned both with resemblance as holding between qualities in the abstract and as holding between those qualities as they occur in particular instances. Upon the whole, I think that he holds very much the same view of the status of qualities, as being both particulars and universals, which I ascribed to Bradley in the last section. Since in the whole of this little exchange both philosophers seem to be concerned with resemblance as holding between qualities as actually exemplified in particular instances rather than in the abstract, and do not distinguish between the resemblance which holds between these qualities and that which therefore holds between the objects said to possess them, I have not tried for an exactitude of expression in this respect which would be foreign to their approach and serve no helpful purpose.)

James allows that there are resemblances of this sort. But there are also resemblances where there is only one relevant quality in each of the two particulars, and where these qualities resemble, without sharing any identical element. This is evidently so when the resembling qualities are completely simple. For here there cannot be two elements in each quality, one of which it shares with the other, while the other is exclusive to it.

---

though different ways of referring to it may emphasise either the identity which sustains itself over a particular type of difference or the difference such difference makes. As to whether identity is always identical with itself that too is perhaps a matter of identity and difference. In fact, in a letter to James of 14 May 1909 he says that his answer to 'the difficulty raised as to identity being different itself in each different case, is "Yes and No"' and that, indeed, it is impossible to think about identity consistently. In this letter he also says that his 1893 controversy with James rested largely on a misunderstanding (see my appendix). However, I hope that my discussion will show that there was some real substance to their dispute. The truth would seem to be that they were somewhat closer by 1909, after James had developed his own conception of identity in difference in PU. See p. 210 above.

14   See PP, I, pp. 490–94 and 530–33.

One reason why this must be the case concerns the nature of series, and here he uses an argument formulated by the psychologist Carl Stumpf.[15]

One main sort of series, as James and Stumpf conceive the matter, is constituted by the fact that the qualities pertaining to it can be arranged in order according to their decreasing resemblance to some one of them taken as a starting point.[16] These degrees of resemblance are in some cases such that one can speak of that quality which differs from a second by the same amount as that differs from a first. It is on this principle (or rather on a complication thereof) that the notes of a scale are ordered. Suppose now that we have a series of qualities J, K, L, M, N, O, in which each quality differs from the preceding one by the same amount. In order that they shall differ in the appropriate way they must also resemble, else they would not be in a series at all. But is the resemblance the presence of some identical element in each case? Maybe sometimes it is. But it cannot be so in all cases.

To see this we are invited to consider a series J, K, L, M, N, and O where there is an identical element present in each. Let X be this common element (and let it include the whole of what is in common to all the terms) and let j, k, l, m, n, and o be that which is different in each term. Then the original series was that of Xj, Xk, Xl, Xm, Xn, Xo, but it is evident that this series is derivative from a more basic one of j, k, l, m, n, o. The relation which determines this latter series, then, is that of decreasing degree of resemblance from a starting point, and of equal degree of resemblance between each term and its neighbour, holding between terms which have no common element. It follows that there is a relation of resemblance, admitting of degrees, which may hold between terms which have no common element and that resemblance is not to be identified with partial identity.

Bradley criticised this view in a short article in *Mind* published in 1893. This produced a reply by James, followed by one by Bradley, followed by one by James, ending in a final brief one by Bradley.[17] The basic dispute was as to

---

15   Carl Stumpf (1848–1936), German philosopher and psychologist, best known for his work on acoustical phenomena, was a good friend and frequent correspondent of James. Husserl was one of his students and dedicated his *Logical Investigations* to him. James's references are to volume I of Stumpf's *Tonpsychologie*, published in 1883.

16   See PP, I, pp. 490–94; 530–33. Presumably series of qualities which stretch infinitely in both directions, and thus cannot be said to have a starting point, could be dealt with along quite similar lines.

17   1893a: F. H. Bradley, 'On Professor James's Doctrine of Simple Resemblance (I)', *Mind n.s*, II, No. 5 (January 1893), pp. 83–88 (Essay XV in CE); 1893b: William James, 'Mr. Bradley on Immediate Resemblance', *Mind n.s.*, II, (April 1893), pp. 208–10 (reprinted in CER and EP); 1893c: F. H. Bradley, 'On Professor James's Doctrine of Simple Resemblance (II)', *Mind n.s.*, II, No. 7 (July 1893), pp. 366–69 (Essay XVI in CE); 1893d: William James, 'Immediate Resemblance', *Mind n.s.*, II, (October 1893), pp. 509–10 (reprinted in CER and EP); 1893e: F. H. Bradley, 'On Professor James's Doctrine of Simple Resemblance (III)', *Mind n.s.*, II, No. 8 (October 1893), p. 510

which of identity or of degree of resemblance or difference is more basic. For James qualitative identity or precise resemblance is simply the minimal degree of a relation of difference (or maximal degree of a relation of resemblance) which does not in other cases have to involve identity at all, while for Bradley identity is basic and degree of resemblance to be explained by reference to it.

Bradley says that James ignores the view which he thinks the right one, namely, that resemblance does involve identity, but that the identical element between resembling qualities is not something detachable from the differing element. Rather the identity and the difference

> are complementary aspects, that the one aspect may be emphasized here, and the other aspect there, but that an attempt to isolate them leads everywhere to an infinite regress.
>
> CE, p. 293

They are aspects of something which is not a synthesis of separable items but the belonging together of the aspect in which the two objects are the same and the aspect in which they are different, neither of these being anything complete in itself.

Bradley does not identify resemblance with possession of an identical quality or element thereof. But it does, as he conceives it, require this. For, according to him, the experience of a resemblance between things consists in an impression that there is such an identical quality or element which is too vague to indicate precisely what it is. But though there must, therefore, be an identical quality or element present in each of two resembling things, it need not be the kind of thing which could be prised off from every fuller and more concrete character, such as includes also that in which the objects differ, so that it might occur, or even be contemplated, in isolation. Indeed, an identical something only can occur or be contemplated amidst such differences.

Bradley makes several other points. He says that the very notion of a simple quality is flawed. Whenever a quality occurs it occurs in a context which enters into its own being, so that it contains both what it is contributing to the situation and what the context contributes. Thus as something which actually occurs a quality cannot be simple.

And as regards the nature of a series Bradley claims that it is absurd to hold that there can be a series in which there is not an increasing or decreasing amount of something which is the very same.

> For how can we have a consciousness of uniform direction if there is not some one element common to all the degrees? How are we to speak with meaning of a 'more' and 'less', if it is to be a 'more' and a 'less' of *nothing*?
>
> CE, p. 289

(Essay XVII in CE).

The suggestion that the series may rest upon degree of resemblance to some quality taken as a starting point ignores the fact that the series is not based merely upon resemblance but upon resemblance of a particular kind.

> But a particular kind of resemblance, degrees of which make the unity of a series, seems to me to imply resemblance in and through a particular point.
>
> CE, p. 289

James begins his reply by saying that the main point does not concern the nature of a series but the possibility of an immediate resemblance which is not a partial identity. Nor is the existence of simple qualities an essential part of James's claim. For whether the qualities which resemble are simple or not, the question still arises whether their resemblance turns on an identical component occurring together with different components.[18] And James continues to argue that it need not. Moreover, he does not see how Bradley avoids the main reason for this claim. For Bradley claims that all likeness must be 'in and through a particular point'. So if two qualities *a* and *b* resemble it must be because there is a 'point' of identity *m* in each. But does the *m* in *a* merely resemble the *m* in *b*, or is it identical with it? If they merely resemble then there must be a more fundamental identical element present in each on Bradley's view. So either it, or some more ultimate point, must be strictly identical, identical, that is, without difference. But Bradley rejects the possibility of this. For he both denies that there can be two objects which are identical in nature and only numerically different (and this is just how the *m* in *a* would have to stand to the *m* in *b*) and denies that there can be sameness of quality apart from difference (such as would hold between *m* and itself in the two contexts).

To this Bradley replies that the point of identity present in resembling objects is not something which can be treated as a separate or even discriminable item about which questions like James's can be asked.

> Identity and difference . . . are inseparable aspects of one complex whole. They are not even 'discernible', if this means that you can separate them in idea, so as to treat one as remaining itself when the other is excluded. And the whole is emphatically not a 'synthesis', if that means that it can be mentally divided, and that its elements then still keep their characters.
>
> CE, pp. 295–96

He urges further that identity is pervasive, for everything is both the same

---

18   James also complains, in a footnote EP, p. 66, that Bradley misrepresents him as thinking of the points of resemblance which form the ground of similarity as separable parts of the similar objects, when all he meant was discernible parts. The main point here seems to be that Bradley misrepresents James's presentation of what he rejects as implying that resemblance requires an identity between separable elements of the resembling things as opposed to discriminable elements thereof.

and different from every other thing, the sameness appearing in different forms. For one thing

> [s]entience, being, or experience (these are all the same to me) is a character in which everything is finally identical.
>
> CE, p. 296

And the world would not be in any way intelligible unless both this most basic aspect of sameness, and other less basic ones, held all things together.[19]

James begins his reply by insisting that he is not trying to deny that there is such a thing as identity.

> Every act of reasoning, every bit of analysis, proves the practical utility and the psychological necessity of the assumption that identical characters may be 'encapsulated' in different things.
>
> EP, p. 69

He is only claiming that there must be some resemblances which are not based on identity. And he insists that, when he says this, he is talking of identity in what he thinks the ordinary sense in which identity is not inseparable from difference. As for Bradley's sort of identity which is

> only one aspect of an integral whole on which you may lay stress for a moment
>
> EP, p. 70

but which becomes self-inconsistent or nothing if you try to separate it out and contemplate it alone, he is so far from being against it that it seems to him simply another word for what he calls resemblance. Stumpf and James himself were arguing that resemblance cannot always consist in the presence of elements which are sheerly identical in the ordinary sense for which Bradley has no use. So far as the kind of immediate resemblance with which James was concerned goes, he now concludes that Bradley is not in the least denying it, but simply preferring to call it 'identity'. Thus the main argument between them seems to have been purely verbal.

In his final reply Bradley is determined not to accept this olive branch. For he is insisting that there is a real point of sameness between resembling qualities such as James denies. And he continues to think it ridiculous to hold that there can be resemblance where 'there is no point in which the things are alike and on which the resemblance is founded'.[20] The reply is very short but it seems that Bradley thinks it utterly wrong to deny that there is a real point of identity or sameness on the ground that it cannot be identified as something which might exist or even be contemplated in isolation.

---

19   See CE, p. 299.
20   CE, p. 301.

§ What should be said about this debate? It cannot have been so merely verbal as James came to think it, for if Bradley's identity were, as James finally suggests, James's resemblance without identity, then Bradley would also be denying the existence of the other kind of resemblance in which James believes, in which there is what James calls 'identity'. (However, there are pressures in James's thought towards the ultimate denial of genuine identity between what occurs in different contexts.) But was he right that by 'identity' Bradley meant what he called 'resemblance'? And if so, is there any reason to think that 'identity' is a better word for it than 'resemblance'?

It is curious that neither of the two mentions what really seems to be the main thing at issue, namely, the existence or being of generic universals as opposed to purely specific ones. It is not surprising that Brand Blanshard, who claimed that there were no such things as generic universals (e.g., colour or even redness) but only specific ones (such as precise repeatable shades of colour) which can be put in groups according to their degree of resemblance, should have declared that James was the victor in this dispute.[21] The points of identity which, according to Bradley, are the basis for any sort of resemblance are, surely, at least in most cases, what others would describe as generic universals. But perhaps Bradley would deny ultimate validity to the distinction between generic and specific universals. For it is based upon the presumption that you can have identity without any difference at all, as say when the same precise shade of colour occurs twice, while for Bradley the most exact reoccurrence of a shade of colour will always go with an element of difference due to the context.

On this point we have seen that the James of PP agreed, at least so far as the repetition of elements within consciousness (as opposed to the world presented thereto) goes. When he later adopted a view for which experience was the only reality, he sometimes thought in terms of natures which do exactly repeat themselves, while at other times he stuck with the earlier view that there could not be exact repetition within experience, this now being the only reality. But upon the whole the holistic view that context always bites into a thing's nature was common property between Bradley and James. However, as this controversy brings out, the implications of this for James are that the basic category for the understanding of repetition and series is that of degree of likeness or unlikeness while for Bradley it is an identity that cannot occur without difference.

Another reason for rejecting James's view that the dispute had become merely verbal is that if one makes degree of resemblance basic, as he does, one is encouraged to regard classification of objects into types as always to some extent optional, while if one makes identity basic with Bradley, then it would seem that, once one has directed one's attention on a definite repeatable quality, there will always be a definite answer to the question whether it is present again

---

21   See Blanshard, *Reason,* pp. 409–14.

in some fresh object. Certainly for Bradley identity cannot occur without a difference, but that does not imply that there can be a real ambiguity as to whether we have the same quality as we had before, as does the suggestion that what we most often mean by the 'same' is a resemblance which is a matter of degree.

§ Bradley had many reasons for thinking this issue of the first importance. For example, he held that the belief in a real identity in the essence which exists in a state of differentiation in each of us, while remaining identical with itself, is basic to morality and religion.[22] Moreover, its denial makes a complete chaos of reality, for it makes nonsense of all explanation (at least at the level of appearance). For causation rests upon the notion of the same thing acting in the same way whenever it occurs, and if identity is replaced by mere resemblance then there can be no exact explanation by law at all.[23] Surely he is right here as against James and, we might add, some of the more fantastic suggestions of Wittgenstein. Laws of nature can have no exact purchase in a world in which there is not a precise truth as to whether some new situation falls under them or not.

One may feel that Bradley's own thought, with its tendency to deny hard-and-fast distinctions, poses the same threats to explanation. However, his attempt, perhaps successful, is to combine insistence that predicates can have a definite meaning which gives them an unambiguous extension, with denial that the universals they designate are simply inert repeatables which slot in with the other ingredients of a situation without mutual modification.

James might have replied that it is indeed the sheer identity which does not involve difference which is essential for the holding of precise causal laws, and that his simple resemblance without identity does not give law the same purchase. But quite apart from the fact that it is not clear how deep his commitment is to such an identity, which, after all, he identifies with maximal resemblance, Bradley would have responded that that sort of blank identity without difference is simply meaningless. Explanation certainly requires a genuine identity, such that what we have identified once is either there or not on a subsequent occasion; nature cannot be explained by concepts of a fuzzy family-resemblance type. But we cannot meet this requirement by postulating a blank identity of what is in no way modified by context, and should appeal rather to the only real sort of identity there could be, one which is inseparable from difference. I am inclined to think that in the end Bradley is right on this.[24]

§ Although seemingly concerned with a matter of rather limited interest this little controversy was for each philosopher an opportunity to show up the inadequacies of a long faulty tradition to which they saw the other as belonging.

---

22   See ES, pp. 334–35, note 1.
23   And, indeed, no inference at all. See PL, pp. 286–87.
24   Bradley's views on identity in difference owe much to Hegel. For Hegel on this see
     Hegel (Miller, trans.), p. 415. For a pithy expression of Bradley's view see PL, pp.
     287–88. The inseparability of identity and difference is also discussed on p. 460, §6.

For Bradley James was just another empiricist for whom bare particulars without a universal content were the basic reality, while for James (who conceived empiricism as the champion of particulars against universals) it provided the opportunity to take up the cudgels against an intellectualist who thought particulars could not relate to each other except via participation in a realm of universals. Thus the dispute is rooted in a pervasive contrast between their two philosophies, which often seems to keep them apart just where one might expect them, on other grounds, to be at one. But it is often hard to know how far this contrast and its consequences is one of rhetoric or real difference of opinion.

This is true, for example, of their respective treatment of identity across time. Both see it as a matter of continuity of existence as well as of identity of character. However, James emphasises especially the way in which one momentary particular merges into the next while Bradley is more concerned to emphasise the identity of the universal present along the series. Again Bradley sometimes seems inclined to make memory basic to personal identity but draws back because he thinks memory derivative from a more basic knowledge of the connection of universals, while for James the memory of past particular facts is more basic than this. Thus their difference over the importance of memory in the constitution of personal identity turns partly on a difference in the meaning they attach to the word 'memory', a difference itself reflecting James's more nominalistic and Bradley's somewhat more Platonic leanings.

One difficulty in saying just how they stand to each other on this is that James's views on universals shifted from a tendency to nominalism to a more Platonic view. However, from Bradley's perspective his final Platonism may have appeared as bad as nominalism, since the universals it endorses are not so much concrete universals as detached abstractions.[25]

§5. *Relations: The Official Arguments*

§ So in chapter two of *Appearance and Reality* Bradley has replaced the notion of a world of things with their qualities, by a world of qualities in various relations to one another. This presumably covers both the relations between the qualities which we would normally regard as belonging to one thing, and the relations between qualities which we would normally regard as belonging to different things. It has also prepared the ground for a general critique of relational thinking through which he seeks to show that 'relations are unreal'. His main formal argumentation to this effect is in the third chapter of the work (though, in fact, its main lines were already there in PL).[26] I agree with Wollheim that to

---

25   It should be remembered, though, that James's later so-called conceptual realism is as much concerned with the status of conceived particular extensions of the given as with universals.

26   See PL, p. 96.

a great extent one can regard this as a criticism of any sort of relational fact, whether the terms of the relations are called qualities or not.[27] It is also to be noted that Bradley often uses the term 'relation' for the *fact* that a relation holds between terms. Moreover, he does not distinguish in any methodical way between the relation R which holds between A and B, and the relational property pertaining to A of being R to B.[28] However, I am not aware that failure to make these distinctions is responsible for any fallacies there may be in his arguments.[29]

In AR, chapter III, Bradley tries to show the incoherence of the conception of the world as composed of qualities (or objects) somehow linked together by another sort of item, called relations, by demonstrating four theses: (1) qualities without relations are impossible, (2) qualities with relations are impossible, (3) relations without qualities are impossible, (4) relations with qualities are impossible. It might seem that (2) and (4) are the same case. However, Bradley is dealing with it first from the point of view of the qualities, then from the point of view of the relations. Thus neither relations and qualities (or objects) can be real as they are required on this scheme.

There is a certain ambiguity as to whether (1) and (3) assert (a) that qualities (or relations) cannot exist without relations (or qualities) or (b) that one cannot form a conception of the one without the other. On the face of it, it might be impossible for the one to exist without the other, but possible for us to conceive of one, that is, to think about one, without thinking about any particular example of the other. Probably Bradley would maintain each of (a) and (b) in some form.

§ (1) However that may be, his first thesis is presented as the claim that '[q]ualities are nothing without relations'. The idea seems to be that one cannot identify anything one could call a quality without using its relations to other qualities as part of one's identification of it. You cannot first identify one quality and then ask how it is related to other qualities. Rather do you have, from the start, to see its relations to other qualities as pertaining to what it essentially is.

If we bear in mind that more or less anything counts as a quality in this connection, we will see how broad the bearings of this claim are. Amongst its more specific targets are, I take it, the Humean notion of the world as a vast collection of distinct sensory existences in external relations to one another. It is striking how especially apt much of his argument seems as an advance critique of Russell's logical atomism. A main target in fact was evidently the German philosopher J. F. Herbart.[30]

Bradley's discussion is so concise, and so short on illustration, that it is not

---

27   See Wollheim, p. 110.
28   The expression 'relational property' in this sense seems to have been introduced by G. E. Moore in 1919 or 1920 (along with the expression 'entails'). See Moore, *Studies*, pp. 280–81.
29   I agree with Wollheim again here. See Wollheim, p. 110.
30   See AR, p. 25, and the note on this passage on p. 539.

at all easy to pinpoint just exactly what in more concrete terms he is getting at. But presumably he has in mind considerations like the two following.

(a) When you identify something in your perceptual field, you never pick it out merely for what it is in itself, but always in part by its spatial or temporal relations to something else. The splodge of green I see before me is not just identified as a splodge of green, but as one to the left of that splodge of blue. You can't, so to speak, concentrate attention on it just for what it is itself: how it stands to other things is always an important part of the way in which it draws your attention.

(b) If you try to characterise a quality to yourself, you are bound to do so in part by considering how it contrasts, or has affinities, or in some other way stands, to the character of other qualities. A shade of colour is identified as lying between two other shades, a musical pitch by its relation to other pitches.

As I have said, Bradley would take such points about the conditions under which something can be identified by us as indications also of the conditions under which it can exist or be at all. It is not, for example, just that we cannot pick out middle C except as a note within a scale (presumably this is true in a sense even for those with perfect pitch) but that it couldn't exist otherwise. Thus the very being of each note is bound up with its relation to others. It couldn't be the case that just middle C existed, and no other pitch; each pitch owes its very being to the way it stands to other pitches. Likewise any particular sensory occurrence in my life can only exist as a historical event because it follows on other such events or is somehow juxtaposed with them.

Bradley, we may note, acknowledges that perhaps there might be creatures 'whose life consists, for themselves, in one unbroken simple feeling'.[31] But he says that such a creature wouldn't be experiencing anything which we could recognize as a quality, for an experienced quality must be experienced as discriminable from other qualities. Thus the quality of its single feeling could not be the same quality as any experienced by a being with a richer range of experience.

My two examples, (a) and (b), concern respectively the need for a quality, qua particular, to be identified by, and have, real relations of juxtaposition to other qualities, qua particulars, and qua universal, to be identified by, and have, ideal relations to other qualities, qua universals. This distinction is one to which Bradley never pays attention, but, as I suggested in chapter one, pp. 268–69, his discussion would often have been clearer if he had. (Ideal relations—some readers may like to be reminded—are such as do, and real relations such as, like those of juxtaposition or influence, do not, consist simply in the contrast or affinity between the characters of things.)[32]

---

31   AR, p. 24.
32   On the face of it, the expression 'ideal relation' covers two things, the relations between forms and qualities merely as such, and the relations between particulars holding merely in virtue of these relations between their forms and qualities. Thus 'brighter than' may refer to a relation between colours or between things which

It is true that Bradley's metaphysics militates against drawing the distinction sharply. On the one hand, he regards space as an ideal construction by which we unite the spaces given in different perceptual experiences into an ideal unity on the basis of the way in which their rims fit together qualitatively, thus effectively making unperceived spatial relations ideal.[33] On the other hand, he tends to view the ideal relations between numbers in such a spatial way that they become as 'real' as the spatial relations between the elements of a perceptual field.

But, even if he would deny the ultimate validity of the distinction, he could hardly deny that it is helpful at the level of ordinary thought. It certainly seems, for example, that there is an important distinction between examining the ideal relations between the systems of two philosophers, perhaps an ancient Indian philosopher and a Western philosopher, and exploring any real historical relations of influence or of derivation from shared sources which may have held between them. Again, there certainly seems to be an important distinction between noticing that a landscape painting presents a scene like one one saw on holiday, and hypothesising that the artist was actually painting the very same place from life.

It is true, as is evident from such examples, that the holding of an ideal relation may often be evidence of, and result from, the holding of a real relation. And Bradley, as we shall see, had a tendency to think that the two were always importantly intertwined. But the *prima facie* distinction between them is clear and Bradley's discussion suffers from ignoring it. Thus one does not know whether, in saying that there cannot be qualities without relations, his main point is that a quality cannot be identified (or even be) except as an element in an ideal system of terms in ideal relations of contrast or affinity (including relative magnitude in such senses as do not make it a matter of actual or possible factual juxtaposition) or cannot be picked out as a particular (or exist as such) except by reference to its position in something like a perceptual or perceptible field. Doubtless Bradley is making both points, and indeed both seem sound. But they seem to require distinct defences.

§ (2) Let us now move on to the second thesis, that qualities are equally unintelligible when taken *with* relations.[34]

The bare bones of the argument are as follows. When you consider a quality together with its relations to other qualities, you find that there are two aspects to it: that part of its nature which gives rise to its relation to the other quality, and that part of its nature which results from this. But these two aspects of each quality must be related to each other, and that implies that they similarly have two related aspects and so on in an endless regress. Unless this regress is, *per*

---

    have the colours. But if we accept the view about particulars and universals I have
    ascribed to Bradley in the previous section, there is no real distinction here, and in
    any case it would be pedantic to insist on it in most discussions.
33   See PL, III, I, V.
34   See AR, p. 25, §2.

impossibile, completed, the requirements for the relation of the two original qualities are not met and they cannot be related.

Thus if quality A is in a certain relation to quality B, there is the AG aspect of A which grounds the relation, and the AR aspect of A which results from the relation. Now it is obvious that AG must be somehow related to AR. But this implies in turn that there are two aspects to each of AG and AR. Take AG. Then there's AGG which grounds the relation of AG to AR, and there's AGR which results from the relation of AG to AR. But these two elements of AG must be related, and that requires a splitting up of each of them in the same way and so on in an endless regress. However, A cannot be R to B unless this regress is completed as it clearly cannot be. It follows, thinks Bradley, that there is an incoherence in the very idea of terms standing in relations to one another.

Unfortunately it is less than clear why Bradley supposes that a relational fact implies that there is a distinction between what it is in the terms which produces the relation, and what it is in them which is produced by it. Why should not the character of A (presumably with the help of the character of B) be such as to set it in a certain relation to B without that fact rebounding on A's character and making some difference to it? In any case, why assume that there is always something 'in' the terms which produces the relation? Why should it not just hold in a manner having nothing to do with what each is within itself?

However my concern at this point is not to criticise Bradley but to try to enter into his thought. I think we may best do this by considering a particular example.

Consider the natural numbers and the sorts of relation which hold between them. Whether Bradley would call numbers qualities or not, they serve to illustrate what I take to be his point rather well.

As I understand him, Bradley would bid us ask ourselves whether the number 7 is the number it is because it comes between 6 and 8, and has all sorts of relations to other numbers, or whether it comes between 6 and 8, and has other numerical relations, because it is the number it is. And I think he would want us to conclude that neither answer is satisfactory. In one way a number seems to owe its nature to the position it occupies in the numerical system as a whole. It just is what fills that slot in the system. On the other hand, it must, surely, be something in its own right, in order to have all these relations to other numbers.

The Bradleyan point, then, is that you have to think of the number 7 as having two aspects, that which it has as an object in its own right, with a character which determines its relation to other numbers, and that which it has qua being in those relations. That being so, there must be some relation between these two aspects of 7, call them 7A (7 in its separate being) and 7B (7 as filling a slot in the numerical system). And that, so Bradley would argue, implies that each of 7A and 7B has two aspects, that which sets it in relation to the other and that which results from its being so related. For surely 7A must be something in its own right, and it must be in virtue of this that it is thus related to 7B. But equally it must be something qua being thus related to 7B and the rest of the system to which they both belong. But this once granted with respect to 7A, and likewise

7B, the same must be granted of each of the aspects into which each of them divides if they are related to each other, as clearly they must be. And so on in an infinite regress. Thus the very idea of 7 being related to other numbers is incoherent, since it requires an endless regress to be completed. For, unless they all hold, none of the terms will be in any relation to any other.

So far as this argument is effective at all it applies to the ideal relations between all qualities. Middle C has to be something in order to be related to the D above it, but it also owes its character to its place in the system of scales. A shade of colour has to be something in itself in order to be related to other colours, but also it can be thought of as owing its very nature to the way in which it is related to other colours.

But if the argument is to show that relations are unreal in general, it must apply to real relations as well as ideal ones. We must not allow Bradley's own failure to note this distinction to let him generalize what may only apply to relations of the first type. Thus even if one allows that the way in which one colour contrasts with another is both determined by and determines the character of each, which therefore divides into two aspects, the determining and the determined, it does not follow that there is any such regress in the offing when a relation like juxtaposition of the different colours on a surface or in a visual field is in question.

Perhaps Bradley would argue that the colours must each have their own distinct private natures if they are to be *capable* of being juxtaposed and a character which they owe to the fact that they *are* juxtaposed. It is not implausible to say that the things presented to experience in any sort of relation must have an initial private nature to be distinct terms, but that the way they are juxtaposed always reacts back on them and modifies that initial private nature. (If one objected that this is only a feature of experience, not of reality, Bradley could reply that we can form no grasp of a relationship which would be different in this respect from the sort of thing we know in our experience.)

What is true of the juxtaposition of colours on a surface or in a visual field is equally true of all perceived or imaginable real relations. (Doubtless much more argument, or at least explanation, is required for this phenomenological claim, but I am simply functioning as a sympathetic exponent here. I say more on this matter in section 7 of this chapter.) So a similar, if not identical, regress may be implicit in real relations as in ideal ones. The terms must both have their private natures which allow them to be terms in a relation, and have their resultant natures. The difference is that in the case of real relations, the private nature of each term is rather something required for the possibility of its standing in that relation, than what sets it in that relation. This is weaker than Bradley's statement but strong enough to serve his purposes. For it would allow him to draw a contrast between the quality considered as something capable of entering into the relation, and as something which has been modified by entering into that relation, and to claim that these must be related. And he could then argue that these two aspects of the quality must be related to each other and that that requires that each aspect has both an aspect which either allows or makes it to be appropriately related to the other and an aspect which follows from its being thus related.

Whether Bradley's argument is convincing or not, its general structure is clear enough. Qualities in relation must have two aspects, that which grounds (determines or makes possible) the relation and that which results from it, and the same must be true of these aspects in relation to each other and so on in an infinite series which requires completion if any quality is to be related to any other.

§ (3) Let us turn now to Bradley's third thesis, that relations *without* qualities are impossible and something of which we can make no sense. He says that 'a relation without terms seems mere verbiage'. His point is that you cannot imagine being merely confronted with a relation such as *on*, *loves*, or *cause* without any items between which it holds. Whereas one may, at least initially, think one could be confronted just with the quality *blue*, one cannot imagine being confronted just with the relation *on* or *to the right of* on its own.

That a relation could not occur as a feature somehow present in the existing world, without having terms, seems undeniable, and that is the main point Bradley needs to establish. It seems to me that he would not be right if he were denying that one can engage in thought about a relation as such, rather than as the relation holding between identified particular terms. Many, including Bradley himself, have addressed themselves to the nature of the causal relation without being especially interested in any particular case in which it is exemplified. And as a universal, belonging to the realm of universals, relations have their own independent identity. Or so at least it will be supposed by those who think in that way about universals at all.

Such qualifications, however, are of little importance in the present context. For the main point is that there cannot be an actually existing state of affairs, or bit of reality, which simply consists in the presence of a relation, without any terms which it relates.

§ (4) So let us turn to Bradley's fourth thesis.[35] This is that relations cannot exist *with* qualities. This is Bradley's most famous argument about relations and is often taken out of context as though it were all he had to say about them. He says:

> But how the relation can stand to the qualities is, on the other side, unintelligible. If it is nothing to the qualities, then they are not related at all; and, if so, as we saw, they have ceased to be qualities, and their relation is a nonentity. But if it is to be something to them, then clearly we now shall require a *new* connecting relation. For the relation hardly can be the mere adjective of one or both of its terms; or, at least, as such it seems indefensible. And, being something itself, if it does not itself bear a relation to the terms, in what intelligible way will it succeed in being anything to them? But here again we are hurried off into the eddy of a hopeless process, since we are forced to go on finding

---

35   See AR, p. 27. It is not given a separate number by Bradley.

new relations without end. The links are united by a link, and this bond of union is a link which also has two ends; and these require each a fresh link to connect them with the old. The problem is to find how the relation can stand to its qualities; and this problem is insoluble.

AR, pp. 27–28

The main point is this. For a relational situation to hold it is not enough merely that the terms and the relation exist. For a cat to be on the mat the existence of *cat, mat,* and *on* is not enough; the three have to be connected. But what connects them, thus making the difference between the three of them just existing and their being in a relational situation? The only answer seems to be that they are linked by a relation, or perhaps by two, one at each end of *on.* But then there is the problem: What links these relations to *on* at one end, and the *cat* or *mat* at the other? It seems that one must postulate fresh relations. And clearly the same question will arise once more as to how these relations are linked to the items so far specified. It follows that the very idea of relations relating qualities is incoherent. For the relations are merely certain further items in the world with no bearing on the qualities unless they are related to them somehow. However, the same applies to whatever relations are supposed thus to relate them and so on ad infinitum.

§ Two main objections have been made to Bradley's arguments, especially the fourth.

(1) It is often said that Bradley treats relations as though they were *things* which themselves stand in relation to their terms. But the job of relations is to relate their terms, not to stand in relation to them.[36]

In putting basically the same objection C. D. Broad says that Bradley is like someone who thinks you can never glue two things together.[37] Glue sticks things together without having itself to be glued to them. Similarly relations can relate things without being related to them.

Bradley has, in fact, implicitly replied to such a criticism somewhat as follows:

Certainly the problem raised in the demonstration of the fourth thesis arises from treating relations as things. But that is not what *Bradley* is doing; it is what is implied in the view of the world he is criticising, namely, that the world consists in qualities linked by something else called relations.

---

36   This is the line of thought of Cook Wilson, Richard Wollheim, Brand Blanshard and others. See Wilson, pp. 255, 692–95; Wollheim, p. 114; Blanshard in Manser and Stock, p. 215. Somewhat similar is the claim that Frege solved the problem by regarding relational expressions (along with one-place predicates and functional expressions) as inherently incomplete, standing for incomplete unsaturated entities. I cannot see that, applied to Bradley's argument, this really adds much to what Cook Wilson and the others have said about it. See Wollheim, p. 120, and Dummett, pp. 175, 255 et ff.

37   Broad, *Examination,* I, p. 85 .

If you are to avoid making relations into things, you should say something about what they are, and the only real alternatives are two.

(a) You may consider the relations part of the character of the terms taken singly, or (b) you may consider them part of the character of the terms taken as making up a whole together. But (a) leaves the qualities quite apart from each other, while (b) packs them so close together that you no longer have distinct qualities at all.[38] Relations are only treated as things by Bradley in the context of trying to find an alternative to these two views. He is trying to show that each of the available alternatives, of which taking relations as thing-like is only one, has insuperable problems.

Thus on view (a) ARB becomes something like 'A has quality R_1, B has quality R_2', while on view (b) it becomes something like 'AB has quality R'. Thus according to (a) 'A is father of B' becomes 'A is a father, B is a son' while according to (b) it becomes 'A+B is a paternity situation'. The problem in the first case is that A and B keep quite apart from, and have no real bearing on, each other, while on the second view they merge and are no longer distinct things between which there can be relations. But the only alternative is the impossible treatment of relations as thing-like.

---

38 Manser effectively takes the doctrine of internal relations as amounting to (b). See Manser, p. 129. And he rightly says that, thus taken, 'there is a sense in which the doctrine of internal relations can be seen as a denial of relations'. But when Bradley talks of a relation as internal, he is operating at the level of relational thought, not at the level at which relations disappear. I see Manser's account as pointing towards an interpretation of the internality of a relation as its being internally holistic in the sense I explain below. However, while Manser sympathizes with Bradley's doctrine of internal relations understood as concerning the unitary nature of the meaning of a judgement, which he associates with the first edition of PL, he regrets the view that this implies a unity in the world as a later metaphysical extravagance. See Manser, p. 133.

There is, indeed, an insufficiently discussed divide between philosophers like Kant, who think of thought as uniting an atomized world, and those like Bergson, who think of it as atomizing a unified world. Bradley's position is, rather, that advanced thought is a struggle to unify a world whose primitively felt unity was broken up by its own earlier analysis. I certainly find the idea that it is only thought and language which bring unity into the world a strange one, and Bradley's doctrine of relations is mainly an attempt to understand the unity of things. In this connection I agree with Manser that for Bradley internal relations are between particulars rather than concepts (Manser, p. 121) and therefore not necessarily *necessary de dicto*, but I doubt if he is right that no sort of *de re necessity* is claimed for them either, at least in what Manser thinks the more respectable purely logical first edition of PL. Manser's approach turns on trying to free Bradley's logical doctrines from any tarnish of what he thinks dubious metaphysics. But ES should be enough to show that Bradley was deeply metaphysical from the start. The effort to keep metaphysics out of PL arose partly from his then uncertainty on certain matters, partly out of a sense of what logic should be, but it was never a very successful, or perhaps in his own terms even desirable, effort.

§ (2) McTaggart (wearing the unfamiliar hat of a man of common sense) contended that Bradley confused vicious and benevolent regresses. He claims that we should distinguish between vicious and non-vicious regresses, and that here we do have a regress, but one which is not vicious. There is a vicious regress where you can't explain a fact without reference to a more basic fact, and that by a more basic, and so forth. A non-vicious regress arises where one fact implies another and that another and so forth, but the later ones result from, rather than explain, the earlier ones. The relational regress is of the second kind, according to McTaggart. If R relates A and B, it follows that R is in a certain relation to A and another to B, and that these new relations are in certain relations to the old relations and terms, and so forth. However, these resulting facts do not explain the earlier ones, but arise from them.[39]

McTaggart is right that Bradley ignores this distinction, which is relevant to the second thesis as well as to the fourth. However, I suspect that Bradley would reply as follows.

First, he would say that an infinite regress is absurd whether it is a presupposition or a consequence and that a fact which cannot hold without presupposing or entailing one is itself absurd. To be at all plausible Bradley would have to distinguish here between a potential and an actual infinite, and say that the relational fact presupposes an actual infinite—not merely a potential one such as the series of natural numbers (conceived as the permanent possibility of counting one more).

Second, he might say relational facts do not merely require an infinite regress but a completed infinite. He could argue this with some plausibility with the regress figuring in the fourth thesis, if not that in the second. Thus he could say that the connectedness of A, R, and B presupposes, and does not merely entail, a relation which links them, and so on in an infinite regress.

§ There is much more that has been said and can be said about Bradley's arguments. However, I shall not examine them further, nor attempt to adjudicate between Bradley and his critics at this level of semi-formal debate. For both his own position and the criticisms levelled at it purport to have a kind of formal validity which is in the nature of the case somewhat specious. If Bradley is saying that we cannot organize relational statements into a logical form which is satisfactory in the sense that we can perform the sorts of logical operations which we wish upon them and use them to describe situations encountered in ordinary life, then he would certainly be wrong (to an extent which is still more obvious now than it was then). But this is not his main or his best point. Rather, since he allows that ordinary thought and language have their own devices by which we avoid confronting what he believes to be their fundamental incoherence, the proper line for him to take is that his critics are merely seeking refuge in these devices. And whether this is true or not cannot really be decided by the

---

39   See McTaggart, I, pp. 88–89; also Wollheim, p. 116.

syntactic validity of the arguments used on either side, since these inevitably use the apparatus under attack.

So rather than enter further into detailed textual criticism I shall conclude this section by summing up what I think the main core of his more formal case, put in a less sophistical-seeming way, and in the next section indicate what I think is really forceful in it:

1. When two terms stand in a certain relation, we must either think of the relation as some kind of distinguishable component in the total state of affairs or in some other way in which it is not given the status of a separable component.

2. If you think of it as some kind of *separable component*, then you have the problem of how the two terms and the relation belong together at all. Certainly there must be more to the state of affairs than simply that the terms and the relation each exist. They must exist in an appropriate combination. But that must mean that the three of them are related in some way. And that calls for some further relation which links them. Thus you get the vicious regress.

3. You may try to escape this by denying that the relation is a *separable component*. But there seem to be only two ways in which you can interpret this.

(a) You may treat the relation as an element in the character of one of the terms. But that spawns various problems. For example, it seems to put the whole of the relation on the side of one of the terms, thus leaving the other term out in the cold. As a result it doesn't show how the terms are related. And it also splits the term in question into two—the term apart from the relation, and the term together with the relation. (That was what Bradley treated under his second head.)

(b) You may treat the relation as an inseparable element in the character of the two terms taken together as forming a single unit. But in that case it is unclear how the terms could have existed apart from that relation, since they and the relation form an inseparable unit together.

4. The trouble, then, about these two alternatives, (a) and (b), is that the first keeps the terms too far apart, while the second glues them together too fast. But if we revert to thinking of it as some kind of independent thing, it requires a relation to link it to the terms, and this yields a vicious regress.

5. Therefore, a relation is an impossibility either as some aspect of the nature of one or more of the terms in the relation, or as a thing in its own right.

6. So the whole way of thinking about the world, as distinct qualities in relation to each other, is incoherent and does not give us the reality of the world.

§ It may be objected that the whole trouble simply arises from refusing to acknowledge that relations form a distinct category from that of particulars and qualities. Thus (2) fails because it tries to treat a relation as a particular, and (3a) and (3b) fail because they try to treat it as a quality. But why expect them to fit into either mould?

To relate this objection formally to Bradley one would have to put it in terms of those views of his about particulars and qualities which we have already discussed. However, taking the objection at a rather impressionistic level, one might offer the following somewhat impressionistic reply on his behalf. In the case of particulars and qualities one does in a sense know 'where' they are supposed to be—the particulars are supposed to be in space and time, and the qualities are supposed to be somehow in the particulars. But with relations any attempt to say 'where' they are effectively forces you back on one of these three alternatives.

§6. *The Real Upshot of Bradley's Argument about Relations*

The upshot of Bradley's investigation of relations is this:

The universe is certainly somehow a variegated whole. As infants we experience it as such but do not really think about it. As we grow up we try to think about this whole, and do so by conceiving of it as independent things or qualities in relation. But this way of thinking is incoherent. For it tries to do justice both to the unity and the variety of the world, yet these two aspects of the world pull apart. Relational thinking is a practically necessary but incoherent and unstable compromise between dealing with things piecemeal and as a whole. 'Everywhere in the end a relation appears as a necessary but a self-contradictory translation of a non-relational or super-relational unity.'[40]

So, for Bradley, the real truth of things is that there are not a whole lot of independent entities in the world. There is really just the universe as a whole, but to get any intellectual or practical grip on it, we have to divide it up into distinct things. However, having thus split it up we have no satisfactory way of putting it together again in our thoughts. We can vaguely sense the possibility of a higher form of consciousness in which the world is again experienced as a unity, but in a way which retains the intellectual advances which take us beyond infancy. Bradley sometimes suggests that art gives us an experience approximating to this, but on the whole his view is that though this is how the universe experiences itself, it cannot be our way of dealing with it.

All in all, it seems to me that Bradley's elaborate arguments about relations are not needed in order to support the really important claim he has to make, and that their sophistical air actually detracts from its defence. Indeed it can be put, as I argued in Part Two, Chapter One, without even describing relations as unreal, as follows:

(1) Things cannot be in relation to each other without belonging to a whole at least as concrete as themselves which they help make up. (Bradley doubtless thinks it must be more concrete, but the essential argument for the Absolute requires only the lesser claim.)

(2) Things cannot belong to a whole together without this being reflected in their individual characters.

---

40   ETR, p. 309, note.

(3) The usual wholes to which things are conceived of as belonging in order to be related are space and time. But the real units of existence, experiences, aren't in space and time. Rather, these are in them.[41]

(4) The only whole to which the world as experienced by different people can be conceived of as belonging is a cosmic consciousness which feels the world through each of us separately and then unifies these experiences in one universal experience.

The real power of Bradley's position lies in these four claims which to me seem irresistible.

§7. *Russell, Bradley, and the Monistic Theory of Relations*

§ I remarked above that much of Bradley's discussion of relations seems like an argument set up in advance against the logical atomism which Bertrand Russell was soon to develop.[42] The general opinion is probably still today that Russell was the sounder thinker on these matters, though there is more respect now for Bradley's point of view than there was some twenty or thirty years ago. I do not think either of these great thinkers ever adequately understood the other. Bradley never really got on top of Russell's emerging philosophy and his criticisms often rest on misunderstanding. But Russell, though superficially he may have had a better grasp of Bradley's thought than vice versa, seems not to have understood the more important aspects of Bradley's claims.

For all that, our understanding of what Bradley did and did not hold can be advanced a good deal by examining Russell's criticisms. Moreover, these criticisms form the background of many still-prevailing views, many of them mistaken, about Bradley's positions and arguments. For just as the criticisms of Moore and Russell paved the way for the light dismissal of James's pragmatism by later thinkers, so did Russell's (and to a lesser extent Moore's) criticism of

---

41   See, for example, PL, pp. 606 and 607. Since my interest is mainly in Bradley's account of reality on its more concrete side, rather than his treatment of such things as numbers, I have concentrated on the implications of his view of relations between existents rather than abstractions. However, it is in the same essential spirit that he holds that the relation of one natural number to another 'is the degraded form in which their ideal continuity is manifest' a continuity only possible 'within the integral whole in which they subsist' (PL, p. 465). Sometimes he speaks as though this integral whole were some vast number of which all other numbers are fractions. Thus, at PL, p. 493, he speaks of 'the one ideal integer in which any given numbers exist as fractions'. Elsewhere, at PL, p. 604, he speaks more helpfully of 'a whole which is the actual complete arrangement of all possible units and integers, so that, in and by this, their identities and differences are visible and grounded'.

42   This and the next section include material previously used in my 'Russell and Bradley on Relations' in Roberts.

Bradley's views on relations set the tone for usual assumptions about this. In truth, the really profound criticism of Bradley came rather from James, but some examination of Russell's criticisms will help clarify some aspects of Bradley's position.

§ According to Russell, incorrect theories about relations had, until his time, impeded the development both of logic and philosophy. The refusal to accept propositions which assert a relation between two or more particulars as having their own distinctive form, no less basic than, and not reducible to, the form of those propositions which ascribe a predicate to a subject, prevented logic from advancing much beyond the Aristotelian stage, and formed the basis of far-fetched metaphysical theories, either of a monadistic kind (in the case of Leibniz) or of a monistic kind (in the case of Bradley).

In *The Principles of Mathematics* and elsewhere Russell cleared the ground for his own treatment of relations by a quite detailed attack upon the two theories of relations which, it seemed to him, had tended to hold the field. On the one hand is the monadistic theory which he attributes to Leibniz, and, with quali-fications, to Lotze, and on the other the monistic view which he associates with Bradley and Spinoza. Our concern is with Russell's discussion of the latter. This is developed in certain sections of *The Principles* and also in the 1906 essay 'On the Nature of Truth'.[43]

In chapter XXVI of *The Principles* Russell tells us that both the monadistic and the monistic view of relations try to reduce relational propositions to ones of subject-predicate form (meaning such as ascribe a predicate to a single subject—for there is a sense in which for Russell himself 'aRb' is a subject-predicate proposition, though one with two subjects).

> Given, say, the proposition *aRb*, where *R* is some relation, the monadistic view will analyse this into two propositions, which we may call ar_1 and br_2, which give to *a* and *b* respectively adjectives supposed to be together equivalent to R. The monistic view, on the contrary, regards the relation as a property of the whole composed of *a* and *b* and as thus equivalent to a proposition which we may denote by *(ab)r*.
>
> *The Principles of Mathematics*, p. 221

This passage comes in a chapter on 'Asymmetrical Relations' and introduces an attempt to demonstrate that neither theory can deal with the logic of these. Leaving aside the discussion of the monadistic theory (in which, I think, Russell largely right) let us turn to what he has to say about the monistic theory which he associates with Bradley. We will turn to the question how far Bradley actually held this monistic view of relations shortly. The brief answer is that he did sometimes seem to advocate it in PL and that his later views remain quite close to it, but that, at least by the time of AR, he did not think it an adequate

---

43   This was first published in PAS in 1906–7; the first two, and most relevant, of its sections are republished as essay VI in Russell, *Essays*.

account of ordinary relational propositions, holding rather, as we have seen, that ordinary relational thought hovered between incompatible elements, including both monistic, monadistic, and other elements closer to those stressed by Russell.

§Russell's first argument rests upon the supposed incapacity of the monistic view to deal with the difference between 'aRb' and 'bRa', where R is an asymmetrical (or, one may add, a non-symmetrical) relation. If 'aRb' ascribes to the whole (ab) a certain predicate which takes the place of R, then 'bRa' will do so likewise, for evidently the whole (ab) is not to be distinguished from the whole (ba), since we are simply speaking of that total object they jointly compose. Thus there will be no difference between 'a is greater than b' and 'b is greater than a', for both will mean simply something like '(ab) contains diversity of magnitude'.

That there is a fairly obvious line of reply on the part of the monist has, I suggest, not struck people because they have tended to think in terms of a proposition 'aRb' where 'a' and 'b' function roughly as what Russell was later to call logically proper names. It is thus overlooked that the material a sensible monist would transform into a predicate applicable to the whole comprises not simply the relation but also the meaning, connotation, or sense of the expressions denoting the terms of the relation.

The monist must interpret the proposition 'This cup is above that saucer' as a characterisation of a certain total situation comprising the cup and the saucer. Now certainly if he took it as the predication of mere *aboveness* of that situation, then indeed he could not distinguish its significance from that of 'That saucer is above that cup'. It is evident, however, that he would take it as the application to a sensibly presented totality of the predicate *being (the totality of) a cup on top of a saucer*, which is a quite different *gestalt* quality from that of *being (the totality of) a saucer on top of a cup*.

The view we are attributing to the monist is close to that advanced in PL, chapter I. Consider, for instance the following:

> We saw that all judgement is the attribution of an ideal content to reality, and so this reality is the subject of which the content is predicated. Thus in "A precedes B," the whole relation A-B is the predicate, and, in saying this is true, we treat it as an adjective of the real world.
>
> PL, p. 28

It is evident that by 'the relation A-B' Bradley means the whole relational situation of A preceding B, not the mere relation of precedence which happens to hold between A and B.

There are two objections to this reply on behalf of the monist which Russell, or one following in his footsteps, might raise.

It might be urged, first, that 'This cup is on top of that saucer', is equivalent to the conjunction of three independent propositions, 'This is a cup', 'That is a saucer', and 'This is on top of that'. Assuming that to be so, let us concentrate attention on the third proposition. Here it does seem that the monist will have difficulty in distinguishing it from the different one 'That is on top of this'. Evidently he could no longer employ a predicate including the notions of cup and saucer. If he made use of any other concepts supposed to be connoted, in this context, by 'This' and 'that', a similar reduction to that applied to 'This cup is on that saucer' would produce three independent propositions of which the third, which we may represent as 'a is above b' would imply nothing whatever as to any difference in character between what is above and what is below.

However, the monist could repel this line of attack by denying that the original proposition can be broken up in this way to yield two propositions ascribing predicates to single subjects and a relational proposition of the form 'aRb' which implies nothing regarding any difference in character between the terms other than that the sense of the relation runs from the one to the other. The Russellian objection to the monistic theory of relations was that the monist can make no distinction between 'aRb' and 'bRa' whereas, in the case of asymmetrical and nonsymmetrical relations, there obviously is a difference. But the monist may insist that 'a' and 'b' must have some distinct sense resting upon some observable or discoverable difference in character between a and b, if there is to be any real difference between its being a which is on top rather than b. To characterise a bit of the world as a cat on a mat, or my cat on my mat, is to ascribe to it a different character from that of a situation which would answer to the description mat on a cat, or my mat on my cat. Maybe the Russellian will insist that a and b may be indistinguishable in character and yet there still be a real difference between a being R to b, and vice versa. If there are two particles, one to the left of the other, the situation is different from that which would have held if their positions had been reversed, even if the particles are absolutely identical in character.

If this is what the Russellian claims, as against the monist, it can hardly be said that the onus probandi lies with the monist to prove him wrong. It is hard to see what observable or discoverable difference there could be between the situations described, for example, by 'a is above b' and 'b is above a', if we suppose no observable or discoverable difference between a and b other than that the one is above and the other below. Moreover, it is of the essence of monism to deny that there can be logically proper names or what, at the time of The Principles of Mathematics, Russell spoke of as names 'which indicate without meaning'.[44]

It is true that if one considers the background history of an observed relational situation, then even if the terms be indistinguishable within the present, one can attach sense to the relation holding the other way round, provided that this implies an observably or imaginably different historical route to the present situation. Finding one particle to the left of another, one can imagine historical routes to that situation which distinguish between the histories pertaining to the particle in each position. But the monist, rather than

44   See Russell, *Principles*, p. 502.

distinguish between its being one rather than the other of two particulars identical in character which occupies a certain position, might distinguish between two alternative spatio-temporal patterns which might have applied to the situation taken as a whole over a certain length of time, which are indistinguishable in their implications for the final state which was all that was actually observed.

§ A Russellian might concede some of this but still argue somewhat subtly along the following lines. Granted, he might say, that if we treat 'This cup is above that saucer' as ascribing to the presented reality the *gestalt* quality of being a cup on top of a saucer, we do indeed distinguish it from 'That saucer is above this cup'; all the same we still do not do justice to the original proposition. For we leave unexpressed the fact that it is this object here which is the cup on top and that object there which is the saucer below.

The point insisted on here is that there are two distinct particulars to which we may attend and note as playing their distinctive role in the total relational situation, and that any suggestion that we only attend to the whole and characterise that misses this point. If one were impressed by this point, but also felt the force of the monistic contention that to observe that certain terms are in a certain relation is to perceive them as constituting a certain sort of totality with its own quality, one might seek to develop a compromise position for which the relational proposition does indeed ascribe a special sort of predicate to the whole, but also indicates the role which each term plays in producing a whole of this character.[45] Yet even this supposition may concede too much to the Russellian. Having noticed that there is a cup and a saucer before me, is there really anything additional to be noted which can be described as its being *this* particular which is the cup on top, and *that* which is the saucer below? If there is not, we cannot object on this ground to the equation of 'This cup is on that saucer' with 'This totality is a cup on a saucer'.

A Russellian might, however, develop his objection to this equation by pointing out that the former contains distinctive references to each of the two particulars which can be taken up by further questioning, as the latter does not. Thus the former may lead me on to the question 'Is it, the cup I mean, chipped?' as the latter evidently could not.

But this is not really true. Whenever a predicate is applied to a subject, one may go on to ask that the description be made more precise in certain respects by the provision of further more determinate predicates. Just as 'scarlet' is more determinate than 'red' so is 'being a chipped cup on a saucer' more determinate than 'being a cup on a saucer', and one could press the line of enquiry supposed to be difficult on the monistic analysis by asking whether the former predicate also applied to the totality in question.

---

45 I developed such a position in Sprigge, *Facts*, pp. 68–70. Apparently James Mill had much the same idea though I cannot now find the reference to it somewhere in his son's work.

§ So far as I can see, then, Russell's claim that the monistic view cannot deal with asymmetrical relations is ill-founded, or, at least, begs the question.

I suppose an objector might say that I have defended the monistic view by reducing it to vacuousness. Of course, he may say, if you introduce not only the relation into the predicate, but also the terms related, you can make the relational proposition ascribe a single, if complex, predicate to a certain totality (perhaps ending up with Reality as a whole as the sole subject), but one can hardly maintain that the possibility of such minor verbal reshuffling shows anything about the logical structure of the proposition.

If there were anything in this, it would follow, not that Russell is right and that the monist is wrong, but that the point at issue between them is an essentially empty one. But the enormous metaphysical implications of the two treatments of relational propositions are enough to show that this can hardly be so. What seems clear, in any case, is that the monistic account of relations is not vulnerable to the charge that it cannot deal with the asymmetry and nonsymmetry of many relations. It only requires that the single predicate which incorporates the terms of the relation must have a meaning which does some justice to the character of the terms related. It was, after all, an essential part of Bradley's view that all ordinary terms of discourse belong logically to the predicate of the judgements in which they occur (a view not without its influence on Russell's theory of descriptions). I do not say that the monistic theory of relations is altogether satisfactory; indeed for Bradley himself it would not do justice to the meaning of ordinary relational thought. But it does not seem vulnerable to this criticism as it stands.

§ So far we have discussed a relational proposition which concerns presented objects indicated by demonstratives. This brought us to fundamentals, since the real question at issue is as to what one becomes aware of, when one perceives that terms stand in a certain relation. However, the same essential points would arise if one considered 'Brutus killed Caesar' (to take the usual heroes of these philosophical debates). On the monistic view this would assert that a certain total historical event had a certain characteristic, that of being Caesar's death at the hands of Brutus. Provided we do not seek to deny connotation to 'Brutus' and 'Caesar' the objection from asymmetrical relations fails in this case too, for there is no reason to identify this character with that of being Brutus's death at the hands of Caesar.

§ In *The Principles of Mathematics* Russell follows up the argument against the monistic view of relations from asymmetrical relations with another concerned with the relation of whole and part. He asks how the monist is to deal with 'a is a part of b' which, if the monistic theory is correct, asserts 'something of the whole composed of a and b, which is not to be confounded with b'.[46] This leads to difficulties. Either the proposition about the new whole is not a proposition concerning whole and part or it is. If the former, we have eliminated the class

---

46   Russell, *Principles*, p. 225.

of propositions about whole and part, and have thereby eliminated the very category of wholes, yet if there are not wholes the monistic theory breaks down. If the latter, we start on an infinite regress of a vicious kind in which each whole and part proposition presupposes the truth of another. Russell then considers the possibility that the monist might hold, after all, that the whole which becomes the subject of the analysans in the monistic analysis of 'a is a part of b' is b itself. But this he regards as incompatible with the monistic denial that the whole is the sum of its parts, and urges that in any case the problem of asymmetry remains. The last point seems a rather weak reversion to the argument from asymmetrical relations.[47]

The monist, I suggest, might reply by proposing two types of analysis for judgements concerning whole and part where these concern things which are perceptible or sensible. First, he might treat 'a is part of b' as really a statement to the effect that a is joined in a certain way to the rest of b. Call the rest of b (i.e. b minus a) 'X'. Then the terms of the relation are not strictly a and b, but a and X. In that case there is no special problem. The relational fact about a and X concerns simply the character of the whole b, in the usual way. On this view, to notice that a tentacle is part of an octopus is to notice that it is joined up in a certain way to an octopus body and seven other tentacles. To notice this relation is to become aware of the character of a certain whole which includes both the terms.

The other, and more formally correct, way of looking at it which the monist might adopt would treat it as asserting a relation not between the so-called part and the rest of the whole, but between the part and the whole itself. In that case the monist must indeed treat the relation of part-whole as a rather special sort of relation, requiring a slightly different analysis from other relations. He will then say that the judgement 'a is a part of b' ascribes to b a certain property which can be expressed as that of containing something of the sort specified by the expression 'a'.

It may be objected that this simply makes use of the relational expression 'containing' and does not explain it. That is perhaps true but it is not really an objection to the theory. For the monist precisely does regard the property of having a certain sort of part as more intelligible than relations are until they are

---

47   It is hardly possible to discuss this alleged incompatibility without going more deeply into rival theories as to the relations of whole and part than space permits. In fact, I believe that some quite various sort of proposition or judgement might be expressed by sentences which say that one thing is part of another. (The distinctions I have in mind are not those made by Russell in Chapter XVI of *The Principles of Mathematics*. It is, indeed, only in his account of his first sense of 'whole' in section 135 that he comes anywhere near talking of whole and part, and this very unsatisfactorily, in the quite simple sense in which my arm is part of my body. This is the sense we should initially have in mind when considering the monistic analysis. Of course, that chapter represents a very early stage of Russell's thought on these topics.) I have discussed the relation of whole and part in connection with a monistic approach to relations in Sprigge, *Vindication*, chapter V.

explained by reference to it. The peculiarity of a judgement predicating the part-whole relation is, then, not that it poses some special problem for the monist but that its form is already a variant of that to which he reduces all relational judgements.

Moreover, the monist may claim even to have cast some light on the nature of statements about the holding of a part-whole relation. For he may claim to have shown that they are not different in essentials from any statement describing a reality by ascribing a property to it. Certainly such a statement as 'This is a triangle' or 'This suit is pin-striped' describe something as a pattern of certain parts. And the monist might claim that the same is true of statements ascribing any sort of quality to something; they say something of the parts which help make it up, and indicate, where necessary, something of the way in which they do so. To say that a tie is spotted or a man bearded is to say something of how they are made up of certain parts. Similarly the statement that a cushion is red picks out a feature which belongs to it in very much the same basic sense as a part does and suggests how it contributes to the totality. In general, to say that something is formed in a certain way of certain parts (or that a certain part makes a particular contribution to its formation) and to say something about what it inherently is can be regarded as the same thing. And it is this basic sort of proposition, ascribing a variegated character to something, which is the monist's clue to the nature of all relational judgements.

But the Russellian may object that it is one thing to say that something is made up in a certain way of parts of a certain sort, and another to say that it contains these very particulars as parts. And this is, indeed, the most serious objection to the monistic analysis as Russell takes it, for such an analysis does seem to eliminate genuine reference to the particulars which we start out with as terms of the relation. Well, if it is to support a monistic theory of reality the monistic theory of relations clearly is bound to downplay the ultimate reality of particulars. We shall be seeing that Bradley himself would agree that it is therefore inadequate as an analysis of ordinary relational thinking. But what is not true is that the part-whole relation itself poses a peculiarly difficult problem for it.

§ It is time to consider the differences between what Russell calls the monistic view of relations and Bradley's actual view.

We have seen that Bradley holds that relational propositions are incoherent because they bid us look at the terms of the relation in two different and incompatible ways. On the one hand, a relational proposition about certain terms bids us think of them as distinct things the nature of which can be grasped independently of each other. On the other hand, it invites us to become aware of a whole which they form together; but this is a whole in becoming aware of which we cease to see the terms as distinct items. Rather do they fall away to be replaced by a variegated character possessed by the whole, a character which precludes us seeing them as distinct things in their own right.

Thus for Bradley relational thinking arises when we try to explain to ourselves how items which we attend to as though they were distinct items in their own right belong together in the same world. In reality they belong together because they are not distinct items in their own right but mere aspects of a greater totality (ultimately of the world as a whole but on the way to this of totalities themselves really abstractions from the whole world) or of the character of a greater totality—for Bradley there is really no distinction between these two—but to recognize this is to give up thinking of them as distinct items in their own right, and this, with our limited grasp of the true wholeness of things, we cannot do. Thus we fabricate the notion of relations binding distinct items together, a notion which cannot be thought through with consistency but which serves as a device to allow us to oscillate between thinking of them as items in their own right and recognizing something of the character of the totality from which they are really mere abstractions.

§ Where Bradley differs most essentially from an atomist such as Russell is in this. For Russell one could identify an individual of some kind A and learn all one could about it as a thing in its own right, then go on to do the same thing with an individual B, and then as a third enterprise study the relations between A and B. This third study would add to one's stock of truth, so that one could formulate lots of truths of the form 'A is R to B', but it would not require abandonment or modification of what one had learnt about A and B in one's original two enquiries.

Bradley would allow that there could be two distinct enquiries centering on each of A and B respectively such as aimed to characterise them in a fair degree of detachment from any larger context (though doubtless he could hardly take seriously the idea that they could be studied in complete isolation). What he would add, however, is that when one studied them in relation, as we must put it, to one another, one would really be studying a whole, call it W, in which they were both included, and that the concept of them which one would then acquire would be incompatible with the concepts of them one acquired in the original separate investigations of each. That is, the study of them together would not merely add new ideas to the old ones, but would require radical modification of the old ones.

If we represent the results of the first two enquiries as FA and GB respectively, then the results of the third enquiry, call it HW, will for Bradley be incompatible with FA and GB, as ARB was not for Russell. However, Bradley acknowledged that we will still frequently need to think of A and B as though FA and GB were true, and this is where relations come in. A proposition of the form ARB represents an attempt to combine the ideas expressed by FA and GB with the incompatible idea expressed by HW, or at least expresses our readiness to oscillate between the two ideas according to convenience. In general there is more truth at the level of HW, but much of the time such truth is too rich and total for practical purposes.

Suppose one made a separate study of each member of the Brontë family, and tried in each case to sum up the very essence of each personality. One might write essays on each one ending 'Such was Emily Brontë', 'Such was Charlotte Brontë', and so on. Subsequently one might study the family as a whole and conclude 'Such was the Brontë family'. Of course, the studies could not really be independent of one another (a point which supports Bradley) but the total impression of Charlotte Brontë given in the one study and in the other would be different. The final study might lead to a vision which (grammar apart) is non-relational, for which the family is a unity from which Charlotte, considered as an individual in her own right, is a mere abstraction, so that all characterisations of her which do not present her behaviour as an aspect of the family's development are distortions. Talking of the relation between Emily and Charlotte is keeping oneself ready to oscillate between these two incompatible viewpoints. They are incompatible because any conception we form of her in relative isolation is falsified, rather than merely supplemented, by correct conceptions we form of wholes to which she belongs.

Another point to bear in mind is that it is not just a matter of seeing some individual, such as Charlotte Brontë, *either* as an individual in her own right *or* as a mere aspect of some larger whole. For she belongs to many different such wholes, and to see her as an abstraction from one is incompatible with seeing her as an abstraction from another. Each of these conceptions of her contains some distortion which could only be finally corrected if we could grasp that ultimate truth which would display her as an abstraction from the one great whole which includes all things. Thus the point of relational thinking is not merely to oscillate between seeing certain items as things in their own right and as mere abstractions from a larger whole. It also allows us to oscillate between the incompatible conceptions of a thing produced by change in the wholes to which we see it as belonging.

§ Cases of social relationship bring out one sort of contrast between Russell and Bradley. But they also clash over the role of relations as they figure in the immediacies of sense experience. Bradley holds, I take it, that to see (for example) an object as an element in a larger perceived totality is to see it as having a character incompatible with that which it has when seen rather as an item on its own, or at least against an only vaguely presented background. The seen character of the cup as element in the unity *cup-and-saucer* is different from that which it has as *this cup*. The relational judgement 'The cup is on the saucer' allows us to retain both visions of the cup as valid, though in fact they annul each other.

§ We have seen that it is no objection to Bradley's claim, as illustrated in these two sorts of example, that the incompatibility between thinking of a thing as an item in its own right and thinking of it as an element in some larger whole cannot be brought out in any ordinary formal logic. For, on his view, this logic is simply the instrument of that discursive relational thought the whole point of which is to disguise it.

It is useful to consider in this connection some views of Bradley's about the meaning of 'and'.[48] For formal logic it is basic that 'A is F and G' is compatible with, indeed entails, 'A is F'. Any hint of a denial of this will seem a mere whimsical confusion of 'A is F' with 'A is merely F'. But for Bradley, if you think

---

48   See ETR, pp. 226–33, including footnotes, especially on p. 231. Cf. James, PU, p. 60.

about A as being F and characterise it in no other way to yourself, you cannot help thinking of it as having a kind of F-ness, different from the F-ness which is merely an element in a richer characteristic which includes G as well. Nor can 'F and G' really be regarded as an adequate representation of such a richer characteristic. Properties cannot be merely conjoined; they must belong together in some distinctive way, and nothing much is conveyed by 'A is F and G' unless some particular mode of being together is implicitly taken as intended.

§ The basic contrast between Bradley's position and that which Russell calls the monist view of relations may be illustrated by a simple example. Suppose we have straight lines, A, B, and C, bound by the three-term relation, call it R, which makes them constitute a triangle. Then Russell's monist identifies the meaning of 'R(ABC)' with 'X is a triangle' (or, perhaps, more strictly, the boundary of a triangle) where X is the relevant totality. Such an example puts the monistic view in a not unfavourable light, but it is not quite Bradley's view. For Bradley 'R(ABC)' would represent a compromise between the state of mind for which what there really is is the triangle X, an individual which certainly is complex but which is not made up of distinct bits (such as could be characterised other than as just the elements which they are in that whole) and that in which we concentrate attention successively on each of A, B, and C and note that they are straight lines. They really only belong visually together so long as they are seen as mere aspects of the triangle, but when we regard them as three straight lines, in relation to one another, we reserve our right to annul the triangle from our consciousness as convenient and see each of them successively as a merely isolated straight line, without the admission that this line has a quality incompatible with that of the line which belongs to the triangle.

For the sake of accuracy I should note here, however, that, somewhat disconcertingly, Bradley holds that relations are essentially two-term.[49] It is not very clear why, but he evidently thought that an awareness of patterns, where more than two terms are being taken special note of, cannot be called a relational awareness.[50] But I cannot find that he makes any important use of this point (except as a rather confused ground for rejecting Russell's view of judgement) and in fact it seems to consort better with his outlook, and even with what he says in these very passages, to contrast relational thinking which employs relations with three or more terms with a proper grasp of the whole the terms form, just as in the case of two-term relations. Moreover, he often himself virtually thinks in terms of three-term relations. Thus his insistence that inference does not have to proceed by relating major and minor term separately to the middle term, and may involve any number of terms synthesised in one constructive act, strongly suggests the notion of multiple relations.[51]

§ Many, of course, will see obscurity or confusion in the claim that there is

---

49   See ETR, p. 306, and CE, essay II, p. 674.
50   See ETR, pp. 306–9.
51   See, for example, PL, pp. 259–60. See also PL, pp. 395–96.

an incompatibility between the character something displays when envisaged as an element in a larger whole and that which it displays when envisaged as an individual in its own right. But granted that, for the reason given, it is not one which ordinary logic can register, it seems to me that Bradley and James are right that the qualities which things exhibit when seen in isolation are incompatible with the qualities they present as elements in larger totalities.[52] There is, of course, sufficient affinity between certain of the qualities exhibited in each case to justify using the same term for them, but there is no genuinely determinate feature which is one and the same in each case.

§ Some who might go along with this as a phenomenological insight might object that it has no bearings on the nature of reality at large.[53] For how can a phenomenological fact about the qualities immediately exhibited to our senses have such vast metaphysical implications as a metaphysical monist like Bradley tries to draw from them? It is most doubtful, after all, that the distinctively visual qualities and forms which alter in character when they play a role in larger *Gestalten* are at all akin to the properties of physical things as they really are in their own independent being. So even if our representations of individual things take on a fresh quality when they come to figure as elements in the representations of larger wholes, it does not follow that the real physical properties of individual things are affected in any corresponding fashion by the larger physical wholes to which they belong.

However, if we cannot *imagine* any whole which does not so permeate its elements that they could not be identically the same within their own bounds outside that whole, the burden of proof seems to be on those who say that there can be components in wholes which remain the same in quite different contexts and do not exhibit something of the nature of the wholes to which they belong within their own bounds. And certainly for panexperientialists like Bradley and James, the phenomenological fact that every imaginable case where an element belongs to an experiential whole is modified thereby within its own bounds must strongly suggest that this is true of the world at large. (This purely metaphysical insight gains additional support, I might remark in passing, by aspects of modern physics.)

If this is so in general it must be true of the way in which finite centres of experience belong together within the Absolute. The character of the Absolute as a whole must so permeate each of these that its character is that of something which could not exist except as just that component therein which it is. This is certainly Bradley's position. However, it does pose the difficult problem how far the character each centre seems to have to itself as it occurs is its true character. It seems to betray the whole notion of a finite centre of experience to suggest that it is not, but it may seem difficult to believe that it provides the

---

52   Compare also Husserl, *Logical Investigations,* p. 699.
53   For example, Santayana. See Santayana, *Essence,* chapter V, and Sprigge, *Santayana,* chapter IV, §4, and chapters VII and VIII.

clue to the character of the Absolute, that is of the Universe in its true being, as a whole.

The difficulty turns largely on the sense in which so-called parts of a greater whole are, for Bradley, merely abstractions from that whole. One has to be careful about the word 'abstraction' here. It tends to suggest that it is *we* who have produced the abstraction by somehow ourselves treating it in isolation from a totality within which it was originally presented to us. Bradley, I believe, should have made it clearer that this is only one case, and that often the relevant wholes to which something belongs are quite beyond our initial experience of it. In that case, though the character of the whole may truly permeate that of the part, the way in which this is so may not be graspable by a mind without independent access to the character of the whole. We shall be considering this point more fully later.[54]

§8. *Russell, Bradley, and the Axiom of Internal Relations*

§ I now turn to another important aspect of Russell's critique of Bradley's views on relations. This occurs mainly in an essay called 'On the Nature of Truth' first published in 1906 or 1907.[55] Here Russell presents a critique of the monistic view of truth developed by H. H. Joachim in his *The Nature of Truth* and of the axiom of internal relations which Russell regards as its chief logical basis. Since Joachim's point of view is closely related to that of Bradley, and Bradley is referred to and quoted by Russell as a supporter of this axiom, we can take it that he is under attack here too.

By the *axiom of internal relations* Russell means the doctrine that '[e]very relation is grounded in the natures of the related terms'.

---

54 See pp. 423–24, and note 61.

55 PAS (1906/7), first two sections in Russell, *Essays*, chapter VI. Russell and Moore did more to lead British philosophy away from Bradley than did anyone else, Moore particularly by his 'External and Internal Relations', cited at note 28 above, which traces the doctrine of internal relations to a confusion between the fact that, necessarily, if a is R to b, then whatever is not so, is, in fact, other than a, with the supposition that if a is R to b, then whatever is not so, is necessarily other than a. Increased clarity on points like this certainly helped introduce more exact styles of reasoning but so far as real relevance to Bradley's position goes Moore's treatment is even wider of the mark than Russell's. All in all, the oft-repeated statement that the new logical techniques of Russell (available to Moore) and Frege put paid to the arguments of the idealists is doubtless correct as a report on how things appeared to their generation but came to be an article of faith rather than an informed assessment of their achievement. See, for example, Thayer, p. 63. It is to James, rather than Russell, let alone Moore, that we must look for a serious critique of Bradley.

It follows at once from this axiom that the whole of reality or of truth must be a significant whole in Mr Joachim's sense. For each part will have a nature which exhibits its relations to every other part and to the whole; hence, if the nature of any one part were completely known, the nature of the whole and of every other part would also be completely known; while conversely, if the nature of the whole were completely known, that would involve knowledge of its relations to each part, and therefore of the relations of each part to each other part, and therefore of the nature of each part.

PAS (1906/7), p. 37; Russell, *Essays*, p. 140

Russell also points out that the converse holds, and that the monistic theory of truth implies the axiom. He then goes on to ask what the grounds are on which the axiom is asserted, and says:

There is first the law of sufficient reason, according to which nothing can be just a brute fact, but must have some reason for being thus and not otherwise.

PAS (1906/07); Russell, *Essays*, pp. 142–43

He quotes Bradley here:

If the terms from their own inner nature do not enter into the relation, then, so far as they are concerned, they seem related for no reason at all, and, so far as they are concerned, the relation seems arbitrarily made.

AR, p. 514[56]

Actually Russell does not consider this grounding of the axiom at much length, since he thinks that 'the law of sufficient reason should mean that every proposition can be deduced from simpler propositions' which consorts ill with the monist's contempt for simplicity. However, Russell is surely right that the law of sufficient reason does loom somewhat vaguely behind those of Bradley's and Joachim's assertions which sound most like the axiom, as in the passage quoted.

Bradley, indeed, goes out of his way to deny that his approach is in any sense axiomatic.[57] It is rather that certain ideas when examined without any formal principles of criticism simply develop themselves in certain ways. But we can still ask whether he actually held the so-called axiom to be a true proposition and, if so, how important a part it plays in his account of relations and the inference therefrom to his monism.

What exactly does the 'axiom' say? Clearly its interpretation turns in great part on the interpretation of 'nature'. If absolutely every truth about a thing counts as a part of its nature, then the axiom is a triviality which no one would deny. We get a more significant proposition if we equate a thing's nature with

56   This is Russell's very slightly misquoted version.
57   See ETR, p. 331.

its inherent character. By this I mean the full character of what it is, so to speak, within its own boundaries. In this sense the nature of the thing excludes what could only be said about it on the basis of an examination of what lies beyond it and includes every feature discoverable within the thing itself such as could be revealed to an awareness of it which did not draw on knowledge of what lies beyond its boundaries. So far as physical things go, their boundaries can be thought of in an essentially spatial way. In the case of non-physical things the notion of boundary becomes somewhat metaphorical. Yet it still seems possible to think in terms of a contrast between as much of reality as constitutes the thing itself, and such reality as is not part of its own being. So by a thing's nature, in this sense, is meant the character it actualises strictly within that part of reality which constitutes it, while by its internal relations to other things will be meant all those the holding of which are somehow grounded in this character. With 'nature' thus understood, the axiom of internal relations says that a thing's relations to things beyond it are somehow grounded in what it is within its own boundaries. If it is true thus taken, it seems to follow that, from separate propositions describing the nature of two things, one could deduce every true proposition as to how they are and are not related to one another. (Such deduction need not be a formal one but the conclusion would have to follow from the premises with the same kind of, in principle transparent, necessity.)

§ Whether the axiom thus taken is true or not, there certainly seem to be some relations which are internal in this sense, namely, those which are merely ideal. (I shall explain the full significance of the 'merely' later.) That there are some relations which are internal in the sense that they conform to the axiom thus taken seems clear. If one patch is brighter in colour than another, that follows from two true propositions each asserting of one of the patches that it is of a certain shade, and these two propositions, taken singly, say nothing of the patch's relation to anything outside its boundaries. The same is true of certain geometrical relations between figures of two different sorts.

§ However, there is still a certain ambiguity in the notion of an internal relation. Is it sufficient for its standing in relation R to B to be internal to A that its doing so follows from A's nature on condition that B exist in possession of *its* nature, or is it required that the very existence of B, with its own nature, as something to which it is R, follows therefrom? Russell is perhaps a little ambiguous on this.

On the one interpretation ideal relations clearly are internal, but on the other, at least as they are ordinarily conceived, they are not. For once granted two things exist, each with its own inherent character or nature, then the ideal relations between them are settled. However, as ideal relations are ordinarily conceived, there is nothing in the inherent character of either term which points to the existence of the other or of anything like it. So, on the face of it, ideal relations are internal in the sense that their holding only requires the existence of each term, each with its inherent nature (so that the relational fact is not some fresh logically independent fact additional to facts about the existence of each term with its own character) but are not internal in the stronger sense that something within either term points intrinsically to the existence of the other as that to which it stands in that relation.[58]

Now the term 'internal relation' is certainly sometimes used in the first way, and indeed for some philosophers it simply means an ideal relation. And some of Russell's discussion suggest that this is how he is taking it. So one might take the axiom of internal relations as the doctrine that all relations are ideal. I shall call this the FIRST interpretation of the axiom and contrast it with some other interpretations which seem more relevant to Bradley.

Has anyone ever held an axiom of internal relations thus understood? It would certainly be a strange view, for it would imply a complete absence of any real connection between different things at all, leaving only the mere contrasts and affinities in character between things with no possible commerce direct or indirect with each other.

Such a view does, in fact, seem to have been pretty well that of Leibniz, and constitutes the heart of monadism. For, in effect, he does not deny relations between his monads, but only real relations. Maybe the forms of proposition he recognized did not allow for assertion of the fact, but the universe he was envisaging was one in which the monads had very complex and interesting ideal relations one to another, such as constituted them highly systematic perspectival variants of one another. (Not that he could quite do without real relations in his system, for God had to be given a more dynamic connection with the monads than they have with each other. Clearly, the relation of *emanation from* in which they stand to him is a real relation, unlike the purely ideal relations which hold between them. Without this common source the fact that they reflect each other in a purely ideal way would be quite inexplicable.) Thus the axiom of internal relations, understood as the assertion that all relations are ideal, leads rather to an extreme pluralism, for which the fundamental things of the world are quite cut off from each other, than to monism.

§ However, Russell makes a show of connecting the axiom, understood either in the FIRST way or in something pretty close thereto, to metaphysical monism. He does this by reflecting on the relation of diversity. If (argues Russell) the diversity of A and B is grounded in their adjectives (such as constitute their natures), this must be in virtue of their adjectives being different. But if difference must be grounded in a difference between the adjectives of the different, then the difference between the adjectives of A and B must be grounded in a difference of *their* adjectives. This leads to a vicious regress, for every difference will have to be grounded in a more basic difference. It follows that, if there is to be a diversity of things, there must be some diversity not grounded in the natures (adjectives) of the diverse terms, and the axiom of

---

58   The point that the other term has to exist for the internal nature of the first term to bring about its ideal relation to it is difficult to formulate in the context of a logical atomism for which it is misconceived to ascribe existence to particulars; however, in some way the point needs to be made.

internal relations falls. *Per contra,* if the axiom is upheld, there cannot be a diversity of things.

One might reasonably object to Russell's argument here that he should not take the axiom as applying in the same way to particulars and universals. A fairer interpretation of it would take it as implying that in the case of two particulars, A and B, ARB must follow from the conjunction of two such facts as that A has a certain quality F and B has a certain quality G, but that in the case of the qualities F and G any relation in which they stand will follow from the conjunction of F=F and G=G. For although the nature of the thing consists in qualities it possesses, the nature of a quality or nature can only reasonably be thought of as consisting in its being itself. This exhibits itself clearly in the example of two coloured patches; the one is brighter than the other in virtue of the shade of each, but the one shade is brighter than the other in virtue of each being just itself. One could doubtless make a somewhat similar distinction even if one took the view I have ascribed to Bradley, that every genuine individual is both a particular and a universal, a particular insofar as it is considered as different from itself, when it occurs in two different contexts, and a universal insofar as it is considered as remaining the same as itself despite such differences.

§ However all this may be, it is implausible to ascribe an axiom of internal relations to Bradley in this first sense. More relevant is the other sense I mentioned in which A's being R to B is internal to it if and only if it follows from the nature of A—from what it is within its own bounds—that B actually exists as that to which it is R. So let us consider a SECOND sense in which the axiom might be taken in which it claims that the very existence of everything else to which it is related, and just how it is related to it, could be read off from what each thing is within its own bounds. (Granted the axiom, there can be no question of a relation between A and B being internal to A, but not to B, so I shall ignore this apparent possibility for the time being.)

It is, indeed, a challenging enough claim that any relations are internal in this sense, let alone that all are. [59] For the holding of such a relation would be an example of that intrinsic connectedness between distinct items of which Hume so famously denied the possibility. Or one could put it otherwise and say that terms between which such relations hold are not distinct existences in Hume's sense. In that case, to hold that all relations are of this sort would imply (at least if taken in conjunction with the principle of universal real relatedness, see Part Two, Chapter One, pp. 268–69) that there are no such distinct existences at all and would clearly imply monism.

---

59   For the believer in such a form of internal relation, a fine question arises as to whether what one term of the relation points to is the existence of something with a certain character to which it is thus related, or the existence of that very particular. Another complication is as to whether that same particular could have existed with another nature. For my own attempts at an exact treatment of such matters see Sprigge, 'Intrinsic'.

The vital distinction between the two sorts of relations which might be called internal is this. Where terms stand in a merely ideal relation, the inherent character of each term contains no indication within it of the existence of the other term, but only settles that, if the other term exists, with its own nature, then it will be in that relation to it. (If one likes to say that it follows that it is thus related to the other term, either as an existent or as a nonexistent, there is still the difference between that case and one where the actual existence of the other term of the relation follows, and it is this which I am supposing to be true in the case of a relation which is internal in the second sense.) In contrast, each term between which there holds a relation which is internal in the second sense somehow points to the existence of the other term as something to which it stands in that relation. (We will see later that there are philosophers who hold that the most important relations between things are internal at one end, in this sense, and external at the other, but Russell and Bradley do not dally with the possibility of that sort of asymmetry.) We might call relations which are only internal in the first sense 'passively internal', and in the second sense 'actively internal'.

Could an ideal relation be actively internal? Well, our definitions do not rule this out. If it followed from the inherent nature of A that B exists, and that A and B contrast in character in a certain way R, then R would be an actively internal ideal relation.[60] But this is so unlike the character of ideal relations as they are ordinarily conceived, that it would be inappropriate to call it 'merely ideal'. For it implies a kind of dynamism absent from this notion. (I am talking here only of ideal relations between particulars, or between individuals qua particulars. Doubtless ideal relations conceived as holding between mere universals do each imply the being [in a Platonic sense] of the other and are thus actively internal in a rather degenerate sense. But the interesting question is whether ideal relations between particulars can ever be actively ideal.)

There are indications that Bradley thought that ideal relations were never merely so, but were always somehow actively internal. However, the more obvious candidates for the status of actively internal relations are real relations of juxtaposition or influence. Thus, upon the whole, the doctrine of internal relations, taken in the SECOND sense, is best interpreted as the claim that the way in which A is juxtaposed to other things, or is causally related to them, is necessarily bound up with its own inherent character.

§ Thus, taken in the SECOND sense, the axiom of internal relations says that all relations are actively internal, so that any terms between which they hold are such that the nature of each points to the existence of the other as something to which it is thus related.

An alternative interpretation with some appeal would take the axiom as saying that all relations are either actively or passively internal. (I shall call this the THIRD interpretation of the axiom.) For we have seen that it would be a

---

60   See pp. 427–28.

sufficient basis for a strong monistic position to claim (a) that there are no items not in real relations to each other, (b) that all real relations are actively internal, while (c) allowing that there are also relations between terms which are merely ideal and only passively internal. However, I believe Bradley's position is better represented as incorporating the claim that even the apparently merely ideal relations have an active aspect.

Active internal relations will seem mere magic to those contemporary philosophers who are still so deeply entrenched in the Humean view, that there can be no necessary connections between distinct existences, that they think such a belief a part of the normal equipment of any rational person. How on earth can anyone really believe, they will demand, that one could read off from investigation of the character of something, just as it is within its own bounds, the existing things beyond it to which it stands in real relations? Surely there must always be some empirical basis for this in past experience.

Interpreted as the claim that all relations are actively internal the 'axiom' certainly takes us a long way towards metaphysical monism. And there are remarks in Bradley which lend some countenance to saying that he did make use of such a claim in establishing his monism. However, in the end, it is misleading to say that he endorses the axiom. For, on the one hand, he holds that conceiving reality in relational terms of any kind is ultimately unsatisfactory, and, on the other, he holds that since we must fall from grace, for purposes of manageable thought, and think in relational terms, it is often best to think in terms of relations which are not internal in any sense. Thus the thesis that all relations are actively or otherwise internal is neither the ultimate truth nor necessarily the best way of thinking about relations for practical purposes.

Still, Bradley also holds that the metaphysician who accepted the axiom as ultimate truth would be more right than one who accepted the existence of external relations as ultimate truth. Thus he would look with some favour on a metaphysics which endorsed the axiom as the claim that all relations are actively internal.

But surely it would be too wild even for an absolute idealist to say that the existence of all things to which any individual A is related, and just how it is related to them, could be read off from what it is within its own bounds. For that would imply that the whole character of the universe is implicit in everything it contains. Would a more modest claim be more promising, that the character of A points to the existence of its more immediate neighbours, the things to which it is more immediately juxtaposed, or related causally, but not to the things to which it is related only indirectly, by their relations to its neighbours, or its neighbours's neighbours, and so on? Thus if A is only related to C via B, then perhaps A's nature settles its relation to B, and B's nature *its* relation to C, and thus the natures of A and B together the relation of A to C. This would confine the axiom to relations which were direct in the sense of not being defined as the ancestral of other relations.

That may sound more plausible. Perhaps my states of mind point intrinsically to states of mind of my friends, and their states of mind to that of their friends, without my states of mind doing so. However, this is only possible if the relations within the character of an individual are external (so that there is a blockage to intrinsic connectedness inside him) and that is in effect ruled out by the axiom, which must apply as much to these relations as to any others.

However, we do not have to take the axiom as implying that even the most powerful finite mind could *infer* the character of the whole universe from any part of it. The claim would only be that nothing *could be* just what it is within its own bounds, without everything else being so, because the character of everything is coloured by that of its neighbours and thus in a more and more indirect way by the character of everything else.[61]

I put the point thus in my *The Vindication of Absolute Idealism*

> The world is like a jigsaw, we may say, in which each piece can fit into one place only, and in which, unlike in an ordinary jigsaw, as ordinarily conceived, each individual piece is such that each part of it is qualified in its character by the shape of the whole piece.
>
> Vindication, p. 266

§ But though this characterisation of Bradley's position is fair enough so far as it goes, it seems to me that we get much closer to the heart of it if we relate it to an axiom of holistic relations, rather than of *internal* relations in any of the senses so far explained. Whether this itself can be regarded as a version of the axiom will be considered shortly. By a holistic relation (a term not used by Bradley himself), I mean one such that its holding between terms consists in the fact that they are mere abstractions from a more genuine individual which embraces them both. Thus an axiom of holistic relations is the holistic principle which I presented as basic to his argument for the Absolute in Chapter One.

To hold that all genuine relations are holistic is very close to acceptance of the monistic analysis of relations. However, it differs in not attempting to transcend the original distinct reference to each term made in a relational proposition. From Bradley's point of view this would doubtless make even the right relational propositions (i.e., those as true as their form allows) further from ultimate truth than they would be on a monistic analysis, but it would also capture more of their actual meaning. For it is essential to this meaning that the unity holding between the terms as aspects of a larger whole is 'degraded' by being conceptualised as a relation.[62] Thus relational thinking is really a prag-

---

61   In short, although intrinsic connectedness, in the sense of all relations between two terms being actively internal, must be transitive, that does not mean that the nature of the first term must be such that one could derive from it the idea of the nature of the second term, but only that it would be evident to an appropriately sensitive mind who knew both natures independently, and perhaps the natures of a series of mediating terms between them, that each could only slot into a universe in which they were thus related. (I put the point in terms of what would be evident to an appropriate mind for convenience of exposition. I am not reducing the necessity of which it would be aware to its awareness of it.)

62   See PL, p. 461.

matic device which allows us to oscillate between two inconsistent conceptions, that of the whole from which the so-called terms of the relation are ultimately mere abstractions, and that of the terms as individuals in their own right. However, it seems to me that Bradley's view is only divided by a hair's breadth from an axiom of holistic relations, and that the latter has the advantage that it does not render the truth of things quite so unsayable.

So even if Bradley would think that even holistic relations are unreal, I suggest that he might have allowed that it is very nearly correct (as I myself believe that it actually is correct) to say that, in ultimate truth, all genuine relations between things are of this kind, even if, for ordinary purposes, we employ modes of thinking which do not take this fact fully on board.

So I shall finish this discussion of the axiom of internal relations by showing how an axiom of holistic relations can, indeed, be regarded as the heart of Bradley's thought, and defended as being actually true in respect of such relations as stand up to an ultimate metaphysical critique. We have, in fact, made most of the relevant points already in Part Two, Chapter One, pp. 266–72, and need only glance at them here.

The essentially Bradleyan defence of an axiom of holistic relations would rest on the claim that one can never genuinely imagine terms standing in a relation without imagining a totality from which they are mere abstractions in the sense that they cannot be imagined apart from that totality without some distortion of their character. The point is not merely the trivial one that, when we imagine things which really do belong to such a totality without imagining it, we are not imagining the whole truth about them. The claim is rather that in doing so we endow them with a positive character actually incompatible with their belonging to it. For, so it is claimed, the characteristic of being just such an element in just such a totality is incompatible with being a complete entity in one's own right, or, indeed, with being an element in a different sort of totality. It is incompatible in the same sense as that in which one shade of colour is incompatible with another; that of not being combinable into a single coherent conception. That people are resistant to recognizing this kind of incompatibility is because the whole logic of our language is designed to divert attention from it. This, it seems to me, is at the heart of what Bradley was seeking to show about relations.

The most evidently holistic relations are those which hold between distinguishable components within a single state of mind. i.e., within the totality of someone's experience at a certain moment. The varied contents of a single experience are not bound together somehow so as to constitute it; rather, the only genuine individual is the whole, and these elements are mere abstractions therefrom. The axiom of holistic relations holds that this is the only way in which we can make sense of any relations at all, at least if thinking in terms of such relations is to be more than a mere pragmatic device.

§ An axiom of holistic relations leads inevitably, as we already effectively saw in Chapter One, to Bradley's basic doctrine of the Absolute. For it implies that the relationship between any two terms requires that there be a more genuine individual from which they are mere abstractions. Now either this more genuine individual is the universe itself, in which case it follows forthwith that the terms are mere abstractions from the universal whole, or it is something lesser. In the latter case, it can only be related to other things so far as it is an abstraction from a more genuine individual still. Sooner or later this process must lead to the universe as the most genuine individual of all, presuming that everything short of the total universe is related to something beyond itself. So, in the end, all things which are in any kind of relation to each other must be mere abstractions from a single totality which, for reasons we have sufficiently considered, must be psychical and thus answer to Bradley's conception of the Absolute. The only alternative is to suppose that there are things out of all relation to each other. Bradley's actual reasons for denying the real possibility of this alternative may not be altogether satisfactory, but it is surely sensible to dismiss it, even if only because we can only reasonably mean by 'the universe', or be interested in the character of the universe conceived as, consisting of all things to which we stand in any relation.

§ At a more concrete level we can reach this view by considering the impossible apartness which we must ascribe to things if we do not conceive them as belonging to some whole together. I am bound to believe, for example, that there are relations between your experiences and mine, and indeed relations which go beyond mere contrasts and affinities of quality. I may believe, for example, that they are simultaneous. If, however, I try to imagine the state of affairs in which this simultaneity consists, I can only do so by imagining a certain sort of totality, in which both experiences figure as elements. And ultimately I must suppose that there is such a totality including the experiences of all persons with whom I am in even the most indirect relationship. This totality may be thought of as a certain portion of space-time, or it may be thought of as a more comprehensive experience or state of mind in which they all figure. However, *prima facie*, there is good reason to doubt the actual existence of either sort of totality; the first because states of mind are not in space, the second because we are unready to believe in the required super-mind or super-experience. Yet if there is not such a totality, there seems no imaginable way in which the two experiences can be related.

Now imagine two physical things in a certain spatial relation. Bradley would claim that you can do this only by imagining a certain spatial totality in which each is a component. The existence of such a totality, *with the full quality you imagine it as having*, is incompatible with there being such other totalities as you imagine when you imagine one of the things on its own (or with the vaguest of backgrounds) or that totality's relations to other parts of space. That is, if X and Y are related spatially because they are essentially components in a portion of space Z, then X cannot be a totality in its own right. And neither can some space larger than X be, for then it would be that, not Z, which you should imagine when imagining how X and Y belong together spatially. More generally, all things in spatial relations with any one thing you start out with must be envisaged as such mere details in a comprehensive space including them all.

Even if a real portion of space is not like anything one can imagine, the general point which these thought experiments are designed to suggest still stands, namely, that it is hard to imagine, or in any way clearly conceive, how things can in any way be related to each other, or what their relations (ideal ones possibly apart) can be other than their constituting or helping to constitute a more comprehensive totality together in which they sink to the status of details contributing their own bit to the total *gestalt*. And if it is suggested that though you cannot imagine it, you can conceive it, the question arises whether your conception of it amounts to anything more than the fact that certain sentences can be appropriately formed which serve the instrumental purposes of language quite well. A conception of things which has any possibility of being a grasp of literal truth must surely do better than this and amount to imagination, taken in a large sense.[63]

§ Actually, there are two aspects to the notion of a holistic relation as we have been describing it. First, they are relations such that for terms to be in them to each other is a matter of the way in which they combine, perhaps along with other things, to form a certain sort of whole. (The one exception will be part-whole relations which are, so to speak, transparently holistic already. Assertions about such relations are about the contribution the part makes to constituting, with the help of other things, that whole.) Second, they are such that the character of that whole always so permeates the individual terms that they could not have been quite the same, even within their own bounds, if they had not belonged to that whole. If a relation satisfied the first condition and not the second, we might call it a weakly holistic relation. Such a relation could not properly be called internal. For it seems misleading to call a relation internal unless the fact of being in that relation is reflected in the term. In the case of terms related by a merely weakly holistic relation, their being in that relation would be a matter of the way in which the terms constitute a whole together, but the whole would not permeate the terms, and would thus be rather a weak whole. In contrast, a holistic relation in which the character of the whole does permeate each term may be called a strongly or internally holistic relation. The form of the axiom with which Bradley may be associated would therefore be the claim, not just that all relations are holistic, but that they are all strongly or internally so.

So one might hold that all relations (except perhaps some merely ideal ones) are in an important sense holistic, without claiming that all are internal and thus without endorsing anything like an axiom of internal relations. Even so much would provide the basis for an argument for an Absolute of a kind, though it would be an Absolute which would not pervade its constituents in the way Bradley believed it did. But it is evident that for his full metaphysical position he needs to claim that all relations are internally holistic. We could call this the FOURTH interpretation of the axiom of internal relations.

Perhaps Bradley does not absolutely require an axiom that absolutely all relations are strongly holistic, or even that all are holistic. For his main meta-

---

63   These points are discussed more fully in my *Vindication*, pp. 22 et ff; 33–38.

physical position might be compatible with allowing that, as well as internally holistic relations, there are ideal relations of mere contrast or affinity which do not require that the terms belong together within a totality. One could still reach the Absolute, as I showed in Chapter One, either by taking it as a doctrine about the universe understood as the totality of all to which we stand in real relationship, or add, as a separate premiss, a postulate of universal real togetherness. One might call this a FIFTH interpretation of the axiom of internal relations. We may note in passing that, while there could be no question of a relation being holistic at one end and not at the other, it would seem *prima facie* possible that it should be strongly holistic at one end, and weakly so at the other. Thus the character of a whole to which the terms A and B of a relation belong might permeate the character of A but not that of B. However, this is ruled out by an axiom of internal holistic relations.

But, though this is a possible position, it would be nearer to Bradley's own to deny that ideal relations could ever be merely ideal. For while he never explicitly discusses how ideal and real relations stand to one another, a view on the matter is implied in what he says about comparison.[64]

There is, in fact, quite a persuasive argument for saying that only elements belonging to the same experienced whole can be in ideal relations to each other. For these relations, it may be said, concern the upshot of a possible comparison, and only what is present to the same mind, or belongs to the same experiential whole, can be compared. (A secondary problem, on which Bradley himself dwells, concerns whether the important possibility is that of an actual comparison or only of some actually experienced contrast or kinship within a whole.)

To this it may be objected that to say that a comparison between A and B is possible is to say that they could be brought into a single experiential whole and compared, not that they are actually together in such a whole. The trouble with this is that if A and B, which belong to different experiential wholes, could be compared by bringing them into the same whole, this could only be because an A and B in the latter unified whole could be the same A and B as they were in the previously separate wholes. But such sameness would have to be an ideal relation between the A in the separate whole with the A in the combined whole, and similarly with B, and this could not itself be reduced to the possibility of their being brought into an experiential whole within which they could be compared.

It follows that if there are ideal relations between the contents of your experience and mine, or even between mine at different times, they must all belong to some over-arching experiential whole. For, if there is any possibility of comparing them, that must be because when brought together for comparison they are the same as they were when unperceived. But *this* ideal relation cannot turn on a possibility of being brought together for comparison but only on their actually being together somehow in a more all-embracing experience within which they can be compared.

---

64   See, for example, AR, pp. 518–21.

The conclusion seems to be that either ideal relations do not imply a possibility of comparison or they can never be merely ideal but must also be holistic. Bradley, it seems, would take the second view. However, as indicated, one could reach a Bradleyan Absolute without agreeing with him here, and accept the axiom of holistic relations only in the FIFTH sense.

§ Whether it is true or not that all genuine relations between things must be internally holistic, or that at least this comes nearer to ultimate metaphysical truth than does the belief that some (or all) relations are external (neither ideal nor strongly holistic), Bradley has, I believe, suggested, if not always very clearly, a case for the claim the force of which was not appreciated by Russell, nor by many subsequent philosophers.

§ In this connection, let us turn back to Russell's suggestion that the axiom of internal relations is rooted in a principle of sufficient reason. If Bradley can be said to accept this principle, it is, it seems to me, as much as a consequence of, as it is as a basis for, the axiom. We have seen that for Bradley one of the problems which shows that relations are unreal is that the nature of the terms between which a relation holds must have two aspects—that which produces it and that which results from the holding of the relation—and that these themselves need to be related. Now if we treat the relation as springing from the natures of the terms, we will tend to accept a principle of sufficient reason, while if we look at the matter in the converse way, we will be less inclined to. But for Bradley, surely, these are just two different ways of looking at the same fact. However, in the case of the ideal relation, it is more natural to think of the natures as coming first, while in the case of the internally holistic relations it is more natural to think of the whole as coming first.

Since it is the latter type of relations which is more important for Bradley, a principle of sufficient reason is not that important to him as a way of establishing his case. Thus if one note is higher in pitch than another, one is inclined to say that this is because each has the character it has. However, if my state of mind exhibits me as in communication with another, one is more inclined to say that its character is due to the relation. (What is in question here is not a contingent causal connection of a type a conventional empiricist might recognize but an actual intrinsic display of my contact with another within my own consciousness.) Bradley would claim that really one can look at it either way in each case. But the second case is more relevant to the main drift of his thought, if I am right that this rests ultimately on an axiom of internally holistic relations.

There is, indeed, another way of taking the principle of sufficient reason which relates it more closely to the nature of discursive thought. As Bradley sees it, the basic unity of things is destroyed by our intellectual discriminations, and this forces the intellect to attempt restoration of the original unity in an intellectualised version by finding discursive reasons why the terms are related. However, the fact that the intellect is intent upon finding an intellectual explanation of the unity of things rests upon the fact that it is the emergence of the intellect which has broken up a more primitive form of unity. And the reason for believing in the existence of that more primitive form of unity lies ultimately in the recognition that all real relations, or perhaps all relations, are internally holistic.

§ To scotch Bradley's monism one would have to show that fully external relations are conceivable, meaning by this relations which are neither ideal nor internally holistic. Indeed to do away with any version of the Absolute one would have to find relations which are also not even holistic in a weak way. The holding of such external and non-holistic relations between two terms would not be equatable with their being merely elements in a more comprehensive totality. In my opinion Bradley has shown that we can form no conception of such a relation, if our conception is to be more than a move in a 'language game' by which we cope with the world in a manner which gives no genuine grasp of how things hang together. At the very least, it should be granted that there is a strand of compelling thought in Bradley's treatment of relations with which Russell never really grappled, and for powerful criticism of which we must turn rather to James.

§9. *Summing Up on Internal and External Relations*

§ It may help the reader if I now bring some of these threads together by summing up, and in some cases supplementing, the main points which have been made concerning the axiom of internal relations and its relation to Bradley's thinking.

It is doubtful whether Bradley ever produces a really clear account of what would be meant by calling a relation internal or external or how far these expressions really help in the elucidation of his thought. However, his name is so strongly associated with the debates about the internality of relations that one can hardly forego some attempt to clarify the issue.

It is usually said that a relation is internal if it is in some way built into the inherent natures of the terms that are in it that they are so, while a relation is external if it is not so built into the terms. Russell thought that all relations were external. Some thinkers believe that some relations are internal, others external. Our special interest is in the claim that in some sense all are internal. Such debates get nowhere so long as we fail to distinguish a number of different senses of 'internal'.

(1) Sometimes the contrast between external and internal relations is equated with one between ideal and real relations. By an ideal relation is meant one which is a matter of contrast, or affinity, or difference of degree, in the inherent characters of things (characters the things possess strictly within their own boundaries either in a spatial or analogous sense). That one apple is rosier in colour than another will be an ideal relation between them (assuming naive realism about colours). (Also describable as 'ideal'—in a sense more or less different according as to how one thinks things stand to their characters—are the corresponding relations between the characters themselves.) Such ideal relations stand in contrast, at least *prima facie*, to what may be called 'real' relations between things, relations of juxtaposition in a common environment, of causation and perhaps of other types similarly not merely ideal.

(2) Most empiricists and realists would have no objection to the idea that some relations are internal in the sense of being ideal, provided these are clearly distinguished from real relations of juxtaposition and influence. What they

typically object to is the idea of a relation which is internal to one or both terms in the sense I have called 'active', that is, is such that the actual existence of the other term, as that to which it is thus related, is implied in its own being. This then provides a second sense of 'internal relation'.

(3) If metaphysical monism is to be based on an axiom of internal relations, it is in the second rather than the first of these senses of 'internal'. However, it could also be based on a third sense, that of their disjunction, provided it was also claimed that everything in the universe is in *some* real (not merely ideal) relation to everything else.

A thing's ideal relations to other things and its real internal relations to other things have (or will have if there really are relations of each type) in common their close involvement with its inherent nature. But they differ, on the face of it, in that the real internal relations would be a partial determinant of its inherent nature, while the ideal relations would merely follow from that inherent nature (though not from it alone, for the other thing would have to exist and possess an appropriate character). Thus if relations of each type are internal, they are so in very different ways, or so at least it must initially seem. If A has a real internal relation to B, the existence and character of B is somehow implied by A's inherent character, but this is not implied by any merely ideal relation it may have to it. It is the real internal relations whose existence is seriously controversial (apart perhaps from the special case of relations between whole and part).

Things are complicated by difficulties in the notion of a thing's inherent nature. I suggest that it is best, and in conformity with Bradley's own approach, to take the inherent nature, in the relevant sense, of a continuant as what it is like within its own bounds so long as it stands in the relation whose type is in question. For discussion becomes hopelessly confused if it is taken for some enduring essence of a continuant which it cannot acquire or lose and such an idea plays no part in Bradley's thinking. Discussion of the whole issue tends to be clearer when the terms of the relation are conceived as events (and although Bradley never considers the contrast between a continuant and an event ontology as such, his approach is in fact much nearer to the latter).

Another thing which has often caused unnecessary trouble in getting the whole issue straight is the tendency of some commentators on Bradley and others sympathetic to the idea of internal relations to confuse *de dicto* and *de re* internality. It is sometimes said that the relation between Socrates and Socrates's wife is internal but the relation between Socrates and Xanthippe is external. This is mere trifling, though we can call it *de dicto* (turning on the way the things are referred to) internality and externality if we wish. The serious question is the *de re* one as to how far these two persons, however referred to, have natures intrinsically bound up with being in these relations. This is sometimes dismissed as an idle dispute as to which of a thing's characteristics pertain to its nature. But if by a thing's inherent nature we understand the character it possesses strictly within its own bounds at the relevant time, the question whether that nature can point to how the thing is related to things beyond it (in the way in which Hume famously maintained it cannot) is a serious and vital one. And it is certainly a *de re* internality of the terms to a relation which is of concern to Bradley.

It should be clear from our discussion in the last section that identification of ideal and internal relations would be most misleading in connection with Bradley and related philosophers. For, in sometimes suggesting a doctrine of the internality of relations in general, Bradley is certainly not meaning to reduce them to relations of mere affinity and contrast as these are usually understood. It would be nearer the mark to say that for him so-called ideal relations are always also in some sense real.

(4) Upon the whole it would, however, seem to be primarily in a fourth sense that Bradley thought all relations internal. (This fourth sense implies the second but is not necessarily implied by it.) A relation is internal in this sense if and only if it is strongly holistic, that is, its holding between things is a matter of the way in which they combine (usually along with other things) to form a certain sort of whole together, with a character to which each makes its specific contribution, and which so permeates each that it could not have existed with just the same character outside just such a whole.

Two things are to be noted about this sense of internality.

(i) A relation is not holistic merely because it holds between parts of a whole. Rather it must actually be the precise way in which the terms form a whole together, perhaps with the aid of other things (or, to allow for the part/whole relation itself, perhaps the precise way in which something contributes to a whole or is a whole thus formed).

(ii) A relation which was weakly rather than strongly holistic would not be internal. To be strongly holistic the whole the terms form, or help to form, must so pervade their inherent natures that they could not exist in the same character outside it. Thus if social relations between people are strongly holistic, the nature of the group they form, or help to form, must enter into what each is individually. Although a weaker form of monism might perhaps be erected on the claim that all relations are holistic, whether weakly or strongly so, Bradley's type of monism requires rather the claim that all are strongly holistic.

(5) Once more, however, it might suffice for his purposes that all non-ideal relations should be so, provided he can also establish that everything in the universe is in some real relation to everything else. In that case he might be content to claim that all relations are internal in a sense the disjunction of the first and fourth sense.

However, the more accurate statement is that for Bradley both internal and external relations are incoherent (however precisely you take these terms) and must be rejected at the level of ultimate truth, but that each of them has their uses for the makeshifts of ordinary daily thought, in which it is convenient to regard some relations as internal and others as external. The most you can say is that thought in terms of internal relations is a bit nearer to ultimate metaphysical truth, but that that often makes it less suitable for the practical purposes of ordinary relational thinking.

(6) For the sake of completeness we should mention a sixth, not very interesting sense in which by a thing's 'internal' relations, is meant its relations

to its parts or the relations of its parts to one another, these being contrasted with its 'external' relations to things outside it. This ordinary usage is not prominent now in philosophy but its lurking presence sometimes confuses discussion of more important grounds on which a relation may be called 'internal', and Bradley himself often uses the expression in this way. [65] If all truth really concerns the Absolute, then doubtless all true relational propositions must concern those which are internal in this sense. (Indeed, even if we think of the relation between two things as turning on their joint contribution to some lesser whole we may regard this as an internal relation of that whole in this sense.) But this is more a confusing way of presenting monism than a basis on which it might be established.

§ Before we leave the topic of internal and external relations, it is worth noting that A. N. Whitehead and Charles Hartshorne emphasised the possibility that relations might be internal at one end and external at the other. [66] In fact that was just how they thought things stood with the most basic sorts of real relation. When an event is individually remembered it is (they held) internal to the memory that it registers that particular past event but not internal to the event that it would be so registered; moreover, properly understood the relation between effect and cause is always of this sort. Hartshorne reproaches Bradley and others for assuming that one must either defend the internality of a relation as holding at both ends or not at all.[67]

This view certainly represents a formal possibility which is too often ignored. However, if one agrees with Bradley that all relations are strongly holistic, and that it is in virtue of the way in which the character of a whole pervades its parts that terms in relation point each within its bounds to the other, one may be doubtful of this suggestion. For the reasons for thinking that a whole must pervade its parts will presumably apply to all parts. However, one might agree that some parts give a clearer indication than do others of the character of the rest of the whole, and that holistic relations may be more perspicuously internal at one end than at the other.[68]

§ As noted above, when Bradley talks of relations he usually means a relation as holding between particular terms rather than as something abstract which holds between many different pairs of terms. I have often followed him in this

---

65   See, for example, PL, pp. 471–72, and note 5 on p. 494; also AR, p. 407.
66   I simplify here and elsewhere by confining attention to two-term relations. This is not because Bradley denied that relations could be three term, a point which we have noticed already consorts rather ill with his main claims but simply for convenience. If we did turn our attention to three term relations we would have to admit the formal possibility of relations which were internal at two of their 'corners' and external at the third, and similarly with relations with more terms still. But neither Hartshorne nor Whitehead, I think, make this point. For a discussion of Whitehead and Hartshorne on relations internal at one end, and external at the other, see McHenry, pp. 87–93.
67   See Hartshorne, *Synthesis*, pp. 83 et ff., 167 et ff., 212, 226.
68   See Sprigge, *Vindication*, pp. 230–32.

in my exposition. The status of a relation in the abstract would be presumably much that of a quality in the abstract, that is, it would be that which is identical amidst difference in different instantiations. Usually the description of a relation as internal or external is with reference to particular terms which it relates rather than merely in the abstract. However, a relation will presumably have the same such status in any instantiation of it, and can be categorized accordingly.

§10. *Conceptual Thinking as Distortive of Reality: James and Bradley*

§ Our two philosophers are at one in the opinion that conceptual thought is more a vehicle for dealing with reality practically than for grasping how it really is. They both think that our concepts distort reality and that this is shown by the paradoxes and contradictions endemic to them.

For James the most basic way in which concepts cannot do justice to reality lies in their inability to deal with its flux. Concepts are static and sharply distinct from one another. In concrete reality, in contrast, one item flows into another without their being either sharply distinct from or identical with each other. Again, concepts cannot capture the kind of continuity which pertains to real change, which manages both to occur all at once and yet not to be jerky in a way we all know intuitively but can never satisfactorily think.

For Bradley it was not so much the flux of reality which eludes our conceptual grasp as the combined togetherness and variety of things. Conceptual thought divides things up into separate units, each intelligible apart, and cannot put them together again in its own terms. As for flux, this is an aspect of experience rather than of reality, for the very concept of a flux is incoherent.

Here then is a major difference: For James concepts of flux and becoming bring us nearer to the reality which concepts distort than do concepts of eternity and being, while with Bradley the opposite is true. Thus for James the solution is to quit conceptual thinking and plunge oneself in some more intuitive way into the sensory flux. Then when one starts thinking again one will have a better sense of what one is talking about, even if one can never adequately capture its nature in talk. For Bradley, in contrast, it lies rather in a determination to think harder, while recognizing that thought must fail to give any final understanding. It is this aspect of Bradley's approach which James thought so unsatisfactory, and from which he turned with relief to Bergson, whom he thought had seen further than anyone else on this.

§ But, in spite of this major difference, they are agreed that the combined togetherness and diversity of the contents of the world frustrates an adequate conceptualisation of it. That is why the concept of relations is particularly problematic for both. Although (as we have seen) James criticises Bradley sharply for alleged fallacies in his demonstration of the incoherence of relational thought, there is much in common in their views about it. Both see it as an essential way of thinking which nonetheless breaks up the continuity of reality in a way which thought can never finally put right in its own terms.

Their shared conviction that our ordinary concepts as much hide reality from us as reveal it, leads to views on truth which are much closer than they may seem superficially. For Bradley the truth required of our ideas for most ordinary purposes is simply a pragmatic one, that of working well for the purpose in hand, technological, moral, spiritual, or even theoretical (when this stops short of attempting an ultimate understanding of reality). It is only in metaphysical ideas that we should look for a truth which goes further and captures something of the literal essence of reality.

§ James's pragmatic conception of truth is much the same as Bradley's of the truth which he thinks appropriate for ordinary purposes. And James likewise believes that there is a way of grasping reality which brings us nearer to its real essence than does pragmatic truth. If he hesitates to call this the possession of ideas which are 'true' in a more absolute way, the contrast with Bradley is more verbal than otherwise. In effect they are at one in contrasting a pragmatic truth consisting in ideas which work, suitable for most of ordinary life, and a deeper grasp of how things are, in which something of their real essence becomes transparent to us. It is such a deeper grasp of the general character of reality which we seek in metaphysics. However, for Bradley access to this deeper insight is essentially an intellectual affair, while for James it is through an intuition which declines the services of the intellect. (That contrast must, however, be qualified. For Bradley too there are non-conceptual ways of relating to reality which put us in touch with things in a manner which is impossible for the intellect. This is the case, he holds, for example with certain sorts of religious and aesthetic experience. He too would decline to speak of 'truth' here.)

§ For both philosophers the basic defect in conceptual thinking is its abstract character. Concepts are somehow too thin to do justice to the concrete fullness of reality. And they agree that the concreteness of reality is one with its experiential character. The failing of physical concepts is typically their tendency to abstract the defining properties of the physical from the experiential embodiment in which alone they can have reality.

They differ, of course, as to where true individual concreteness lies. For James it pertains only to finite individuals, ultimately to single pulses of experience, while for Bradley it pertains only to the universe as a whole. But even in this contrast there is an affinity. For both of them we get our grasp of what genuine individuality is from noting the character of such pulses of experience. But for James this character is true individuality while for Bradley, in contrast, the concreteness of such finite experiences is merely a clue to the more genuine concreteness of reality as a whole. They relate to each other here almost exactly as did Leibniz to Spinoza. Both start from the notion of a substance as an individual thing, but for the one we are such substances while for the other only the universe is.

§ These two thinkers, then, share these three important (and in my opinion true) beliefs: (1) that our ordinary concepts distort reality and that this is shown in the paradoxes they breed when pressed too far; (2) that a large part of the problem with our concepts is that they treat features which can only be real as elements in some more concrete whole as fully real items in their own right; (3)

that such a concrete whole or wholes must in some sense be experiential or psychical. The great disagreements between them are (4) as to whether reality is more deeply a flux or an eternal changeless one; (5) as to whether concrete individuality in the fullest sense belongs to individual finite experiences such as we live through from moment to moment, or only to one single cosmic experience. I shall conclude this chapter with some comments on these points of agreement and disagreement.

Granted they are right about ordinary concepts, are they right that concepts *must* distort reality? Is not the fault simply one of our present concepts? Perhaps Whitehead, who agrees on many points with our thinkers, was right that the problems stem from the concepts (like substance) of one particular philosophical tradition and that we can develop metaphysically better ones which will not distort reality. On this I am inclined to agree with him, though the concepts I would recommend as replacements for the traditional ones are not so much his as ones I would cull from James and Bradley themselves.[69]

In particular, I would agree with Bradley that we cannot coherently think through the notion of a purely external relation, and yet that it is essential for ordinary life. But I incline to think that the notion of relations which are internally holistic is one which holds literally of reality. And maybe something like Whitehead's epochal view of time will resolve what is valid in the Zeno-type problems about flux which James and Bradley press.

For there is something rather odd in the claim that concepts *must* distort, rather than simply that our usual ones are in various ways inadequate. If the complaint is simply that concepts—or conceptual symbols—are not the same (special cases apart) as that to which they apply, that is true enough and must remain true. But to complain about concepts in this way is rather like eating the menu at a restaurant and complaining that it isn't up to the meal you expected; one 'does not dine off the bill of fare', as A. J. Ayer put it.[70] Or we can recall Mephistopheles's remark to Faust:

> Grau, teurer Freund, is alle Theorie
> Und grün des Lebens goldner Baum
>
> Goethe's *Faust*, lines 2038–39

Or we may quote Bradley himself:

> The shades nowhere speak without blood, and the ghosts of Metaphysic accept no substitute. They reveal themselves only to that victim whose life they have drained, and, to converse with shadows, he himself must become a shade
>
> ETR, p. 14, note

---

69   See Whitehead, *Process*, Part III; Hartshorne, *Synthesis*, p. 83 and passim. See also McHenry, chapter III on Whitehead as trying to conceptualise what Bradley and James thought could not be. I have only had the text of this fine work since completing mine, but I have often benefited from discussing such things with the author.

70   See Ayer, *Metaphysics*, p. 205. Compare VRE, p. 500, and Perry, p. 683.

Maybe, but that does not mean that all theories and metaphysical propositions are false (roughly the point Bradley himself is making in that context).[71]
Certainly there must be more to a reality, and more to our encounter with it,
than mere conceptual thinking (though as Bradley always emphasises, and
James sometimes seems to forget, there is little human experience that does not
owe a large part of its value to the conceptualising of what we are living through
or encountering). But that is not to say that our concepts are inadequate ways
of grasping it intellectually. And to the extent that they are, do we not discover
this precisely because we are fumbling towards ones which are more finally
adequate?

Yet perhaps Ayer's witty saying is not the end of the matter. For after all
there is a sense in which to experience something directly (in some appropriate
sense) is to know it, and to know it in a fuller way than that of mere conception,
though one to which all conception in a manner aspires. Santayana criticised
such an ideal of adequate knowledge in his aphorism that knowledge is a salute
not an embrace. Bradley and James might reply, however, that it is the salute
of someone who would rather embrace, and claim to be showing why this is
impossible.

We shall discuss Bradley's belief that genuine reality is always psychical in
the next chapter (section 2). We have already discussed James's version of this
doctrine at length.

However, for Bradley, as for James, even when we recognize that reality can
only be genuinely concrete, in the way it must be, if it is psychical, we have not
found an adequate way of conceiving it. For concepts are abstractions and what
corresponds to them in the reality to which we apply them must be indissolubly
one with a larger context in a way to which they, as isolated units, cannot do
justice.[72]

It may be objected that concepts are not isolated units for Bradley, but
discriminated features in the flux of our consciousness. However, they are
discriminated in order to serve as descriptions of what lies beyond. As such,
they are but thin ghosts of being, lacking, so far as thought is concerned, both
the flesh and blood reality of its own subjective existence and that which, if the
thought is true, they must have in its object.

It is to be noted, in this connection, how strikingly empiricist Bradley's
account of thinking really is. We can only think of a reality possessing a certain
character to the extent that that character can occur as an element in our own
experience. The problem is, however, that this character must be modified
somewhat differently by the two distinct contexts in which it occurs, as element

---

71　Thus though for Bradley conceptual thought must always in a manner distort
　　reality, metaphysics must remain a conceptual affair and be satisfied that the
　　degree of success it can obtain in its own terms is one of the functions in which the
　　Universe fulfills itself. For James, in contrast, metaphysics must move rather to
　　Bergsonian intuition. See Part One, Chapter Four, section 1(d).
72　See, especially, his attack on empiricist views in PL, pp. 95–97.

of our thought, on the one hand, and as an actual character of the object thought of, on the other. Traditional empiricists dream of no such problem because their conception of experience and of thought and its objects, is insufficiently empirical. They treat it as a mosaic of bits which can change their context without changing their character and Bradley, just like James, thinks one has only to direct one's attention at experience itself to see how wrong this is.

Thus Bradley's most basic reason for saying that conceptual thought distorts lies in his view that abstraction of any element from a whole distorts it, and his ground for this is, at least in part, empirical. This is close to James's view that concepts distort because they are discrete while reality is continuous.

The most striking difference between them is over points (4) and (5) above. For James we come nearer and nearer to a grasp of reality in its real essence the more we see it as a flux, whereas for Bradley its apparently flux-like character is one of the most striking indications that we are not grasping it properly. And this is closely tied up with his view that only reality as a whole can be a genuine individual. Who is right on these matters? Our final answer must await further investigations of Bradley's thought, in particular his views on time, to which I shall turn in section 3 of the next chapter.

4

The Absolute

§1. *Towards the Absolute*

§ To say that the Absolute exists is to say that reality as a whole and as it really is (as opposed to how it is convenient to think of it for certain limited purposes) has a certain character which earns it the title of 'the Absolute'. This character is that of being a single unified, but in some manner variegated, experience of which everything else which in any sense is is a so-called 'appearance'.

What does 'appearance' mean here? It seems at least initially helpful to distinguish two senses in which an item can be an appearance of the Absolute. In the first sense it is something which some finite mind posits as part of the conceptual scheme by which it tries to understand the reality to which it belongs. (Since no such positing is entirely without worth as a form of understanding, there will always be at least a degree of pragmatic truth to the assertion that such a thing exists and this can be expressed by saying that it has a certain degree of reality.) In the second sense something is an appearance of the Absolute if it is an actual component in that unitary experience which is the whole of what truly is, and such that all concepts of it which do not grasp the way in which it belongs thereto represent a partial distortion of its character. Appearances in this second sense pertain to it in a more part-like way, though Bradley would deny they could properly be called parts, since this implies that they are more fundamentally distinct from one another than they are.

Bradley does not himself explicitly distinguish these different senses of 'appearance', and indeed on his principles they slide into one another. There are two reasons for this. (1) That which is an appearance to a finite mind in the first sense must be something such that the experience of encountering it will be an appearance of the Absolute in the second sense, and, since Bradley denies any sharp distinction between a thing and the experience of it, he would conclude that the thing itself is an aspect of the absolute experience. Moreover, since for the Absolute all finite centres of experience are simply aspects of itself, it may, and Bradley thinks it does, unite their deliverances into a single deliverance. Thus when many finite centres posit some common object each from its own perspective, their positings of it are combined at the level of the Absolute to give a single deliverance which will be as truly a 'part' of it as they are. (2) Appearances in the second sense are up to a point only our constructions, since we cannot help conceiving them as more sharply distinct from each other than they are, even though 'we' can only explain what 'our' means by reference to them.

Nonetheless the distinction between these two senses of 'appearance' is a helpful one for clarifying Bradley's system. A finite centre of experience is surely more a 'part' of the Absolute than is the British constitution, whose being is that of a shared posit of many such centres. And, if 'nature' only exists as a presentation to finite minds, then its components too are much less like 'parts' of the Absolute than these minds are.

§ We have already seen that the two most basic premisses for Bradley's argument for the Absolute are two.

(1) Relations are unreal because 'things' have a togetherness with each other to which relational thought cannot do justice. Wherever, from the point of view of relational thought, two things are related, there is a more comprehensive whole of which they are parts or aspects and which is so much more of a genuine individual reality than they are, and which so permeates them, that they are necessarily to some extent misconceived when conceived apart from it.

(2) In the end there is nothing but experience. 'Experience' covers both total states of experience, such as we live through from moment to moment, and everything which is presented perceptually or conceived within them.

To these we must add two supplementary premisses which will perhaps be granted more readily than the first two.

(3) The most adequate account of the world in relational terms would maintain that everything in the universe is related to everything else.

(4) A whole whose parts are all experiences, and which is more of a genuine individual than any of the experiences it contains, must itself be a single experience with a variegated but intensive unity of which our own momentary states give us the best available clue.

From this it clearly follows that reality as a whole is a single all-inclusive experience of the kind the expression the 'Absolute' is meant to designate.

§ I have suggested[1] that the most important part of Bradley's argument could be retained if one replaced (1) and (3) by:

(1a) The real relations between things are all of them internally holistic, that is, are such that their holding consists in the fact that the terms jointly constitute, or help constitute along with other things, a whole whose nature so permeates

---

1   See Chapter One, §2, and Chapter Three, §8, pp. 424–29.

each of theirs that things with just those natures could not have existed outside it. Moreover, this whole is always more of a genuine individual than are either of the terms.

(3a) Everything is related to everything else by real relations.

I also believe that it would be an improvement in the expression of Bradley's basic point of view to replace (2) by:

(2a) Nothing really exists except experience. This covers all units comparable to total states of experience such as we live through from moment to moment and the experiences they contain. However, though this is all that exists in literal metaphysical truth, there is much else of which it is useful to posit the existence for various purposes and which therefore exists as an appearance in Bradley's first sense. Now while our common belief in such things is an experience, and an experience which really exists in the Absolute, the things themselves need not therefore be regarded as experiences as Bradley seems sometimes to conclude. It is, however, a possibility to be taken seriously that some of them have an experiential inner nature which is an appearance of the Absolute, in the second sense.

I have also suggested that a rather weaker doctrine of the Absolute could still be established if we weakened the premises so that they insisted only that the whole constituted by terms in relation, or which are together in the way we represent to ourselves as their being in relation, must be *at least as much* of a genuine individual as is each term and if the claim that the nature of the whole must always permeate the nature of the terms or parts were dropped (so that relations which are only weakly holistic were not ruled out). The advantage of this would be that the premisses thus modified might seem more compelling. And once this weaker doctrine of the Absolute were granted, it would be difficult to avoid moving onto Bradley's stronger doctrine. For surely the general orderliness of the cosmos shows that, if it is a single unitary experience at all, it is a better organized and more truly individual one than are our momentary states of consciousness or any other such finite unit. I shall not, however, trouble further with this weaker argument and doctrine.

Of these various premises we have now sufficiently discussed all except (2) and (2a). The next section will consider the case Bradley makes for the panexperientialism they present, a position very close to James's. After that, I shall consider what Bradley did and, as I see it, should have said, about time, in order to justify and make sense of the claim that the Absolute is an eternal unchanging experience rather than one which alters.

§2. *Panexperientialism*

> We perceive, on reflection, that to be real, or even barely to exist, must be to fall within sentience. Sentient experience, in short, is reality, and what is not this is not real. We may say, in other words, that there is no being or fact outside of that which is commonly called psychical existence. Feeling, thought, and volition (any groups under which we class psychical phenomena) are all the material of existence, and there is no other material, actual or even possible.

This result in its general form seems evident at once; and, however serious a step we now seem to have taken, there would be no advantage at this point in discussing it at length. For the test in the main lies ready to our hand, and the decision rests on the manner in which it is applied. I will state the case briefly thus. Find any piece of existence, take up anything that any one could possibly call a fact, or could in any sense assert to have being, and then judge if it does not consist in sentient experience. Try to discover any sense in which you can still continue to speak of it, when all perception and feeling have been removed; or point out any fragment of its matter, any aspect of its being, which is not derived from and is not still relative to this source. When the experiment is made strictly, I can myself conceive of nothing else than the experienced. Anything, in no sense felt or perceived, becomes to me quite unmeaning. And as I cannot try to think of it without realizing either that I am not thinking at all, or that I am thinking of it against my will as being experienced, I am driven to the conclusion that for me experience is the same as reality. The fact that falls elsewhere seems, in my mind, to be a mere word and a failure, or else an attempt at self-contradiction. It is a vicious abstraction whose existence is meaningless nonsense, and is therefore not possible.

AR, pp. 127–28

There could not be a plainer statement of the claim that there is nothing but experience.[2] As for argument in favour of this claim, as opposed to exploration of its implications, Bradley never really has much more to say than is said here. The proof rests entirely upon the claimed impossibility of genuinely thinking of anything other than experience. Bradley claims never to have been able to think of anything but experience, however hard he tried, although he can recognize a confused state of mind in which he might describe himself as thinking of something other than experience. And it is implicitly suggested that no one else has ever really succeeded, or could do so, in thinking of anything other than experience.

§ There are, in fact, three main questions raised by this passage.

(1) Suppose it were true of Bradley that he could not think of anything except as experienced, would it be reasonable for him to conclude that it was true of human beings in general?

If this question can be answered positively, we can then raise the question:

(2) Was it really true of Bradley that he could not (and therefore in the light of a positive answer to the first question, is it not true of human beings in general that they cannot) really think of anything except as experienced?

If these two questions can be answered positively, we may ask:

---

2   It is amusing to compare this with a statement of Bradley's archenemy, F. C. S. Schiller: 'it was not without difficulty I seemed to discover two fundamental points of initial agreement which would, I think, be admitted by nearly all who have any understanding of the terms employed in philosophic discussion. The first of these is that the whole world in which we live is experience and built up our of nothing else than experience' (Sturt, p. 51). The second is that reality is a construction which we build up out of experience with certain assumptions, connecting principles, etc.

(3) Does it follow from this fact about human beings that there could not be, and therefore is not, any reality other than experienced reality?

§ Consider first (1). It is obvious enough that it could not be valid in general to argue from the fact that Bradley had never succeeded in thinking of something of a certain kind, or even from the fact that he could not do so, to the conclusion that no human being ever did or will, or could. And the same would hold whatever other human one put in the place of Bradley here. Bradley, presumably, never thought about helicopters, but that does not show that no one ever will or would. Perhaps this was no real incapacity, just lack of opportunity. But if, say, Bradley tried to think of Gladstone as a benefactor of his country, but was quite genuinely unable to do so, he might not altogether unreasonably take that as a ground for denying that Gladstone was a benefactor of his country, but one would not be much impressed if he concluded that no one could so think of him. Or again, if there were certain mathematical concepts simply beyond Bradley's grasp, he would hardly have argued that therefore those who think they grasp such concepts are deluding themselves. But there does seem to be something different about the effort to think about something as general as unexperienced reality.

It is surely not a very plausible hypothesis that Bradley and certain fellow idealists come to their views on the basis of an unusual incapacity, relating to thinking about unexperienced things. Presumably the person who counters Bradley by saying that he can think about unexperienced things believes not only that Bradley and the like could, but that they do, think about them, though philosophical confusions prevent their realizing this when they philosophise. To which the Bradleyan idealist may reply that his opponent never really does think about them but only thinks he does in the course of confused philosophising.

For must not we all, on whichever side of the philosophical debate we stand, at least acknowledge the truth of this proposition?:

(A) It is either true that no ordinarily functioning human beings can ever think about anything other than experience or true that all can.

If so, it is reasonable for anyone to come to his view as to what human beings are capable of in this regard by examining his own capacities. And this will be true even if we cannot satisfactorily explain why we are so sure of (A). However, something should be said about what grounds there may be for holding it. One could carry on for a long time arguing about this but the essential point seems to be as follows.

If some people do and some people do not have the power to form the concept of a reality quite distinct from sentient experience, it may be that it is the first group or it may be that it is the second group who are in the majority.[3] And it may be, or it may not be, that anything exists answering to the concept of something distinct from sentient experience. Let us consider the four possibilities to which this gives rise. And let us concentrate on the question whether

---

3   It seems hardly worth working out the case where the two groups are equal.

people exhibit such a power when they do what they would describe as thinking about physical things. For those who claim to be able to think about things other than sentient experience would usually proffer their power to think of these as at least the main example, even if they might add an ability to think of other such things, perhaps abstract objects and noumena, for good measure.

Case One: *Most people do, but a minority do not, have the power to form the concept of something other than sentient experience, and do so when they do what they would regard as thinking about the physical world. Moreover, this concept truly applies to something with which they are then engaging.*

In this case the minority would be suffering from a most remarkable incapacity, and one would expect it to show up in some striking incompetence in their dealings with reality. But I am not aware that those who, when they look into it, think that, when they do what is naturally called thinking about the physical world, they are really always thinking about actualities or possibilities of sentient experience, are particularly incompetent in their dealings with the environment.

Since that does not seem to be so, it is more likely than that this case holds that in fact either the minority or the majority, as this claims them to be, have been misdescribed or misconceived either by themselves or others.

Case Two: *A minority of people do, though most people do not, have the power to form the concept of something other than sentient experience, and do so when they do what they would regard as thinking about the physical world. Moreover, this concept truly applies to something with which they are then engaging.*

In that case the minority would have a remarkable insight into the world lacking to the others, and an insight which is strictly unavailable to the majority, an insight which comes into play in all their ordinary thought. One would expect some remarkable powers in dealing with the world to follow from this, but there is no evidence of the existence of such a peculiarly insightful minority of this sort.

Since that does not seem to be so, it is more likely than that this case holds that in fact either the minority or the majority, as this claims them to be, have been misdescribed or misconceived either by themselves or others.

Case Three: *Most people do, but a minority do not, have the power to form the concept of something other than sentient experience, and do so when they do what they would regard as thinking about the physical world, However, this concept does not truly apply to anything with which they are then engaging.*

In that case those who have the better view of how things are have the smaller conceptual capacity. Perhaps this is not so strange. Seventeenth-century rationalists thought that the more rational one was, the less one could imagine.[4] However, the same argument applies, namely, that in that case one would

---

4   See De Deugd, pp. 70–71, 74–75.

expect the less confused minority to be more effective in their dealings with reality. But this does not seem to be so.

Since that does not seem to be so, it is more likely than that this case holds that in fact either the minority or the majority, as this claims them to be, have been misdescribed or misconceived either by themselves or others.

Case Four: *A minority of people do, but a majority do not, have the power to form the concept of something other than sentient experience, and do so when they do what they would regard as thinking about the physical world. However, this concept does not truly apply to anything with which they are then engaging.*

In this case one would expect the minority of physical realists, as one might call them, to show a peculiar incompetence in their dealings with the ordinary environment.

Since that does not seem to be so, it is more likely than that this case holds that in fact either the minority or the majority, as this claims them to be, have been misdescribed or misconceived either by themselves or others.

In concluding that it is most unlikely that some people do and some people do not have the capacity in question, I am far from suggesting that we all have the same basic conception of the physical world. That we do not is strongly suggested by the fact that philosophers differ so much in trying to analyse what they think of as the common sense concept of the physical. The truth seems to be, rather, that there are various alternative conceptions which, for practical purposes, come to much the same but nonetheless have a genuinely distinct cognitive content. However, the divide now in question would not be merely between actual conceptions but between fundamental conceptual capacities and would, moreover, be of a more fundamental kind than seems plausible among comparatively normal people.

Thus it seems reasonable to generalize from one's own case in such a matter.

§ (2) In the light of this we can ask our second question in the form: 'Was Bradley right in holding that we cannot conceive of anything except as experienced?' (understanding by 'we' human beings in general, and taking it that each person can answer the question by reflection on his own abilities).

Bradley's main reason for saying he could not conceive of such a thing seems to have been simply that he failed to do so when he tried. How reasonable a form of inference is that? Well, surely there can be no better grounds for saying that one cannot do something, than that one honestly tries to do so again and again and fails. Doubtless it is not conclusive proof; moreover, 'cannot' is not without ambiguity. But upon the whole it seems a reasonable basis for a fairly confident conclusion.

However, there is something of a problem in saying what exactly Bradley claimed he could not do. For surely there is a sense in which he obviously could think about a reality which was quite distinct from experience. Otherwise how could he know what it was that he could not do? There is a paradox in the very form of words 'I am not thinking about X' and likewise in 'I cannot think about X'.

§ If such claims make any sense, we must be able to distinguish between thinking and thinking. For there is evidently some sense in which Bradley could quite well think of something existing independently of all experience. In some sense he knew what it was which he found inconceivable here and attributed some sort of meaning to it. So he needed a distinction between a sense in which he could, and a deeper sense in which he could not, conceive of such a thing, perhaps akin to the contrast between the sense in which one can and cannot conceive a square containing five internal angles. And when he moved from claims about what is conceivable to what is possible or impossible he needed to claim that it is conceivability in this deeper sense which is relevant. For it is only in talking of what we can conceive in this deeper way that we have even a putative case of the kind of grasp of how things are which a metaphysician seeks. Although he does not make such points expressly, they are quite in line with the main contours of his thought.

§ Bradley might be following in the footsteps of some empiricists and saying that he could not imagine something quite apart from experience, or he might be saying that he could not form a clear and distinct idea of such a thing in something like the Cartesian sense. Perhaps these two are not as far apart as they have sometimes seemed. For to form a clear and distinct idea of something in the seventeenth century sense meant to perform a mental act in which the essence of the something was clearly and distinctly exemplified in an 'objective' fashion, while to imagine something means in some manner to actualise its character within one's mind. Both refer to a kind of thinking in which one does not merely have a symbol designating or specifying something within one's mind, but somehow brings home its character to oneself, by some kind of presence thereof within one's own consciousness. Surely it that sort of thinking of something which Bradley finds impossible in respect of a reality quite unexperienced. I shall call thinking in which the character of that of which one is thinking is thus brought home to one 'intuitively or imaginatively fulfilled thinking'. Such fulfilment, it should be emphasised, is a matter of degree.

The suggestion that the clear and distinct ideas sought by the rationalists, and the iconic images typically sought by empiricists, are essentially the same thing may be thought strange, since rationalists, such as Descartes and Spinoza, were so anxious that one should not confuse conceiving something clearly and distinctly with imagining it. However, in part what they objected to under the heading of imagination was a type of thinking not rationally unfolding through its own inner logic but determined by non-rational psychological processes such as the association of ideas. It is not so clear that the actual achievement of a clear and distinct idea did not involve a kind of imagining. For certainly it did involve the essence of the thing thought of having some kind of so-called 'objective' presence within the mind, and that is a very reasonable account of what *imagining* is, understood in the broadest sense.

Descartes, however, says that while one can clearly and distinctly conceive a chiliagon, one cannot imagine one, as one can a triangle. So what is the difference between the two cases? What is the difference between the presence in the mind of the form of something one imagines and that of something one only conceives? (I shall concern myself here only with imagination of a type of reality or thing, rather than of a particular thing, as only the former concerns us here.)

§ The distinction which seems to me primarily important here is that I adumbrated in Part Two, Chapter Two, §2, between directly imagining something and indirectly imagining something. (1) When one imagines a type of reality or thing *directly*, it is specified for one by a universal actually present as the character of some element of one's stream of consciousness, and singled out by an act of attention as a property one attributes to a reality beyond present consciousness or, in the case of explicit fantasy, plays at thus attributing. (For Bradley, as we have seen, the latter case came to be thought of as the ascription of universals to a special imaginary realm of reality, but that need not especially concern us here.) Perhaps one should also allow, as a less full sort of direct imagination, cases where a universal strongly suggestive of the universal in question is thus singled out and felt about somewhat as it would be if it were present to the mind. (2) When one imagines a type of thing *indirectly*, it is specified for one by a universal identified by its ideal relations to a universal which one can imagine—either directly or indirectly.

Both types of imagining contrast with purely verbal thinking of a thing. In this case one merely has symbols for the universal in question and thus no genuinely presently realized sense of the character of that of which one is thinking. In contrast, imagining in either sense may be said to give one a clear and distinct idea, of the sort the metaphysician must insist on being able to conjure up, of that in the existence of which he seriously believes.

Presuming one can imagine a four-sided plane figure directly, and can imagine the relation of *being a plane figure with one more side than*, then one can indirectly imagine a plane figure of any number of sides. For a five-sided figure can be specified by this ideal relation to a four-sided figure, and a six-sided figure can be specified by its ideal relation to this, and so on.

In the light of this I suggest that metaphysicians who have tried to give an account of the world which they think they really understand in a deep way have been trying to describe it by way of features which they can imagine either directly or indirectly, and that this is true even of proclaimed enemies of the imagination as a form of understanding. Even if this is rejected as a general claim about metaphysicians, there is plenty of evidence that it is true of Bradley. For even if he presents no express account of anything like indirect imagination, it seems an appropriate and indeed essential development of what he does say. It also seems implicit in some of his discussion of various particular examples of things of which he can and cannot form an idea. For example, his account of the kind of idea one can form of the Absolute presents it, in effect, as something which we can imagine indirectly, whereas the mental process of not being able to conceive of unexperienced reality here seems only to make sense as a description of an unsuccessful attempt to imagine it, even perhaps indirectly. For surely he is not denying that such a reality is verbally describable, but only that it cannot be thought of in the fuller way which metaphysics requires of what it will count as real. . And I do not see what that fuller way could be except some sort of imagining, direct or indirect.

§ Certainly a close association of conceiving with imagining is wholly in line with Bradley's account of judgement. For judgement, on his account, as we saw in Chapter Two, involves the occurrence of the universal ascribed as a predicate as an actual element in one's own state of mind.

> It should be a commonplace that ideas are psychical realities, and we cannot represent without using a psychical fact. Further, what represents a pain must be a pain, and so again with pleasure. It is not true that the idea of the greater pleasure or greater pain must itself be a stronger pleasure or pain, but to think of a pain or a pleasure without *in some degree* feeling them is quite impossible.
>
> CE, pp. 253–54

> [R]ight as it is to say with Lotze that ideas are not what they mean, it is also true that ideas can mean nothing but that which they are. For unless a thing has, and to that extent is, a quality, I cannot myself understand how it goes about to show it. The idea of the extended has extension, the idea of the heavy has weight, the idea of the odorous has smell, and the idea of pleasure, beyond all controversy I should have thought, exists and is so far pleasant.
>
> CE, pp. 334–35 (from an 1895 essay; see also his footnotes)

To the extent that he ever revises such claims it seems to be in the direction of allowing that some thought is more like that which I have described as indirect, as opposed to direct, imagining of the situations it affirms to exist. But it seems necessary for him to admit also that some thought is purely verbal and that such thought can be divided into that which can be intuitively fulfilled, directly or indirectly (in a more or less mutually coherent set of ideas of it) and that which must remain at best a more or less adequate verbal technique for coping with the world. If so, only the former could be a serious contender for truth of the type sought in metaphysics, since the latter would convey no genuine opinion of how things are, such as could be even a candidate for insight into any real truth about the world.

§ So I suggest that, in effect, what Bradley is really claiming is that he, and thence human beings in general, cannot imagine anything existing unexperienced, and cannot do so either directly or indirectly. For the universal one ascribes to reality in any imaginatively realized judgement is experiential, that is, specifies its instances as indissolubly one with experience.

Since this is supposed to be something one discovers in the attempt, rather than proves abstractly, it would be inappropriate to seek a proof. It is not a matter for argument but for what Bradley calls 'ideal experiment'. We should simply see that whatever it is we imagine is really something involving sentient experience. However, the idealist and his opponent are likely to charge each other with mistakes as to what has really been imagined resting on alleged confusions which can only be removed by discursive reasoning in words. Bradley must claim that in all judgements or imaginations in which one seems to be ascribing a universal which is not experiential, really elements are present which show themselves, when examined, to be clearly psychical in character and that one cannot prune off these psychical elements and obtain an imaginable universal with nothing peculiarly psychical about it. And his opponent must claim that he can really imagine directly or indirectly an unexperienced reality, not merely that talk of such a thing has a pragmatic use.

There are two main sorts of cases where Bradley's claim is likely to be disputed: first, those in which what is imagined is specified as physical; second, those in which what is imagined is, *prima facie*, a so-called abstract object.

Let us consider briefly the second and less important case. Cannot one imagine the number seven as something existing in a Platonic way without being presented to any sentience?

In my own opinion an abstract object is a universal which might be exemplified in concrete reality. To think of it simply as an abstract object is to imagine it instantiated, while recognizing that, whether it is so or not in fact, it remains a form that concrete reality *might* take. The relevant question here, then, is whether one can imagine abstract objects whose instantiation might be by something non-psychical. Thus the question of the imaginability of an abstract object is the same as the question of whether a concrete situation involving it is imaginable.

§ So let us turn now to the more important case in which we normally suppose that we can think of something existing independent of experience, that of the physical world in its 'independent' being. Is it really true that we cannot conceive, in a genuinely fulfilled way, of anything here which 'does not consist in sentient experience'? Many people will say that, even if the imagery by which we think of physical things, insofar as our thought is 'fulfilled', depicts them with qualities they can only have for a subject, we can abstract the truly physical qualities from the 'subjective' ones and conceive of a physical world characterised only by the former. Thus even if the shape (or weight or movement) which one imagines is always shape as presented to a person from a certain position, viewing or feeling something with certain emotions and intentions, one can abstract from these subject-implying features and thereby conceive of the shape pure. Or if shape, conceived visually as we normally imagine it, is still dubbed subjective, perhaps by a further abstraction one can arrive at a purely structural concept thereof which is free from any subject-implying quality. Such a possibility may well seem allowed for on Bradley's own account of judgement, which insists that only a selected element of the 'mental' idea pertains to the 'logical' idea.

It cannot be said that Bradley's brief treatment of the matter supplies any full answer to such claims. But I suggest that a reply can be given which is essentially Bradleyan in character.

Certainly for Bradley judgement and imagination can be of a highly abstract nature. One can judge or imagine that something exists characterised by some fairly unspecific universal, without bothering about the specific way in which it does so. (Indeed one could never expect to know the full specific nature of anything thought of as actually existing, though it must have some such nature.) For example, I can judge that someone is suffering without imagining the full specific nature of his suffering. This occurs because one abstracts suffering in general from one's own image of suffering and applies this to the situation beyond.

This opens the possibility, so it would seem, that even though one's own image of a situation beyond has itself a psychical character, one abstracts from it (to use in judgement) only the non-psychical elements which determine just one particular species of something more generic. But, and here is a point on which Bradley himself does not develop things adequately, it may be that one can abstract from the psychical in the sense that nothing particularly psychical is attributed to what lies beyond. But that only means that one is not positively characterising it as psychical, something quite different from characterising it as non-psychical. For this one needs something in the universal which one attributes which marks any instance of it as something non-psychical (not something which merely fails to mark it as psychical). And it is this which I think Bradley could argue one cannot do.

Put abstractly, the point is this. There is a difference between imagining something to which one does not attribute either X or not-X, and imagining something to which one attributes not-X. The first can be done on the basis of an image which is itself X, for one can abstract from its X-ness. But to do the second one needs an image which has a kind of 'positive' non-X-ness to it. And Bradley might have done well to have said that, while one can perhaps imagine something with a character which does not of itself mark it as psychical, one cannot imagine something with a character which actually marks it as non-psychical.

Thus one can imagine the occurrence of seven somethings, leaving it quite vague whether it is seven psychical or seven non-psychical elements. But this is not the same as imagining seven non-psychical elements. For that requires that one imagine seven things which are specified by one's image as positively non-psychical. And it seems to me that Bradley would be right to say that that is impossible.

§ It may be said that one can imagine the unexperienced indirectly. One thinks of things which are less and less psychical and the non-psychical is some kind of ideal limit which has the relation of *being less psychical than* in the maximal degree to everything we can directly imagine. But to this there are two objections. First, it is not at all clear that one can in fact identify such a relation. Secondly, even if one could, the maximal degree of that relation would seem rather to specify something which was minimally psychical than something which was not psychical at all.

However, such details are probably less important than the force of the ultimate thought experiment to which Bradley invites us. I have suggested that we interpret this as the claim that if we try to realize in imagination the idea of something divorced from all experience we will fail and only say that we succeed, if we do, through confusion, and that the same applies if we try to give ourselves some kind of less direct realization in imagination of this idea by specifications rooted in what we can imagine.

§ The claim that one can only imagine what is experienced must not be confused with the claim that one can only imagine things as experienced by oneself. Even if Bradley at times confuses these questions, there is nothing in his main line of thought, nor in my development of it, which implies the latter claim. And there is very little to be said in its favour. One can certainly imagine an experience one supposes someone else to have, without imagining oneself having that experience. So one cannot establish that what one imagines always belongs to *experience* on the ground that it is always imagined as belonging to *one's own experience*.

One can imagine, for instance, an image which is not in one's own mind. For to be an image in one's own mind is for it to belong to a stream with a certain character. What that character is is open to much dispute. But suppose it is that of being permeated with a certain emotional quality distinctive of one's own interests. Then surely one can so drain one's imagery of that personal emotional quality that it serves as an icon of something with a different personal emotional quality. Thereby one can use it to imagine an experience not one's own. And the same will be true in the case of any other sensible proposal as to what make an experience one person's rather than another's.

But surely if it is drained of one's own personal emotional quality, it is not an image occurring in one's own mind. The answer is that, though that emotional quality will be there in the background, the foreground can contain something which positively repels it and which, abstracted from that background, serves as an icon of what lacks it. If one is to imagine something which is altogether non-psychical, then one must do so by having an image which has characteristics which go some way positively to repel the psychical characteristics and which, abstracted from all subject-implying features present in the background, serves as an icon of what lacks them. But I would support Bradley in holding that on examination one will never find any characteristics in one's imagery which have any tendency to repel the psychical characteristics. Rather do they seem to summon them to complete what is lacking in the purely abstract universal if it is to be exemplified in a full concrete fashion.

§ We must also sharply distinguish the Bradleyan case from an argument sometimes attributed to Berkeley, who is sometimes thought to have said that we cannot imagine something unperceived because whatever one imagines is thereby being 'perceived' in imagination by us. Actually, I think he was not so much using this dodge to prove that we cannot imagine the unperceived as simply dealing with an apparent exception to a claim supposedly already proved. In any case, to argue that one cannot imagine something unexperienced on the ground that what one imagines is always part of one's experience, simply as being something one imagines, is hopelessly sophistical. It rests on a confusion between the state of affairs imagined and the experience of imagining it. Imagination always postulates (either as a reality or as something being feigned) something which lies beyond one's present experience.

§ There are perhaps occasional suggestions in Bradley of reasoning of these fallacious sorts which try to prove that we can conceive of nothing except as an element in our own experience. If so, they are to be utterly rejected. But it is not the main basis of his case and, upon the whole, he quite clearly rejects it.

> To transcend experience and to reach a world of Things-in-themselves, I agree,
> is impossible. But does it follow that the whole universe in every sense is a

possible object of *my* experience? Is the collection of things and persons, which make *my* world, the sum total of existence? I know no ground for an affirmative answer to this question.

AR, p. 190

He does, however, contend for something which might be confused with this fallacious line of thought. For he says that unless I was somehow *one with* reality beyond me, I could not think about it. And he sees this as supporting his view that reality at large must be a unitary experience, since my oneness with it can only take the form of the experience which constitutes my personal being belonging to reality at large as an element falling within a more all embracing and unitary experience the character of which pervades all its elements.

This must be understood in relation to his theory of judgement as the ascription of an idea to reality, where an idea is a universal abstracted from present experience and reality is a larger and more truly individual whole of which present experience feels itself to be a mere fragment. Thus judgement requires that we experience ourselves as somehow intrinsically directed onto a larger reality with which what we are experiencing now is essentially continuous. And Bradley holds that such continuity between present experience and a greater beyond is only possible if that beyond is itself experiential in character.

I believe that this argument, if not conclusive, gives strong support to the Bradleyan view that reality at large, in any sense in which we can be directed upon it, is of this character. At the least one can say that its being a unitary experience makes such directedness more intelligible than it would be otherwise. But that is not the fallacious argument sometimes ascribed to Berkeley, nor even that of our present concern.

§ (3) Let us now turn to our third question: Granted that people in general cannot conceive of anything unexperienced, in the full sense of 'conceive' which requires something like imagination, does it follow that such reality is intrinsically impossible and therefore nonexistent?

There are two main questions about the relation between conceivability (in the sense of direct and indirect imaginability) and modal concepts such as possibility and impossibility: (A) Is the fact that something is conceivable proof that it is possible? (B) Is the fact that something is not conceivable proof that it is impossible?

§ (A) A first thing to note is that if indirect imagining is allowed, matters are less straightforward than if we stick to direct imagining. There is a good deal to be said for Hume's view that whatever can be imagined is possible. For basically that means that the universal which specifies the object of imagination can be exemplified in the stuff of our own experience, and therefore cannot consist of clashing elements incapable of exemplification. It is true that, strictly speaking, it is always rather an approximation to, rather than full exemplification of, the relevant universal in the mind, so that it can never quite be ruled out that something intrinsic to it would stop its complete exemplification. However, the closer to full exemplification imagination comes, the more reason there is to think that we are homing in on the intrinsically possible. In the case of indirect imagining, however, there may be some intrinsic impossibility in something ideally related in some imaginable way to what we can imagine directly. However, that line of thought suggests that there may be impossibilities which seem possibilities to us, rather than the more relevant case of possibilities which seem impossible to us. The relevance of indirect imagination here is rather in suggesting that there may be things which are too readily classified as unimaginable because imagination is given an unhelpfully narrow sense. Thereby we may either be too precipitate in denying their possibility or in denying the relevance of what is imaginable to its modal classification.

§ (B) It is the second question, however, which is more relevant here. In taking inconceivability as an argument for impossibility Bradley, I suggest, could argue like this. If you cannot even indirectly imagine that of which a proposition asserts the existence, or cannot combine your imaginings of it into any single coherent conception, that proposition says nothing which a metaphysician can take seriously. For he wants to know what the world is really like and that means forming a genuine idea of it such as can figure in an intuitively fulfilled and coherent judgement about it. Claims which cannot yield this can therefore only be stimuli to useful behaviour and are irrelevant as attempts to characterise the world in a way which metaphysics can take on board. Such a proposition may be good enough, indeed, for daily life or even for such theory as does not claim ultimate truth. For much of our ordinary thinking about the world consists in the manipulation of verbal formulae, or of oscillation between images which cannot be combined into a coherent picture, which work more or less well as guides to practice or even for certain theoretical satisfactions. But they cannot possibly give that sense of the real essence of things sought by the metaphysician.

That the metaphysician is seeking the deep grasp of reality which could only be given by direct or indirect imagination does not show that this is attainable. But it does show that application to the world of predicates of which one has no such grasp must be rejected by the metaphysician. For these do not even purport to make the essence of the world transparent to us. So if unexperienced physical reality is unimaginable its postulation is not even a candidate for the kind of truth the metaphysician seeks.

However, it is not primarily verbal descriptions which leave a mere blank in the mind when one tries to imagine (directly or indirectly) what they describe which are of interest here. For ordinary descriptions of physical things supposedly implying that they are not being experienced are not of this sort. What are relevant, rather, are cases where the more full we try to make our conception of something the more baffled we become or where a fully realized imagination of something requires that we combine the imagination of features between which we normally oscillate by what Bradley calls 'rapid shuffling'. And this is the character which Bradley thinks belongs to all attempts to think of things as unexperienced.

§ This argument does not restrict the character of the world to something imaginable by us. We may allow that the world may contain much that lies beyond that kind of deep grasp the metaphysician seeks while disallowing that it could contain *unexperienced physical objects* (or anything else unexperienced). For if something answers to an expression in our language, it must answer to the conception this conveys *for us*. And if Bradley is right that this expression conveys for us no intuitively fulfillable conception of any character anything might really possess, it can only be a pragmatically useful formula.

To a great extent I endorse this line of thought. However, even if the only positive conception of the world that is metaphysically viable is a panexperientialist one, more needs to be said to defeat the agnostic alternative that the nature of things in themselves must remain opaque to us. In my own defence of absolute idealism I have tried to deal more adequately with such agnosticism.[5] My argument was briefly this. First, we should give some preference to views of reality which render it knowable if they do seem to supply an adequate account of things. It seems perverse to prefer the hypothesis that reality is unknowable to available accounts which make a good job of characterising it in more positive terms. Secondly, I suggested that the only ground we ever have for supposing that something is impossible is the increasing bafflement we feel in trying to conceive it the better we seem to understand what is at issue. So the fact, if it is a fact, that this is so with unexperienced reality is good, even if not quite decisive, evidence for saying that it is intrinsically impossible.

It may be objected that our discussion has put too much emphasis on imagination and not enough on direct experience. Surely one knows better what loneliness is by experiencing rather than imagining it. But, apart from the fact that I am following Bradley here, it may be replied that the imaginable presumably includes all that one can actually experience, and more besides, so that reference to it effectively covers both. (Or if this is not quite true, and there are some things whose essence only reveals itself to direct experience, references to what we are in a position to know about through imagination should be taken as qualified by the addition of 'or direct experience'.) The metaphysician can accept whatever he has directly experienced without demur as pertaining to reality. But if he thinks that there is more to reality than he can directly experience, it must be something he can imagine directly or indirectly.

§ Bradley's reasons for panexperientialism are very similar to James's, and it is here that they are at their closest. But are they not both grossly anthropocentric in taking the fact that we cannot conceive something unexperienced as showing that there cannot be such a thing? Surely, after all, an agnosticism about the matter is more becoming, for which there may be a thing-in-itself, or

---

5   See my *Vindication*, pp. 87–90, 125–30.

things-in-themselves, behind our experiences, the nature of which we cannot know. James, as we saw, allows this and claims only that a positive philosophical account of the universe should ignore such a *ding-an-sich,* since it is an idle possibility which can contribute nothing to our conception of the universe we inhabit. Bradley is more forthright in his denunciation of any such idea. My own suggestion that the impossibility of imagining something non-psychical gives some, but not conclusive, reason for thinking it intrinsically impossible lies somewhere in between. But I would still argue that accounts of the universe which do not appeal to such a doubtful conception are to be preferred provided they give a characterisation of it which is complete in its own terms.

§ But can we really resist Bradley's stronger claim that the idea of unexperienced reality betrays itself as simply vacuous when properly examined? For how can there even be an idea in my mind of the possibility of things of which neither I nor anyone else can form any conception?

Well, one can imagine what it must be like to be deaf and to have no conception of sound. For one can produce imagery of a life filled by material from the other senses in which sound is lacking, and see this as bringing with it a lack of all idea of sound. Of course, one's imagery of this situation occurs in a mind pervaded by awareness of sound, but in the imagery on which the act of imagination is based there is something which would tend to repel or exclude ideas of sound if left to itself. So it seems one can imagine a situation in which (a) X exists and (b) a type of mind exists which is quite unable to conceive of X. If one abstracts this rather general feature from that of the relation of the deaf to sound, one can imagine its applying to all human minds (perhaps even all minds) with respect to something else and even suppose it very likely that it does. But that does not mean that one can imagine something specified as non-psychical, for that requires a positive imagination of it *as* non-psychical not simply *as* something unimaginable by oneself. The characteristic of being unimaginable by us is a character we can abstract from something we can imagine, and thus itself imagine in a broad sense; there is no similar situation from which we can abstract the character of being non-psychical.

It is more than likely that there are things in the world of the specific nature of which no human can form any conception. But that leaves it open whether they *are* or *are not* such as could only occur as forms or contents of experience. If they are, then, though inconceivable by us in their specific nature, they do have a generic nature which we can conceive.

But what of the second case? Is that a genuine alternative at all? How can we even attach sense to the supposition that they are non-psychical if none of us can imagine (directly or indirectly) what something non-psychical would be like? The only answer, I think, must be that they might be such that, if we could imagine them, we would somehow find the expression 'non-psychical' suitably applied to them, though we cannot conceive what it would be about them which would solicit that description. Now while we cannot perhaps absolutely dismiss the idea that there are such qualities, it does seem to me that our inability to form any idea of a reality which would solicit the application of such an expression, gives good, if not absolutely conclusive, evidence that it is impossible that there should be such a thing. For it is an inability which seems to grow stronger, not weaker, the more one grasps what is at issue.

§ It may be objected that this whole argument is quite specious, since it simply trades on the fact that we are bound to use psychical material to think of the non-psychical and that obviously we cannot obtain a positive picture of something non-psychical from psychical material. That would show an impossibility in imagining something which is positively non-psychical which would hold however much of the non-psychical there may be, and can hardly therefore be used to show that there is nothing non-psychical.

To this I reply that if one is to say in a serious way that there is, or may be, non-psychical reality, one must be able to cash the idea of it somehow in imagination. Otherwise one is saying merely that there may be something we cannot imagine. This is not the claim that there may be non-psychical reality, but the quite different claim that there may be things of which we know nothing. We should not confuse agnosticism about aspects of reality with a positive belief as to its possible non-mental nature.

§ In treating both Bradley and James as having held that propositions which refer to something unexperienced cannot possess the kind of ultimate truth the metaphysician seeks, and can only be useful pragmatic fictions, I may seem to ascribe to James a distinction between genuine and pragmatic truth which is alien to him. Verbally this objection may sound right, but it misses the essential agreement between our two heroes on the main point. James may have regarded the pragmatic sort of truth as truth in the proper sense, but this was coupled with a search for a deeper metaphysical grasp of things than such truth can give. This is an aspect of James it is easy to document, however much it is ignored by those who see him as a kind of logical positivist.[6]

§ Among writings which mark the decline of idealism in twentieth century philosophy, G. E. Moore's 1903 article, 'The Refutation of Idealism',[7] is especially prominent. It is still worth considering as a serious attempt to refute such claims as we have just been examining, especially as it also stands in a rather interesting relation to James's occasional 'new realist' position.[8]

Moore claims that, with careful attention, one can distinguish within, say, the sensation of blue two distinct elements, consciousness and the present object of consciousness, blue, of which the former is psychical, and the latter not. Of these the former is admittedly somewhat elusive. For that reason it is easy to slip into simply identifying blue and the sensation of blue, and conclude that, since a sensation is mental, blue cannot exist apart from mind. But once

---

6   Bergson was very good on this aspect of James. See his introducton to the French
      translation of *Pragmatism* at Bergson, p. 1449.
7   *Mind n.s.*, XII (1903); reprinted in Moore, *Studies*. See, in particular, p. 13 et ff.
8   I have attempted to rebut some similar more recent arguments against a claim like
      Bradley's in my *Vindication*, pp. 131–40.

they are distinguished, Moore argues, the apparent difficulty there is in conceiving of blue as existing apart from anything mental disappears.

Moore supports this contention by arguing that, since consciousness is present both in the sensation of blue and in the sensation of red, it must be something distinct from both. As Ayer has pointed out, you might argue similarly that there might be a waltz without dancing since dancing is present also in a tango.[9] Moore is ignoring the possibility that red and blue are *species* of consciousness. But despite this bad argument, we may still see him as inviting us to a thought experiment akin to Bradley's, but with the contrary result of finding that we can form a perfectly good idea of blue existing apart from any experience of it.

Which, then, is carrying out a more reliable thought experiment, Bradley or Moore (assuming on grounds we have canvassed that the disagreement should not be put down to different conceptual capacities)? I am compelled to support Bradley here. For I can find no difference between imagining blue and imagining consciousness of blue. Having imagined the former I find no more to do to imagine the latter.

However, a different conclusion might be drawn from this than the Bradleyan one. May it not show that, though blue and the consciousness or sensation of blue, are one, what this one thing is is a simple quale, which counts as mental in one context and physical in another, while remaining intrinsically the same? That is, of course, the 'new realist' version of James's radical empiricism discussed in Part One, Chapter Three. So even if this is not quite Moore's own position, maybe he has led us back to it as the genuine alternative to idealism which James at one time thought it.

So is this quale inherently mental or is it only mental in contexts not essential to it? James himself somewhat complicated matters by still calling such neutral items 'experiences' even when he temporarily inclined to the view that they were not essentially mental. The real question is whether they are necessarily experiences in some more pregnant sense.

I suggest that such a quale as blue can only occur as what is properly called an experience in a properly mental sense. For you can only imagine blue by imagining a totality (even if one which has nothing to it except a vague extensity of blue) which could be the consciousness of some organism, as that which one would have to imagine to know what it was like being it. Maybe such a totality could exist without being the mental state of an organism, but as being the kind of thing which could be, it is something essentially psychical.

As a means of deciding whether something is a mental state or not, asking whether it could be the what-it-is-like-being-it of some organism, provides simply an idiomatic pointer to what consciousness is, not a definition.[10] The real question is: Is it a specific form of some generic essence one can call sentient

---

9   See Ayer, *Russell and Moore*, pp. 147–48.
10   Cf. Sprigge, 'Final', p. 166 et ff., Nagel, *Mortal*, chapter XII.

state of affairs ceasing and giving way to another. They do not deny that the experiences which seem to constitute my unfolding conscious life over time exist. Each total experience of a moment is really part of the universe. However, it is a part containing a misunderstanding of its own status. For it seems to itself to have taken over from a previous moment of experience, which has simply dropped out of being, and to be itself falling out of being as it is replaced in turn by another. And that is not how things truly are. Rather, each experience is simply eternally there with just the quality it feels itself as possessing, joyful, painful, cognitive, volitional, emotional, and transitory, when these are understood as referring to its own inherent character. In virtue of these qualities it seems to itself to be flanked by experiences belonging to a kind of *demi-monde* of the *was* and the *will-be* from which it has itself briefly escaped but in truth it is just eternally there, as these other experiences are too (merely imagined ones apart), each with its own precise sense of its own ephemerality.

Such philosophers, then, admit the existence of experiences which seem to themselves to be temporal but deny that they really are temporal. And they may or may not also admit that something of the same sort pertains to merely physical events.

I shall be elaborating on this view in what follows. I believe that it is the true view of how things are, and the view to which Bradley is basically committed. But he did not embrace it in any very clear fashion, and did not argue for or explain it very well.

These first two views are not incoherent in themselves, even if sometimes presented in a confused fashion.

(3) There is, however, a third group of philosophers who regard time as unreal or phenomenal who do seem to be very confused. For they seem to think that time is an illusion or appearance experienced by beings whom they go on conceiving in essentially temporal terms. There is at least some ground for thinking of Kant as belonging in this group, as also Schopenhauer. And sometimes Bradley seems to be thinking along these lines.

Some of the thinkers in this third group are perhaps in a state of oscillation between the first and second positions.

§ In what follows I shall develop four themes in turn.

(1) Bradley's attempt to show that the concept of time is contradictory or incoherent and that therefore time must be unreal;

(2) Problems about motion and change and the perception of time;

(3) The fact that what Bradley's theory really needs is the statement that time is unreal in the second sense listed above, but that while he sometimes makes this clear enough he also speaks at times as though he were a philosopher of the third type; and

(4) The fact that there was available to him a simple proof and clarification of the meaning of the unreality of time in the required second sense.

(b) Attempts to Prove the Unreality of Time

§ The main formal demonstration of the unreality of time is in chapter IV of *Appearance and Reality*. It is preceded in that chapter by a would-be demonstration of the unreality of space at which it will be convenient to take a brief look here.

Bradley says that space cannot be coherently conceived either as a mere relation or as something other than a mere relation. He means that the existence of space cannot be successfully reduced to the holding of relations between terms and yet, on the other hand, that that is all there seems to be to it.

That space cannot be a mere relation is shown by the fact that the only terms between which such a relation could hold would themselves be spatially extended. But if the terms of spatial relations are themselves already spatial, then space cannot consist merely in the relation between them. Besides, the piece of space whose existence is supposedly constituted by the relation between certain items is always as much a thing as they are and not therefore reducible to the mere holding of a relation between them.

That space is nothing but a relation is shown by the fact that nothing is needed for 'a space' to exist except that the things within it be in certain spatial relations.

Bradley's main point seems to be this. A space seems to be a mere set of terms in relation but these terms themselves are a set of terms in relation, which latter terms seem to be only a set of terms in relation, and so on *ad infinitum*. Thus we never come to any final terms. Yet unless there are final terms the relations between which constitute space, there can be no space.

I shall not add to the mass of literature on relational versus substantival views of space by attempting my own evaluation of this line of argument. Basically Bradley is simply exploiting the familiar problems of infinite divisibility. It seems doubtful if these really justify calling space unreal. If it is to be so called, it must be upon the basis of the other idealist arguments for the merely phenomenal nature of physical reality along with the space pertaining to it.

§ Bradley begins his discussion of time with the rather inauspicious remark:

> Efforts have been made to explain time psychologically—to exhibit, that is to say, its origin from what comes to the mind as timeless.
>
> AR, p. 33

He decides not to consider the issue of the origin of time. However, he does not dismiss such a notion as absurd. Yet it is hard to see what can be meant by the question about the temporal origin of time[12] itself as opposed to a child's first idea of it. But if he means, not time, but the sense of time, should he not say so? Or is he already implying—what is really the main point of his discussion—that time has no reality except as the illusory deliverance of some experience? If so there is really no time in which the sense of time can begin.

He remarks that time is often conceived 'under a spatial form . . . as a stream' with an ambiguity as to whether past, present, and future co-exist or not.

---

12   Cosmic speculations about the beginning of time with the 'big bang' would scarcely be relevant here.

Bradley does not develop the significance of this metaphor though he had used it himself in PL.[13] It is surely not a purely spatial metaphor, since the stream is thought of as in motion. The properly spatial metaphor for time (to which Bergson especially objected) depicts it simply as a straight line in which each event has its definite place. For that view there is no problem as to whether past, present, and future co-exist. *Now*, for any instance of thinking, is the cross-section (or short stretch) of the line at which it occurs, and the past consists of the line as it stretches away from this in the direction of what is remembered, while the future consists of what lies along it in the direction of expectation. Instants, as represented by the cross-section of the line are not simultaneous in the sense implied by this analysis, but they all are ultimately just equally there as realities. The trouble with time as common sense conceives it, surely, is that it seems both to require and to reject some such spatialisation of time.

Bradley next remarks on the way in which, as he sees it, time is vulnerable to the same critique as space. Is it merely a relation or is it something more thing-like than that? In short, is the existence of time simply the fact that certain elements stand in certain relations to each other, or is it, rather, something within which things exist?

If time is taken as a relation, we must ask whether the terms between which it holds have duration themselves, and are thereby temporal, or not. If not, then the whole time, being made up of what is timeless, must itself be timeless, so that this account removes temporality from time, and defeats itself. But if the units do have duration, then time is not simply the relation between units. If it is said that the units are indeed temporal, but that this is a matter of the way in which their existence consists in relations between more ultimate units, then the fact of time becomes a relation between terms whose own existence consists in a relation between further items, and so on *ad infinitum*. In this way we never get any account of what time is which can be completed.

Bradley's rejection of the first limb of this seems fallacious, resting on the fallacy of composition. It is like saying that the existence of a club cannot consist in the members being related in certain ways, since they are not themselves clubs, an argument for social holism which none would think holds water. Why should not the existence of time consist in the holding of certain relations between elements which are not separately temporal? If there are objections to this view, Bradley has not given them. And, as for the other limb, many would deny that such a regress is vicious. One may doubt, then, whether Bradley has shown that the existence of time cannot consist in the holding of certain relations, such as that of being earlier than, or simultaneous with, between events.

However, rightly or wrongly, Bradley thinks he has shown that time cannot be a relation. And he claims also that it must be a mere relation. For to think otherwise is to ignore what he holds to be the evident fact that nothing more is

13   See PL, pp. 54–55.

required for time to exist than that events should occur which are related in these ways. It follows, he thinks, that time involves a contradiction.

§ Bradley's whole argument at this point is impressionistic and none too impressive. James, basing himself on Zeno and Bergson, makes a better show of exhibiting the problems of time which spring from infinite divisibility. So far as there are real problems here it seems to me that an epochal view of time, such as James adumbrates, and Whitehead developed more fully, will solve them.[14]

Basically, the idea of such a theory is that any process in time is a succession of certain ultimate events with a certain wholeness and discreteness to them. They are not, however, durationless instants and that for three reasons. (1) There is an aspect of before and after within them, and yet they do not include smaller and genuinely distinct temporal units. Thus there is no meaningful question as to the number of such units. (2) Each event occupies a certain stretch of clock time. Now though there is in fact just one such event pertaining to that period it is logically possible that there might have been a succession of them. Thus, as Whitehead puts it, time is not infinitely divided but is infinitely divisible. (3) Finally, we must emphasise that on this view, foreshadowed by James, the successive events, although each has its own unity, are also continuous with each other in the sense that the end of one in a manner melts into and merges with the next.

I do not, however, find Whitehead's account altogether satisfactory. I am inclined to agree rather with James that there is something about the character of specious presents (on the model of which all ultimate events must be conceived), and the way in which they dissolve into one another, which defeats cut and dried conceptualisation and that we must simply be pointed to the reality by metaphor. Still the ephocal view seems sufficiently clear to suggest how the problems of infinite divisibility can be met, and undercuts a demonstration of time's unreality based upon them. In other ways, however, I think it very helpful for the development of an essentially Bradleyan thesis about the unreality of time, as we shall be seeing.

§ So far Bradley professes to have been dealing with time conceived spatially. He moves on from this to attempts to understand it rather as it is actually experienced or presented. What is actually presented, he says, must presumably be a *now*. Yet the problems of understanding such a *now* are insuperable.[15]

Does such a *now* contain a before and after within it? A negative answer would seem empirically false. Surely we experience things in the actual process of change. (We see the flag flapping, the cursor on the word processor pulsating.) And logically it might seem odd too. For it would imply that time is made up of the timeless (though I have noticed a certain feebleness in this as an argument).

If it does, then, contain a before and after it must include at least one or both

---

14 See Whitehead, *Process*, Part II, chapter II, §2; Part II, chapter X; Part IV, chapter I.
15 See PL, *Terminal Essays*, pp. 654–55, for a further discussion of these problems.

of past and future, for presumably it includes the present, and what is before or after this will be past or future. One view is that it contains all three, but Bradley inclines to think that it contains only 'the present changing into the past' and that the future is a 'construction'. (Provided the before-after relation is actually experienced within a specious present we can define the concept of the future in terms of what is empirically given even if we never experience anything future, but only what is past and present.[16]) However, Bradley does not insist on this, for all that matters is the acknowledgment that the now must contain a 'process' within it.

To say that it contains a process within it is to see it as consisting of a series of contained moments, which are, so to speak, little 'nows', the most genuinely *now* of which will be the true present. But the old questions arise about these *nows*. If they are ultimate, they are not really temporal, but if they are not ultimate, then we really have no *now* at all, since every putative *now* is made up of more genuine *nows*, in an infinite regress which cannot terminate in any real *now*.

Here, as before, Bradley rejects, without any adequate argument, each of two alternative views. On the first, the *now* would be a timeless instant. No real reason is given for rejecting this view beyond the fallacious argument that then time would consist in a sequence of what is timeless. On the second, any moment which for certain purposes might be called a *now* would be infinitely divisible and the occurrence of that moment would consist in the fact that included moments stand in certain relations to each other, and this would be true of each of those included moments and so on *ad infinitum*. The real objection to this second view is surely the one which James takes from Zeno, that in order that the whole moment shall come into being, first its first half has to do so, and before that the first half of that, and so on. It follows that reality can be added to only by way of an infinite series of increments which can never be completed. This difficulty is not met by pointing out that mathematically there is an infinitely divisible time within any stretch of time, within which this task can be completed. For the problem is not how a process can have room to occur within a pre-existent time, but how reality can be added to. Bradley could have made a better case for the incoherence of our notion of time by reference to this problem than in fact he did. However, if he had, he would have had to show that it cannot be resolved in anything like James's way, as it seems to me it can be, or perhaps in some other way, perhaps Husserl's.[17]

Actually towards the end of this chapter, Bradley does, in effect, give an objection to any view which denies 'time's continuity', by which he seems to mean something rather like the epochal theory. He objects to it on the ground that, if time consisted of distinct moments, there would be successions which represent the quickest possible rate of change and that, he says, is absurd.

---

16   Compare Ayer, *Essays*, pp. 177–80; Ayer, *Knowledge*, pp. 170–71.
17   See Husserl, *Time*, I, §§1–2; also *Ideas*, §81.

However, the epochal view can cope with this perfectly. For it maintains that, though every process consists in a series of undivided moments, there is no limits to the number of such moments that could have occupied its duration as measured by clock time.

§ Bradley ends the chapter by pointing out that the present must be related to past and future. But that raises the general problem of relations over again. And he briefly makes the point (really the same as that concerning the 'co-existence' of past, present, and future) that 'the existence, not presented, of past and future seems ambiguous'. In the end it seems to me that this is the only one of Bradley's reasons for regarding time as unreal which has much force, one which needs a much fuller development than he ever gives it.

(c) Motion and Change, and Their Perception

§ In the next chapter Bradley takes things a little further by offering some discussion of motion, change, and the perception of them.

He opens with typical robustness and paradox. 'Motion has from an early time been criticized severely and it has never been defended with much success' soon noting that the basic problem is that '[m]otion implies that what is moved is in two places at one time; and this seems not possible' .[18]

The problem of motion is just one case of the problem of change, and that is just one case of the problem of relations in general and of the unity of the thing amidst its various different features and relations. Just as at any one time a thing has to be somehow one in spite of its different qualities, so over time it has to be one amidst its different successive states.

Suppose A passes through states A_1, A_2, A_3, then either we have just three different things or we must treat the thing as out of time and thus distinct from each of these states. But in that case we have not got a changing thing. If we are not to remove change altogether then we have, standing in 'unintelligible relation with the timeless A, a temporal change which offers us our old difficulties unreduced'.[19] Change requires a permanence which underlies the changing states. But that implies that the permanent is something apart from these states and thus stands apart from them in a way which renders its relation to them unintelligible.

Although a good deal of what he says on this topic seems rather sophistical, he is right, surely, that there are real difficulties in explicating and justifying our ordinary thinking about continuants which undergo change while remaining the same. In effect, his point is that we must choose between a thing ontology and an event ontology but that each poses insuperable problems. The first distinguishes the thing from its passing states but cannot explain how the two stand to each other. The second cannot explain what links one moment of the world's history to the next, since this requires that there be absolutely

18   AR, p. 37.
19   AR, p. 39.

identical things whose persistence supplies the bond between them. Thus our conceptions of change and movement require a combination of the notions of identity and difference (between what is there at different moments) which we cannot render stable or coherent and can only manage by oscillating between these incompatible elements.

The problem is a genuine one, though I have already suggested that Bradley has a doctrine of concrete universals which, in fact, provides a sufficient solution of it.[20] For Bradley, however, its insolubility shows that the concepts of change and movement are incoherent and that these are therefore mere appearances. And I take it that for Bradley, since the notion of time without change is incoherent, the incoherence of change is another reason for dubbing time unreal.

§ These troubles arise not just with the changing thing but with the time in which change occurs. This has to be both a single time and a series of different times. Bradley's point seems to be this. In order to be an imaginable event a change must occur in a unitary moment which could be apprehended as a whole. But if such a moment really is unitary, there can be no change within it, for real change requires that one distinct moment succeed another. Altogether change is 'an artifice by which we become blind' alternatively to one or other of the two incompatible elements of sameness and difference

> to suit the occasion; and the whole secret consists in ignoring that aspect which we are unable to use. . . . And our compromise consists in regarding the process mainly from whichever of its aspects answers to our need, and in ignoring— that is, in failing or in refusing to perceive—the hostility of the other side. . . . But change, as a whole, consists in the union of these two aspects. It is the holding both at once, while laying stress upon the one which for the time is prominent, and while the difficulties are kept out of sight by rapid shuffling.
>
> AR, p. 40

§ Contradictory as change and succession are, we do have the experience of perceiving them, and Bradley tries to say something as to how this is possible.[21] However, much of his discussion seems rather to be a demonstration of how it is impossible.

It is generally agreed, he says, that succession could only be perceived in connection with some kind of unity. But what is this unity? One view is that a succession is 'apprehended somehow in an indivisible moment—that is, without any lapse of time—and to be so far literally simultaneous'. Bradley finds such a proposal incoherent for a variety of reasons. The apprehension is an event in history and must therefore occupy a time, and this it can only do if it is stretched out in time and thus lacks the unity claimed for it.

Moreover, it is unclear how such a unitary experience could present the

---

20   See PL, pp. 291–94. Compare my 'Personal and Impersonal Identity'.
21   See AR, p. 41 et ff.

element of difference essential to change. It purports to explain the unity of the experience in which a succession is presented by saying that it is not itself successive but a single unit. And Bradley objects that this exaggerates the extent to which 'ideas are not what they 'mean''.[22] One cannot be aware of a feature of reality through experiences which do not in some way possess it themselves. Apprehension of red can only be through an experience in which red is an actual ingredient and the same is true of an apprehension of change.

The claim that an experience can only be of things whose character it itself somehow possesses is, as we have seen, an important feature of Bradley's methodology springing from his account of judgement. In judgement we attribute a universal to reality which we find as an actual element in our own subjectivity. This seems to me correct, as I have sufficiently argued, so far as the type of intuitively fulfilled judgement sought in metaphysics goes.

However, it is not so much judgement as perception which is in question here. How does the principle apply to it? Digging below the surface a bit, we may say that, for Bradley, perception is attention directed at some actual ingredient of one's present this-now, which, in virtue of synthetic judgements of sense, is taken to be a bit of a larger extended world. Thus what is strictly perceived is an actual part of one's experience. It follows from this that a succession cannot be perceived except by an experience which includes a real succession and thus has a before and after within it. So succession cannot be perceived in a moment in which there is no lapse, and yet one which does contain a lapse seems not to be a single experience. (Among those who would deny this is Husserl, who claims that we perceive change at each durationless instant of flowing time through a retention of what has been perceived previously.[23] However, I do not see how retention can give a real experience of succession unless that succession is somehow given as a genuinely occurring element within our present experience.)

Might not the solution be that the total experience is unitary on the self side and successive on the not-self side? Bradley himself, it seems, favours something of that sort, but believes that we cannot form a really coherent conception along these lines. For so great a contrast between the self and not-self would seem incompatible with their belonging to a single experience.

The upshot seems to be that there is something incoherent in the very idea of an experience of change. For it must be single if it is to be a genuine experience of anything and must be successive if it is to be of a succession.

§ Bradley seems to have arrived at an impasse. It is not just real succession and change which are impossible but any kind of experience which *seems* to be of them. Yet it is absurd to say that we do not have even such a seeming experience of them.

He tries, however, to derive an account of the nature of the experience of

---

22   AR p. 43
23   See Husserl, *Time*, p. 44 et ff.

change and succession from his account of what it is that is incoherent in the
concept of them. The trouble with that was that it attempted to combine
incompatible elements of identity and difference. For we can think about them
only through an oscillation between incompatible elements which works fairly
well in practice but does not yield a single coherent concept.

This give us our clue to the perception of succession. This is a piece of
changing experience in which the lapse is not noticed, and the unitary aspect,
which also belongs to it, is emphasised.

> We found that succession required both diversity and unity. *These could not*
> *intelligibly be combined,* and their union was a mere junction, with oscillation of
> emphasis from one aspect to the other. And so, psychically also, the timeless
> unity is a piece of duration, not experienced *as* successive. Assuredly every-
> thing psychical is an event, and it really contains a lapse; but so far as you do
> not use, or notice, that lapse, it is not there for you and for the purpose in hand.
> . . . Presence is not absolute timelessness; it is any piece of duration, so far as
> that is considered from or felt in an identical aspect.
>
> AR, p. 44 (My italics in second sentence)

But who is it who fails to notice the lapse in the perception of change, an
outsider who describes the experience as a perception of a series, or the person
for whom it currently is such a perception? Presumably it is the latter, for
Bradley is trying to explain the actual character of such an experience. That
implies that for there to be a perception of change there must be an experience
with two contrasting felt characteristics: it must be and feel itself to contain a
lapse, in order that there be a change to be perceived, and it must feel and be
unchanging, in order that the change be grasped in a single synthetic grasp.

What is really troubling about this is that he says that these characteristics
are incompatible. That seems to imply that the experience of change is no more
of a reality than is real change. Evidently its very existence consists in its failure
to register its own impossibility!

§ Could it possibly be true that it is not only the concepts of change and
succession which are incoherent, so that there is really no such thing, but that
the same is true of the very experiences in which they seem to be presented?
The philosopher who claims that some familiar feature of reality, as we ordinarily conceive it, is unreal is, surely, obliged to explain what it is about our
experiences which make us normally postulate such a thing. Many think that
that cannot be done in the case of change, since the experiences in question can
only be conceived in temporal terms. I believe that there is an adequate answer
to this which Bradley's account of finite centres of experience makes available.
But this seems to require that, even if change itself is unreal, there really are
experiences in which change seems to be present. If such experiences are
themselves unreal, and merely useful posits of that of which there can be no
coherent conception, then there is no home either for the experience of time or
even for the conceiving of such an experience.

For when space and time or physical reality in general are said to be unreal
what is meant (I have suggested) is that nothing really answers precisely to our

concepts thereof. And the point now seems to be that nothing really answers precisely to the concept 'perception of change'. Doubtless we can still say that there is some reality which suggests our concept of such a perception but it will no more really be such a thing than is the reality which suggests our concept of the physical really physical.

In my discussion of Bradley's view of physical reality I have assumed that our experience of the physical is real even if the physical is not. The one is something posited in a judgement, the other is the judgement's psychological home and experiential basis. But now we seem invited to believe that the experiences in which we posit the various things Bradley calls appearances are themselves simply appearances.

Some of the difficulty stems from Bradley's unacknowledged use of 'appearance' in two *prima facie* distinct senses, even if he is not aware of it, for an inevitable but incoherent posit and for a component in a whole which lacks independent individuality. (We noted above that these senses are not sharply distinct, for on Bradley's view we cannot form a correct conception of any such component without a correct conception of the whole, such as is impossible for us. But there must, surely, be at least a difference of degree between them, so that the reality corresponding to an appearance in the second sense is much less remote from our conception of it that in the first case).

There is no great difficulty in holding that the temporality of an experience is an appearance in the first sense if this means that it is not really a member of any series properly called temporal. For the existence of a temporal series of experiences can be interpreted as a posit made from within one or more experiences supposed to belong to it. But to hold that the experiences within which the construction is constituted, together with whatever experience of change they extend by such a construction, are appearances in this sense (except in a very qualified way) is deeply puzzling. That Bradley does seem to hold this may reflect his confusion of the two senses of 'appearance'.

If experiences are appearances primarily in the second sense and only appearances in the first sense to a limited degree, then it should be possible to go some way to conceiving them satisfactorily and in a way which explains their apparently temporal character. And Bradley does, after all, seem to hold out some hope of this by suggesting that we distinguish between the character of the perception of time and the validity of its content. Thus he says that it is one thing

> to see how a certain feature of our time-perception is possible. It is quite another thing to admit that this feature, as it stands, gives the truth about reality.
>
> AR, p. 44

This is surely to allow that the experience is real in a sense in which its deliverance is not. However, if this is to provide an explanation of the unreality of time compatible with the upshot of even the most superficial introspection, one must distinguish that part of an experience's temporal deliverance which can be cut off from its own nature and that which cannot. Perhaps its sense of itself as belonging to a temporal series of similar moments belongs to the first, and its sense of itself as containing a lapse within it to the second. For it is hard to see how the latter could be a delusion even from the point of view of ultimate metaphysical truth.

§ Once again I suggest that Bradley is reaching for an epochal view of time close to that of James. That would allow him to say that the perception of change comes in a unit containing a *before* and *after*, which, however, are not distinct items related by a relation, but inseparable aspects of its unitary but variegated character. This coheres well with the main lines of Bradley's philosophy and seems to be the notion with which he sometimes effectively operates. But the actual account of this perception given in chapter V of AR is the more obscure one that it is an experience which must have a false feeling of its own character.

(d) What Corresponds to Time in the Absolute?

§ Rightly or wrongly, Bradley thinks that he has shown time to be unreal. But quite apart from the force or otherwise of his arguments, what does the claim amount to, and what is the reality behind the appearance of time supposed to be?

There are some passages which suggest that the sense in which Bradley regards time as unreal is the first, the Platonic and Indian one, of those listed in section 3a of this chapter.

> Everything that is worth our having is (you may say) our own doing, and exists only so far as produced by ourselves. But you must add that, in the whole region of human value, there is nothing that has not come down to us from another world—nothing which fails still to owe its proper being and reality to that which lives and works beyond the level of mere time and existence.
>
> PL, p. 724

This suggests that the temporal flux is a transitory and, in some sense, unreal manifestation of an underlying timeless reality. And Bradley does tend to think of the temporal as somehow owing both its being and its value to the way in which it manifests something non-temporal. But much of what he says implies the (to me) more interesting second sense in which time may be regarded as unreal, namely, that the very events in the temporal flux are somehow—in a way in which I shall try to explain—elements of a timeless reality and in the last resort themselves really timeless. I shall call this view eternalism.

§ It is this view which finds expression in chapter XVIII of Part Two of AR, which is supposed to be about Reality rather than Appearance. Here Bradley tries to show how the unreality of time and change, as required by the doctrine of the Absolute and supposedly demonstrated by the arguments we have considered, is compatible with their undoubted existence as appearances. By such existence, I have contended, Bradley means the being a necessary posit in our ordinary way of dealing with things. However, as we have seen, there is a peculiar difficulty in regarding time and change as mere appearances in this sense, for they seem to be immediately given in experience. Bradley, indeed, asks us to distinguish between an experience and its deliverance. However, in this case, they seem peculiarly close and we shall have to see how far he meets this point.

§ Bradley begins by noting that time itself struggles to give way to something non-temporal. 'Thus, in asserting itself, time tries to commit suicide as itself, to transcend its own character and to be taken up in what is higher'.[24] What this colourful statement evidently means is that the more developed our thoughts about temporal fact, the more we characterise it in terms tending to the timeless. We cannot conceive of change without an underlying permanent which unites its successive phases. Moreover, the scientific account of the world 'treats past and future as one thing with the present'.[25] It reaches for statements of law which do not change their truth value and thus lie beyond time.

These reflections seem rather questionable. The belief that change takes place according to unchanging laws has little in common with the belief that it is unreal. But perhaps Bradley is right on two points. We have already sufficiently considered the first and have not found that it provides much of a case for dubbing change (and hence time) unreal. The other, only rather vaguely implied by some of what he says, is much more powerful in this connection and, as I have already hinted and shall argue at length in the next section, gives a really good argument for the unreality of time in the sense in which the doctrine of the Absolute requires it. (1) Ordinary thought about change and time both requires and renders problematic the notion that the same thing exists at different times. For, on the one hand, we tend to think of different times as different parts of the universe in which we cannot find exactly the same existents, while on the other hand identity of things across time seems necessary to knit one moment of time to another. (2) We cannot think of temporal fact without treating past and present (though normally not the future) as realities on a par with one another, while yet we betray our ordinary concept of time if we think that reality contains the past, just as it does the present.

§ If the Absolute, or Universe in its true being, is timeless, there must still, surely, be something about it which explains the existence of time as an appearance. Bradley, however, disclaims any obligation to explain what this is. He is content to show that there is nothing about time as an appearance which precludes its ultimately illusory character. He does this partly by drawing attention to certain features of time as we conceive it 'which help to weaken our belief in time's solidity.'

1. Normally we think of there being just one time within which every event stands in a definite temporal relation to every other. But a little thought shows that there could be many different time series, such that events within one are in no temporal relation to events within another. Indeed, this is true of events within different dreams or fictions, for we should not confuse the date within

---

24   AR, p. 183.
25   AR, p. 183.

the time pertaining to these with the dates we ascribe to the thoughts through which we posit them.[26] All events, Bradley notes, must be felt together in the Absolute, but it need not unite them all by temporal relations.

2. It is quite conceivable that time goes in a different direction for different minds. There may be events a b c d occurring in the experience of two beings, but for one the order may be a b c d and for the other d c b a (or even b a d c, or c d a b). For 'the direction, and the distinction between past and future, entirely depends upon *our* experience.'[27] In short, for any one momentary experience the past is that from which it feels itself to have arisen, or what it constructs upon the basis of that feeling, and the future is what it feels itself to be moving into. So if there are two experiences of b as present, one may feel itself to be arising out of an experience for which a was present and moving on to one for which c is present, while for the other it may be the other way round.[28]

But are not such alternative orderings ruled out by causal considerations, and are not these what really determine our beliefs about temporal order?[29] Well, Bradley claims to have shown already that causation is unreal. It turns on the assumption that when one state of affairs X becomes Y, it must do so for a reason R. But if there must be a reason for one state of affairs becoming another, there must also be a reason for X, together with R, becoming Y, and hence another reason R_2. Thus events can only follow on each other in virtue of causal relations if an infinite series of causal necessitations is completed—which Bradley takes to be impossible.

I do not think there is much to be said for this argument. Whatever the difficulties in the concept of causation, the main contenders for a satisfactory analysis raise no such problem. More forceful is his suggestion that the usual causal explanation of events is so complex that it is unreasonable to assume that an event can only be explained in one temporal direction. And he might have added that the idea that the direction of time is entirely a causal matter ignores the extent to which it is also derivative from the nature of our memory experiences, feelings of anticipation, and so forth, and that it seems conceivable that these might point in different directions for different minds. Moreover, even if an adequate account of causation would rule out some of the possibilities Bradley plays with, they would certainly not rule out the most important, which is that there may be quite different time systems totally cut off from each other.

Personally I think the main possibilities Bradley describes (in much more detail than has been done here) are real ones. However, their being so seems rather to be a deduction from the unreality of time in the ordinary sense than something which can be used in support of it. A philosopher firmly committed to the reality of time in that sense will simply dub them impossible.

---

26   See AR, pp. 186–89.
27   SSee AR, pp. 189–92.
28   See AR, p. 192.
29   For a careful working out of a causal account of temporal order, see Mellor.

§ The upshot of all this would seem to be as follows:

The conscious history of any finite sentient being consists in a series of total experiences (that is, of momentary centres of experience or this-nows) and their forming a temporal series turns on two related factors. First, that each comes with a sense of having emerged out of previous ones, which thereby constitute its past, and of issuing into others which thereby constitute its possible future. Thus they feel to themselves to be passing away and as mere transitions between what precedes and follows. Second, that within each total experience a larger world is posited to which they belong and within which events are arranged in temporal connections definable in terms of *before, after,* and *simultaneity.* The meaning of these expression lies partly in their association with immediate feelings of *emergence from* and *passage into,* partly in the kind of causal story into which they are woven.

All such total experiences (and any other kindred experiential units there may be) whether, from the point of view of *this one here,* they are *past, present,* or *future,* or in another time system, are just eternally there as elements in that one total experience which is the Absolute. They are included there with precisely whatever feeling of their own transitoriness, and relation to a larger world, they have for themselves, though the Absolute feels them in a unison with other experiences which may give them a quite different significance for it in their total upshot. Thus they are all present there with their own feelings of temporality and of transitoriness, and with their felt positing of other events to which they stand in temporal relations of one kind and another. Nonetheless, from the point of view of the Absolute, they do not come and go, but are eternal elements (each with precisely those features which make it a part of a temporal world in its own eyes and of other finite experiences in community with it) in that one eternal experience which it feels or knows itself to be.

Such a view, I suggest, is what Bradley must believe, and could believe, and therefore did believe. But that is to say only that it is what he ought to have believed. However, there is much that seems to make it clear enough that this was his actual position. Consider, for example, such passages as the following:[30]

> Is there, in the end and on the whole, any progress in the universe? Is the Absolute better or worse at one time than at another? It is clear that we must answer in the negative, since progress and decay are alike incompatible with perfection. There is of course progress in the world, and there is also retrogression, but we cannot think that the Whole either moves on or backwards. The Absolute has no history of its own, though it contains histories without number. These, with their tale of progress or decline, are constructions starting

---

30   The first passage comes just after the statement famously chosen by Ayer in *Language, Truth and Logic,* p. 36, as a prize piece of metaphysical nonsense chosen at random, that the Absolute 'enters into, but is itself incapable of, evolution and progress'.

from and based on some one given piece of finitude. They are but partial aspects in the region of temporal appearance. Their truth and reality may vary much in extent and in importance, but in the end it can never be more than relative. And the question whether the history of a man or a world is going forwards or back, does not belong to metaphysics. For nothing perfect, nothing genuinely real, can move. The Absolute has no seasons, but all at once bears its leaves, fruit, and blossoms. Like our globe it always, and it never, has summer and winter.

AR, p. 442

[S]uppose, for instance, that the lapse of time were ultimately real in our experience, then what on such a view would have become of our past? To us it could be nothing, unless indeed we possessed a miraculous 'Faculty of Memory'. If there is not, present in this passing 'now', a Reality which contains all 'nows' future and past, the whole of our truth and knowledge must be limited to the 'now' that we perceive. For to reach a larger Universe by transcendence would really be nonsense.

ETR, p. 332

The exact meaning of saying that the Absolute contains all histories is rather complex. All moments of experience in which temporal processes are presented are certainly elements in the Absolute, but it does not follow that they are strung out there in a quasi-temporal series in which their positions correspond to the positions in time which they ascribe to themselves and to each other. Time only exists as posited within single total experiences and the organization of individual experiences within the Absolute may have little correspondence to it. The Absolute contains histories without number primarily in the sense that it contains the experiences in which they are posited. This leaves it open how far its own unification of all finite experiences is in patterns isomorphic to any of these histories.

But surely some of what is posited within a single moment of experience about other experiences supposed to have occurred in the past is correct in literal truth. If I remember what I did yesterday I believe that among past events there is one answering to the description I give myself of that experience. And surely in most cases such an experience, indeed the very one I posit, is one of those total experiences which belongs together in the Absolute. Bradley can hardly be denying this. What he is denying, rather, is that it is genuinely true that that experience which I describe to myself as one I had yesterday is really 'in the past'. For pastness is something which only belongs to events from a beholder's point of view.

§ In some respects Josiah Royce gives an account of the relation between the Absolute and time which seems more intelligible than Bradley's.[31] For him the absolute experience is comparable to one of our specious presents and within it the experiences which make up the world have quasi-temporal relations

---

31   See Royce, *World*, I, pp. 424–27: II, p. 141.

comparable to those which hold for us within these. Just as each of our specious presents is an experience of some A changing into B so will the absolute experience be of a total historical process which includes all our experiences. What sets it quite apart (in addition to its inconceivably vaster comprehensiveness) from one of our specious presents is that it will have no sense of itself as an ephemeral transition point between a preceding and a subsequent experience.

There is much less suggestion in Bradley that the absolute experience has this quasi-temporal internal character. Indeed, it might seem even precluded by the fact, first, that it probably contains experiences pertaining to quite separate historical systems and, second, that what is felt most closely together within it may not be experiences which we see as temporally contiguous but rather ones which have a common deliverance. But I see no reason why he should not have thought that the individual historical systems are felt about somewhat in this way. Moreover, in taking our *this-nows* as our best model for the unity of the Absolute he seems to imply that it is something like a frozen specious present. This seems to me the best clue we have to the Absolute's nature. However, the main point is that the Absolute is a unitary experience which is simply eternally there and which includes all finite total experiences within it in an eternal present. And this view seems to be undoubtedly Bradley's.

§ It may be objected that, for Bradley, none of our total experiences belong as such to the Absolute, since that contains only a transmuted version of them.

Though Bradley sometimes seems to be saying this, it can hardly be quite what he means. His view is rather that, from the point of view of the absolute experience, they do not have the sorts of relations to each other which they seem to themselves to have. This is not to deny that they belong to the Absolute as just what they are for themselves. If he were denying that, he would be admitting that there is something which falls outside of the Absolute. He would be acknowledging the point made against absolutism by James (and later withdrawn) that an experience described as composed of total experiences A, B, C, is really a fresh experience synthesising the deliverances of these three experiences into one experience, but not literally containing them. But Bradley must deny this if he is to have the Absolute all-inclusive.

There are, clearly, problems in understanding the way in which Bradley thinks our experiences belong to the absolute experience. Maybe he is incoherent here. I am inclined to think that he is, and that a more successful absolute idealism must correct him by making it clear that experiences do not lose (or rather, eternally fail to possess) their own private characters as elements in the Absolute. And, in fact, the whole thrust of Bradley's metaphysics implies that all total experiences really are eternally there in just their own felt character in the Absolute. It is not as though this experience occurs twice, once as mine and then again as the Absolute's, still less that these occurrences are successive, as Bradley's talk of things becoming transmuted in the Absolute suggest. If absolutism is true there is no duplication of our finite experiences, with one the experience as it is for us, the other as it is for the Absolute. Rather there is the single experience which feels itself and which as feeling itself is part of the one absolute experience.

So, upon the whole, I think we must take it that, for Bradley, all total experiences, of which it is ever true that they are taking place, have taken place, or will take place, are just eternally there in their place in the Absolute. That place may not be temporal as we conceive time but there they are nonetheless, and in many cases they are there with knowledge of each other's being and to some extent character. Certainly absolutism, of a Bradleyan sort, requires that the past and the future are real in a rather strong sense, inasmuch as all my so-called past and future experiences are eternally there in the absolute with the same throbbing presentness as is this so-called present one in which these thoughts are finding expression.

§ It must now be admitted that there are passages in which Bradley seems to deny the reality of the past and still more of the future as an independent reality in its own right rather than as something posited in present experience. For example, in discussing various views of the self, he says that to take the soul as 'those psychical events, which it both is now and has been' is, though proper enough for ordinary purposes, to qualify 'something by adjectives which are not, and to offer it as an expression of ultimate truth would be wholly indefensible'.[32] And shortly after this he says 'Past and future, and the Nature which no one perceives exist, as such, only for some subject which thinks them'.[33] Likewise in a letter to James of 1910 he says: 'You seem (e.g.) to ask me to believe in a real past fact independent of present experience. Of course I reject such a thing. Of course I at once ask you how, even if it existed, you could know that it existed and get it into your mind.'[34]

In PL, in particular, he several times insists that the past has no existence except as a present construction and there is no suggestion that this is a view later superseded.

> [E]vents past and future, and all things not perceived, exist *for us* only as ideal constructions connected, by an inference through identity of quality, with the real that appears in present perception. In what character (if any) these things really exist *for themselves*, is a question for metaphysics.
>
> PL, p. 75

And again on p. 587 he says:

> For unless we think that phenomena can be real, though they appear to no one,

---

32   AR, p. 275.
33   AR, p. 279.
34   Bradley to James in a letter dated 2 January 1910, quoted in Perry, II, p. 641. Compare also PL, pp. 55 and 719. The letter, however, continues in a vein which seems to suggest that, if one once acknowledges that time is unreal (as James would not), the reality of the past is saved.

we must hold that the past, *at least as we know it*, has no existence outside reproduction. . . . We thus either have relinquished the presumption that reality lies in what is *given* to sense, or are compelled to admit that a *serial* reality is itself a bad inference.

PL, p. 587–88[35]

However, it is hard to believe that he means that experiences, such as I correctly think I had, have no status in reality except as useful posits. So perhaps he only means that I am wrong in conceiving them as past rather than as fellow components in the Absolute. For to suppose that, apart from our thought of them, past experiences are nothing is to adopt a 'philosophy of the present', which is certainly not Bradley's view. Likewise his denial at times of the reality of the future must mean that future events are not real qua future, but are, so far as they have a being beyond our conceptions, realities which in themselves are nows.[36]

However, uncompromising as some of these statements appear, it is hard to see how they can be taken at face value. Their point must surely be that past and future experiences are *for us* nothing except as thought about, while Bradley holds in reserve his doctrine that in absolute truth they are all eternally there in the Absolute.[37] If so, this is one of those cases where a philosopher talks about a limitation in the objects of human thought while clearly having an inconsistent belief in them in reserve himself. As such it is not a very satisfactory aspect of his treatment of time. The best sense I can make of them would be as explorations of the implications of common sense.[38] For common sense the past is, up to a point, regarded as nothing and yet inconsistently a thing's past is regarded as part of its character. Some of Bradley's obscurities stem, I suspect, from the fact that while he was committed to an eternalistic view, he thought

---

35 Bradley is insisting in such passages that we must not, as empiricists do, treat a series of experiences as though it were a given fact. The past, qua past, is never known immediately. But as for what the past is, when metaphysics gives its answer, surely it is (like the present and future) immediate experience eternally located in the Absolute.

36 An early treatment of this matter occurs in *The Presuppositions of Critical History*, reprinted in CE. Here Bradley insisted on the unavailability to us of, and meaninglessness of looking for, a past which is not what we construct from accessible data on our own principles, and thus on the fact 'that the past varies with the present, and can never do otherwise, since it is always the present upon which it rests' (CE, p. 20). However, the argument fits in well with the view, if it does not quite say, that while human experiences only make up a narrative, perhaps only have a definite order, insofar as collected in the thoughts of a thereby later mind, nonetheless the experiences themselves took place independently of being thus collected (see CE, pp. 7–8).

37 Thus the passage just quoted from his letter to James is illustrating the point that for Bradley *'knowledge* or *belief* beyond experience is impossible' (my italics).

38 This seems to me in accord with such remarks as that at PL, p. 587, about the past.

it more 'way out' than we are inclined to do since Einstein and so often reverts to discussing things from a supposedly more common-sense perspective for which only the present is real. [39]

In any case, however we parse such passages, he can hardly be denying that such experiences as actually occurred in the past, temporally speaking, together with those which lie in the future, all belong eternally to the Absolute along with this *now*. For,

> In the Absolute, there is neither mere existence at one moment nor ideal construction. Each is merged in a higher and all containing Reality.[40]

While such an assertion is hardly crystal clear, it is naturally read as implying the eternalistic view which is essential to Bradley's metaphysic.

(e) Eternalism of the Type Bradley's System Really Requires

§ I believe that the essential truth of what I shall call eternalism, the view that there is a total reality which does not change and in which all moments of time are eternally present as 'nows', can be demonstrated on the basis of certain considerations about truth. To demonstrate this is not of course of itself to demonstrate the existence of Bradley's Absolute. However, it is to demonstrate that reality as a whole has one of those characteristics which Bradley ascribes to it. Whether it has the others is to be assessed on the basis of an evaluation of Bradley's panexperientialism and his position on relations.

My demonstration owes much, indeed almost everything, to the work of George Santayana.[41] Santayana was no absolute idealist, indeed he was the sworn enemy of any such view. Moreover, he professed himself a believer in the reality of time. I shall say something briefly about his actual position later. For the present I merely wish to make the acknowledgement, while emphasising the distaste Santayana might have felt for seeing his work used to supplement a Bradleyan metaphysics.

§ We may begin by asking how a plain man, if there is such a thing, reacts to the question: Are past, present, and future all equally real? He would say, I think, that the present is the one thing which is fully real, the past has a kind of secondary reality, and the future no reality at all.

If he did so, what would he have taken 'real' as meaning? Well, perhaps as: *absolutely determinate in character.* This would coincide with a current usage,

---

39   Somewhere, I seem to recall, he speaks of 'daring' to believe in the reality of past and future.

40   I have searched for the location of this passage I once copied down, but cannot find it.

41   See Santayana, *Matter,* chapters IV and V, and *Truth,* chapters IX and X; also Sprigge, *Santayana,* chapters VIII and, especially, IX, and Sprigge, 'Immortality'. Some of the material in the present section was used in Sprigge, 'Unreality', and Sprigge, 'Hartshorne'.

introduced by Michael Dummett, for which a theory about things of a certain type is *anti-realist* if it rejects the law of bivalence with reference to them (so that certain propositions about things of that sort are neither true nor false) and *realist* if it accepts it (so that all propositions about them have a definite truth value). Personally I think this use of 'realist' somewhat unfortunate, as there are views about things which are realist in this sense but not realist in more traditional senses of more interest for our purposes. In the present context, in particular, it is important not to identify too readily the claim that past and present are equally real with the claim that they are equally determinate, though I think the first claim will imply the second on any reasonable interpretation of it.

However, if that was all that was meant by 'real' in this context, and if one succeeded in making it quite clear to him that the question was not about the availability of evidence about the matter now, but of sheer truth, I suggest he might well move to the view that the present and past are both equally real, but that the future is less real. For the usual view is, surely, that present and past are absolutely determinate, while the future is to a great extent indeterminate or open. Let us call this *the standard view* about the determinateness or otherwise of these three regions.

§ The standard view has been challenged by some philosophers. For example:

(1) Some philosophers say that the future is just as determinate as past and present. All have a determinate character. The only difference is that a human knows less of what lies before, than of what is over. It will be convenient to call this *determinationism.*

(2) Other philosophers say that the past is not determinate. It is there only in the sense that it is recalled, reported, or evidenced in an unambiguous way. Where evidence as to what happened is non-existent, then there is no definite truth of the matter. Let us call this *the philosophy of the present.* According to this philosophy, the past only exists insofar as it is in some way recorded or posited in the present, and the future doesn't exist in any definite way either.[42]

There is a tendency for the philosophy of the present to turn into the view that propositions about the past are hypotheses about what evidence is discoverable about it. This is better called *predictionism* since it makes propositions about the past into predictions as to what will be observed as a result of certain researches. However, I shall largely lump predictionism and the philosophy of the present together in what follows since I shall have much the same to say about each of them.

The two most explicit predictionists of whom I know were C. I. Lewis and the early A. J. Ayer.[43] While it does not appear that they took predictionism

---

42   This is the view advanced in Mead. In an odd way Schopenhauer also sometimes seems to have espoused it.

43   See Ayer, *Language,* pp. 101–2, and C. I. Lewis, *Mind,* pp. 150–53.

as implying that the past was indeterminate, it would, in fact, make it quite likely that it is so, for we can hardly be confident that all propositions about the past are verifiable as true or false. Michael Dummett has some sympathy with predictionism, and for him it certainly is associated with the so-called anti-realist position about the past according to which in certain respects there may be no definite truth about it.[44]

So in what follows when I talk of predictionism I shall take it as leaving open the possibility that some properly formed propositions about the past are neither true nor false because there is no way of verifying their truth or falsehood by tests we can hope to make in the future.

§ The philosophy of the present and predictionism are such weird views that I doubt whether many people really hold them. I shall try to bring out their strangeness by a little story. If I am successful, I will have persuaded the reader that the serious alternatives are either determinationism or the standard view. The Bradleyan eternalist is, of course, bound to side with determinationism, but we are still a long way from establishing such eternalism. At this stage what I want to establish is simply that the serious options are the standard view and determinationism and that no sensible person will accept either the philosophy of the present or predictionism.

Suppose a man alone on a raft, after a shipwreck, decides that he is not going to survive for long, so he decides to cut the agony short by drowning himself. But before he does so, he recites a favourite poem out aloud, and no one hears him. And he also says to himself that it will always be true that he showed that act of defiance to fate, since what has once been so cannot cease to be so.

Now can one really resist the admission that he is quite right in thinking that it will then remain true, for ever after, that he did so, so that the manner of his death is for ever part of the world's history, however undiscoverable?

If you deny this, think of some trivial fact about a present or recent experience of yours, which you plan to keep private, and which it is evident no one will ever find out about in the future, or probably have any interest in finding out about. Can you really say to yourself that one day it won't even be the case that you had that experience—not of course, that it will be the case that you did not have it, but simply that nothing of that sort will be the case at all?

§ If you are persuaded, as I think you should be, that such an idea is absurd, you will have to agree that the past can possess quite determinate features which no one can now or henceforth ever know about.

It may be suggested that one might reject this view on the idealist ground that facts about matters never put to the test, and no longer open to testing, never were and never will be determinate. However, the relevant contention is not so much that the past is entirely determinate as that there are at least parts of it which are so even when it is no longer possible to know about them. And in any case the idealist of any sense will only hold that it is only matters of

---

44   See Dummett, *Truth*, chapter XXI.

physical fact which can be thus indeterminate. Maybe there are facts about my physical environment which are indeterminate because no one ever makes the appropriate check. That is a plausible view for one who thinks that there is really nothing but experience, and that the physical is a pragmatic construction. But he will still think that there is an absolutely determinate truth about the existence and character of my present experience and that it cannot one day cease to be true that it occurred and had that character.

The important thing, then, for determinationism and the standard view is that there is a certain class of facts about the past which are determinate, even though they may be beyond the reach of knowledge henceforth and that these include all facts about the experiences anyone has ever had. And it is in denying this that the philosophy of the present and predictionism seem so absurd. For it is really unbelievable that it may one day cease to be true that someone ever had the experiences they are now having.[45]

§ In view of the strangeness of denying that it will always remain true, once one has had a certain experience, that one did so, it seems reasonable to take the proposition that the past is as determinate in character as the present as a premiss in our further reasonings. The question which now stands out is this: Is the future indeterminate or open in some sense which is not just a matter of our ignorance of it? Or is there just as determinate a truth about all aspects of the future as there is about the past?

Is there, for example, an absolutely precise truth as to what each of us will do tomorrow in the sense in which we now agree that there is an absolutely precise truth as to exactly what each of us did yesterday?[46] In short, which is correct, the standard view or determinationism?

---

45 But might not a Bradleyan argue that while there is an absolutely determinate truth about what experiences will ever have taken place (or perhaps more accurately about what experiences pertain timelessly to reality) there is not a determinate truth as to their temporal ordering or as to which are past, present, or future from the point of view of other experiences, since this is more a matter of construction from within centres than of what is actually experienced in any centre? If so, there will not be a determinate truth about the past, for it will not be determinate which experiences belong to the past nor as to how one experience followed on another. This is correct. But such a view remains basically a form of determinationism, for truths about the actual character of all individual experiences which it will ever be correct to say have taken place will be timelessly true, whatever indeterminacy there may be as to their order or as to which are properly to be called past and future by judgements occurring in a particular centre.

46 That the present is determinate may be taken as common ground to all three views. It seems to me, indeed, that it is our awareness of the definiteness of present fact from which we get the very idea of determinacy. Leemon McHenry has argued, as against this, that it is only the past, and neither present nor future, which is determinate for a Whiteheadian, for whom the present is the unfinished process of determining what will be. (McHenry, pp. 151–53.) I admit that I find it hard to take this on board. Incidentally, if there is some unclarity in the notion of the

Determinationism holds that the sorts of proposition about the past, however exactly we define them, which have a determinate truth value also have it when they concern the future. Or what comes to the same thing, the propositions which will have a determinate truth value when they become propositions about the past have that determinate truth value already, or, as some might prefer to say, have it timelessly. The standard view, in contrast, holds that there are propositions about the future, of the sort which could not be indeterminate if they concerned the past, and cannot remain so once the appropriate time elapses, which do not have any truth value. (The temptation to express the point by saying that they do not have it *now* should be resisted. That suggests that they do have it at some other time. The point is simply that they do not have a truth value, though one day they will.) [47]

§ In examining the rival claims of determinationism and of the standard view it is unnecessary to tie the argument closely to any particular view about the sorts of items of which 'true' and 'false' are most basically predicated: subsistent propositions, sentences, ideas, or judgements. I shall assume with Bradley that it is judgements which are true or false in the most basic sense, though including under this head not just judgements actually made, but also possible judgements, that is, acts of judgement or thought which would be true or false if made. Thus in saying that there is a definite truth about something I shall mean that various possible acts of judgement or thought would be true if made. (They are in a sense true even if not made, but only in the sense that if they were made they would be correct or incorrect, true or false.) However, the main points I shall be making could be adapted to each alternative. They do, however, presuppose that the truth of such items must lie in their 'corresponding' in some sense to what they are about. We have seen that Bradley himself holds this, so far as the truth of judgements acceptable in metaphysics goes, and I shall be

---

present, neither determinationism nor the standard view need be worried by that too much. The point is that they do not allow that anything one might call the present has a privilege over what one might call the past in terms of determinacy. If there is a problem in settling what is meant precisely by the present or by 'now', these are difficulties for the philosophy of the present, rather than for the standard view or determinationism. Since determinationism treats past, present, and future very much on a par, a difficulty in settling their precise boundaries can easily be taken on board, while the standard view can deal with it provided it can make a sharp separation between present and past together from the future. But the philosophy of the present has a grave problem in deciding just how long that moment lasts at which the determinants of all current factual truth must exist. It is difficult to say quite what the requirement of predictionism are on this matter.

47   A more radical view might even say that there will one day be true propositions about the past such that there is not at present even an indeterminate proposition about the future corresponding to them, on such grounds as that propositions about persons need an existing or having existed referent. This is sufficiently close to the standard view, as I have specified it, not to need separate treatment.

trying to reinforce the reader's commitment to this in the course of the discussion.

Discussion of Bradley's own precise position is complicated by his conception of truth and falsehood as a matter of degree. To take account of this one would have to interpret the debate between the standard view and determinationism as over the extent to which judgements which were once judgements about the future, but are now about the past, already had *then* whatever degree of truth they have *now that they are about the past* and that those *now about the future* already have whatever degree of truth they are *ever* going to have. However, it will simplify matters if we ignore the doctrine of degrees of truth. Such a simplification is justified because, if the argument I shall give for eternalism goes through on the assumption that truth and falsehood are a more definite affair than that doctrine implies, it will equally go through when qualified so as to take account of it. Moreover, it seems to me that an eternalist view of time is much more important for establishing a Bradleyan account of the Absolute than the doctrine of degrees of truth and is better discussed without the special complications that that doctrine brings to the discussion.

§ It is important in this discussion not to confuse *determinationism* either with *determinism* or with *fatalism* as that term is most naturally understood. For it is very important to distinguish the question whether the future is determinate, from the question whether it is determined (causally determined). Determinationism is different from determinism.

The determinist holds that the future is determined by what has preceded it. To hold that the future is causally determined is to say that there are laws of nature such that the character of the future could, in principle, be read off from the character of the present and future by means of them. This is by no means implied by the determinationist's view that there is a determinate truth about the future.

This can be seen from the fact that the determinateness of the past does not depend on its being connected with what has gone on since then in such a way that it could be read off from the present, with proper knowledge of laws of change. And we can grasp the point also by the consideration that if you think of space as divided into two halves, common sense will assume that at any one moment there is a determinate truth about what exists in each half, but is not thereby committed to holding that what exists in one half could be read off from what is present in the other half.

The distinction between determinism and determinationism may be illustrated thus, with alphabetical order depicting the unfolding of events according to strict law, its absence depicting a degree of unlawfulness, and letters of the alphabet standing for determinate events, with the large N standing for *now*:

(1)   G H I J K L M N O P Q R S T U

Contrast with:

(2)   Y D M S L R W N A P F U M T C

In both cases the right hand part of the line is just as determinate as that of the left part, but only in the first case could you read the one off from the other. So our question is not whether the truth is more like (2) than (1), but whether it is more like one or other of these than like either (3) or (4) below where the dots represent gaps, either such that there are in principle discoverable grounds for very precise anticipations of how they will be filled, or such that the precise filling they will eventually have could not be reasonably surmised on the basis even of unlimited information.

(3)   G H I J K L M N ....

(4)   Y D M S L R w N ....

§ So the question: Is the future determinate? is not the same as the question: Is it determined? It could be determinate without being determined. Moreover, there is even a sense in which it could be determined without being determinate. It could be that determinism is true of the world so far, and can be expected to be true in the future, without this being as yet an actual truth about the future as opposed to something it might be reasonable to guess at for one with sufficient information both about particular events and the laws to which they have conformed so far. Even if those laws are supposed to have a certain necessity to them, there is still a difference between being sure that, as a real necessity, it will continue to hold in the future, and thinking that it is actually true now that those events will conform to it. (Thinking the future settled because one believes laws of nature are necessary is different from thinking it determinate because truth about the future has the same status as truth about the past.)

§ A more vulgar fallacy than confusion of determinationism with determinism is its confusion with a certain sort of fatalism. Such a fatalism is not often clearly stated, but it is presumably the real gist of 'what will be, will be' when it figures as a piece of popular wisdom.

The fatalist, in the sense I have in mind, believes that all really important events in one's future are settled, in their broad character, and that the choices one makes can only alter the details of the way in which they happen. Either your number is up today or it is not, so there is no point in being careful. No need to cross the road carefully—it's either your death day or it's not.

So for fatalism you have no choice as to what will happen so far as that seriously matters, because these things are doomed to happen whatever you do. No such claim is made either by determinism or determinationism. Fatalism says: 'Do X or do Y, it cannot make a difference whether Z will occur', where Z is something important. Determinism says: 'Whether Z will occur or not, often depends on whether you do X or Y. However, it's already causally settled whether you will do X or Y.' Determinationism says: 'Whether Z will occur or not, may well depend on whether you do X or Y. However, it's already true that you will do X, or true that you will do Y (though it need not be causally determined, or be predictable, which you will do).'

If fatalism were known to be true, it really would be sensible to be much more casual in the planning of our affairs than we normally are. In this way it contrasts sharply with both determinationism and determinism, each of which admits that what you do makes a difference to what happens even if it is in some sense settled what you will do, either because it is causally determined or because the future is there with its own definite character just as the past is. Doubtless there is some difficulty in thinking out clearly how these two doctrines relate to fatalism. But they are certainly distinct from it and do not in the least imply that carefulness in life is wasted.

Fatalism, in this sense, certainly seems absurd (though Tolstoi's view of history could be thought a version of it) and it is hard to see anything in its favour. However, it needed to be characterised to distinguish it firmly from determinism or determinationism.

§ Sometimes philosophers speak of what they call logical fatalism. This is conceived as a doctrine about the settled nature of the future supposedly derivable from the law of excluded middle (or of bivalence). This is taken as implying such things as that, for every day in the future, the proposition that you will die on that day is either true or false, so that it's settled 'already' when you will die.

It may be thought that logical fatalism is just the same as determinationism, as I have specified that.[48] But they are really quite distinct. Even if their central claim were the same, the ground for its support would be quite different. Moreover, if the logical fatalist really accepts it in the sense in which the determinationist intends it, he has no right to do so. His argument only establishes it, if it establishes it at all, in a much weaker sense in which it is of little consequence.

For the logical fatalist's point is simply this. There is a rule of language according to which any well-formed proposition must be described as 'either true or false, though not both'. Thus 'Timothy Sprigge will die on 11 December 2001' must be, as a matter of convention, regarded as having a truth value, though one which is unknown. When that date comes, then (if not before) people will be able to say that they now know which truth value it had. It will be inappropriate to say that it has now acquired that truth value, for it is simply linguistically more correct to say that it has now been found to have that truth value.

Thus if the logical fatalist is right that there is such a rule of language (and I am not particularly concerned with the question whether there is or not), that has no real implications for the determinacy of the future in any metaphysically important sense. For philosophically one could still hold that there is no *deep* way in which Timothy Sprigge's death on some particular day is a fact in the sense as that in which the death of Charles Dickens on a certain date is. For, so

---

48   See Alan White, *Truth*, pp. 48–56.

one may say, all it amounts to is that, when Timothy Sprigge eventually dies, it will be more correct to say that it has turned out that certain propositions about when he would and wouldn't die have turned out to have been true, rather than that they have become true. (One might even claim that a like convention applies to 'fact'.) There is a vast gap between speaking of the future as determinate on the basis of such an alleged linguistic convention, and saying that it is determinate because the future really is a region of reality as definite in itself as the past. So we must neither reject determinationism because we think logical fatalism specious, nor suppose ourselves to have accepted it because we think logical fatalism sound.

§ There may be other senses of fatalism. Perhaps sometimes it is the view that something beyond ourselves makes everything happen, and we have no real part in it, though what this something makes happen includes the degree of care we take. On this version of fatalism it is not true that whether I take care or not makes no difference to the occurrence of events which are really important for me, but nonetheless it is fate which settles how much care I will take, and with what results. Neither determinism nor determinationism implies any such thing. For the first, the various causal sequences in the world all unroll and intermingle in a necessary fashion, but that does not deprive human caution of efficacy. There is too much efficacy around in the world, if you like, rather than too little. It is absurd to think of determinism as making me entirely the victim of things outside me, for at least to some extent what happens outside me is just as truly a victim of what happens inside me, including the internal determinants of my movements. Similarly determinationism says that the future *me*, exercising such care as it does, exists in the future as the past and present *me*, exercising such care as they do, exist in their time. There is no suggestion that their caring activities are not playing their eternal part in settling how things eternally are. Maybe determinism and determinationism can each be combined with various forms of fatalism, as they can be combined with each other, but they are quite distinct doctrines, and the chances are that fatalism (unless perhaps in the vacuous logical sense) is simply false. In contrast I believe determinism may well be true, and as I shall try to show, determinationism is certainly true.

§ Now at last we may move on to the case I am to make for determinationism. I need first to establish some points about the nature of the past which, as it seems to me, are implied by the belief that the truth about it is determinate.

The nature of truth is of course as much debated as is any other in philosophy. But to me it seems certain that there can be no genuinely true judgements or propositions, at least about matters of concrete fact, unless there is some bit of reality whose existence and character make them true. This much is acknowledged by various theorists who would not typically be called adherents of a correspondence theory of truth. Thus James thinks that a judgement is true about a bit of reality if and only if it puts us into fruitful relations with it. And Bradley tends to think of reality as somehow accepting the adjective we ascribe to it. In either case the reality must have some sort of being; it cannot be nothing at all. And of course the hodgepodge of theories labelled correspondence theories require that there be something which is the thing, fact, or whatever in virtue of which the judgement, belief, proposition, sentence, or whatever is true. Different theories will put the same essential point in different ways, and develop it along different lines, but virtually all grant something of this sort. And, even if they did not, I would feel it quite certainly true. To think correctly about some particular matter of fact is to be right about the existence and character of something, and something cannot be nothing.

As a special case (or perhaps as the main case) of this general point, we may say that a judgement about a past matter of fact which is true must be so because in some way it identifies something and characterises it, and that this something cannot be merely nothing. Now some philosophical views of judgements about the past effectively proffer as that something the so-called present physical or psychical evidences for the past occurrence, or the evidence which will become available to us if we enquire. But such views have two disadvantages. First, it is surely the very past event, or individual or individuals as they used to be, which is the something which our thoughts about the past correctly identify and characterise if they are true. The evidence is only an indication to us that we have succeeded in doing this, not that which the judgement is true in virtue of successfully identifying and characterising. Second, such theories make judgements about the past susceptible of indeterminacy in truth value and thus lapse back into that philosophy of the present or predictionism which we have found to be absurd. Thus the something which our judgements about the past, when they are true, succeed in identifying and characterising correctly must be the very past events (or individuals as they used to be) which they state to have occurred (or existed).

So if a judgement about a past event is true or false, that must be because it either succeeds in identifying and correctly describing such a past event or it does not.[49] In the simplest case the judgement will ascribe some property to a past event and, if it is true, that property must really inhere in that event, while if it is false, either there will be an event which has been identified but which does not have that property, or there will be no such past event at all. (It does not matter whether we do or do not allow these two different sorts of failure as forms of falsehood, for the argument could be put entirely in terms of the situation which must hold when a judgement is true.) It seems evident that that past event can only have or lack that property if it is a reality. In short, no sense can be made of judgements about the past being true unless we grant that reality in the largest sense includes the past, that past events are realities.

§ The use of tenses is very problematic in these discussions. It is important

---

49   Henceforth I shall simply talk of past events as that which judgements about the past concern, but those who regard events as secondary to individuals may translate such statements into something such as 'So if a judgement about how things were is true or false, that must be because it either does or does not succeed in identifying some individual, or group of such, which there at least used to be, and correctly describing how it was at some past time'.

therefore to emphasise that I am not saying that the event must still be a reality, in the sense that it must be a reality existing in the present. For the past event certainly isn't a reality existing now; it is a reality then. What I do say is that the *then* and its contents, to which this event belongs, must still somehow belong to reality.

We must stick close to these two points:

(1) The past event no longer exists, that is, it does not belong to *now*;

(2) The past event belongs in its own time, and is real there.

One might perhaps put the matter thus: It is certainly not true that the event still exists. It belongs to the past, not to the present. However, it is still true that it did exist. And this can only be because it is still somehow just as much one of the independent realities, which present thought might be true by somehow corresponding to, as are things which are occurring or which exist now.

Suppose that it is a truth about the past that I had a toothache at a certain time (characterised perhaps as the time when I had certain other experiences). Then the truth that I had the toothache lies in the fact that any subsequent judgement to that effect somehow identifies and correctly characterises that particular experience. In some sense such judgements correspond to that past state of affairs involving toothache. There can only be such a relation of correspondence if the toothache is somehow still a reality, or somehow included in reality.

§ I now ask: How can reality include a past toothache? What kind of thing is a past toothache? A toothache is an experience of a painful kind. Some people think that past events continue to be part of reality because they somehow take on a kind of quality of pastness. But I would say that it is of the essence of an experience to be vividly present as an element in some consciousness, and that an event which lost this quality of presentness would not be an experience. In consequence, it could not be a toothache.

I conclude that the toothache can only be there as a part of reality if, somehow from its own point of view, or that of the consciousness which contains it, it is still there as a present reality. The reality which makes our judgement true must have the *throbbing presentness* of an actual experience. The reason I don't feel it now is because its *locus* is in another *part* of the universe, which from the point of view of *this* part of the universe is called *then* or *past*.

I may be told that it is absurd to say that it is still there in the past, as if this added anything to saying that it occurred. But this is simply to avoid the issue of the ontological status of the past. If it is to be the objective correlative of our judgements, it has to be something. Say by all means that it is sufficient that it *was* something. The problem remains what 'was' means. If there is no sense in which *that which was* is, then it is sheer nothing, and cannot provide the role of such an objective correlative. If we avoid unsatisfactory views, according to which the past has become something that it was not when present, and exists now as some kind of metaphysical shadow of what once was, we must say that it is in some sense still there in its own time. Doubtless it is much better to say that it is eternally there in its own time, than to say that it is so still. But that immediately raises the question what this eternal form of being is. It can only be, so far as I can see, the eternal being possessed by reality as a whole.

We are not concerned with the eternal being possessed by abstractions, but with that which must be possessed by thoroughly concrete events, or thoroughly plangent experiences, that of eternally belonging to a whole which contains all times without itself being in time. And it is not enough that some *version* of it should exist eternally within that eternal reality, for it itself, in its very presentness, must be part of what makes up that eternal being. For if it is said that only some eternal version of it exists there, the question arises: Of *what* is it a version? If there is nothing other than the version, then there is no reality of which it is the version. No, it must be the event itself which belongs to the eternal being, and thus that eternal reality must be composed of events which from their own point of view are temporal, such as this very sense of trying to get my meaning across, without getting bogged down in verbal tussles, which I am 'now' feeling.

The view of the past to which these reflections force us is that all past events are eternally present events from their own point of view. In particular, every total experience is an element in the universe which feels present to itself, but which may be remembered or inferred by thoughts contained in later total experiences which regard it as past.

§ Once this is accepted, it is impossible coherently to avoid taking a similar view of the future.

For in taking this view of the past one is taking it that the series of one's experiences up to this moment consists in a series of pulses or states of experience, each of which is present from its own point of view and in itself, but past to others. Those experiences I call past (i.e., the ego of this moment calls past) are, in themselves, and as they really are, present experiences of their own momentary egos.

Now from the point of view of what we may call the momentary ego having those experiences which the ego of this moment calls past, this ego which is me now, together with its experiences, is future. That is, if they have any knowledge of them, it is anticipative knowledge of them as something to come.

This shows that an experience which is present from its own point of view (this one) can be future from the point of view of another.

The crucial point is this. This present moment is a future moment from the point of view of moments which in themselves are eternally present and can never really cease to be present. Moreover, the events the ego of this moment calls past, are past only in relation to other moments such as this. In themselves they are eternally present. But granted that this present event is future from the point of view of other events, and so is both future and present, future for other events and present for itself, it seems an unavoidable conclusion that events which, from the point of view of this present ego, are future, are also present realities from their own point of view. Both futurity and pastness must then be something which belongs to events from the point of view of other events. But every event *must be present from its own point of view, and as it really is*—because it knows itself as it really is.

These points apply most obviously to events which are experiences. The Bradleyan holds that this is true of all real events. But essentially the same point would apply to unexperienced events, even if its application to them is less easy to state. (Thus Santayana, from whom I have derived this argument, was quite hostile to the view that all events are experiences.)

§ The general vision of the universe implied by this argument—at least if taken in conjunction with panexperientialism, while something pretty close to it follows even without this—is that the universe consists of innumerable states or moments of experience. Each of these is eternally just there and cannot really cease to be. However, each of them—or at any rate the ones we know about— feels itself as something which is a transition point between two other experiences. It feels as though it is in the process of emerging from, and passing into, other experiences.

It by no means follows that the feeling which each experience has of emerging from and passing into other experiences is entirely an illusion. Personally I am convinced that there is a sense in which this feeling is quite correct. For surely an experience must have a very special relation to what we call its predecessors and successors, of which this feeling is a sign. And I am not sure that even Bradley really wants to deny this.

Still, if our conclusions are correct, there is an element of illusoriness in the feeling of transition, for it goes with a feeling that somehow past, present, and future are radically different sorts of reality, whereas the truth is that present-ness is eternally the true character of every event, and that each is eternally there in precisely its own locus in the whole temporal series.

If this is the truth about the universe, it justifies us in saying that to some extent time is an illusion. However as I see it, one could equally say that it presents an alternative account of time showing us what time really is. Perhaps I would diverge somewhat from Bradley here. But the main point stands in any case, namely, that it supports a Bradleyan view of time, for which all moments of experience are eternally there in the Absolute. Of course, one might well accept the eternalism established by our argument and not believe in anything like Bradley's Absolute. For one might reject both his panexperientialism and his account of relations. But it does establish that reality has one feature which it requires to answer to Bradley's description of the Absolute.

§ I have noted that my reasoning here largely follows that of Santayana.[50] Oddly enough, however, Santayana is particularly insistent that time is real. But what he really means to insist on by this, I think, is that, contra the

---

50   See Santayana, *Matter*, chapters IV and V; *Truth*, preface and chapters IX and X; *Character*, chapter V. See also Sprigge, 'Ideal Immortality', *Southern Journal of Philosophy*, 10, No. 2, special issue on Santayana, and Sprigge, *Santayana*, chapter IX. Among recent philosophers who have expressed somewhat similar views see Seddon. What is unique in Santayana's presentation of this view is the care and success with which he deals with the sense of nowness and of temporal passage.

pragmatists, the past is real and determinate, and that therefore the future is so too.

For the strange thing is that the more one endeavours to establish the reality of past and future, the more one demolishes the reality of time as we ordinarily conceive it. Although Santayana does not like putting it in this fashion, it is, I believe, the real upshot of his view. And though for him it was associated with a hostility to absolute idealism, in fact it provides reason for accepting an essential part of Bradley's metaphysics better than anything he says himself.

§ There is an objection to the view of past, present, and future for which we have argued which merits consideration. [51] It is said that, if each event is simply eternally there in its own position in time, and its pastness is just its being before *this* utterance, then there is no genuine sense to such feelings as are expressed in a statement like 'Thank God, that's over', said when some pain ceases, or of regret for the fact that something has slipped into the past. For it can hardly mean 'Thank God, that that experience eternally belongs to a time before this utterance' or 'How sad that those experiences belong to a time before those utterances.' For those propositions, if true, were always or equally true (so at least the eternalist will hold). What one is pleased at, or regrets, is that an experience is in the past, not that it precedes some other event.

There are two replies to this point, taken as an objection to the eternalism in question here.

(1) These utterances express gladness or sorrow on the part of the ego of one time that it is not it, but the ego of another time, to which a certain experience pertains. Just as I can be pleased or envious at the fact that it is you, not I, who is having a certain experience, so the I of one time can be pleased or envious of the I of another time because it is it, rather than itself, to which a certain experience pertains. If it is objected that this does not explain the difference of feeling towards the future and the past, there is a double reply. First, the future is known about less than, or on a different basis from, the past, and this produces some change of emotion. Secondly, the objector may be referred to the next point.

(2) It is true that some philosophers have tried to analyse the conception of past, present, and future in terms of the relation in which they stand to the utterance in which these expressions are used.[52] But what has been presented here is, not an analysis of the ordinary meanings of 'past', 'present', and 'future', but an account of the real status of the realities to which these predicates are applied. These expressions, as ordinarily used, convey not just facts about their temporal relations to other events, but ascribe a certain status to them. But what

---

51   See A. N. Prior, 'Thank Goodness That's Over', *Philosophy*, XXXIX (1959), p. 17.
52   Or if not to analyse the concepts thus, at least to explain the functioning of tensed statements as turning on the temporal relation between their utterance and states of affairs which in themselves include nothing of the nature of presentness, pastness, or futurity. See Mellor, p. 6.

is this status? In the end I think no clear meaning can be given to it which is consistent with still more basic convictions we have about there being a genuine truth value to descriptions of past events.

For what mainly constitutes the properties of pastness, presentness, and futurity, as we ordinarily conceive them, are, I believe, certain emotional feelings which we project on to events, with the impression that they possess them as they really are. These feelings are not easy to describe and are some-what complex, but basically they are those of regret, nostalgia, relief and so forth, and of hope and fear. There is no denying that we feel differently about the events we believe to be there in the time before this from what we do about those we think may be there in the time beyond. This is connected with the fact that our present conations (those occurring with the utterances which dub events as past, present, or future) are differently related to each of these. These conations are genuinely part of what is moulding the future; it is eternally true that later events are partly due to them. And they in turn are partly the result of, while unable to influence, events earlier than them. So it is quite appropriate that we should feel differently about these different events. Thus the emotional timbres which partly define pastness, presentness, and future have some suitability to things as they really are.

§ Thus, though Bradley never puts forward quite this argument, it supports, better than anything he actually said, the view of time he requires for his main metaphysical purposes. And it is in accord with at least one of the main things he means to say when he calls time unreal. For certainly part of what he means by this is that there is an element of illusion and incoherence in the notion of 'ceasing to be' and it is just this which eternalism denies as a genuine feature of reality.

True, Bradley also implies other things when he says that time is unreal, things with which I do not agree. For, first, I think a reasonable view of the Absolute will hold that reality is laid out for it in a more temporal way than Bradley is inclined to allow. Royce seems nearer the likely truth in holding that the experiences of all sentient beings fit into the absolute experience in temporal relations of the kind which hold within a specious present, and in a way isomorphic with the way in which we think of them as ordered. And, secondly, I believe that the problems about infinite divisibility and so forth, which play such a role in Bradley's attempt to demonstrate the unreality of time, can be solved along lines James adumbrated and Whitehead developed. Still, if time as we ordinarily conceive it can be demonstrated to be unreal in the way I have outlined, then the Absolute has just that kind of eternal unchanging being which Bradley ascribes to it.

§ The argument for eternalism which I have offered may be summed up thus. Past events, in particular past experiences, can't just be nothing. Having hap-pened, they must be eternally there, else there could be no truth about them. But if the past is real, it must be present from its own point of view, and we must be future from *its*. So futurity and pastness are properties belonging to events from the point of view of other events which are eternally and essentially present.

Some philosophers who take an essentially eternalist view of the past and future deny that it implies that time is unreal. For they hold that the reality of time requires only that things change, not that events do. Indeed, to ask whether an event ever genuinely ceases to be is, they say, to ask an absurd question. It is things, such as plants and trees and planets, which do so. To talk about events in this way is to speak neither truth nor falsehood but nonsense.[53]

Such philosophers may have failed to absorb the full force of their own position, and the extent to which it challenges what we normally believe in when we believe in change. For the truth is, as others have argued, that for time to be real (as some of them think it is and others deny) it is not enough that things cease to be, in the sense that there is a time such that they are not present at subsequent times. Rather, it requires a real passing-away and coming-to-be of events. And it is this which the eternalism which I claim to have established in this section, and which is essential for Bradley's doctrine of the Absolute (however cloudy his pronouncements on these matters sometimes are), denies.

(f) Theories of Becoming

§ Bradley's doctrine of the Absolute requires an eternalist conception of time, and I have now offered what seem to me conclusive reasons for adopting it. But such a conception will, for a variety of reasons, stick in the throats of many. So to round out the case I have made, on Bradley's behalf, for eternalism, I shall now consider how one might attempt to resist the thrust of the argument of the last section.

The pattern of my argument was this. I contended that the three serious alternative views about the respective status of past, present, and future were: (1) the philosophy of the present (or the predictionist view to which it is closely allied); (2) the standard view; (3) determinationism. I then rejected the philosophy of the present as absurd and went on to contend that the realist view of the past common to both the standard view and determinationism requires, when properly thought through, an eternalist conception of time which is a version of determinationism.

If one is anxious to reject this line of thought, one may attempt first to resist my bluff dismissal of the philosophy of the present and predictionism as being incredible. However, I do not think any such attempt can be convincing. For they are not merely incredible but self-defeating.

For the philosophy of the present and predictionism the proposition that there is a real past there to be corresponded to makes no sense. There is really no such thing as truth or falsehood about a real past—the past is nothing at all. Or rather it only exists as the creation of our present memories or of our present beliefs on the basis of so-called present evidence of it, or (for predictionism) of

---

53   This is roughly the argument of J. J. C. Smart in Flew, *Conceptual*, p. 222 et ff., though he associates it with a rather special treatment of the notion of an event. Similarly Mellor, p. 103, and Seddon, pp. 47–48.

memories or beliefs which may occur in the future. There is nothing in the real world which these memories or beliefs report either truly or falsely beyond their own content and the presently existing, or in the future discoverable, states of affairs said to provide their evidence. But presumably it is allowed that there were real past events, even though they have now passed out of being, leaving no definite truth about themselves. For to deny that there *were* past events is to deny that anything really happened before the present moment, and this is hardly a serious philosophical position, since it would have to be advanced as a fresh and different claim each time it was propounded. But that granted, we may now ask to what one is referring when one says that there were such events. If past events are to be objects of reference (or values of variables) in even this minimal way as things which have passed out of being, it can't be true that the past has become strictly nothing. For if it is *nothing*, then the expression 'the past' has no reference. There would be no truth even of the general sort: 'There were *events* prior to this present time' and we have seen that no philosopher can deny this. However, once granted that the past events which there were, and to which we can still refer (or which can still be values of our variables) when we say that there is no definite truth about them, are not mere *nothing*, reasons such as we have given against the standard view must eventually lead us to admit that the only actual something they can be is events which are eternally present in their own time, however much they are nothing from our point of view. And that is to adopt eternalism.

§ But perhaps we have been too facile in our insistence that there is no satisfactory conception of a status which past events can have as objects of reference other than that ascribed to them by the eternalist theory. In order to meet this charge I shall now examine what I believe to be the only really serious attempt to meet the challenge as to what past events are without embracing eternalism. This is a version of the standard view which I shall call the theory of absolute becoming. C. D. Broad upheld a view of time under this label, and Whitehead and Hartshorne have each developed views of the same broad type. Something of the same sort was also held by Bergson, for whom life is conscious becoming and matter what this changes into when it is past and unconscious.[54] It is also the view, I think, which we must take James as implicitly holding.[55] Broad expressed the view thus:

> There is no such thing as *ceasing* to exist; what has become exists for ever. When we say that something has ceased to *exist* we only mean that it has ceased to be *present*.
>
> Broad, *Thought*, p. 69

He also says:

---

54   See, for example, *L'Évolution Créatrice* in Bergson, pp. 703–8.
55   See Part One, Chapter Four, note 41.

Nothing has happened to the present by becoming past except that fresh slices of existence have been added to the total history of the world.

Broad, *Thought*, p. 66

Broad's notion is that reality is continuously getting larger. As time moves on, all events which have ever happened are still there, the only alteration to them, once they have occurred, consisting in the fact that, while at first there were no events which came after them, thereafter they steadily acquired more and more successors.

The following diagram gives the idea.

E's moment of presentness:
————————————————— E

F's moment of presentness:
——————————————E————————F

G's moment of presentness:
——————————————E————————F————————G

When E comes into existence there's nothing after it.

When F comes into existence E has successors but F does not.

When G comes into existence both E and F have successors, but not G.

So, according to Broad, it is *still* true at F's moment of presentness that E comes before F and is a reality, but it is not *yet* true at F's moment of presentness that G is a reality which comes after F. For that, we have to wait till G's moment of presentness.

But what kind of reality is E at G's moment of presentness?

One cannot say that it is an experience which is present from its own point of view, and only past from the point of view of F. For if so, you return to the thesis that this present moment is a future event from the point of view of an event which is itself present from its own point of view, and we have the eternalist theory that past, present, and future are purely relative.

The proponent of absolute becoming must say, rather, that, as events cease to be present, they are still there but with a quality of pastness. In short, they *do* change as *more* is added, contra Broad.

So far as I can see there are only two senses which can be given to this.

(1) It might mean that when an event ceases to be present a kind of shadowy version of it is still left.

The simplest version of this view holds that it is stored in a cosmic or divine memory, which, ever afterwards, recalls just what happened.

This is the very explicit view of Charles Hartshorne and close to the view of

Whitehead. We should add, however, that both philosophers hold that events may continue not only as objectively immortal within the consciousness of God, but within the later consciousness of finite beings. So there could be *some* real past even without God, but not the whole of it including what no finite being recalls. The essential point is that the past is literally present in the consciousness of one who remembers it in a really concrete way.

The trouble is that it is hard to see how it can be denied that, in that case, the past event has undergone a change in virtue of having thrown off what Whitehead called subjective immediacy, and acquired the status of an object for, or within, a later consciousness. And that being so, it is clear that the past as thus retained, in an objective form, only does its job if it is an objective version of what once was subjectively immediate, in short, if the objective version of the event corresponds to the original subjectively immediate version of it. And that requires that the subjective version of the event is eternally there in its subjectivity in eternal reality. (Hartshorne says that he does not think of the event as losing subjective immediacy, but I do not really see how this can be avoided without turning it into a genuine present of which we are the future.)[56]

In general, one may say that any attempt to make the past real as something remembered by God, or retained in some way in finite consciousness, founders on the fact that a later memory, however concrete and full, and even infallible, is only worth anything if it corresponds to the original fact—otherwise it's not a memory. The omniscience of God may be a necessary fact but if it is to be a fact at all his beliefs must be true by correctly characterising what they are about. So his memory can only be the metaphysical guarantee that there is a definite truth about the past if it is a correct memory of what actually happened. Unless there is a real past such as he remembers, there is nothing here that he knows. For if the memory *corresponds* to the fact, it can't *be* the fact. And the fact must have some kind of reality in itself. And once we ask what this kind of reality is, we must answer that it can only be that of being eternally there as a present event from its own point of view.

It would be a mistake to suppose that a similar objection could be brought against the doctrine that the Absolute contains events belonging to all times. For the claim is not that the Absolute gives the event an everlasting status by being everlastingly aware of it, but that it contains the event itself with its own ephemeral presentness which eternally pertains to it. And there is no question of any change of status from subjective immediacy to objective fact.

(2) The alternative is that events don't just leave *shadows* of themselves, but somehow *themselves* fade, or acquire a certain quality called *pastness* in a more and more extreme form. But then we may ask: If the events can fade in this way, why should they not change in other ways, so that, for instance, an event which was once a present pleasure becomes a past pain? This may sound absurd, but

---

56   I have examined his position, for which I have much admiration, though I cannot quite agree, in my contribution to Hahn (for which also see Hartshorne's reply).

once one allows that the sense in which they remain parts of reality for ever is compatible with their changing in one way, it is hard to see how one can be confident that they may not change in other ways too.

The real trouble, indeed, lies in the very conception of 'a past experience'. To think of an experience as a reality is to think of it as present. Presentness is, in truth, one and the same as being real, and one can only think that the past is real by taking the eternalist view that it is eternally there as present in itself, while past and future in relation to other events.

So we return to the point that, rather paradoxically, the more real you make the past, the more you make time unreal. The past can only be made real if one regards the distinction between past, present, and future as not ultimately valid. That goes against treating time and transition as real. On the other hand, make the past *unreal* and you have no real truth possible about it. This also goes against our ordinary notions.

The conclusion—or so it seems to me—must be that our ordinary conception of time is so incoherent, that it's not unreasonable to say that Time, as we understand it, is unreal. The truth is that every moment is eternally present, and only seems past and future to other events. Its real character is that of being eternally present, however much it seems to itself to be passing away.

(g) A Side-glance at McTaggart

It would be strange to conclude without some remarks about the most celebrated attempt to prove the unreality of time, that of McTaggart. His positive position is close to eternalism though he has his own very peculiar and, as I believe, quite incoherent conception of a C series which is the reality behind the appearance of temporal order.

A brief outline of McTaggart's much discussed argument for the unreality of time will have to suffice.[57] For time to be real both what he calls the A series and what he calls the B series must be real. The B series consists of events ordered according to the earlier-later relation; the A series of events ordered according to their degree of pastness, presentness, or futurity, so that the series points from the more distant past events, through present events, to more and more future events.

McTaggart says that theories which try to define temporal facts in purely B series terms deny any genuine change, and thus time. For each event is just there in its position in the series and nothing changes. We only have real time if the A series is real, and constantly changing, not in its order, but in the predicates which determine that order, so that what was a future event eventually becomes first a present one, and then a more and more past one.

In arguing thus McTaggart is agreeing with the proponents of absolute becoming on what the reality of time would require. Some critics have claimed that this is a misconception.[58] The reality of time, they say, requires that things

---

57   See McTaggart, *Existence*, II, chapter XXXIII, and McTaggart, *Studies*, essay V.
58   See note 53 above.

change, not that events do. And things change if there are predicates applicable to them at one time which are not so at others, while to speak of events as changing is without relevant meaning. (Those who criticise McTaggart thus typically wish to define temporal facts in terms of the B series alone. Their position is essentially an eternalist one, but they deny that eternalism makes time unreal.)

It seems to me that McTaggart is essentially right in holding, as against such critics, that the reality of the A series, as well as that of the B series, is required for the reality of time. For it is only through the conception of the first that we ascribe to past, present, and future that radically different status which they must have if time, in anything like the sense in which we ordinarily believe in it, is to be a reality. However, McTaggart himself hardly does justice to the difference of status we normally attribute to past, present, and future. For we ordinarily suppose that it is an essential part of this difference that the future is indeterminate in a manner in which the past and present are not. (Even determinism, in any sense which is compatible with the reality of time as ordinarily conceived, must hold that the determinacy of the future is different in kind from that of the past.) McTaggart's account of the A series, however, treats all the events pertaining to it as quite determinate, though they are continually changing their temporal character, so that the past ones become more and more past, the present ones past, and the future ones become less and less future until they are present and then past. However, the main burden of his argument could be altered to allow for this by somewhat altering his account of the A series.

Our argument, on behalf of Bradley, against the reality of time has essentially been an argument for the unreality of the A series. And McTaggart's argument for the unreality of time is similar. However, the argument is not the same, McTaggart's being more question begging.

According to McTaggart, the upholder of the reality of time must say of a given past event that it *is* past in the sense that it *is past now*. It is not enough to say simply that it is past, for after all, from the point of view of events before it, it is future. So unless we add 'now' we must say of every event that it is past, present, and future. For this is true of every event viewed from the appropriate perspective. And yet this cannot be right, for present, past, and future are contraries. Not to see them as contraries is to abandon the view that time is real.

But, McTaggart asks, what does 'now' mean when it is said that by a past (present or future) event we must mean one which is so *now*? And he answers that it must mean *now from the point of view of an event which is present*, for example the speech act to which this occurrence of 'now' belongs. The trouble is, however, that this event is itself as much present, past, and future as any other. So to nail it down, as simply present, we must add once more 'present now'. However, this 'now' can again only be cashed as meaning *now from the point of view of an event which is present*. So we are launched on a hopeless regress and this regress is vicious rather than benevolent since it must be terminated to give sense to what we are saying and is not merely an infinite series of consequences of what we have said.[59] Thus we must conclude that time is unreal, since there is no way of finishing what must be said in order to show how an event can answer to one of the mutually incompatible temporal predicates, 'present', 'past', and 'future', without answering to them all.

McTaggart claims next that, since the A series is unreal, the same must be true of the B series. For the earlier-later relation, if it is to be a genuinely temporal relation, must be defined by way of the predicates of the A series, not conversely. 'Event A is earlier than event B' means 'A is past when B is present'.

In spite of the unreality of both A series and B series there is good reason, according to McTaggart, for supposing that events belong to some real series, which we may call the C series, having the same abstract structure. It seems to me that a Bradleyan should agree with that general point, though I think McTaggart's own actual account of the C series (as what he calls an inclusion series) is quite absurd, however ingenious.[60]

More appropriate to Bradley's metaphysics is an account of the C series along lines we have found in Josiah Royce's metaphysics. According to this, it is ordered by relations in the absolute experience, which are somewhat like the before-after relation which pertains to the elements of our specious present. However, these are not properly temporal relations since they are not elements of an event which emerges from, or passes into, any other event or even feels itself to be doing so.

§ I should be pleased if McTaggart's argument were sound, but I have my suspicions of it. The first step, in particular, seems highly suspect. The assumption is that every event must be regarded as past, present, and future, and thus as answering to contrary predicates, until it can be saved from this by the qualifier 'now'. But the believer in the reality of time has no reason to accept this. If he says of the beheading of Mary Queen of Scots that it is past, he is not saying that it is past now, just that it is past. Similarly if he says that the first British election of the twenty-first century is future, he does not mean that it is

---

59   See McTaggart, *Existence, p. 89 and note.*

60   McTaggart suggests that a possible view, though one he rejects, is that the A series and B series are both unreal, and that there is no C series isomorphic with that. (See McTaggart, *Studies,* p. 130.) Sometimes it seems that Bradley's view amounts to this. But it it a much more reasonable Bradleyan view to hold that there is a C series, though not the one McTaggart describes (according to which apparently earlier events are really eternally just parts of later ones) but rather one determined by position within something akin to an eternal specious present eternally experienced by the Absolute. There is an unfinished essay in manuscript, among the Bradley papers at Merton College, on the absolute theory of time. Its drift is by no means clear but the point seems to be one which could be expressed in McTaggart's terminology thus: An eternalist account of time, simply in terms of the B series, does not capture the essence of time; to do so we need the absolute becoming and flow provided by the A series. The A series, however, is ultimately unreal. (See Notebook in Box III, B 115, Bradley papers, Merton College.)

future now, just that it is future. And similarly when he says that he is up to something or other now, he does not mean now from the point of view of now, but just now. Of course, he is fully aware, indeed insistent, upon the fact that the past event was once future, that the future event will be present and then past, and so forth. But all these propositions are asserted without the need of any kind of qualifier. They are, indeed, what have been called fugitive propositions. But to say that they are only true fugitively is not to say that they concern the temporal relations of what they assert to their own utterance. They state an absolute fact, though one which does not last.

As a believer in the unreality of time, I do not accept this as an adequate account of the matter but it is doubtful that McTaggart's argument suffices to show this. This is not to deny the fruitfulness of his distinction between the A series and the B series, nor of his idea of a C series, however inadequate his conception of this may be.

But whether McTaggart's argument is sound or not does not matter too much. For the more natural line of argument presented in the last section is independent of it and suffices to establish, as it seems to me, that reality, in the largest sense, eternally holds all events together whether they are what I-now must call present, past, or future. It is unchanging in just the sense that Bradley's Absolute is meant to be.

It may be said that even if it is eternal, it is vastly misleading to call it unchanging. Such a predicate is only applicable to something like a Democritean atom which was supposed to survive through change of relations while remaining just the same in itself as the aeons pass.

True, it would be wildly wrong to see reality as a whole (or the Absolute if it meets the other criteria for being so called) as persisting through time without changing. It is simply the container of all times, so far as it is proper to talk of time at all, and itself not an event in time. But this does not make it wrong to say that it is unchanging. For that means no more and no less than that it does not change, and that is, indeed, the truth about it, if the arguments advanced in this and the last section have been correct.

§4. *The Absolute Achieved*

§We can now marshal the basic Bradleyan case for the existence of the Absolute.

The Absolute is the Universe or whole of reality. This whole is more truly an individual than anything within it, it is composed of experience, and it is not properly speaking temporal, though it includes all times.

(1) Bradley takes it fairly much for granted that there is such a thing as the universe or reality as a whole. Perhaps most will be ready to take it for granted with him; however, James's pluralistic metaphysics may seem its denial. (See Part One, Chapter Four, §2(b).) Bradley's reply would doubtless turn on his theory of judgement according to which all thought is ultimately an attempt to characterise that great Reality in the midst of which we sense ourselves as existing. And James's own concern, after all, was to decide whether the Universe was pluralistic or monistic. So both can converge on the question whether

the Universe has the character it needs to be properly called the Absolute. Is it, for example, a genuine individual or is it just a mass of individuals in relation?

(2) His treatment of relations gives the case for saying that the universe is a single individual. It contains everything there is, and every thing is in some relation to every other thing, so far as it is appropriate to talk of relations at all. However, where at the level of relational thought it is appropriate to speak of two things as related to each other, the deeper truth is always that they are aspects of some larger whole, more truly individual than themselves, which they help to make up, and the nature of which as a whole so pervades them that they could not exist other than as aspects of it. Thus starting with any two individuals, A and B, one can see that there must be a larger whole, more truly individual than themselves, of which they are both aspects in this sense. Unless that whole is the Absolute itself it must be related to another individual, and that means that it and that other individual are aspects of some larger whole, more truly individual than themselves. Similarly, unless that whole is the Absolute itself, it must be related to some further individual, and that has the same implication over again. Eventually one must reach the universe or whole of reality in this way. And everything in the universe will then have turned out to be simply an aspect of that larger whole which will be a more genuine individual than these its aspects. For clearly the aspect of an aspect of something is an aspect of it.

Should someone think that the case had only been made for an argument along the above lines in which 'more truly individual than' is uniformly replaced by 'as truly an individual as', he would still have the conclusion that the universe is *as* truly an individual as anything else there is. All those many theories will be wrong, then, which depict it as less truly individual than some of what it contains.

(3) That the universe or Absolute is composed of experience and nothing else follows from the arguments for panexperientialism considered in section 2. Since experience comes in those total experiences which Bradley often calls finite centres of experience, it follows that the Absolute is made up of such total finite experiences, and that they belong to it as aspects of a whole which is more truly individual than they are themselves. It is left as an open possibility that there are intermediate wholes of experience, including finite centres within them, and themselves included in the Absolute. This could, theoretically, occur at a series of different levels.[61] But see (7) below.

(4) The Absolute is timeless. For the notion of total experiences passing away, being replaced by others, or coming to be, are simply our confused way of registering certain features of the total experiences themselves and the likely way in which they belong together in the Absolute. Felt transitoriness, and felt

---

61 I have in mind the possibility of something like Fechner's conception, most readily accessible from James's description in PU, chapter V. For Bradley on Fechner see AR, p. 240, and Perry, II, p. 638. See also ETR, p. 436, note.

occurrence as the replacement of another experience, is an actual quality of the total experiences with which we are familiar in our own case and by insight into the consciousness of others. It is an open question to what extent the togetherness of our total experiences in the absolute experience echoes the temporal relations we think of them as having.

The reference to what *we* think does not introduce selves into the universe as some additional element. The thoughts which 'I' am calling *ours* are thoughts which occur in certain total experiences which feel themselves to be phases in the unfolding life of persons. The status of persons will be more fully discussed in the next chapter.

§ Such, as I see it, is the heart of Bradley's case for the Absolute. But some further points should also be noted which either qualify—as do points (7) and (8)—or supplement it—as do the remainder—in important ways.

(5) Bradley speaks of the Absolute as infinite, but in just what sense is it meant to be so?

Let us consider first whether the number of total experiences in the Absolute is or might be infinite in a strict mathematical sense.

Bradley would surely answer negatively, though I do not think he ever gives a direct answer to the question and would perhaps have objected, if pressed, that numerical concepts cannot apply to reality as it really is. But he was an enemy of the mathematical infinite, agreeing with Hegel in thinking of it as the bad infinite and in denying that the number of constituents of some defined kind within a concrete reality could ever be infinite in this sense.[62]

My own inclination is to agree with them on this. (See again Part One, Chapter Four, §2b.) But if one does think that there can be a strictly infinite number of individuals of some fully concrete sort, then I see no reason why they should not all be contained within a single Absolute. Certainly some metaphysical monists have thought along these lines, Spinoza, for example.

If the Absolute is not infinite in a mathematical sense for Bradley, it is so in what he considers a more important sense. It is not bounded by anything else, and, as self-determined in what it contains, it could not conceivably have contained more. It therefore lacks nothing which conceivably might have pertained to reality. 'Finite' for him means conditioned by something beyond it, and the Absolute is not finite in this sense.

(6) For Bradley the Absolute is perfect. But what is meant by this? He denies that it means that it is good. Goodness pertains to the finite, as badness does, although goodness is a better indication of the Absolute as a whole.[63] The claim is rather that it is in some sense harmonious to the maximal possible degree and contains no conflicts other than those essential for its having the most comprehensive sort of harmony there could be.

---

62   See, for example, PL, pp. 228–29, §§52–54; pp. 233–34, §§57–59; p. 241, note 46.
63   See AR, chapters XVII and XXV.

In this connection Bradley poses the rather disconcerting question of whether the Absolute is 'happy'.[64] His answer is that it cannot be strictly demonstrated that it is so or even that it is not unhappy. But the reasonable view is that it is 'happy'. Basically the reason for this is that an experience which is not felt as that of an individual itching to be on to the next thing must be satisfying. There cannot be any kind of striving within it to pass on to something else. Every total finite experience feels itself to be in transition to something beyond, and this is reflected in greater or less dissatisfaction with its own character. There can be no such feeling of transition to the absolute experience as a whole, though it contains all feelings of transition, and, without a sense of transition, Bradley is inclined to believe, there can be no dissatisfaction. Once this is granted, one can hardly avoid thinking it must be enormously, indeed in Bradley's sense, infinitely satisfying, since it contains 'infinite' riches.

A word should be said here about Bradley's attitude to 'the problem of evil'.[65] He confesses to no such problem in the usual theological sense, for there is no God who has freely chosen how things should be. The Absolute is what it is because that is how it has to be, there being no intelligible alternative.

But surely once one concludes that the Absolute is 'happy', one must conclude that all evil is, in some manner beyond us, contributory to that happiness and this does seem to pose something of a problem of evil. Bradley recognizes this as the question how evil ministers to the Absolute's perfection (though this also includes a more abstract logical harmony) and it cannot be said that he deals with it very satisfactorily. (A much more satisfactory treatment of the relation of the Absolute to evil is that of Josiah Royce.)[66]

To me it seems perfectly possible for an absolutist to deny that the evil in the world adds to the happiness, or, as I would rather say, final satisfactoriness of the universal experience as a whole. One can say simply that it has to be there, and that, nonetheless, the final upshot is on balance satisfying. Bradley, however, is more inclined to think that everything positively ministers to the perfection of the universe, and this seems to include contributing something to its happiness. It must be admitted that he does not do much to allay the horror of James[67] at such a claim, which does not seem necessary to his main case.

I now turn to some points which qualify, rather than supplement, the summary statement of Bradley's doctrine of the Absolute given in points (1) to (4). These are not needed, in my opinion, for the cogency of his case but they are parts of it as it actually stands.

(7) It could be misleading to say that the Absolute is made up of finite centres.

(A) A first reason for saying this is that Bradley thinks it possible that the Absolute contains a margin of experience which 'is not filtered through finite

---

64   See AR, p. 473.
65   For this see mainly AR, chapter XVII.
66   In Royce, *Religious Aspect,* chapters XI and XII.
67   See, for example, PRAG, chapter I.

centres'.[68] That is, the Absolute may contain, alongside all the momentary centres of experience or this-nows which there are, a mass of experience which neither is, nor contains anything which is, itself a unity of that sort. Thus the contents of the Absolute may consist in finite centres of experience a, b, c, d, . . . and together with these X, which is psychic in character but not a unitary experience. (The contents of X would of course belong to a unitary experience, namely, the absolute experience itself, but they would not belong to any lesser unity as do the contents of a finite centre belong to it.) Bradley thinks this unlikely to be so, but he does not entirely preclude it. He even suggests that X might be that which appears to us as nature.

(B) A second, more important reason is this. The objects perceived and thought about within different centres of experience belonging to the same community typically dovetail into, and complement and cohere with, each other. Thus I may be thinking of my home, 14 Great Stuart Street (identified as that of which certain sensory contents within my centre are the given part) and how it relates to an only vaguely sketched 16 Great Stuart Street, while my neighbour may have a much fuller idea of 16 Great Stuart Street (similarly identified as partly given within his centre) and how it relates to an only vaguely sketched 14 Great Stuart Street. Now if our thoughts could be combined, they would constitute the thought of a fuller state of affairs into which the descriptions each of us gives fit harmoniously. Well, for Bradley, if I follow him correctly, this is just what happens at the level of the Absolute. So this more comprehensive thought is not a mere logical function of the thoughts within the separate centres but an actual piece of thinking within the Absolute. That is, the thoughts pertaining to different finite centres are experienced in a unity within the Absolute in such a way that they constitute more comprehensive thoughts than occur in the mind of any one finite individual. And these thoughts may be more important articulations into which the one absolute experience divides than are any thoughts belonging to any one centre.

We have seen that for Bradley it is likely that many of the most worthwhile such comprehensive thoughts within the Absolute arise from the combination of thoughts of finite creatures who are at some distance from each other in the phenomenal or posited world of space and time (or perhaps do not even belong to the same space time system). Thus many of the thoughts of Leibniz may combine more importantly with thoughts occurring in the mind of Einstein than with those in the minds of his physical neighbours.

The superior unity of connections which are not spatio-temporal to those which are is, we saw, part of what Bradley means when he speaks of time as unreal. As against this I have urged that the absolute idealist should not only assert, but emphasise, that the absolute experience must have a structure which is isomorphic with our best accounts of the way things are arranged in space and time. Perhaps Bradley would not seriously disagree but only insist that

---

68   See AR, pp. 241–44, 467; ETR, pp. 350–51, note.

such a structure would not be the most important one in which the contents of the Absolute fall. But however this may be, he certainly rejects the individualistic view that the most significant articulation of the Absolute is into finite centres of experience, even if the stuff from which, so to speak, it weaves its own total experience has to be found in the contents of these.

(8) But is it altogether correct to say that for Bradley the Absolute consists only of experience quite apart from whether its only or most significant articulation is into finite centres or not? For an experience commonly includes judgements which posit the existence of things other than itself. Let us call these its deliverances. (The phrase 'intentional object' is too closely associated with approaches other than Bradley's to be used here.) Now the deliverance of an experience, as opposed to the judgement which posits it, is not exactly a part of it in the way in which what is strictly perceived of an object is a part of the experience to which the perception belongs. Nor, so it might seem, need it be part of any other experience. Yet surely the deliverances of experience, including such things as number systems, belong to the Absolute as truly as do the experiences themselves, especially when they are posited in bodies of thought which are combined to form the major units of significance within it in the manner we have just been considering. So it seems that the Absolute thinks of there being things which are neither part of its own psychical stuff nor necessarily even thought of by any finite individual. And because the Absolute thinks of there being such things, in an important sense there *are* such things. For, as Bradley sees it, that which is postulated in a satisfying and harmonious thought can properly be described as having *being*. Such being pertains not only to our physical environment, but to such other things as the abstract entities of mathematics, philosophical systems, hierarchies of value, and other such deliverances of a variety of experiences. And surely these deliverances do pertain to the Absolute, which, therefore, seems not to be solely experiential in character.

A possible answer might be to distinguish between the actual constituents of the Absolute and what pertains to it without being in the same way part of what makes it up. On this view *to be* is *to be thought or to be experienced* but it is only that which is experienced and not merely thought which is an actual constituent of the Absolute, though the latter pertains to it.

But that cannot be quite correct. For Bradley's panexperientialism implies that at the level of the Absolute all judgements which posit something not experienced must be corrected by judgements which ascribe an experiential character to these posits. And what is more he holds that the very distinction which holds for us between actually experiencing something and merely thinking about it is somehow transcended in the Absolute.

To understand this we must recall his account of judgement as the alienation of some feature of one's own experience from its home therein to become a concept which is projected onto reality beyond. Thereby (as Bradley sees it) it becomes a mere wandering adjective. For it has been deprived of its original home in the experience of the thinker without having been given a proper home in the beyond onto which he projects it.

This is somewhat puzzling. On the one hand, it has not really lost its home in the mind of the thinker, and, on the other, if the thought which predicates it is literally true, it does have a home in the beyond. But perhaps Bradley means that for us it has been deprived of its status as an element of the concrete fact of our own experience, but that, since we have no direct access to its home in the beyond, it is not presented to us as a genuinely concrete reality there but only as something characterized in a rather abstract way. In the Absolute, however, the contrast between a universal as a predicate of what is thought about and a character present in the judging thought itself somehow disappears.

This is fairly straightforward where thoughts about the character of another's experiences are in question, but it is difficult to see how it is to be interpreted in relation to the thought and perception of the physical. Bradley's doctrine here has been well expressed by Dawes Hicks (commenting on Bradley's remark that 'Nature may extend beyond the region actually perceived by the finite, but certainly not beyond the limits of finite thought'.) [69]

> Somehow, what we merely think must, in the Absolute, be perceived; and the nature which we know conceptually will in the Absolute, where all content is reblended with existence, gain once more the form of being immediately felt or sensed, i.e. an intuitional (*anschauliche*)form.
> 'Mr Bradley's treatment of Nature' in *Mind*, XXXIV (1925), p. 61[70]

Thus suppose I am holding a torch and thinking that there is a battery within it. Then the universal which specifies the character and location of the battery is, indeed, exemplified in my experience, but it is attributed to a reality beyond. Thus it has two distinct loci, one of which I experience but have to ignore in order to think, the other which I think about but do not experience directly. But the Absolute experiences the identity amidst difference of the universal in these two loci and thus heals the division between its felt occurrence as a character of concrete experience and its merely abstractly thought occurrence as a feature of the object.

I do not see how else we can understand the coming together of the conceived and the immediately experienced in the Absolute. Yet it has apparent implications to which Bradley denies he is committed. For it suggests that there is something within the Absolute, with a certain distinctness from my own experience, which is what that battery I am thinking of really is. What could this be? For panpsychism it might be the group of feelings which constitute the 'in itself' of the ultimate physical units making up the battery. (Though it would only be to a very limited extent that these would exemplify precisely the character I ascribed.) Another possibility is that it would be an element in that margin of experience, X, unfiltered through any finite centre, which Bradley

---

69   AR, p. 277.
70   Compare AR, p. 146.

acknowledges might be the 'in itself' of nature. But Bradley insists that he is not committed either to panpsychism or to the existence of such a margin. Yet without one of these, it is hard to see how the battery can be anything more substantial than a shared posit, that is the common deliverance of judgements united in the Absolute. And that leaves it unclear how the Absolute can heal the breach between thought and felt being. Or rather, it would limit it to the case where the object of my thought of the battery can be equated with the battery as actually perceived by someone else. It is true that Bradley plays with the idea that everything physical is perceived by some finite mind,[71] but he is no more committed to this than to the other possibilities just canvassed, and that means that, insofar as I think of what no one perceives, even the Absolute cannot heal the breach between perception and thought. It seems it could only do so if it was given a much more Berkeleyan role than Bradley seems mostly willing to give it as a universal perceiver of physical nature.[72] For more on this see sections 5 and 6 of the next chapter.

(9) The contradictions of the ordinary world of appearance are meant to be resolved at the level of the Absolute. A word should be said in summary of what that means. We may distinguish two main claims.

(a) Our ordinary conceptions of reality are full of contradictions. But reality as it really is, that is to say, the Absolute, can only answer to these conceptions in a revised form in which their internal and mutual contradictions are resolved.

But how does Bradley know that reality is not self-contradictory? Well, a good answer was available to him on the basis of his account of basic logical laws. These say very little concretely about reality themselves but remind us that there *are* predicates which cannot be combined in certain ways as characters of things and advises us to avoid trying to combine them thus in our thoughts, if we want to think truly. Thus the law of contradiction tells us to avoid trying to combine F and G if they really cannot combine; it does not tell us which properties are examples of F and G. (Remember that for Bradley not-F is a mere stopgap for some G which is a contrary of F.) It follows that reality cannot be self-contradictory, for that would be to say that it combines what cannot be combined. (It may be objected that to suppose that it cannot do this, is simply to invoke the law of non-contradiction. This may be true. But at least it is now invoked in a form which makes it appear very foolish to wonder whether reality may not be self-contradictory, as some have wondered.)

That suggests that the truth about reality could be given in concepts free from contradiction. But Bradley thinks that in the end there is no such truth. So in

---

71   see AR, p. 244.
72   Bradley speaks rather scathingly of Berkeley's conception of the role of God. See AR, p. 250, note. But it was the conception of the divine and human mind as external to one another to which he objected. There is nothing contrary to his metaphysics in including perception of all physical reality within the Absolute.

what sense is reality free of contradictions if even the most coherent concepts cannot describe it with absolute truth? The answer is, presumably, that the Absolute possesses an immediate non-conceptual understanding of its own nature which is the ideal limit on which increasingly coherent (and that means also, increasingly comprehensive) accounts converge.

Bradley's attempts to show the self-contradictory nature of ordinary concepts seem of varying quality. Perhaps the most important are his critiques of relational and temporal thought. I have suggested that the main points of his metaphysics could have been retained without his total condemnation of these. Thus I have argued that it might have been better to have claimed that all real relations are internally holistic, and that the reality corresponding to time is the holding of certain quasi-temporal relations within the Absolute between finite experiences, analogous to those which hold between successive elements within a specious present. But I agree with him that much of our ordinary thought about the world is self-contradictory or incoherent and needs to be revised, for the seeker after literal truth, in favour of a vision of reality akin to his of the Absolute.

(b) Bradley also treats the resolution of contradictions in the harmony of the Absolute as including a kind of moral resolution of divergent values. While I can see that the overall character of the absolute experience must be satisfying rather than unsatisfying I find much that he says in this connection unconvincing. Thus I doubt whether his elaborate attempt to show that what answers to a coherent description must be strife-free works.

(10) In view of the importance of the notion of a necessarily existing individual in theological and metaphysical thought it is important to know just in what sense the Absolute possesses necessary existence for Bradley. There is also the distinct question how far every truth about it in detail is supposed to be a necessary truth. On the face of it, Bradley is committed to the necessary existence of the Absolute, in general and in every detail: however, his treatment of modality in PL is not altogether as favourable to such a view as one would most naturally interpret it. For he treats necessity as essentially a relative notion so that no truth is necessary *tout court* but only relative to others. But one still wants to ask whether the Absolute is necessary in the more absolute sense in which the necessary is simply that which could not possibly have failed to be the case. I suggest that Bradley's position implies the following answer:

(a) The proposition that the Absolute exists is a necessary truth. For what this proposition means is this. (i) There *is* a whole of things, or universe, and (ii) it is 'a single [and we may add timeless] Experience superior to relations and containing in the fullest sense everything which is'.[73]

On the face of it (i) might have failed to be true in two ways. First, because nothing existed at all. Second, because though various things existed, they did not make up a universe. But, on Bradley's analysis of existential propositions,

---

73   ETR, p. 246.

to say that X does not exist is to say that the universe is X-less. So the universe must exist for other things not to exist, while it would be impossible for the universe itself not to have existed for this would have been for the universe to be universeless which is nonsense.

I am inclined to agree with the main upshot of this argument, even if it is hardly conclusive just as it stands. For I agree with those who have argued that the idea of nothing at all existing is senseless, and that there must be a totality of some sort of what does exist. However, the conclusion reached by such reasoning is very weak, for it does not establish that the universe has any very strong kind of unity, still less the character ascribed to it in clause (ii). However, we have, in effect, seen at length the Bradleyan case for the necessity of (ii), granted the necessity of (i).

If the only form of being which is possible is experiential being, as Bradley holds, then the Universe must be experiential. And if everything in the universe must be related to everything else, then the universe must be more truly individual, or at least as much so, as anything in it, and this implies that it must itself be a single experience. Only so, could it be more, or as truly, individual as any experience which it contains. Moreover, if the eternalist view of time can be established, it must be a timeless unity containing all experiences. And such a single timeless experience embracing everything is just what is meant by the Absolute. From all of which it follows that Bradley's metaphysics implies, and in my opinion constitutes an excellent case for, the necessary existence of the Absolute even if Bradley's own account of necessity adds complications to the saying so.

(b) But it does not immediately follow that everything about it is a necessary truth. Yet Bradley seems effectively to think that this is so. Has he any good reason at his disposal for such a claim? There are perhaps two reasons, both deductions from that perfection and happiness which it is supposed must pertain to the Absolute.

The first runs thus: The universe is necessarily an overall, satisfying experience; it is pleased with itself on balance. However, it could not be pleased with itself if the evils it contains could have not existed. Therefore the evils in it necessarily exist. But it could not be pleased with itself if it could have been better. Therefore it is necessarily just what it is, for otherwise it could have been better.

Another argument for the necessity of all truth is rather nearer the surface of his thought. According to this, thought is essentially an effort to understand things as necessary and can never be satisfied with mere facts which, so far as it can see, might not have obtained at all. It follows that if the whole detailed character of reality is not necessary, there is no resolution in the absolute experience of the dissatisfaction we feel at our lack of understanding. If so, the Absolute cannot be 'happy' for it must contain our attempts to understand it without any resolution of their dissatisfaction. And since it must be happy it follows that its detailed character is necessary.

These arguments may look rather specious at first but further reflection should suggest that they are quite hard to avoid, once the existence of the

Absolute is accepted as established. However that may be, I believe that the most important and compelling part of the doctrine of the Absolute is that summarised in (1)–(4) above.

To finish our account of Bradley's metaphysics, I turn now to a fuller treatment than I have so far given of his views of individual persons and of the nature in which they take themselves to be living.

5

The Self and Its World

§1. *The Self in* Ethical Studies

§ Idealist thinkers have often argued for the unreality, or merely phenomenal nature, of the physical world, in order to present an account of reality in which selves or egos, the core referents of personal pronouns, are its basic constituents. This is true, for example, of Berkeley, Kant, and Fichte. With the last of these, however, and still more with Hegel, the individual ego was tending to give way to a single absolute cosmic ego. And with Bradley we have a complete repudiation of the reality of the self, which is brought to its knees on the basis of criticisms as fierce as those launched at space, time, and physical reality in general. Indeed the critique of the self is considerably more thorough, just because Bradley was aware that many sympathetic to his attempt to give a spiritual interpretation of the universe would balk at this form of destruction.[1]

Denial of the reality of the self is strange in any thinker, doubly so in an idealist. For surely when a thing, credited with existence by common sense, is denied we must still assume a self as that for which it seemed to be real and which is to be persuaded of its unreality. However, there is no real objection to Bradley's position here. He is not denying that there are thoughts, only claiming that the pragmatically useful conception they contain of an individual thinker whose thought they are is too incoherent to be that of a genuine reality. If we insist on an answer to the question who or what is really doing the thinking, and finding it useful, each of these three answers has some appropriateness:

---

1   The main sources for Bradley's eventual views on the self are: AR, chapters IX, X, XV, XXII, XXIII, XXIV, XXVI; ETR, chapters I, XIV–XVI. Also relevant are chapters XXVI–XXIX of CE and chapters I–II of PL.

there is no thinker but the thoughts themselves; the thinker is a finite centre of experience which cannot be equated with a self; the thinker is the Absolute.

§ Bradley's later denial of the self must have seemed particularly strange to readers of *Appearance and Reality* (1893) who recalled the highly positive and interesting account of what it is in *Ethical Studies* (1876) and how self-realization is there made the basis of ethics. So let us start with a brief account of the view of the self taken there.

The work opens with a valuable contribution to the debate about free will, determinism, responsibility, and retributive punishment, focused on the question: 'When is a man responsible?' One answer is that he is never really responsible for what he does, for the universe is governed by an iron law of causation in virtue of which his every deed was already necessitated by events which preceded his birth. And Bradley agrees with this much, that if all a man's doings were settled before he came into existence, he could never be to blame for anything. That makes it look as though we can only defend moral responsibility by denying the truth of any such determinism. The trouble is that such a defence seems to imply that people are responsible for their actions only to the extent that they occurred by sheer chance. But that is absurd, for what occurs by 'chance' cannot be truly attributed to us as anything we have genuinely done.

§ He made the same point to James in 1897 in a letter written about his *Will to Believe*.

> I have always supposed that I am not morally responsible for mere accidents. You seem to tell me that these are all I am responsible for. But you offer me no sort of explanation. I do not understand this at all. . . . All that the ordinary man asks, so far as I see, is that his act should come from himself and not be extraneous. I think this demand is fully satisfied by the view that the self, once in being, is an internal principle and agency—not the same with selfless conditions, nor the same even with what it is conscious of. But what has all this to do with chance? I cannot see.
>
> Perry, II, pp. 238–39

However, Bradley congratulates James on his unusual frankness in simply identifying freedom with chance. And surely James was exceptional here. What he disliked in determinism was not the threat it posed to responsibility. For, as he confessed to Bradley in his letter in response, even after reading Ethical Studies many years previously it always seemed to him '(doubtless from the lack of some quickening on the subject) that this whole aspect of ethics is relatively unimportant'.[2] His concern rather was that if determinism were true, there was small chance that the world would develop into a better state. For it suggests that the determinants of evil doing will remain for ever with us, rather than be superseded by the free, that is, the chance, development of a morally improved humanity. Bradley, it would seem, had scant sympathy with this line

---

2   Kenna, p. 316. Compare PP, I, p. 349.

of thought, holding rather that human life would be emptied of moral significance if what seems most important in it is really the product of mere chance. Certainly it is not in this that the 'plain man' believes, when he believes in human responsibility.

§ Bradley is, surely, right that most opponents of determinism have been in a fix. For not wanting to identify freedom with chance, they have had difficulty in finding any coherent alternative.

The dilemma arises, he suggests, from the misconception that there are only two alternatives: (i) that phenomena develop one from another according to causal laws which are uniform throughout nature, including human nature; (ii) that some events occur in a purely chance way without explanation. This ignores a third alternative, which Bradley thinks that implicitly held by the plain man: (iii) that one's personality is a universal which in particular circumstances requires particular actions in order that it shall be actualised, but that it cannot be reduced to a formula from which one's behaviour in any circumstances could be read off mechanically.

This view is developed in relation to the question how far it is, or would be, disconcerting to have one's actions predicted by another. Bradley says that it would horrify the man in the street if his total character and behaviour (or presumably if large parts of it) had been predicted in detail before his birth on the basis of a rational deduction 'from the elements of his being, from his original natural endowment, and the complication of circumstances which in any way bore on him'.[3] What would shock him, however, would not be the mere fact that his behaviour had been predicted, but that it had been calculated from general facts and laws which made no reference to his personal individuality. Thus he has no objection to the fact that people who know his character, as an existing factor in the world, can largely predict his behaviour in various circumstances. Indeed, he would often be upset if that were not the case, if, for instance, it could not be predicted that he would remain honest in a position of trust whatever the temptations. Such prediction is quite acceptable, for it rests on knowledge of what he is and does not deduce his behaviour and character from laws which make no reference to his special individuality. Indeed, even supernormal prediction, if there be such a thing (whether antedating or subsequent to his birth), based upon some actual vision of the future in its full concreteness would not upset him in the way that a rational scientific prediction of it would do. For it would not be a deduction of his character and behaviour from something other than himself.

In thus contrasting the plain man's view of himself and that of the scientific determinist Bradley is careful not to insist that it must be the plain man who is right. Still, in this work Bradley treats the plain man with considerable respect, implying that he is likely to be wiser on the matter than the abstract theorists whom Bradley contemptuously refers to as 'advanced thinkers'. (There is

---

3   ETR, pp. 15–17.

something of a contrast here with the poor view of common sense taken in the later metaphysics.) Yet there are, surely, considerable difficulties to the plain man's view, as Bradley describes it. For, supposing it to be true that it is one's distinctive personality which produces one's actions, so that they neither occur by sheer chance nor through the operation of impersonal laws, we may still ask whether that personality itself came into existence by 'pure chance' or as a result of the chain of events leading up to one's conception, birth, or emergence as an individual. The former risks associating human freedom with randomness, contrary to the gist of the previous argument, yet the latter seems rather too like scientific determinism. For it still suggests that, however genuinely novel a reality my personality may be, it was an in principle predictable novelty. However, I take it that Bradley's reply on behalf of the plain man would be that one's personality could not have been predicted by use of the concepts appropriate for describing what preceded its existence, such as one's genetic endowment and early circumstances, even if it arose therefrom with a kind of necessity, and itself necessarily issues in certain behaviour once there.[4]

§ However that may be, a human personality is what Bradley calls a concrete universal. It is a universal in the sense that one's every particular experience and piece of behaviour is an instance of it in somewhat the same way as every colour (or coloured surface) is an instance of colour in general. And it is concrete, rather than merely abstract, for several reasons. (These, in fact, seem to be conceived by proponents of the concrete universal as features of all genuine universals. For the doctrine of concrete universals, as propounded by such as Bradley and Bosanquet, does not really concern one special type of universal called 'concrete', which they contrast with another called 'abstract' but is presented as the correct account of all genuine universals as opposed to the more usual but inadequate account of them as merely abstract.)[5]

(i) It is not merely passive in the sense in which so-called abstract universals are presumed to be. If there are two objects of the same shape, the explanations of why they are thus shaped may not connect up at all. One chain of events may have led to the one having that shape, and another to the other doing so. Having developed as they have, they both fall under that universal, but there is no sense in which it actively operated to give them their shape. A concrete universal, in contrast, is more like a law of nature. (Indeed, Bradley would regard laws of nature as themselves concrete universals.) Certain sequences of phenomena exemplify a concrete universal in that the way in which they develop can be understood as their taking whatever form circumstances require if it is to continue to be actualised. Moreover, the fact that each one falls under the universal is in some way due to and/or productive of the fact that another among its instances does. In saying that a human personality is a concrete universal in this sense, Bradley is in effect making the human personality much

---

4   There are some reflections bearing on this at CE, p. 44.
5   See, for example, PL, pp. 186 et ff. and 486–87.

what the individual essence of a finite mode was for Spinoza, an essence with a intrinsic conatus to persist in its own being.

(ii) It is not merely a common feature found in a great many things but something which calls out be actualised in a range of such instances, and which could not be fully itself unless it were.

The ordinary philosophical view is that we grasp the universal 'man' (='human person') as an abstraction from the various men we have encountered by noting that there is a common element present in this man, that man, ourselves and the other, and calling anything by the same word in which we note it again. The true way of looking at it, however, is that man-ness is something a full grasp of which would point much more positively to all the possible ways in which it might be specified.

Consider the simpler case of the universal *triangle*. Triangularity, taken as a concrete universal, is not just some common element in each precise sort of triangle. Rather, one can see from the very definition of a triangle, from a grasp of what it is for something to be one, that it is capable of all these various specifications.

(iii) Not only has it not been fully actualised in the world until all possible particular specifications of it have been so, but the history of its instances is somehow the history of its pressure to actualise itself thus fully.

§ The analytic philosopher may, with some justice, think that the notion of a concrete universal trades on a confusion between the relation in which a generic universal stands to the more specific universals which fall under it and the relation in which it stands to particulars which exemplify it. For surely even if *triangle* in some sense generates *isosceles, scalene,* and so forth, that is only to say that this generic universal is intrinsically such that these more precise determinations fall under it. In no sense does it generate the particular existing triangles. Similarly, one might agree that a divine mind could move from a conception of the generic essence of man to a conception of every possible type of man, or even of every possible precisely individualised version of it. But again, that would not be to see their concrete actualisation as somehow necessary.

If the charge were simply that the notion of a concrete universal assimilates the relation of determinate to determinable with that of particular to universal, Bradley might reply that there is no real distinction between these. For we have seen that, for him, particulars simply are their natures as they occur in particular contexts which bite into their character. However, that would not show that the actual existence of these particulars or natures followed from the generic universal under which they fall.

Perhaps the concrete universal is to be conceived neither as merely a possible genus of which its so-called instances are the possible species, nor as something producing the very existence of its instances, but rather as a kind of teleological law governing certain phenomena, that is, a pattern which these phenomena present in the most satisfactory form permitted by their context. The idea of universals which are concrete in this sense seems coherent and even promising.

What may be challenged is the idea that all the genuine universals actualised in the world are thus concrete. Surely there are things which are similar in some definite respect without that respect providing any dynamic linkage between them. That my actions all exhibit a certain personality may show that the phenomena which constitute my life all fall under it as a kind of common law, and that they are also in some sort of dynamic connection with one another. But if there is a man on another planet with just my sort of character, that might well be mere coincidence, our existence springing from causes in no dynamic connection with each other.

That is doubtless the common-sense view of the matter but Bradley would not endorse it. For he seems to have thought that in the end identity always ultimately implies some kind of dynamic connection.[6] At any rate, Bradley held that an action which truly is a certain individual's action, and for which he can properly be called responsible, is an instance of the concrete universal which is his personality. This so pervades an individual's life that everything he does is the specification of it appropriate for those circumstances. Such actions are in principle predictable for one who knows that personality, but they are not derivable from impersonal natural laws containing no reference to it.

Bradley always insisted that this account does justice to any proper sense in which humans are ever sensibly thought to be free.

> And if I am told that I deny Freedom, not only is such a statement contrary to fact, but (what is of more importance) I ask the Irrationalist [his current opponent] to produce any positive aspect he connects with that word, which I have failed already to include in my own account. [Note: See my *Ethical Studies*, and cf. *Essays*, pp. 131–32, and, on the other side, James, *Pragmatism*, pp. 115 ff.] What more does the Irrationalist ask than that every volition should be able to be taken as a new creation from the individual self? Certainly I do deny that mere Chance is anything positive; but I deny also that any one who wants Freedom, and who understands what he is saying, really can desire to have chance.
>
> PL, Terminal Essays, p. 679

§ There is a good deal of resemblance in this to the position on free will of Schopenhauer. According to him all phenomena are explained by the combination of preceding circumstances and a basic force of nature characterisable in a statement of law; the movements of the planets, for example, by their previous position and the force or law of gravity, and the behaviour of a lion by her particular circumstances and the force or law of lionhood. What distinguishes the human case is simply that there is a different force or law for each of us. Our actions are thus determined, but not by the same laws as govern nature at large, or even other human beings.

Schopenhauer holds that the basic forces or laws operative in the world are the Platonic Ideas manifest in the phenomena they govern. So this thesis about human behaviour is presented as the claim that there is a distinct Platonic Idea expressed in each human life. On this basis he claims that, at the noumenal

---

6   See PL, p. 508 and elsewhere.

level, our behaviour expresses the free choice exercised out of time by the universal Will to introduce our distinctive Platonic Idea into the world. And since each of us is ultimately identical with that Will, each of us is ultimately the kind of person he is as a result of his own free choice, at the noumenal level, to exist in a world governed deterministically by the law of motivation corresponding to his particular Idea. That a human being with my character should be the result of the physical processes which generated me was unpredictable on the basis of the laws operative in the world till then, but, granted I am here with that character, my behaviour follows in a strictly deterministic way from the situations I find myself in. Clearly there is a good deal in common here with Bradley's view in ES.

§ However, there is no talk in Bradley of any such grand cosmic choice behind the scenes. In ES he eschewed such high-flown metaphysical enquiries. His later metaphysics implies that the being of each actual person was required by the ultimate nature of the Absolute but he would not have said that it *chose* to manifest it. Rather, its nature requires it as one of its specifications just as my individual actions are a specification required (or required in particular circumstances) by the overall personality which is me. In any case there does not have to be any choice of my personality for me to be free. I am my personality, and am free to the extent that what I do is the specification of my personality required in the circumstances.

§ However, what my personality requires in any particular circumstance cannot be predicted mechanically. For not only can the wholeness of my personality only be grasped by a concrete intuition of it but so with each fresh whole which it forms together with each fresh set of circumstances. Such wholes are no mere recombinations of unchanging parts. My behaviour can only be confidently predicted, then, by one who can form a concrete idea of these wholes and find it as a necessary feature thereof, something which is often impossible before the event.

This is simply a special case of the view Bradley later developed of inference in general. This is not a matter of applying mechanical rules but of constructing a whole in our minds and finding it in possession of certain novel characteristics of which we could have had no conception beforehand. To infer how someone will act in a certain situation one must imaginatively construct a fresh whole in which his personality figures and read off his behaviour by inspection. The inference will be correct to whatever extent one has really grasped his personality and those circumstances.[7] (We may note in passing that Bradley says similar things about moral judgement. Moral principles are not rules to be mechanically applied, but requirements whose implications can only be seen when we construct a vision of their application to a total situation.)

---

7   It is, however, a question for Bradley how far the real world operates in conformity with what we can thus read off about it by inference. For the merely conceptual cannot quite register the richness of actual life. See above at Part Two, Chapter Two, §3(c).

I have been speaking as though whenever I act at all my personality fully actualises itself in what I do. But that, as Bradley sees it, is more an ideal than a constant reality. For first, I do not have a full concrete personality from the start. And second, as one develops, one's soul becomes the scene of its struggle with a chaos of contrary patterns which collectively form the bad self.

Thus one's moral development consists in the gradual building up of a main personality. But the 'psychic stuff' from which it is built is never made quite conformable to it, for some of it remains outside in various lesser personalities, or rather mere recurrent moods, impulses, and desires. Bad behaviour is the capturing of the organism by the material which has not entered into the main system. The ideal is a main system sufficiently comprehensive to leave only a little of such dross and sufficiently harmonious to be an effective unit. This is akin to Spinoza's view that bad behaviour typically springs from the *conatus* of a part rather than the *conatus* of the whole. For Bradley the basis of ethics lies in self-realization because each of us is a concrete universal which acts in the way which will best preserve itself and thereby move towards an ever more comprehensive and harmonious version of what it is so far. Self-realization is our inevitable aim, and the morals of our society and our own further development of them specify a large part of what such self-realization requires.

It seems an obvious objection that the self in this sense might not be at all a good one. But Bradley takes it that 'bad behaviour' is necessarily destructive of wholeness of personality.

Having seen something of the basic role of the self in ES, we must now move to the more negative account of it in AR. However, the contrast must not be exaggerated. On the one hand, already in ES, the nature of the self is seen as paradoxical. One must lose oneself to save oneself, and the struggle between self-sacrifice to the demands of a larger whole and the quest for self-fulfilment is endemic to human life. And, on the other hand, the self is still regarded in the later work as an appearance of especial importance. There is a high degree of truth to the conception of the world as a scene of self-development or 'soul making'.

§2. *The Unreality of the Self*

§ By chapter IX of *Appearance and Reality* Bradley has satisfied himself that *space* and *time*, *causation*, and *things*, particularly *physical things*, are unreal. He then turns to the self to consider the claims of that to reality. Many idealists have thought that the universe is basically composed of selves, but Bradley will not have it so. Even in the self we cannot find reality.

What exactly is Bradley's target? Ordinary people may not use such abstract phrases as 'physical object' or 'causation' but we know well enough to which of the things they talk about these terms are meant to apply. But talk about selves seems more removed from ordinary thought and speech. We talk about men and women, but we do not talk about selves. Nor is the philosopher's use of 'self' merely a synonym, it seems, for 'man or woman'.

Presumably the target of a discussion of the reality of the self is the supposed referents of such words as 'I' and 'you'. Each of us (whatever 'we' are) thinks that he is referring to something by the word 'I', and does not typically think that this is simply the physical organism from which his speech comes forth. For one thing some of us believe that we will still be there in some form after our death and that our deceased friends are somewhere behind the veil waiting for us. Ultimately intelligible or not, that has been a common belief (more so in Bradley's day than ours, perhaps, so far as the 'West' goes, but still a common belief) and suggests that we do not identify ourselves in any simple fashion with our bodies. And it has seemed clear enough to the majority of philosophers that a self (the sort of thing which can call itself 'I') is not simply the living physical organism. Upon the whole, then, I suggest we can understand by 'self' 'the sort of thing which can call itself "I" '.

§ Bradley opens his discussion of the reality or unreality of the self by a chapter (chapter IX) listing seven meanings of 'self' and follows it with a chapter on the reality of the self. The material in these chapters is not very well organized, and it is, in fact, chapter IX, rather than X, which contains the more interesting material.

Bradley lists seven meanings of the self, that is, I think, not seven ordinary meanings, but seven alternative philosophical accounts of how it is best to take the term.

(1) The self is sometimes thought of as the total contents of experience at any one moment, i.e., everything experienced in one single moment.

(2) The self is sometimes thought of as 'the constant average mass' of contents of experience such as are usually there when (and presumably only when) the self in question is supposed to be there. Thus understood one's self is one's typical moods, feelings, and style of thought.

(3) The self is sometimes thought of as some background core of experience which is always there.

(4) The self is sometimes thought of as a 'monad', i.e., as something not itself experienced but which has all one's experiences.

(5) The self is sometimes thought of as whatever engages a particular type of concern, or personal interest, and which is especially bound up with pleasure and pain.

(6) The self is sometimes thought of as what stands in opposition to the not-self as subject to object. Bradley calls this sense 'most important', and I shall be taking it as his main positive account.

(7) The self is sometimes thought of as consisting of those subjective factors which interfere with our attempt to think about something in a manner we might call 'objective'.[8] (This is not so much a theory, I suppose, as an approach to the matter implicit in some ordinary thinking, of a kind which Bradley, indeed, approves.)

---

8   See also PL, p. 41.

§ The following chapter seems meant to show that the self is unreal in each of these senses. However, Bradley seems to confuse two distinct lines of objection to them. Sometimes he seems concerned to show that they do not give an account of it in which it lives up to our expectations of what a self should be. But in other cases he seems concerned to question their adequacy, not so much as accounts of the self, but as accounts of anything genuinely real at all. Let us start by considering what he has against each of them as accounts of the self.

(1) This account fairly obviously fails this test. For we expect a self to be something which persists through time.

(2) This fails because it implies that I cease to be myself when my mood shifts sufficiently, something which we are not willing to admit. Bradley also urges that what I am in this sense alters with changes in my environment. This goes against our sense of the self as a separate thing in its own right.

Bradley's discussion here reflects his opposition to political individualism and tendency to think that one's nature is so bound up with one's community that purely personal interests are a myth or a disease. Thus politically he joined with other absolute idealists in rejecting the notion that the state is simply a device to protect purely individual interests. Each individual emerges as a fresh phase in the life of his community, not as something with an independent being. The organs of the state are there, indeed, to serve the community but we shouldn't think of this as a matter of their serving the interests of individuals as isolated units.[9]

(3) This fails because if there is any constant core to one's experience it is probably some background bodily tone quite lacking the significance which we expect a self to have.

(4) This fails the test because it falls so outside our experience that it cannot be what we care about when we care about our destiny. If, indeed, we had a clear concept of the self at the empirical level the monad might at least be considered as an attempt at a deeper explanation of a familiar phenomenon. However, the defects of the other senses of 'self' show that we do not. In any case, it would be a hopeless explanation for it is quite unintelligible how something unchanging and simple can stand to the flux of our experience.

> But if the monad stands aloof, either with no character at all or a private character apart, then it may be a fine thing in itself, but it is mere mockery to call it the self of a man.
>
> AR, p. 75

Here we have Bradley in his insufficiently recognized role as a proto-logical positivist.

(5) and (7): The self, if it were understood in either of these ways, wouldn't be an individual reality at all, such as we expect a self to be. And it would be too miscellaneous in its contents to be the permanent entity it is meant to be.

---

9   See, for example, CE, p. 150, and ETR, p. 435.

(6) Bradley thinks this a very important sense of self. In effect he utilises it through much of his philosophy. But he supposes that it doesn't quite answer to what one normally expects of the self because like sense (2) it makes the division between self and not-self highly unstable, whereas the self is thought of as something with quite definite and constant boundaries as against the rest of reality.

These considerations don't show that what these senses specify is unreal, only that they are not what we mean by the self. Thus vindicating their reality, were it possible, would not be vindicating the self's reality. But are they themselves real or unreal?

§ We have suggested above that Bradley calls things unreal for two apparently distinct reasons—first that the concept of them is finally incoherent, however pragmatically useful, and second that they are essentially only aspects of something else (as a two-dimensional plane figure of a three-dimensional object).

On the face of it, this gives 'unreal' two distinct meanings. But perhaps for Bradley the second meaning is simply the most important case of the first. For he thinks that in picking out something and giving it a name we treat it as though it has a distinctness which it could not have as mere aspect of something else. In consequence, there must be incoherences in our concept of it. And this may be the main reason for the incoherence of our concept of most things. At any rate, it supplies sufficient reason for dismissing as unreal the referents of all the purported senses of 'self' which do not qualify immediately as unreal in the first sense, as we have already in fact seen the self as monad—sense (4)—did. This is obvious enough and I shall confine my discussion to senses (1), (2), and (6).

The self in sense (1) is the total present contents of experience. This seems to be the same as a momentary centre, described with less emphasis on its unity. Bradley does, indeed, up to a point think of such centres as the very 'stuff' of reality. However, if we think of the centres in too thing-like a way, we divorce them from the context of historical process from which they emerge, and from other such centres, and thus our concept of them becomes incoherent. In the end you can only describe them properly by saying how they relate to other centres and to the public world posited by acts of judgement within them.

The self in sense (2) ('constant average mass') is unreal in much the same way. You can't ultimately make sense of my personality as an individual thing in its own right apart from how I stand to other personalities.

As for sense (6), the self as opposed to not-self, the mere fact that we can only say what it is by describing how it stands in contrast to something else shows that the real thing is the unity of self and not-self in which the self is embedded like a plane figure in a three-dimensional object.

§ An apparent objection to the whole discussion is that the description of these different senses of self often seems to presuppose an unexplored common-sensical background assumption concerning the identity of the self over time (such as Bradley seems to deny especially in his discussion of the self as monad). For example, sense (2) must presumably mean the usual contents of one particular person's experience over time. Likewise the self as constant background of experience—sense (3)—seems to mean 'background of the experience of the person in question', for certainly it doesn't mean the constant background of all the experience that there is. To this I offer two replies on Bradley's behalf.

1. He might say that there is a certain continuity between total experiences which makes it fair enough to think of them as phases of a single enduring *centre of experience* but that this enduring centre is not what we mean by the self.

For this he could have given two reasons. (A) He might have said that there's not a genuine identity across time here of the sort we expect of the self. It's just a mere series. This answer, it must be said, stands in striking contrast to the view of the self taken in *Ethical Studies*. (B) So far as the centre is a genuinely identical something persisting across time, it's rather a particular version of the world than something in the world. But the self is rather something in the world than a version thereof.

2. He might have said that he was making the usual assumption that the experiences associated with a particular organism belong to one self, and then showing that we cannot identify anything which is the self in question. (He would have needed to back this up with the usual reasons for saying that the self is not simply the organism itself, namely, that we do not think that the life of the self has to be coterminous with the life of the organism.)

Neither of these answers seems quite satisfactory. Upon the whole I think the first is the better from a Bradleyan point of view. Indeed, I think he would have done better if he had started with an account of the sense in which a centre of experience can endure through time, and then gone on to show that such an enduring centre is (a) not itself quite real and (b) not what we ordinarily mean by the self.

§3. *Finite Centres and the Self*

§ So the self bites the dust along with physical things, space, time, causality, and so forth. Yet, for Bradley, reality and unreality are a matter of degree and the self scores better here than does the merely physical. And though it is unreal it certainly exists, that is, thought which posits it is essential for good ordinary purposes. Moreover, just as it is possible to reinterpret the statement that time is unreal as a claim about what time really is, so one can take what he has to say about the self as a claim about what the self really is, or about the correct analysis of the ordinary concept thereof. In particular, the sixth of his seven senses, together with discussions of the self or subject in some of his psychological writings, adumbrates an account of the self which deserves to be taken seriously.

Yet saying just what that account is is complicated by the fact that like all other concepts which are pragmatically useful but metaphysically unsatisfactory there is bound to be a good deal of incoherence to it. Thus while most philosophers today regard it as a fault in an analysis of an ordinary concept, if it exhibits it as incoherent, pretty well the converse holds for Bradley. Thus doing justice to Bradley and, if he is right, to the self itself, may require some incoherence in our account.

However, it is something of a problem to know what sorts and degree of incoherence are to be regarded as tolerable and what not in the explication of an ordinary concept from a Bradleyan point of view. For example, he insists that religion suffers if its practitioners are too concerned with coherence in their beliefs, since, like science and common sense, it must work with practical makeshifts, and should not fear inconsistency.[10] Yet Bradley would not, one imagines, have been patient with any and every contradiction on the part of a religious apologist.

Despite all this, it does, in fact, seem possible to extract from Bradley an account of the self susceptible of a reasonably coherent statement. Such an account will draw substantially on ETR, especially XIV–XVI, but will be based mainly on his account of the sixth sense of self in chapter IX of AR.[11] The essence of this view is that a centre of experience (in cases familiar to us, at least) has two aspects, a self or subject aspect, and an object or not-self aspect, of which the most obvious case is the physical world as presented to our senses. Thus the self is that aspect of the centre which is conscious of the rest, the immediately given not-self, and contains acts of projection which extend the not-self in conception.

§ To follow this one must bear in mind that Bradley distinguishes between something's being experienced and its being an object of consciousness. The whole centre of experience including all its elements and the 'relations' between them (a way of putting it, of course, not finally satisfactory) is experienced at each moment, but only the not-self side of it is an object of consciousness, an object, that is, to its self-side, which is experienced but not normally the object of consciousness. (It may, however, become object for another layer of self. But there must always be a final layer of self which is experienced without being an object of consciousness.)

§ But if the self is not what has experiences, as an element within experience, what is it which does *have* the experiences? Well, perhaps the question is misconceived, but if it is pressed, the Bradleyan answer might be that in one sense each total experience experiences itself and in another sense it is experienced by the Absolute, though this only means that it is included in the one absolute experience.

Is it somehow absurd to speak of the centre as experiencing itself? Well, I believe that this is an apt formula for capturing a fact of which there is no absolutely satisfactory verbal statement. In a sense it does seem that the very being of our total experience at any moment is one with its non-conceptual knowing of itself, and that this constant self-knowing is distinct from that explicit knowing which one part of the centre may have of another.[12]

---

10   See ETR, p. 431; Perry, II, p. 640, etc.
11   See CE, pp. 596–97; AR, pp. 185–89; ETR, pp. 446–47.
12   See AR, pp. 94, 153–54; CE, p. 224; and ETR, pp. 159 et ff.

Though Bradley finds some incoherences in this concept, he evidently thinks it has a place even at quite profound levels of thought; moreover, it is a conception which either under the head of 'self' or 'subject' one can hardly avoid using in presenting Bradley's view of the world. Thus it contrasts with the other senses of 'self' in which it is either a creature of bad metaphysical theory or something of only peripheral significance to his thought.

§ According to this view, then, the world (not the object world, but the actual Universe in its true, or almost true, colours) consists of innumerable centres of experience, but these are not selves. For a self is just one aspect of a centre of experience which confronts its other not-self aspect. (By a centre of experience here I mean an enduring centre, or soul. Something will be said about the trans-temporal identity of both self and centre in the next section.) Thus the existence of selves, *qua* subjects of experience, who are aware of a world of surrounding objects, rests on, or consists in, the following facts.[13] Centres of experience of the kind with which we are familiar (though we can conceive of centres of which this is not true, as may perhaps be the case with those of babies and lower animals) have two aspects, an object aspect and a subject or self aspect. That is, their contents divide into those which form a sub-unity which is the core of the self, and those which form a sub-unity which is the core of the world in which that self seeks its fortunes.

The contents which form the core of the object world are certain sensory or perceptual presentations (though they only earn the term 'perceptual' through playing the role we are to describe) which form the basis of a construction in which they are conceived of as supplemented by indefinitely more material of essentially the same kind, organized on spatial principles which they themselves suggest.[14] Thus we think of the extreme left of our visual (or perceptual, see next section) field as continuing on with further visibilia of a kind we may conceive more or less definitely; similarly the right side and the top and the bottom (and stretching out beyond us in the depth dimension in a manner suggested by various experiences of handling of things).

As for what distinguishes the self aspect, Bradley from time to time indicates several features.

(a) The self is experienced without being an object of consciousness. This sense (6) of AR, chapter IX, is certainly the most important.

(b) The self aspect is sometimes distinguished as that which is most strongly imbued with hedonic qualities.[15]

(c) His discussions of *will* suggest that the self or subject consists above all of ideas which tend to actualise themselves.

(d) The centre as a whole somehow identifies itself with some of what it

---

13 See ETR, p. 350, and AR, pp. 241–43 and pp. 466–69. In ETR Bradley refers back to the AR passages by the pagination of the Allen and Unwin edition.
14 See ETR, pp. 46, 461, and CE, essay XXI, etc.
15 See CE, p. 222.

includes in a way which it does not with the rest, the former being the self, the latter the not-self. The idea of the whole somehow carrying out such an operation is somewhat obscure, for the operation would seem to be just another of its contents, and therefore part of what it needs to operate upon. Perhaps therefore we should regard this feature as needing analysis in terms of the previous three.

(e) We should also bear in mind the respect Bradley shows for the seventh alleged sense of 'self' and of 'subject' in which the subjective is the irrelevant, what has to be pushed aside if one is to follow a train of thought through—e.g., in working out one's opinions on a philosophical matter, questions of the rewards which come more readily to those who take a certain viewpoint would be subjective considerations irrelevant to the problem.

Upon the whole it seems that it is (a) and (b) which are the most important of these. (c) is to a great extent a derivative of (b), (d) is probably in the end reducible to other features, and (e) does not pick out any sense of self in which it could be called an entity. So let us examine the first four features, dropping a remark or so about the fifth *en route*.

§ (a) The suggestion that the self is that to which the world is presented, and which is experienced without itself normally being an object of consciousness, strikes me as excellent. However, his detailed development of the point seems rather unsatisfactory.

It would have been best, I believe, to have developed it somewhat as follows.

The contents of experience divide into two classes, which we may call active contents and passive contents. The distinction between them consists in the fact that the first are directed upon other contents of experience, which may be called their objects, while the second are not. (Such direction might be upon them for their own sakes or as symbols of other things lying outwith experience.) The first constitute the self and the second the not-self. Of the first we may say that they are lived through but are not objects of consciousness. The second, when they are the objects of the first, are objects of which we are conscious. There is not, however, some stable contrast between the active items forming the self and the passive ones forming the not-self. Active contents may become objects to other contents, and in doing so may become more passive. Moreover, there may be passive items which are not objects of consciousness, experienced without being attended to. (We shall consider shortly whether these belong to the self or the not-self.)

It is tempting to ascribe this view to Bradley. However, he was intensely suspicious of such words as 'active' and 'passive' in such a context, supposing that philosophers and psychologists who talk about 'activity' are usually quite unclear what they mean by it.[16] Still, such expressions are not entirely alien to him. Thus in PL he criticises empiricist psychology for giving too passive a

16   See, for example, CE, pp. 226–27, 247, etc.

picture of the workings of the human mind, and insists that judgement is 'our act' not a mere passive result of associations.[17] And apart from this, there seems no reason why he should object to a contrast between *active* and *passive* characterised in the above terms. For to say that the active contents are directed upon the passive only means that they are some mode of felt dealing with them or responding to them, whether this be primarily intellectual, emotional, or the experience of directly handling them. And surely Bradley allows that emotions may be felt as directed upon other contents of experience, while his whole view of judgement implies that there is a way of feeling towards another content of experience which alienates it from its actually experienced context and projects it onto an unexperienced beyond. Moreover, his talk of consciousness as being an experienced relation, and of the self as being confronted with the not-self, seems to imply a notion of such 'directedness upon'.[18]

§ But though Bradley sometimes seems to be taking some such view his actual account of the contrast between subject and object in AR, chapter IX, is that the self consists in such components of experience *as lie in the background of experience.* The idea seems to be that the sole distinguishing mark of the subject is that it is not an *object* of consciousness.

One problem here is as to what being an object of consciousness amounts to if it does not mean being the object of certain mental activity. But perhaps a notion of experience as having a foreground and background can be developed which meets this point.

§ More serious is the strange implication that any unnoticed background element of experience pertains to the self. This would include not only background somatic sensations—which suit the thesis quite well—but any background noises, smells, sights, sounds, warmths, such as the noise of the traffic outside, the table I see out of the corner of my eye, the faint smell of roses in the garden, etc. Surely this is not very satisfactory. For these are contents which would belong to the not-self if noticed, and it seems inappropriate to say they belong to the self as long as they are not. It seems equally plausible to say that all passive contents belong to the not-self whether or no they are presented as objects.

---

17   See, for example, PL, p. 478, p. 482. On activity see also PL III, I, VII, where Bradley speaks of the mind without any embarrassment about the notion of activity and comes near to identifying the self, even in one of the additional notes, written after AR, with the active side of the centre of experience. Thus in note 5 on p. 516 he says: 'The view which was taken by me in this Chapter may be stated as follows. Every change in feeling is an incoming disturbance which involves a reaction on the side of that which is changed. This reaction shows itself within every feeling as an integral and also distinguishable aspect. And the felt group which habitually reacts is a central core which is later the basis of what we call self.'

18   It is worth noting here that Husserl, whose view is close to that I am recommending, strongly rejects the idea that mental acts are 'active' in any sense involving free will, spontaneity, or other such things to which Bradley might have objected. See Husserl, *Logic,* II, p. 563.

§But is not Bradley right about somatic sensations in the background? Well, perhaps the best view would distinguish between the 'I' and the 'me' rather as James did. (The fifth sense of 'self' in AR, chapter IX, was, in effect, a characterisation of the 'me' as opposed to the 'I'.) Then one might say that the *I* consists only in the active contents, and that all passive contents belong to the *not-I*. This, however, divides into the *me* and the *external not-self* according to the type of concern with them shown by the active elements, or such as they would receive if made objects thereof.

(b) How far does feature (b) coincide with feature (a)? Is it the active (as opposed to object) side of experience which is the most strongly imbued with pleasure and pain?

To make them coincide, it would be necessary, I suggest, to distinguish the pleasure or pain which one takes in some other element of experience, from that which is an object of attention for itself. Only the first would belong to the self in the sense of subject.

But surely all my pleasures and pains are very much a part of me. Well, here again, a distinction between *I* and *me* seems called for, and the distinction of both from the world I experience as external to myself. Beauty has well been called objectified pleasure. A beautiful scene is strongly imbued with pleasure, but it is pleasure experienced as pertaining to the scene itself.

Pleasures and pains felt in the body, I suggest, may belong either to the *I* or the *me*. So far as they are ways in which I mind what is happening in the body, functioning as triggers for action to protect it, they are my way of caring about it and belong to the *I*, while the body belongs to the *me*. But if they become objects of attention on their own account, they are rather parts of the *me*. Indeed, if distanced from our active core by a special effort, they may become rather part of the external world than of the *me*. Equally it would seem, the beauty or ugliness of my surroundings become part of my *I* to the extent that they determine my behaviour.

I am not sure how satisfactory this is in detail. But something along these lines would fit in well with Bradley's main positions and certain difficulties in our distinctions would support his view of the instability of the contrast between self and not-self.

§ (c) Bradley's discussion of will, in his psychological essays, is of considerable interest.[19] Basically his view is that it consists in the tendency of certain ideas, with which the centre especially identifies itself, to actualise themselves in the world. Their tendency to do so is to some extent a function of their pleasantness, or of the pain experienced in the contrast felt between their content and what is currently given as actual. It is hard not to take this as part of a doctrine of the self. However, it can perhaps be reduced to the operation of the other features. Certainly ideas which tend to actualise themselves in the world can be regarded as *active* contents, in my sense, directed threat.

---

19   See CE, essays XXIII and XXVI–XXVIII.

§ (d) The notion of the whole centre identifying itself with one of its parts is rather puzzling, as I noted above. For surely any such operation will simply be one of the elements within it, and it is unclear why this will be more especially its operation as a whole than anything else it contains. Here again Bradley's position seems to make better sense if we make use of the idea of active and passive contents of experience, and of the distinction between the *I* and the *me*. We can then regard the active contents of experience as peculiarly representing the main thrust of the centre's being, and as that with which it identifies itself as 'I', while that at which these are directed can be regarded as thereby made into self in the sense of 'me'.

On this account, and allowing for Bradley's view that contents of the self can always pass over into the not-self, it seems that an experience, say of feeling angry at someone via direction of an angry experience upon some presentation of him, can itself be objectified and thereby ceases to belong to the I. Indeed, if we bring our anger before us an object of curiosity rather than personal concern it may even take on the character of a part of the external world rather than either of the *I* or the *me*. (Somewhat Spinozistic conclusions might be drawn from this, about the value of achieving clear ideas of our emotions in order that we shall not be dominated by them.) Thus it is not the case that attention to acts of the ego—as on some views—leads to a splitting of the centre into two egos, one regarding the other, but that what was once ego is de-ego-fied.

§ Whatever the detailed truth of the matter, Bradley's account, particularly in relation to feature (d), has the merit of not identifying the self, either as *I* or *me*, with anything experienced as peculiarly mental. For that with which the centre identifies itself will typically include the experienced body as its main core, along with such more spiritual things as qualities of character, social status, reputation, and so forth.

This is obvious enough in the case of the *me*. More interesting is its application to the *I*. This, on such an account, will consist to a very great extent of one's body as felt in physical activity. When acting upon the world physically, my 'lived' body (to use the phenomenologist's jargon), and to a great extent the physical implements it employs, is experienced in its direction upon the external reality to be transformed. Thus the self, in this sense, includes both my thoughts and feelings about perceived or conceived things in the object world, and also my body as engaged in action within it. Though Bradley does not insist on this explicitly, it is implied by his contention that no 'content' belongs essentially to the self or not-self. Each is self so far as it is part of that to which the world is presented, and it is not-self (perhaps in the form of 'me') to the extent that they are the world presented.

If this is right, the self aspect of experience is content, which may be 'physical' or 'mental', but which has other contents as its object. Whether 'physical' or 'mental' it is, of course, experience. The physical components of our experience, for Bradley, are those which can be fitted into a larger spatio-temporal construction forming the world of things in an abiding space and single time series, together with all that is conceived of as belonging to the thus constructed reality. The mental is what has no clear place in such a construction. Since what is experienced as subject often has the potential for being included in such a construction the division between self and not-self does not coincide with any possible divisions of reality into the mental (or rather 'my' mental) and the physical. To the suggestion that there is no clear boundary between the mental and the physical in this sense Bradley would give unequivocal assent.

§ All in all, I do not think that Bradley offers as satisfactory a conception of the self as his philosophy has the resources to provide, mainly on account of his fear of the notion of *activity*. But the general point that the self is an aspect of a centre of experience, rather than something unexperienced which yet somehow 'has' the experience, seems eminently acceptable.

§4. *Trans-temporal Identity of Self and Finite Centre*

§ It is to be noted that the not-self lies partly in experience, partly outside as something merely posited (so far at least as that centre of experience is concerned). For most of the not-self is a conceived extension of the given not-self. That suggests the question: Does not the self also extend beyond the self-aspect of the centre as a posited *more* thereof? For is there not within the centre the construction of a larger and fuller self of which what is actually experienced is just the tip? One could find grounds for saying both yes and no in Bradley.

Clearly the answer is positive so far as the temporal dimension goes. Each momentary centre, in the standard case, contains a sense of a history to which the present self is heir, provided by something akin to a synthetic judgement of sense. (Theoretically, one should distinguish between this history of the self and that of the centre conceived as a continuant.) But is the self to be thought of as having more to it at each moment than what is experienced of it, as is the object world? Such an extension might be conceived as one's *unconscious* in something like a Freudian sense. However, there is no suggestion of this in Bradley, though in some form it could well be grafted onto his view, either as a theoretical posit or as, with James, a further experience existing in detachment from the dominant stream.

What is more to the point is Bradley's contention that a person is as much an object in the centres of experience or personal worlds of others as it is something pertaining to its own.[20] Thus you are a figure in my world as much—or more—than in your own. As such you have features beyond those ever pertaining to your actual experience.

However, it is rather doubtful whether one's person, or *persona*, is supposed to be something of which the self side of one's centre is the presented part, supplying the basis for the construction of the rest. For it is a figure in the object world, rather than one of the subjects to which that is presented. If so, it would seem that the self is wholly immanent in experience while the *persona* is rather a part of the not-self.

---

20   See especially ETR, chapter XIV.

§ Some of what Bradley says might suggest that another, as he is for me, must be person or *persona*, rather than inner self. And that looks dangerously like that foolish sort of solipsism from which we have sought to dissociate him above.[21] Surely I can conceive of 'your' centre, and of its self-aspect, and use 'you' to refer to the latter rather than to your *persona* as it figures in the object world. Bradley seems to be denying this when he says that I can only think of that which can enter into my own experience. However, such remarks must be understood in connection with his equation of a thing with its character and his views on identity and difference. For if there is nothing to a thing except content, as he puts it, meaning its character, and if in thinking of it I partly realize its character within my own experience, then, in a sense, the thing itself partly enters into me.[22] This may not be a very satisfactory view but it is not solipsism.[23] Moreover, for Bradley, the thing in my experience is both the same as, and different from, itself as it exists beyond my experience. And he also believes, of course, that the Absolute is in some sense immanent within our every experience, in the sense that our experience intrinsically points to its being a fragment of that larger whole and suggests its position within it.

We may say, then, that for Bradley, you and I, in at least one fundamental sense of such pronouns, are certain aspects of centres of experience considered as enduring through time, but realized at any one moment in single total experiences. The not-self is part of a larger not-self; the self is not a part of a larger self.

§ Most discussions of the nature of the self in philosophy are concerned with the conditions of its trans-temporal identity and we must now dig somewhat deeper into Bradley's views on this.

That a self is not the same as a finite centre of experience, but only an aspect of one, does not necessarily mean that there is a separate question as to what it is for a self to endure over time and for a soul (that is, a centre of experience *qua* enduring entity) to do so. For the same facts may determine whether the same centre is here now as was there then as determine whether it is the same self which they contain. However, Bradley sometimes seem to suggest that there may be a different self pertaining to the same soul at different times (whether the converse can hold is less clear.) And there is some suggestion that the identity of a soul across time is a more definite matter than that of a self. Thus, as we saw, his critique in AR of the self's self-identity over time sometimes seems to presuppose that the identity of the soul is unproblematic.[24] But, upon the whole, it seems that the factors which make for the identity of the self and

---

21   See pp. 450–52.
22   See ETR, p. 426.
23   The idea that what I think of is somehow present within me, through the exemplification of its nature within my experience has some affinity to the Whiteheadian thesis of the entry of one actual entity into another, perhaps also to the Thomist view of thought.
24   See above, pp. 521–22.

for that of the soul over time are the same, and that, if their identity diverges, it is simply because some have *more* to do with the self and some *more* to do with the soul. It is, therefore, best to assume at first that their identities correspond, and then add such qualifications as may be necessary.

§ We saw above (in Part Two, Chapter One, §3) that, while it is tempting to suppose that, for Bradley, the identity of soul or self across time is determined mainly by memory relations, he at times denies this on the ground that memory is derivative from more basic mental functions.

However, the function from which he thinks memory derivative is itself what many thinkers would describe as a form of memory, namely, the way in which we presently move from the thought of one universal to the thought of another as a result of the way in which they were connected in past experience. Thus when Bradley insists that memory is inferential, he is not interpreting it as consisting in inferences from the present by way of principles possessing a timeless validity of a kind accessible to all sufficiently rational minds, whatever their past experiences. (He is quite happy to regard q as inferred from p, where this relation has been set up by past experiences which I do not recall, a use of 'inference' which allows him to pack much more under this head than seems proper). Rather is he deriving it from what, following Sir William Hamilton (because, as he unkindly said, he found nothing else to take from him), he calls 'redintegration'.[25] This is his version of the association of ideas. For, in spite of the fame of his attack upon associationist psychology,[26] Bradley was very much an associationist himself, and his objection was at bottom only to the confused notion that the association was between particular mental atoms rather than universals.[27] This change once made, one could hardly expect to find a more rigid associationist than Bradley. For he tries to explain all the usual mental activities as complications of the basic fact that mind has a disposition to supplement experienced contents by contents previously associated with them.[28]

If one is to explain the development of memory and other mental powers in this way, one must presuppose the notion of the continuation of a single mind or consciousness, or at least a unitary and distinct stream of consciousness, through time. On the face of it—though Bradley sometimes seems to fudge this fact—it is only elements previously experienced by *this* mind together which serve to reinstate each other within it. One can either infer from this that it is because it is the same individual mind that redintegration occurs later under the influence of the previous experience, or that the identity of a mind across time is constituted by such relations of influence. Bradley, I believe, would take the second option. Thus his view of the identity of a mind or consciousness across time is not so very far from a memory account.

---

25   See PL, p. 304.
26   PL, II, II, I.
27   See CE, p. 209.
28   See CE, essay XII, etc.

Sometimes, Bradley seems to hold that it is only when redintegration has produced memory in what he thinks the proper sense, in which it provides knowledge of particular past events, that it constitutes personal identity proper. So perhaps his view is, in effect, that the trans-temporal identity of a soul is constituted by trans-temporal influence of the redintegration type but that it is only when this leads to memory of particular events in that soul's past that a continuing self is thereby constituted. But he is not very clear on these matters, perhaps because he thinks these concepts essentially fuzzy. (Matters are complicated further by his tendency to treat the past as something created by our positing of it—as a result of processes of redintegration! But we have seen that his whole eternalistic account of the Absolute collapses if such a suggestion is taken too seriously.)

Despite these complications, the upshot of his account seems to be that there is a continuing individual centre of experience to the extent that there is (in a timeless sense of 'is') a set of momentary centres which form a temporal series in virtue of relations of influence, memory, or some other not too dissimilar relation. And sometimes he does not seem so far from the Jamesian idea that this involves either each (a first one perhaps apart) taking over from one other in the set as its predecessor, in virtue of an act of identification with it, or acts of taking over of other moments as predecessors of a less immediate kind, whereby certain distinct series constituted by immediate such takings over latch onto each other to form a single series.[29] However, we should probably add that, for Bradley, it is not so much that a soul or centre *now* takes over from one which is anyway in *the* past, as in *its* past, but that it is only *past* at all (rather than future, past, or present) because thus taken over as in its past.

It would be a mistake to think that for Bradley an enduring centre is a series of momentary ones. Rather is it something supposedly one and the same present in each moment of that series which is its history. To the extent that there really is something one and the same, and distinct from what is present in members of other such series, the enduring self is a concrete universal, that is, what is the same is an element of character or content or whatness, forming a concrete rather than a merely abstract universal because of the historically explanatory relations in which its instances stand to one another. To the extent that there is not something thus one and the same, talk of an enduring centre turns upon the fiction that there is. This, I believe, is what Bradley's position amounts to even if it is not set out so bluntly.

§5. *Nature: A Comparison with Husserl*

§ Consideration of this view of the self, understood as subject, must go hand in hand with Bradley's view of the phenomenal not-self which is the world the

---

29   See 'On Our Fear of Death and Desire for Immortality', ETR, chapter XV, Supp. Note B, especially p. 454. I discuss this in §6 below.

self feels itself to be living in. The not-self consists for the most part in what Bradley sometimes calls the object world sometimes 'my real world'.[30]

The word 'my' suggests a purely personal environment, but Bradley is not denying that my real world can be the real world of other selves as well. In this connection we should remember that for Bradley the answer to the question whether different persons have the same 'real world' may be truly both yes and no, since, on his account, identity and difference are opposite sides of the same coin and 'it takes two to make the same'.

§ There is much that Bradley leaves very vague about the relation between the constructed object world and the presentations which form its basis. What, for instance, is supposed to be the status of the third dimension? Surely Bradley would have done well to draw on James here and say that the visual field has sensible depth and stretches away from a point of view which is not itself visible. Then he could have said that the essential construction is that of an indefinite more which stretches out in all directions beyond the actually given.

A charge sometimes made against views of this kind is that they conceive the world in too purely visual a manner. However, Bradley's view that analysis is always a breaking up of a whole more real than the elements thus produced militates against any idea that we live in a number of different sense worlds which are merely correlated. It suggests rather that, at least for the post-infantile mind, the visual is simply the most sharply obvious of the distinguishable aspects of a single sensory plenum in which the different sensory modalities are merged. Although Bradley does not make this point himself, it fits well with his general principles.[31]

The object world, then, as it is for us, consists of a sensibly given core of spatially patterned sensory quality together with a conceived indefinitely larger *more* of which this is taken as a fragment. This is as much as to say that the physical world is there for us essentially as that which is specified in the analytic and synthetic judgements of sense of PL. The only truth, however, of which these judgements are capable is pragmatic rather than literal. For, if we try to think them out fully, they exhibit all manner of incoherences. Thus we have to think of what falls inside our experience as of the same nature as what exists outside it or anyone else's, and such as might have thus existed itself. Yet it is coloured inside our experience by features which we cannot, and yet must, think of as present outside it.

§ The object world only exists, then, insofar as it is presented within finite centres of experience, either as immediately experienced contents therein facing the self aspect of experience or as an extension of these contents posited in synthetic judgements of sense. This gives such centres of experience a certain basicness in his ontology even if it can be misleading to say, without qualification, that they are what the world is composed of.

This view of things was compared by T. S. Eliot in his doctoral dissertation

---

30   Especially in ETR. See index.
31   See, again, CE, essay XXI.

to the monadism of Leibniz.[32] There is some justice in the comparison, though Bradley's centres of experience are anything but windowless. (He says that there is no such thing as real privacy in the universe, though he also says that centres of experience are not directly pervious to one another.[33])

In some ways Bradley's position is closer to that of Husserl, with his view of reality as consisting of a community of monads who constitute a shared public world by their convergent intentional acts. In Part One, Chapter Three, §6, we found it fruitful to compare the views of James and Husserl on the physical world and a comparison between Bradley and Husserl should also be illuminating. It may help, for one thing, win recognition of Bradley's contribution to phenomenology, in something approximating to Husserl's conception thereof as *an examination of the world strictly as it is for consciousness*. In particular, there is a good deal to be learnt from a comparison of Bradley's views of nature, and of what he calls 'my real world', and the concept of *the life world* as developed by Husserl and later phenomenologists.[34]

I must first deprecate any suggestion that Bradley is merely a primitive phenomenologist adumbrating themes which are better developed by Husserl. For in some ways Bradley seems the better phenomenologist. (One turns, however, to the wonderful sharpness of outline of Husserl's world view with a certain relief from a certain murkiness in Bradley's *Weltanschauung*.) I am not, however, concerned to distribute merit marks but to suggest that the two thinkers have convergent views on the self and its world which can be usefully combined. This is particularly true of what each has to say about nature as understood by science and as experienced in daily life.

§ Both thinkers are concerned at the impoverishment of our conception of nature which sets in if we contrast the nature described by physical science, and in terms of it alone, with the sensibly presented nature of daily experience, and regard the latter as a merely subjective appearance of the former. For Husserl, especially in his later writings, the surrounding world, conceived of as composed of those very things which we directly encounter in perception, and with their encountered properties, are the actual environment. Scientific descriptions either provide an extension of our conception of this world, or a particular kind of idealised set of concepts in which to construe it for special purposes. So far from annulling the validity of the life world these descriptions only have point insofar as they improve our technological, or other peculiarly scientific, dealings with it.[35]

Bradley's position is not so dissimilar, though he develops it less fully

---

32   See Eliot, *Bradley*.
33   See AR, pp. 306, 416, 464.
34   The comparison of Bradley and Husserl which follows uses material from my contribution to Manser and Stock.
35   This is the main theme of Husserl, *Crisis*, but is prefigured in Husserl, *Ideas*, and elsewhere.

and precisely. [36] He insists that, even if the conception of nature, appropriate for scientific enquiry, is an abstract mathematical one in which it is stripped of the so-called secondary qualities, aesthetic qualities, qualities presented to emotional response, and the inner felt life of organisms, they are nonetheless absolutely essential to our non-specialist idea of what that very nature is which science makes its own special, but limited, contribution to controlling and understanding.

In Bradley's day, as in ours, the appropriateness of various emotional responses to nature was a subject of some discussion. The trouble with such discussions, says Bradley, is that it is usually left unclear what is meant by 'nature'. (Surely this is true of much discussion in our own day of environmental ethics.) If by 'nature' is meant the nature of the scientist, then it is a useful construction rather than a concrete reality to which we can respond with much feeling. But though this construction is legitimate and important for limited ends, the nature of the ordinary observer, and still more of the loving naturalist (as opposed to scientific theorist) is a much less misleading abstraction from the total reality to which we all belong.

> The Nature studied by the observer and by the poet and painter, is in all its sensible and emotional fullness a very real Nature. It is in most respects more real than the strict object of physical science. For Nature, as the world whose real essence lies in primary qualities, has not a high degree of reality and truth. It is a mere abstraction made and required for a certain purpose. And the object of natural science may either mean this skeleton, or it may mean the skeleton made real by blood and flesh of secondary qualities.
>
> AR, p. 438

However, if one sets out to correct the misleading abstractness of the natural scientist's account of nature by adding features which he will dismiss as merely human subjective response thereto, the point at which one stops will either be arbitrary or become rather an account of the life of spirit in its fullness than of nature. For the concept of nature is an essentially unstable one in which we cannot help either including more of its human significance than we feel appropriate or less. Thus that ordinary conception of nature, which is brought to its highest fruition in nature descriptions which celebrate it in a manner which lies between poetry and science, belongs to a half-way house between scientific materialism and idealist metaphysic. We must still cling to it, however, if we are to avoid that alienation from the world, and impoverished conception of it, which merely scientific conceptions of reality bring, for the metaphysics which provides its intellectual correction is not a viable conception for daily use. (We might add—and Bradley would not disagree—that the metaphysical grasp of the spiritual nature of reality likewise risks distorting reality by its excessive abstractness. However correct it may be as abstract truth, more naturalistic descriptions may keep us in better touch with the concreteness of real existence.)

---

36   See, especially, AR, pp. 435–39.

This half way house conception of things with which Bradley would have us normally approach reality is very much the same as Husserl's life world, though, unlike Bradley, he does not think of it as ultimately incoherent.

Although there is much that is similar in Bradley's account of the relation between the emotionally rich nature of daily life and the abstract nature of the scientist and Husserl's of the relation between the life world and the idealised world of natural science, Husserl depicts the life world primarily as the environment as we experience it in practical activity while Bradley's emphasis is more on nature as presented to somewhat rarefied aesthetic contemplation. But, if Bradley would have done better to have put more emphasis on what Heidegger calls its 'ready-to-hand' features, Husserl, whose life world is a bit townily banal, could with advantage have done more justice to the status of natural beauty and sublimity, the mountains and the cataract. Heidegger's work might be held to mark an advance on both, though I think only if interpreted in an idealist way which most commentators think misconceived.[37]

Perhaps a Heideggerian or a Marxist might complain that Bradley's musing sense for the wonders of nature sometimes suggest the passive aestheticism of one who, removed from physical labour, forgets that for most men, nature is experienced as something to be struggled with in hard toil if they are to survive. However, while his economic position and life style may betray themselves in the somewhat lordly and Shaftesburyan reflections on nature, and on man's place in it in AR, chapter XXII, his philosophy has the resources for reinstating what he tends to neglect in such rhapsodies. And indeed to some extent they are so in remarks in ES and ETR. Thus in ETR, chapter XVI, he emphasises that the natural world is, for me, what surrounds my body and what I must act on through it to survive and do my duty.

Another criticism which might be levelled at Bradley's treatment of nature here is that he belittles the richness and formal beauty of the world as presented by science. Bradley might reply that the scientist who makes a metaphysic of his work must insist that there is nothing in his subject matter corresponding to his own sense of wonder and intellectual excitement at it and thus that there is no true beauty or wonderfulness there. And, even if Bradley does less than justice to the wonders of what science reveals, it remains true that an effort to think of a nature devoid of all properties besides the traditional primary ones, or other such supposedly purely 'physical' properties as more recent science may add, is an attempt to purge our conception of it of most of what is attractive in it for ordinary experience. Such an attempt is both pointless and, as we should all long since have learnt from Berkeley, vain.[38] (This, indeed, is even more obviously true today than in the past, since the properties ascribed to matter by modern physics can only be understood in the most abstract way as structures which reality must fill out somehow in ways that physics cannot grasp.)

§ For Bradley, then, the physical world is only there for consciousness, and

---

37   See Sprigge, *Theories*, chapter VIII.
38   See AR, chapters I and XXII.

we cannot, and should not, strive to improve our concept of it by divesting it of everything interwoven with our own subjectivity. For thereby we only arrive at what is not really there in any proper sense at all.

But am I to think of the physical world as only there for my consciousness, or as there also for the consciousness of other beings with whom I can communicate? Surely the latter.

Perhaps Bradley would have accepted the distinction Husserl made between my initial 'ownmost' world and the inter-subjective world which emerges when different egos identify figures in their respective 'ownmost' worlds as conscious subjects, and develop a sense of a world, common to them all, of which these are merely subjective versions.[39] In fact, something along these lines is suggested in Bradley's early work, *The Presuppositions of Critical History*, first published in 1874.[40] The sharing of a real world in the fullest possible sense is there said to require the ability of each such sharer to possess himself adequately of the consciousness of others on the basis of his own observations. Though he never develops the matter very fully we can take it that something like this continued to be his view.

§ But whether it is for my consciousness or the consciousness of others too, what does this being of a physical world for consciousness amount to? Does it imply that I cannot truly speak of anything physical existing of which no one will ever have been actually conscious? For Husserl, at least, the answer seems clear.

> The statement "It is there" means rather that from actual perceptions and their background of real appearances *possible* series of perceptions lead up under *motives* that are constant and continuous and girt about (as unnoticed backgrounds) with ever-changing fields of things; and so further till we reach those systems of perceptions in which the Thing in question appears and is apprehended. In principle we make no essential alteration here when in the place of a single Ego we consider a plurality of Egos. Only through the relation of a possible reciprocity of understanding can I identify the world of my experience with that of others, and at the same time enrich it through the overflowings of their experience. A transcendence which dispensed with the aforesaid systematically motivated connexion with my existing sphere of actual perception would be a completely groundless assumption; a transcendence which dispensed with the same, *on principle,* would be *nonsense.* The presence of what is actually not perceived in the world of things is then of this type, and is essentially different from that mode of Being of which we are intrinsically sensible, the Being of our own inward experiences.
>
> Husserl, *Ideas*, §45, pp. 142–43

Thus unperceived things are there for someone if the perception of them

---

39 See Husserl, *Meditations* (Meditation 5); also, besides Husserl, *Crisis*, see Husserl, *Ideas*; Husserl, *Psychology*; Husserl, *Experience*.

40 See at CE, pp. 28–31.

would be the result of certain experiences of kinaesthesia, whether he knows it or not.[41] And their existence can be equated with the holding of certain conditional truths about what I, or in a fuller sense of the physical, what someone, would perceive under certain conditions.

Husserl's phenomenology thus includes a phenomenalist position about the physical, for which physical things exist only so far as they are perceived or are available to be perceived. Where Husserl may differ from typical English-language phenomenalists, like early A. J. Ayer or C. I. Lewis, is in his views about the character of perceptual experience. For, according to him, our perceptual experience is of physical objects themselves rather than of mere sense data. Thus the conditional facts which figure in the phenomenalist analysis, concern experiences which can only properly be described as of physical things. What this seems to mean is that the content of perceptual experience is intrinsically coloured by the conditional facts about perceptual experience which we are ready to infer from it. But this marks no difference between them on the essential point that the existence of physical things consists in if-then facts about the experiences of appropriate observers.

If Husserl was a phenomenalist in this sense, what about Bradley? Certainly he avoids typically phenomenalistic formulations, especially such as are associated with the position of the detested John Stuart Mill, of whose talk of a permanent possibility of sensation he is scathing on the ground that appeal to the potential is typically the way out of difficulties for superficial thinkers.[42]

Bradley's contempt for the notion of matter as a permanent possibility of sensation may not really be directed at a phenomenalist analysis of statements about the physical into conditional statements about what we would perceive if we gave ourselves the experience of certain movements. For I suspect that he thought the notion of the potential was supposed to have a meaning not thus cashable in conditional statements. If so, I believe he was wrong about Mill's phenomenalism and certainly his objections would not apply to that of Husserl.

Some philosophers object to a phenomenalist account of the physical world, for which categorical statements about it are equivalent to conditional statements about what one would perceive if one gave oneself the experience of moving in certain ways, on the ground that the meaning and truth value of conditional statements in general is too unclear for them to be used in such an analysis. (Husserl seems never to have been troubled by this problem.)

It is doubtful if this can be the case with Bradley. For him a conditional statement reports a relation forced on adequately informed minds by genuinely actual features of reality, and, as such, is susceptible of as definite a truth-value as he could wish statements about physical reality to have.

Perhaps, however, Bradley thought the actual reality which would have to

---

41   The importance of bodily experience of kinaesthesia is more emphasised in Husserl, *Crisis*; see, for example, pp. 107, 161–67.

42   See, for example, PL, pp. 209–19, §§23–25; also in 1910 letter to James, Perry, p. 641.

provide the categorical underpinning of the conditional statement would be such that to grasp its nature would be to see the impossibility of doing justice to reality by physical conceptions. Thus the attempt to explain the real significance of our conception of the physical would undermines it. Such a contention would have an odd affinity amidst difference to the position of those physical realists who have argued that phenomenalism is circular because its conditional statements rest on a categorical basis which can only itself be conceived as physical.[43]

But I cannot see good grounds here for Bradley to reject an equation of statements about the physical with statements about what one would perceive if one gave oneself the experience of moving in various ways. For even if one could not grasp the categorical basis of these conditional statements without seeing it as better reported in another way, it could still be the basis of such meaning and definite truth value as our statements about the physical have. And, in fact, this seems highly appropriate as an interpretation of Bradley's view of the status of the physical.

But perhaps he regards our construction of the physical world as incoherent precisely because its only intelligible interpretation is in phenomenalist terms which clash with the categorical meaning we want to give it. Thus its unsatisfactory nature may lie in our unavoidable unclarity as to whether physical things are there because available for perception or available for perception because there.[44]

I would sympathise with this line of thought. But perhaps Bradley's position is, in fact, better understood as a form of constructivism close to that which A. J. Ayer developed in his later work.[45] On this view, the physical world is a posited larger whole of which our perceptual presentations belong as elements. Where Bradley would differ from Ayer would, then, be in his insistence that such a construction cannot give the literal truth of things. Ayer will not brook any notion of how things really are which can challenge such a construction. Bradley, in contrast, thinks the conception too riddled with incoherences to be supported as a final view of how things are by a metaphysician.

§ Despite the differences we have noticed, there is a good deal in common between Bradley's conception of my 'object world' and Husserl's of 'the life world'. Thus they agree that human, and to a some extent animal, minds share a system of corresponding sensory presentations which form the basis of the construction or constitution of a common physical world. They agree that natural science is a special development of this construction of great pragmatic use and intellectual value, but with a tendency, which we must resist, to turn against the ordinary conception of the physical world of which it is a special outgrowth and in terms of which its uses must be charted. For both agree that *the world of daily life*, with its sensible fullness and its cultural significance, is

---

43 See Armstrong, *Perception*, pp. 56–68.
44 See AR, pp. 241–44 and 338–43.
45 See Ayer, *Problems*.

more real than *the artificial idealisations of science*. While neither can exist except as an object of consciousness (possible if not actual) our constant consciousness is only of the former so that it is in terms of our role in it that we must make sense of our lives.

The two philosophers disagree, however, on some interesting points. Thus Husserl believes that there can only be one constituted spatio-temporal world, and that there can be no monads directed onto any other world. He denies, therefore, that there can be a multiplicity of space-times forming the object world of distinct groups of centres or monads unable to communicate with each other.[46] His essentially verificationist reason is that a transcendental ego can only know of other egos as animating organisms in its surrounding world. Thus it is senseless for me to suppose that there may be egos experiencing other worlds to that which I inhabit. (Husserl also thinks that we know *a priori* that the general structures found in our experience must be common to the objects present to any mind whatever.)

Bradley, in contrast, urges that there may be non-communicating alternative societies of souls or selves whose space and time (if they have such) may be out of any spatial or temporal relation to each others', something which may, but need not, prevent any form of communication, or other type of influence, between their inhabitants (for some selves may, in their own subjective time, move between them).[47] Some spiritualistic phenomena (for which, however, Bradley had a marked distaste) just might be a case of this.[48]

Thus, though Bradley thought that the idea of an unexperienced reality was absurd, he was quite at odds with a verificationism which would limit the reality of which I can meaningfully speak to that which I might experience myself. Of course such alternative spaces and times, and the centres in which they were presented, would belong to the one cosmic experience of the Absolute.[49] Perhaps this is a kind of cosmic verificationism, but it is not verificationism of any usual type. At any rate, he seems right, as against Husserl, as to the conceivability of a plurality of such non-communicating space-time systems.

§ Another matter on which it is interesting to compare Bradley and Husserl is as to the phenomenology of perception, a matter on which I believe Bradley beats Husserl on his own ground. I have already made the same point about James and Husserl.[50] Both James and Bradley believe that a perceived physical thing, as we ordinarily conceive it, is in part actually a part of our experience, rather than something merely presented by some such part. In virtue of this,

---

46   See Husserl, *Ideas*, §48, and *Meditations*, §60; also, I seem to recall, in *Crisis*.

47   See CE, pp. 596–97; AR, pp. 185–89; ETR, pp. 446–47.

48   Anthony Quinton does less than justice, I think, to Bradley's exploration of this theme in his 'Spaces and Times', *Philosophy*, XXXVII (1962), where he gives the impression that Bradley was concerned only with the alternative time systems of fiction or dreams.

49   See AR, p. 186.

50   See Part One, Chapter Three, §6.

their account does justice to the point insisted on by Husserl that in perception, as opposed to thought, the thing is present *in propria persona*, as Husserl himself put it.

Husserl, however, also insists that the physical world is utterly transcendent of consciousness. No part or element of it can intelligibly be identified with any element which is a literal (*reell*) ingredient in one's stream of consciousness.[51] When I see something, feel its hardness or weight, or hear the sound it makes, then the thing, its hardness, weight, or sound, must not be identified with any sense datum in my consciousness. Rather does the awareness of it consist in a mental act which bestows a perceptual sense or meaning upon the sense datum in virtue of which it presents a transcendent thing which is no part of consciousness.

§ Husserl's view of perception rests on a general view about the basic structure of mental acts. And his description of this structure is very persuasive in all other cases. He is, surely, right that in memory the past event is not itself in consciousness, but 'presented' by something which is. The same is true in all cases where I merely think of something. Thus when I imagine a non-existent unicorn, that unicorn is no more a part of my consciousness than a past event which I remember, though there is an image there which presents it. But when he analyses perception along the same lines, he seems to deny his own claim that it has a unique directness in virtue of which the thing itself is actually present to one.

So far as he offers any real explanation of this, it is that the validity of all thought claims is to be tested by some most basic form of experience which is the final arbiter of their truth, and that, in the case of the physical, it is perceptual experience which plays this role. But this still leaves a gap between the 'hyletic' datum and a thing perceived which does not do justice, as it seems to me, to his own claim that the thing itself is really present there.

One reason why he insisted so strongly on this was, doubtless, that he thought no truth about what is in consciousness at any moment entails that a physical thing exists. But this would only show that the truth which makes a thing in consciousness a physical reality must concern its relation to what lies beyond (especially those quantitatively exact properties which are a matter of its relations to various instruments of measurement rather than its more basically sensible form and qualities).

§ Some of the differences in Bradley's and Husserl's phenomenology of perception stem from the fact that Husserl is committed to endorsing its validity, while Bradley is more than happy to give it a significance which is finally incoherent.

Bradley, of course, finds plenty of incoherence in the status of the things we

---

51   Husserl's use of the word 'reell', and its relation to his use of the German word 'real', causes a lot of pother among readers, translators, commentators, but translation of it as 'literal' or 'literally' in the present context—and I believe most others—seems to me to convey its full meaning. See, for example, *Ideas*, §41.

regard ourselves as perceiving and of our relation to them. It is curious, however, that his views on identity and difference, and on concrete universals, provide him with more resources for combatting charges of incoherence here than are available to most philosophers. For the main objection to the conception of perception of Hume, James, and Bradley, as the actual partial presence of the object in our experience, turns on the transitivity of identity. If the sense data of two people seeing the same part of the same object are each identical with the object, then they must be, if identity is transitive, identical with each other. Yet there are good grounds for saying that they are different. For one holding to fairly traditional logical views like Husserl this objection was perhaps insuperable.

However, for Bradley this should pose no great problem. For he could interpret a physical thing as a concrete universal whose instances are its presentations in different minds. As such, we may say, it occurs as identically itself amidst systematic differences which change together in a lawful manner. This is quite akin to the identity of a thing with itself at different times.

Such an account would explain how the very same physical object can be identically the same in the minds of two different persons who perceive it. Certainly there is a difference between them, and it is this which we emphasise when we speak of them as distinct mental events. But they are also identical, for the concrete universal which the physical object is remains identical in all its different appearances.[52] Since physical things are continuants this account makes them concrete universals twice over. That is, the thing at a moment is a concrete universal more or less fully present in each of its appearances, and a thing over time is a concrete universal present in each of its temporal stages.[53]

§ Bradley's position fits in, as Husserl's does not, with the great trump card of empiricism, the insistence that we cannot understand the concept of something unless we either have direct acquaintance with things falling under it, or it is constructed out of such concepts by way of relations, or forms of unity, with examples of which we have direct acquaintance. Only when such direct acquaintance means the actual (though clearly only partial) presence of a thing as an ingredient in our stream of consciousness does it really amount to anything.

In taking this view Bradley (like James) is at one with Hume in his account of the non-philosophical conception of bodies, according to which the bodies

---

52   It may be said that there is no genuine identity here, since the presentation of a thing from different points of view or for different senses may have no sameness of character. Thus there is no abstract character to become the concrete universal in virtue of the systematic causal relation of its instances. But I do not think this true. There are both constant structural features and a common quality due to the permeation of each presentation by suggestions of other perspectives on the same thing. This account, of course, is not meant to apply to some presumed thing in itself behind the appearances, but to the relation of the appearances to the constant thing at a phenomenological level.

53   Cf. AR, pp. 248–50.

are essentially perceptions, thought of as capable of existing even when detached from experience. Bradley's more holistic conception, however, allows a better description of how we imaginatively fill out the ingredient actually present in perceptual consciousness with a quality in the depth dimension which is not merely attached as a separate particular to the presented but blends with it. Thus the physical object of common sense is not reduced, as with Hume and James (in his rather atomistic ERE writings), to a system of discrete percepts but to a continuous totality supposed to spread out smoothly from the given. This is surely a better account of our ordinary concept of it.

§ However, if Husserl fails to explain the apparent presence of the thing itself in perceptual experience, Bradley may seem deficient in explanation of its absence in thought. If a thing cannot be distinguished from its *what* or nature and this is present in our thought, as much as in our perception, then it seems that it is genuinely partially present in both cases.

Bradley does, indeed, sometimes speak of anything we think of as being an element in our experience. However, the absence of a thing thought of is implied in his basic account of judgement as the alienation of a universal from its exemplification in present experience and its application to something beyond, not itself given but continuous with what is. Both belong to a reality of which my centre feels itself to be a mere fragment, but the perceived part of that reality is immediately present within my experience as the merely thought about is not.

So for Bradley the physical world in which we ordinarily believe is an extension of our perceptual fields, and these are genuinely parts of it—though not exactly physical parts of it, for no physical part of an object can be present other than partially—not merely representative thereof. As such, it is not finally real, for there are radical incoherences to any possible conception of it. Its final status is, therefore, only that of a practically effective posit. But it is the world we, as it were, inhabit, and as such is properly regarded as more 'real' than a world supposedly purged by science of all that is subjective.

§6. *Bradley and Panpsychism*

§ As a phenomenological account of how we do, and for most ordinary purposes should, conceive the physical environment I find Bradley's account most convincing. Surely it is true that the physical world of our ordinary belief is an indefinitely larger imagined totality of which our perceptual fields, and felt bodily states and activity, are simply the parts currently most immediately present to us. And surely we cannot substitute any alternative for this as our day-to-day manner of conceiving the world in which we live.

But, however practically effective and inevitable the conception of such a physical word is, its incoherences are such that there cannot be a reality concerning which it provides the literal truth. Among various reasons for saying this two stand out. (1) Although it is imagined as a whole containing, and similar to, our perceptual fields, it is of the essence of our conception of it that any of its parts can exist outside anyone's perceptual consciousness. But the elements of our perceptual fields have features which for various reasons we think of as subjective. These are supposed only to belong to things when they fall within a perceptual consciousness and drop off from them when they exist unperceived. But no satisfactory principle can be found for determining which features of things, as they occur in our perceptual field, are and which are not, thus 'subjective', while however they are distinguished we can form no coherent picture of things without them. (2) Each perceptual field spreads out from a bodily centre and its distance from this affects the inherent character of everything within it. The same must be true of any imagined extension of such a field. Yet that extension of it which constitutes the physical world must spread out from a multiplicity of such centres, since it is supposed to contain the perceptual fields of many different persons. But we cannot imagine a physical thing whose inherent character reflects its different distances and spatial relations to a variety of such centres. Thus the unity of the physical thing breaks down and we are left with a multiplicity of subjective perspectives belonging to extensions of different perceptual fields. If there is anything real of which they are the perspectival representations, it cannot be found in the physical world of this conception.

Despite these and other incoherences our most basic conception of physical reality does seem to be of that character. But for reflection it tends to give way to the conception of a purely objective world in which things have only the traditional primary qualities or some more sophisticated successors thereto. The scientific account of this vastly increases our control of our environment, whatever that really is, and must point to something true about it. But it either gives us no imaginative sense, such as metaphysics seeks, of the nature of that to which it applies or only one as stubbornly incoherent as the other. And, in fact, we cannot make use of it except by bridging principles through which it yields information about the physical world of the first more naive conception.

Upon the whole, it seems to me that Bradley's treatment of these themes is excellent. But I would put more emphasis on the need for an explanation of the fact that our experiences are sufficiently congruent with one another, and with those of others, to ground the conception of a unitary physical world which works well enough in practice whatever its ultimate incoherences. Bradley simply pleads ignorance of details here while appealing to the unity of the Absolute for the basic explanation.

§ If no such explanation can be discovered, it might be reasonable to content oneself with this, but one should not do so without a search for something more positive. A hypothesis which seems promising here is that science, as it advances, specifies with increasing refinement the structure of a reality to which we belong (and whose grosser features are already implied in the common-sense conception) but either tells us nothing of, or misinforms us concerning, the concrete nature of what exemplifies it. Combining this hypothesis with panexperientialism points to a panpsychist view of the reality which presents itself to us as nature. This can be identified either with a part or with the whole of the Absolute, according as to how much of it exemplifies that structure.

§ To develop Bradley's views in this way is to see him as closer to Whitehead and Hartshorne than to Husserl. And in many ways he is so in any case. Whitehead acknowledged the influence of Bradley's account of feeling on him.[54] And if my interpretation of Bradley is correct, they held quite similar views on the way in which the being of a continuing consciousness is constituted by a series of momentary experiential wholes taking over from each other. And even without panpsychism Bradley's vision of a universe composed of finite centres has considerable affinities with Whitehead's of it as composed of actual occasions which pass into each other and constitute continuants insofar as they form societies possessing 'serial' order.[55] (That it is to some extent misleading to speak of the universe as, on Bradley's view, 'composed' of centres of experience has been admitted.)[56] What Whitehead adds is that the actual occasions are so related to each other as to constitute the world described by physics. My suggestion is that Bradley's position would be improved by a movement in this direction.

We have seen that views of this kind are the upshot of James's metaphysics too. Thus Bradley, James, and Whitehead are, upon the whole, much closer to each other in their views of experience and consciousness than any of them are to Husserl. The analogy with Husserl, on the part of Bradley, and to some extent James, is rather in their views of the phenomenal physical world. But for Husserl that is the only world, there is no reality underlying it. James finally conceded the unsatisfactoriness of this by supplementing it with a panpsychist view of the underlying reality. Our present suggestion is that Bradley would have done well to do the same, though perhaps his doctrine of the Absolute made the need less crying. Of course, he differs from the other three in his belief that all those innumerable centres or monads are aspects of a single supra-relational absolute experience.

§ So let us pursue the possibility of a panpsychist development of Bradley's metaphysics a little. On such a view there exists within the one absolute experience a system of streams of experience whose interweavings conform to a structure which science is gradually revealing more fully but which is substantially adumbrated in the structure of the ordinary object world as we imagine it. This system of streams of experience is the 'in itself' of the nature of both ordinary and scientific thought. It is the source of the experiences which produce our belief in it and it is the really existing thing which has the structure ascribed to it.

It is worth noting that this leaves it open whether our own experiences belong wholly or partly to this structure or wholly or partly to a larger structure which outruns that distinctive of the physical. Bradley would, surely, take the second view, but a more Spinozistic development of his thought might be possible which took the first, regarding the mental as the inner being of a system

---

54   See Whitehead, *Process*, p. 63, and for a discussion of this, McHenry.
55   See Whitehead, *Process*, part I, chapter III, §II; part II, chapter III, §11.
56   On pp. 503–7. Cf. AR, pp. 468–69.

whose structure is pervasively physical. However, quite apart from the status of our own mental life, Bradley's suggestion that there may be more than one space and time implies that whether or no the Absolute is more than nature, it is more than just one nature.

§ One cannot say that Bradley held any such panpsychist view. He is, however, ready to admit the possibility that panpsychism of some form is true. Thus he parries the complaint that it is extravagant to think that nature can only truly exist as perceived by saying that more things in nature may be 'organisms' than we realize and therefore more things objects of perception; it may even be that nature is entirely composed of organisms. This points to a form of panpsychism not unlike that we have described. And that he thought of it in this way is shown by his reference to Fechner in this connection.

An alternative to such a panpsychism to which he seems somewhat more inclined is that the 'in itself' of nature is a margin of experience in the Absolute which is not 'filtered through finite centres'. It seems to me, however, that this requires much more of a break with his usual assumptions.[57]

His general attitude to panpsychism, then, is that it is possible but that there is no very strong reason for believing in it. He was perhaps influenced in this guarded stance by Bernard Bosanquet's hostile attitude to panpsychism.[58] The alternative seems to be that the part of the Absolute constituting us and our world consists in a system of experiences relating to each other in ways which divide them into the histories of distinct individuals whose experiences have the right kind of congruence to allow for the construction of a common object world. That suggests that it is only in the exchange of thoughts with one's companions, and not in labour upon one's environment, that one is dealing with a real not-self continuing beyond one's own centre. To me that seems incredible. For this and other reasons I can only take seriously a panpsychist version of Bradleyan idealism.

Among other reasons for taking this as congruent with the main spirit of Bradley's thought is the extent to which it is suggested by a certain vein of pantheistic feeling about nature to which he sometimes gives expression. This certainly suggests that he tended to think that we are confronted in nature with more than the not-self sides of human and animal experiences.[59] Consider in

---

57   See AR, pp. 238–41 for his dallyings with panpsychism of a Fechnerian sort. In a letter to James of 3 February 1909 he declares himself unimpressed by Fechner's advocacy of planet souls, but says that Fechner had helped him move away from Hegel's too humanistic view of the world, and was conclusive as 'to the possibilities of non-human organic life' (by 'organic' he means, in effect, 'sentient'; see AR, p. 239). See Perry, II, p. 638. See also his letter to him of 15 October 1904 at ibid., p. 488. For the idea that the Absolute may contain a 'margin of content', not filtered through finite centres, and that these may be the backing of nature as it appears to us, see AR, pp. 241–44 and 467, and ETR, p. 350, note 1, noting that his page references back to AR are to the Allen and Unwin second edition.

58   See Bosanquet, *Individuality*, p. 362 and passim.

59   See, for example, the additional note on ES, p. 330; see also the passage about

this connection the following passage expressing a preference for a pantheistic view of nature against one in which it is an external eject created by a God not present in it. This defence of pantheism makes much better sense if each individual part of nature is the presentation of some distinct aspect of the total absolute experience as it will only be if his absolutism is taken panpsychistically.

> A God who has made this strange and glorious Nature outside of which he remains, is an idea at best one-sided. Confined to this idea we lose large realms of what is beautiful and sublime, and even for religion our conception of goodness suffers. Unless the Maker and Sustainer becomes also the indwelling Life and Mind and the inspiring Love, how much of the universe is impoverished! And it is only by an illusion which is really stupid that we can feel ourselves into, and feel ourselves one with, that which, if not lifeless, is at least external. But how this necessary 'pantheism' is to be made consistent with an individual Creator I myself do not perceive.
>
> ETR, p. 436

§7. Religion

(a) Bradley and James

§ Like James, Bradley had a father who was, so to speak, an official religionist. Bradley's, however, was of a more orthodox cast than James's, for his father was a minister of the Evangelical school. At any rate, it is one goal of the philosophy of Bradley, just as it was of James, to provide a defence of a spiritual view of the universe against the apparent threat to it from developing scientific knowledge. But while each was concerned to produce a theoretical account of reality which would be essentially spiritual, each also thought religion itself more a matter of practice than of belief.

There is also a certain similarity in their rather ambivalent relation to Christianity. Both of them believe firmly in the Protestant tradition as opposed to the Catholic, but for neither does the figure of Jesus seem to have loomed very large, nor do they show any great interest in such distinctively Christian dogmas as that of the Trinity. On the face of it their religious conceptions relate to Christianity only as the most familiar form of theism

Despite these resemblances, they differ more on what is important in religion than they do on almost any other topic.

James, we saw, thought that religious belief could not be arrived at intelligently by *a priori* arguments. Its support must come from the evidence of religious experience and our will or right to believe where evidence is not conclusive and decision is obligatory. And if it is to be worth much, it must be more than a mere habit of conceiving the natural world in the glow of certain

---

animals and inanimate nature I quote from an unpublished manuscript in §7(f) below.

abstract metaphysical concepts; genuine religion, rather, requires a *crass* or *piecemeal* supernaturalism, for which the divine is distinct from the mundane and capable of acting upon it as one agency among others. And among religious conceptions, the best, for James both morally and evidentially, was that which postulated a finite God whose victory in the world was not guaranteed but which we could freely participate in making probable.

Bradley's position was almost totally opposed to this. A spiritual view of the universe was, for him, at least *qua* philosopher, something arrived at on the basis of metaphysical argument. He despised attempts to base it on alleged particular matters of fact. Thus in his first published work he was as scathing upon the topic of miracles as Hume. And while James believed that spiritualistic phenomena might support a religiously relevant piecemeal supernaturalism, Bradley thought that, even if true, they had nothing of religious value. Moreover, Bradley's Absolute might well be thought the apotheosis of that metaphysical substitute for a living God which James sought to combat through his idea of a 'finite' one. Similarly Bradley well exemplifies that tendency to treat 'all evil as partial good' which James deplored as an implication of monistic idealism.

§ This blank opposition is only to a small extent offset by some points of agreement.[60] Thus Bradley thought that religious belief was primarily a practical and ethical matter, and that religious creeds were to be evaluated, not for their ultimate metaphysical truth but as working ideas stimulating the spiritual and moral life. From this pragmatic point of view, he was prepared to grant that there was some place for thinking of God as having goals not guaranteed of fulfilment.[61] However, he held that this must be combined, even at the level of ordinary religious working conceptions, with a sense that the final goal was guaranteed, and indeed somehow already eternally reached. For the idea that the supremacy of good in the world was only a possibility genuinely at risk seemed to him incompatible with an adequate religion.[62]

§ It is more difficult to get a balanced picture of Bradley's attitude to Christianity than James's. This is partly perhaps because it was more ambivalent. Certainly on the face of it his published writings seem to show somewhat shifting attitudes on the matter. These are to some extent cleared up by an unpublished paper which I examine in §(f) below. But it remains doubtful, so

---

60   Though his scornful remarks on Matthew Arnold's attempt to replace religious belief by 'morality tinged with emotion' reflect an impatience with a reduction of the religiously supernatural to an attitude to this world somewhat similar to that of James with refined supernaturalism. See 'Concluding Remarks' in ES.

61   His letter to James of 14 May 1909 has some bearings on this. See Perry, II, pp. 638–40. See also ETR, p. 429–30. See also his earlier letter of 21 September 1897, quoted in my Appendix, where he confesses his own failure to find a satisfactory personal gospel.

62   See ETR, chapter XV, with notes and Supp. Note A.

far as my own researches go at least, how early in his life he came to the
conclusions formulated there, or quite what form his own religious life took.[63]
The key documents for Bradley's attitude to Christianity and religion in general
would seem to be:

> *The Presuppositions of Critical History* (1874) [CE]
> *Ethical Studies* (1876)
> 'The Evidences of Spiritualism' (1885) [CE]
> *Appearance and Reality* (1893)
> 'Some Remarks on Punishment' (1894) [CE]
> 'The Limits of Individual and National Self-sacrifice' (1894) [CE]
> *Essays on Truth and Reality* (1914)

To these should be added the important unpublished essay

> 'A Note on Christian Morality' (evidently written between 1909 and 1912).

(b) Religion in The Presuppositions of Critical History

§ *The Presuppositions of Critical History* of 1874 was the first of Bradley's published works. It is perhaps his most thorough treatment of a purely epistemological
issue. In it he discusses the circumstances under which the critical historian may
accept historical records as factually correct. Its main thesis is that all belief must
be an interpretation of one's own experience on the basis of one's own preconceptions, and that this means acceptance of the testimony of others only to the
extent that one can work out what one would oneself have concluded from their
experience. Thus one should take their testimony at face value only to the extent
that their outlook is rational by one's own lights. Consequently there are strict
limits to the extent to which one should accept records of events which clash
with one's own preconceptions.

> [A]ny narrative of 'facts' which involves judgements proceeding from a relig-
> ious consciousness or a view of the world which , as a whole or in respect of
> the part in question, differs from ours, cannot have such force as to assure us
> of any event un-analogous to present experience.
>
> CE, p. 31

These points have some similarity to Hume's treatment of miracles (to which
he does not refer). However, Bradley is careful to avoid the implication that
testimony cannot give one grounds for believing in facts of a type one previously thought impossible. What one must not do is accept testimony to such

---

63   It is striking that, writing to his sister Marian on 24 January 1922 about the disposal
      of their father's papers, he said: 'Of course, as to the religion in which we were
      brought up, my feeling was and is and always will be one of loathing—with regret
      for certain persons so far as they accepted it.' See also his letter to James of 14 May
      1909 where he says: 'I am not myself an orthodox Christian,—far from it' (Perry,
      II, p. 640).

an effect when it comes through minds with whom one cannot identify and presume to have sifted things as one would have done oneself.

Although written in the context of controversies over the 'higher criticism' of his day, Bradley does not directly conclude anything about the acceptability of the traditional accounts of the historical Jesus (or of Old Testament narratives) though this was presumably his main concern. But it emerges clearly enough that he was quite unsympathetic to forms of Christianity in which particular historical claims are central. Insofar as Christianity requires belief in such events as the resurrection Bradley was quite alienated from it. Thus the only sort of Christianity in which he had a positive interest was that which offers an interpretation of the significance of human life in whatever particular events it unrolls.

The epistemological position of this essay is not so far from James's. For its stress on the need to interpret present experience by rational reflection on past experience is quite close to James's view of the way in which putative new truth must meet the test of assimilability with the bulk of old truth. However, its more specifically religious message is totally opposed to the piecemeal supernaturalism James favoured. (Though James's enthusiasm for this does not seem to have gone with any particular interest in the Gospel miracles, the virgin birth, the resurrection, and so forth. However, he does claim that his finite God is effectively that of the ordinary religious believer.[64])

It would be a mistake, indeed, to suppose that Bradley thought history unimportant for religious thought. For it is the study of the concrete development of human life, of 'the tradition and the tale of the deeds and sufferings of *men*'. As such, it contrasts with science. And testimony is only testimony to matters historical insofar as it springs from that interest.

> In more simple language, the interest at the basis of scientific testimony is to use the particular case just so far as to get the universal *out of it*; the concretion of life is worth having solely for the sake of the abstract relations it contains. But the interest which gives birth to historical testimony is a human interest, an interest in the particular realization. Our common nature, which is personal in us all, feels in each one of us 'that nothing human is alien to ourselves'. Our interest in the past is our feeling of oneness with it, is our interest in our own progression; and because this human nature to exist must be individual, the object of historical record is the world of human individuality, and the course of its development in time. For scientific testimony the man is a mere example, for historical never: he is a new incarnation of the same felt substance, the manifest individualization, it may be, at highest, of a stage in progress (but on this point we wish to express no opinion). For the universal *as such* the historical witness cares not at all; at most it concerns him to see it embodied in a single person or the spirit of a nation.
>
> CE, p. 36

---

64   See, for example, PU, p. 311.

There is, perhaps, a certain tension in Bradley's position. On the one hand, he endorses our remaining so wedded to the preconceptions of our own time that we cannot take seriously the possible occurrence of phenomena which would challenge them. On the other hand, he sees it as a central human concern to grasp how man has changed through the ages. Although there is no formal incompatibility here, one may suspect that a grasp of past or alien cultures is harder for those who cannot take beliefs opposed to their own seriously.

Philosophers tend to divide into those, like Hegel, for whom reality in its most important aspects is essentially historical, and those, like Schopenhauer, for whom the essential facts about all time are much the same. It is not too easy to classify Bradley in either way. On the one hand the historical is the concrete and it is only the concrete which can be fully real for Bradley. On the other hand the scientific is the only phenomenal realm in which truth appears to possess that unchanging quality which is the goal of rational thought. This is perhaps one of the antinomies which show that the objects of human thought are appearance rather than reality, for genuine reality must be both concrete and unchanging.

> The interest of science is the discovery of the laws of what *is*, neither past nor present nor future events, nor events at all, but only the abiding. The interest of history is in the recalling of a course of events which *are not*, which neither exist nor will exist, but which *have* existed. The object of the one is 'the permanent amid change', the object of the other 'the changes of the permanent'; facts to the one are illustrations, to the other are embodiments; the individuals of the one are limited to be abstracted, of the other are incorporated to be realized.
>
> CE, p. 36

In the light of this Bradley can only be said to agree partially with James that individual historical facts about what sentient subjects thought or felt are the sole object of literal truth. For he has some tendency to the scientific approach, as he conceives it, for which particular facts are only of interest as illustrations of universal truths. Yet he also shares the view that such truths concern unreal abstractions and are of interest only so far as we see them concretised in the particular. Doubtless the Absolute grasps the details of its being in a way which does justice to both these ideals.

(c) *Religion in* Ethical Studies

§ Turning to *Ethical Studies* we find Bradley taking a very positive attitude to a Christianity in which piecemeal supernaturalism stays in the background. Its passionately intense last chapter is the one place where Bradley seems to endorse a religious point of view which he regards as essentially Christian. In it he explains how religion resolves certain contradictions which pertain to morality as such. It is not that religion necessarily comes after morality, either in the race or the individual, but that moral experience points intrinsically to a form of experience in which its own contradictions are mended.[65] Morality without religion leaves man stuck in a 'region of weariness, of false self-approval and no less false self-contempt', something with which the human race as a whole will never rest content. It requires a sense that the goodness to which it aspires is somehow at the heart of things.

In believing that religion provides a guarantee of the ultimate goodness of things Bradley gives it a role which James thinks, upon the whole, corrupting of morality. For, as he sees it, manly moral thought requires the sense that God and the good may lose the battle, and that we must give them a hand if things are not to end in ultimate wreckage (or at least their final victory be delayed). Bradley, in contrast, insists, here and elsewhere, that morality requires the support of faith in such an ultimate guarantee.[66]

What are the contradictions supposed to pertain to morality? One is that morality must strive for a state of affairs in which what it most values would have no role. For the elimination of evil which it seeks would remove all opportunity for exercise of the good will. Morality is also described as contradictory in its conception of the relation between the real and the ideal. For it seeks both to root itself in what is and to stand apart therefrom as its critic. Thus it bids us both think of our society as that to which we must conform our private will, and as that which, composed of paltry beings like ourselves, we must rise above.

There is also a contradiction in the self as that exists for moral experience. Sometimes he seems to conceive this simply as the clash between the good self and the bad self, between the main steady personality as that develops through moral education and the chaos of impulses which are never quite integrated into it. That suggests the Hegelian identification of contradiction with a war between real features of the cosmos rather than with a defect in our conception of a universe which is necessarily consistent as it truly is. However, Bradley comes nearer to the latter view when he presents the contradiction as between two conceptions we have of ourselves, as the good self over against the bad self and as a totality which is the scene of their battle (and perhaps even of their final reconciliation through recognition of their need for each other).

All in all, the nature of these contradictions is not stated very clearly. The heart of them is a theme which recurs in Bradley's later writings, namely that there is something incoherent in the very idea of a good which is not realized. One is inclined to object that there is no incoherence in the proposition that things are not as they ought to be. In AR Bradley does, indeed, say that one cannot simply take it for granted that the non-contradictory nature of the real precludes it from being bad, but, by rather tortuous reasoning, he does in the end reach this conclusion, and seems always to have found it inviting and natural.[67] Thus he seems always to have inclined to see a clash between ideals

---

65   See ES, p. 314.
66   See Bradley's letter to James of 14 May 1909 in Perry, II, pp. 378–79.
67   See AR, pp. 132–33.

and sense of fact as a source of unease essentially akin to that we feel in embracing a logical contradiction and which we have the same necessary nisus to remove. I do not find it easy to follow him here, though, doubtless, once the existence of the Absolute is taken as proved, its nature must be supposed harmonious in a way which goes beyond mere logical consistency.

At any rate, for Bradley, religion is required to resolve the contradiction between the ideal and the real, for it experiences the real as a universal will of which our own is an articulation. We are real only so far as we are the good self and, as such, we are identical with the reality which manifests itself in the world at large. Evil, both as it occurs in our bad self and as it exists in the world outside, is an unreality, and, as such, all the more detestable. Religion consists in the faith that this is so. By 'faith' is not meant a state of mind less than that of certainty, but one in which we have absolute confidence in a reality not immediately present to us.[68]

> Faith then is the recognition of my true self in the religious object, and the identification of myself with that both by judgement and will; the determination to negate the self opposed to the object by making the whole self one with what it really is. It is, in a word, of the heart. It is the belief that only the ideal is real, and the will to realize therefore nothing but the ideal, the theoretical and practical assertion that only as ideal is the self real.
>
> Justification by faith means that, having thus identified myself with the object, I feel myself in that identification to be already one with it, and enjoy the bliss of being, all falsehood overcome, what I truly am. By my claim to be one with the ideal, which comprehends me too, and by assertion of the non-reality of all that is opposed to it, the evil in the world and the evil incarnate in me through past bad acts, all this falls into the unreal: I being one with the ideal, this is not mine, and so imputation of offences goes with the change of self, and applies not now to my true self, but to the unreal, which I repudiate and hand over to destruction.
>
> ES, p. 328

Bradley says that he is here endorsing the Protestant doctrine of justification by faith and of the necessity by which true faith issues in good works.[69] Mere belief in certain theological or metaphysical views is not religious faith. It consists rather in such a sense of one's identity with the universal will that one strives with all one's being to be in the day-to-day world what one truly is in ultimate reality.[70] This is not the claptrap of Matthew Arnold that 'religion is simply morality tinged with emotion'. This could only be true if it meant, tautologically, 'with religious emotion'. And such emotion has a cognitive content. For it includes the confidence that the ideal for which we strive is more deeply rooted in reality than what seems to obstruct it.

Religious practices, whether in the form of private prayer and meditation,

---

68   See ETR, p. 327.
69   See ES, p. 325.
70   See ES, p. 329.

or of public worship and ceremonies, have a properly religious value only insofar as they promote religious faith, and its issue in good works, in the true sense.

> We maintain that neither church-going, meditation, nor prayer, except so far as it reacts on practice and subserves that, is religious at all.
>
> ES, p. 337

In fact,

> [y]ou can have true religion without sacraments or public worship, and again both without clergymen.
>
> ES, p. 339

The object of true Christian faith, then, is a universal will, present as identically the same, though in a state of difference from itself, both in the individual and in his community and, indeed, in the world as a whole and such that all that appears to conflict with it is an unreality which we must grasp as such by overcoming it.

There is some kinship here with the religion of mankind promoted at that time by the Comtian positivists, but Bradley is careful to insist that humanity, conceived as a mere collection of particulars, cannot be the object of properly religious feeling.

> Unless there is a real identity in men, the 'Inasmuch as ye did it to the least of these' becomes an absurdity.
>
> Original note 2 to ES, pp. 334–35

In stressing the common essence present in us all Bradley's position chimes in somewhat with the ethical thought of Schopenhauer. But, from his more Hegelian perspective, he must have thought that Schopenhauer paid insufficient attention to the difference which is essential to the identity. We must have a sense of the different roles we each have to play in the scheme of things. For the concrete universal of humanity at large is articulated into a system of distinct roles each grounding partly different duties, as well as those which spring from the sheer identity of the common essence. Moreover, from a religious point of view, it is the ideal self, rather than one's whole chaotic personality, which is identical with the ultimate single reality present in all things. If there is some incoherence in looking at things in this way, that is, nonetheless, the religious way of experiencing the world. [71] Metaphysically, this presumably means that it is only our ideal self which gives us a clue as to how things would look if we could see them as a whole.

(d) Religion in Appearance and Reality

Bradley says that, as a metaphysician, he is concerned neither with charting the

---

71   See ES, p. 322.

origin of religion nor with forecasting or attempting to influence its future.[72] For metaphysics is an enquiry into the nature of reality aiming solely at the intellectual satisfaction of understanding, and not at providing a substitute religion or guide to life. Its concern with the religious consciousness is clarification of its phenomenology and assessment of the ultimate validity of its claims. And, while there are many different forms of religious consciousness, Bradley is concerned with what seems to be its fullest development in the Christianity of his own day. (Bradley never seems to show much interest in religions other than the Christian, though he does emphasise that there are genuine religions which do not teach belief in a personal God.[73])

If we are to examine the claims of religion, we must be clear as to what we are meaning by the term, for it is used to cover some very different things. Some people use it to denote 'any kind of practical relation to the "other world", or to the supersensible generally'.[74] Thus understood, the possibility of communication with 'spirits' is a central religious issue. Others take it as a particular way of relating to things, whether they belong to another world or to this. For Bradley it is the latter usage which is the right one. Thus to him '[t]he question as to life after death or as to the possibility of spirit-rapping or witchcraft, is really not in itself in the very least religious'.[75] What is essential in religion is that there should be 'a fixed feeling of fear, resignation, admiration or approval, no matter what may be the object, provided only that this feeling reaches a certain strength, and is qualified by a certain degree of reflection'.[76] In fact, thinks Bradley, religion requires a specific combination of fear and approval towards its object, and an effort 'to please, or at least to submit our wills to, the object which is feared'. And in the highest forms of religion, with which alone Bradley is concerned, this combination takes the form of 'devotion to' something which can be regarded as 'the one perfect object which is utterly good'. Being in love is a form of religious experience in this sense, though an incomplete one. For a complete form of religion, the one perfect object must in every sense be conceived as the supreme reality, supreme both in goodness and in power.

The most familiar object of the religious consciousness thus understood is God as Christians conceive Him. But, as Bradley sees it, the God to which such religious consciousness is devoted is ultimately an appearance, just as are the objects of science or of ordinary practical thinking. For religion cannot provide a coherent account of how the finite self stands to God or God to the finite self. God, as the ordinary Christian conceives Him, cannot simply be identified with the Absolute, for such identification deprives Him of his otherness. Moreover, Bradley's critique of relations has shown that the conception of things in

---

72 See AR, p. 388, note; ETR, p. 446, etc.
73 See ETR, p. 432, including note.
74 AR, pp. 388–89.
75 The same point is often repeated. See, for instance, ETR, p. 440.
76 AR, p. 389, note.

relation is at best an attempt to grasp the character of a whole which transcends the terms and cannot be accepted as metaphysical truth as it stands.[77] Thus for metaphysics the conception of the human self and its relation to God gives way to the notion of an Absolute which includes them both, while ordinary religious thinking requires that we think in terms of our relation to God rather than of our oneness with the Absolute. Yet religious feeling itself cannot rest in this purely relational view and requires that we also somehow think of God as present in oneself and oneself as present in God. For the relationship between God and the worshipper is experienced within a centre of experience and the religious consciousness somehow includes the experience of both sides of the relation.

That the object of religious consciousness is appearance rather than reality no more counts against it than it does against science that its posits are so. The aim of science is technological and its concepts are to be evaluated not for their metaphysical truth but for their technological utility. Similarly the concepts of religion are to be evaluated for their service to the aim of religion, not for their metaphysical validity. And that aim is 'to express the complete reality of goodness through every aspect of our being'. Thus religion is essentially ethical striving united with the faith that goodness is somehow at the heart of things, or rather (since *goodness* itself is said to be appearance), that at bottom reality is *perfect* and that just because evil, as a genuine danger to that perfection, is *not* real, there is all the more reason to attack it.[78] This belief is something which Bradley's metaphysics purports to give reason for endorsing. But it may not, and need not, endorse the particular form of it which is most helpful religiously. Maybe, for some, an absolutism of Bradley's sort can play this role, but most people need religious concepts of a less monistic kind and these will be 'true' for them in the only sense they need be. However, Bradley sometimes hints that more monistic or pantheist religious concepts may in the end replace orthodox theism. But, if so, it will not be because they possess a superior metaphysical truth, but because they promote religious feeling better. It remains to be seen how far it will be anything like a traditional Christian theism which will serve humanity's aims best in the future. Bradley is content to leave it to time to decide on this. But religion in some form, although it has been the source of many evils, and takes many appalling pathological forms, is too much of a human need for it to be desirable to dispense with it.[79] Bradley, however, although possessed of his own steady view of how Reality truly is, does not wish to step forth with any personal recommendation as to the conceptual system which will best serve the proper ends of religion.

§ How much of a real change is there between ES and AR? Certainly the spirit of the former is much closer to the ordinary Christian feeling of Bradley's time than are his later writings. Thus it is only there that he speaks of sin as a felt

---

77   This point is made sharply at PL, pp. 96–97, §66—see also the note.
78   See AR, p. 392.
79   See AR, p. 393.

alienation from that ideal self which is what we truly are, and of the atonement as the highest formulation of the ultimate identity of man and God.[80] However, the difference may be less a change of viewpoint than a difference in what he was doing. For in this part of ES he was not so much presenting his own view of reality as describing how things present themselves to the Christian consciousness; still, a general impression of endorsement is given.[81] How far, then, can we take the deliverance of that consciousness, as he describes it here, as in accord with his final metaphysics?

The additional notes he added in old age to ES, and his remark in AR that that work still represented his views in the main, suggest that it was so (though he expressed regret for the rather contemptuous tone with which he refers at times to Roman Catholicism). He says, however, that he would now insist more firmly than before that the divine is to be found not only in human life but in nature at large. 'The whole of Nature must, *in some sense*, be included and itself will the Divine, e.g., "My brother the sun"', he says in one of the additional notes.[82] And although he does not say so here, we may add that the divine is now conceived rather as a pervasive feeling coursing through the universe than as a Will.

Still the essential message concerning the validity of religious experience is the same and might be put somewhat as follows. There is an all-containing and all-pervading universal mind. Although this includes all that is bad in us as well as all that is good, the good is a better clue to the character of the whole, and to how every detail would look in the light of the whole, than is the bad. So the religious man's sense that he is most at one with reality when he acts out of devotion to the divine perfection is correct. In ES, however, the perfect whole tends to be talked of as a divine *will* rather than as a mind, while in the later metaphysics it is not a mind in the sense of a changing continuant or subject aware of objects external to itself. However, this is a change of emphasis and expression rather than of doctrine.

The change is more marked in the treatment of the self. Though the self, as experienced in morality, is, indeed, said to be unreal in ES, it is treated with far more respect than in the later metaphysics. But here again the difference may reflect the differing purposes of the texts rather than any great change of doctrine. ES is concerned with the phenomenology of the moral and religious life, AR with the ultimate truth, as opposed to the human appropriateness, of the conceptions essential to it.

So we may take it that there is no real change between the two works concerning the validity of religious faith. In ES he writes sympathetically of religious faith as the sense that it is the 'ideal' which is finally real. For the metaphysics of AR such faith is essentially correct inasmuch as, though both goodness and badness play an essential role in constituting the perfection of

---

80   See ES, p. 323–24.
81   See ES, p. 330.
82   ES, p. 330.

the whole, the former is a much better clue to it. And the point that the sense of the religious person that it is his ideal self which is what he truly is is again stressed.

In both works Bradley exemplifies that feature of monistic idealism which most repelled James. For James's hearty moral feeling found it corrupting and repellent to reconcile oneself to the more ghastly features of human and animal life by conceiving them as ministering to the perfection of the Absolute. I share James's feelings here. Persuaded as I am by Bradley's main argument for the Absolute I can only conclude that evil is a necessary part of the necessarily existing Absolute, and that the overall character of this is good and worthwhile though it is not improved by the evil it must contain. (Of course, though there is no alternative to the Absolute, there are alternatives to things as they are now; there have been such in the past, and there will be such in the future, and it is to be hoped that the best are still to come. But these are all parts of the one reality, to which there has never been an alternative, which embraces all times.)

The religious implication of absolute idealism which is most accessible to my own temperament are two: on the one hand, the deep identity which links us all so that the sufferings of another can only be dismissed as not our concern through a false sense of apartness, and, on the other hand, the fact that all phenomena whatever are the more-or-less transparent appearance of an inner life pertaining to nature as a whole. Both of these find expression in Bradley and it seems to me that they can survive the acknowledgment of the existence of sheer evil in the world.

(e) Darwinist Critique of Christianity

§ Thus in AR, as in ES, Bradley seems essentially sympathetic to Christianity. But not long after its publication we find him speaking of Christianity in a quite negative way. Thus in 'Some Remarks on Punishment' (1894) he discusses the extent to which Darwinism should alter our moral outlook and suggests that its main message concerns the means appropriate for promoting a moral end which modern man has already placed above the Christian one.

> For in the ordinary moral creed those means seem estimated on no rational principle. Our creed appears rather to be an irrational mixture of jarring elements. We have the moral code of Christianity, accepted in part and in part rejected practically by all save a few fanatics. But we do not realize how in its very principle the Christian ideal is false. And when we reject this code for another and in part a sounder morality, we are in the same condition of blindness and of practical confusion. It is here that Darwinism, with all the tendencies we may group under that name, seems destined to intervene. It will make itself felt, I believe, more and more effectually. It may force on us in some points a correction of our moral views, and a return to a non-Christian and perhaps a Hellenic ideal.
>
> CE, p. 149

An adequate view of society and morality should already have taught us that 'the community, though it may have grown naturally to be what it is, should now more or less consciously regulate itself, and deliberately play its own Providence'.[83] What Darwinism can help us see more clearly is that once the original primitive struggle for existence has been so tamed that inferior types are not weeded out naturally, the community must instead act as its own providence and take on this task itself for the sake of the chief good, which is 'the welfare of the community realized in its members'. In doing so it needs to get beyond outmoded ideas like that of the rights of the individual and the Christian view of the sanctity of human life.

For Christianity

> [t]he individual in the next world has an infinite value; the things of this world, our human ends and interests, are all alike counted worthless, and the rights and duties founded on these interests, of course, bodily disappear. The good of the whole, worthless in itself, can therefore confer no right to interfere with its members; and each individual, on the other side, is, so to speak, the preserve of Providence. Violence, immoral in itself or, at least, immoral for us men, is forbidden us, and is left in the hands of the Deity. Now to criticize this view, otherwise than by stating it, seems here not necessary. Once admit that life in this world is an end in itself, and the pure Christian doctrine is at once uprooted. For, measured by that end and standard, individuals have unequal worth, and the value of each individual is but relative, and in no case infinite. And the community, we have seen, is itself its own Providence, and therefore against its rights the individual is not sacred. With this we may pass from the Christian error, and may proceed to consider a fresh form of delusion [a doctrine of individual human rights based on an erroneous view of the individual as having reality and value apart from his place in the community].
>
> CE, p. 157

Bradley draws certain conclusions from this about punishment. Although a place must remain for retributive punishment (which he still conceives as at the time of ES as 'the reaction of the moral organism against a rebellious member')[84] allocated only on the basis of desert, there must also be a field in which, irrespective of any moral blame, types of humanity detrimental to the good of the whole are weeded out by 'social surgery', that is, it seems, by compulsory euthanasia. The community must be able to say:

> 'You and you are dangerous specimens; you must depart in peace.' It would probably add, 'There are some children here over and above what we want, and their origin, to say the least, is inauspicious. We utterly decline to rear these children at the public cost and, so far as we can judge, to the public injury.'
>
> CE, p. 162

This, admits Bradley, will outrage much moral feeling, rooted in feelings of compassion essential to a civilized community. But we must choose which is the less of various evils. As a moral philosopher rather than a practical reformer

---

83   CE, p.150
84   CE, p. 153.

he will not say just where the balance should be struck but there are feelings he will not try to hide.

> I am oppressed by the ineffectual cruelty of our imprisonment. I am disgusted at the inviolable sanctity of the noxious lunatic. The right of the individual to spawn without restriction his diseased offspring on the community, the duty of the state to rear wholesale and without limit an unselected progeny—such duties and rights are to my mind a sheer outrage on Providence. A society that can endure such things will merit the degeneracy which it courts. More and more on certain points we seem warned to return in part to older and to less impracticable principles of conduct. And there are views of Plato which, to me at least, every day seem less of an anachronism and more of a prophecy.
>
> CE, pp. 163–64

Bradley's attitude to Christianity here is quite Nietzschean. Christianity has located value in an afterlife rather than in this, and regarded all men as equal in the sense that the salvation in an afterlife of each matters equally. As a result it has not concerned itself with the means necessary to develop the best type of man and puts sentimental barriers in the way of improvements of the human type.

Seen in context these remarks may not be quite as harsh as they seem. Bradley is not concerned, like Nietzsche, only with the development of an elite but with the welfare of a community in which all capable of fulfilment through the social life it provides have a positive share. He has none of Nietzsche's contempt for the mediocre, but he does envisage a humane weeding out of those who can only participate in society as wreckers. So far as capital punishment, or non-punitive extermination, of such beings as the Moors murderers goes, one may agree or disagree with Bradley, without charging him with any grotesque failure in humane sentiment. In the case of what he says about the children born in inauspicious circumstances, one must suppose a failure on his part to think through the practicalities of what he seems to be saying. Indeed, it is doubtful how far he had really imagined what it would be like even to tell the homicidal psychopath that he must depart in peace.

The same negative view of Christianity is apparent in another paper published in the same year, 'The Limits of Individual and National Self-sacrifice' of 1894. Here he again attacks the 'Christian' view that self-assertion and violence towards enemies is always wrong in both the individual and the state, while he also attacks those who preach unfettered individual or national selfishness. Since he speaks here of 'Christians' rather than Christians it might be thought that he was not criticising Christianity as such. However, he leaves us in no doubt of his negative view of a lot of what is quite properly called Christian.

> If 'Christianity' is to mean the taking the Gospels as our rule of life, then we none of us are Christians and, no matter what we say, we all know we ought not to be. If Greek morality was one-sided, that of the New Testament is still more one-sided, for it implies that the development of the individual and the state is worthless. It is not merely that it contemns victory over the forces of nature, that it scorns beauty and despises knowledge, but there is not one of

our great moral institutions which it does not ignore or condemn. The rights of property are denied or suspected, the ties of the family are broken, there is no longer any nation or patriotism, and the union of the sexes becomes a second-rate means against sin. Universal love doubtless is a virtue, but tameness and baseness—to turn the cheek to every rascal who smites it, to suffer the robbery of villains and the contumely of the oppressor, to stand by idle when the helpless are violated and the land of one's birth in its death-struggle, and to leave honour and vengeance and justice to God above—are qualities that deserve some other epithet. The morality of the primitive Christians is that of a religious sect; it is homeless, sexless, and nationless. The morality of to-day rests on the family, on property, and the nation. Our duty is to be members of the world we are in; to be in the world and not of it was their type of perfection. The moral chasm between us is, in short, as wide as the intellectual; and if it has been politic to ignore this, I doubt if it is politic any longer. We have lived a long time now the professors of a creed which no one consistently can practise, and which, if practised, would be as immoral as it is unreal.

CE, pp. 173–74

On the face of it these articles represent a considerable shift in Bradley's view of Christianity. But perhaps there is less difference than might appear. For it may be that in these articles he was concerned with moral issues, the treatment of psychopaths and the rights of nations to defend themselves, on which he was less Christian than he was in his sense of how the ordinary decent citizen should conduct his life. Even so, the difference of tone is quite startling.

(f) Bradley's Unpublished Paper on Christian Morality

The Bradley papers at Merton College include an unpublished essay called 'A Note on Christian Morality', together with two addenda to it on separate sheets.[85] There is also a correspondence between Bradley's sister, Mrs Marian de Glehn, and H. H. Joachim, as to whether it, as also the essay 'On the Treatment of Sexual Detail in Literature', should be included in the *Collected Essays* which was published in 1935 with a short preface under their two signatures. In the event the latter paper was included but not the former.

The article sets out to clarify Bradley's attitude to Christianity and to reply to criticisms of what some had taken as the anti-Christian tone of what are referred to as 'the two foregoing papers'. What were these papers? Mrs de Glehn says that she had originally thought they were essays XV and XVI of ETR, namely 'On God and the Absolute' and 'On My Real World', particularly Notes A and B to the former. However, she continues, Bradley himself in his

---

85   These are to be found in IIB9 (chest II, Pile B9) in the Bradley collection held at Merton College along with the correspondence between Bradley's sister and H. H. Joachim referred to below. I have used the fair copy made by his sister. (I have learnt at the last moment that this paper was in fact published in *Religious Studies*, 19, 1983, pp. 175–83, edited by Gordon Kendal. Thanks to Mr Guy Stock for this information.)

Instructions to his executors said that the article was written in 1909, and, that although this may have been a slip and it may have been written in 1912, when he had the article on Sex in Literature typed out, both dates rule this out. She then jots down the suggestion that the articles in question were 'Some Remarks on Punishment' and 'The Limits of National Self-Sacrifice', both published in 1894 in the *International Journal of Ethics*. This, indeed, seems much more probable from the content of the discussion. Poor Mrs de Glehn was in agonies as to where her duty lay, to publish or to suppress, and evidently non-publication was the final decision. One of her worries was the offence it would cause to Dean W. R. Inge, who in a later work apparently often cites Bradley with admiration but whose *Contentio Veritatis* is held up to some scorn in this piece. In general, Mrs de Glehn was worried at the shock it would cause to 'good people' who found Bradley's work an inspiration and she remarks that, after all, he had had plenty of time to have published it himself had he wished to do so.

However all that may be, the piece does a good deal to clarify Bradley's mature attitude to Christianity.

The moral teaching of Jesus, as presented in the New Testament, must be judged, Bradley insists, like any other moral teaching, by the moral consciousness as it has developed through history to where we stand today. Thus judged, it is so hopelessly one-sided that it would be positively immoral to attempt to live one's life by it today. Essentially the original Christian teaching was appropriate only to a sect and could not possibly become the pervasive moral code of a society without radical modification. Such modification it received in practice, but whenever men have attempted to go back to the original source and take their morality straight from that, mental confusion and hypocrisy have been the inevitable result. 'The fact is that the morality [of] early Xtianity is that of a mere sect while ours is that of citizens in a state and the world.' The matter is different, however, if one takes Christianity as a principle which first appeared in a one-sided form with Jesus and the early Christians but has now developed into a moral consciousness which can recognize the limitations of vision associated with its source. As to the historical Jesus, Bradley's position (in the spirit of *The Presuppositions of Critical History*) holds that his real character and life must remain a matter of intriguing speculation. But if Christ is to remain the central symbol of an adequate morality we must dissociate him as an ideal more and more 'from the historic Jesus. This disconnection seems to be essential and to be really a matter of life and death for Christianity.' Yet there are grave problems in developing a religion of the book in this way.

The advice often given to Christians to take Christ as one's 'model in all the relations of life' (as Dean Inge had put it) is hopeless. For it would frequently either be no guide or a bad guide. How unhelpful or downright immoral it is to '[i]magine Jesus of Nazareth plunged into our social and political life, and then take him as a model, no matter what the situation may be'! Bradley instances the worthlessness of the guidance one might get on military conscription, on behaviour in war, on salary negotiations, and so forth.

Bradley especially contrasts the morality of primitive Christianity with the morality endorsed by decent people today on three matters, private property, our duty to the state, and sexual morality. In the course of the discussion he expresses a profound contempt for pacifists and for those who denigrate patriotism. He recognizes that better values are endorsed by the Christian Church in history and in particular today, but the attempt to present readiness to die for one's country as a component of Gospel teaching is absurd.

> [W]here in the Gospels is the patriot applauded or even recognised? How could there be a duty of patriotism when the framework of society was to go, and the world itself soon to pass away? The idea is absurd, and the actual fact, to any one who is not blind to fact, is certain. To profess here to follow Jesus as a model is not possible except to the injury or the ruin of one's own moral honesty.

Then again New Testament teaching on sex is thoroughly corrupting and has led our society to a double code neither aspect of which is acceptable: on the one hand, a counsel of chastity as the ideal, and marriage as 'a second-rate means against sin', and on the other, a 'man of the world' morality which is 'confused and void of principle and [anything else than] inspiring'. Thus the young man in a Christian country has no proper guide as to how he should deal with his sexuality, and how he should distinguish between the misuse of sex as a trivial pleasure and fully human sexual fulfilment. At the worst he is subjected to the horrors of the non-conformist conscience, for which 'robbery and murder weigh like feathers and one adultery like lead'.

Does all this imply that Bradley is against Christianity? Yes, if Christianity means an attempt to live by the actual teaching of the New Testament. Christianity thus understood can only be described as something 'it is the duty of every honest man to hate' as the source of endless hypocrisies and miseries. The same is true, indeed, of every religion which puts the precepts of a historical book above the lessons of the developing moral conscience. 'It is these sacred books which to us, like our fellow sufferers of Islam, threaten, if we cannot subordinate them, to become an intolerable hindrance.'

The question is different, however, if by Christianity is meant a developing principle with which it is appropriate especially to associate Jesus 'while reserving your right to treat any or even every utterance attributed to him as morally one-sided and defective'. How far it is really appropriate to associate Jesus with any such principle, as Bradley can conceive it, he leaves open but he can formulate a principle which will make him a Christian if it can be so regarded.

> The principle is that of the positive immanence and realization of the Divine in the Human or rather in the world of finite mind. It is negatively the denial of any good outside of the world of finite mind. It is again the denial of any breach or split in this world. It is positively the assertion of Good as the self-realization of this world as a whole. And for the individual the self-reali-

zation of this so far as it is given him to see it both in and beyond his own personal existence.[86]

Developing this further Bradley stresses what he calls the principles of autonomy and autocracy summed up jointly as 'We are our own providence'. The first concerns the positive value of self-affirmation and the need for autonomous moral thinking unbound by traditional or external authority; the second affirms the in principle unlimited right of the Whole to control the individual in the interests of its own improvement.

The principle of autocracy belongs, we may note, to that aspect of absolute idealism in the tradition of Hegel which has most disturbed people, especially in the light of subsequent history, for its apparently totalitarian implications. It also shows the striking moral difference between Bradley and James, who would never have agreed that the individual only matters as a means to the perfection of his society or other whole to which he belongs. As this work is not concerned primarily with the moral thinking of our two philosophers I shall not dwell on this matter further, beyond remarking that we must always remember that for all his talk of the over-riding importance of the needs of the 'Whole', the good of a social whole for Bradley can only take the form of the maximal self-realization of its members, so that the upshot is really not so far from a perfectionist type of utilitarianism.

It is also worthy of remark that in his fragmentary development of his two principles Bradley shows a concern for animals and nature which is somewhat contrary to that which undue attention to his hostile attitude to sentimental humanitarianism might suggest.

> Positively the right and duty of self-assertion on the part of the Whole and lesser Wholes and again the individual follow. And of course the use of force where required follows, (force as compulsion of others).[87]
>
> This self-realization is to have no limits—no higher region of any kind which is separate and has more than a relative value.
>
> Hence no denial of right to exist to any class or part of the finite world. Early Xtianity assailed [affirmed?] this principle though only of all *human* beings—mainly on a mistaken ground. But we cannot stop there. We cannot exclude what we call the lower animals. We cannot even exclude what we call the inanimate world. There is no downward limit. To treat these things as matters of indifference is not moral.
>
> Nothing is excluded but on the other side all is a matter of degree. There are no equal rights in the human world or outside it. You must sacrifice the welfare of part to whole within that world—and also outside it. It is monstrous to say that for us man has no more right than lower animals or inanimate nature. It is also monstrous to say that these have no right as against him. The covering

---

86   I have ironed out some slight confusion in the text.
87   Added here in pencil: 'Immorality of peace-mongers'.

a hideous world with the greatest possible number of inferior beings so long as they are human is not the end—even for us.

Bradley concludes the main article by acknowledging that he does not know what the best path to follow is for thinking people at the present time. On the one hand people like him have no wish to separate themselves from the moral community to which they feel themselves to belong by making a public show of throwing 'off in public the incubus of the holy books', while on the other hand, 'silence may be taken as a condonation of that which I am forced to abhor'. In general, one may take it that he wished to remain associated with his society's main institutional expression of a spiritual view of reality as against material-ism, while regretting the hypocrisy this tended to produce in those who, fortunately, recognized the inadequacy of the outlook associated with its origins. This was clearly an especial problem for one who believed that human fulfilment required participation in a community and did not at all share James's view that institutional religion was only a pale shadow of its fount in individual inspiration. In fact it was his dislike of 'sects', which distance their members from their own community, which underlay both his negative atti-tude to the early Christian church and his reluctance to break his ties with it as an institution central to the life of his nation.[88]

(g) God and the Absolute

§ Bradley's ideas about religion receive a final statement in 'On God and the Absolute' in ETR. This is a peculiarly sensitive statement of his position, mainly echoing what was said in ES and AR. It reiterates his view that religion proper has little to do with belief in another world and everything to do with how we experience the presence and demands of the eternal good in this world.

Bradley insists on a fundamental inconsistency at the heart of theistic relig-ion. For such religion must both tend to identify God with the Absolute and conceive Him in terms which such identification makes impossible. For, if God is the total reality, he is not an other to which we can relate; moreover, once we think in terms of the Absolute we must suppose that reality as a whole is perfect, and that may reduce our sense that our bad will must be overcome if the good is to be realized. But to make God something less than the Absolute is neces-sarily to deny Him perfection and infinitude. Bradley discusses the possibility of a religion, like that recommended by James, in which God is conceived as finite. And he acknowledges the heroic nobility of a commitment to helping a finite 'God in his struggle, more or less doubtful and blind, with resisting Evil'.[89] But, on the other hand, a 'principal part of religion is the assured satisfaction of our good will, the joy and peace in that assurance, and the added

---

88   His sister remarks that it was also his loyalty to Merton College which accounted for his not wishing to scandalise by distancing himself too explicitly from the faithful. Compare the letter of James of 21 September 1897 quoted in my appendix.

89   ETR, p. 429.

strength which in the majority of men can come perhaps from no other source'. So upon the whole the doctrine of a finite God can only occur in an incomplete version of religious faith.

What we must escape from, insists Bradley, is the unnecessary concern with consistency. This is no more needed in religion than in science, since both often need 'useful mythology' rather than absolute truth, and this does not require it. Our religious ideas must, ideally, be fitted to the world as it really is, and an adequate religion will find justification for the character of its working ideas in an adequate metaphysics, but that is far from saying that the ideas must be the same.

> If the object of religion is to realize in the fullest sense in my will the supremacy of goodness, then the ideas and the practices called for by this object are true and right.
>
> ETR, p. 431

So religious ideas should be judged only for their appropriateness for promoting this religious goal. A central question here is as to the degree and nature of the personality to be ascribed to God. Metaphysically it cannot be ultimately true that a personal God exists, but then it is not ultimately metaphysically true that finite persons exist. Both finite persons and God exist as presentations or posits the Absolute gives itself within finite centres of experience. God is as much a reality there as are individual persons. When a man prays to God, or struggles with him, both man and God are elements within the felt whole. That a personal God does exist as an appearance in this sense is indubitable. But there are forms of religion in which no such personal God appears and it is an open question for Bradley whether they do so in the highest form, or that to which mankind may best move in the future.

The whole question of personality is, indeed, far from clear. A God might be personal as a metaphysician understood the terms without being personal in the way he is conceived as being by religious believers.

> The personality, for instance, that is proved in a philosophical treatise, may, so far as religion is concerned, be no more than impersonal. And it is not simply the reality perhaps of a special Providence, but the whole matter of personal intercourse, love and friendship, which is really here at stake. 'It is not merely one of the doctrines of religion, but the central doctrine, the motive for all religious exercises, that God cares for every one of us individually, that he knows Jane Smith by name, and what she is earning a week, and how much of it she devotes to keeping her poor paralysed old mother.' [Bradley's footnote tells us he is quoting Hamerton, *Human Intercourse,* p. 166.]
>
> ETR, p. 450

Bradley offers no opinion as to what sort of personality should be ascribed to God in religious belief, and is content to acknowledge the existence of different types of religion, many of which have their own validity. He is inclined to think that humanity needs a new religion and hopes that one may arise which, without being identical with an adequate metaphysics, will have leading ideas which can receive some kind of justification therefrom. But he can play no part himself in promoting such a religion, and it will only arise after his own time.[90]

It is difficult to be satisfied with Bradley's statement that God, though only an appearance, exists for the religious consciousness. He realizes that some readers will think he is prevaricating, that for them

> a thing must be real or unreal, that, whatever things are real, are real alike and equally, and that, in short, with regard to reality it is always a case of Yes or No, and never of more and less.
>
> ETR, p. 448

and they may wish to know whether Bradley holds God to be real or not in this sense. But in any such absolute sense Bradley must reply that indeed God is not real, any more than is Bradley or the reader. However, to infer from this that God is less real than us would be an absurd mistake. On the contrary, if

> I am allowed to hold to degrees in reality, the conclusion at once is different. God to me is now so much more real than you or myself that to compare God's reality with ours would be ridiculous.
>
> ETR, p. 448

But Bradley himself allows that belief in a personal God is an optional element of religion. Does he really think that the existence of individual human persons is an optional concept in this way? It would be hard to go along with him if so. Whatever some bold writers say about the invention of the individual in the Renaissance, there surely could not be a community of language speakers which dispensed with any version of the category of persons, but there may, surely, be ones which dispense with any concept of God. And does not that make persons more real, in a sense, than God? Perhaps Bradley might contend that under some name or other every culture has its 'object of ultimate concern' (as Tillich put it) and that this is its category of the divine. But a society's object of ultimate concern, if, indeed, it must have one, cannot properly be called God in all cases. So, even if God can be the most real of appearances for some cultures (that is, the concept of Him be the most indispensable for them of all) He is a less real appearance for men in general (as being a more dispensable concept) than that of themselves. (Things may be different for any thinking there may be which simply cannot be conceived as the thinking of persons, but, the overall thinking of the Absolute apart, Bradley shows no wish to invoke this.)

It follows, I think, that if Bradley is to maintain that God is a more real appearance than we are, it is not because the conception of Him is more inevitable, but because it is an approximation to a concept of the Absolute, and

90   See ETR, p. 446–47.

that this is more real than any thing to which the concept of a person is an approximation (such as a finite centre) in the sense that it is the concrete whole from which any such thing is a mere abstraction (an appearance in the second sense we distinguished above).

Despite his interest in the possible development of a new religion, Bradley's negative feelings towards Christianity seem to have been in abeyance in this article. For he seems to be looking with sympathy on the religious experience of straightforward Christian believers in his own day, and may have found it not so far from his own experience. Perhaps the truth is that what he objected to in Christianity was a certain kind of sentimental humanitarianism, as he saw it, into which it had grown and a limited conception of human good which it encouraged, but that he continued to endorse the religious faith of the ordinary Christian, so far as this is concerned more with his carrying out God's will in this world than with his fate in another, as the most satisfactory way of relating to reality yet found.[91]

(h) Life after Death

§ I shall conclude my discussion of Bradley's views on religion by considering his attitude to the question of life after death, though the main thing he has to say about it is that it is not religiously important. (His treatment of this topic will, however, be seen to fill out the views on personal identity treated in §4 above.)

Treated as a purely factual question the issue of personal survival seems always to have been regarded by Bradley as open. He insisted, however, that the truth may not be expressible as a stark 'yes' or 'no'. And the view that the question is not of primary importance for religion, or indeed for metaphysics, seems to have been constant with him.

In an article published in 1885, called 'The Evidences of Spiritualism' (chapter XXIX of CE) he offers a critique of some claims made in A. R. Wallace's *Miracles and Modern Spiritualism*. He says that the spiritualist must prove three things: that his 'phenomena' are real, that they are not the abnormal work of human spirits, and that, if they are the work of intelligences other than those incarnated in human bodies, they are the spirits of the dead existing, as Wallace claims, without dependence on any sort of material body. And Bradley insists that, even if we granted that the first two had been demonstrated, the spiritualist would still be in no position to establish the third. For the intelligences in question may well be dependent on some other form of matter than ours (and the reports of spiritualist phenomena suggest that this is so) and, what is more, they may only be masquerading as our dead.

For, after all, what sort of souls are these which manifest themselves in spiritualistic phenomena if there really are such? Bradley asks first whether the

---

91   A. E. Taylor insisted on Bradley's essentially Christian outlook in his personal life
      in an article he published in *Mind* on Bradley's death. See Taylor, 'Bradley'.

bodies they seem to have provide them with 'a higher life than ours', and answers with pleasant irony.

> Like ourselves they have bodies, and these bodies at least are presumably mortal, but can we know more? Is there anything to tell us if, as compared with ourselves, they are higher or lower, more or less spiritual? If we consider first their material performances, it is clear that they do much which we cannot do. And this certainly has weight. On the other hand, when we ask if they can do the things which we accomplish, the evidence fails us. And if, further, we inquire if our ordinary life may not seem to them extraordinary and even miraculous, we have no information. We are not able to tie knots in an endless cord, or to pass through a keyhole, and that is in their favour. On the other hand, they have never made anything useful or done anything great; and so far as we know, they could not if they would. Again, living as we do in two different worlds, what is common in one may be astonishing in another. If they pass through our keyholes perhaps we pass through theirs, and should bewilder them if, like ourselves, they were wise enough to wonder, or if our high matter could affect their gross bodies. But these are all idle fancies, worthless imaginings.
>
> CE, p. 599

He continues by asking about the nature of these beings *qua* souls and suggests that all the evidence is that they are vastly inferior to ourselves.

> To the damning evidence of the so-called Spirit-Teachings no answer can be made. It would be unfair to say that the best of them are twaddle, and they perhaps may be compared with our own pulpit-utterances. They are often edifying, and often reasonable, and sometimes silly, and usually dull. Still, to mention them in the same breath with the best human work would be wholly absurd. And it is an inferior race which can produce nothing better.
>
> CE, p. 600

He concludes that even if spiritualistic phenomena were proved genuine, any religion based upon them would 'conflict with the best aspirations of the soul in a way in which modern materialism does not', inasmuch as it would be concerned with communication with spirits inferior to ourselves.

As for the claim that these spirits are our dead, it can only be dealt with on the basis of far clearer ideas about the nature of personal identity than the spiritualists have ever yet produced.

Bradley argues, first, that we have no reason to believe anything that such spirits say, inasmuch as the normal conditions on which we can rely upon the testimony of others do not hold. We have no way of finding out whether they wish to speak the truth, or whether they are competent witnesses or sufficiently understand what they are talking about to speak with sufficient care. So, Bradley argues, we should believe nothing out of line with what we should have believed anyway on the basis of what they say, just as he had with recorded historical testimony.[92] In fact, if by any chance they really are 'our'

92   See CE, pp. 601–6.

dead, they may be existing in a state so inferior, and so close to a final dissolution, that there would be little religious comfort in the reality of such survival.

Moreover, the very meaning of survival is unclear, for the main criterion of this, bodily identity, used in this life, cannot apply. How far this actually constitutes personal identity, Bradley seems to leave open here. He suggests that continuity together with identity of character is required for personal identity, but the discussion is somewhat inconclusive. The only essential point is that the establishment of personal identity becomes virtually impossible when this criterion is unavailable and we are concerned with a realm where none of our ordinary ideas about what is and what is not possible may apply. Thus we cannot know what the limits of possible deception are in a world of spirits of whose powers we know nothing.

All things considered, it is more congruent with genuine religion to believe that after death we continue only in what we have achieved in this life.[93] Bradley is quite open to the possibility that something supernatural is going on in the spiritualistic séance. But whatever it is, it has no genuine religious interest, though he says some polite things about the actual spiritualists of his day. If there is a spirit world it may well be so inferior a world that humanity has risen precisely because it has detached itself from it.

§ There is a brief and eloquent discussion of the issue of immortality (or of a finite period of personal survival after death) at the end of chapter XXVI of AR.[94] Special metaphysical arguments set aside, Bradley contends that some form of survival, whether with or without a body, is a bare possibility, but no more. He repeats his rejection of spiritualistic evidence, emphasising even more strongly than before that it is far from established that there is communication here with spirits of any sort, let alone with our dead. As for the usual metaphysical arguments they are all radically flawed. The best argument would be one which showed that the perfection of the Absolute requires our personal survival, but no such argument holds water. The universe has needed me in this life, but why should it need my survival? It may be said that without it, virtue would have no adequate reward and evil no sufficient punishment. Quite so, but all we can be sure of, on the basis of Bradley's doctrine of the Absolute, is that the evil in the world is somehow made good. To assume it must be made so, for the particular person who suffers it, gives a metaphysical centrality to the individual person pertaining to an inferior form of religion which we should move beyond. The best side of a belief in a life after death lies not in the concern we may have at our own cessation, but in the wish we have to see our loved ones again. But this could be a mixed blessing, when we consider the complications of relationship which arise between those who survive after a loved one's death. Still, if it comforts someone to believe that there is a bare epistemic possibility (to use modern jargon) that there is a life

---

93   See CE, p. 612.
94   AR, pp. 444–52

after death, so much can certainly be granted him. But it can corrupt both religion and morality to rest their validity on a belief which upon the whole the educated world is losing.

§ A rather more positive tone towards the possibility of life after death is adopted in 'On God and the Absolute' and in its second appendix, and still more so in 'On My Real World'. Altogether ETR shows more sympathy with the other worldly note in religion than most of the earlier writings.

He does, indeed, still insist that 'mere personal survival and continuance has in itself absolutely nothing to do with true religion. A man can be as irreligious (for anything at least that I know) in a hundred lives as in one'.[95] But if a doctrine of personal survival is the one way in which people can formulate the conviction that at our best we are identical with something which transcends time, then he is not without sympathy with it.

§ In 'On our Fear of Death and Desire for Immortality' (Supplementary Note B to 'On God and the Absolute') one of Bradley's most moving pieces, he discusses the lack of precision in the whole question of personal survival. For it is not at all clear what has to exist in a future time for it to be true that I survive. (He has things to say here which are relevant to recent debates concerning the proper objects of egoistic interest. Should we fear pain under anaesthetic if we thought that the anaesthetic only cut it off from public expression and later recall?[96]) Of all the various possibilities, however, the only one in which I can take anything properly called a personal interest is one in which the future being looks back upon me as I am now with a personal interest.

> Suppose after my death a man to exist who is to be very like myself. Certainly I prefer to feel that I have now perhaps helped such a man rather than another man less like me. And suppose that I myself am to exist after death and am to be altered considerably, the more I am altered the less and less personal concern do I now feel, until a point is reached where my interest really ceases to be special. The only personal identity which seems to count here is the degree and the amount of likeness in the felt self. From the other side, though felt sameness in character is wanted in order to have continuity recognized between myself now and then, this by itself is not enough. If I am to have an individual personal interest, I must suppose also a memory in the 'then'. I must imagine, for instance, a man after my death reading what I myself write now, and saying to himself, 'Yes, I wrote it.' He must not only feel it to be the expression of his self, but must make that self continuous in the past (even if there are intervals) with my own. Here is the identity in which I can now take interest as personal to me myself. In whatever falls short of this I can feel a concern which, though never individual, may be special, special until by lessening degrees we arrive at that which is merely general.
>
> ETR, p. 454

---

95   ETR, p. 440.
96   See ETR, pp. 454–56.

Upon the whole Bradley thinks that a special concern with my own future rests upon an illusion. And the fear of annihilation may arise partly from the confused belief that it is an extreme version of those forms of partial annihilation which really are objectionable.[97]

But may not lovers wish to survive as lovers for ever? Rather, thinks Bradley, in the most passionate love the question becomes irrelevant.

> Something has been revealed which is beyond time and sports with the order of events. There never was a before, and God has made the whole world for this present.
>
> ETR, p. 457

Thus in moments of completest fulfilment we live as though in an eternal now, and that moment is, then, indeed one of the eternally present peaks of the absolute experience. This theme is taken up again in 'On My Real World'.

> 'For love and beauty and delight', it is no matter where they have shown themselves, 'there is no death nor change'; and this conclusion is true. These things do not die, since the Paradise in which they bloom is immortal. That Paradise is no special region nor any given particular spot in time and space. It is here, it is everywhere where any finite being is lifted into that higher life which alone is waking reality.
>
> ETR, p. 469

Such passages (anticipative of the *Four Quartets*) exhibit an increasingly Platonic insistence that the world of phenomenal flux is of value only for the eternal forms which are actualised in it from moment to moment (though in holding that they are only actual as thus actualised he is, perhaps, more Aristotelian).

In all this Bradley is very much the 'refined' supernaturalist criticising the crass supernaturalism of which James was the avowed champion.[98] There may be a crass supernatural but what is spiritually significant is as present in this world as it could be in any other. In all equally there can be the expression of goodness, truth, and beauty, and all must equally play their role in constituting the absolute experience.

My own sympathies are mostly with Bradley here. The idea that the great questions of how to live turn to any great extent on whether we will later live in a world beyond this seems as wrong-headed as he thought it, and he is right, surely, that beauty, truth, and goodness are as valuable in this world as they could be in any other. Yet it must be said that in his somewhat mystical Platonic raptures Bradley manages to turn his mind away from the horrors which are so pervasive in this world too. As I have already said, his lack of concern with evil deserves James's strictures on absolute idealism.

---

97   See ETR, p. 456.
98   See VRE, pp. 520–21.

6

Conclusion

We have now surveyed the main teachings of both James and Bradley on truth and reality. In the process I have said most of what I have to say as to the way in which the ideas of these two thinkers, usually considered diametrically opposed, share many main premises and some main conclusions, while the contrasts between their views are all the more interesting just because they share so much. I have also indicated my own acceptance of the bulk of what they have in common and tried to persuade the reader of its rightness. Anyone who agrees with me on these points will agree that one of the great choices in philosophy can be put in the form of 'James or Bradley?' that is, as the choice between a monistic or a pluralistic form of panexperientialism.

There is not much which remains to be said, but a summary may be helpful.

The greatest affinities between our thinkers are five. In summarising them here I shall assume such qualifications and refinements as are made in the main text, and, for ease of comparison, shall not trouble especially to preserve the special mode of formulation of either thinker.

(1) They both agree that the stuff of the universe is entirely psychical. That is, concrete reality is composed of innumerable pulses of experience. In the cases with which we are familiar these occur in streams which constitute them the lives of sentient continuants. If anything else concrete exists at all (apart perhaps from groups of, or components in, such pulses or the continuants they constitute when they occur in streams), it too is psychical in essentially the same sense as these are. Everything else which can properly be said to exist does so only as a useful posit.

In the case of James we must qualify this by recalling that at times he says only that this is the sole reality with which the philosopher can concern himself. If there is anything beyond, it belongs to a realm of things-in-themselves about which we can know nothing and by which we can explain nothing. And in the case of Bradley we must recall that he ascribes quite a high degree of reality to much that exists only as something constructed from within one or more centres of experience.

This panexperientialist doctrine has been held by many thinkers, and should recommend itself, as I see it, to serious metaphysicians, but it must remain eccentric in the eyes of many. Of course, we speak as though there were other things, and, to the extent that these serve as useful posits for coping with the world, we may say that it is pragmatically true that they exist. However, if, as metaphysicians, we wish to know the ultimate truth, we must specify the world in panexperientialist terms.

My own reasons for holding this view have been expounded more fully in another book as is true of my own reasons for holding most of the other doctrines which I endorse in this section.[1] But a good deal in favour of them, culled from James and Bradley, has been said here too.

(2) Experience is not ultimately best understood as the experience of a self, soul, mind, or whatever. Selves, the things referred to by personal pronouns, are not substances in any traditional sense but either aspects of pulses or streams of experience or constructions made by thoughts occurring within them. The view I sympathise with most is that the self at any given moment is the self side of a total experience, and that, *qua* continuant, it is a concrete universal actualised in successive such momentary selves. This formulation is more Bradleyan than Jamesian but the basic idea is common to them. Upon the whole, I think it is more satisfactorily worked out by James, though I believe a really adequate view needs the Bradleyan notion of a concrete universal.

(3) Both thinkers had some inclination to a panpsychist view of nature, for which the physical things of common sense or science are the appearances to us of flows of experience, or of an interwoven system of such. This sort of view has been developed most fully by A. N. Whitehead and Charles Hartshorne, and I have made some contribution to it myself. It implies that nature, at some level of articulation, consists in individuals which are sentient, in the sense that there is a stream of sentience which is what they are in themselves while in the case of objects, like most ordinary things, which are the appearances of a complex of streams rather than a single stream, there may or may not be a dominant stream which is the consciousness of the whole. Our own sentience may be a peculiarly dominant one among the streams of experience which are the reality of our brains, or it may be a distinct reality which they somehow either generate or are currently in special *rapport* with.

James seems finally to have adopted a view of this kind, while Bradley regarded it somewhat gingerly as a possibility. To me it seems essential if panexperientialism, either of James's pluralistic or Bradley's monistic variety, is to be credible.

---

1   See Sprigge, *Vindication*.

(4) The phenomenal physical world, that is the world as we usually and for ordinary purposes properly conceive it, consists in certain components of the experiences which constitute our conscious lives together with a postulated extension of them into an indefinitely larger space and time within which they are supposed to be included. Thus it is not *represented* by our sensory presentations but composed of them and their posited extension.

James is ambivalent at times about just what sort of truth the belief in a physical world thus conceived possesses. Upon the whole he probably ascribed it a pragmatic truth falling short of a deeper metaphysical truth provided by the panpsychist account. For Bradley, much more obviously, its truth is only pragmatic, but his view of the literal truth of what lies behind it, is, as we have seen, less clear. It cannot, however, concern a genuinely unexperienced realm lying behind the sensory structure.

(5) Both thinkers hold that the discrete nature of concepts means that they cannot do justice to the world's unity. However for Bradley the unity is ultimately that of an eternal *Nunc Stans*, while for James it is that of a perpetual flux. For both of them reality is composed of units which seem to themselves to be replacing, and giving way to, others, but for James this sense is our best clue to how reality is in general, while for Bradley it is an illusion endemic to their character.

In addition to these five major points of substantial accord there are two further points of less complete affinity.

(6) There is some overlap in their views of truth. Each holds that what such thought as does not aim at metaphysical finality needs is ideas which are useful for its purposes rather than revelations of reality. For example, science mainly needs ideas useful for technological control, while religion mainly needs ideas which encourage such sense of oneness with a power for good at the heart of things as may best sustain our moral aspirations.

There is less agreement on the truth to be sought in metaphysics. For Bradley it aims at such revelation of reality as ideas may bring. The main tests of their doing so are their coherence and comprehensiveness. These criteria are relevant in non-metaphysical thought too, but should not be pressed there too thoroughly. James's position is less clear-cut on the truth to be sought in metaphysics. Much of the time he seems to have thought of metaphysics as distinguished only by the generality of its subject matter and not by its aiming at some special type of truth distinct from that of forwarding human purposes. But he also came to think of it as aiming at a specially intimate grasp of the essence of reality and thus (in effect, if not in so many words) at a special peculiarly literal sort of truth. But, whereas for Bradley this is to be sought through pressing reasoning to its limit, for James it is to be sought rather by its abandonment in favour of a thought-cleansed attention to the flux of our experience. But even here there is some affinity. For Bradley thinks reasoning only a preparation for something more intuitive.

(7) Bradley's main affirmation is of the existence of the Absolute, a single infinite experience of which everything finite is an aspect, and much of James's

thought is devoted to the critique of such a claim. Yet he came to believe in a single mother sea of consciousness which all finite consciousness emerges from, and returns to, with enrichments won when separate. This is not the Absolute, since as long as we are separated individual subjects we are not part of it, but it is not as far apart from it as all that, especially in the light it is supposed to cast upon the nature of religious experience. However, for James the existence of the mother sea of consciousness was an empirical hypothesis whereas for Bradley it was a logical necessity. In any case James's mother sea is not the heart of his metaphysics as is the Absolute of Bradley, and is given an interpretation which still leaves the world fundamentally a *many* while for Bradley it is a *one*.

So much for the main affinities between our thinkers. Let us now consider the great divides between them, where he who follows them both so far must choose between them.

(8) A first contrast is that between their views on particulars and universals. James likes to insist that the heart of the empiricism to which he subscribes is that particulars are more fundamental to knowledge and reality than universals. Bradley in contrast, constantly complains of the primacy which empiricists give to particulars.

Their divergence on this shows itself mainly (1) in their contrasting accounts of reasoning, and (2) in their debate over identity and similarity. Its presence is also felt (3) in their treatment of personal identity. For James this turns primarily on the memory in later moments of experience of particular occurrences pertaining to one's past. This cannot quite be so for Bradley for whom memory of particular events is derivative from the acquisition of knowledge of the relation between universals. I have discussed the second and third of these in the main text. Adequate treatment of the first would require more attention to their respective accounts of inference than I have had space for.

At times this difference seems to be more a temperamental one than a real difference of doctrine. For when the qualifications each philosopher has to make to his initial statements are taken into account the difference often seems to be less important than one might first think.

How important are their respective views on particulars and universals for their fundamental monism and pluralism respectively? A pluralist, it may be thought, is bound to emphasise the importance of particulars, which, since Hume, are thought to be quite loose and disconnected, whereas a monist is likely to emphasise universals which supply a bond between much that is superficially most distant. Yet when one considers that, for James, the particulars of the world melt into each other, while universals are a principle for carving up the world into the sharply distinct, one becomes aware of so many qualifications to such a suggestion that it does not appear a very fruitful way of explaining their main metaphysical divergences.

The most interesting contrasts between them turn on Bradley's belief in what James detested as a 'block universe' with no free play between its elements, and no genuine indeterminacy or openness. Although I do not accept James's view that our choice between metaphysical systems is bound to be as much temperamental as rational, he is clearly right that his own attempt to establish pluralism was to a great extent motivated by this. Closely related is his objection to what he sees as the absolute idealist's attempt to reconcile us to evil.

(9) The most obvious contrast of this sort lies in their positions on freedom of the will. James related this to an element of indeterminism or 'chance' pervasive in the universe and was not prepared to accept the blandishments of a 'soft' determinism professing to give us all we ordinarily want of free will without sacrificing the universality of causation. And certainly no determinism could have given him what he wanted. For his concern was not primarily to establish moral responsibility, still less the desirability of retributive punishment, but rather that there is an element of spontaneity in things, and that time is not simply the working out of processes every detail of which was always settled. What he wanted was not so much moral responsibility as a universe with parts not so tightly bound up with one another that one cannot think one thing good or bad without thinking everything so.

In contrast to this, Bradley did, effectively, support a form of soft determinism or compatibilism. Certainly he thought that moral responsibility would fall, if human actions were explicable by the same laws as suffice to explain purely physical phenomena. But once grant that a new principle occurs when a new person is born, he still thought that that principle arose inevitably, if unpredictably, from what came before, and that what a man, whose behaviour is governed by such a principle, does follows from it of necessity. Though this aspect of his thought was less emphatic in later works, it can be said that, while James did not approve retributive punishment but did believe in contra-causal free will, Bradley did not believe in contra-causal free will but did believe in retributive punishment.

(10) More fundamental, though less clearly discussed by either thinker, are their opposing views on time and eternity. For Bradley, though there is some unclarity in his statement of the point, there is ultimately just the eternal Absolute which contains all experience, that is, all that there is. From the point of view of any one pulse of experience, of the sort with which we are familiar, the rest of the reality of which it knows either belongs to the past or the same present time, and has a settled character, or exists only as one among other possibilities in the future. But from the point of view of the Absolute, and of the ultimate truth, all moments of time are just eternally there, each just what it eternally is, with whatever feeling of transitoriness it has. Thus the idea that there is a genuinely open future is an illusion.

James totally rejected this. He does not always seem very clearly aware of the strongest form of, or strongest kind of argument in favour of, the eternalistic point of view to which he was opposed (though his friend Josiah Royce was perhaps its best exponent). He tended to think of the absolutist as believing that it is somehow already settled how the future will unfold, not adequately realizing that, for absolutism, the main point is not that how things will be is settled already, but that, in real truth, the very notions of past, present, and future are flawed, and that all times are just parts of one eternal now to predicate change of which is simply senseless. Thus he attacked the notion of the closed future mainly by insisting on the looseness of fit between one moment and another, whereas the more ultimate question is whether every moment be not eternally there with its own definite character, whether this be settled for it by 'earlier' moments or not. But whatever the rights and wrongs here, this is one of the biggest divides between a Bradleyan and a Jamesian conception of things.

(11) The issue on which our two thinkers clash most explicitly concerns the nature of relations. For Bradley the truth which underlies what we conceive as the relatedness of two things is always the existence of a whole of which they are each so essentially mere aspects that it could not exist without them or they without it. Amidst all the tortuosities of his dialectic the key point is that one can only envisage things as related by envisaging such a whole and that, since everything is somehow related to everything else, ultimately there must be one single unitary whole in which all things participate.

James was much more aware of the force of the monist case as advanced by Lotze, Bradley, Royce, and others than any other critic (except perhaps Santayana) of whom I know. It had impressed him most in Royce's version where it rests on the claim that even error requires that thought have an object which is present with it in an absolute consciousness. However, he also addressed himself to arguments more typical of Bradley. He sometimes dismisses these as resting on a naive confusion between concepts and things. But his recognition of a profounder case for holding that related terms must be mere aspects of a larger unity fired his attempt to conceive the relation between different experiences as a real partial merging of elements which, however, leaves them distinct individuals such as can be conceived, and could have existed, apart.

(12) Their metaphysical differences go with a basic ethical contrast in their thought, though it would be hard to say, in either case, whether it is the metaphysics which follows the ethics or vice versa. James was a thorough individualist for whom what really mattered was what individuals feel. Ethics arises because a sufficiently enlightened individual can enter imaginatively into the felt life of another and see that there is real joy and sadness there on a level with his own, which he cannot properly acknowledge without feeling the need to take account of it in his own behaviour. But he quite rejects the idea that human fulfilment requires a sense of belonging to something which matters more than oneself.

> I am against bigness and greatness in all their forms. . . . The bigger the unit you deal with, the hollower, the more brutal, the more mendacious, is the life displayed.
>
> James, *Letters*, II, p. 90

For Bradley, in contrast, the individual person can only find fulfilment as conscious element in a larger whole, most often that of a human community. He does, however, qualify this typically absolutist theme in important ways. The individual may, in solitary pursuits of an intellectual or artistic nature, fulfil himself in detachment from any human community, and only vaguely be aware of some larger spiritual whole enriched by his activity. Moreover, metaphysically, there are strains of individualism in Bradley. The finite centre, even the momentary centre, of experience sometimes threatens to become the most truly individual thing within the universe, more real than the intermediate units between it and the Absolute. But though this might suggest an atomistic hedonistic ethic any such conclusion is checked by his envisaging these centres rather as the loci in which what really matters must be actualised, than as themselves what really matter. Moreover, they are so shot through with their relations that they cannot be conceived as mere isolated throbs of sentience.

(13) Our thinkers differ sharply in their attitude to evil. James believes that there are components of the universe which are sheer loss adding nothing to the sum of positive value. It would have been much better if much of the wickedness and suffering in the world had never been and we should not attempt to reconcile ourselves to their existence. Granted the reality of time, moreover, one can hope eventually to make it as though they had never been and work towards their simply dropping out of reality. (However, unlike Dewey, James sharply denied that the truth about the past could change.)[2]

For Bradley it was senseless to think that anything could drop out of reality. And since the Absolute is necessarily perfect, the evil in the world must ultimately minister to a higher good, or, since he thinks the word 'good' inept in this connection, to the perfection of the Absolute. (Actually he admits that the perfection of the Absolute, in any sense relevant to religion and morality, cannot be finally proved, but that it is much the most reasonable supposition.)

(14) With these contrasting attitudes to evil go contrasting attitudes to religion. For James the Absolute, if it existed, would not be an appropriate object of religious feeling, since it would be radically flawed. Only a finite God, who battles against real evil and waste outside Him, and whom we can aid with our own endeavours, can be an adequate religious object. Moreover, the existence of such a being is a reasonable way of interpreting the phenomena of religious experience, once granted that monistic interpretations are metaphysically and morally objectionable.

For Bradley, too, the Absolute, conceived strictly as such, is, indeed, not a proper object of worship. It is so, however, conceived incoherently, as a divine will with which we can co-operate against evil. But while this implies a partial agreement with James on the phenomenology of religious experience, it implies a fundamental disagreement over its explanation. Moreover, James thought that a 'manly' religion requires belief that the final victory of good is an uncertain thing to be fought for, while, for Bradley, assurance of the final or rather eternal victory of the best is an essential (and metaphysically correct) part of the most satisfactory religion.

(15) Still more important is James's belief that it is only the crassly or piecemeal supernatural which is worth much religiously. Since the divine is

---

2   See Perry, II, pp. 476–78.

properly thought of as one element in reality, rather than the character of the whole properly understood, it is quite proper for the religious person to be interested in the possibility of special effects due to the divine, perhaps in the form of special providences and miracles, but, more importantly, in the form of special saving experiences of a mystical kind.

For Bradley, in contrast, the truly religious mind sees the divine as necessarily present in all phenomena, and as available in the whole range of experiences and situations in which a man could ever find himself, not as requiring the existence of dubitable empirical facts for its demonstration or actualisation.

(16) This last point exemplifies what may seem the most obvious contrast between the two thinkers, that of empiricism versus a certain sort of rationalism. For Bradley, the most important truths about the universe are necessary and knowable through reasoning (indeed all truths are necessary in some sense, though not transparently so for us) whereas for James they might have been otherwise, and can only be ascertained empirically.

However, Bradley explicitly dissented from any Hegelian attempt to characterise the world from the resources of sheer thought, and believed that even to think of it as basically one great *thought*, as other absolute idealists had done, was one-sided, since experience cannot be reduced to intellectual process. Doubtless the great truths about the Absolute are necessary and knowable *a priori*, and doubtless the aim of thought is to see necessity in all things. But, in practice, we cannot know why the details of the world are as they are and can only know them empirically. In fact, his rationalism is so qualified that not too much should be made of this contrast between our two thinkers. Moreover, their detailed methodological recommendations and practice have much in common.

Should I end by saying which of James and Bradley I believe most right? To give myself the last word may seem arrogant. Yet, after so long an examination, it would be false modesty to hide my own conclusions many of which are clear already.

On free will I side more with Bradley. I doubt whether anything of supreme importance is saved for the universe by believing that there is an element of causal slack within it. But I agree with Bradley that the distinctively human must enter into the explanation of what we do if we are to be genuine agents.

So far as time and eternity go, I believe the arguments for an eternalistic view of time, such as Bradley's Absolute requires, and which James rejects, so conclusive that whether one likes it or not, there is no option for a rational person but to take this view. But though he is certainly committed to eternalism Bradley speaks at times in ways which seem at odds with it. In any case, James's description of the phenomenology of temporal experience is better than Bradley's. Moreover, there is no need to deny that reality has a spatio-temporal structure, in the sense that apparent neighbours in space and time are real neighbours in reality, and James is more helpful on such neighbourhood than Bradley. But, in the end, we must admit , reality is a *Nunc Stans* the overall nature of which is distorted for each of its components by their sense of being in flux.

On relations Bradley is tortuous and obscure but presents, I believe, a core of argument that is irrefutable. James's alternative account of relations is a valiant effort to resist monism, in fact, the best alternative on offer. But his pulses of experience, merged with their predecessors at one end and their successors at the other, and perhaps their neighbours at their sides, are inevitably either pulled apart into two components requiring to be related or so merged with these other experiences that they are also merged. The logic of monism is inexorable. One may not like the idea of a monistic universe, but that seems to be how things must be.

If monism is logically irresistible, is the universe something which our better feelings must rebel against, as James would then think it?

Let us first consider the moral implications, so far as ethical individualism versus collectivism go. Here I think the truth must lie in a synthesis. What matters is the quality of experience genuinely lived through in the world, and lived through, so far as any experience with which we have much concern goes, by finite individuals. Thus, from one point of view, individualism must be the final truth. Goods not realized in the experience of individuals are only false goods. But to hold this is quite compatible with an element, if not of collectivism, then of communitarianism. It may well be that individuals are so bound up with each other that their main satisfactions can only be that of members of a community and that purely private selfish pleasure can never finally satisfy. Here then it seems to me that there is no need to make some simple choice, and, in fact, this would be echoed by both thinkers, though more especially by Bradley.

Does the absolute idealist have to believe all evil a positive contribution to the perfection of the universe? Like James, I find that idea repellent and implausible. So here I side with James against the suggestions of absolute idealists like Bradley.[3] But I do not think this shows that there must be some flaw in the dialectic leading to the Absolute. Rather must one say that the Absolute necessarily includes, along with what makes the whole thing worthwhile, elements which are simply bad, but which cannot fail to be there in their own position in the whole. Of course, it is sheer confusion to think that we must reconcile ourselves to any evils being there *for ever*. We can hope that their place is in the past more than in the future and work to that effect.

This might suggest that the absolute idealist could identify something less than the Absolute, like James's finite God, as the divine portion of the whole. But I incline to agree with Bradley that nothing short of the Absolute can really satisfy a developed religious sense, even if it has to be conceived in mythological

---

3   It should be noted, however, that Bradley himself thought it a repellent feature of theism that it postulates a creator 'who planned the evil of the world and is responsible for it' (letter to James of 21 September 1887—see appendix). See also AR, p. 174. So perhaps his real view was not so different from mine, in spite of his having to hold that every evil somehow ministers to the Absolute's perfection.

ways for religious purposes. Besides, there is good reason to believe in the Absolute and little for believing in a finite God, unless the term is simply used à la Matthew Arnold, for the main forces in the world tending to goodness.

Although I think that the universe or Absolute must contain elements which are sheer badness or waste, the case for saying that as a whole it is supremely good is strong. The Absolute must grasp its own nature, and must be satisfied with being what it is. For, if it were not, it would be straining on to something else and the true Absolute would be the whole including also the future onto which it is in movement. But, if the Absolute is satisfied with its nature, it must be one in which omniscience can acquiesce with pleasure, which seems as much as to say that it must be good. However, the Absolute may be pleased with its overall character, while still unreservedly deploring, to speak anthropomorphically, much that it contains. For it may know that there was no alternative to its existing with just that character, except the meaningless alternative of nothing, and so be glad of that, without in any way being glad at the horrors it contains. That is, in fact, the attitude to the world of most of us. We believe that it is better that the world should exist as it is, even with its horrors, than not at all, but we do not think the horrors improve it. An absolute idealist sympathetic to a finite God might also have some sympathy with piecemeal supernaturalism as an important component of religion. But I myself would agree with Bradley that a religion worthy of modern man must not base itself upon hazardous judgements as to what happened in history or on the reliability of witnesses to the apparently paranormal.

So far as the rivalry between rationalism and empiricism goes I will only say this. No one in their senses will deny the extent to which our knowledge or reasonable beliefs must be grounded on observation and experiment, either our own or what we take to be reliable reports upon or inferences from those of others. The sole question is how much may be known *a priori*. To this I think one must adopt an experimental approach. If something is claimed to be true on the basis of an *a priori* demonstration, one must either absolve oneself from an opinion on the matter, or choose someone one thinks more intelligent than oneself in this matter and be guided by him, or, and much better if one has appropriate competence, assess the validity of the proof for oneself. If one finds it conclusive, one is unreasonable not to accept the conclusion; if one finds it faulty, one has no reason to be swayed by it. If nothing seems provable *a priori*, then it is sensible to believe nothing on this basis. But I have found that certain propositions of some considerable importance as characterisations of the cosmos do seem to have conclusive *a priori* proofs, among them the existence of the Absolute and the truth of eternalism, so here I go along with Bradley. As to whether everything is necessary in some ultimate sense, certainly its being so would provide the basis for a solution of the problem of evil not otherwise available. The belief that most important things just must be contingent rests essentially upon the belief that distinct existences do not necessarily imply the existence and character of each other, and we have seen reason to think that Bradley has shown that this is false. That being so, one bit of the universe may necessarily imply the rest of it. The only question is whether the whole thing might somehow have been quite otherwise, with quite other ingredients, thus excluding oneself and all one loves, or perhaps not have existed at all. I am inclined to think that the possibility of nothing having existed is a meaningless one, and that alternatives only have reality as postulations occurring within the one thing which necessarily is.

Though I accept the basic monism of Bradley and thus his overall characterisation of the world, I am in greater sympathy with James on most points of greater detail, for example, on the character of the stream of consciousness, on his final panpsychist view of nature, and on the nature of moral sensitivity. In short, while I think Bradley right upon the whole about the whole I think James right in very large part about the parts. So even if that would hardly please James, I think a Bradleyan account of the universe can only stand when filled out and qualified in Jamesian ways. And James remains its best critic and his philosophy its best alternative.

APPENDIX

The Correspondence of William James and F. H. Bradley

Although Bradley and James never met they carried on a fairly extensive philosophical correspondence and exchange of proofs and offprints. The letters from Bradley are more frequent and longer; as he said, in his letter of 8 February 1905, he had more time. The following is a list of the known extant letters between them. The letters from James to Bradley are held in the Bradley papers in Merton College library. They were published as 'Ten Unpublished Letters from William James, 1842–1910 to Francis Herbert Bradley, 1846–1924' with introduction and notes by J. C. Kenna, in *Mind*, LXXV, No. 299 (July 1966). Page references to this are to Kenna. The letters from Bradley to James are in the Houghton Library at Harvard. Substantial extracts from some of these were published in *The Thought and Character of William James* ed. R. B. Perry, vol. II, as indicated by references to Perry below. (Perry did not know that James's letters to Bradley were still extant.)

I do not believe that the correspondence contains anything of philosophical importance not adequately expressed in what James and Bradley said about each other in published works, but it certainly gives enjoyable additional expression to it and adds something to our picture of their personalities, especially that of Bradley (in particular, of how his health disturbed his philosophical work). They also show Bradley regularly referring to himself as a 'pantheist'.

For my access to Bradley's letters to James via photocopies I have to thank the Curator of the Houghton library (Mr Rodney Dennis), and also Dr I. K. Skrupskelis (who is editing a twelve-volume edition of *The Correspondence of William James* for the University of Virginia Press). The following is, I believe, a complete list of at least the extant correspondence, with some notes upon its contents and quotations.

Letters between James and Bradley

4 June (and 16) 1895   Bradley to James

'Dear Sir'. Bradley opened the correspondence between himself and James with this letter about James's article, 'The Knowing Things of Things Together', which had appeared in *The Psychological Review* that year (and of which perhaps James had sent him an offprint, though his reply to this shows he had not written). Among other things, Bradley argues that James is unclear what it means for an idea to point to its object. Can a dog understand a signpost? He encloses two papers, evidently 'What Do We Mean by the Intensity of Psychical States?', and 'In What Sense Are Psychical States Extended?', both published in *Mind* [1895], reprinted in CE, essays XIX and XXI.

9 July 1895   James to Bradley   [Kenna, pp. 311–14]

'Dear Mr. Bradley'. James emphasises the sense of smooth continuity experienced between an idea and an object which answers to it. Years ago (in 'The Function of Cognition') he had argued that this was the key to understanding 'intending' and 'pointing' and, though Royce temporarily beat him out of it, 'further pondering has bro't me back to wallow in the same mire'.

> I look forward to my future dealings with your *Appearance and Reality* as one of the great tasks of the rest of my life. I have only read it once, and must confess to a temperamental mistrust of the dialectics and inner inconsistencies of things and their relations, the 'between' business, etc. Nevertheless that is the central pivot of metaphysics and you have for the first time brought it fairly and squarely into the middle of English philosophy, from which henceforward it can never be removed.

22 August 1895   Bradley to James

'Dear Professor James'. About his style as a writer (re a comment by James on the greater friendliness to opponents shown by his letter than in his publications) and response to James's suggestion that his account of mental intensity implies the mind dust theory (in which case it would certainly be wrong).

21 September 1897   Bradley to James   [Perry, pp. 238–40]

'Dear Sir'. A long letter about free will and chance, and theism versus pantheism, evoked by reading James's *The Will to Believe*. Also some remarks about psychical research and the defects of F. W. H. Myers.

> I dont believe that morality ever accepted chance except as a refuge from fate, or ever in its own character. I believe it always means by freedom an internal principle not moved by the extraneous nor a mere external result of and dependency on anything but itself. Now this is not chance at all nor has anything to do with it. If I am once started on my own bottom and with a nature of my own, I believe that this is all morality asks for for freedom, and that it is perfectly consistent with the strictest law. To ask "Could it have been otherwise when *all* the conditions are taken in?" is, I believe, not a *moral* question at all,

nor one ever raised by morality. My self once there is part of the conditions and is what it is and is responsible for what it does. That is how I read the moral consciousness.

The trouble, I believe, has been mainly caused by the moral (or immoral) Creator. Once tell a man that another fellow, however big, has made him to be and do what he is and does, and of course he throws it on the other fellow, and his poor morality goes to the devil or may do so. I dont understand a word of what you say about "possibilities," in connection with this other fellow, unless you mean to say that he's not a "Creator" at all, but somehow a limited struggling sort of chap like ourselves only bigger and better and loves us and tries to help us and we ought to stick to him. *That's* a moral doctrine if you like, and you may even say too He tried to make us to be like him as well as he could and he knew how—and that's moral or not *un*-moral again. But go further and I dont think you'll save either the morality of the personal God—or ours either, so far as we take him seriously and look on ourselves as his pottery. You must forgive me, but when I kicked the personal God off *my* premises, if I may say so, it wasn't wholly on intellectual grounds, and there is a pretty long bill against him on other accounts. I dont say he *cant* be whitewashed, though I doubt if that is one of the "all things" that are possible with a personal God—but I dont believe *I* shall ever see it done. But "blasphemy is not argument" you are perhaps remarking to yourself. Only I get indignant when I see it assumed right and left that what is called "pantheism" is nowhere morally, compared with theism and find it difficult not to break out in print. But I won't do that for I dont want to do harm and God knows I have no gospel (I wish I had) either for others or myself. And I know very well that a creed is practically what one makes of it justly or unjustly, and what matters so long as one "saves one's soul" as they say? So I try to say nothing—having hardly saved mine, if at all. . . .

Of course (to return to the moral creator) I too believe that it is natural and necessary in religion to relate oneself to a Will which desires and wills what is right. I think this attitude is also justifiable. It is also true, I believe, that the same Power, which appears as this Will for good, is also that to which our being and the being of the world is due. But it is *not* true, I think, that these aspects can be lumped together so that you can say "The God that speaks to my conscience did *as such* make me and the world." And here I am at a loss altogether what to say to the non-philosophical. He, unless he saves himself (as he usually does) by mere confusion, is led naturally to doctrines which I find abominable e.g. that a moral agent designed sinners like myself and in short planned the evil of the world and is responsible for it. For from that conclusion you most assuredly cannot escape logically unless you will degrade the Creator to a limited moral Demiurge and so break wholly with Christianity and the predestination to sin which it entails. Yes and by Theism I would say things are even in one way made worse, for the Christian distinction of persons within the Deity is the one safe road, if it could have [been] followed out rationally. So that for my part I say nothing, only I feel inclined to protest against a moral Creator, I who in youth was "vexatus toties" by him and his—almost as badly as you seem to have been vexed by Hegel and his disciples. I dont think much of the disciples myself.

3 January 1898   James to Bradley   [Kenna, pp. 314–17]
Dear Brother Bradley,
—If you will allow this familiar mode of address from one who in spite of the

extremity of *odium metaphysicum* feels much nearer allied to you than to the non-metaphysical herd . . .

On the sense in which he believes in objective chance; its importance is not as underpinning moral responsibility but as showing that evil is not intrinsically necessary to the universe.

> . . . I confess that even after reading the chapter in your Ethical Studies (many years ago) my mind did not grow quite clear. In fact it has always seemed to me (doubtless from the lack of some 'quickening' on the subject) that this whole aspect of ethics is relatively unimportant. The *deep* questions which the moral life suggest are metaphysical: 1) Is evil *real*? 2) Is it *essential* to the universe? If these questions are to be answered with a yes I care not who is responsible, or may be called so.

24 February 1898   Bradley to James
'Dear Brother James'. Mainly about James's unsatisfactory and surely, to the ordinary man, unappealing belief that chance is fundamental in the universe.

> I think probably I am not clear in my mind as to the ultimate qualitative diversity of the Universe, and I venture to doubt if you are wholly clear about Chance. It is, I presume, certain that the tidings that the last things in the world go, or may go, by chance, would be received by "the plain man" with horror.

4 July 1904   Bradley to James   [Perry, p. 486]
'Dear Professor James'. This explains that some of the animadversions in Bradley's 'On Truth and Practice' about to appear in the July issue of *Mind* inadvertently show less respect for James's work than he intended. It is his distaste for James's fellow pragmatist, F. C. S. Schiller which lies behind this.

16 July 1904,   James to Bradley   [Kenna, pp. 318–20]
'Dear Mr. Bradley'. No need to 'stroke my fur down' over 'On Truth and Practice' of which Stout sent him a proof and to which he has sent a response ('Humanism and Truth', *Mind* [1904]). Defends Schiller from Bradley's charge of constant self-advertisement and urges Bradley to integrate pragmatism into his absolutism as Royce has done. James kept a copy of most of this letter. It is headed 'Extracts from letter to Bradley of June [sic] 16, 1904' and is now in the Houghton library collection.

> The doctrine of your Admirable *Logic* is that reality is the primal *that* of which all our *whats* are determinations . . . The ultimate that, according to Schiller, is a ὕλη which, as you say we rarely 'encounter', and which we handle by our predicates,—as best we may. This is perfectly compatible in my eyes with your Absolute, since you expressly deny that our predicates *copy* the latter; and your notion of 'truth' as relative to the final *amount of translation* into Absoluteness which all our predicates in the end require, can simply *add* itself to the humanistic notion thereof. I do not believe in your Absolute, neither does Schiller; but nothing debars you from believing in our humanism, bag and

baggage—you need only throw your Absolute round it, and give yourself the richer world you require.

27 July 1904   Bradley to James

'Dear Professor James'. On Schiller and on the meaning of 'man' in humanism.

15 October 1904   Bradley to James   [Perry, pp. 488–99]

'Dear Professor James'. Remarks on James's 'Humanism and Truth' (published in *Mind* [1904]) of which James had sent him a proof.

> Certainly I agree very largely with your view, that is, with a large amount of it. You must remember that I was brought up in that development of Kantianism which ended in Humanism or at least was said to end in it. That there was no reality beyond human experience and no possibility of copying or following anything from the outside was a sort of watchword even. "No Transcendence" in short.
>
> For myself I have had in some respects to diverge from this "Humanism" as I received it.

6 November 1904   James to Bradley   [Kenna, p. 321]

Wrongly dated 6 October. Opens 'My dear Bradley (can't we drop the handles to our names?)'. Again urges Bradley to incorporate some of the relativism of humanism into his absolutism.

16 November 1904   Bradley to James

'My dear James'. Expresses unclarity as to how pragmatism, humanism, and relativism are meant to be related. Bradley stresses the difficulty of a conception for which human experience is identical with reality.

> Of course I, for instance, hold that, to be true or good for me, something must prevail in me. About two years ago I e.g. wrote a chapter (of a book which will never I fear be written) the thesis of which was that for me my last judgement is infallibly true. [This would seem to be ETR, chapter XIII, first published in *Mind* in 1908.] But the question is whether this is all there is in it, and whether you must not either hold to something more than *mere* prevalence, or else give up in your theory the whole world of "objective values", which no one outside of theory is going to give up.
>
> You can of course fall back on the gattungsbewusstsein and take that seriously, but here your pluralism is in danger at once, and in any case there are terrible difficulties in the way of identifying humanity and reality, and I don't see how you meet them.
>
> Where I am with you wholly is that the end for man is the realization of human nature and that nothing else can interfere. I think it likely that I am with you very largely otherwise, but it is hard to know where you are at present.

25 November 1904   Bradley to James   [Perry, p. 637]

'Dear James'. Comments on James's 'Does Consciousness Exist?', and 'A

World of Pure Experience', which James has sent him (both just published in *Journal of Philosophy* [1904]). James misrepresents the conception of the Absolute by overemphasis on unity at the cost of differentiation. And his view of objective reference 'it seems to me, will never do'.

> I can't admit that I don't know about New York because I am never going there. I know *now* if I know at all. And the introduction of "virtual" doesn't help me.

22 January 1905   James to Bradley   [Kenna, pp. 322–23]
   'My dear Bradley',

> I duly got your highly interesting letter of Nov. 25th, but delayed answering it till I should be able to send also a reprint of an article criticizing *you*, the bogey and bugbear of most of my beliefs. But the article ['The Thing and its Relations', *Journal of Philosophy* [1905]] hung back, and is only now sent, so the letter can go too.

His objections to the Absolute may apply more to Royce than to Bradley.

2 February 1905   Bradley to James
   'Dear James'. Thanks him for three articles he has sent (evidently 'The Experience of Activity', *Psychological Review* [January 1905]; 'The Thing and its Relations', *Journal of Philosophy* [January 1905]; and possibly 'How Two Minds Can Know One Thing', to be published in *Journal of Philosophy*, in April). Unfortunately his kidney inflammation too bad for much philosophising.

8 February 1905   Bradley to James
   'My dear James'. Will take account of Schiller's views (as James had urged him to do in the letter of 22 January) if they are ever clearly stated.

28 April 1905   Bradley to James   [Perry, pp. 489–90]
   'Dear James'. Thanks him for all the papers sent. Hopes to attend seriously hereafter to the two papers mostly about himself, presumably 'The Thing and Its Relations' and perhaps 'The Experience of Activity'. A long critical discussion of James's radical empiricism follows. Bradley complains (1) that the meaning of experience is unclear and that the appeal to possible experience only fudges things; (2) that the relation between different selves is unclear; (3) that the possibility of transcendent knowledge and avoidance of solipsism is not solved. (James sent this letter to Schiller and Schiller's notes on it are attached to the letter.)

> The finite selves [on James's view] seem to be constituted by the presence at certain parts of the great flow (of the One Experience) of other elements. The identity of the contents of the Universal Stream plus the addition of floating superimposed diversities (bubbles or eddies) *makes* the finite selves, while they really and veritably arise and perish utterly.

This you *cannot* mean, but this is what arises in my mind as I read you. Of course we have here no Pluralism but an extreme Monism—only the Absolute here is a Stream or Flux. . . .

If the ordinary Pluralist who stands on Experience is asked "Here are you James, with a felt experience of your own. How are you going to transcend it so as to speak of the Universe of other persons and things and talk about it as one"? This ordinary Pluralist is in a difficulty. At least I am accustomed to think so.

If however he can say 'As I already *am* the others' world as well as my own, I have not to transcend my contents in order to know the Universe[']—he is in a very different position. The interesting thing is that he is, so far, exactly in the position of the 'Absolutist.' For he, (though you will not have it so) is not leaving his own actual experience to seek the Absolute (the real World). He has the Absolute there in experience from the first, and the only question with him is as to how far the first experience he has is merely a first experience to be replaced by a fuller one. As to going outside or looking outside—that believe me or not believe me—is to him out of the question. It is one of his condemned heresies.

And so it will interest me not a little to see how this Real Identity of the One in the Many in Being and Knowledge is going to be used so as to forward your conclusions. But again I imagine myself here to be under a misapprehension. What I fail to see is how you answer the question as to how you or I is able to talk about the Universe and how you dispose of Solipsism?

Have we one great immediate experience containing all things and selves? If so, how does the one self among others know the whole?

24 May 1905   Bradley to James
'Dear James'. Bradley resists a suggestion that his letter of 28th April be published.

3 June 1905   Bradley to James
'Dear James'. This thanks James for a note he had evidently left for Bradley while spending one night at Oxford. (James was only in England for a couple of days on his return from a philosophical congress in Rome.) Bradley regrets that bad health on both their parts prevented a meeting. He continues to resist the idea of publishing his letter of 28 April, though James may quote it without naming Bradley if he wishes.

10 April 1907   Bradley to James
'Dear James'. About his article, 'Truth and Copying' (ETR, chapter V) which has just come out in *Mind* and of which he will be sending an offprint.

22 April 1907   James to Bradley   [Kenna, pp. 324—25]
'Dear Mr. Bradley'. Succinct statement of some of the differences between them; will be sending his volume *Pragmatism*.

I believe that your general conception of truth in the singular as a sort of entity trying to identify itself with reality, and of reality as a ditto trying to idealize itself into truth, is a perfectly true description of the state of affairs that exists, but too abstract a description to do much work of detail withal, and issuing (I think in your own case) only in a sort of divine discontent.

6 May 1907   Bradley to James

'Dear Professor James'. Thanks James for sending two articles, apparently 'Pragmatism's Conception of Truth' (*Journal of Philosophy* [1907], later chapter VI of *Pragmatism*) and 'The Energies of Men' (*Philosophical Review* [1907]). He finds it hard to say whether he is a pragmatist or not. There seems to be an ambiguity as to whether a true idea must work for the individual or only in the long run. Bradley is virtually a pragmatist if the latter is meant. Is struck by what James has to say in the other article by how little is known about this aspect of human psychology.

> I am myself quite lost when I begin to wonder how much of the energy which the average European man takes in is wasted, and how much his output could be increased . . . . Experiments like Xtian Science are bound to kill a few people I suppose but the result may be worth it. But I begin to maunder.

14 July 1907   Bradley to James

'Dear Professor James'. Thanks for the copy of *Pragmatism* James has sent him.

21 March 1908   Bradley to James

'Dear Professor James'. Thanks him for 'The Meaning of the Word Truth' (privately printed, published in *Mind* in July) and 'The Pragmatist Account of Truth and its Misunderstanders' *Philosophical Review* [1908]. He still finds it hard to know precisely what pragmatism claims. Has at last finished his 'On Our Knowledge of Immediate Experience', *Mind* [1909], ETR, chapter VI—'a beastly obscure subject and I have an uneasy feeling that I have been manufacturing further obscurity instead of helping to dispel it'.

3 February 1909   Bradley to James   [Perry, p. 638]

'Dear Professor James'. Some remarks on spiritualism but mainly about James's paper on Fechner (*Hibbert Journal* [1909]; later chapter IV of *A Pluralistic Universe)* and how Fechner weaned Bradley from too humanistic a view. How does this stand to James's 'humanism'?

> Fechner's arguments to my mind don't *prove* much more than does Shelley's Sensitive Plant and the visions of the later part of his Prometheus. But so far as I was concerned they helped to take me back to a wider form of pantheism. I don't see *any* connection in principle between Absolute Idealism and the giving the highest place to human beings. That strikes me as a onesidedness which came historically but is not logical at all.

25 March 1909   Bradley to James   [Perry, pp. 490—91]

'Dear Professor James'. Thanks James for sending his review of Marcel

Hébert's book on pragmatism (*Philosophical Review* [1908]; *The Meaning of Truth*, chapter XII). Still does not know whether he (and Hegel) were pragmatists. The true is, indeed, what works best in the long run, but it may not be best for the individual, even though his life is part of the Absolute's fulfilment. This, indeed, was really Hegel's view, and it avoids subjectivism as pragmatism does not. Another difference lies in pragmatism's calling ideas true when their 'working' is not theoretical. But the issue here may be partly verbal, in which case pragmatists should not be so sharp with their opponents.

4 May 1909   Bradley to James
'Dear James'. What counts as practice—'wretched' word? Do aesthetically pleasing ideas work practically as such?

14 May 1909   Bradley to James   [Perry, pp. 638]
'Dear James'. A long letter on James's *A Pluralistic Universe,* which James had kindly sent him. Suggests that in their old controversy on identity they quite misunderstood each other because Bradley thought James was denying identity altogether, while James thought Bradley was arguing for an abstract identity which excludes difference. Bradley's view is that identity and difference are incoherent but necessary ideas.

Bradley also points out that for many pantheistic monists the Absolute is no mere witness of the universe. Thus for Hegel it is also its substance and will. There is also much discussion of the idea of a finite God. Bradley suggests that James's view is more a form of Manichaeanism than of Christianity, though he also finds traces of a monism inconsistent with this. It is unclear, at any rate, how far he really believes in fully external relations 'which make *no* difference to their terms'; they seem to be incompatible with the stress on continuity which he shares with his supposed monistic opponents.

30 May 1909   Bradley to James   [Perry, pp. 491—92]
'Dear James'. Remarks on James's 'On a Very Prevalent Abuse of Abstraction' which James had sent him. (*Popular Science Monthly* [1909]; reprinted as 'Abstractionism and "Relativismus"' in *The Meaning of Truth*). Does the thesis that thought is moving to a consensus which is truth absolute have any firmer basis than observation of the experience 'of a few passing parasites on a speck of dust'?

30 June 1909   Bradley to James
'Dear James'. Thanks him for his letter (evidently lost). This continues to challenge James as to whether his humanism implies that reality is identical with human experience:

> I understand more or less, I think, the position of a man who identifies reality with human history either absolutely or to the extent of saying that nothing else matters in any sense. But it is an extreme paradoxical doctrine, I should say, and the breach between it and ordinary views is wide. And if I attributed this doctrine to you I should certainly be told I was wrong.

On the other hand nothing *less* than this paradox is of any use to you so far as I see.

17 September 1909   Bradley to James
'Dear James'. Note accompanying copy of *Ethical Studies* sent simply for him to recall Bradley's views on freedom and character in chapter I.

17 October 1909   Bradley to James
'Dear James'. Thanks James for sending him a copy of *The Meaning of Truth*. Will be sending him offprints of 'On Truth and Coherence' and 'Coherence and Contradiction' (published that year in *Mind* [ETR, chapters VII and VIII]; also writing, with difficulty, the supplementary note on Russell to 'On Appearance, Error and Contradiction', *Mind* [1910; ETR, chapter IX]).

23 November 1909   James to Bradley   [Kenna, pp. 326—27]
'Dear Bradley'. There is an emotional divide between them as to whether ideas or experience are more important.

25 November 1909   James to Bradley   [Kenna, pp. 327—28]
'Dear Bradley'. How well equipped Bradley is to be the Moses to lead English thought from the wilderness of intellectualist error towards knowledge through immediate feeling à la Bergson—the idea James expressed later in 'Bradley or Bergson?'

14 December 1909   Bradley to James
'Dear James'. Bradley admits that he may sometimes in his publications have

laid too much emphasis on the imperfection of all truth and all reality, forgetting perhaps at times that I believe quite as much in relative degrees of perfection and of our power and duty to produce these, both in the intellectual world and also outside it.

23 December 1909   James to Bradley   [Kenna, p. 329]
'Dear James'. Is sending him a proof of 'Bradley or Bergson?' (This was published in *Journal of Philosophy* [1910].)

2 January 1910   Bradley to James   [Perry, p. 641]
'Dear James'. On various aspects of *The Meaning of Truth* and on the status of past and future for radical empiricism and pragmatism.

You seem (e.g) to ask me to believe in a real past fact independent of present experience. Of course I reject such a thing. Of course I at once ask you how, even if it existed, you could know that it existed and get it into your mind.... You hint at a solution in the future by the arrival at a point where the past is swallowed up and so becomes accessible.... But (i) this seems to me to carry the unreality of Time, and (ii) It does *not* solve the problem of how, *before* this happens, you can get at the past in any sense. For that you want a present experience and reality in and by which the past is. And how can *you* accept that?

4 January 1910   Bradley to James   [Perry, p. 643]
'Dear James'. Thanks for the proof of 'Bradley or Bergson?' He is not aware of any sufficiently clear cut issue to be able to reply to it.

17 January 1910   James to Bradley   [Kenna, pp. 329–30]
'Dear Bradley'. Sadly acknowledges the great gulf that divides them as thinkers, after he had been hoping for a coalescence.

> It is enough to make the angels either weep or explode with laughter to see how hard it is for two philosophers to coalesce. You had seemed to me lately in so 'promising' a state of mind that I actually began to have hopes of your reaching port on the pragmatist tack before I should have time to overtake you! But what foolish hopes! Your two letters of the 2nd and 4th arrive today, and pulverize them. I realize from what, a different (and to me unapproachable) centre of thought you take your aim . . .

28 January 1910   Bradley to James   [Perry, p. 644]
'Dear James'. James should not mind so much as 'philosophy gets on quite as well by misunderstandings as by anything else'.

10 February 1910   Bradley to James
Opens directly. He is not replying to 'Bradley or Bergson?' beyond writing a note to the *Journal of Philosophy*, disclaiming any originality in breaking away from the Kantian notion that immediate feeling is disconnected, as he owes it to Hegel. (This was published in the *Journal* in March, and may be found at CE, p. 695.)

James died in August of that year, Bradley in 1924.

Bibliography and Chronology

1. Abbreviations of the Works of James

BC   *Psychology: Briefer Course*. London: Macmillan and Co., 1892.

CER   *Collected Essays and Reviews*. London: Longmans, Green and Co., 1920.

ECR   *Essays, Comments and Reviews*. Cambridge, Mass.: Harvard University Press, 1987.*

EP   *Essays in Philosophy*. Cambridge, Mass.: Harvard University Press, 1978.*

ERE   *Essays in Radical Empiricism*. New York: Longmans, Green and Co., 1922.

ERM   *Essays in Religion and Morality*. Cambridge, Mass.: Harvard University Press, 1982.*

Kenna   'Ten Unpublished Letters from William James, 1842–1910 to Francis Herbert Bradley, 1846–1924' with introduction and notes by J. C. Kenna, in *Mind*, LXXV, No. 299 (July 1966).

Letters   *The Letters of William James*. Edited by his son Henry James. 2 vols. London: Longmans, Green and Co., 1920.

MS   *Memories and Studies*. New York: Longmans, Green and Co., 1924.

MEN   *Manuscript Essays and Notes.* Cambridge, Mass.: Harvard University Press, 1988.*

MT   *The Meaning of Truth.* Cambridge, Mass.: Harvard University Press, 1975.*

Perry   *The Thought and Character of William James: As Revealed in Unpublished Correspondence and Notes, Together with His Published Writings.* By R. B. Perry. 2 vols. Boston: Little Brown and Company, 1935.

Perry 1948   *The Thought and Character of William James: Briefer Version.* By R. B. Perry. Cambridge, Mass.: Harvard University Press, 1948.

PRAG   *Pragmatism: A New Name for Some Old Ways of Thinking.* New York: Longmans, Green and Co., 1937.

PP   *The Principles of Psychology.* 2 vols. London: Macmillan and Co., 1901.

PU   *A Pluralistic Universe.* New York: Longmans, Green and Co., 1909.

SPP   *Some Problems of Philosophy: A Beginning of an Introduction to Philosophy.* New York: Longmans, Green and Co., 1928.

VRE   *The Varieties of Religious Experience: A Study in Human Nature.* Edited by John J. McDermott. Harmondsworth: Penguin Books Ltd, 1985.

WB   *The Will to Believe and Other Essays in Popular Philosophy.* New York: Longmans, Green and Co., 1923.

* In the series of The Works of William James, ed. Frederick H. Burkhardt, et al. (Cambridge, Mass.: Harvard University Press). The pagination of all other editions used is that of the first edition. The Harvard Works indicate how their pagination is related to this.

2. *James Chronology*

The following lists the dates of first publication of the main books and articles by William James referred to in the text with dates of first publication, indicating collections in which articles can be found. (Articles largely incorporated into books proper, rather than collections of papers, are not listed.) For details of original publication see *The Writings of William James*, ed. John J. McDermott

(Chicago and London: The University of Chicago Press, 1977), and *William James: Writings 1902–1910,* ed. Bruce Kuklick (New York: The Library of America, 1987).

1842	BIRTH
1878	'Remarks on Spencer's Definition of Mind as Correspondence' [CER and EP]
1879	'The Sentiment of Rationality' [WB and EP]
1881	'Reflex Action and Theism' [WB]
1882	'On Some Hegelisms' [WB]
1884	Introduction to *The Literary Remains of the late Henry James* [ERM]
1885	'The Function of Cognition' [MT]
1890	*The Principles of Psychology*
1891	'The Moral Philosopher and the Moral Life' [WB]
1892	*Psychology: Briefer Course*
1893	'Mr. Bradley on Immediate Resemblance'[CER and EP]
1893	'Immediate Resemblance' [CER and EP]
1895	'The Knowing of Things Together' [CER and EP]
	This includes what became 'The Tigers in India' [MT]
1896	'Address of the President before the Society for Psychical Research' [partly reprinted WB as 'What Psychical Research has accomplished']
1896	'The Will to Believe' [WB]
1897	*The Will to Believe and Other Essays in Popular Philosophy*
1898	'Philosophical Conceptions and Practical Results' [CER]
	Human Immortality; Two Supposed Objections to the Doctrine. The Ingersoll lecture at Harvard University, 2nd ed. with additional material published 1899 [ERM]
1899	*Talks to Teachers on Psychology: and to Students on Some of Life's Ideals*
1902	*The Varieties of Religious Experience: A Study in Human Nature*
1903	Review of *Personal Idealism,* ed. H. Sturt in *Mind* [ECR]
1904	Introduction to M. C. Wadsworth's translation of G. T. Fechner's *Little Book of Life after Death* [ERM]
1904	'Does Consciousness Exist?' [ERE]
1904	'A World of Pure Experience' [ERE]
1904	'Humanism and Truth' [MT]
1905	'The Experience of Activity [ERE, and partly in PU]
1905	'The Thing and its Relations' [PU and ERE]
1905	'The Essence of Humanism' [MT]
1905	'How Two Minds Can Know One Thing' [ERE]
1905	'Humanism and Truth Once More' [ERE]
1905	'Is Radical Empiricism Solipsistic' [ERE]
1905	'The Place of Affectional Facts in a World of Pure Experience [ERE]
1905	'La Notion de Conscience' [ERE]
1905–8	'The Miller-Bode Notebook' [MEN]
1906	'The Mad Absolute' [1920–21 and EP]
1906	'Mr. Pitkin's Refutation of "Radical Empiricism" [ERE]

1907	'A Reply to Mr. Pitkin' [ERE]
1907	'A Word More about Truth' [MT]
1907	'Professor Pratt on Truth' [MT]
1907	'The Absolute and the Strenuous Life' [MT]
1907	*Pragmatism: A New Name for Some Old Ways of Thinking*
1908	'The Pragmatist Account of Truth and its Misunderstanders' [MT]
1908	'"Truth" versus "Truthfulness"' [reprinted in MT as 'The Existence of Julius Caesar']
1908	'The Meaning of the Word Truth' [MT]
1909	*A Pluralistic Universe*
1909	'Two English Critics' [MT]
1909	'On a Very Prevalent Abuse of Abstraction' [in MT as 'Abstraction and "Relativismus"']
1909	'The Confidences of a Psychical Researcher' [in CER as 'Final Impressions of a Psychical Researcher']
1909	*The Meaning of Truth: A Sequel to "Pragmatism"*
1910	'Bradley or Bergson?' [CER and EP]
1910	'A Suggestion about Mysticism' [CER and EP]
1910	'A Pluralistic Mystic' [in CER and EP]
1910	DEATH
1911	*Some Problems of Philosophy: A Beginning of an Introduction to Philosophy*
1911	*Memories and Studies*
1912	*Essays in Radical Empiricism*
1920	*Collected Essays and Reviews*
1975–	*The Works of William James*, Harvard Critical edition.

3. Abbreviations of the Works of F. H. Bradley

AR	*Appearance and Reality: A Metaphysical Essay.* Oxford: Clarendon Press, 1930.
ETR	*Essays in Truth and Reality.* Oxford: Clarendon Press, 1968.
PL	*The Principles of Logic.* 2nd ed., 2 vols. Oxford University Press, 1963. The 1922 second edition includes additional notes and *Terminal Essays.*
ES	*Ethical Studies.* Oxford: Clarendon Press, 1927.
CE	*Collected Essays.* Oxford: Clarendon Press, 1969.

4. Bradley Chronology

The following lists the dates of first publication of the books and articles by F. H. Bradley referred to in the text with dates of first publication. The articles are all reprinted either in ETR or CE as indicated; for details of original publication see CE, pp. 698–99.

1846	BIRTH
1874	*The Presuppositions of Critical History* [CE, essay I]
1876	*Ethical Studies* (1st ed.)
1883	*The Principles of Logic* (1st ed.)
1885	'The Evidences of Spiritualism' [CE, essay XXIX]
1887	'Association and Thought' [CE, essay XII]
1888	'On Pleasure, Pain, Desire and Volition' [CE, essay XIV]
1893	'On Professor James's Doctrine of Simple Resemblance', I, II, and III [CE, essays XV, XVI, XVII]
1893	*Appearance and Reality: A Metaphysical Essay* (1st ed.)
1894	'Some Remarks on Punishment' [CE, essay VII]
1897	*Appearance and Reality: A Metaphysical Essay* (2nd ed. with an appendix)
1899	'Some Remarks on Memory and Inference' [ETR, chapter XII]
1901	'Some Remarks on Conation' [CE, essay XXIII]
1902–3	'The Definition of Will', I, II, and III [CE, essays XXVI, XXVII, XXVIII]
1904	'On Truth and Practice' [ETR, chapter IV]
1906	'On Floating Ideas and the Imaginary' [ETR, chapter III]
1907	'On Truth and Copying' [ETR, chapter V]
1908	'On Memory and Judgement' [ETR, chapter XIII]
1908	'On the Ambiguity of Pragmatism' [ETR, chapter V; Appendix 1]
1909	'On our Knowledge of Immediate Experience' [ETR, chapter VI]
1909	'On Truth and Coherence' [ETR, chapter VII]
1909	'Coherence and Contradiction' [ETR, chapter VIII]
1910	'On Appearance, Error, and Contradiction' [ETR, chapter VIII]
1911	'On some Aspects of Truth' [ETR, chapter XI]
1911	'On Professor James's *Meaning of Truth*' [ETR V, chapter; Appendix II]
1911	'Reply to Mr Russell's Explanations' [ETR, chapter IX; Supp. Note 3]
1911	'Faith' [ETR, chapter II]
1914	*Essays on Truth and Reality*
1922	*The Principles of Logic* (2nd ed.)
1924	DEATH
1924	'Relations' (first published as CE, essay XXXII)
1927	*Ethical Studies* (2nd ed.)
1930	*Aphorisms*

5. *Bibliography*

References in the text to these books or articles are by name of the author alone in capitals, where only one work by him is listed, or accompanied by some obvious abbreviation of its title where more than one is so.

Abbreviations:

| PAS | *Proceedings of the Aristotelian Society* |
| PASS | *Proceedings of the Aristotelian Society, Supplementary Volume* |

Allard, James. 'Bradley's Principle of Sufficient Reason' in Manser and Stock.

Allen, Gay Wilson. *William James: A Biography*. London: Rupert Hart-Davies, 1967

Austin, J. L. *Sense and Sensibilia*. Oxford: Clarendon Press, 1962.

Armstrong, David. *Perception and the Physical World*. London: Routledge and Kegan Paul, 1961.

———. *A Materialist Theory of the Mind*. London: Routledge and Kegan Paul, 1968.

Ayer, A. J. *Language, Truth and Logic*. rev. ed. London: Victor Gollancz, 1946.

———. *Russell and Moore: The Analytical Heritage*. London: Macmillan, 1971.

———. *Philosophical Essays*. London: Macmillan, 1954.

———. *The Central Questions of Philosophy*. London: Penguin Books, 1973.

———. *The Foundations of Empirical Knowledge*. London: Macmillan, 1940.

———. *The Origins of Pragmatism: Studies in the Philosophy of Charles Sanders Peirce and William James*. London: Macmillan, 1968.

Baldwin, Thomas S. 'Phenomenology and Egocentric Thought'. PASS, LXII (1988).

Bergson, Henri. *L'Évolution Créatrice* (first published 1907, reprinted in *Oeuvres*).

———. *Essai sur Les Données Immédiates de la Conscience* (first published 1889, reprinted in *Oeuvres*).

———. *Les Deux Sources de la morale et de la religion* (first published in 1932, reprinted in *Ouevres*).

———. *Oeuvres*. Paris: Presses Universitaires de France, 1959.

Bird, Graham. *William James*. London and New York: Routledge and Kegan Paul, 1986.

Bjork, Daniel W. *The Compromised Scientist: William James in the Development of American Psychology*. New York: Columbia University Press, 1983.

Blanshard, Brand. *Reason and Analysis*. London: Allen and Unwin, 1962.

————. 'Bradley on Relations' in Manser and Stock.

Bode, Henry. '"Pure Experience" and the External World'. *Journal of Philosophy*, II (March 1905): 128–33. [ERE, chapter IX: 'Is Radical Empiricism Solipsistic?' is a reply to this.]

————. 'Cognitive Experience and its Object'. *Journal of Philosophy*, II (November 23, 1905).

————. 'The Concept of Pure Experience'. *Philosophical Review*, XIV (November 1905).

Bosanquet, Bernard. *Knowledge and Reality.* London: Kegan Paul, Trench and Co., 1885.

————. *Logic or the Morphology of Knowledge.* 2nd ed. London: Oxford University Press, London, 1911 (1st ed., 1888).

————. *The Principle of Individuality and Value.* London: Macmillan, 1912.

Brentano, Franz. *The True and the Evident.* Edited by Oskar Kraus; translated by R. M. Chisholm, et al. London: Routledge and Kegan Paul, 1966.

————. *Psychology from an Empirical Standpoint.* Translated by A. C. Rancurello, et al. London: Routledge and Kegan Paul, 1973. First published 1874.

Broad, C. D. *The Mind and its Place in Nature.* London: Routledge and Kegan Paul, 1923.

————. *Scientific Thought.* London: Routledge and Kegan Paul, 1923.

Browning, D. S. *Pluralism and Personality: William James and Some Contemporary Cultures of Psychology.* Lewisburg, Penn.: Bucknell University Press, 1980.

Candlish, Stewart, 'The Truth about F. H. Bradley'. *Mind,* XCVIII (July 1989).

Čapek, Milič. 'The Reappearance of the Self in the Last Philosophy of William James'. *Philosophical Review,* LXII (1953).

Carroll, Lewis. 'What the tortoise said to Achilles'. *Mind,* N.S. IV (1895).

Cook, Daniel J. 'James's "Ether Mysticism" and Hegel'. *Journal for the History of Philosophy* (1977).

Davies, Martin. 'Perceptual Content and Local Supervenience'. PAS, XCII (1991/92).

Davidson, Donald. *Inquiries into Truth and Interpretation*. Oxford: Clarendon Press, 1984.

Dennett, Daniel C. *Consciousness Explained*. Boston: Little, Brown and Company, 1991.

Deugd, C. De. *The Significance of Spinoza's First Kind of Knowledge*. Assen, The Netherlands: Van Gorcum & Co., 1966.

Dummett, Michael: *Frege, Philosophy of Language*. London: Duckworth, 1981.

———. *Truth and Other Enigmas*. London: Duckworth, 1978.

Eisendrath, Craig. *The Unifying Moment: The Psychological Philosophy of William James and Alfred North Whitehead*. Cambridge, Mass.: Harvard University Press, 1971.

Eliot, T. S. *Knowledge and Experience*. London: Faber and Faber, 1964.

Evans, Gareth. *The Varieties of Reference*. London: Clarendon Press, 1982.

Fechner, Gustav T. *Little Book of Life after Death*. Translated by M. C. Wadsworth. Introduction by William James. Boston: Little, Brown and Co., 1904.

Feigl, Herbert, and Sellars, Wilfred, eds. *Readings in Philosophical Analysis*. New York: Appleton-Century-Crofts Inc., 1949.

Flew, Antony, ed. *Essays in Conceptual Analysis*. London: Macmillan and Co., 1960.

Flournoy, Th. *The Philosophy of William James*. London, New York: H. Holt and Co., 1917 (translated from the French of lectures given in Switzerland in 1910).

Ford, Marcus. *William James's Philosophy: A New Perspective*. Amherst: University of Massachusetts Press, 1982.

Geach, P. T. *Love, Truth and Immortality*. London: Hutchinson and Co., 1979.

Grayling, A. C. *Berkeley: The Central Arguments*. London: Duckworth, 1986; La Salle, Ill.: Open Court, 1986.

Grogin, R. C. *The Bergsonian Controversy in France, 1900–1914*. Calgary, B.C.: The University of Calgary Press, 1988.

Grossmann, Reinhardt. *The Structure of Mind*. Madison: University of Wisconsin Press. 1965.

Hahn, Lewis E., ed. *The Philosophy of Charles Hartshorne*. Library of Living Philosophers. Vol. 20. La Salle, Ill.: Open Court, 1991.

Hartshorne, Charles. *Creative Synthesis and Philosophic Method*. London: SCM Press Ltd, 1970.

———. 'The Case for Idealism'. *Philosophical Forum*, I, No. 1. n.s. (1968).

———. *The Logic of Perfection*. La Salle, Ill.: Open Court, 1962.

Hegel, G. W. F. *Science of Logic*. Translated by A. V. Miller. London: Allen and Unwin, 1969.

Hertz, Richard A. 'James and Moore: Two Perspectives on Truth'. *Journal of the History of Philosophy* (April 1971).

Hicks, Dawes. 'Mr Bradley's treatment of Nature'. *Mind*, XXXIV (1925).

Hobart, R. E. (Dickinson Miller). 'Freewill as Involving Determination and Inconceivable Without It '. *Mind*, XLIII (1934).

Holdcroft, David. 'Holism and Truth' in Manser and Stock.

Holt, Edwin, et al. *The New Realism: Cooperative Studies in Philosophy*. New York: Macmillan, 1912.

Honderich, Ted. *A Theory of Determinism: The Mind, Neuroscience, and Life-Hopes*. Oxford: Clarendon Press, 1988.

Hume, David, *Treatise of Human Nature*. Edited by L. A. Selby-Bigge. Oxford: Clarendon Press, 1888. First published 1739.

Husserl, Edmund. *Cartesian Meditations*. Translated by Dorion Cairns. The Hague: Martinus Nijhoff, 1969.

———. *Experience and Judgement*. Translated by J. S. Churchill and Karl Ameriks. Evanston, Ill.: Northwestern University Press, 1973.

———. *Formal and Transcendental Logic*. Translated by Dorion Cairns. The Hague: Martinus Nijhoff, 1978.

————. *Ideas, General Introduction to Phenomenology.* Translated by W. R. Boyce Gibson. London: Allen and Unwin Ltd, 1931.

————. *Logical Investigations.* Translated by J. N. Findlay. 2 vols. London and Henley: Routledge and Kegan Paul, 1900.

————. *Phenomenological Psychology.* Translated by J. Scanlon. The Hague: Martinus Nijhoff, The Hague, 1977.

————. *The Crisis of European Sciences and Transcendental Phenomenology.* Translated by David Carr. Evanston, Ill.: Northwestern University Press, 1970.

————. *The Phenomenology of Internal Time Consciousness.* Translated by James S. Churchill. Bloomington: Indiana University Press, 1966. First published in 1928.

Huxley, T. H. *Methods and Results.* Vol. IV of *Collected Essays.* London: Macmillan and Co. 1893.

Joachim, H. H. J. *The Nature of Truth.* Oxford: Clarendon Press, 1906.

Johnston, Mark. 'Is there a Problem about Persistence?' PASS (1987).

Kallen, H. M. *William James and Henri Bergson.* Chicago: University of Chicago Press, 1914.

Krauth, Robert. 'Varieties of Pragmatism'. *Mind,* XCIC (April 1990).

Kripke, Saul. *Naming and Necessity.* Oxford: Basil Blackwell, 1972, 1980.

Kuklick, Bruce. *The Rise of American Philosophy.* New Haven, Conn.: Yale University Press, 1977.

LePore, Ernest, ed. *Truth and Interpretation.* Oxford: Blackwell, 1986.

Levinson, H. Samuel. *The Religious Investigations of William James.* Chapel Hill: University of North Carolina Press, 1981.

————. *Science, Metaphysics and the Chance of Salvation: An Interpretation of the Thought of William James.* Missoula, Mont.: Scholars Press, 1978.

Lewis, C. I. *Mind and the World Order: Outline of a Theory of Knowledge.* New York: Dover Publications Inc., 1956. First published 1929.

Lewis, David. *Counterfactuals.* Oxford: Basil Blackwell, 1973.

Lovejoy, Arthur O. 'The Thirteen Pragmatisms'. *Journal of Philosophy*, V, Nos. 1–12 (1908).

Manser, A. *Bradley's Logic*. Oxford: Basil Blackwell, 1983.

Manser, Anthony, and Stock, Guy, eds. *The Philosophy of F. H. Bradley*. Oxford: Clarendon Press, 1984.

McDermott, John, ed. *The Writings of William James*. Chicago: University of Chicago Press, 1977.

McGinn, Colin. *Mental Content*. Oxford: Basil Blackwell, 1989.

McHenry, L. *Whitehead and Bradley: A Comparative Analysis*. Albany: State University of New York Press, 1992.

McNiven, Don. *Bradley's Moral Psychology*. Lewiston/Queenston: The Edwin Mellen Press, 1987.

McTaggart, J. M. E. *Philosophical Studies*. Edited by S. V. Keeling. London: Edward Arnold and Co., 1934.

———. *The Nature of Existence*. 2 vols. Cambridge University Press, 1921 and 1927.

Mead, George H. *The Philosophy of the Present*. La Salle, Ill.: Open Court, 1959. First published 1932.

Mellor, D. J. *Real Time*. Cambridge University Press, 1981.

Miller, Dickinson. 'Is There Not a Clear Solution of the Knowledge Problem?' (1937) in Miller, 1975.

———. *Philosophical Analysis and Human Welfare*. Edited by Lloyd Easton. Dordrecht, Holland: D. Reidel Publishing Company, 1975.

Moore, G. E. 'The Conception of Reality' in Moore, 1922.

———. *Philosophical Studies*. London: Routledge and Kegan Paul Ltd, 1922.

———. 'Professor James's "Pragmatism" '. PAS (1907–8). Reprinted in Moore, 1922.

———. 'The Refutation of Idealism'. *Mind*, N.S. XII (1903). Reprinted in Moore, 1922.

————. *Some Main Problems of Philosophy.* London: George Allen and Unwin, London, 1953. Text of lectures given in 1910–11.

Myers, F. W. H. *Human Personality and its Survival of Bodily Death.* 2 vols. New York: Longmans, Green and Co., 1903.

Myers, Gerald. *William James: His Life and Thought.* New Haven: Yale University Press, 1986.

Nagel, Thomas. *Mortal Questions.* Cambridge University Press, 1979.

Parfit, Derek. *Reasons and Persons.* Oxford: Clarendon Press, 1984.

Passmore, John. *A Hundred Years of British Philosophy.* London: Gerald Duckworth and Co. Ltd., 1957.

Peirce, C. S. *Collected Papers of Charles Sanders Peirce.* Edited by Charles Hartshorne and Paul Weiss. Vol. 4. Cambridge, Mass.: Harvard University Press, 1934.

Pettit, P., and McDowell, J. *Thought and Context.* Oxford: Clarendon Press, 1986.

Pratt, J. B. *What is Pragmatism?* New York: Macmillan, 1909.

Prior, A. N. 'Thank Goodness That's Over'. *Philosophy,* XXXIX (1959).

Putnam, Hilary. *Reason, Truth and History.* Cambridge: Cambridge University Press, 1981.

————. *Realism and Reason.* Cambridge University Press, 1981.

Quine, W. V. O. *Word and Object.* Cambridge, Mass.: MIT Press and New York: John Wiley and Sons, 1960.

————. *From a Logical Point of View.* Cambridge, Mass.: Harvard University Press, 1953.

————. *Methods of Logic.* London: Routledge and Kegan Paul, 1952.

Quinton, Anthony. 'Spaces and Times'. *Philosophy,* XXXVII (1962).

Rescher, Nicholas. *The Coherence Theory of Truth.* Oxford: Clarendon Press, 1973.

Roberts, George W., ed. *Bertrand Russell Memorial Volume.* London: Allen and Unwin, 1979.

Rorty, Richard. *The Consequences of Pragmatism*. Brighton: Harvester Press, 1982.

Royce, Josiah. *The Religious Aspect of Philosophy*. Gloucester, Mass.: Peter Smith, 1965. First published 1885.

——. *The World and the Individual*. First and second series. New York: Dover Publications, Inc., 1959. First published 1899 and 1901.

Russell, Bertrand. *Logic and Knowledge*. London: Allen and Unwin, 1958.

——. *Philosophical Essays*. London: George Allen and Unwin, 1960. First published 1910.

——. *The Principles of Mathematics*. London: Allen and Unwin Ltd., 1937. First published 1899 and 1901.

Santayana, George. *Character and Opinion in the United States*. London: Constable and Company Ltd., 1920.

——. *Scepticism and Animal Faith*. London: Constable and Company Ltd., 1923.

——. *The Realm of Essence*. London: Constable and Co., 1928.

——. *The Realm of Matter*. London: Constable and Co., 1923.

——. *The Realm of Truth*. London: Constable and Co., 1937.

——. *The Life of Reason*, Vol. V. *Reason in Science*. New York: Charles Scribner's Sons, 1906.

Scheffler, Israel. *Four Pragmatists*. London: Routledge and Kegan Paul, 1975.

Schiller F. C. S. essay in Sturt, 1902.

——. *Humanism: Philosophical Essays*. London: Macmillan and Co., 1903.

Schopenhauer, Arthur. *The World as Will and Representation*. Translated by E. J. Payne. Vols. 1–2. New York: Dover Publications Inc. 1966. First published 1818 and 1844.

Seargent, David A. J. *Plurality and Continuity: An Essay on G. F. Stout's Theory of Universals*. Dordrecht: Martinus Nijhoff, 1985.

Seddon, Keith. *Time: A Philosophical Treatment*. London: Croom Helm, London, 1987.

Smart, J. J. C. *Philosophy and Scientific Realism*. London: Routledge and Kegan Paul.

———. 'The Stream of Time' in Flew.

Sperry, Roger. *Science and Moral Priority*. Oxford: Basil Blackwell, 1983.

Sprigge, T. L. S. 'Bradley and Russell on Relations' in Roberts, 1979.

———. *Santayana: An Examination of his Philosophy*. London: Routledge and Kegan Paul, 1974.

———. *The Vindication of Absolute Idealism*. Edinburgh: Edinburgh University Press, 1983.

———. 'Final Causes'. PASS, XLV (1971).

———. 'Intrinsic Connectedness'. PAS (1987/88).

———. 'Personal and Impersonal Identity'. *Mind* (January 1988).

———. 'Personal and Impersonal Identity: Reply to Oderberg'. *Mind* (January 1989).

———. 'The Unreality of Time'. PAS (1992).

———. 'Hartshorne on the Past' in Hahn.

———. *Facts, Words and Beliefs*. London: Routledge and Kegan Paul, 1970.

———. *The Rational Foundations of Ethics*. London: Routledge and Kegan Paul, 1988.

Stevens, Richard: *James and Husserl: The Foundations of Meaning*. The Hague: Martinus Nijhoff, 1974.

Stout, G. F. 'Are the Characters of Particular Things Universals or Particulars?' PASS, III (1923).

———. *The Nature of Universals and Propositions*. 1921 British Academy Lecture, reprinted in Stout, 1930.

———. *Studies in Philosophy and Psychology*. London: Macmillan, 1930.

———. *God and Nature*. Cambridge: Cambridge University Press, 1952.

Strawson, P. F. *Individuals: An Essay in Descriptive Metaphysics*. London: Methuen and Co., 1959.

Strong, C. A. *Why the Mind has a Body*. New York: Macmillan, 1903.

Sturt, Henry. *Personal Idealism: Philosophical Essays by Eight Members of the University of Oxford*. London: Macmillan, 1902.

Tarski, A. 'The Concept of Truth in Formalized Languages'. In Tarski, A. *Logic, Semantics, Metamathematics*. Oxford: 1965.

———. 'The Semantic Conception of Truth' in Feigl and Sellars, 1949.

Taylor, A. E. 'F. H Bradley'. *Mind* N.S. XXXIV (1925).

———. *The Elements of Metaphysics*. London: Methuen, 1903 and 1961.

Thayer. *Meaning and Action: A Critical History of Pragmatism*. Indianapolis: Bobbs-Merrill, 1968.

Trine, Ralph Waldo. *In Touch with the Infinite*. London: G. Bell and Sons, Ltd, 1939. First published 1897.

Walker, R. C. S. *The Coherence Theory of Truth*. London and New York: Routledge, 1989.

White, Alan R. *Truth*. London and Basingstoke: Macmillan, 1970.

Whitehead, A. N. *Process and Reality*. Corrected Edition. New York: The Free Press, 1978. First published 1929.

Wiener, Philip P. *Evolution and the Founders of Pragmatism*. Cambridge, Mass.: Harvard University Press, 1949.

Wild, John. *The Radical Empiricism of William James*. New York: Doubleday and Company Inc., 1969.

Williams, Bernard. *Problems of the Self*. Cambridge University Press, 1973.

Wilshire, B. W. *William James and Phenomenology*. Bloomington: Indiana University Press, 1968.

Wilson, John Cook. *Statement and Inference*. 2 vols. Oxford: Clarendon Press, 1926.

Wollheim, Richard. *F. H. Bradley*. Harmondsworth: Penguin Books, 1959.

Woodfield, Andrew, ed. *Thought and Object: Essays in Intentionality*. Oxford: Clarendon Press, 1982.

Index